Women and the Periodical Press in
Twentieth Century

In this major new collection, an international team of scholars examine the
relationship between the Chinese women's periodical press and global modernity in the late nineteenth and twentieth centuries. The essays in this illustrated
volume probe the ramifications for women of two monumental developments
in this period: the intensification of China's encounters with foreign powers
and a media transformation comparable in its impact to the current Internet
age. The book offers a distinctive methodology for studying the periodical
press, which is supported by the development of two bilingual databases of
early Chinese periodicals. Throughout the study, essays on China are punctuated by transdisciplinary reflections from scholars working on periodicals
outside of the Chinese context, encouraging readers to rethink common
stereotypes about lived womanhood in modern China and to reconsider the
nature of Chinese modernity in a global context.

MICHEL HOCKX is Professor of Chinese Literature and Director of the Liu
Institute for Asia and Asian Studies at the University of Notre Dame.

JOAN JUDGE is Professor in the Department of History at York University in
Toronto, Canada.

BARBARA MITTLER is Professor of Chinese at the Institute of Chinese
Studies and Director of the Heidelberg Centre for Transcultural Studies at
Heidelberg University.

Women and the Periodical Press in China's Long Twentieth Century

A Space of Their Own?

Edited by

Michel Hockx

Department of East Asian Languages and Cultures, University of Notre Dame

Joan Judge

Department of History, York University

Barbara Mittler

Institute of Chinese Studies, Heidelberg University

CAMBRIDGE
UNIVERSITY PRESS

CAMBRIDGE
UNIVERSITY PRESS

University Printing House, Cambridge CB2 8BS, United Kingdom

One Liberty Plaza, 20th Floor, New York, NY 10006, USA

477 Williamstown Road, Port Melbourne, VIC 3207, Australia

314–321, 3rd Floor, Plot 3, Splendor Forum, Jasola District Centre,
New Delhi - 110025, India

79 Anson Road, #06-04/06, Singapore 079906

Cambridge University Press is part of the University of Cambridge.

It furthers the University's mission by disseminating knowledge in the pursuit of
education, learning and research at the highest international levels of excellence.

www.cambridge.org
Information on this title: www.cambridge.org/9781108419758
DOI: 10.1017/9781108304085

© Cambridge University Press 2018

First published 2018

Printed in the United Kingdom by TJ International Ltd. Padstow, Cornwall

A catalogue record for this publication is available from the British Library

ISBN 978-1-108-41975-8 Hardback

For Harriet Evans
An inspiration to all of us

Contents

Figures

Contributors

MARIA AF SANDEBERG is a Senior Teaching Fellow in the Department of the Languages and Cultures of China and Inner Asia at SOAS, University of London, and a freelance writer and translator. Her research interests include gender studies and the literature and literary debates of China's Republican period.

JULIA F. ANDREWS is Distinguished University Professor in the History of Art Department at the Ohio State University. In addition to many articles in journals, exhibition catalogues, and anthologies, among her previous publications are *Painters and Politics in the People's Republic of China, 1949–1979* (1994), which was awarded the Levenson Prize; *A Century in Crisis: Modernity and Tradition in the Art of 20th Century China* (1998); and *Art of Modern China* (2012), which received the Humanities Book Prize of the International Convention of Asia Scholars. She is currently completing an exhibition catalogue, *Painting Her Way: The Art of Fang Zhaoling (1914–2006)*, for the Asia Society Hong Kong Center. Her research has received vital support from the NEH, NEA, ACLS, Fulbright Program, Chiang Ching-kuo Foundation, and, most recently, a Guggenheim fellowship.

PAUL J. BAILEY is Professor of Modern Chinese History at the University of Durham (UK), having previously taught at Lingnan College (Hong Kong) and the University of Edinburgh (UK). His previous publications include *Reform the People* (1990); *Postwar Japan* (1996); *China in the Twentieth Century* (2001); *Gender and Education in China* (2007); *Creative Spaces: Seeking the Dynamics of Change in China* (2012, co-editor and contributor); and *Women and Gender in Twentieth-Century China* (2012). His forthcoming book, *Chinese Overseas Labour in World War One France: Migrant Workers, Globalisation and the Sino-French Connection*, will be published by Routledge. His current project is a study of female crime and socioeconomic change in twentieth-century China.

MARGARET BEETHAM's publications include A *Magazine of Her Own? Domesticity and Desire in the Woman's Magazine, 1800–1914* (1996);

Victorian Woman's Magazines: An Anthology (2001), with Kay Boardman; *The Women's Worlds: Ideology, Femininity and Women's Magazines* (1991), with Ros Ballaster, Liz Frazer, and Sandra Hebron; and numerous journal articles, chapters in books, and edited or co-edited volumes. She was an Associate Editor of the *Dictionary of Nineteenth-Century Journalism* (2009) and is Senior Advisor to the Boards of the Research Society for Victorian Periodicals and ESPRit (the European Society for Periodical Research). She is an Honorary Research Fellow in the School of Arts and Media at the University of Salford, Manchester, having retired from the English Department at Manchester Metropolitan University.

NATHALIE COOKE is Associate Dean of McGill Library (rare and special collections) and professor of English at McGill University in Montreal. Her publications focus on the shaping of culinary and literary taste. She is the author of two books on the writing of Margaret Atwood, the founding editor of the journal *CuiZine: The Journal of Canadian Food Cultures: Revue des cultures culinaires au Canada* (2009–), and the editor of *What's to Eat? Entrées in Canadian Food History* (2009). She is the co-editor of *Mrs. Johnson's Receipt Book: A Treasury of Cookery and Medicinal Receipts, 1741–1848* (2015) and of *Catharine Parr Traill's* The Female Emigrant's Guide, *Cooking with a Canadian Classic* (2017), which includes resource materials to make this publication a toolkit for those exploring historical cookery.

HARRIET EVANS is Professor Emeritus of Chinese Cultural Studies at the University of Westminster. She was recently appointed Visiting Professor in Anthropology at the London School of Economics. She has written extensively on the politics of gender and sexuality in China and on visual culture of the Mao era. Her main publications include *Women and Sexuality in China: Dominant Discourses of Female Sexuality and Gender since 1949* (1997); *Picturing Power in the People's Republic of China: Posters of the Cultural Revolution* (co-edited with Stephanie Hemelryk Donald, 1999); and *The Subject of Gender: Daughters and Mothers in Urban China* (2008). She is currently completing *Beijing from Below*, an oral history of a disadvantaged neighborhood in Beijing. She is also coming to the end of a three-year research project, funded by the Leverhulme Trust, on "Conflicts in Cultural Value: Localities and Heritage in Southwestern China."

GRACE FONG is Professor of Chinese Literature in the Department of East Asian Studies, McGill University. She is Director of the Ming Qing Women's Writings digital archive and database project (http://digital.library.mcgill.ca/mingqing/); author of *Herself an Author: Gender, Agency, and Writing in Late Imperial China*; and co-editor of *Representing Lives in China: Forms of Biography in the Ming–Qing Period, 1368–1911* (Cornell East Asia Series, forthcoming 2018). She is currently conducting a genealogical study of the filiality of daughters in late imperial China.

JENNIFER GARLAND is an Associate Librarian at Rare Books and Special Collections, McGill University and curator of the Blackader–Lauterman Collection of Architecture and Art and the John Bland Canadian Architecture Collection. Her recent research interests include visual literacy, the history of book illustration, and engaging new audiences with special collections. She is also part of a team currently developing the McGill Library Book Arts Laboratory, a hands-on space for teaching the history of the book using the tools of the hand press period. She serves on the Executive Board of the Art Libraries Society of North America (ARLIS/NA) as Canadian Liaison (2016–2018).

MICHEL HOCKX is Professor of Chinese literature and Director of the Liu Institute for Asia and Asian Studies at the University of Notre Dame. He has published widely on modern Chinese literary communities, their practices and values, their printed and digital publications, and their relationship to the state. His latest monograph, *Internet Literature in China* (Columbia University Press, 2015), was listed by *Choice* magazine as one of the "Top 25 Outstanding Academic Titles of 2015."

RACHEL HUI-CHI HSU received her first Ph.D. in Chinese history in 2001 and her second Ph.D. in U.S. transnational history in 2016. She has taught in Mingdao University (2001–2003), Tunghai University (2003–2014), and Loyola University Maryland (2016). She is a two-time Fulbrighter and has published two books, *"Nala" zai Zhongguo: Xin nüxing xingxiang de suzao ji qi yanbian, 1900s–1930s* 「娜拉」在中國：新女性形象的塑造及其演變, 1900s–1930s ('Nora' in China: The image-making and evolution of the new woman, 1900s–1930s; 2003) and *Gudu xinmao: Qianduhou dao kangzhanqian de Beiping chengshi xiaofei* 故都新貌：遷都後到抗戰前的北平城市消費 (1928–1937) (New looks of an ancient capital: Urban consumption in Beiping from 1928 to 1937; 2008), as well as more than twenty peer-reviewed articles. She is currently a research fellow in the Department of History, Sun Yat-Sen University, Guangzhou, China.

SIAO-CHEN HU is a Research Fellow at the Institute of Chinese Literature and Philosophy in Academia Sinica, Taiwan. A specialist in early modern Chinese literature, especially Ming–Qing narrative and women's literature, she is the author of *Xinlixiang, jiu tili yu bukesiyi zhi shehui: Qing-mo Minchu Shanghai 'Chuantongpai' wenren yu guixiu zuojia de zhuanxing lixiang* 新理想、舊體例與不可思議之社會–清末民初上海「傳統派」文人與閨秀作家的轉型現象 (*A conflicted new world*; 2011); *Cainü chuyeweimian: Jindai Zhongguo nüxing xushi wenxue de xingqi* 才女徹夜未眠–近代中

國女性敘事文學的興起 (*Burning the midnight oil: The rise of female narrative in early modern China*; 2003), and *Ming Qing wenxue zhong de Xinan xushi* 明清文學中的西南敘事 (*The Southwest in Ming–Qing literary imagination*; 2017). She is also the co-editor, with Wang Ayling, of *Jingdian zhuanhua yu Ming Qing xushi wenxue* 經典轉化與明清敘事文學 (*Transformations of literary canons and Ming–Qing narrative literature*; 2009), and with Wang Hongtai, of *Richang shenghuo de lunshu yu shijian* 日常生活的論述與實踐 (*Discourse and practice of everyday life*; 2011). She has published widely in essay collections focused on Chinese women's literature, including *The Inner Quarters and Beyond: Women Writers from Ming through Qing* (edited by Grace Fong and Ellen Widmer, 2010) and *Text, Performance, and Gender in Chinese Literature and Music* (edited by Maghiel van Crevel, Tian Yuan Tan, and Michel Hockx, 2009).

JIN-CHU HUANG obtained her Ph.D. in Chinese Literature from National Taiwan University (1992). She is Professor of Chinese Literature at National Chung Cheng University, Taiwan, and her academic interests include late Qing and early Republican fiction and fiction theory and modern women writers, as well as gender studies. Her publications include *Wan Qing shiqi xiaoshuo guannian zhi zhuanbian* 晚清時期小說觀念之轉變 (The development of the concept of fiction in the late Qing period; 1995); *Wan Qing xiaoshuo zhong de xin nüxing yanjiu* 晚清小說中的新女性研究 (A study of "new women" in late Qing fiction; 2005); *Wu Meicun xushishi yanjiu* (A study of narrative poetry of Wu Meicun; 2008); and *Nüxing shuxie de duoyuan chengxian: Qing-mo minchu nüzuojia xiaoshuo yanjiu* 女性書寫的多元呈現：清末民初女作家小說研究 (Multiple presentations of female writing: A study of the fiction of late Qing and early Republican women writers; 2014). She is currently doing research on women's newspapers and magazines.

JOAN JUDGE is Professor in the Department of History at York University in Toronto, Canada. She is the author of *Republican Lens: Gender, Visuality, and Experience in the Early Chinese Periodical Press* (2015); *The Precious Raft of History: The Past, the West, and the Woman Question in China* (2008); and *Print and Politics: "Shibao" and the Culture of Reform in Late Qing China* (1996) and the co-editor of *Beyond Exemplar Tales: Women's Biography in Chinese History* (2011). She is currently engaged in a project with the working title "Quotidian Concerns: Everyday Knowledge and the Rise of the Common Reader in China, 1870–1955."

BARBARA MITTLER is Professor of Chinese at the Institute of Chinese Studies, and Director of the Heidelberg Centre for Transcultural Studies (Asia and Europe in a Global Context) at Heidelberg University. She is the author of

Dangerous Tunes: The Politics of Chinese Music in Hong Kong, Taiwan and the People's Republic of China since 1949 (1997); *A Newspaper for China? Power, Identity and Change in China's News-Media, 1872–1912* (2004); and *A Continuous Revolution: Making Sense of Cultural Revolution Culture* (2012), which won the Fairbank Prize 2013. She is also the editor of *Asian Punches: A Transcultural Affair* (with Hans Harder, 2013). Currently, she is finishing another book-length study on women's magazines and a joint book with historian Thomas Maissen on the Renaissance and China.

NANXIU QIAN is Professor of Chinese Literature at Rice University and the author of *Politics, Poetics, and Gender in Late Qing China: Xue Shaohui (1866–1911) and the Era of Reform* (2015) and *Spirit and Self in Medieval China: The Shih-shuo hsin-yu and Its Legacy* (2001). She is also co-editor of *Different Worlds of Discourse: Transformations of Gender and Genre in Late Qing and Early Republican China* (with Grace Fong and Richard J. Smith, 2008); *Chinese Literature: Conversations between Tradition and Modernity* (with Zhang Hongsheng, 2007); and *Beyond Tradition and Modernity: Gender, Genre, and Cosmopolitanism in Late Qing China* (with Grace Fong and Harriet Zurndorfer, 2004). Her current book project is *'Exemplary Women' (Lienü) versus 'Worthy Ladies' (Xianyuan): The Two Traditions of Representing Women in the Sinosphere.*

JENNIFER SCANLON is the William R. Kenan Jr. Professor of Gender, Sexuality, and Women's Studies at Bowdoin College. She has written extensively on women's magazines and consumer culture, including two books, *Inarticulate Longings: The Ladies' Home Journal, Gender, and the Promises of Consumer Culture* and *Bad Girls Go Everywhere: The Life of Helen Gurley Brown*. Her most recent publication, *Until There Is Justice: The Life of Anna Arnold Hedgeman*, is the first biography of the acclaimed civil rights worker.

LIYING SUN is a cultural historian who focuses on early-twentieth-century Chinese visual media history and popular culture from transcultural perspectives. She received her Ph.D. from Heidelberg University in 2015; her dissertation is entitled "Body Un/Dis-covered: *Luoti*, Editorial Agency and Transcultural Production in Chinese Pictorials (1925–1933)." In Heidelberg, she worked as content manager and co-editor of the database projects "Chinese Women's Magazines in the Late Qing and Early Republican Period" and "Early Chinese Periodicals Online." Sun is presently an Andrew Mellon Postdoctoral Fellow of Digital Humanities at the University of Southern California, Los Angeles. Her current project deals with historical audiences and transcultural receptions of silent films in China.

DORIS SUNG is Assistant Curator for Exhibitions and Research at the Peabody Essex Museum in Salem, Massachusetts. Prior to joining PEM, Sung was an adjunct professor of studio art and Chinese and East Asian art history at York University and the University of Toronto. Her publications cover topics ranging from women's art practices in early-twentieth-century China to contemporary performance art. Sung earned her Ph.D. in Humanities from York University in June 2016. She is also a visual artist and holds an M.F.A. in visual arts.

ELLEN WIDMER is the Mayling Soong Professor of Chinese Studies at Wellesley College. Her research fields include Chinese women's literature of the Ming and Qing dynasties, history of the book, missionary history, and traditional Chinese fiction and drama. She is the author of three monographs: *The Margins of Utopia: Shui-hu hou-chuan and the Literature of Ming Loyalism* (1987); *The Beauty and the Book: Women and Fiction in Nineteenth Century China* (2006); and *Fiction's Family: Zhan Xi, Zhan Kai, and the Business of Women in Late-Qing China* (2016). Volumes she has edited include *From May Fourth to June Fourth: Fiction and Film in Twentieth-Century China* (with David Wang, 1993); *Writing Women in Late Imperial China* (with Kang-i Sun Chang, 1997); *Trauma and Transcendence in Early Qing Literature* (with Wilt Idema and Wai-yee Li, 2006); *China's Christian Colleges: Cross-Cultural Connections* (with Daniel Bays, 2008); and *The Inner Chambers and Beyond: Women Writers from Ming to Qing* (with Grace Fong, 2010).

XIA XIAOHONG is a Professor of Chinese Literature at Peking University. She is the author of numerous works, including *Jueshi yu zhuanshi – Liang Qichao de wenxue daolu* 觉世与传世 – 梁启超的文学道路 (Awakened and transmitted worlds: Liang Qichao's literary trajectory; Zhonghua shuju, 2006); *Wan Qing wenren funü guan* 晚清文人妇女观 (Late Qing literati views of women; Zuojia chubanshe, 1995); *Wan Qing nüxing yu jindai Zhongguo* 晚清女性与近代中国 (Late Qing women and modern China; Beijing daxue chubanshe, 2014); *Liang Qichao: Zai zhengzhi yu xueshu zhijian* 梁启超：在政治与学术之间 (Liang Qichao: Between politics and scholarship; Dongfang chubanshe, 2014); and *Wan Qing nüzi guomin changshi de jiangou* 晚清女子国民常识的建构 (The construction of late Qing female citizens' common knowledge; Beijing daxue chubanshe, 2016).

Acknowledgements

This volume has been a long time in the making. It is the product of a conference entitled "Gender and Transcultural Production: Chinese Women's Journals in their Global Context, 1900–2000," which was held at SOAS University of London in May 2011. We are extremely grateful to the American Council of Learned Societies, which awarded us a conference grant under its "Comparative Perspectives on Chinese Culture and Society" program, and to the Chiang Ching-kuo Foundation for International Scholarly Exchange, which funds the program. In addition to funding the conference, the ACLS/CCK grant also provided a generous publishing subvention that has greatly facilitated the publication process and enabled us to include all of the images we wanted to appear in the volume. We must also acknowledge the many other agencies and institutions that helped subsidize various aspects of the London conference: the SOAS Centre of Chinese Studies, the Social Science and Humanities Research Council of Canada, and the Heidelberg Centre for Transcultural Studies, HCTS (Asia and Europe in a Global Context) at Heidelberg University.

The conference, which included 24 participants from six countries, would have been a logistical nightmare without the support of Alicia Filipowich at the York Center for Asian Research, York University, Toronto. Alicia managed flight details and reimbursements with unfailing efficiency and good nature. We also want to thank Jane Savory and her team at SOAS, who provided invaluable local assistance.

The London meeting was not merely a standalone conference on the Chinese women's periodical press. It was also the culmination of a three-year international collaborative project on "Gender and Cultural Production: A New Approach to Chinese Women's Journals in the Early 20th Century," funded by the Social Science and Humanities Research Council of Canada and the German Alexander von Humboldt-Foundation's Transcoop Programme. The conference was an opportunity for the six members of the project who attended (Michel Hockx, Joan Judge, Barbara Mittler, Grace Fong, Liying Sun, and Doris Sung) to share their research and to further refine the project's methodology for reading the periodical press. It was also the occasion for the launch of the digital component of the project, the database "Chinese Women's

Magazines in the Late Qing and Early Republican Period" (womag.uni-hd.de), and its follow-up, the "Early Chinese Periodicals Online Database" (ecpo.uni-hd.de). We owe a tremendous debt of thanks to our digital team, who constantly refined the database's functionality, uploaded data, and organized metadata. We are immensely grateful to our database technician, Matthias Arnold of the Heidelberg Research Architecture (HRA), Heidelberg University, and to our two former database program managers, Liying Sun and Doris Sung, both contributors to the volume, who have now moved on to exciting new stages in their professional careers.

The transition from vibrant conference to coherent volume would not have been possible without the support of Cambridge University Press. Lucy Rhymer showed enthusiasm for the project from the moment we presented her with the idea, and she continued to offer thoughtful support as we navigated the publication process. We also want to thank the various members of the Cambridge team: Melissa Shivers, Ian McIver, Laura Blake, Anamika Singh, Shubhangi Tripathi, and our conscientious copy editor, William H. Stoddard. We also owe deep thanks to the two readers for the press. We greatly benefitted from their detailed and insightful suggestions and criticism of the original manuscript. Their input has strengthened the final volume in innumerable ways. Last but not least, we want to thank Ms Wai-hing Tse of the SOAS Library for assisting us in getting a high-quality image for the book cover.

We owe a huge intellectual debt to those who participated in the conference as discussants but who are not represented in the volume. They include Jan Bardsley, Parnal Chirmuley, Natascha Gentz, Andrea Janku, and Francesca Orsini. We have special thanks for Jennifer Scanlon, who launched the conference with her illuminating keynote lecture, "Ephemeral, Material, Instrumental: Meditations on Women's Magazines."

Our final round of thanks is for the contributors to the volume. These include our "outside experts," who were willing to grapple with the particularities of the Chinese case, and our "China experts," who were willing to think hard about the methodological challenges and transcultural dimensions of the Chinese women's periodical press. Each of them has endured multiple rounds of revisions and long periods of wondering if their essays were ever going to make it into print. The volume would never have come together without their fine work, energy, and commitment to the project.

Note on Sources

Two databases provide online access to digital copies of many of the journals discussed in various chapters in this volume. Their search and browsing features offer researchers access to indices of articles, illustrations, advertisements, key terms, and personages appearing in these journals.

Chinese Women's Magazines in the Late Qing and Early Republic (WoMag: womag.uni-hd.de)

This database of the Heidelberg Research Architecture (HRA) is a key component of a collaborative project first funded by the Social Science and Humanities Research Council of Canada and the German Humboldt Foundation, and further expanded with additional funding from the Chiang Ching-kuo Foundation. It is a joint project, conducted by researchers at York University, Toronto; Academia Sinica, Taiwan; and the Heidelberg Centre for Transcultural Studies. The focus is on four seminal women's or gendered journals – a key genre of the new media – published between 1904 and 1937: *Nüzi shijie* (Women's world, 1904–07), *Funü shibao* (The women's Eastern times, 1911–17), *Funü zazhi – The Ladies' Journal* (1915–31), and *Linglong – Linloon Magazine* (1931–37).

The database facilitates research on these periodicals. It highlights the journals' pictorial material, including materials normally excised in reprinted or digitized editions, such as advertisements. It provides online access to digital copies of the journals from cover to cover, and its search and browsing features offer researchers access to indices of articles, illustrations, advertisements, key terms, and personages. It therefore mobilizes and interrelates various bodies of data (e.g., visual and textual) within the same tableau, enabling its users to create horizontal and vertical narratives and interconnections between them. The database is ultimately not simply another electronic archive, but can serve as the basis for new forms of historical research. It is of interest to scholars of cultural history and of Chinese cultural, print, literary, women's, and art history.

Early Chinese Periodicals Online (ECPO: ecpo.uni-hd.de)

ECPO was originally created by the Heidelberg Digital Humanities Unit, the Heidelberg Research Architecture (HRA), in collaboration with Taiwan's Academia Sinica. It joins together several important digital collections of the early Chinese press and makes them available to scholarly communities around the world.

Developed jointly by many of the authors of the book, this database is distinguished from all other existing databases of Chinese periodicals in that it not only provides image scans, but also preserves materials often excluded in reprint, microfilm, or digital (even full text) editions, such as advertising inserts and illustrations. In addition, it incorporates a sophisticated body of metadata in both English and Chinese, including keywords and biographical information on editors, authors, and individuals represented in illustrations and advertisements. By framing the journals with this body of metadata, ECPO enables researchers to establish interconnections between, for example, specific individuals, topics, or illustrations over the entire run of a particular periodical or across different periodicals. These capabilities open new horizons in Chinese studies. Using ECPO, the researcher is able to nuance, challenge, and potentially refute existing narratives of historical and cultural change.

Illustrations

High-resolution color versions of the illustrations in this book are available at https://doi.org/10.25354/2017.06.1
Most images contained in this book can also be found in the two databases introduced above, WoMag and ECPO.

Online Resources

All online resources cited in this volume are permanently available through the Digital Archive for Chinese Studies (http://www.zo.uni-heidelberg.de/boa/digital_resources/dachs/). We have created a repository for this volume.

Conventions

In discussions of Chinese periodicals, the first mention gives the pinyin transliteration of the title, followed by the English translation: for example, *Nüzi shijie* (Women's world). Subsequent mentions use the English translation: for example, *Women's World*.

If publishers gave a journal an English name we use that name as our translation. At the first mention, we give both the Chinese and English titles. Subsequent mentions will give the English title: for example, *Funü zazhi – The Ladies' Journal*; *Linglong – Linloon Magazine*.

Preface: The Role of Gender in Defining the "Women's Magazine"

Margaret Beetham

"Women's magazines? Old women's magazines? Are there any?" People's responses when I answer a question about what I am studying often betray surprise and more or less politely concealed contempt at the idea of scholarly attention to a form so ephemeral, so marginal. They never ask, "What are women's magazines?" or "How do you study them?" There is a common-sense view that we already know the answers to these questions and could all recognize a women's magazine at ten paces and, as for reading it, nothing could be easier. As I and all the authors in this volume have discovered, such "common sense" fractures under critical scrutiny. We have to answer the implicit question "Why study women's magazines?" – a form that until recently was below the horizon of the academic gaze. However, even more basically and surprisingly for my hypothetical questioner, we have to define the object of our study. What is a women's magazine? What is it that the writers in this volume see as the object of their study, a study mostly of the recent past of China, a country not normally associated with this particular print genre?

Historians have often turned to periodicals of various kinds, including magazines, for facts about, or contemporary views of, a particular period; literary critics have extracted poetry or fiction; art historians have looked for visual material. However, the magazine is a slippery kind of form, not single-authored but multivocal, heterogeneous in terms of genre, and with a particular relationship to time that complicates periodization. It juxtaposes different kinds of writing or textual and visual representations, it mixes voices, and, because it comes out at regular intervals over a period of time, it resists closure – even as it presents each number as self-contained. If we ignore these formal qualities and try to treat the magazine simply as a repository of facts, or of literary gems from the past, we miss the particular qualities that the form can bring to our historical understanding. All the characteristics of the magazine listed above open up the complexities of the past as no single-authored or single-genre work can, but these characteristics also present methodological problems. They challenge our modes of reading. Of course, I and others engaged in this field would argue that it is precisely this complexity that makes the magazine such a potentially wonderful resource for historians of all kinds – literary, cultural, and social.

And this is abundantly demonstrated in the range and variety of scholarship represented in this volume.

What happens when we add gender to this already rich mix? Katherine Shevelow, among others, argues that the rise of the magazine in the anglophone world at the end of the seventeenth century was inextricably bound up with gender, as it was with class.[1] Scholars of the nineteenth-century press, particularly Brake and Fraser *et al.*, though coming at periodical study from different perspectives, argue cogently that periodical forms, such as the magazine, are intrinsically gendered, though the way gender works in and through them is not stable.[2] However, the "women's magazine," as we now understand the term, makes the role of gender central and explicit. This is what distinguishes it.

The "women's magazine" has its roots in the late eighteenth century/early nineteenth century, and by the late nineteenth century and early twentieth century had become an important part of the magazine press globally, as the chapters in this volume attest. However, as I have suggested, despite a commonsense understanding of what we mean by the term, it is not easy to define for scholarly research. *The Ladies' Magazine*, which was launched in England in 1770 and lasted through mergers and title variations until 1847, may be seen as the earliest example of the form, and it defined itself as a magazine written exclusively "by ladies." However, even a rapid reading shows that this claim is hard to sustain. For one thing, most of the contributors were anonymous or used pseudonyms, a practice that continued and continues to make it difficult for scholars to know the gender of a magazine. Later women's magazines have almost always employed men as well as women writers, and some of the most famous nineteenth-century English journals, such as *The English-woman's Domestic Magazine* (1852–1877) and *Woman's World* (*Lady's World* 1886–1887, then *Woman's World* –1890) were openly edited by men (Samuel Beeton and Oscar Wilde, respectively) or edited by men who concealed their gender under female pseudonyms, as did the future novelist Arnold Bennett when he edited *Woman* (1890–1912) in the 1890s. Of course, some women's magazines that were explicitly concerned with women's rights did make a point of employing women at all levels of the processes of production, from writing articles through to the print room (see, for example, Emily Faithful's *The Victoria Magazine*, 1863–1880), but generally the gender purity of production is uncertain, ambiguous, and shifting. This is in part because of the nature of the magazine as a polyvocal, multiauthored work.

---

[1] Shevelow, *Women and Print Culture*. See also Ballaster, Beetham, Frazer, and Hebron, *Women's Worlds*, 43 ff.

[2] Brake, *Subjugated Knowledges*. Fraser, Green, and Johnston, *Gender and the Victorian Periodical*.

Recent scholarship, including some in this volume, situates particular magazines within communities of writers, editors and artists, which further complicates the importance of gender as a defining concept of the women's magazine.
In terms of production the magazine is more like a film than a novel; that is –
even with a powerful editor or "auteur" director – it is the product of a team.[3]
And beyond the immediate editorial team may well lie other networks of fellow
writers, fellow artists, and – of course – readers who bring their own gendered
and classed identities to bear.

Turning to readership, then, can we define the "women's magazine" in terms
of an exclusively female readership? We can usually find out who the target
readership of a magazine is or was, though even that may be unclear. However,
I think we can safely say that women's magazines can be defined as aiming
to be read by women and usually to be read by a particular group of women
defined by social status, education, political persuasion and so on, as well as
by gender. This is crucial. Discovering who in point of fact read, or even reads,
any kind of published work is extraordinarily difficult. Proving who were the
actual readers of magazines is particularly so. Contemporary media research
shows that substantial numbers of men read magazines designated for women.
Historically, we may look to extraneous information from diaries, letters or
other such sources, but these are hard to find. Where there is correspondence or
advice columns in the magazines themselves, we can look to see what propor-
tion of those who wrote in to the magazine defined themselves as men, though
all the cautions about anonymity and pseudonyms apply.[4] The methodological
challenges are great indeed.

There is a further aspect of readership that both complicates and enriches our
research, and that is the way the magazine characteristically seeks to blur the
line between readers and writers, rhetorically inviting the reader into the circle
of the magazine's community or even inviting actual readers to become writers.
This is a function of the way the magazine comes out over time and therefore,
in common with other forms of serial, has the potential not only to enter the
life of the individual reader in a time-extended way but also to create real or
"imagined" communities of readers who are linked through the publication.[5]
To sum up, we can define the women's magazine as having a target readership
that is exclusively female, but we cannot prove that its readership is exclusively
defined by gender – in fact, evidence suggests the contrary.

Where does this leave us? We may either decide at this point to go and find
an easier research topic or, like the writers of this volume, press on to develop

---

[3] See Leary, *The Punch Brotherhood*, for a detailed examination of this in relation to *Punch*.

[4] For an extended discussion of these problems see Beetham, *In Search of the Historical Reader*.

[5] The concept of the "imagined community" in relation to periodical readers was coined by Benedict Anderson in *Imagined Communities*, and has been widely used, and perhaps abused, in periodical studies.

a more nuanced methodology. Such a methodology must, I suggest, take the foregrounding of gender in the woman's magazine as a starting rather than a finishing point. In identifying women as its target readers, the women's magazine presents these imagined readers with material appropriate to what Judith Butler has called the "performance" of femininity.[6] Whether it concentrates on domestic matters, on the upbringing of children, on fashion or on family, it is defining an "appropriate" gender role for its readers.

If, as argued above, the magazine is always already gendered, then the presence of women's magazines in a print culture where there is no equivalent flagging up of the masculine as a writing or reading position shows that "woman" here represents the "other" to a norm, assumed to be masculine. The binary of gender means that address to femininity always involves, whether articulated or not, an equivalent masculine norm. Women's magazines, therefore, not only delineate a particular cultural and historic femininity but by implication, by omission, or sometimes by direct admonition can also reveal much about the masculinity that is the cultural norm against which "woman" is defined.

Of course, some of the magazines, including some of those studied here, deliberately sought to challenge accepted definitions of appropriate femininity by offering new models. In particular, the very act of allowing, or even encouraging, women to appear in print might itself be a challenge to traditional concepts of a valued femininity as confined to the private or the domestic. The ambiguous nature of the magazine as a print space that is simultaneously public and yet private is important here. For, as the magazines discussed in this volume show, the unsettling of gender definitions is one of the marks of modernity, like the appearance of print media. The women's magazine, with its interactive and multivocal form, emerged globally in the late nineteenth/early twentieth century as a site in which shifting gender roles could be debated, enacted, or denounced.

There are other methodological problems that the study of women's magazines in a historical context raises. These range from the practical difficulties of finding and delimiting the historical sources to wider questions of what critical and theoretical models are useful for the study. Material problems in relation to historical women's magazines are Janus-faced, often presenting us simultaneously with lack and overabundance. Because magazines are of their moment, ephemeral, they were not always preserved as were more valued literary objects, or, if kept, they were often in partial and fragmented form. Even digital resources, which open up so much for us, cannot completely solve this. They may, however, contribute to the converse problem, which is that, where we can find runs from the past – either material or digital – even a single magazine can provide a daunting quantity of material over the course of just a few

---

[6] Butler, *Gender Trouble*, is the work where she first developed this theory.

years. In seeking to draw on appropriate reading strategies for these texts, we
may turn to draw on different theoretical models from elsewhere, including
those of philosophers and social theorists, such as Bourdieu and Foucault, or
we may look to a Bakhtinian model.[7]

However, whatever the other problems we encounter in our study of the
women's magazine, we need, I suggest, to keep the role of gender central, along
with the qualities of the magazine. Whatever the body of material to be studied,
whatever theoretical models we draw on to develop our research and reading
methods, we need to address the complexity of the "women's magazine" in
relation to both terms, to genre and gender and to the dynamic between them.[8]
The chapters in this volume show some of the ways in which that task can
fruitfully be carried out.

[7] See Liddle, *The Dynamics of Genre*. See also the discussion in *Victorian Periodical Review*, 44:3
(2011), 291–300.

[8] See Beetham, *A Magazine of Her Own?* 1–14 and passim; see also Gough-Yates, *Understanding
Women's Magazines*, 6–25 for an overview.

Introduction: Women's Journals as Multigeneric Artefacts

Joan Judge, Barbara Mittler, and Michel Hockx

Chinese women's journals offer unparalleled access to the intricacies of China's gendered past.[1] Their value as a source lies in their inherent complexity as multigeneric artefacts – repositories of fiction and poetry, of photographs and cover art, of advertisements, essays, and letters. Unlike single-authored texts, these multivocal, multigeneric, and multiregistered materials create spaces of experimentation – testing grounds for new cultural forms, scientific ideas, and – our focus in this volume – gender roles. Defined by their serialized temporality, they are both fleeting and continuous. As discrete publications with finite runs, they capture the actors, issues, and publishing practices of particular historical moments. As participants in broader conversations within a worldwide web of periodicals, they illuminate the ways Chinese gender concerns were inextricably linked to the knowledge, perceptions, or imaginings of the world at large. They are porous documents that bring historical actors to life: transforming readers into writers in interactive columns and viewers into photographed subjects in illustrative sections. As sites into which the self and family extend, the state may intrude, and global norms and images are introduced, they create rich amalgams of ever-shifting identities.

Over half a century ago, Raymond Williams declared that periodicals provide access to "actual culture" and demand careful study.[2] A discrete field, "Periodical Studies," has, however, only recently begun to come into its own. Scholars of various disciplines and geographic areas are no longer merely instrumentally using periodicals to serve other research agendas, but identifying them as valid objects of scholarly inquiry in and of themselves. They are increasingly recognizing the remarkable possibilities these materials open up for deepening our understanding of history, literature, art, commerce, science, and the intersections among them.

In the "Introduction" to *The Journal of Modern Periodical Studies*, launched in 2010, two prominent scholars in this emerging field, Sean Latham and

---

[1] See Beetham's Preface to this volume for reflections on the ability of periodicals to "open up the complexities of the past."
[2] Williams, *The Long Revolution*, 70.

1

Mark S. Morrison, note that mass culture first dawned not in film nor on the radio but on the newspaper stands and bookstalls that operated in the "golden age of print culture": the late nineteenth and early twentieth century. While these bookstalls offered readers novels and books, their hottest-selling commodities were magazines. The periodicals published between 1880 and 1950 were both pervasive and deeply influential. In Latham and Morrison's words, they shaped modernity, in deep but still unexplored ways.[3]

This volume endorses Latham and Morrison's claim, while complicating their conception of modernity by stressing the relationship between the Chinese periodical press and a global modernity, or "modernity in common."[4] A grammar with different inflections rather than a single model with national alternatives, this modernity is a process of change that has developed and resulted in important commonalities worldwide. These commonalities include two phenomena that are the focus of this volume: the rise of the periodical press, on the one hand, and the advancement of women, on the other. Our focus is on one important and heretofore underexplored aspect of the (women's) periodical press: the coincidence of its rise with the dawn of global communications.

Global Contexts

The period generally designated as the beginning of "modern" Chinese history is inextricably tied to two monumental developments: the intensification of China's encounters with foreign powers both within and outside of East Asia, and a radical media transformation comparable in its impact to the current Internet age. This globally mediated transformation of Chinese print culture began with the introduction of the missionary press into China in the early nineteenth century, and led to the adoption of letterpress printing and lithography by the end of the century.[5] China's first Chinese-language daily newspaper was founded by a British tea merchant in 1872, and by 1937 some 1,500 newspapers – dailies, weeklies, and monthlies – had been published in Shanghai alone.[6] Similarly, the number of periodicals increased exponentially

---

[3] Latham and Morrison, "Introduction."

[4] Carol Gluck has elaborated on this concept, urging us to place particular histories in their global context – in the context of "modernity in common." She notes, "Just as the modern history of a society cannot be explained in isolation from the world, it is also possible to explore the history of the modern world from the vantage point of any particular place in the existing 'globeful of modernities.' [Each particular place] shares commonalities and connections with other modern societies, [offering] the opportunity to think about the 'modern' on empirical bases different from the European experiences that underlay earlier theories of modernity." Gluck, "Modernity in Common."

[5] On the missionary press see Zhang, *The Origins of the Modern Chinese Press*; Kurtz, "Messenger of the Sacred Heart." On the adoption of letterpress and lithography, see Reed, *Gutenberg in Shanghai*.

[6] See Jia Shumei, *Shanghai xinwenzhi*, 236–63.

over the early years of the twentieth century. Considering Chinese women's journals alone, an estimated forty-four were published in China and Japan between 1898 and 1911, another thirty appeared between 1912 and 1915, and close to 250 more by the late 1930s.[7] These media changes marked a radical transformation in terms of the quantity of available information, the range of usable print forms, and the expansion of opportunities for readers to participate in public culture. They also signaled the globalization of the Chinese print world.

From its inception in the late nineteenth century, the Chinese periodical press was the direct product of global interactions. The majority of journal editors, contributors, and illustrators had been exposed to Japanese and Western publications and models while studying abroad (most often in Japan) or at foreign-run institutions in Shanghai (such as the Jesuit Tushanwan Art Studio). The format of Chinese journals often mirrors those of Japanese or Western publications, and the cover art references foreign visuals and styles. At the same time, a large part of the content of the journals was taken directly from foreign sources. This includes the photographs of, for example, Japanese or Javanese women that opened the journals and the translations of a range of materials that filled their pages: from German scientific articles and British fiction to biographies of such diverse cultural icons as Joan of Arc and Clara Bow.[8] In addition to direct translations, references to foreign heroes, practices, and events appear in all of the journals, and conceptions of women's new roles are foreign-influenced. Western lawyers, engineers, and teachers serve as prototypes for imagined professional Chinese women, and Hollywood celebrities as models for Chinese film stars. Of critical importance as well, the very language of the journals was a highly hybridized amalgam of Japanese loan words, Western names and terminology, and newly imported grammatical forms.

While much has been written about popular women's magazines in specific national and cultural contexts, an approach that takes a transcultural perspective and thus emphasizes the dynamics of cultural flows rather than focusing on static "receiver" and "sender" relations is still rare.[9] There are very few substantial enquiries into how women's magazines in different countries engage one another and how ideas and concepts move from one place and context to another. In this book, in contrast, we examine these flows and connections, disruptions and disconnections in the production, dissemination, and consumption of China's gendered journals. While all of the chapters are concerned with women's magazines in China, the authors discuss the transit of ideas, images,

---

[7] Maeyama, "Chûgoku no josei muke teiki kankôbutsu ni tsuite," "Fu 3."

[8] See Xia, Bailey, and Mittler in this volume and Judge, *Republican Lens*, Chapter 3.

[9] See, for example, Moeran, "On Entering the World of Women's Magazines"; Frith, "Portrayals of Women in Global Women's Magazines in China"; Fahad and Karande, "A Content Analysis"; Skalli, *Through a Local Prism*.

and thoughts across the globe and through the medium of the gendered magazine, often attempting to trace the particular routes of these exchanges. Thus, engaging with the world of Chinese women's journals in a global context, we are also able to offer a perspective on what one could call a female modernity in common.

The book is further punctuated by reflections by scholars who are experts on periodicals outside of China, beginning with Beetham's preface. These transdisciplinary interventions emphasize general points to be made about women's reading and writing in the periodical press in the context of the twentieth century's shared modernity.

An Emerging Field

Scholars of China have made important, if as-yet unacknowledged, contributions to the emerging research field of "Periodical Studies."[10] Numerous monographs on particular Chinese newspapers and journals have been published over the last decade and a half, and a journal entitled *East Asian Publishing and Society* was launched in 2011.[11]

Periodical studies have an even longer history in Chinese-language scholarship. To date, most emphasis has been on periodicals that played a role in the New Culture Movement of the late 1910s and early 1920s, a movement that has been deemed a historical watershed and a crucial precursor to the 1949 Communist Revolution. Indeed, one single magazine, *Xin qingnian* (New youth), published at Peking University, is traditionally credited with having raised virtually all significant questions underlying Chinese modernity, including "the woman question" (*funü wenti*). Periodicals were also considered the main drivers of the anti-imperialist "May Fourth Movement," which grew out of the New Culture Movement. A standard three-volume textbook on "May Fourth" journals was edited in 1979 by the same Party office that translated and edited the works of Marx, Lenin, Engels, and Stalin.[12] Introductions to periodicals linked to other revolutionary moments, most particularly the 1911 Revolution, were also published at approximately the same time.[13]

---

[10] As noted above, this development culminated in the foundation of the *Journal of Modern Periodical Studies* in 2010.

[11] For scholarship in English on Chinese newspapers, see Judge, *Print and Politics*; Mittler, *A Newspaper*; Wagner, *Joining the Global*. On literary journals, see Gimpel, *Lost Voices of Modernity*; Hockx, *Questions of Style*. On entertainment journals, see Wang, *Merry Laughter*. On pictorials, see Ye Xiaoqing, *The Dianshizhai Pictorial*; Pickowicz et al. on *Liangyou huabao*. The journal *East Asian Publishing and Society*, edited by Peter Kornicki, is not exclusively concerned with the periodical press, but is a new journal dedicated to the study of the publishing of texts and images in East Asia, from the earliest times up to the present.

[12] Zhonggong, *Wu si shiqi qikan*.   [13] For instance, Ding Shouhe, *Xinhai geming shiqi qikan*.

Throughout the 1980s, Chinese libraries rapidly expanded access to a much wider variety of pre-1949 periodicals, including many not directly linked to the revolutionary movement. This led to increased scholarly interest in the late Qing period (1850–1911), as well as the urban popular culture of the Republican era (1912–1949). Many important periodicals from these eras were reprinted in the 1980s and 1990s, and large reference works listing all available journals in a specific field were subsequently published.[14] More recently, large-scale digitization projects have reduced the need for publication of such printed reference works. The Shanghai Library, which has the most extensive holdings of periodicals in the country, has made scans of over 25,000 of the pre-1949 periodicals in its collection available, linking the digitized versions to an earlier electronic index of tables of contents.[15] The National Library in Beijing is engaged in similar efforts. Some newspapers, most notably *Shenbao* (Shanghai journal), have also been made available in full text.

An important number of landmark cultural and historical studies by Chinese scholars, including Professor Xia Xiaohong from Peking University, whose work is included in this volume, have been based predominantly on periodical materials. These scholars also include the study of periodicals in their basic training of Chinese graduate students. Professor Xia's work has inspired many of the other contributors to this volume with her wide-ranging studies of periodical culture of the Late Qing period, including a number of publications dealing with women.[16]

Much relevant scholarship has also been produced by scholars in Taiwan, as evidenced by the contributions to this volume by Siao-chen Hu, Jin-Chu Huang, and Rachel Hsu. Taiwan has produced reprints of significant overseas student, general interest, and women's journals as well.[17] A recent Japanese–Taiwanese project on one of the seminal Chinese women's journals, *Funü zazhi – The Ladies' Journal* (1915–1931), which several authors discuss in their contributions to this collection, produced both a series of scholarly essays and a detailed print and online catalogue of the journal.[18]

---

[14] Reprints published in China include *Tuhua ribao*, *Beiyang huabao* and *Liangyou*. Reference works in the field of literature include Liu Zengren's study of literary periodicals, which provides a complete list of all available literary journals of the 1919–1949 period. Several other publications provide complete lists of tables of contents. Cf. Liu Zengren, *Zhongguo xiandai wenxue qikan*. See also Tang Yuan, *Zhongguo xiandai wenxue qikan*, and Wu Jun, *Zhongguo xiandai wenxue qikan*. A more general collection of journal content tables is Shanghai tushuguan, *Zhongguo jindai qikan bianmu*.

[15] Shanghai tushuguan, *Quanguo baokan suoyin*.

[16] For instance, Xia Xiaohong, *Wan-Qing nüxing yu jindai Zhongguo*.

[17] Taiwanese reprints of overseas student journals published by the Zhongguo guomindang, Zhongyang weiyuan hui, Dangshi shiliao bianzuan weiyuan hui, all in 1968. They include *Hubei*; *Hansheng*; and *Jiangsu*. Taiwan reprints of women's journals include *Zhongguo xin nüjie zazhi*.

[18] Special issue: *Jindai Zhongguo funü shi yanjiu;* Murata Yûjirô, "*Fujo zasshi*"; "*Fujo zasshi*" *sômokuroku*.

A Gendered Genre

This volume builds on recent work on Chinese periodicals in East Asia, North America, and Europe over the past decade and a half and has greatly benefited from recent East Asian reprinting and digital remediation projects. It marks an important step towards the consolidation of a subfield focused on the study of Chinese periodicals. It comes directly out of an ongoing international collaborative project on early Chinese periodicals, which has three principal aims: to advance intensive research on specific periodicals, to develop new methodological approaches to the study of periodicals, and to create an "intelligent" electronic archive of important periodicals. This comprehensive database offers exhaustive data and metadata on the full contents of specific periodicals – including not only their articles, but their cover art, photographs, and advertisements.[19] A crucial instrument for facilitating our methodology and advancing our research, the database has been used by a number of authors in this collection.

This volume marks the culmination of the first phase of this project, which has focused on women's journals. The women's press constitutes an important subfield within the field of Western periodical studies, and we are honored to have the doyenne of this field, Margaret Beetham, as the author of the preface to our volume.[20] Scholarly studies of Western women's magazines in different countries began several decades ago with feminist approaches focused on representations of women in the 1970s and 1980s.[21] More recently, the emphasis has shifted towards questions derived from sociology and media studies. Scholars have increasingly analyzed women's magazines as consumer objects central to processes of ideology and identity formation.[22] The field continues to thrive,

---

[19] Funding for the first phase was provided by the Social Science and Humanities Research Council of Canada and by the Humboldt Foundation's TransCOOP program. The database can be accessed at http://womag.uni-hd.de/. Funding for the second phase has been provided by the Chiang Ching-kuo Foundation. For a description of the database see Sun and Arnold, "TS Tools"; Sung, Sun, and Arnold, "The Birth of a Database of Historical Periodicals."

[20] Cf. Beetham, *A Magazine of Her Own*; Beetham and Kay, *Victorian Women's Magazines*.

[21] Braithwaite, *The Business of Women's Magazines*; Christmann and Leppert, "Das Bild der Frau in den deutschen Frauenzeitschriften"; Eskridge, *How the Psychology of Women Is Presented in Women's Magazines*; Hüntemann, "Der schöne Schein in der Massenkommunikation" Keller, "Mothers and Work as Represented in Popular American Magazines"; Linden, "Media Images of Women and Social Change"; Millum, *Images of Woman*; Probst, "Frauenzeitschriften"; Röser, *Frauenzeitschriften und weiblicher Lebenszusammenhang*; Suleiman, "Changing Attitudes towards Women in Egypt"; White, *Women's Magazines*; Winship, *Woman Becomes an "Individual."*

[22] Attwood, *Creating the New Soviet Woman*; Baron, "Readers and the Women's Press"; Clark, "*Ms. Magazine*"; Endres, *Women's Periodicals in the United States*; Gough-Yates, *Understanding Women's Magazines*; Johansson, "Chinese Women and Consumer Culture"; Skalli, *Through a Local Prism*; Whitethorne, *Cosmo Woman*.

as recent international conferences and the ongoing publication of monographs attest.[23]

The chapters in this volume contribute to this body of scholarship in examining the women's periodical press as a space for the implicit expression and explicit articulation of fundamental moral, cultural, and political concerns at key moments in China's long twentieth century. The collection's focus is on the first three decades of the century, but it also traces manifestations of women's engagement in the periodical press through and beyond the Mao era (1949–1976). Without claiming to be exhaustive either chronologically or thematically, the volume has two central objectives. The first is to develop and showcase methodologies that approach women's journals as complex material and historical objects. Comprising different genres of textual and visual media, they are deeply embedded in both distinctive print cultures and specific historical and political conjunctures (Part I and throughout the volume). The second objective is to use women's journals to explore key issues in Chinese women's history. These include the unprecedented public expression of female subjectivities in the full range of genres featured in women's journals: poetry, painting, fiction, essays, and letters (Part II). They also include the crucial role of foreign concepts and images, i.e., the global context, in the constitution of these emerging female subjectivities (Part III).

Our overriding aim in developing new methodologies and exploring new manifestations of female subjectivity on the pages of China's women's magazines is to enrich, nuance, or challenge conventional historical narratives. While the early twentieth century has been recognized as a formative period in Chinese history, scholars have emphasized intellectual, institutional, and political changes: efforts at thoroughgoing administrative reform from 1901, the abolition of the civil service examination system in 1904/1905, and the demise of the imperial order in 1911. Our focus on the emergence of women on the public pages of the periodical press reflects an equally fundamental shift. Integral to the unprecedented movement of women towards work and study outside the home, women's engagement with the periodical press was central to what Susan Mann has characterized as "the most significant and sweeping change in China's sex–gender system in centuries."[24]

---

[23] A conference on "Women in Magazines: Research, Representation, Production and Consumption" was held at Kingston University, London, in June 2012, for example, and recent publications among the many that focus on women's journals include DiCenzo, Delap, and Ryan, *Feminist Media History*; Chapman and Mills, *Treacherous Texts*. For China, see articles in this volume by Qian, Xia, Mittler, and Judge. See also Judge, *Republican Lens*. Mittler is finishing a manuscript on women's magazines in China's long twentieth century, entitled *Portrait of a Trope*. One volume that is a survey of Chinese women's journals is Ma, *Women Journalists and Feminism in China*.

[24] Mann, *Gender and Sexuality*, xvii.

In creating "A Space of Their Own," women's magazines not only documented but advanced and mediated changes in the realm of women's work and most particularly in the sphere of women's education. The first Chinese women's journal was founded in conjunction with the first Chinese-run women's school in 1898, and subsequent early women's journals were staffed by educators, featured writings by female students, published investigations of various schools, offered descriptions of female students and teachers, and promoted the institutional development of women's education.[25] The government heeded these early demands in 1907 when it finally sanctioned formal public education for women. According to incomplete statistics, the number of female students increased almost twelvefold over the next five years: from 11,936 female students in 391 schools in 1907 to 141,130 students in 1912 to 1913. Over the course of the next decade that number would nearly triple again: by 1923, there would be 417,820 female students attending school.[26] For the young female students who attended these schools over the course of the twentieth century, women's journals constituted a new public space serving the unprecedented unfolding of the long-sequestered world of women's culture, the open discussion of women's bodies and sexuality, and encounters with Japanese, Western, and non-Western Others in texts, images, and advertisements.

The multivalent nature of women's encounters with the foreign in the periodical press highlights the multigeneric and multiregistered quality of the medium. The study of these textually, visually, and materially complex materials requires an approach that is both flexible enough to accommodate their layered content and rigorous enough to make sense of it. One of the prime objectives of our international collaborative project was to move beyond existing approaches to the periodical press by refining a methodology that would mobilize good scholarly practices to address the complexities of the periodical medium specifically. The chapters in this volume provide various examples of this methodology in practice, and the three papers in Part I highlight key components of our approach.

To address the complexity of the materials at hand, we engage in four different (and more or less established) modes of reading the journals: "horizontal," "vertical," "integrated," and "situated."[27] The first, a horizontal reading, is

---

[25] On the first women's journal see Qian in this volume; for more on the journal and this school, see Qian, *Politics, Poetics, and Gender*. Women's schools had been founded by missionaries in China since 1844.

[26] These numbers are compiled from Bailey, *Gender and Education*, 84–85; The Chinese National Association, "Bulletins on Chinese Education," 6. On the distribution of girls' schools by *xian*, see The Chinese National Association, "Bulletins on Chinese Education," 7, and by province see Bailey, *Gender and Education*, 86–90.

[27] The concept of "horizontal reading" was first introduced by Michel Hockx in *Questions of Style*. This method is further explicated and applied in Judge, *Republican Lens*.

based on the premise that a journal is much greater than the sum of its parts, and that what journals do is much more complex than what they declare they will do. A horizontal reading involves a close examination of all materials (texts, images, advertisements) included in one issue of a particular journal. We read cover art in relation to textual columns and photographs in conjunction with readers' letters; we place classical lyric poems in conversation with polemical essays, and advertisements with treatises on health. This arguably brings us closer to the reading experiences of the historical readers of these magazines. It also encourages novel interpretations of texts and images through unusual juxtapositions of material traditionally considered to belong to different genres or categories. The horizontal approach is complementary to a more common scholarly practice that we call vertical reading – and that several authors in the volume use in conjunction with other approaches. A vertical reading traces a particular genre or theme over time in one journal, without necessarily taking other parts of the contents into account (for instance, reading all the fiction in a particular journal but ignoring the poetry).

In an effort to reconstitute the immediate cultural context in which these journals and their contemporary audience were located, we further engage in what we call "integrated readings." Such readings examine women's journals as part of a wider print culture, holding them up against contemporary periodicals and other publications. These include their commercial competitors and "sibling" works published within the "families" of journals that were commonly produced by publishers in twentieth-century China. This approach allows us to see how particular tropes or images were differently purposed within the same print moment. It also highlights networks of authors and readers, by, for example, allowing us to map the various publications to which a certain author contributed, or the various journals to which a reader submitted her photograph.

Another facet of our approach is situated reading. In the new historicist manner, such a reading extends the study of a particular journal to other source materials that informed its broader context. These materials could include official documents, biographies, memoirs, films, and literature, as well as artistic and material objects. In conducting a situated reading, we view the journals as nodes of broader networks of cultural critics, educators, readers, writers, editors, artists, illustrators, and photographers. This approach allows us to better understand the dissemination and impact of specific topics, tropes, and ideas and to observe discourse formation in the making.

In adopting and combining these different reading strategies, we are able to capture the individual reading experience of the historical reader flipping through a magazine (horizontal reading), to trace the sedimentation of discursive ideas in cultural memory (vertical reading), to map the parameters of the readerly and writerly communities of journals (integrated reading), and to deepen our knowledge of particular journals' sociohistorical context (situated reading). Deploying these various reading strategies, we are ultimately better able to understand the multilayered historical act of perusing a periodical.

The Chapters

The authors of the chapters in this volume apply this methodology variously. Most combine at least two kinds of readings, depending on the type of argument they are making and the nature of the specific women's journals they are analyzing. In their totality, the chapters demonstrate the ways in which this stratified approach can maximize the potentiality for reading women's journals as valuable historical sources.

The volume is structured around the notion of women's journals as a multipurpose space, a laboratory for the exploration of gender ideas, the assertion of gendered identities, and the investigation of both historical and more recent foreign and Chinese gender norms. Few of the journals examined here were actually edited by women. As a result, a number of these male-edited and female-focused publications became a site where, as Joan Judge notes in her paper, "the once sequestered female figure could become an object of public discussion, public spectacle, public commerce, and public scrutiny." At the same time, however, even male-driven journals made space for women's textual and visual contributions, and, as several authors suggest, these contributions often extended this newly created space in unanticipated ways.

Part I of the volume, *Methodologies: Framing, Constituting, and Regulating the Space of the Women's Journal*, highlights different methodological approaches to the women's periodical press. The three chapters provide examples of the methodology developed throughout the book. Each demonstrates the ways a particular reading (or combination thereof) – horizontal, vertical, integrated, or situated – deepens our understanding of how the journals functioned in their particular visual, historical, print, and political contexts.

Julia F. Andrews's chapter, "Persuading with Pictures: Cover Art and *The Ladies' Journal* (1915–1931)," explores the ways the space of the woman's journal, and most specifically, of the influential *Ladies' Journal*, was visually framed. Covering the entire history of this long-running journal, Andrews reads the cover images, some created by male artists and others painted by women themselves, against the journal's changing content and shifting editorial objectives. Combining this horizontal method of reading with a vertical reading, to emphasize the complexity not only of the covers but of the genre of women's journals themselves, and across time, Andrews highlights the disjunctions between the aims and capabilities of commercial artists, their publishers, and their prospective public.

In "Engendering a Journal: Editors and Nudes in *Linloon Magazine* and Its Global Context," Liying Sun offers an integrated reading of the pictorial entertainment journal *Linglong – Linloon Magazine* (1931–1937). Focusing on the important concept of editorial agency, Sun juxtaposes the textual and visual content of *Linloon Magazine* with that of other journals edited by the same company. Through this integrated reading, Sun directly confronts the question of the kind of space the male editors of *Linloon Magazine* sought to create: was this "women's magazine" designed for women's edification or male titillation? The presence of often foreign-derived nude photographs in the journal is central to Sun's analysis and to her concept of a "global database" of material available to Chinese editors in the Republican era. The complex ways these photographs were framed further complicates questions of editorial agency and projected audience.

Michel Hockx's chapter, "Raising Eyebrows: The Journal *Eyebrow Talk* and the Regulation of 'Harmful Fiction' in Modern China," offers a situated reading of the journal *Meiyu* (Eyebrow talk, 1914–1916), which, like *Linloon Magazine*, included nude and suggestive photographs and which, as Jin-Chu Huang demonstrates later in the volume, was a space for the fictional expression of female desires. Placing *Eyebrow Talk* in its broader political, moral, cultural, and commercial context, Hockx documents official efforts to limit and control the expanding space of the periodical press in the early twentieth century by banning the journal. He maps a genealogy of the terminology employed to categorize transgressive publications from *Eyebrow Talk*'s day through the Internet age at the turn of the twenty-first century. He further highlights the connection between the representation of women in printed or digital space and the perception of moral transgression by regulating authorities. In addition to this situated reading of the journal in question, the chapter also offers an integrated reading of parts of the journal in relation to a famous essay by the literary author Lu Xun, who was directly involved in the censoring of *Eyebrow Talk*.

Ellen Widmer's coda, which closes the section, offers another method of approaching not so much the content but the perception of late Qing women's journals in their own day. She uses contemporary fiction to illuminate a range of views on the utility and the danger of the periodical press.

The authors of chapters in Part II, "A Space of Their Own: The Woman's Journal, Generic Choice and the Making of Female Public Expression," use the various modes of reading introduced in Part I in analyzing women's efforts to inhabit and push the parameters of the new space of the woman's journal. In her opening reflection, Jennifer Scanlon, an expert on the American magazines *Ladies Home Journal* – which served as a template for the Chinese journals *Funü shibao* (The women's Eastern times, 1911–1917) and *The Ladies' Journal* – and *Cosmopolitan*, urges us to excavate the experience of the women who wrote for women's journals or who read them.[28] Although many of these publications were founded and edited by men who promoted specific political and social agendas, we have to be attentive to the often subtle ways women "talked back." In establishing particular relationships with journals as poets and painters, as authors of fiction, essays, and letters, women contributed to the crafting of both the journals and themselves.

In "Radicalizing Poetics: Poetic Practice in *Women's World*, 1904–1907" Grace Fong explores the complexities of this process of self-crafting. She closely examines the ways the traditionally gendered genre of women's poetry was reconfigured in the pages of one of the earliest Shanghai women's journals, *Nüzi shijie* (Women's world). Using a situated and vertical reading that is attuned to the shifting cultural status and political import of poetry in this period, Fong demonstrates that *Women's World* functioned as a space in which poetry was transformed from a mode of personal response and expression to a form of public and progressive communication. At the same time, her close readings of the poetry reveal the ways authors used conventional imagery to convey new ideas.

Doris Sung examines the ways two important women's journals, *The Women's Eastern Times* and *The Ladies' Journal*, became a space for creating the discourse on "women's art" in early-twentieth-century China. In "Redefining Female Talent: *The Women's Eastern Times*, *The Ladies' Journal*, and the Development of 'Women's Art' in China, 1910s–1930s," Sung discusses the changing attitude of and towards newly mobile and internationally recognized women artists, emphasizing the ways these women were represented and represented themselves in the pages of these journals. As spaces where the private practice of women's painting became public in unprecedented ways, these publications created a new forum in which artists and writers, both female and male, expressed and shared their opinions on issues related to women's art and women *in* art. At the same time, her reading, which combines horizontal and vertical approaches, shows how the journals reinforced and extended the contemporary emphasis on aesthetic education in the curriculum for the new public education of women.

The women's periodical press also functioned as a space in which female authors could express their subjectivities through fiction. In "Constituting the Female Subject: Romantic Fiction by Women Authors in *Eyebrow Talk*," Jin-Chu Huang argues that the founding of the women's press and particularly of the largely female-run journal *Eyebrow Talk* opened an unprecedented space for women to rethink the meaning of women's rights. The romantic fiction they published in *Eyebrow Talk*'s pages – the material that raised the ire of the cultural authorities Hockx discusses in his chapter – became a prime vehicle

---

[28] Scanlon, *Inarticulate Longings*; Scanlon, *Bad Girls Go Everywhere*.

for the expression of women's own fantasies about love and desire. Huang's careful vertical reading of female-authored fiction from different issues of the journal, as well as her integrated reading of contemporary fiction authored by men, illustrates how important it is to look beyond the text on the page of a given journal in order to decipher the frustrations and aspirations that echo between the lines.

Rachel Hsu examines a more direct and contentious form of women's writing that emerged in the pages of the women's press in the early 1920s. It was in these pages that female authors first began to adopt the genre of the polemical essay as a vehicle for the articulation of their opinions on love and marriage. Examining the woman's journal as a site of direct gender contention and focusing on instances when women contributors took issue with male editors on intimate matters, her chapter, "Rebellious Yet Constrained: Dissenting Women's Views on Love and Sexual Morality in *The Ladies' Journal* and *The New Woman*," traces the often vigorous interplay between male editorial agency and female authorial subjectivity – highlighting, in her integrated reading, the differences between certain journal environments in this regard.

Siao-chen Hu traces the public transformation of two other genres of women's writing – intimate letters between close female friends and autobiographical writing – in "Voices of Female Educators in Early-Twentieth-Century Chinese Women's Magazines." In her vertical and integrated approach, Hu shows how reading and writing for women's magazines transposed the late imperial mode of epistolary friendship into the new medium of the periodical press. Journals such as *The Ladies' Journal* and, more importantly, *Zhonghua funüjie – The Chung Hwa Women's Magazine* (1915–1916), opened up a networking space for women and changed their sense of self and community. Hu further demonstrates that women's journals functioned as a pedagogical space where women were instructed (by male teachers) on a range of themes and where they could be taught the mechanics of expository writing.

In addition to functioning as a new pedagogical space, women's journals also advocated the transformation of the household into a new pedagogical space. In "'Room for Improvement': The Ideal of the Educational Home in *The Ladies' Journal*," Maria af Sandeberg examines the mediating role of the women's periodical in encouraging readers to reconsider (and ultimately, rearrange) their most intimate physical spaces: their own homes. Committed to making the home one of the prime sites for the education of China's future citizens, reformers used the pages of *The Ladies' Journal* to diagram and describe the necessary configuration and furnishing of the ideal domestic "classroom."

The physical space of the early-twentieth-century Chinese home and the discursive space of the early-twentieth-century Chinese journal were both constituted within the global context and contributed to the formation of global modernity. This is a central theme in the third section of the volume, "Gendered

Space and Global Context: Foreign Models, Circulating Concepts, and the Constitution of Female Subjectivities." In their opening reflection, Nathalie Cooke and Jennifer Garland, experts on the Canadian women's journal *Châtelaine*, for which they have created an intriguing database of advertisements, emphasize that the idealized self projected in women's journals can only be constructed in relation to an "Other."[29] In twentieth-century China, it was the global Other – in the form of successful Western nations, upright Japanese educators, intrepid French heroines, hygiene-savvy German bodies, but also Indian, African, and Southeast Asian counterfoils – that served as the transcultural backdrop to the expanding geographic and imaginative space of Chinese women's journals.

In "Competing Conceptualizations of *Guo* (Country, State, and/or Nation-State) in Late Qing Women's Journals," Nanxiu Qian highlights the multiplicity of global resources available to Chinese reformers at the turn of the twentieth century and the divergent political ends to which these resources could be put. Her focus is on the concept of *guo*, which could be translated as country, state, or nation, and which became increasingly salient in Chinese discourse in the face of international aggression from the mid-nineteenth century. In her integrated and vertical reading of two journals, Qian scrutinizes deliberations on the term in the first Chinese woman's journal, *Nü xuebao – Chinese Girl's Progress*, published in 1898 and its radical 1902–1903 successor, *Xuchu Nübao/Nü xuebao* (Continued publication of women's journal/Journal of women's learning). She argues that while the former drew on foreign intellectual resources in forging a cultural and humanitarian sense of *guo* and *aiguo* (to love the *guo*, i.e., patriotism), the latter took a more confrontational approach based on the Japanese Pan-Asianist notion of Social Darwinian conflict between the white and the yellow races. She thus illustrates that while the concepts of country, state, and nation-state were reconstituted within the new grammar of modernity, their local inflections were manifold.

Xia Xiaohong makes an important contribution to our understanding of the often vague notion of global cultural flows not only by tracking the presence of foreign figures in early-twentieth-century women's journals but also by tracing the route by which they traveled from the West via Japan to the pages of the Chinese periodical press. She thus draws our attention to second- and third-hand mediations in global modernity's grammatical inflections. Her focus in "Western Heroines in Late Qing Women's Journals: Meiji-Era Writings on 'Women's Self-Help' in China" is on what became a ubiquitous genre in women's journals: "biographies of foreign women." Their function in the language of modernity was to serve as models, but the way they were translated showed much variation. In her rich vertical, integrated, and situated reading, Xia highlights

---

[29] http://chatelaineads.mcgill.ca/browse.php. See also Cooke and Garland, "Putting Questions to Images."

the role of Japanese collections of Western heroines in expanding the geographical and historical space of the Chinese women's journal and, by extension, the imaginary of their female readers.

Joan Judge also traces concrete global flows of knowledge in "Foreign Knowledge of Bodies: Japanese Sources, Western Science, and China's Republican Lady." Her focus is on triangulating discourses on women's reproductive health that were often generated in Europe, mediated by Japan, and rearticulated in the Chinese women's press. Combining horizontal and situated perspectives, Judge examines both visual and discursive texts including foreign-influenced cover art, photographs of Western women, and translated texts on such topics as menstruation and childbirth. She argues that these foreign materials helped to make the female reproductive body a valid topic of inquiry in China's early-twentieth-century print media. They also implicitly acknowledged the complexity of women as physical and sexual beings.

Paul Bailey makes an important global detour in his chapter on "'Othering' the Foreign Other in Early-Twentieth-Century Chinese Women's Magazines." Rather than focus on the more familiar and pervasive Japanese sources and Western heroines, he examines how non-Western (particularly Asian) women were discursively represented in several women's magazines. In a combination of integrated and vertical readings, Bailey questions whether such representations might have been echoes of an early-twentieth-century Chinese revolutionary identification with China's Asian neighbors and, if so, how they might further suggest a questioning of "Euro-American centrality" and of the notions of Western "civilization" and "progress." This again illuminates the ways inflections of a particular global modern grammar come into being.

The last article in the volume demonstrates how the expanded and expanding space of the women's journal continued to develop into the early twenty-first century. Barbara Mittler examines how the newly established space of the women's magazines and the discursive options it had contributed to cultural memory would serve to expand the parameters of imagining the "New Woman" in the long twentieth century. In "The New (Wo)man and Her/His Others: Foreigners on the Pages of China's Women's Magazines," she scrutinizes the presence of foreigners on the pages of a series of women's magazines that are as generically diverse as they are chronologically distant – from *Women's World* in the first years of the century, through *Linloon Magazine* in the 1930s, *Zhongguo Funü* (Women of China, 1949–) founded at the inception of the People's Republic of China, and *Nongjianü baishitong – Rural Women Knowing All* (1993–) of relatively recent vintage. In her horizontal, integrated, and vertical readings, Mittler questions how the image and status of foreigners changed over this period of time and what this change can tell us about evolving perceptions of (wo)manhood (and the women's journals involved in its creation).

Harriet Evans, a prominent scholar of gender and sexuality in modern and contemporary China, reprises a number of the volume's themes in her conclusion. Evans also raises critical questions about the ultimate limits of the space of twentieth-century Chinese women's journals. This space was the site not only for new inclusions – most notably of global concepts, heroines, and images – but for longstanding exclusions. The ideal of Chinese woman that emerges in the pages of these publications was a restricted rather than a generic ideal, an ideal defined by a class and urban-centered silencing and absenting of the rural – in spite of the attempts by journals such as *Rural Women Knowing All* as discussed by Barbara Mittler. Instead of diminishing the importance of twentieth-century Chinese women's journals, her cogent observations further illuminate – as does the volume itself – the nature, the specificity, and the significance of a gendered "modernity in common" in the long twentieth century.

The Journals

The numerous women's journals discussed over the course of this volume both reflect and challenge received narratives about the unfolding of Chinese history from the late nineteenth through the twentieth century. Their close reading in the following chapters highlights a number of the major turning points in this period of unprecedentedly rapid change. It also illuminates the complexity of women's history, which was not merely affected by but integral to the profound political, social, cultural, and epistemological shifts in this era. Because the organization of the volume is not strictly chronological and because such a range of periodicals are discussed in different chapters, we provide a brief chronology and a bibliographic overview of the journals here for readers' reference. Further data on the various periodicals are available in the Appendix, as mentioned in detail below.

The first Chinese women's periodical, the 1898 *Chinese Girl's Progress*, appeared at a moment of opening to the idea of fundamental administrative, institutional, political, and educational change, a moment known as the One Hundred Days Reform. Founded at the height of this movement in the spring of 1898, the journal closed shortly after the Empress Dowager Cixi's September coup, which put an end to the hopeful one hundred days. Consistent with the ideals of the 1898 reform movement, *Chinese Girl's Progress* promoted a gradualist notion of reform that seamlessly drew on elements of the Confucian and Daoist traditions, together with newly imported Western ideas.

Four short years later, in the aftermath of the disastrous Boxer Rebellion (1900–1901), a more radical approach to both political change and women's roles within it emerged. This shift is salient in the *Continued Publication of*

Women's Journal/Journal of Women's Learning published in 1902 to 1903, in *Women's World* (1904–1907), and in a number of subsequent journals published up through the 1911 Revolution. These include the *Zhongguo xin nüjie zazhi* (Magazine of China's new world of women, 1907) and *Tianyi bao* – Journal of natural justice (1907–1908), both published in Tokyo. They also include *Nübao* (Women's journal), published in China in 1909, and *Shenzhou nübao* (China women's news, 1911–1912), which was published in the early hopeful months following the October 1911 Revolution.

The radical edge apparent in the journals published in the first decade of the twentieth century was attenuated both in political tone and in aspirations for women in what has been touted as China's first commercial women's journal, *The Women's Eastern Times* (1911–1917). Founded shortly before the October Revolution, *The Women's Eastern Times* and its imitators and successors, *The Ladies' Journal* (1915–1931) and *The Chung Hwa Women's Magazine* (1915–1916), were restricted by the harsh regulation of the periodical press under President Yuan Shikai in the early Republic. *The Ladies' Journal*, the longest running of these early Republican journals, outlived Yuan's regime, however, and became a barometer of subsequent political and cultural changes through the early 1930s.

The first of these changes was the New Culture Movement (1915–1925) and the related May Fourth Movement of 1919, which gave rise to a new cultural iconoclasm, a fervent social radicalism, and a new brand of Chinese nationalism. These changes are evident in the new editorship of the *Ladies' Journal* in the early 1920s and in the journal *Xin nüxing* (The new woman), which continued the *Ladies' Journal*'s radical agenda from 1926. After the Nationalists had some success in unifying warlord-torn China in 1927, beginning a period known as the Nanking Decade, the female-run and Nationalist affiliated *Funü gongming* (The woman's resonance) was founded in 1929.

These more politically focused women's journals had to compete with commercial entertainment journals in the 1930s, most notably the wildly popular *Linloon Magazine* (1931–1937). At the other end of the ideological spectrum, the Communists, who were resisting Nationalist rule in a number of base areas in the early 1930s and who would further consolidate their power after the completion of the Long March in 1935, founded their own women's journals. These include, most notably, *Women of China*, which was first published between 1939 and 1941 and then reappeared in a number of different iterations after 1949. The world of women's journalism has diversified significantly since the 1980s, and both franchise magazines such as *Elle* and specialized magazines, only for rural readers, such as *Rural Women Knowing All* came into being.

Appendix I contains basic bibliographical information about the Chinese women's journals referred to in the various chapters in the volume (and in the chronological overview above). Information provided includes the titles of the journals in Chinese and in English, the lifespans of the journals, places of publication, names of editors, and references to the chapters where particular journals are discussed in detail.

Part I

Methodologies: Framing, Constituting, and Regulating the Space of the Women's Journal

This section offers examples of three key methods of reading women's journals, or any other genre of periodicals. Julia F. Andrews reads the covers particularly of *The Ladies' Journal* over the span of two decades. Rather than simply employing a vertical reading, she uses the horizontal method in reading cover art against the respective journals' contents. In so doing, she not only traces an artistic trajectory but also highlights shifting editorial objectives over time. Liying Sun uses an integrated approach. Closely examining one particular family of journals, she demonstrates that "editorial agency" can only be fully understood if we read journals not as discrete works but as part of a larger constellation of publications. Michel Hockx offers a situated reading, which demonstrates the ways particular journals illuminate their broader historical context and the ways cultural politics have informed the historical reading of particular periodicals. His focus is on censorship and pornography: he specifically probes what the censorship of one allegedly obscene journal, *Eyebrow Talk*, tells us about the cultural politics of the time and enduring perceptions of pornography in China.

The brief reflection by Ellen Widmer that concludes this section of the book proposes another intertextual method of approaching women's journals. She does not focus on the content of actual women's periodicals but instead uses another genre of materials altogether – novels – to probe questions related to the perception, reception, and actual production of women's journals.

The method Ellen Widmer explores could potentially be used across the period covered in the volume – from the turn of the twentieth through the turn of the twenty-first century. Her focus is, however, on one brief moment at the beginning of this longer history. At this time, as later chapters by Grace Fong and Nanxiu Qian demonstrate, the Chinese "women's journal" was quite radical in tone and thus opened up and closed off certain spaces for women's reading and writing. Widmer uses three "women's novels" to gain insight into how this type of women's magazine was received.

1   Persuading with Pictures: Cover Art and *The Ladies' Journal* (1915–1931)

Julia F. Andrews

The covers of magazines are often dismissed as inconsequential wrapping paper, soon torn and tattered as they protect the more important contents within. Most libraries, indeed, discard them when they send the magazines to the bindery, and many reprint editions of historical materials fail to include them. The vivid effect of the object's transitory encounters with glancers and readers is thus lost in this transformation from the ephemeral into the permanent, as the conventions of preservation necessitate the conversion of magazines deemed worthwhile into hardbound books or microfilm.[1] This chapter, by surveying covers of women's magazines of the early Republican period, seeks to draw attention to the significance of these publications as material objects, and particularly to explore the visual images with which editors and publishers conveyed their ideas to their readers. *Funü zazhi – The Ladies' Journal*, as the longest running of these magazines (1915–1931) presents a good case for examination of the intersection between the concerns of magazine publishers and larger trends in society of the day (Figure 1.1).[2] These intersections become most apparent when we do an integrated reading of the covers of various magazines, a situated reading of the covers in the context of the shifting Chinese art world, and most importantly in the analysis that follows, a horizontal reading of *The Ladies' Journal* covers against its content.

The Object

The Ladies' Journal, published by the Commercial Press, was one of nineteen new journals created by the press shortly before and after the 1911 Republican revolution to satisfy and profit from public demand for reading matter on

---

[1] Digitization of as yet unbound and unmicrofilmed magazines has the potential for preserving the color images, but it obviously cannot bring back those already discarded. Our project database, "Chinese Women's Magazines" (womag.uni-hd.de), attempts to retrieve lost covers for the journals under scrutiny there.

[2] This essay has relied upon original issues of the magazine in the collections of the University of California and Shanghai Municipal Library, a reprint edition in 72 volumes (Shanghai Funü zazhi she, ed,), as well as on photographs and scans collected from libraries around the world by the project's intrepid research assistants, Doris Sung and Liying Sun. See the project database, "Chinese Women's Magazines."

Fig. 1.1 Cover of *The Ladies' Journal*, 1:1 (1915): painting by Xu Yongqing

modern subjects. From about the turn of the twentieth century, the expanding use of modern printing technology and Western paper by Chinese publishers introduced new formats and sizes, yielding tactile and visual changes that presented editors with unprecedented potential, as well as challenges. Most notably, with the birth of magazines on the Western model and their stiff paper covers came the opportunity, and the competitive necessity, for cover images and text that would most effectively communicate with the magazine's anticipated readership. Over its seventeen-year history, the editors and artists of *The Ladies' Journal* evolved a range of conceptual and practical responses to the challenges presented by the new cover format and new technological possibilities.

Until the twentieth century, Chinese books were generally printed on soft Chinese paper from large wooden blocks, with the individual pages folded at the outer edge. Each fascicle of the book was tightly bound with thread and usually protected by a plain paper or cloth cover. On the exterior, there was little to distinguish one volume from another, other than the vertical paper label on which the title might appear, usually in hand-brushed calligraphy.[3] Volumes

---

[3] Paper covers were usually off-white or indigo blue. Occasionally, elite bibliophiles might use figured brocades for their outer wrappers, but most books had a practical plain blue or beige fabric.

Fig. 1.2 Cover of *Dianshizhai Pictorial*, 128 (1887.8.xia)

in a set of books were usually protected on four of their six faces with stiff wrappers constructed from hand-made paperboard that was lined with good paper and faced on the outside with blue cotton. The sets were distinguished only by a paper label and the bone, ivory, or jade fasteners used to close the wrapping case and were shelved horizontally so that one would see the exposed white ends of the pages rather than the binding or the cover.

Some of the earliest modern periodicals produced in China, such as the *Dianshizhai Pictorial* (1884–1898), which was photolithographically printed on soft Chinese paper, were distributed with pages unbound and folded in a colored paper wrapper that was printed with the periodical's title, price, and issue number and a brief advertisement of its contents (Figure 1.2). Periodicals of the next generation, in contrast, began to present readers with an aesthetic founded on international models, but modified to the extent deemed necessary by its editors. *Women's World* began by closely following Japanese periodical design of the day, with an attractive but simple two-color design printed in red and

Fig. 1.3 Cover of *Women's World*, 1 (Jan. 1904)

gold on a white background (Figure 1.3). Curved lines and two small clusters of flowers frame the large characters of the magazine title, hand-brushed from right to left in a legible but relaxed *kaishu* (standard script). This cover, its imagery similar to that of Art Nouveau commercial art in the United States, Europe, and Japan, is elegant, refined, and stylish. The influence of a European enthusiasm for Japonisme in the formation of Art Nouveau makes this style modern in a way that is simultaneously international and Asian. Although the text of the magazine's title, *Women's World*, states its intention, it does not, in its inaugural issue, yet speak to gender in visual terms.

The Women's Eastern Times broke new ground in the conceptual richness and visual coherence of its full-color cover designs.[4] With its first issue, published just before the Republican revolution, the editors established a standard for the

---

[4] Carol C. Chin ("Translating the New Woman") has taken note of these covers to address a different argument. They are also closely analyzed in Judge, *Republican Lens*, Chapter 3. For color images of many of the covers, see our repository at https://doi.org/10.25354/2017.06.1 and the database "Chinese Women's Magazines."

Fig. 1.4 Cover of *The Women's Eastern Times*, 1 (June 11, 1911): painting by Xu Yongqing

magazine's subsequent imagery and design. Commercial artist Xu Yongqing (1880–1953), who was trained in the Jesuit painting atelier associated with the orphanage at Xujiahui, depicted two girls looking happily at the cover of the inaugural issue of *The Women's Eastern Times* (Figure 1.4). A full-page color reproduction of a watercolor painting, it carries a strong sense of narrative – as though caught in a spontaneous moment, one girl has tucked a small Western-style book under her arm and is avidly listening to her friend, who holds the magazine with two hands to better display and inspect its cover. That cover, of course, is the same one, depicting the same two girls looking at it. If carried to its logical conclusion, the image would repeat infinitely, like a hall of mirrors. The difference between this fictional self-portrait of the magazine and that implied optical reality is that here the present and the future coexist in the same space. Moreover, as spectators, our viewpoint is identical to that of the cover girls who are looking at the magazine, suggesting that we are they, or vice versa.

In simplest terms, this striking conceit simultaneously signifies both the potential readership of the magazine, literate young women, and its subject matter. Indeed, as a marketing statement, Xu Yongqing's cover image conveys to potential buyers and subscribers how completely *The Women's Eastern Times* aims to serve its readers, with this visual trick totally eradicating the distinction between contents and audience, the magazine world and that of reality.

A systematic cover program reinforced this visual definition of the magazine – that it was both for and about young women. Each issue of the journal bears a different image, but the entire run, at least through 1916, shares a consistent theme – images of young Chinese women enjoying their daily lives – and a consistent Western style of illustration.[5] These are young women who do not always stay at home, and the covers demonstrate in pictorial terms the many possibilities, from reading to aviation, that might occupy the minds and lives of readers at the dawn of China's new era. The cover of issue four continues the publisher's clever self-promotion, with an image of a girl relaxing in a garden chair reading a newspaper, probably intended to be the magazine's sibling, the daily *Shibao – The Eastern Times*. Continuing to emphasize the desire of modern girls to read modern periodicals, the visually reduplicative cover of issue 13 (1914) takes as its subject a well-dressed young woman gazing intently through a shop window at two rows of magazines on display (Figure 1.5). Readers will immediately recognize that the objects of her interest, depicted with legible cover images, are prior issues of *The Women's Eastern Times*. The successful establishment of the visual identity of the brand is proclaimed in this painted image. Those who conceived and approved these covers, whether the publisher, his editors, or an art editor such as Xu Yongqing, clearly emphasized the communicative potential of the visual on their covers.

These were not the only Shanghai publishers of the day to headline their editorial agenda with cover design. A more flamboyant effort that survived for fourteen months and seventeen issues was *Zhenxiang huabao* (True record), founded by artists and revolutionary activists Gao Jianfu and Gao Qifeng early in 1912.[6] Lavishly printed on high-quality paper, its complex covers, printed in rich colors and even gold, survive as extravagant celebrations of the victory of the revolutionary movement (Figure 1.6). Printed by the Shangwen printing house, the covers created a grand impression that emphasized the seriousness of the publishers' political and artistic agenda. This idealistically conceived periodical took its cultural mission as primary and financial concerns as secondary. Faced with loss of their subsidy from the Nationalist Party after Yuan Shikai

---

[5] Some of the later illustrations were done by Shen Bochen (1889–1920), who was also trained at the Jesuit painting workshop, and whose style of cover illustration is similar to that of Xu Yongqing. In the final publication year, 1917, the editors used a Chinese painting of figures in antique garb on the cover of issue 21. On Shen and on this final cover see Judge, *Republican Lens*, Chapter 3.

[6] Although the magazine is considered influential, its editorial approach, combining politics and art, seems to better reflect the editors' personal interests than those of a larger Shanghai audience. Perhaps most difficult, from the perspective of its commercial viability, were its expensive production values.

Fig. 1.5 Cover of *The Women's Eastern Times*, 13 (April 1, 1914): painting by Xu Yongqing

Fig. 1.6 Cover of *The True Record*, 12 (1912): painting by Gao Qifeng

began centralizing his power, however, its editors were forced to close it after the March 1913, issue, when funding collapsed.

The Company

In contrast to this important but short-lived publication effort, *The Ladies' Journal* survived for a decade and a half (1915–1931). The history of its parent, the Commercial Press, from 1897 to 1948, spans the birth and development of graphic design in China, and the evolving appearance of its publications testifies to the growing importance of a professional practice that operated at the intersection of art, commerce, and persuasion. Over the decade of its Sino-Japanese partnership, 1904 to 1913, the press experimented with letterpress and advanced photographic printing, and it subsequently expanded its repertory to include color lithography, copper engraving, collotype printing, and three-color copper engraving.[7] Technicians from Japan and the United States were engaged to develop the capacity for sophisticated use of color with newly purchased equipment. By the time *The Ladies' Journal* was established in 1915, the press had a decade of experience with the highly successful *Dongfang zazhi – The Eastern Miscellany*, established 1904, and *Jiaoyu zazhi– The Chinese Educational Review*, established 1909.[8] In 1909, Commercial Press even produced its own *kaishu* type fonts. Its magazines, printed with moveable type on Western paper in the modern magazine format, had stapled bindings and stiff paper covers.

The First Designer

In 1913, after the appearance of Xu Yongqing's striking covers for *The Women's Eastern Times*, the Commercial Press engaged him to head its illustration department (*tuhuabu*).[9] Xu had co-authored a middle school drawing textbook for the firm as early as 1902.[10] At this chronological junction, however, it may have been more important that he had developed the appealing visual image that gave the cover of *The Women's Eastern Times* its look. When the new

---

[7] Reed, *Gutenberg in Shanghai*, 199; Reynolds, *China*, 121–3; Ip, "A Hidden Chapter," 23–44.

[8] See Zhang Jinglu, "Shangwu yinshuguan," 557–9.

[9] Soon after he was hired as head of Commercial Press's illustration department in 1913, Xu Yongqing began teaching interns at the press to do watercolor painting and drawing. His two earliest disciples, He Yimei and Ling Shuren, succeeded him as leaders of the publisher's art department in 1915 when Xu left to join the faculty at Shanghai Art Academy. Other students included men now famous for their *yuefenpai* tobacco advertisements, such as Hang Zhiying, Jin Meisheng, and Jin Xuechen, as well as renowned illustrator Ge Xianglan. *Shanghai meishu zhi*, 406. Also see Chen and Feng, *Old Advertisements*, 25–29.

[10] See Laing, *Selling Happiness*, 127, for reference to Xu Yongqing and Odake Takunobu, *Zhongxue yong qianbi huatie*; see also Chen and Feng, *Old Advertisements*, 27.

magazine *The Ladies' Journal* appeared on the stands, it announced its intention to compete with *The Women's Eastern Times* in unmistakable terms: its cover images in the first year were a series of twelve images by the same experienced illustrator, Xu Yongqing, which featured young women engaged in various activities of daily life.

Although the Chinese title of *The Ladies' Journal* was placed in the margin above the illustration rather than superimposed on the image, as in the earlier journal, the hand of the artist was unmistakable and the compositional concept identical. Perhaps the only thing that differentiated the young women on the first twelve covers of *The Ladies' Journal* from their sisters on the first twenty issues of *The Women's Eastern Times* was the somewhat less adventurous nature of their activities.

Readers of *The Women's Eastern Times* had encountered many cover images of women who were outside the home, and engaged in specifically modern activities – walking to school, playing tennis, walking dogs, photographing, fishing with rod and reel, posting a letter, donning white gloves, and watching an airplane. The covers of this magazine thus generally describe a world of modern women who were literate, creative, independent, athletic, and mainly urban. The texts on the interior pages are further supplemented by an assortment of images to inspire the imagination – princesses, concubines, female artists, and woman aviators.

Over the course of the first twelve issues of *The Ladies' Journal*, Xu Yongqing presented a spectrum of more ordinary women and differentiated the look of *The Ladies' Journal* from that of *The Women's Eastern Times* by his concentration on images of women at home. The first issue announces itself and its potential readers with a girl reading in an urban garden, the red brick wall behind her suggesting that the setting is a modern city and her calm concentration testifying to her enjoyment of the solitary pleasure offered by the book in her hand (cf. Figure 1.1). Although to our eyes today her clothing looks "traditional," in the context of her time, and in contrast to many of the cover illustrations to subsequent issues, her garments are particularly colorful and stylish – the green fabric of her skirt is echoed in the artfully exposed inner face of her tunic's high collar, displaying it as a carefully designed matched set. On all twelve covers of volume one, the same masthead, *Funü zazhi*, proceeds in large standard script calligraphy from right to left across the top margin of the page. The date, volume, and issue number are arrayed vertically in the left margin and the government registration and publisher's name appear at right. Below the illustration is printed in four small characters a poetic Chinese title for the cover image. In a small font, the alternate title *The Ladies' Journal* is printed in English below the illustration title.

The young woman on the cover of issue two, even more colorfully garbed, is painting, her tools at her side and her watercolor paper tacked to her tilted

Fig. 1.7 Cover of *The Ladies' Journal*, 1:2 (1915): painting by Xu Yongqing

drafting board (Figure 1.7). She works in a Western-style interior, with an electric light overhead and an ornate clock on the wall. Equally significantly, she is painting in the Western manner, and tacked on the wall to her right appears a completed watercolor landscape painting. Beside her on the table is a square, indicating her familiarity with geometry, a subject introduced in the previous issue and considered the most important scientific foundation of Western perspective. A pamphlet at the edge of her table suggests the benefits of using instructional manuals of the kind that Commercial Press offered on the market and that the cover artist had himself authored. Artist-designer Xu Yongqing has simultaneously brought to the attention of readers a number of his editors' stated goals: to promote women's art – a topic discussed at length in Doris Sung's chapter in this volume – to emphasize useful scientific principles, to facilitate understanding of Western culture, and to demonstrate the varied occupations of women. "Art," the editors declared in issue one, "is our national essence, but women's art, particularly that of modern times, rarely reaches readers. If the magazine can collect examples of their artistic achievements it will be a grand event for women." Moreover, the editors noted that they had added an additional column on art to their original plan of twelve thematic sections, and particularly sought submissions of painting, calligraphy, embroidery, epigraphy, and music.[11]

Bridging the gap from ideas with the authority of antiquity to those that might herald modernity was still an awkward process for the editorial team in the second decade of the twentieth century. Moreover, the definition of the newly translated term for art, *meishu*, remained in flux.[12] Perhaps acknowledging that Europe prized artistic activities that had never achieved significant status in China, the art (*meishu*) section aimed to expand the boundaries of Chinese critical theory beyond the high arts of ink painting and calligraphy. In issue one, editor Chunnong (Wang Yunzhang) stated that his project was inspired by shortcomings in the two earlier histories of women's artistic accomplishments, *Yutai shushi* (Calligraphy from the jade terrace) by Li E (1692–1752) and *Yutai huashi* (Painting from the jade terrace) by Tang Shuyu, which were limited to women's painting and calligraphy.[13] He thus combed the art (*yishu*) section of the *Siku Quanshu* (The complete library in four sections) for additional examples. The result, organized biographically into the same categories as its source, still included many women famous as calligraphers and painters, but also three Qing dynasty artists in other fields – Gao Mei, a composer for the *qin* (a seven-stringed zither), Han Yuesu, a seal-carver, and Gu Erniang, an ink-stone carver – along with three more ancient women, Gongsun Daniang, a Tang dynasty sword-dancer, Huang Daopo, a Yuan dynasty weaver, and Lu Meiniang, a Tang dynasty embroiderer. Issue two summarized biographical entries for eleven painters and calligraphers, along with one composer, one seal carver, and one embroiderer. The articles may have served their purpose of informing young women of these earlier histories and of the names and notable reputations of a few of their predecessors, but they did not succeed in expanding upon the Jade Terrace histories in any significant way and were dropped in later issues. The question of women's artistic production remained

---

[11] The essay begins by noting that the magazine was planned with twelve columns, but had added two more: *meishu* (art) and *jizai* (reports). Two other thrusts of the essay were investigation of the status of women's schools and translations that would bring information about Western culture.

[12] The word *meishu* was a Japanese adaptation (*bijutsu*) of the European "Fine Arts" that is believed to have first appeared in 1872 in Japanese instructions for the Vienna Exposition. It appeared in Japanese institutional names, the Kobu bijutsu gakkô (Ministry of Technology School of Fine Arts), established in 1876, and the Tokyo bijutsu gakkô (Tokyo School of Fine Arts), established in 1889. By 1911, a major art-historical anthology, *Meishu congshu*, which would later include ceramics and textiles, had begun publication in China, and the following year the awkwardly named Shanghai tuhua meishu yuan (literally, Shanghai Fine Arts Academy of Painting, hereafter called Shanghai Art Academy) was established. As Ogawa (13–14, 17) noted, "Asia did not have a concept of fine arts that encompassed painting, sculpture, architecture, and craft until the modern era."

[13] Li E, *Yutai*; Tang Shuyu, *Yutai*. For an article on the Jade Terrace texts, see Ma Yazhen, "Cong 'Yutai shushi.'"

Fig. 1.8 Cover of *The Ladies' Journal*, 1:3 (1915): painting by Xu Yongqing

important to the editorial agenda, however, and pages with black-and-white or color reproductions of paintings by female artists were bound into each issue, along with photographs of girl's school principals and other notable figures in the world of literate women. These pages were printed on more expensive coated paper for better results than could be obtained on the rougher paper used for the text.

In issue three, the art section was given over to a three-part series on embroidery, and Xu Yongqing's cover again highlights the contents of the journal by depicting a young woman earnestly bending over her needlework (Figure 1.8). The setting is the interior of a traditional house, its floor paved with rectangular grey tiles, the embroiderer's work mounted on a simple frame and illuminated by diagonal rays of natural light that filter into her high-ceilinged room. We move outside on the April cover, where pink blossoms in the distance evoke springtime and, to continue the theme of silk working, a young countrywoman picks mulberry leaves to feed silk worms. Expanding the female occupations rendered on previous *The Ladies' Journal* covers, Xu Yongqing depicts a pair of girls picking tea leaves on the cover of issue five, suggesting their contributions to the gustatory pleasures of the urban population (Figure 1.9).

Fig. 1.9 Cover of *The Ladies' Journal*, 1:5 (1915): painting by Xu Yongqing

Injecting the most prosaic housework with a touch of romance in issue six, a girl washing clothes on the bank of a stream is depicted gazing poetically at the flight of distant geese. We return to the domestic interior in issue seven to find a girl spinning thread in an expansive home with grey tile floors of traditional architecture (Figure 1.10a). The settings in the cover illustrations for issues eight through eleven may be metropolitan, but are sufficiently generalized to be typical of the aspirations of a wide range of potential readers. Ensuring that cuisine is not neglected, issue eight's cover girl slices vegetables in a comfortable but simply furnished Chinese kitchen, with a steaming wok behind her (Figure 1.10b). The cover images return to a thoroughly Western interior and a new Western occupation with issue nine, on the cover of which appears a nurse, garbed in crisp white uniform, preparing medicine (Figure 1.10c). Like all the interiors depicted on these covers, the setting is clean and hygienic. The matron on the cover of issue ten sits in a tidy room with dark woodwork, a hardwood floor, and a stone outdoor patio, presumably an elegant urban residence (Figure 1.10d). The labor of the cover girls on the last three issues of the year returns to textile production. The one on issue eleven stitches fabric, her basket and scissors at her side. Finally, on the cover of issue twelve, a pretty girl

Fig. 1.10 Covers of *The Ladies' Journal*, 1:7–10 (1915): paintings by Xu Yongqing

婦 女 雜 誌

(聲機影傻)
THE LADIES' JOURNAL (Issued Monthly)

Fig. 1.11 Cover of *The Ladies' Journal*, 1:12 (1915): painting by Xu Yongqing

wearing the blue tunic and black skirt typical of Xu Yongqing's traditionally attired women turns towards us from her seat at a large loom (Figure 1.11). The oil lamp behind her contrasts with the electric light illustrated on the cover of issue two. Six of the images are rendered in modern metropolitan settings: the other six women are placed in more traditional Chinese rooms that could be almost anywhere in the Yangzi River valley area – in Shanghai's old city, in Suzhou, or in any one of the prosperous smaller cities of the region.

Although published in Shanghai, and painted by an artist who had grown up in the rural suburbs of the city, the generalized images on the covers of this first volume are not primarily urban and seem targeted to the wider geographic reach of the Commercial Press's network of thirty-six branch booksellers in cities, large and small, throughout China. Indeed, Xu Yongqing's illustrations echo the editorial postscript to the first issue. Perhaps most important, their variety and careful balance of setting and occupation suggest the national scope of the publication's aim: "Our country is very large, and the situation in every different region is different. We will be grateful to writers who can carefully explain the customs and professions of your areas."[14]

Equally important, Xu Yongqing's covers are directly related to topics specifically mentioned by the editors in the respective issues of the journal – hygiene, home management, handicrafts, and cuisine – and they echo the mutually reinforcing relationship between the magazine's contents and the advertisements for Commercial Press publications on its pages. Reading horizontally, we realize that in the first issue the ads introduce texts specifically for girls on Chinese literature, moral cultivation, and choral music, as well as a range of general textbooks – elementary arithmetic, Chinese, and ethics, and secondary science, geography, history, mathematics, and Chinese – along with edifying works on hygiene and poetry, an English–Chinese dictionary, travel guides for China, Shanghai, and West Lake, diaries, household budgets, handicraft and sewing manuals, letter-writing manuals, reproductions of Tang, Song, Yuan, and Ming calligraphers' writings, maps of the European war, and art products – art and photography albums, art reproductions, and postcards.

The first year's covers for *The Ladies' Journal* thus established an identity for the magazine, displaying the range of modern and traditional women who would form its subject matter. Whether all of them, the pickers of tea and mulberry leaves, the embroiderer, the spinner, and the weaver, were likely to read this magazine is less certain, but the images created by Xu Yongqing and the magazine's claims that art is the national essence both aimed to elevate the status of women's work in the eyes of male and female readers alike.

A distinctive, and sometimes even disorienting, new cover look was introduced for every one of the first five years of the magazine, and each, in its own way, contributed to the editorial agenda. In the second year, 1916, the focus of the color images changes from women as subject matter to art made by women. Each of the covers features a rectangular full-color reproduction of a Chinese painting framed by a complex botanical arabesque. Like that of the first year, the design is essentially Western, but it now assumes a hybrid form. The Chinese masthead appears in the decorative clerical script popular among enthusiasts of epigraphy in Shanghai, balanced below by its large English title set in a curvilinear Art Nouveau font to match the background ornament (Figure 1.12).

The artist of the bird-and-flower paintings on the cover of issues seven and eight (Figure 1.13) was Jin Zhang (Jin Taotao; 1884–1939), the British-educated daughter of a prominent Zhejiang family (also discussed in Sung's chapter). She had studied in Shanghai, England, and France by this time, but was talented in Chinese painting, thus exemplifying a certain ideal of the well-educated cosmopolitan Chinese woman. Her older brother, the legal expert Jin Cheng (1878–1926), a former Qing official who continued to serve in the new

---

[14] *The Ladies' Journal* 1. 1 (1915): 202 (yuxing 14).

Fig. 1.12 Cover of *The Ladies' Journal*, 2:6 (1916): painting by Lou Tong

Fig. 1.13 Cover of *The Ladies' Journal*, 2:8 (1916): painting by Jin Zhang

Republic, recruited her to teach in the vigorous traditionalist painting group he led in early Republican period Beijing. She would go on to exhibit her paintings in major national and international exhibitions of the 1920s and 1930s and was best known for her paintings of fish. Flower paintings such as this were well regarded as well.[15]

Oddly, although the artists of the painting reproductions that appear in the magazine are usually listed in the captions and the table of contents, those who painted the cover images are rarely identified, and, as is more common, the art editor in charge is never mentioned. The artist of the central cover image for the first half of 1916, six different bird-and-flower album leaves, may be read from signatures and seals as the still unidentified, but possibly female, Lou Tong (sobriquet Hongye ciren, Poet of Red Leaves). Xu's and Jin's paintings also bear legible signatures, but most cover paintings and designs are anonymous. Nevertheless, by virtue of the signed paintings on some covers, the theme of women artists is conspicuous, and a Western Art Nouveau design is established as the magazine's new look. This pattern survives into 1917, when black-and-white reproductions of Chinese narrative paintings become the ornamental centerpiece of the fussy floral design (Figure 1.14).

In the issues of 1918 and 1919, however, there is a conceptual shift in a more Asian aesthetic direction. The featured artist in volume four, 1918, was the famous woman painter Wu Shujuan (1853–1930) (Figure 1.15). Primarily a painter of landscapes, a traditionally masculine genre, she was paired by admirers with the renowned male painter Wu Changshi (1844–1927) as "the two Wu."[16] Her reputation was furthered by the selection of her work for exhibition in an international exposition held in Rome in 1910. These twelve covers thus demonstrate the accomplishments of a Chinese woman artist notable on the international stage.[17]

Thematically, therefore, the covers take Wu Shujuan as a model to demonstrate the potential of women creative artists, but simultaneously put forth a larger argument about the position of Chinese culture in the international milieu. Moreover, from an artistic perspective, they mark a shift in approach that parallels larger trends in the Shanghai art world of the day. Unlike the paintings on the covers of volumes two and three, which were subordinated to a dominating Western-style commercial design, the Wu Shujuan covers foreground her work, monumental Chinese landscape paintings, as high art. The

---

[15] Reproductions of Jin Zhang's paintings appear frequently on the pages of *Yilin xunkan*, *Yilin yuekan*, and *Hushe yuekan*, publications of art societies with which she was associated, as well as in the women's magazines. Her 1922 treatise on fish painting, *Haoliang zhile ji*, was reprinted in 1985. For more on her career see Lü Peng, "Hushe yanjiu," 16, 63, 133.

[16] Ho, *Biographical Dictionary*, 234.

[17] For a preliminary study of this aspect of Wu Shujuan's career, see David, "Making Visible Feminine Modernities."

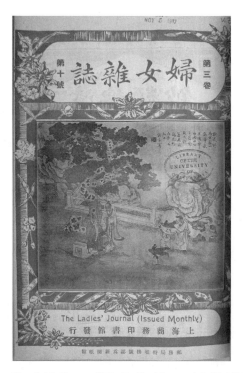

Fig. 1.14 Cover of *The Ladies' Journal*, 3:10 (1917)

cover has now banished the previous Art Nouveau ornaments, replacing them with a plain background design that, in totality, suggests the effect of a Chinese painting. Around the black and white vertical landscape image is printed a simple border of textile patterns in a single subtle hue of green, yellow, or grey, as though to form the silken borders of a traditionally mounted painting. The Chinese masthead is in a plain, handwritten standard *kaishu* script, and the English title has retreated to a small strip below the painting.

This emphasis on fine arts over commercial art on these covers shows changes occurring in the Chinese art world making their way into the pages of the journal. The Shanghai Art Academy, which opened in 1913, was founded as a school of Western painting, but in practice, this meant commercial art – the skills in drawing, watercolor, and oil painting that would enable artists to work as illustrators and designers in the new Shanghai publishing industry and theatre world. From 1915, its faculty included Xu Yongqing and Shen Bochen. However, with the increasingly widespread acceptance of Cai Yuan-pei's theories of aesthetic education, which were published in 1917, as well as the return from study in Japan of several men who taught at the academy,

Fig. 1.15 Cover of *The Ladies' Journal*, 4:7 (1918): painting by Wu Shujuan

the modernizers in the Shanghai art world quickly realized that this school for commercial art did not fulfill the more elevating role of an academy of fine arts.[18] From 1918, Shanghai Art Academy, which began to supply the publishing industry with talent, also took the lead in promoting new style art education. It was soon followed by establishment of the Beijing Art Academy and the implementation of co-education in both schools in 1919.

In accordance with these developments, the journal's focus on fine art covers in 1918 would continue in the 1919 issues, which reproduce figure paintings by the famous nineteenth-century Shanghai-school painter of elegant women Hu Xigui (1839–1883). The two volumes of *The Ladies' Journal*, which reproduce high-quality Chinese paintings rather than commercial art on their covers, are thus in harmony with both the overall aims of the magazine and broader trends in art circles of the day.

[18] For one such text see Cai Yuanpei, "On Replacing Religion with Aesthetic Education."

Fig. 1.16 Cover of *The Ladies' Journal*, 6:5 (1920): painting by Zhou Li, dated 1801

Perhaps considering that bird-and-flower paintings were common subjects for female painters, the art department turned back to this theme as the central cover image of the 1920 issues, publishing paintings dated 1801 by Zhou Li (Figure 1.16). By 1920 the interior pages were more fully decorated with line drawings, and almost every section or article was supplied with an ornamental header. Even the photographs of paintings on the covers are now ornamented with a pale figural border, somewhat incongruously depicting little boys holding sets of string-bound books overhead as they dance on fluttering ribbons. The covers of volumes four through six (1918–1920) span the three major genres of Chinese classical painting, namely landscape, figures, and birds-and-flowers. In May of 1919, Luo Jialun published a scathing critique of the Commercial Press magazines, including *The Ladies' Journal*, which led the press to reconsider its editorial strategy.[19] During this period, 1919–1920, Wang Yun-zhang implemented a shift from classical Chinese to the newly fashionable *baihua* (colloquial) language, and, to satisfy demand for new content, staff

---

[19] Nivard, 39–40. Luo Jialun, "Jinri Zhongguo."

Fig. 1.17 Cover of *The Ladies' Journal*, 7:5 (1921)

writer Shen Yanbing (best known under his pen name Mao Dun) was asked to contribute articles on women's issues.[20] Wang Yunzhang's last two years as editor of the journal, however, show no dramatic break with the magazine's previous graphic design.

The Radical Era

In contrast, the term of new editors Zhang Xichen and Zhou Jianren in 1921 was launched by a strikingly ornamental cover, a single image used for an entire year (Figure 1.17). The magazine's designers turned away from the focus on the high art of Chinese painting that had dominated recent volumes and returned to an image made as a commercial ornamentation. The elegant drawing, a peacock framed by the moon, is decorative and cosmopolitan, suggesting an exoticism in which East Asian and Western viewers might equally partake. Most conspicuously, it is not identifiably Chinese. The most radical change in the magazine's look, however, occurred in the following year, 1922, with more experimental and less consistent visual ideas at work and a conspicuously greater emphasis

[20] See Wang, *Women in the Chinese Enlightenment*, 78–84.

Fig. 1.18 Cover of *The Ladies' Journal*, 8:4 (1922): special issue on divorce

on text than image. The table of contents began to appear on the cover for the first time, even replacing the cover image. Issue four of volume eight announced a special issue on divorce with a plain but bright red-and-white checked cover on which no other image was attempted (Figure 1.18).

Reading horizontally, one sees that these changes on the cover are congruous with changes inside the journal: Under Zhang Xichen, the magazine shifted to more controversial aspects of feminism, including women's sexual emancipation, while deemphasizing the practical aspects of family life, child-rearing, and housekeeping that were found in earlier issues.[21] This stance, developed in the context of New Culture theoretical and social ferment and in response to attacks on the magazine for conservatism, is not directly reflected by images on the magazine's covers. What may be notable is what is *not* on the covers. First, the revival of Chinese paintings as cover motifs between 1916 and 1920 completely ceases. For 1923, editors Zhang and Zhou settled on a stark unfigured cover. As though needing nothing to attract readers beyond its sophisticated contents, the cover eschewed visual complexity and had no decoration other

---

[21] Shiao, "Printing, Reading, and Revolution," 61.

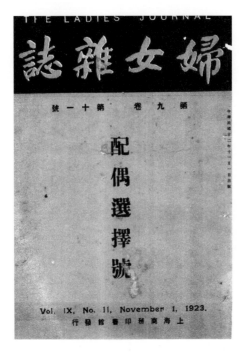

Fig. 1.19 Cover of *The Ladies' Journal*, 9:11 (1923): special issue on choosing a spouse

than plain color and straightforwardly laid out words. An editorial innovation of this period was the frequent publication of thematic special issues. Number eleven of 1923, for example, announced the title of one such number – Choosing a Spouse, in black type against a bright blue background (Figure 1.19). It is not currently known who designed such covers, but they are broadly in keeping with the simplified functional designs promoted by the Bauhaus and other European proponents of modern design in the same period.

The last two years of Zhang and Zhou's editorship were devoted to pushing the boundaries of conventional thinking even farther, but the pair chose not to carry forward a similar revolution in cover design. All twelve issues of 1924 (volume 10) were decorated with comfortable images of paired birds on a flowering branch signed by the male artist Li Licheng (1881–1942) (Figure 1.20). Li, a contemporary painter from Shaoxing, was a maternal cousin of the magazine's editor Zhou Jianren and his more famous brothers Lu Xun (Zhou Shuren) and Zhou Zuoren.

The year 1925 opened with the special issue that would eventually cost Zhang Xichen his editorship – The New Sexual Morality. The covers of some

Fig. 1.20 Cover of *The Ladies' Journal*, 10:2 (1924): painting by Li Lichen

of the 1925 issues were strikingly new – bold and lyrical versions of Art Deco botanical motifs possibly stimulated by art world excitement about the International Exhibition of Decorative Art soon to open in Paris (Figure 1.21).[22] This Asian version of Art Deco was most brilliantly displayed in the designs of Sugiura Hisui (1876–1965), the lead designer for the Mitsukoshi department store and a pioneer of Japanese graphic design. Work such as his seems to have inspired a number of Japan-oriented Shanghai designers, including Feng Zikai (1898–1975). This striking and innovative cover style suggested similarly forward-looking contents.

The magazine covers chosen during the term of Zhang Xichen and Zhou Jianren are as simple as the ideological issues raised in the magazine's text are profound. In contrast, the interior pages followed a course of increasing visual complexity. The upper margin of the table of contents typically published lyrical landscape drawings, and almost every section and in some cases every article was decorated by an ornamental line drawing, usually in an Art Nouveau style. The most elaborate chapter headings drew attention to articles by Zhang

[22] The cover of *The Ladies' Journal* 11.3 (1925) is signed by an as-yet-unidentified artist, Ke, and no. 11 by Xiang, perhaps Commercial Press staff artist Ge Xianglan, who had trained under Xu Yongqing.

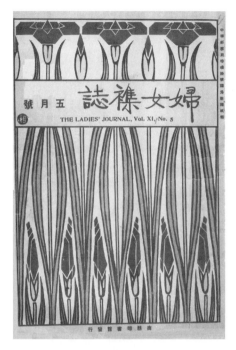

Fig. 1.21 Cover of *The Ladies' Journal*, 11:5 (1925): design by "Xiang"

Xichen himself: "What Is the New Sexual Morality?"[23] in the special issue of the same title (Figure 1.22) and "The Female Student's World View," in the special issue on woman students.[24] Special issues routinely had additional title pages, which were often ornately decorated. They were not particularly avant-garde by international standards, some reminiscent of Aubrey Beardsley, but they remained entirely "Western" in look.

Modern graphic and book design began to separate themselves somewhat from illustration and advertising in the mid- and late 1920s. With the appearance of Art Deco, and later Bauhaus- and Constructivist-inspired designs, the second half of the 1920s was the period when a fully cosmopolitan modernist look began to appear regularly in Shanghai publications.[25] Zhou Jianren's brother, Lu Xun (1881–1936), was one of the earliest editors to concern himself seriously with cover design.[26] He had insisted on providing his own

[23] *The Ladies' Journal* 11.1 (1925), special issue on the New Sexual Morality, 16.
[24] *The Ladies' Journal* 11.6 (1925), reprint, 662.
[25] For good examples, see Minick and Ping, *Chinese Graphic*.
[26] The completeness with which Lu Xun's diaries survive has enabled reconstruction of a particularly good picture of his activity. For further sources see Andrews, "Commercial Art," 191–192.

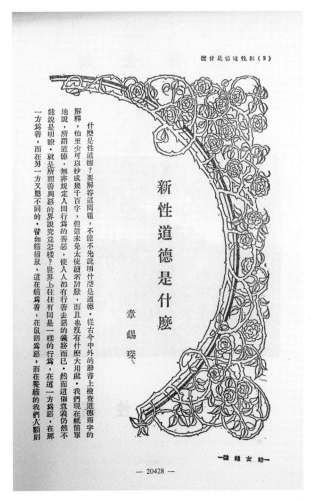

Fig. 1.22 "What Is the New Sexual Morality?" *The Ladies' Journal*, 11:1 (1925)

cover designs for some of his early book publications, including his 1909 *Stories from Foreign Lands* and his 1923 translation *Peach-Colored Cloud*, and soon after began commissioning young artists to design covers for some of his books and magazines. One of his favorite designers was Tao Yuanqing (1893–1929), whose work was simple and direct, sometimes with a slight Japanese flavor, and who avoided the fussy Victorian styles that characterized early-twentieth-century Chinese magazines, including *The Ladies' Journal* issues of

Fig. 1.23 Cover of *The Ladies' Journal*, 11:3 (1925): design by "Ke"

the 1910s. The 1925 covers of *The Ladies' Journal* are similarly in the new, more direct and simple cosmopolitan style (see Figure 1.23).

By end of the 1920s, when the journal was edited by Du Jiutian, *The Ladies' Journal* began to solicit individual covers from commercial artists of the day. The seventh issue of 1929 (vol. 15) devoted an entire issue to the First Ministry of Education National Fine Arts Exhibition, with a particular focus on female artists whose work was selected for the show. Extensively illustrated, and filled with biographies of women who exhibited in the Shanghai exhibition, this special issue made a greater contribution to recording and publicizing the careers of female artists than any other in its seventeen-year history. The striking cover was adorned with an Art Deco image in which a female nude towers over the earthly globe on which she stands, gracefully raising her arms toward a celestial orb (Figure 1.24). Not designed specifically for the magazine, this was one of five "designs" by the male artist Jiang Zhaohe that had hung in the applied arts section of the national exhibition. Critic Li Yuyi singled it out for particular praise as representing women's spiritual liberation, calling attention to the bonds that tie her ankles to the earth, the shackles of family and society that the young woman must resist. She extends her bound hands toward the auspicious light of the moon, toward the goddess of beauty in her lunar palace,

Fig. 1.24 Cover of *The Ladies' Journal*, 15:7 (1929): design by Jiang Zhaohe

yearning for freedom.[27] While the eye-catching quality of the image and the critic's enthusiastic explication may bring attention to this ambitious special issue, the artist's addition of a cupid in the upper right is a diversion from the issue's main theme, the seriousness and success of women artists of the day. The remaining covers of 1929, possibly selected, like this, from pre-existing designs rather than commissioned for the journal, are varied in style and theme in an almost random way.

The Final Phase: A New Cosmopolitanism

The strategy Commercial Press used at the end of 1929 to reestablish a more coherent visual identity was similar to that employed in its inaugural issues – it simply borrowed talent from its competitors. The covers of the 1930 issues

[27] Li Yuyi, "Jiaoyubu." The image was also reproduced in smaller scale on the pages of *Liangyou* 45 (1930): 28 and elsewhere as an example of design. Jiang's central image of a sinuous figure on tiptoe is extremely close in design to that of a bronze female figure sculpted by Max le Verrier, *Clarté*, in which a young woman standing on a stepped pedestal holds an illuminated globe. Created in Paris by the prize-winning art deco designer in 1928, and marketed in various sizes, it is possible that its image, if not one of the lamps itself, made its way to Shanghai. For the sculpture, see www.maxleverrier.com/english/sculpteur.htm (accessed July 11, 2015).

Fig. 1.25 Cover of *The Ladies' Journal*, 16:11 (1930): design by Qian Juntao

all feature the same bold and attractive Art Deco design (Figure 1.25). Beginning in that year, and continuing through the first half of 1931, drawings and decorations on the interior pages of *The Ladies' Journal* bear signatures such as Baceo, Bacceo, and J Pacco (see Figure 1.26). All were part of the artist Qian Juntao's (1906–1998) playful transformations of his artistic and editorial identity. The Chinese characters of the artist's studio name, on which these signatures are based, look as though they should be Japanese (白川尾 Mandarin: Baichuanwei). In these versions, however, he has romanized his pseudonym in an Esperanto version of its pronunciation in his native Zhejiang dialect.[28] The result now looks European, not Japanese. On other occasions, particularly in his work for his primary employer, Kaiming Book Company, he published under female pseudonyms – a common practice, as Grace Fong explains in her chapter, in early-twentieth-century poetry as well.

When Qian Juntao announced his public launch into the field of graphic design in 1928, he began a long career that would mark him as one of the most consistently accomplished of the Japan-oriented modernist designers in

---

[28] Personal communication with the artist, Shanghai, 1995.

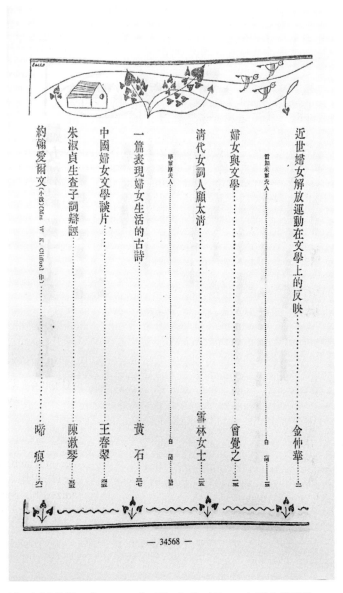

Fig. 1.26 Table of contents for *The Ladies' Journal*, 17:1 (1931): ornaments by Baceo (Qian Juntao)

Shanghai, and one of the first to openly and consistently claim design as his primary profession.[29] Following the pattern commonly seen among Chinese professional painters, he asked his teacher,Feng Zikai, to draw up a price list for his designs. In this public recommendation, Feng praised his student highly for his gifts as a graphic designer and pointed out the significance of book design in influencing the mood of readers – "it may symbolize the contents, and it can prepare people's mood and attitude for the reading before they even open the book. Like the overture of an opera, it can stimulate the feelings of the viewers, and get them in tune with the drama . . ." The price list was published in *Dushu zazhi* (Readers' magazine) in 1932, as well as in *Xin nüxing* (New woman) and as a flyer.[30] Qian Juntao worked freelance for a number of Commercial Press publications, including Xiaoshuo yuebao (Short story magazine), *Eastern Miscellany, The Educational Review*, and *Xuesheng zazhi* (Student magazine), throughout this period, although he later listed his editorship at the Kaiming Book Company as his primary job.

He brought a very modern sensibility to his work, both in design and lettering, and his covers therefore speak of a cultural world that is fully up to date, flowing forward in the same aesthetic stream that carried the artists of the West and Japan. This is evident in his introduction of modernist lettering and abstraction to the masthead of *The Ladies' Journal* (see Figure 1.25). Qian provided most of the cover designs and ornamentation for the interior features for *The Ladies' Journal* throughout the magazine's final two years.[31]

Qian Juntao's designs for the journal were generally more lyrical than was his abstract design for *Student Magazine* (Figure 1.27) (and more often signed with a Chinese seal, Juntao, than with Esperanto). He often used floral motifs, which were closely related to Japanese design and were a hallmark of his style in the 1920s. The 1930s would bring a more global look to Qian's work, as it did to Chinese publishing as a whole. Designs inspired by Egyptian archaeology brought a more exotic form of Art Deco imagery into his covers for the first three issues of *The Ladies' Journal* in 1931.

While Qian Juntao stopped work for *The Ladies' Journal* after its chief editor, Ye Shengtao, departed in the spring of 1931, the magazine continued to

---

[29] Qian made a substantial contribution to recording the history of the profession and made a point of reconstructing his own portfolio (predominantly with Kaiming shudian covers, and a few from Commercial Press) in the last years of his long life. Unlike some commercial artists who deemphasized their publishing careers after reintroduction of China's fine art market in the 1980s and 1990s, Qian remained proud of his role as a professional designer. Qian Juntao, *Qian Juntao*.

[30] For one example of this text, see the unpaginated advertisement at the end of *Dushu zazhi* 2: 11–12 (1932).

[31] Qian Juntao was credited for cover design in the table of contents, 1930, no. 9, and Zhang Lingtao in 1931, no. 7. Qian also published a number of articles on Western art history in the journal's pages in this period.

Fig. 1.27 Cover of *Student Magazine*, 18:1 (1929): design by Qian Juntao

run equally striking cover designs by Qian's younger colleague, Zhang Ling-tao, and other designers in the second half of 1931. In the magazine's last years, with these innovative modern designers, *The Ladies' Journal* reassumed the cosmopolitan look with which it had begun. International standards had changed dramatically since 1915, however, with the widespread adoption of modernist forms in commercial design, and the decision makers at Commercial Press chose *The Ladies' Journal*'s designers from those who worked in this new international style.

When a brief war with Japan broke out in Shanghai on January 28, 1932, one of the first casualties of the battle was the headquarters of the Commercial Press, located adjacent to the Japanese district of Shanghai. In addition to raining bombs on the printing factory, arsonists burned to the ground the building in which the magazine offices were located. This could not have come at a worse time, after the great stock market crash of 1929 had plunged much of the world, and thus some potential advertisers, into financial crisis. Publication of *Eastern Miscellany* was soon resumed despite the great practical difficulties faced by the press, but *The Ladies' Journal*, having recently lost much of its staff, was never revived as an independent publication. The last issue of 1931, its cover an abstracted image of a fair-haired girl and a dove, was its final appearance.

The Commercial Press, which survived for more than half a century, was more notable for its economic success than for innovations in aesthetic language or high production values. Yet the seventeen-year run of *The Ladies' Journal* spans a crucial formative period of China's magazine industry, one in which the various goals of edification and entertainment, modernization and profit, were pursued against the unpredictable background of contemporary political and economic events. The look of the magazine, as defined by its cover, was crucial to its identity. The lyrical images of gentle, industrious women that greeted readers in 1915 spoke to a new regard for women as cultural consumers and as a focus of educational, economic, and social concern. While women as participants in constructing a new society are demonstrated by some covers in the magazine's first half decade, their real or imagined tastes for floral and figural fine arts imagery become dominant in its first transitional phase as the press implemented a radical linguistic shift from classical Chinese to the modern written language in 1919 and 1920. This break with the past was marked in 1922 by covers of the new *The Ladies' Journal* that consistently rejected traditional Chinese imagery.[32] By the end of the 1920s, as pictorial magazines such as *Young Companion* (Liangyou huabao) and tabloids like *Pictorial Shanghai* emerged as potential competition for the attention of Shanghai readers, Commercial Press reaffirmed the importance of the visual by seeking eye-catching imagery. Covers for 1928 and 1929 span rather backward-looking figural images in watercolor, conservative Japanese-style floral imagery, epigraphic-style calligraphy, Art Deco designs and lettering, and finally even photography.[33] This diversity may be construed positively as trying to offer something for every class of reader, or negatively as lacking necessary coherence. In terms of the editorial message, the increasing exposure for work by women artists was also part of a message the magazine as a whole was trying to convey. In its last phase, under the editorship of Ye Shengtao (who had signed the price list for his designer friend Qian Juntao in 1932), the magazine sought clarity of cover design, with a consistent focus on Art Deco images that speak to a gentle cosmopolitan stylishness.

By its very final months, which corresponded to the dawn of Shanghai's great era of 1930s graphic design, the publisher consistently ran striking modern cover designs on *The Ladies' Journal*. The September 1931 issue presents a young woman, her fashionably cropped hair blown in the wind, who bends her torso expressively as she turns to gaze through a window (Figure 1.28). But the vivid black and white pattern of her short dress extends over her whole form, including her head, converting the woman into a patterned silhouette. Over her

---

[32] The only anomaly is the 1924 cover program, with traditionalist paintings by a cousin of the editor.

[33] *Funü zazhi* 15:9, cover.

Fig. 1.28 Cover of *The Ladies' Journal*, 17:9 (1931)

head, as she looks out the window, grows a tree. Is she indoors or out? Is it night or day? The modish pattern of her garb and the elegance of the tall, European-style window beside which she stands are the utmost in high style, a quality that the surrealistic puzzle of the image and the modernist masthead only empha-size. This pictorial ambiguity, with a woman standing intensely alert, lost in thoughts we cannot read, suggests a more complicated agency for this female subject than the more straightforward pictures of her sisters who read, painted, sewed, or cooked on the covers of *The Ladies' Journal* a decade and a half before. Indeed, while obviously not the intent, this uncertain image might even be read as foretelling the end of *The Ladies' Journal*. While it was certainly the destruction of the Commercial Press facilities in 1932 that precipitated the magazine's demise, the publishing boom of the 1930s, with the appearance of so many more beautifully designed and printed modern magazines, as well as the increasingly numerous and diverse possibilities for culture, profession, and life-style that this decade of prosperity brought to Shanghai, may have made it impossible for a magazine like *The Ladies' Journal* to continue to try to speak to or for "all Chinese women," as it had attempted for seventeen years.

Just as the concerns of its potential audience and the editorial agendas of the press and its editors evolved over the seventeen-year run of the magazine, so did its visual identity. Though it was assumed to target an audience of women, many of its readers were, in actuality, like the majority of its editors and authors, men for whom the situation of women in modern China was of personal, social, or intellectual concern. Its artists and editors triangulated the diverse desires of its publishers and its public against their own ideals and practical compromises. The evolving and often contradictory standards that it set for itself represent major trends in the Chinese publishing world and in the rapidly evolving culture of which it was a part.

Reading horizontally, we realize that the cover images developed at the Commercial Press for *The Ladies' Journal* usually pushed forward its editorial agendas. No doubt they were also affected by certain practical limitations, ranging from personnel to budget to schedule, and, as we have seen, reading situatedly, by the relationships between managers, editors, and artists; nevertheless, the conspicuous changes over the years give visual form to transformations in the rapidly modernizing domestic and international environment in which the magazine was published. However one may wish to evaluate the changing editorial approaches that might appear on its interior pages, whether to consider the journal's approach more or less progressive in the context of its time, the cacophonous nature of the early twentieth century debates about women,[34] along with the social transformations then under way, are well reflected in its cover design. From its coherent initial imagery in 1915 to the visual diversity of its final year, 1931, *The Ladies' Journal* offered its readership a convincing demonstration of the centrality of the Chinese woman in a modernizing and internationally oriented urban world.

---

[34] On the significance of the debates of this era as "cacophonous," see Chiang, "Womanhood, Motherhood, and Biology."

2 Engendering a Journal: Editors and Nudes in *Linloon Magazine* and Its Global Context*

Liying Sun

Introduction

In the first three decades of the twentieth century, the development of the Chinese publishing industry benefited tremendously from the active circulation of textual and visual materials around the globe. These materials included large quantities of photos, books, newspapers, and magazines from all countries, which constituted a veritable "global database" of world print culture. This database offered inspiration for cultural brokers in China, namely publishers, editors, writers, artists, and translators, to create (trans-)culturally inspired products.[1] Magazines preserve particularly rich evidence of this editorial practice of promoting an early "globalization." This chapter focuses on one such magazine, *Linglong – Linloon Magazine* (1931–1937),[2] and uses integrated and situated readings to explore the following questions: How did local cultural brokers consciously select certain images, series, or discourses from a global setting, and how did they use these materials to address local issues of body, femininity, and gender relations? If a journal was gendered, how did the selection reinforce the gendered nature of the publication? Did the

* An early version of this paper was presented at the conference "Gender & Transcultural Production: Chinese Women's Journals in their Global Context, 1900–2000," May 13–15, 2011, SOAS, London. I am thankful for the invaluable comments by Professors Nathalie Cooke, Barbara Mittler, Joan Judge, Michel Hockx and two anonymous reviewers. I am also grateful to Matthias Arnold, Annika Joest, and Li Yu-Chieh, who have been closely working with me on *Linglong – Linloon Magazine* in the database "Chinese Women's Magazines." Some materials regarding the background of *Linloon Magazine* and *Sheying huabao* have been included in one of my Chinese articles, "Cong *Sheying huabao* dao *Linglong*."
[1] The concept of "cultural brokers" is drawn from Rudolf G. Wagner; see his "The Role of the Foreign Community"; "Joining the Global Imaginaire." For earlier scholarship see Hagedorn, "A Friend to Go between Them" and Richter, "Cultural Brokers."
[2] The Chinese word *linglong* literally means "small, cute and smart," "exquisite," "petite," and the magazine is also referred to in English as *Petite*. It describes the important features of *Linloon Magazine*. On the one hand, the actual magazine was pocket-sized, and it was designed to be easy to carry around; on the other hand, the title *Linglong* personalized the magazine and made it emotionally more accessible to its readers. For a detailed discussion of the possible meanings of the title *Linloon*, please refer to the introduction to *Linloon Magazine* in the WoMag database Website: http://kjc-sv013.kjc.uni-heidelberg.de/frauenzeitschriften/public/linglong/characteristics.php?magazin_id=3.

selection and interpretation contribute to the manipulation of a gendered voice? And what can we learn from our findings about whether *Linloon Magazine* as a "women's magazine" was in fact written in a "genuine" female voice?[3]

As early as a decade ago, Leo Ou-fan Lee had already recognized the value of *Linloon Magazine* as integral to the collective pursuit of modernity in the metropolis of Shanghai.[4] Since the digitization of *Linloon Magazine* conducted by Columbia University, scholars have benefited from accessibility to the journal and have examined *Linloon Magazine* from multiple perspectives.[5] Barbara Mittler explored the discourse of "new (wo)men" as well as gender relations in the journal. She pointed out that the journal was "polyphonic, sometimes internally contradictory" and suggested the need for future research on the individuals and institutions behind the journal in order to understand its internal contradictions and multiple voices better.[6] In another study on *Linloon Magazine*, she further complicated the question by investigating the construction and function of particular (non-)gendered genres in *Linloon Magazine* and other women's magazines.[7] More recently, Gary Wang has explored the journal's editorial group, and thus is able to offer a new understanding of the representational tensions in the construction of heteronormative marriage in *Linloon Magazine*.[8] Hsiao-pei Yen, Yunxiang Gao and, most recently, Louise Edwards have further examined *Linloon Magazine* in studies on its discourse of beauty and morality in relation to larger calls of nationalism and feminism.[9] While all of these essays grapple in some way or other with the question of the "female voice" in *Linloon Magazine*, the question of who the editors were and whether it was thus a women's magazine just in name, remains somewhat unresolved. At the same time, nobody appears to have read *Linloon Magazine* against either other Chinese periodicals by the same publisher, or other non-Chinese magazines circulating at the time.

This study takes up precisely these two questions and thus goes beyond conventional readings of the journal. The first of two sections introduces the background of the main editors and discusses the extent to which *Linloon Magazine* was a "women's magazine" (ideally designed for women, read by women, and perhaps also edited by women) and whether its gendered voice

[3] On the complexity of the "women's voice" in women's magazines, see Beetham, *A Magazine of Her Own?*

[4] Lee, *Shanghai Modern*, 86–88. See also Li Keqiang, "*Linglong zazhi.*"

[5] See "*Linglong* Women's Magazine."

[6] Mittler, "In Spite of Gentility."   [7] Mittler, *Portrait of a Trope*, chapter 1.

[8] Gary Wang, "Making 'Opposite-Sex Love.'" Gary Wang's article is based on his MA thesis. A few other MA theses on *Linloon Magazine* have been produced in the last few years, both in Taiwan and in mainland China, such as Kong Lingzhi, *Cong Linglong zazhi kan.*

[9] Yen, "Body Politics"; Yunxiang Gao, "Nationalist and Feminist Discourses on *Jianmei*"; and Edwards "The Shanghai Modern Woman's American Dreams."

and prominent style of "attacking men" (*xiang nanzi jingong*) was determined by its "female editorship." I argue that in the first two years (1931–1933), *Linloon Magazine* was first and foremost a commercial product targeting both men and women, and that the gendered voice was only eventually created by male editors. The second section focuses on the circulation of nudes, as a particular type of visual material published in *Linloon Magazine*, and uses an integrated approach to explore the editorial practice of addressing different readerships with the same visual materials. I will argue, first, that the entire discourse of body representations and gender relations in *Linloon Magazine* had a transcultural dimension, which reflected the editors' efforts to "promote globalization." Second, I will contend that visual and textual materials are not gendered *per se*, and they both can be used by more or less gender-specific magazines. At the same time, however, the materials can contribute to or reinforce the shaping of a gendered voice through editorial practice.

I   Gender Matters on the Editorial Board – Lin Zecang and Chen Zhenling

Existing scholarship has offered very little information on the background of the members of *Linloon Magazine*'s editorial board. Consequently, the journal has been viewed as a finished product, isolated from the dynamic process of production. An investigation of the agents behind the magazine can, however, help us understand why and how *Linloon Magazine* was created. In fact, only a few figures remained central to the editorial group, although many editors joined the team for short periods. Lin Zecang (1903–1961, male, founder, chief editor) and Chen Zhenling (allegedly female, copy editor, later responsible for the column Women/*Funü*) were key figures on the editing team.[10] In the following section, I first introduce Lin Zecang's educational background and social networks and show his skill as a cultural broker. I then problematize the understanding of *Linloon Magazine* as a "women's magazine" by identifying the puzzling "female editor" Chen Zhenling and examining the journal's targeted readers.

---

[10] A number of well-educated and talented young graduates supported Lin's achievements in publishing and photography as contributors or editors. Many of them were Lin's relatives, who received elite education and were exposed to "Western" culture. For example, Lin Zemin (d. 1938, male, editor of photography) and Lin Zeren (?–?, male, editor of the column Common Knowledge/*Changshi*) were Lin Zecang's younger brothers; Gao Weixiang (b. 1906, male, contributor) was his cousin. Other editors were Zhou Shixun (male, editor of the column Entertainment/*Yule*), Huang Shiying, Ye Qianyu (1907–1995, male, editor responsible for Fine Arts/*Meishu*), Liang Xinxi (b. 1908, female, copy editor from 1932), Cao Lengbing, Zong Weigeng, and Liang Yongfu.

Lin Zecang: A Cultural Broker

Born and raised in a prominent Christian family from Gutian, Fujian Province, *Linloon Magazine*'s founder Lin Zecang received his Bachelor of Commerce from Kwang Hua University (*Guanghua Daxue*) in Shanghai in 1926.[11] He seems to have been fully bilingual and able to read original English-language materials fluently. Skilled at combining knowledge and practice, culture and market, Lin's extremely well-developed instinct for new products and potential markets was clearly shown in his later publishing and editorial enterprises. He was representative of a group of cultural brokers in 1920s and 1930s Shanghai who were interested in introducing Western culture for both educational and commercial purposes.

As early as January 1922, when he was still at the university, Lin founded the San Ho Company (Sanhe gongsi). Later in 1925, he established the China Photographic Society (Zhongguo sheying xuehui) in Shanghai.[12] The society greatly contributed to the early development of Chinese photography and established important links to international photographic organizations, including the Royal Photographic Society of Great Britain and the French Photographic Society.[13] These connections explained the source of "foreign" images in *Linloon Magazine*, which I will discuss later in this essay. Unlike the China Photographic Society, the San Ho Company was not labeled as a cultural institution, but as a commercial body to deal with "all trades."[14] It extended its business to publishing in 1925, and founded *Sheying huabao – Pictorial Weekly* (1925–1937, hereafter SYHB) in the name of the Chinese Photographic Society that same year. The pictorial positioned itself as part of entertainment tabloid (*xiaobao*) culture in Shanghai, although it reserved space for discussions of photographic technology. From that time on, Lin made great efforts to build up his publishing empire. He founded a series of illustrated newspapers and magazines in addition to *Pictorial Weekly*: *Changshi – Common Knowledge* (1928–1931), *Linloon Magazine* (1931–1937), *Diansheng* (the abbreviation for two periodicals: *Diansheng ribao – Movie Radio News*, 1932–1933; *Diansheng zhoukan – Movie Tone: The National Movie*

---

[11] Lin first went to study at St John's University in 1921 and then Kwanghua University after the May Thirtieth Movement in 1925. St John's University enjoyed great fame for its high-quality education, its English-speaking environment, and its high tuition. It was one of the most prestigious (church) universities in Shanghai, or anywhere in China at that time. See Xiong Yuezhi and Zhou Wu, *Sheng Yuehan daxue shi.*

[12] At the beginning the English name was "China Camera Club." It was changed to "China Photographic Society" in 1926. See Lin Zecang, "Sanhe gongsi."

[13] Lin Zemin, "Canguan Yingguo huangjia sheying xuehui."

[14] As Lin commented in 1937, three kinds of products were regularly sold by the company from the very beginning: table tennis equipment, photos of movie stars, and photographic devices. See Lin Zecang, "Sanhe gongsi," 80. Of the three, "photos of movie stars" were possible sources of images used for reproduction in *Linloon Magazine*.

Weekly, 1934–1941), *Jinghua zhoukan – Essence Weekly* (1940s), *Zhongwai yingxun – Chinese and Foreign Movie News* (1940s), and others.[15] It is notable that *Pictorial Weekly* had existed for almost six years when *Linloon Magazine* was established. The two periodicals coexisted until August 1937. Bearing a "pre-history" and viewed as a "little sister," *Linloon Magazine* was not a stand-alone cultural carrier, but part of a commercial and cultural publishing system.[16] In the system, *Pictorial Weekly* was *Linloon Magazine*'s "parallel text." It offers rich historical materials for decoding the editorial strategy practiced in *Linloon Magazine*. Whereas *Linloon Magazine* holds a privileged position in terms of preservation, digitization, and accessibility, *Pictorial Weekly* has not received sufficient scholarly attention. I will therefore juxtapose these two journals in this essay through integrated and also situated readings.

Chen Zhenling: "She" in Question

In addition to the male editors, two women's names appeared in *Linloon Magazine*'s colophons. One is Liang Xinxi, who was first a contributor to *Linloon Magazine*, and then became the official copy editor from issue 77 on (December 7, 1932). About a year later, she married Lin Zecang and acted as editor of *Diansheng ribao*, a tabloid focused on gossip surrounding Hollywood and Chinese movie stars.[17] The other woman's name was "Chen Zhenling," or more often "Ms. Chen Zhenling" – "Chen Zhenling nüshi."[18]

---

[15] *Changshi* issue no. 13 is dated Feb. 1, 1928. Since the newspaper was published every three days, it was perhaps founded at the beginning of January 1928. The newspaper existed for four years, and later was incorporated into *Linloon Magazine* as a column; see *Linglong* 1.4 (1931): 126. Lin Zecang's name usually did not appear in *Movie Radio News* as editor, but as founder (*chuangban zhe*). The publisher was given as San Ho Company. There is no known scholarship on the relation between *Movie Radio News* and other publications founded by San Ho, to my knowledge. The information on *Chinese and Foreign Movie News* and *Essence Weekly* appears in Zhu Junzhou, *Shanghai tushuguan*. However, the information is not easy to find, because the Chinese name of the San Ho Company contains a typo, and no editor's name is listed.

[16] An editor's note in *Pictorial Weekly* literally said that *Linloon Magazine* "is our journal's little sister" after *Linloon Magazine* published two issues. The female personalization of *Linloon Magazine* shows how Lin initially designed and positioned *Linloon Magazine*. See SYHB 6.281 (1931): 247.

[17] See *Linloon Magazine* 1.30 (1931): 1138. Lin and Liang were married in 1932; see *Linglong* 2.70 (1932): 953. Most scholarship so far has assumed that Liang Xinxi was male.

[18] Both Gary Wang and I myself have individually tried to identify Chen Zhenling over the past years. Except for a few books of the *Linglong Series* (*Linglong congshu*), we discovered very little about Chen's further publications. Nor did we find any photos. As Gary Wang points out, *Linloon Magazine* published a huge number of photos of female authors and readers, and it is unlikely that Chen's photo would not have been published if she was a real person. Moreover, in a group photo of editors employed by the San Ho Company in 1937, no female editors can be clearly identified. See "Sanhe gongsi shiwu zhou jinian quanti zhiyuan sheying." Judging from the hairstyle and the outfit, such as long jackets and suits, most people should be male, but the sex of the person in the first row in the left corner, for example, remains unclear. However, even

"Chen Zhenling nüshi" was also the name of the "editor-in-chief" of *Funü ribao* ("Women's Daily"), a supplement to *Movie Radio News* around 1932.[19] The column *Zhenling xinxiang* ("Zhenling's Mailbox") was concurrently published in *Funü ribao* and in *Linloon Magazine* over the course of its print run. Even after *Linloon Magazine* ceased publication in 1937, Zhenling's Mailbox continued to appear in *Movie Radio News* until at least 1940. The only biographical information that we can find about Ms. Chen Zhenling, however, is a frequently quoted statement published in the first issue of *Linloon Magazine*. According to this statement, getting out of school, Chen had immediately started to work as editor for *Linloon Magazine*. She "wishes to be the mouthpiece (literally the 'throat and tongue') for her female compatriots."[20]

Chen Zhenling was the only name to appear in every single issue of *Linloon Magazine* throughout its seven years of publication. But who was Chen Zhenling? Gary Wang creatively conjectures that Chen Zhenling might not actually have been a real person, but the pseudonym for one, or even a whole group of (male) editors: why else would the name "Zhenling" (preciously elegant) tally so perfectly with the journal's self-fashioning remarks? This becomes even more plausible as "Chen" if pronounced in Shanghai dialect actually sounds like "cheng" – meaning "to become." Accordingly, Chen Zhenling could mean "becoming preciously elegant" – an aim the readers of *Linloon Magazine* were expected to aspire to – and their editor, Chen Zhenling, appeared thus as the perfect model for them.[21]

Let me carry Wang's attempt to decipher Chen's name by examining its contemporary and local pronunciation even further: What if Chen Zhenling was one of Lin Zecang's female pseudonyms? In contemporary Romanization, his name Lin Zecang was transcribed as "Tse Tsang Ling" (T. T. Ling). Read in reversed order ("Tsang Tse Ling") and in Shanghai dialect this actually becomes "Chen Zhenling." What is more, the "cang" in his name is a homonym with "cang" meaning "to hide"; the name could also be read as "hiding (cang) genuine Ling."[22]

Before female editor Liang Xinxi officially joined the editing team in December 1932, the editorial board was exclusively male, then. It is possible that Liang Xinxi continued the work under the name of Chen Zhenling after December 1932. But it is also possible that "Chen Zhenling nüshi" continued to be used

---

if the person was female, it should be Liang Xinxi, as she was the editor-in-chief of *Diansheng* at the time.

[19] *Women's Daily* is preserved in very poor condition together with *Movie Radio News*. As part of *Movie Radio News* 545 (Nov. 10, 1933), *Women's Daily* was marked as Issue 301. Further research is necessary.

[20] *Linglong* 1.1 (1931): 5. The rhetoric "throat and tongue" was recurrently used in later advertisements for the journal, and presented one of the foci of the journal's self-representation.

[21] Gary Wang, "Making 'Opposite-Sex Love,'" 247.

[22] For more detailed information see my PhD dissertation "Body Un/Dis-Covered."

as a composite of Lin Zecang and other male editors who used Chen's byline to "attack men," as a successful marketing strategy aimed at convincing readers that *Linloon Magazine* was indeed the "one and only mouthpiece for women."[23]

Linloon Magazine: *A Magazine of Her Own?*

Linloon Magazine targeted female readers, and, edited by a "Ms." Chen Zhenling, has been taken as a source for discussing an "alternative," a "women's voice" on such issues as gender relations, bodies and femininity in relation to modernity and nationalism.[24] However, *Linloon Magazine* was *not* strictly a "women's magazine" – certainly not in its first two years (March 1931– beginning of 1933). The journal was not exclusively designed for, edited by, or read by women. Rather, it was a new product created by the San Ho Company to stimulate the market. This can be seen when self-definitions in *Linloon Magazine* and its "parallel text," *Pictorial Weekly*, are compared. *Linloon Magazine* was initially designed in March 1931 to be a lifestyle and leisure magazine aimed at both educated female and young male readers, although female readers were emphasized. As stated in its publishing goal from its very first issue, *Linloon Magazine* was conceived as an exquisite combination of addressing the "women question" and offering "sophisticated entertainment."[25] In August 1931, *Pictorial Weekly*, the "parallel text" to *Linloon Magazine*, proclaimed that it was "especially welcomed by women, but even more admired by young people [of both sexes]."[26] Similarly, *Linloon Magazine* did not forget its male readers. It even launched a short advertisement from September 2, 1931 to January 1, 1932, that addressed this *male* reader: "*Brother Ying*, if you want to have a perfect love life, a happy family, and find a job successfully, you should read 'Linloon Magazine' regularly."[27] In addition, both the Chinese and English titles of *Linloon Magazine* constantly changed from 1931 to 1933, alternately including and excluding the term *funü* (literally: women) or "ladies."[28]

---

[23] It is one of the slogans repeatedly advertised; see, for instance, *Linglong* 1.5 (1931): 147.

[24] See, for instance, Gao, "Nationalist and Feminist Discourses," 548.

[25] The publishing goal was "to promote women's 'elegant and beautiful' lives, and encourage 'sophisticated entertainment' in society." See, for example, *Linglong* 1.1 (1931): 13.

[26] SYHB 7.302 (1931): 12.

[27] My emphasis. The advertisement was published from September 1931 to January 1932 in the following issues: *Linglong* 1.25 (Sept. 2, 1931): 915; 1.28 (Sept. 23, 1931): 1024; 1.31 (Oct. 14, 1931): 1209; 1.39 (Dec. 9, 1931): 1510; 1.42 (Jan. 1, 1932): 1661.

[28] The Chinese title of the journal included *funü* (women) for the first time in vol. 3, no. 96 (May 24, 1933), and it continued to be used sporadically until the Chinese title was finally stabilized from vol. 3, no. 107 (Aug. 23, 1933). The English title of the journal was first "Linloon Magazine" from vol. 1, no. 1 (March 18, 1931) to no. 25 (Sept. 2, 1931); then it was changed to "Ladies' Magazine" from vol. 1, no. 26 (Sept. 9, 1931) to no. 29 (Sept. 30, 1931). Then vol. 1, no. 30 (Oct. 10, 1931) changed to "Lin Loon Magazine" again, exactly when the advertisement targeted male readers. This situation continued until vol. 2, no. 62 (Aug. 10, 1932), and vol. 2, no. 63

Only between September 1932 and August 1933 did Lin Zecang begin to focus on female readers in *Linloon Magazine*, whereas *Pictorial Weekly* targeted male readers – and this was advertised aggressively. Thereafter, as a result of marketing and interaction between editors and readers, *Linloon Magazine* became a more gendered magazine that clearly targeted female readers. It is difficult to find hard evidence to explain why the publishing strategy was unstable at the time, but most likely Lin Zecang was trying to maximize readership and profits. It seems that once Lin knew that *Linloon Magazine*'s female readership was stable, he began to divide its readership by suggesting that *Pictorial Weekly* was for men, while *Linloon Magazine* was for women. When the editors of *Pictorial Weekly* realized in August 1931 that, although the journal targeted young people of both sexes, its major readership was *female*, it tried to direct female readers to purchase *Linloon Magazine*.[29] An advertisement in January 1932 stated, "If men read *Pictorial Weekly*, [then their] happiness is incomparable; if women read *Linloon Magazine*, [then their] worries disappear."[30] Also, in January 1932, *Pictorial Weekly* published an announcement in *Linloon Magazine*, entitled "Speak Up against Unfairness towards Men." It says that although it was fairly "reasonable" for *Linloon Magazine* to "attack men," the magazine ridiculed men so much that "male readers were unsatisfied." *Pictorial Weekly* would, therefore, start a new column called "Speak Up against the Unfairness."[31] Even more radically, Lin later openly advocated a style of "attacking," which purposefully encouraged the two pictorials to compete with each other, claiming that *Linloon Magazine* was "to discuss women's issues, promote elegant and beautiful lives, and *attack men*,"[32] whereas SYHB was designed to "*attack women*."[33] These examples clearly reflect Lin's marketing strategies, and explain why *Linloon Magazine* shows a prevalent tendency of "misandria" (while keeping up some misogynist attacks as well), as Mittler pointed out.[34]

Both in *Pictorial Weely* and in *Linloon Magazine*, advertisements reveal elements of "attack" against both sexes. For example, one advertisement in *Pictorial Weekly* claims on the one hand to "attack women," while on the other, it states that the journal is "most welcomed by young people and women,"

(Aug. 17, 1932) started to add "the Ladies' Journal" to "Lin Loon Magazine." A few months later, vol. 3, no. 90 (April 5, 1933) replaced the title with "Lin Loon Ladies' Magazine," which lasted to no. 217 (Dec. 25, 1935). The English title disappeared from no. 221 (Jan. 22, 1936) on.

[29] Gao Weixiang, "*Sheying huabao*."   [30] See advertisement in SYHB 7.324 (1932): 188.

[31] *Linglong* 1.46 (originally misprinted as 45) (Jan. 27, 1932): 1873.

[32] *Linglong* 1.48 (April 27, 1932), 1941.

[33] See advertisement in SYHB 7.352 (1932): 308. The advertisement claims to "attack women" on the one hand, but also claims to be enjoyed by women and youngsters on the other. I analyze it later in this chapter.

[34] Mittler, "In Spite of Gentility."

as well as "deeply favored by fashionable women, and greatly admired by fashionable young men."[35] I would argue that simultaneously attacking and welcoming (wo)men was precisely one of the editorial strategies that Lin successfully used. Satire becomes an "editing style" that could potentially draw both male and female attention.

In the first two years of its publishing history, then, *Linloon Magazine* was not exclusively designed for women, nor was it edited by women, or only read by women. This was so in spite of its misandric rhetoric, in spite of its being personalized as a female "little sister" of other magazines, in spite of its female voice (albeit by male and female editors) and in spite of the fact that as a "gendered" journal, it focused on femininity and gender relations.[36] Yet women did become the journal's most important and openly targeted readers after 1933. The choice of particular visuals and their framing on the pages of *Linloon Magazine*, to be discussed in the second part of this chapter, may illustrate how *Linloon Magazine* eventually did become "a magazine of her own" – by and through editorial agency.

II   The Circulation of Nudes: Reading *Linloon Magazine* against *Pictorial Weekly*

Both *Linloon Magazine* and *Pictorial Weekly* used visual materials, and indeed, visuality was essential to their market success. Depictions of nudes, and especially nude photographs, were important elements in shaping both *Linloon Magazine* and *Pictorial Weekly* as modern and artistically sophisticated journals.[37] What is the function of nudes in *Linloon Magazine* and how is it different from that of those found in other periodicals, such as *Pictorial Weekly*, however? To what extent would the difference in representation of the nudes in the two journals, if any, reflect a different implied readership? This section compares how nudes were displayed in the two periodicals through an integrated reading.

Female Nudes: Healthy or Scandalous?

An identical image published in both journals gives us a good basis to compare. Figure 2.1 is a stand-alone nude photograph published in *Linloon Magazine*,

---

[35] SYHB 7.302 (1931): 12.

[36] Similar examples of how male editors manipulated the "female voice" and female authorship can be found in Victorian magazines; see Beetham, *A Magazine of Her Own?* 188.

[37] In this chapter, "nude" or "nudes" will be used merely as a technical term to refer to images of (1) totally unclothed bodies; (2) upper bodies unclothed; (3) bodies scantily clad with transparent materials. The theoretical debate over "nudity" and "nakedness," which is not directly relevant to the situation in China at the time, is dealt with in my PhD dissertation.

Fig. 2.1 A semi-nude, *Linloon Magazine*, 1:39 (1931), 1534

depicting the upper body of a female nude. The darkness of her hair and background is contrasted with the lightness of her body. It is presented as an artwork with specific aesthetics; yet the caption relates the nude to notions of "health and beauty" (*jianmei*).[38] It says, "Women in our country are always satirized for being either healthy without beauty, or beautiful without health. The picture above is a healthy and beautiful woman. Who, then, can say that women cannot have healthy and beautiful physiques?"[39] The caption thus attempts to draw the readers' attention to the discourse of *jianmei* rather than the aesthetic values of the nude, although readers might have "resisted" this suggested reading.[40]

Yet this image was not necessarily bound to the *jianmei* discourse. Half a year later, it was used in *Pictorial Weekly* (Figure 2.2). After describing the woman's "graceful posture and medium stature," the caption explains, "Li Li, a dancing girl from Peking, used to be an actress in the Peking Qingtian Film Company. She has moved to Shanghai now, and is one of the famous dancing girls in Shanghai. This is a photo of her in the semi-nude." Instead of commenting on her physique, the explanation concentrates on her profession as a movie actress and famous dancing girl, and offers ambiguous associations between

[38] Cf. Gao, "Nationalist and Feminist Discourses."
[39] *Linglong* 1.39 (1931): 1534.   [40] Cf. Fetterley, *The Resisting Reader*.

Fig. 2.2 A semi-nude, Li Li, *Pictorial Weekly*, 8:366 (1932), 49

her semi-nude photograph and her profession. More sensationally, a long story entitled "Sixty thousand *yuan* for a dancing girl; Li Li's whole lovelorn story" occupies the entire front page next to her picture. It recounts one of Li Li's scandalous affairs, and explains why she had the semi-nude photo taken:

At first, Li Li was renowned in the circle of dancing girls in Peking. She had broad social contacts, and did not care much about social conventions. Therefore, she didn't reject the invitation to take nude photos of her. She came to Shanghai after the 9·18 Incident, and met Zhu Lide, employee at the post office, at the old Carlton Dance Hall . . . [41]

Unlike the caption in *Linloon Magazine*, the story emphasizes not Li's beautiful physique but her carefree attitude about social conventions, which allowed her to have the photo taken. The photo serves to illustrate this social gossip, full of sex and crime. To avoid the combination of the semi-nude image and the related scandal around her not being considered "sophisticated" enough, he added an "Editor's Note," questioning "how those lechers and married men would think about it?"[42] His question functions as a warning, which prevents the report from being entirely scandalous. As analyzed in the first section of this chapter, *Pictorial Weekly* had begun to focus more on male readers from

[41] SYHB 8.367 (originally misprinted as 366) (1932): 49.   [42] Ibid.

January 1932. Li's nude photo was obviously used to attract this readership's "male gaze," to bring men "incomparable happiness (*kuaile wubi*)."[43]

An identical nude image was thus used as an instructive figure for an implied, mostly female audience in *Linloon Magazine*, while it was interpreted as an ambiguous illustration to a report on sex and scandals prepared especially for the male palate and gaze in *Pictorial Weekly*. In fact, circulating identical or similar photographs – not necessarily nudes – between *Linloon Magazine* and *Pictorial Weekly* was a common phenomenon (see Figure 2.3). Generally speaking, *Pictorial Weekly* connected these images to social activities or current affairs, or used them to satirize women, while *Linloon Magazine* deliberately related these images to fashion, health and beauty and used them as part of their instructive advice, or sometimes as a way of "attacking men." The phenomenon suggests that images are not intrinsically gendered, and that the same images can be used and read differently in different journals. Editors would use captions and stories to frame and interpret one and the same image differently in different journals, guiding implied male/female readers to diverse – sometimes even opposite – ways of seeing. I call this the power of "editorial agency."[44]

Male Nudes: Good Example for Physical Training?

The style of "attacking men" in *Linloon Magazine*, as we might predict, could easily be taken as reflecting the female voice: a style created by and for women, and thus published in a women's magazine. Yet "attacking men" was not a unique attribute of *Linloon Magazine*, nor was it necessarily voiced by and for women. Figure 2.4, for instance, is one of three male nudes (out of forty-five standalone nudes) published in *Linloon Magazine* between 1931 and 1934.[45] It represents an aesthetics of strength and masculinity, or "cuirasse ésthetique" as art historians would put it. The caption reads, "It is most important for men to train their bodies, [thus] not only can [their] spirit be delighted, but also [they] can dispel illness and live longer. This image clearly shows the fully developed muscles of a physically healthy man. Who knows how many men from our country have such a physique?"[46] The last sentence disparages the physiques of Chinese men, well known in contemporary discourse on the "sick man of Asia," while referring to the discourse of "health and beauty." In the context

---

[43] See Sanjiaojia, "Li Li pai luoti zhao." According to gossip, Li Li's semi-nude photo was taken by Chu Baoheng, a professional photographer who allegedly had an affair with her.

[44] See Sun, "Body Un/Dis-Covered."

[45] The image is counted as a "nude" in spite of the briefs worn by the man. Few photographs of male nudes were published in pictorials from the 1910s to the early 1930s. The majority either posed in briefs or exposed only their upper bodies. See Sun, "Body Un/Dis-Covered."

[46] *Linglong* 1.17 (1931): 606.

Fig. 2.3 Examples of photographs circulated between *Linloon Magazine* and *Pictorial Weekly*

男子身體之鍛鍊。最為重要。不特矯
矯愉快。且可却病延壽。此影足示健
美男子肌肉之飽滿。未知吾國男子具
此體格者有幾人。

Fig. 2.4 A male nude in *Linloon Magazine*, 1:17 (1931), 606

of *Linloon Magazine*'s "attacking" style, the critique can be understood as a female satire of men.

The colophon of the seventeenth issue shows, however, that a man, Zhou Shixun, was the editor of the "Entertainment" section, in which Figure 2.4 appears. He therefore should have been responsible for the editorial decision. Even if he was aided by other editors, only Lin Zecang and Lin Zemin's names were listed on the colophon; both of them were male. The only supposedly female name, Chen Zhenlin, was not even listed as an editor on the colophon, but on the page of the "Woman" section. The voice of *Linloon Magazine* was therefore again controlled by male editors.

Was *Linloon Magazine* the only magazine that satirized men or male nudes, in order to evoke a sympathetic response from female readers? The male nude in Figure 2.5, which was published in SYHB, is similar to the nude in Figure 2.4. The image was included in the column "Photography Studies" (*Sheying yanjiu lan*) in *Pictorial Weekly* in 1930, more than one year before the publication of Figure 2.4 in *Linloon Magazine*. Typically edited by Lin Zecang (sometimes by Lin Zemin), the section was a fixed space for both (male) professional and amateur photographers to exchange information on photo-chemistry, exposure settings, photographic masterpieces, and the activities of

Fig. 2.5 A male nude in *Pictorial Weekly*, 5:250 (August 9, 1930), 399

the China Photographic Society. The fact that the male nude was included in this section indicates the editors' appreciation of its artistic value. The caption of the image is almost the same as the caption of Figure 2.4. Comparing these two captions, we can see that the caption of Figure 2.4 in *Linloon Magazine* was based on the one in *Pictorial Weekly* (Figure 2.5) published a year before: the disparaging sentence is identical. The only difference is that one sentence that is absent in *Pictorial Weekly* has been added in *Linloon Magazine*: "not only can [their] spirit be delighted, but also [they] can dispel illness and live longer."[47] The additional sentence in *Linloon Magazine* emphasizes how men can benefit from physical training. This is in accord with our observation of Li Li's semi-nude and its presentation in *Linloon Magazine*: Here, the images would stress the ideology of beauty and health rather than eroticism. In this case, however, the image was gendered by a female voice in a gendered journal.

The Global Context

The (mostly Western) nudes in *Linloon Magazine* were part of the global circulation of visual materials between periodicals, reproducible photographs,

---

[47] The complete caption of Figure 2.5 is, "It is most important for men to train their bodies. This image clearly shows the fully developed muscles of a physically healthy man. Who knows how many men from our country can have such a physique?" SYHB 5.250 (1930): 399.

and photographic albums. In the pre-*Linloon Magazine* era, Lin Zecang was already aware of the circulation of nude images, and had established his taste, criterion, and channels for selecting and publishing nudes.[48] He announced that he would not publish images of Chinese nude models from the very beginning of *Pictorial Weekly* in 1925. Yet he never rejected Western nudes, especially "world photographic masterpieces" of nudes, which he often published in the column "Photography Studies." Before 1931, all the nudes he selected for publication were not "full nudes" in his understanding. To Lin, "a full nude photo" would mean a completely exposed (usually female) nude who posed very close to the camera. In the summer of 1930, after his publishing enterprise suffered from the global economic crisis, he started to "reform *Pictorial Weekly*." His new policies included focusing more on women-related content, and publishing more images that displayed "healthy female physical beauty."[49] His San Ho Company started to openly advertise its desire to trade artistic nude photos, imported from the West. Not long after he introduced these new policies, *Linloon Magazine* was founded. Therefore, *Linloon Magazine* was very likely a consequence of the economic crisis, and it was created to increase his market-oriented publishing business. The integration of nudes, thus, could neither be isolated from the journal's commercial purposes, nor from its global context.

In the 1920s and 1930s, the publication of popular journals was a huge business not only in China, but also in Europe and North America. Large numbers of foreign magazines were imported into China, but very little is known about them. In many cases, we must assume the nudes in *Linloon Magazine* were reproduced from reprints of photos, photographic journals and fan magazines from around the world; the satirical images in *Linloon Magazine* were reproduced from French or American journals, although sometimes we lack sufficient evidence to identify precisely from which journals, or how the editors acquired them. What we do know is that foreign bookstores such as Kelly and Walsh in Shanghai, for example, provided readers with periodicals such as *The Illustrated London News*, *Punch*, *The New Yorker* and *Vanity Fair*.[50] Importing magazines might also have been good business for companies. In an advertisement in *Linloon Magazine*, the Dahua Magazine Company (Dahua Zazhi Gongsi) claims, "our company transported more than two thousand kinds of novels, magazines and newspapers from Britain, America, Germany and France." In addition to direct sales, the company also offered subscriptions to any foreign magazine.[51]

---

[48] For detailed information on Lin's attitude toward nudes as well as the sources of nude photographs selected for publication in *Linloon Magazine* and SYHB, see Sun, "Body Un/Dis-Covered."

[49] SYHB 5.248 (1930): 377.

[50] Huang Haitao [Calvin H. T. Wong], "Biefa yanghang kao," 232.

[51] *Linglong* 1.30 (1931): 1130.

Lin Zecang understood that foreign magazines were an extremely rich source for his publishing enterprise. He was also aware that a number of his well-educated readers were interested in these magazines. In an Editor's Note in 1929, he encouraged readers to "translate the essence of magazines from all over the world, and then send them to us together with the original copy. [Readers] could also send the original copies and copperplate pictures."[52] It would not be surprising if certain readers thus became contributors to *Pictorial Weekly* and collected miscellaneous materials for the journal. *Linloon Magazine* continued the tradition, and aimed at "collecting the essence of various magazines in the world."[53]

Conclusion

This chapter has examined gender issues and the use of nudes in *Linloon Magazine*. It appears that the birth of *Linloon Magazine* was more a commercial event than an effort to create a purely "feminized space." This means that in studying gendered journals, we should consider the role of male editors, or male "editorial agency," more carefully. A particular style of "attacking men" in *Linloon Magazine* was not necessarily adopted because *Linloon Magazine* was a "women's magazine," nor was it purposefully done by "female editors." On the contrary, in many cases, it was male editors who manipulated the female voice for commercial purposes; the gendered target of a journal could be as much of a construction as the gender of women or men is. After examining the circulation of nudes in *Linloon Magazine* and *Pictorial Weekly*, I further found that images are not intrinsically gendered, but rather gendered through editorial framing. Editors selected and interpreted the same materials in different ways for variable implied audiences, in shaping the styles of their journals. In *Pictorial Weekly*, female images were often connected to social activities, to current affairs, or sometimes to satirizing women, while in *Linloon Magazine*, female images were deliberately associated with fashion, health and beauty (*jianmei*), instructive advice, or sometimes "attacking men." Generally speaking, nudes in *Linloon Magazine* often emphasized the ideology of beauty and health rather than eroticism. All of these findings complicate the question of what can or must be called a "women's magazine" or a "gendered journal"; to what extent is our assessment of these publications affected by our assumptions of the gender of the editors? Finally, this chapter asserts the value of engaging in carefully integrated and situated investigations in our study of these multifaceted texts.

[52] SYHB 5.207 (1929): 49.   [53] *Linglong* 1.48 (1932): 1977.

3 Raising Eyebrows: The Journal *Eyebrow Talk* and the Regulation of "Harmful Fiction" in Modern China

*Michel Hockx**

The journal *Meiyu* (Eyebrow talk), published from 1914 to 1916, was the first modern Chinese literary magazine edited by and targeting women. It also has the dubious honor of being the first modern Chinese literary magazine to be banned for being obscene and harmful. This paper examines exactly how the banning of this journal came about and how this affected its later reputation and its scholarly treatment up to the present day. I focus on the terminology employed to categorize transgressive publications and on the regulatory and censorial mechanisms involved in limiting their distribution. At the same time, I highlight the significant connection between the representation of women through modern print culture and the perception of moral transgression by regulating authorities.

Although the modern movement in Chinese literature positioned itself largely in opposition to traditional morality, I argue in the main body of the paper that the banning of *Eyebrow Talk* represents a crucial moment when certain ways of representing love and desire were banished from the realm of cultural acceptability, while others were elevated to the level of elite respectability. I show that gender was an important element in this process and, moreover, that the rising popularity of magazine publishing made the need for state regulation more acute. Towards the end of the paper, I will show that, in present-day China, the boom in online fiction has led to similar concerns and similar types of state intervention, once again aimed particularly at fiction produced by and for women.

Exemplifying the need for "situated" and "integrated" readings of journals, this chapter reads *Eyebrow Talk* against historical sources that shed light on its significance in discussions about morality and education. I also show how moral verdicts on *Eyebrow Talk* played a role in its dismissal by literary critics and how these dismissive comments affected scholarly treatment of the journal for many decades. I specifically focus on the role played by a misleadingly

---

* Part of this chapter is based on ongoing research carried out jointly with Liying Sun. See also her contribution to this volume.

formulated reminiscence by the famous author Lu Xun, whose involvement with *Eyebrow Talk* I demonstrate to have been much more intricate than he himself ever cared to admit. Although I do not provide a "horizontal reading" of any of the issues of *Eyebrow Talk*,[1] the censorship documents I examine provide conclusive evidence that, in the eyes of their contemporaries, journals such as *Eyebrow Talk* needed to be defined and assessed in terms of the entirety of their contents, including texts, illustrations, covers, and all the other elements that one would normally include in a horizontal reading.

I begin with a brief introduction to erotic fiction from premodern China, as a reminder that concerns about moral transgression in literature existed in China prior to the introduction of modern mechanized print culture.

Premodern Pornography

In her oft-quoted introduction to the collection *The Invention of Pornography*,[2] Lynn Hunt emphasizes the importance of the link between the spread of print culture and the emergence of pornography as "a regulatory category ... invented in response to the perceived menace of the democratization of culture."[3] Referring to Walter Kendrick's *The Secret Museum*, another classic study of the history of pornography, Hunt situates pornography in "the long-term context of the careful regulation of the consumption of the obscene so as to exclude the lower classes and women."[4] Hunt's introduction asserts a direct link between pornography and modernity. Not only did pornography as a "category of understanding" emerge around the same time as Western modernity, but its producers, according to Hunt, belonged to a "demimonde of heretics, freethinkers and libertines" that was integral to Western social and intellectual developments including "the Renaissance, the Scientific Revolution, the Enlightenment, and the French Revolution."[5]

The 1910s and 1920s in China were the period *par excellence* when Western modernity made its way into China, and terms such as "renaissance," "revolution," "science," and "enlightenment" are part and parcel of intellectual and cultural debates of the period. The introduction of these modes of thinking into China within the space of a few decades has been noted by many scholars. Most studies of Chinese literary culture of the period have not, however, paid much attention to the link between this high-speed introduction of modernity and the development of heretic or libertine genres of literary expression.

---

[1] When I introduced the concept of "horizontal reading" in 2003, one of the examples I gave at the time was a horizontal reading of part of the contents of the first issue of *Eyebrow Talk*. Cf. Hockx, *Questions of Style*, 134–36. A "vertical reading" of women's fiction from the pages of *Eyebrow Talk* is provided in Jin-Chu Huang's chapter in this volume.

[2] Hunt, "Introduction."   [3] Ibid., 13.   [4] Ibid., 12.   [5] Ibid., 10–11.

Before further exploring potential similarities between Hunt's observations about European pornography and Chinese print culture of the early twentieth century, it is important to acknowledge that China already had a print culture, and indeed pornography, well before the early twentieth century. Giovanni Vitiello, who has done extensive research on late Ming (early seventeenth-century) Chinese pornography, notices similarities between Chinese and European cultural history in that period. Referring to the work of Lynn Hunt, Vitiello writes that "[t]he history of pornography in China parallels that of European pornography."[6] Rather than looking at developments in China as outcomes of Western influence, Vitiello perceives historical symmetries in the sixteenth century that are unrelated to direct contact. These include the rise of the novel and the development of commercial printing, as well as new philosophical attitudes towards feelings and desire that are integral to late Ming Neo-Confucianism. Vitiello prefaces this analysis, however, with the comment that the history of pornography in China is short-lived. By the early eighteenth century, the Qing dynasty had firmly established a regulating category (*yinshu* or "licentious books"), which, according to Vitiello, rooted out the practice of pornography until the gradual demise of Qing power in the late nineteenth century.[7]

Dealing also with the late Ming, an essay by Paola Zamperini sets up a direct and detailed comparison between a Chinese pornographic novel and one of the French novels featured in Lynn Hunt's collection. Following Hunt and also referring to Foucault, Zamperini suggests that the historical modernity of European pornography, especially in the early period, lies in its "transgressive nature," that is, its ability "to challenge existing authority and to suggest new paradigms of thought, identity, and behaviour."[8] Zamperini emphasizes that this ability to shock and challenge the dominant culture is what gives pornography its power, in Hunt's understanding, and also what necessitates its regulation or suppression. In the late Ming novel she studies, Zamperini notes little transgressive potential, since the main female protagonist undergoes a lengthy Buddhist purification to atone for the "sins" of her younger days – although the fact that atonement is at all possible might constitute some sort of challenge to authorities who might have considered harsher punishment.

It seems, therefore, that the first rise of pornography in China did not set in motion the kind of sustained development of a transgressive, anti-authoritarian literary and visual practice and category of understanding that Hunt has outlined for the European case. Whether this is because the early development of the genre was cut short by harsh government intervention (Vitiello) or because the genre itself was less transgressive than its contemporary European counterpart (Zamperini) is hard to say. For the purposes of this paper, however, it is

---

[6] Vitiello, "The Fantastic Journey," 296.
[7] Ibid., 295.   [8] Zamperini, "Canonizing Pornography."

important to bear in mind that a pornographic tradition, as well as regulatory jargon (the category of *yinshu*), did exist in China prior to the advent of modern mechanized print culture.

Central to this premodern regulatory discourse about pornographic writing was a moralistic discourse about women. If *yinshu* or "licentious books" were the opposite of proper publications, then *yinfu* or "wanton woman" was, as pointed out by Keith McMahon (citing Ding Naifei), "the obscene antithesis of the chaste remarkable woman." The category of *yinfu* was epitomized by Pan Jinlian, the female protagonist of the Ming dynasty erotic novel *Jin Ping Mei*.[9] McMahon's work on late Qing fiction provides plenty of examples of positive and negative gender stereotypes within the wider context of the late imperial cultural ideal of polygyny (i.e., men entering into simultaneous relationships with multiple women, including a wife, several concubines, and courtesans and prostitutes). By the time *Eyebrow Talk* came out, in the third year after the fall of the Empire, modern urban elites had started to oppose polygamy. In fact, as we will see, one of the characteristic features of *Eyebrow Talk* is its celebration of the strictly monogamous relationship between the editor Gao Jianhua and her husband Xu Xiaotian. The banning of *Eyebrow Talk* therefore heralds a new chapter in the history of Chinese transgressive fiction, as its repression and regulation become intertwined with concerns about general education and women's enlightenment.

Popular Education and Problematic Women

In September 1916, the sale and reproduction of *Eyebrow Talk* were banned by order of the Ministry of the Interior (Neiwu bu), acting on advice obtained from the Ministry of Education. That ministry in turn had acted on the advice of the Popular Education Research Association (Tongsu jiaoyu yanjiuhui), a committee established by the Ministry of Education itself in order to supervise and control the distribution of popular literature (fiction, drama, and records of public speeches).

As pointed out by Paul Bailey, the discussions at the regular meetings of the Association (the minutes of which are still available and will be referred to later) focused especially on the fight against "sexual corruption." Bailey notes that many of the books proscribed by the Association were "stories of sexual adventures." What is interesting in the current context, however, is that most of the banned books mentioned by Bailey have the word "women" in the title and that, according to Bailey, "intimate adventures of women students" later even became a separate category of obscenity meant to be banned.[10] Clearly,

---

[9] McMahon, *Polygamy and Sublime Passion*, 18.
[10] Bailey, *Reform the People*, 189.

state concerns about sexual corruption were not gender-neutral and the mere mention of women in the title of a publication could potentially attract censorial attention.

The emphasis on women in *Eyebrow Talk* went well beyond its title and manifesto. First and foremost, its editor-in-chief was a woman, Gao Jianhua, who also used the name Gao Qin. Gao's dates of birth and death are unknown, but she was most likely born in the late 1880s. She grew up "at the borders of the West Lake" (i.e., in Hangzhou), was educated at Beijing Women's Normal College, and had returned to Hangzhou in the summer of 1914, where she married her cousin Xu Xiaotian (Xu Jia'en, Xu Zehua, 1886—1948), who had apparently been her childhood sweetheart. Xu, who hailed from Shangyu in Zhejiang and came from a respected literary family,[11] had been an active revolutionary during the last years of the Qing empire and a member of the anti-Qing revolutionary Restoration Society (Guangfu Hui), which was active in the Zhejiang area between 1904—1907. The female revolutionary Qiu Jin (1875—1907) was its most famous member. Both Gao and Xu are described as having been close to Qiu Jin, and both joined the Restoration Society again when it was revived in the 1940s.[12] By all accounts, Gao Jianhua and Xu Xiaotian were a close couple, and they were involved in many other publishing ventures throughout the 1920s and 1930s.[13] Xu Xiaotian died in 1948 in a traffic accident. Gao Jianhua is said to have been still alive in Shanghai in 1965. It is not clear when she died.[14]

The appearance of such a magazine would seem to be a logical outcome of a process that was set in motion about a decade earlier, namely the trend towards the open advertisement of female authorship of fiction. As Ellen Widmer has shown, the popularity of fiction written by, or presented as written by, female authors increased rapidly from 1904 onwards. Such fiction was valued especially for its purported ability "to combat women's seeming ignorance of the world."[15] In other words, women's fiction was considered part of the drive

---

[11] Xu Xiaotian's grandfather Xu Zhengshou passed the *jinshi* examination in 1829. Xiaotian's brother Xu Jiaxing (Chia-hsing Hsü) was active in Shanghai as an educator and translator and contributed to many publications of the Christian Literature Society (Guangxue hui). More information about the Xu clan can be found on the home page of Mr Xu Baowen, grandson of Xu Jiaxing and great-nephew of Xu Xiaotian.

[12] That Xu Xiaotian was an associate of Qiu's is mentioned in all biographical sources about Xu, most tracing back their acquaintance to the Datong school in Shaoxing, where Xu worked under Qiu as principal. In 1929, Xu wrote one of the four prefaces for Qiu Jin's collected posthumous works, edited by her daughter Qiu Canzhi. Gao Jianhua is referred to in most sources as "the youngest of Qiu's sworn sisters (*jiebai jiemei*)."

[13] Some of their later journal publications were similar in style to *Eyebrow Talk*. Although there were no subsequent instances of banning, some of their projects were met with mistrust and suspicion by others in the magazine world. Cf. Hockx, *Questions of Style*, 205.

[14] Information based on private correspondence with Xu Baowen, July 17, 2011.

[15] Widmer, *The Beauty and the Book*, 253.

towards enlightening those previously denied formal education. As such it came under the remit of the regulators of "popular education."

Widmer's observations about authorship raise the question of authenticity: to what extent was women's fiction written by "real" women?[16] In scholarship to date, *Eyebrow Talk* has suffered especially from suspicions pertaining to the gender of its contributors. Consequently, its pioneering status has only recently been recognized. In English-language scholarship, the *locus classicus* (in fact the only reference to *Eyebrow Talk* in English scholarship prior to 2003) is a comment by Perry Link, who stated that Gao Jianhua was "a *pro forma* editor . . . whose real purpose was to attract attention to the idea of the new-style woman in a magazine written mostly for men" and that most of the fiction published under female names was in fact penned by men.[17] Recent scholarship, especially the work of Jin-Chu Huang included in this volume, has refuted this assumption.

Most Chinese-language scholarship on *Eyebrow Talk* prior to 2004 also cites a brief description of the magazine by Lu Xun (pseudonym of Zhou Shuren, 1881−1936), the most canonical of male writers associated with the "New Culture" movement. In a 1931 essay where he passes a scathing verdict on vulgar, commercial Shanghai culture, Lu Xun gives a sarcastic description of 1910s popular fiction, which he characterizes as superficial romances of the "scholar + beauty" variety. He then mentions *Eyebrow Talk*:

The monthly journal *Eyebrow Talk* appeared at a time when the Mandarin-Ducks-and-Butterflies-style literature was flourishing. Although *Eyebrow Talk* was later banned, the power [of this style] did not wane at all. It was challenged only when *New Youth* started to become popular.[18]

In view of the canonical status of Lu Xun in socialist China, this brief comment and the concomitant verdict on the entire genre was sufficient to prevent serious scholarship on *Eyebrow Talk* for decades. Yet one would have expected that, from the 1980s onwards, as Lu Xun's status diminished and his former nemeses were given ample attention as "alternatives" to the "New Culture" mainstream, someone would have gone back and looked at *Eyebrow Talk*. This has, however, hardly happened.[19] Moreover, Lu Xun's account raises a question: if *Eyebrow*

---

[16] For an extensive discussion of how notions of authenticity and sincerity affected literary thought about women's writing during the Republican period, see Maria af Sandeberg, "Gender in Chinese Literary Thought."

[17] Link, *Mandarin Ducks and Butterflies*, 171.

[18] Lu Xun, "Shanghai wenyi zhi yipie," 294.

[19] Apart from the research by Jin-Chu Huang, represented in this volume, the most notable exception is the work done by Shen Yan for her MA thesis. See Shen, "20 shiji chu Zhongguo nüxing xiaoshuo zuojia yanjiu." An otherwise path-breaking study by Xue Haiyan devotes a long section to tabulating works of fiction written by women and published in early Republican journals, but it overlooks *Eyebrow Talk*. Cf. Xue Haiyan, *Jindai nüxing wenxue yanjiu*. A later article by

Talk was representative of such a strong popular current in modern Chinese literature, then why was it banned?

Lu Xun's Lie

When reading about *Eyebrow Talk* in secondary sources, even recent scholarship recognizing its contribution to women's fiction, it is very difficult to get an impression of the reason it was banned. Things become clearer when one looks at actual original copies of the journal, which are held in various libraries in China, and can be found sporadically in libraries elsewhere. Anyone who is familiar with the general style of literary journals of the 1910s cannot but be somewhat shocked, or surprised, when encountering the cover of the first issue of the journal, which features a woman with one exposed breast.[20] The surprise continues in leafing through the pages following the cover. As with most journals of the time, those pages are devoted to reproductions of photographs and paintings, but in the case of *Eyebrow Talk*, many of those reproductions are images of female nudes or semi-nudes.[21] In the 2006 reprint edition of the journal, the quality of the reprint is such that the nudes are hardly visible. Moreover, the reprint does not include the most provocative cover images, but instead has included the "cleansed" covers of later editions (about which more below). Therefore, although access to the contents of *Eyebrow Talk* is now much more convenient than before, because the reprint has been bought by many libraries, it is still difficult to get a full impression of the visual impact of the original journal. Moreover, even those Chinese scholars who undoubtedly did consult the original remain silent about the dominant presence of nude images in it. Apparently, scholars in China are still reluctant to discuss nudity publicly, making it all the more important that scholars outside China take the lead in studying this particular journal.

At this point it is necessary to point out that nothing in the content of *Eyebrow Talk* constitutes "pornography" in the absolute sense, as captured in Lynn Hunt's definition of pornography as "the explicit depiction of sexual organs and sexual practices with the aim of arousing sexual feelings."[22] There are no sexual organs on display anywhere in *Eyebrow Talk*. Even when fully unclothed women appear in images in the journal, the sexual organs are always covered

---

Xue indicates that she has now taken notice of Shen Yan's research, and of *Eyebrow Talk*, and calls for a larger project that might provide a more comprehensive overview of early modern Chinese women's fiction. Cf. Xue Haiyan, "Minchu (1912–1919) xiaoshuo."

[20] The image in question was painted by Zheng Mantuo (1888–1961), who is also famous for having introduced semi-nudes in advertisement posters around the same time. See Laing, *Selling Happiness*, 115.

[21] In most cases they are photographs of Western women, reproduced from so-called "erotic postcards." Cf. Sun Liying, "An Exotic Self?" 276–277.

[22] Hunt, "Introduction," 10.

Fig. 3.1 Nudes in *Eyebrow Talk*

in some way (see Figure 3.1).[23] The texts in the journal refer to sexual practices through allusion and innuendo, but they never describe such practices directly. To reiterate, what interests me in this paper is the role that *Eyebrow Talk* may have played in the development of a more relative definition of pornography as a regulatory category representing sexually oriented cultural material considered unsuitable for popular consumption. And my special interest is in how such a category is constructed in the specific case of the regulation of women's magazines.

By early 1915, i.e., not long after the founding of *Eyebrow Talk*, the Chinese Ministry of Education seems to have started to take a stronger interest in the regulation of literary journals. The March 1915 issue of *Jiaoyu zazhi* (The Chinese educational review), a widely read commercial journal that routinely reproduced official Ministry announcements and other policy-related news, contains the text of a Ministry document signaling specific concerns about the lack of good quality literature in China. The text focuses its criticism on "despicable, deviant fiction journals that are harmful to customs" (*weibi guaili you shang fengsu zhi xiaoshuo zazhi*).[24] The document makes special mention of the use

---

[23] Although, as pointed out to me by Joseph McDermott in response to a presentation of this research at Cambridge University, it might have been shocking to readers at the time that in many images the women's *feet* are not covered.

[24] "Da shi ji." According to one Chinese scholar, writing in the 1960s, this document was authored by Zhou Shuren (Lu Xun) in his capacity as Ministry official – about which more below. See Shen Pengnian, "Lu Xun," 35.

Fig. 3.2 Original and "cleansed" covers of *Eyebrow Talk* 1

of "obscene" (*yinwei*) front covers, even by fiction journals whose contents are not objectionable. The document ends by calling upon authors and publishers to clean up their act.

Possibly in response to such criticism, new print-runs of the first four issues of *Eyebrow Talk* that came out after January 1915 carry "cleansed" covers – although the contents were not changed, leaving in place the nude images in the opening pages of each issue (see Figures 3.2, 3.3, and 3.4). Still the journal continued to associate its brand with nudity in different ways, for instance, through an advertisement in the *Shenbao* of October 13, 1915, which shows an unclothed woman with one breast exposed, while the other breast and her sexual organs are covered by the two characters for "eyebrow talk" (see Figure 3.5). Moreover, as became clear in the process banning *Eyebrow Talk* in 1916, the publication of nude images was not considered to be its only transgression. Below I shall take a closer look at that process.

In July 1915, the Popular Education Research Association was founded by the Ministry of Education. Its members were Ministry officials as well as representatives from educational institutions in the capital and police representatives. The Association's main task was to judge the quality of literary publications, drama performances, and public speeches, with the explicit aim of determining which publications and performances may or may not be harmful to the general

Fig. 3.3 Original and "cleansed" covers of *Eyebrow Talk* 2

Fig. 3.4 Original and "cleansed" covers of *Eyebrow Talk* 3

Fig. 3.5 *Shenbao* advertisement for *Eyebrow Talk*

public. The Fiction Section (Xiaoshuo gu) of the Association, to which I shall limit myself here, was not simply a censorship office; i.e., it was not just in the business of banning books. It also gave prizes to books it considered especially noteworthy and provided advice about which books to include in free "popular libraries" (*tongsu tushuguan*) across the country.[25]

Although it is a well-known fact, it is still especially salient in this context that the individual chairing the Fiction Section of the Popular Education Research Association was the Ministry official Zhou Shuren, i.e., the future canonical author Lu Xun, whose reminiscence about *Eyebrow Talk* played such a key role in later scholars' perceptions of the quality of the journal. Although there has been ardent debate in China as to whether Lu Xun participated voluntarily in the banning of books or was only half-heartedly following orders, and although it has been pointed out that by the time *Eyebrow Talk* was banned Lu

---

[25] Bailey, *Reform the People*, 205.

Xun had already stepped down from his position, the minutes of the meetings he did chair in the second half of 1915 make it clear that he was the architect of the classification system by which *Eyebrow Talk* and other similar publications were later banned. Even scholars who have attempted to downplay Lu Xun's involvement in the Association have confirmed that he created the classification system that they considered to be a positive example of his stance against the "Mandarin Ducks and Butterflies" school.[26] None of the scholars taking part in these debates have attempted to consult *Eyebrow Talk* or to form an independent opinion about the journal.

An overview of the classification system for fiction, designed by Lu Xun for the Popular Education Research Association, was published in *The Chinese Educational Review* in December 1915.[27] The system proposes that the Fiction Section assess all works of fiction published in China, including both book publications and journals, in terms of a three-tier ranking: upper-rank, middle-rank, and lower-rank. Criteria are provided for what constitute upper-, middle-, or lower-rank works in eight different genre categories, defined by subject matter (education, politics, philosophy or religion, history or geography, concrete matters and science, social issues, fables and jokes, and miscellaneous writings). In most cases, the lower-rank categories are defined in terms of what is unscientific, superstitious, immoral, harmful to customs, or lewd and obscene. The document points out that the Association sees it as its task to try and promote all works assessed as "upper-rank" and that it will seek to "limit or ban" all works assessed as "lower-rank." The last sentence states that all related visual material (cover images, inside images, and illustrations) will be assessed according to the same criteria.

As part of its regulatory work, the Fiction Section compiled lists that were passed on to the Ministry, to regional associations and libraries, and later also to publishers. These lists are included in the Association's annual reports (*baogaoshu*) and, when examined with the present context in mind, they draw attention to two further important details about the censorship system. First, the lists create two additional ranking categories, namely a top category called "upper-rank with award" (*shangdeng gei jiang*) and a bottom category called "lower-rank and banned" (*xiadeng jinzhi*). Second, the lists show that fiction magazines were assessed as a whole; i.e., a single verdict was made on the basis of one or more issues of the journal and no individual verdicts were made about works of fiction included in those journals.

Throughout 1916 the Fiction Section, by then no longer chaired by Lu Xun, applied these principles to their readings of and discussions about fiction submitted for assessment by the publishers themselves, as well as fiction found on

---

[26] Cf. Chen Shuyu, "Lu Xun yu tongsu jiaoyu yanjiuhui," 75.
[27] "Tongsu jiaoyu yanjiu hui," 108–9.

sale in Beijing. Although 1916 witnessed a significant change in government, with Yuan Shikai's attempts to restore the monarchy thwarted and Yuan himself dying soon after, the policy towards popular education and the regulation of fiction seems to have remained relatively consistent throughout. In this context, Paul Bailey observes that Chinese educators involved in regulating fiction between 1912 and 1918 only criticized work considered to have "a damaging effect on sexual morality."[28] Unlike later critics associated with the post-1918 New Literature movement, these educators and regulators did not take an overall dismissive stance towards what would later be called "Mandarin Ducks and Butterflies" fiction. This is presumably what Lu Xun meant when he wrote in his later reminiscence that the style of fiction epitomized by *Eyebrow Talk* remained popular until it was challenged by the *New Youth* group.

It is indeed the case that the Fiction Section made no attempt at all to exercise a blanket ban on works of the "butterfly" variety. In fact, only a very small number of works were banned, and even fewer magazines, which makes the case of *Eyebrow Talk* all the more interesting. It confirms that those holding real power to regulate the publication of literary work considered *Eyebrow Talk* to be on the wrong side of a dividing line between work that was substandard but harmless and work that was substandard and dangerous, and therefore to be outlawed. Seen in this light, *Eyebrow Talk* represents not the epitome of "butterfly fiction," but something considered *worse* than "butterfly fiction." This might also explain why, in spite of the general rehabilitation of "butterfly fiction" in Chinese academia and more widely in Chinese culture since the 1980s, *Eyebrow Talk* has remained in obscurity.

Censorial Considerations

As mentioned above, *Eyebrow Talk* was officially banned only five months after its last issue had come out. It may be that the journal had stopped publication for other reasons, entirely unrelated to the later banning. In my view, however, it is more likely that the publisher, the New Learning Society (Xinxue huishe), which had sales branches in all major cities in China and appears to have derived most of its income from the sale of textbooks, i.e., from educational activity, was sensitive to the policies coming down from the Ministry of Education and closed down the journal pre-emptively. Moreover, the investigation may have taken longer than usual due to the political turmoil that summer. Be that as it may, when the final verdict came in September 1916, the censors' opinion, as reproduced in the following month's *Jiaoyu gongbao* (Education gazette), was very clear. *Eyebrow Talk* was banned because

---

[28] Bailey, *Reform the People*, 190.

its language and topics seem specifically aimed at destroying moral barriers and harming social standards. It is the most offensive of all the fiction journals . . .

The *fiction and images* printed in *Eyebrow Talk* are largely of an obscene nature and of ridiculous intention. They seem to have no idea of the meaning of respecting human dignity.[29] [emphasis added]

The same issue of the *Education Gazette* also reproduces the directive from the Ministry of the Interior in which it states its approval of the request for banning and decrees that all sales and printings of the journal must be repressed.[30]

As suggested in my joint research with Liying Sun,[31] the wording of the banning order is important: *Eyebrow Talk* was not banned just for its images, but also for its fiction. Although no concrete examples are provided, it is possible to speculate which specific content would have been considered, in the words of the banning order cited above, "aimed at destroying moral barriers and harming social standards." One of our preliminary conclusions is that, apart from the nudity, it was also the description of romantic and physical intimacy, in some cases with sexual overtones and often amplified by the presence of illustrations featuring intimate couples (including same-sex couples),[32] that may have been considered transgressive at the time – although as mentioned above, none of the descriptions or illustrations feature explicit sexual activity. Transgressiveness might also have been found in the many texts devoted to celebrating the intimacy between the editor Gao Jianhua and her husband Xu Xiaotian, including a very early occurrence of the "new love-letters" (*xin qingshu*) genre, as well as references to hugging and kissing.[33] These may seem innocuous nowadays but may have been considered harmful in the mid-1910s, especially in the context of a genre (fiction) and a type of publication (illustrated magazine) that was widely perceived at the time as playing a crucial role in popular education.

Further evidence that transgressiveness was found not only in the images but also in the fiction in *Eyebrow Talk* emerges when reading through the 1917 annual report of the Popular Education Research Association. First and foremost, the report refers in several places to a new journal, entitled *Shuoye* (literally: Speaking of the armpit), edited by Xu Xiaotian and published by the New Learning Society, of which seven issues were found to be in circulation. The report indicates that although *Shuoye* appeared to be in book format, it was in fact a journal reprinting large amounts of fiction previously published in *Eyebrow Talk*. There is no mention of images in the report, yet once again

---

[29] "Zi neiwu bu."   [30] Ibid., 50.   [31] Hockx and Sun, "Women and Scandal."
[32] For a brief discussion of some images of same-sex intimacy in *Eyebrow Talk*, see Sang, *The Emerging Lesbian*, 1–3.
[33] Xu Xiaotian, "Xin qingshu shi shou."

a decision is taken to ban the publication. Just as *Eyebrow Talk* was the only banned journal on the 1916 list published by the Fiction Section, *Shuoye* is the only banned journal on its 1917 list.

During its March and May 1917 meetings, the Fiction Section discussed the case of individual works of fiction that had previously appeared (presumably serialized) in *Eyebrow Talk* and were now published as books. The question was raised if every single work that ever appeared in *Eyebrow Talk* should automatically be banned, and the conclusion arrived at was that this should not be the case. Fiction Section member Gao Buying presented the consensus opinion as follows, as recorded in the minutes of the meeting: "Mr Gao Buying stated that in the past our Association had banned *Eyebrow Talk* on the basis of its editorial principles [or perhaps 'editorial layout,' *bianji tiaoli*]. It was never said that all fiction in it should be banned."

In relation to other cases discussed at the meetings, the censors also expressed concern about the effect of their decisions. They showed themselves well aware of the fact that their banning orders might in fact create more interest in "harmful fiction" (*buliang xiaoshuo* – the term most frequently used to describe their target), resulting in more illegal copies being distributed. Their lists, which were published in the media and presumably circulated to libraries around the country, might become free advertisements for the substandard works they were trying to suppress. They also showed concern that they could only limit the circulation, but had no means of rooting out the production of "harmful fiction," because many of the publishing houses were safely ensconced in the foreign concessions in Shanghai, where the Ministry had no jurisdiction. They even went so far as to send a letter to the Jiangsu provincial authorities (responsible for governing the nonforeign parts of Shanghai), asking them to help find a solution. The reply from Jiangsu was simple: they had absolutely no authority over what went on in the foreign concessions. The discussion about this problem also points up another subtle distinction: it is noted that the foreign concessions do carry out their own policies regarding the suppression of obscene (*yinhui*) material, but that they have no interest in addressing potential harm to "customs" (*fengsu*). Clearly, the Chinese regulators wished to see a wider category of publications suppressed than their European counterparts who governed the concessions.[34] In the case of fiction, their concern was that this genre, considered at the time in China as the most promising form of

[34] A relevant context here is constituted by the international treaties concerning the "repression of obscene publications," the first of which dates from 1910. This might have been the basis on which the foreign concessions regulated pornography. China was at this time not yet a signatory to this treaty (it joined in 1923) but seems to have opted for even stricter domestic legislation. National differences in interpretation of what did or did not constitute an "obscene publication" appear to have thwarted the implementation of such treaties for many years. A fuller treatment of this aspect awaits further research.

writing for inspiring and educating the general populace, could become a danger to popular education if it were to focus on transgressive topics.

The content of *Eyebrow Talk*, however, is by no means solely focused on attempts at transgression. In terms of visual content, the journal's editors demonstrate a comprehensive interest in the lives of women, publishing an extensive series of photographs of Chinese women in different settings and practicing different occupations (see Figure 3.6). In some of its fiction, such as Gao Jianhua's short story "The Words of the Nude Beauty,"[35] the theme of nudity is employed to comment on the vanity of adornment and embellishment and the fate of women who functioned only as "pretty property" of their husbands in patriarchal society. Another strong interest of the journal is in the so-called "New Drama" (*xinju*) movement, which, among other things, promoted the practice of male and female actors appearing together on stage.

Interestingly, many of these themes (romantic love, the position of women, the aesthetic appreciation of the nude, new drama) were later taken up by the "May Fourth" generation, including Lu Xun himself. The members of that generation, too, were accused of immorality by cultural conservatives, but somehow they managed to cultivate a "serious," "detached" attitude that allowed them to establish themselves as *connoisseurs*, rather than as *profiteurs*. In contrast, their distaste for and distrust of journals such as *Eyebrow Talk* stems from their suspicion that its publication was first and foremost a commercial venture, selling libertinism to the uneducated masses without considering the consequences. The trade-off appears to have been that the "May Fourth" generation was itself largely unable to reach out to any readers outside their own circles. Whether *Eyebrow Talk* really had a much wider readership than, say, *New Youth* is difficult to verify. What seems clear, however, is that the *suspicion* that it might reach a wide audience, including a large female audience, together with the topics it chose to address and the often rather playful manner in which it chose to address them, combined to push *Eyebrow Talk* towards what Bradford Mudge called the "cultural nether world," while the "May Fourth" generation forced itself to "ascend to the transcendent heights of 'high art.'"[36]

Transgression and Regulation in Today's China

In the contemporary People's Republic of China, a postsocialist state with a strongly moralistic government, the issues addressed in this paper are unfolding in fascinating ways on a new playing field: the Internet. Pornography, now defined as the graphic depiction of sexual acts, is banned in China on the basis of a comprehensive moral argument: it is considered "harmful" to all citizens, regardless of age, as opposed to the situation in most Western countries, which

[35] Gao, "Luoti meiren yu."   [36] Mudge, *The Whore's Story*, xiii.

Fig. 3.6 Photographs of women's everyday lives in *Eyebrow Talk*

stipulate an age-limit of eighteen for legal access to pornographic material. Regulation is most apparent with regard to "popular" media such as film and especially television, but the increasingly popular Internet is much more difficult to regulate. In recent years, online entrepreneurs have begun to undermine the state-owned publishing system by setting up commercial websites for popular genre fiction. These websites function as publishers: they contract authors to serialize their novels on their websites, and they charge online readers for access to those writings. In doing so, they circumvent the regulations of the print-based publishing system, which requires every publication to be preapproved by government censors through the "book number" (*shuhao*) system.[37]

Women writers (or male writers using female avatars) appear to have taken the lead in this industry by creating several hugely popular forms of transgressive erotica, which are said to cater to literally millions of predominantly female readers. The most well-known of these genres is *danmei* (known in English as "Boys' Love" or BL for short): erotic stories featuring pretty, young, male homosexual partners, often presented as fan fiction based on characters from popular novels, films, or TV series.[38] So important is female participation in this industry that literally all the main websites now show, at the top of their home pages, very prominent direct links to the "women's writing" section.

Although strong female participation in the production and consumption of genre fiction is the norm in other parts of the world as well, as is the presence of erotic elements in such fiction, the Chinese case is interesting because the authorities are still hesitant to accept the more erotically tinted works as harmless entertainment, and continue to worry about its effect on China's citizens. In 2007, the General Administration of Press and Publication (GAPP), which regulates the Chinese publishing industry, announced that it would seek to eradicate "online obscene and pornographic fiction" (*wangluo yinhui seqing xiaoshuo*). Since 2009, GAPP has been publishing regular blacklists of websites that feature "obscene and pornographic content."[39] Although the word "fiction" now no longer appears in the title of those lists, the actual websites listed are predominantly fiction sites. The uncertain status of the issue is emphasized by the fact that the websites are blacklisted as a form of "naming and shaming"; i.e., it is made public that they carried pornographic content, which they have been asked to remove, but the sites themselves are not closed down.

---

[37] This system is circumvented by some print-based publishers as well, but arguably not so easily. For a study of the so-called "second channel" in traditional publishing in the PRC, see Kong, *Consuming Literature*.

[38] For a pioneering study of this genre in China and its main website, Jinjiang, which is entirely focused on women's writing, see Feng, "Addicted to Beauty."

[39] I am grateful to Ashley Esarey for pointing me in the direction of this material. For an example of such lists, preserved by the Internet Archive Wayback Machine, see http://web.archive.org/web/20121108011729/http://www.gapp.gov.cn/cms/html/21/413/201105/716458.html.

Unsurprisingly, the same sites end up in the Top Three of the lists every time they are published.

The term *buliang xiaoshuo* (harmful fiction), referred to above as the term of choice to describe transgressive journals such as *Eyebrow Talk* by the Chinese government of the 1910s, is still in use today. Morally bad fiction is still seen as a force that might corrupt the general populace. Interestingly, the term has also been adopted by netizens wanting to read such fiction and actively roaming the forums to ask if anyone knows where they can download harmful fiction. Some of the genre fiction sites have latched onto this trend by featuring all kinds of works with the word *buliang* in the title and even floating potential future genre categories such as *haokan de buliang xiaoshuo* (well-written harmful fiction).

Almost a century after the banning of *Eyebrow Talk*, Chinese netizens, many of them female, are using a wide range of playful and creative methods to undermine the long-cherished and long-defended link between fiction and morality, as well as the government's authority to regulate both. If the *Eyebrow Talk* material were to appear on the Internet in China today, most likely nobody would raise an eyebrow (pun intended). In time, this will hopefully result in this journal also receiving at least some measure of dedicated scholarly attention in China itself. As I hope to have shown through this situated reading of the journal, *Eyebrow Talk* is unique in its ability to shed light on a set of moral and literary standards, as well as a set of educational policies and censorship policies, that have continued relevance to the study of Chinese culture today.

Coda: Women's Journals through the Prism of Late Qing Fiction

Ellen Widmer

My recent book, *Fiction's Family: Zhan Xi, Zhan Kai, and the Business of Women in Late Qing China*, examines three novels in which women's journals play a crucial role: *Nü yuhua* (Female jail flower), published in 1904 by Wang Miaoru, *Nüwa shi* (The stone of goddess Nüwa), by Haitian Duxiaozi, published in the same year, and *Nüzi quan* (Women's power) by Siqi Zhai (pen-name of Zhan Kai, 1861?–1911?), published in1907.[1] These novels are part of a much larger group written specifically for women readers between 1904 and 1907[2] and they significantly reflect the changing relationship between women and fiction at this time. Whereas traditional fiction was often risqué and hence mostly off limits for proper women, reformers of the late Qing obviously hoped to upgrade the form and use it as a vehicle of social change.[3] In this fiction, the female figure engaging with women's journals at the time would become an object of public discussion and public scrutiny.

Wang Miaoru's *Female Jail Flower* is generally accepted as the work of a woman. After a few dramatic adventures, one of the novel's heroines, Sha Xuemei, comes across a group of women dedicated to the idea of improving the world from a women's point of view. One among the group is an editor of a women's paper (*nübao*), whose title is unspecified. The magazine's rhetoric is uncompromising in its call for improving conditions for women, including by violent means. It is also quite anti-male. When a part-time contributor to the magazine falls ill, Xuemei steps in. Eventually she writes a whole novel, *Choushu* (The book of revenge), for the newspaper. As events in the novel unfold, Xuemei and her group of radical agitators take their own lives after an abortive attempt to improve conditions for women.

Female Jail Flower casts women's journals in a rather ambiguous light. It is partly thanks to them that Xuemei acquires the ideology to cope with her desperate situation. Although she is presented as a positive character, the novel is

---

[1] Widmer, *Fiction's Family*. *Women's Power* is the second of two reformist novels by this author, both published in the same year: the title of his earlier novel is *Zhongguo xin nühao* (China's new heroines).

[2] For a fuller list of such titles see Aying, *Wanqing*, 120–33.

[3] See David Wang, *Fin-de-siècle Siecle*, 23–30.

clearly of the view that she can never fit comfortably in the real world surrounding her. Her methods are too violent, her point of view too uncompromising, and her attitudes toward men too negative. The novel sees more of a future for another female character, Pingquan, who is depicted as more gracious and ladylike and who is able to contemplate marriage, even though she does not finalize plans to marry before the novel ends. The text suggests that education and medicine are safer careers for women than journalism. Journalism, the novel seems to say, can raise important ideas, but it cannot always control the way women readers will respond, and it can lead them into dangers that could threaten their lives.

The plot of the second novel, *Goddess Nüwa's Stone*, is quite different, but the attribution to women of explosive reactions to women's periodicals is similar. The point is made already in the first chapter. There, a seemingly peaceful woman, Qian Yifang, is provoked by her reading of European history to write a poem and article and submit them to a journal entitled *Nü xuebao* (Journal of women's learning). The story of Cleopatra, in particular, rouses her to action. She is outraged to think that China's current plight is related to men's predominance in positions of power. Were women to have the right to hold office, they could do a much better job of ruling the country and bringing it out of its current state of humiliation, she believes. Qian's two pieces are quoted in the text, the poem in full, the essay in part. Their radical tone is typical of articles in the actual women's journal of this name (the *Journal of Women's Learning* discussed in Chapter 10), but the writings are invented.[4] Soon Qian Yifang disappears from the unfinished novel and a crew of amazons appears. With this move, *Goddess Nüwa's Stone* transfers the action to a more fantastic plane.

Although *Female Jail Flower* never provides a title for the magazine that energizes Sha Xuemei, the fictional magazine she reads and writes for must have been more or less like the *Journal of Women's Learning* in *Goddess Nüwa's Stone* in its uncompromisingly radical stance and its unwillingness to work with men. Both novels pose a contrast between more and less radical strategies, and they assign the fictional women's periodicals and the space they provide to the more radical side. Without these periodicals as outlets for women's frustrations, it seems, neither crew of amazons would have been as fully activated.

In the third novel, *Women's Power*, there is again a contrast between radical and peaceful strategies, and again this is one in which women's journals play a big role. Unlike Zhan Kai's earlier novel of the same year, entitled *Zhongguo xin nühao* (China's new heroines), this one has no violent women among its main characters, and the plot has been softened in at least one other way: Yuan Zhenniang (this novel's heroine) is pursued by her male friend (she does not

---

[4] I am indebted to Nanxiu Qian for help with this point.

actively pursue him). I believe this moderation was intended to reassure read-ers and censors that the novel's agenda conformed to "proper" boundaries for women.

A key turning point in the novel is when Zhenniang meets a woman who has connections in the newspaper world. She asks Zhenniang whether she would like to try her hand at writing an editorial on women's rights. Zhenniang's first draft is cogently argued, and the woman sees to its immediate publication. Without asking permission, she affixes Zhenniang's name to the document, and Zhenniang becomes famous all over China. She happens to be on her way to a school in Beijing at the time of publication. Once she arrives, her fellow stu-dents convince her to found a women's newspaper. It will be called the *Nüzi guomin bao* (Women citizens' news). She and the students who will work with her on this project decide upon a set of rules for incorporation. These provide important insights into how women's periodicals at the time may have been run. (Zhan Kai was a journalist and knew the profession well.) The rules per-tain to the name of the paper; the amount of money stockholders must raise; the timing of publication (daily); the language to be used (half vernacular and half classical); the election of chief officers by stockholders; the content of the newspaper (editorials, fiction, and news); the establishment of distribution cen-ters in every province; the exemption of articles and letters from publication fees if they help women; the printing only of advertisements that pertain to women; the exclusive employment of women; and the distribution of profits to stockholders, with any extra being used to set up branch offices.[5] After suffi-cient funds are raised through Zhenniang's schoolmates, who represent every Chinese province and can appeal to women's schools in their home areas, per-mits are obtained from the necessary government ministries, the newspaper is incorporated, and a headquarters is found.

The paper attracts a good deal of attention. Yet trouble arises when women readers extend the space of the journal to real space and attempt to set up clubs and societies in response to this publication. The phenomenon of clubs of female newspaper readers is an interesting offshoot of the newspaper cul-ture described by Zhan Kai. In Hunan interest spreads like wildfire. When the journal advocates freedom from male control, a provision with which Zhen-niang disagrees, corrections are made to the charter of *Women's Citizens' News*: it becomes less anti-masculine and the radical groups in Hunan also simmer down. A worse problem erupts in Xinjiang. There, women's groups lose con-trol altogether and attack legal authorities, killing several people in the process. Significantly, the violent women are not friends of the heroine but emerge from fringe groups lying well outside her acquaintance.

---

[5] See p. 34 of the first edition in the Shanghai Library. Amy Dooling calls this part of the novel a "how to" manual for setting up a newspaper. See her "Revolution."

With this development, reprisals against Zhenniang's newspaper begin. The authorities disband affiliated clubs all over China. As the person in charge, Zhenniang is in danger of being arrested. However, by this time her father has taken a position of political authority in Beijing. Out of courtesy to his rank, the authorities decide not to arrest Zhenniang, but instead put her under house arrest at the newspaper office. The associate editor is then asked to stand in and take the blame. However, she is of frail constitution and dies in prison. Zhenniang is understandably depressed by this sad outcome. When her father asks her to give up newspaper work she accedes. The newspaper will go on, but without Zhenniang at the helm. We later learn that the newspaper continues to attract interest and subscribers, but under another woman's control.

As in *Female Jail Flower* and *Goddess Nüwa's Stone*, the fictional newspaper in *Women's Power* plays an ambiguous role. It makes many credible points, and there is no doubt that its editor, Zhenniang, is reliable (in the author's opinion), in the sense that she is a moderate progressive and believes women reformers should work with and not against men. But whether because its readers are not sophisticated enough, or because of the incendiary nature of the subject matter, women's journals cannot always keep issues from spinning out of control. Even with as reliable a leader as Zhenniang at the helm, *Women's Citizens' News* still has the potential to cause violence in outlying areas such as Hunan and Xinjiang. Zhenniang is on much more solid footing, in the author's mind, when she pursues other methods of achieving reform. One possibility is the *Zhongguo furen hui* (Chinese Women's Organization) that is brought to readers' attention in an appendix to the novel.

The question can be asked at this point of whether the *Women's Citizens' News* was based on any existing periodical, and if so, which. Other than *Journal of Women's Learning*, there were several newspapers or magazines at the time with progressive enough agendas to have served as models. Among these are Qiu Jin's (1875–1907) *Zhongguo nübao* (Chinese women's news). As a person whose journalism made her well known, Qiu Jin's experiences are quite likely to have informed Zhan's novels, and it is conceivable that the toned-down quality of *Women's Power* (in contrast to Zhan's earlier novel) was a response to her arrest and execution.[6] However, it does not seem that she or any other woman editors were unique influences. For example, the charter guiding Qiu's *Chinese Women's News* contains points that are similar but not identical to those

---

[6] Qiu died on July 15, 1907, by the Western calendar. This is the sixth day of the sixth month by the lunar calendar (the sixth month runs from July 10 to August 8 on the Western calendar). Both of Zhan's novels were published in the sixth month of Guangxu 33. *China's New Heroines* was printed at the beginning of the sixth month; *Women's Power* was printed in the sixth month, not necessarily at the beginning. Adding this evidence together, we come up with the possibility that *China's New Heroines* came out before Qiu's death and *Women's Power* came out afterwards.

for *Women Citizens' News*,[7] and Qiu's struggles to raise funds for her publication contrast with the perfect ease with which funds for *Women Citizens' News* are raised. Additionally, *Women's Power* is more interested in employment for disadvantaged women, whereas Qiu Jin focuses on the basic indignities faced by all classes of women.

Setting aside the question of which real women's journals may have been models, we find that Zhan's own rhetoric follows that in *Goddess Nüwa's Stone* quite closely. Thus, his novel suggests that a women's journal can create excessive disruption as well as raising useful questions. A far less incendiary route for women is to work in professions like education or medicine, or join clubs like the Chinese Women's Organization. Unlike *Female Jail Flower* and *Goddess Nüwa's Stone*, Zhan does not present amazon-like heroines in his second novel, but his more toned-down female leaders imply a belief that women make their best contributions through professions that do not aim to arouse readers.

We know from the prefaces to his novels that Zhan Kai was quite progressive for his time. He believed that women's rights, including voting and employment rights, were necessary if China was ever to become whole. But he also thought that a strong push in this direction would have to wait until constitutional government was firmly in place, and that women should always work in concert with men. Furthermore, the events his novels describe are set roughly forty years in the future. He does not imagine such reforms occurring any time soon. In these provisos, he is far less radical than Wang Miaoru, not to mention Qiu Jin and He Zhen.

The way readership is portrayed in these novels is also of interest. It is telling that in *Female Jail Flower* only the more radical Xuemei is shown to be deeply immersed in reading a woman's journal. This selectivity allows the journals to be seen as appealing particularly to radicals. Likewise, when Qian Yifang is outraged by her reading of European history, it is to a woman's journal that she turns. Had her feelings been less inflamed, would Cleopatra's story have led her to submit writings to such an outlet? Similarly, Zhenniang never sought to enter the newspaper business, and she eventually left it behind. Can we deduce from this evidence that calm women, women with sophisticated reading skills such as Zhenniang, would prefer to stay away from women's journals? Or was it rather that the novelists wanted to oversimplify, portraying these journals as intent on rupturing the status quo and thus coding them as more incendiary than they really were? This second alternative accords with the iconography by which women's journals were linked to amazons and violence in *Female Jail Flower* and *Goddess Nüwa's Stone*. If Zhan Kai deliberately removed amazons from his second novel, whether or not in response to Qiu Jin's fate, he may have done so advisedly, with a sense that some woman readers preferred

---

[7] On Qiu's draft charter see "Chuangban," 10–11.

quieter modes of self-expression or that censors would find less to object to in what he had to say. The overriding point is that in our novelists' view women's periodicals provided the space to foster incendiary reactions. Circumspect, progressive women might prefer face-to-face encounters as a less risky means of contributing to progressive change.

These possibilities suggest that women's journals had an impact not only on women readers, who may or may not have known how to handle them, but also on male literati, who worried about their impact – the space these journals opened up to women had not been calibrated sufficiently. It is in the case of a woman author, Wang Miaoru, that they play the most positive role, even though they largely disappear once Pingquan appears on stage. Both male writers, Haitian Duxianzi and Zhan Kai, are clearly more worried about the power of women's journals to lead women astray. Yet none of our authors cast such concerns in terms of their own anxieties. Instead we are shown the "objective truth" that women's journals would provoke disaster if proper precautions were not exercised. Considering that our novelists wrote on the eve of, or even after, Qiu Jin's arrest and execution, we might agree that they had a point about disaster. But this consideration does not fully explain their tendency to write their own fears and cautions into their novels. If we sought the full truth of what it meant to have radical women's journals on the scene in the late Qing, we would want to go beyond the novels considered here.

Our three novels tell us something about what happened when new journals for women emerged during the late Qing. Even if we look only at the fears they generated, we can conclude that their impact was profound. In addition, *Women's Power* is of value for its detailed information about the steps one had to take to launch such a journal, although it sometimes makes the process sound easier than it was. As long as one remembers that they are fiction, these three novels lend useful insights into how early women's journals were received by contemporary readers. They draw a map of the unsettling thoughts that these journals' pioneering opening of new space for women's articulations and women's concerns had engendered.

Part II

A Space of Their Own: The Woman's Journal, Generic Choice and the Making of Female Public Expression

Our volume is structured around the notion of women's journals as multipurpose spaces that offered both old and new avenues of expression for women. The chapters in this section of the book use horizontal, vertical, integrated and situated readings to illustrate the variety of uses to which these new spaces were put. They deliberate on the complexities of female public expression by focusing on the range of generic choices available to women in this new medium. The prime organizing principle of these chapters is the generically varied deployment of women's voices in the pages of the periodical press.

Grace Fong examines female self-crafting through established as well as changing poetic modes. Jin-Chu Huang demonstrates how the women's media opened avenues for rethinking women's (sexual) possibilities through romantic fiction. Rachel Hsu shows the importance of the polemical essay – a radically new genre of female self-expression – in articulating women's views on love, marriage and sexuality. Siao-chen Hu traces two familiar genres of women's writing – intimate letters between close female friends and autobiographical writing – that took on new salience in the periodical press. She highlights the extent to which the women's press established lasting networks of public communication between women while also serving as a new pedagogical space.

Women's journals, as other chapters indicate, taught almost everything. They offered instruction in how to reform one's home, as Maria af Sandeberg discusses. They also helped women refashion themselves, as did the women artists featured in Doris Sung's chapter. Closely reading women's contributions across a range of genres and magazines from the late Qing and early Republic, the chapters in this section also show examples of women "talking back" – to men and to existing norms and conventions – a point to which Jennifer Scanlon draws our attention in her opening reflection.

Reflection
Writers and Readers: Constituting the Space of Women's Journals

Jennifer Scanlon

Women's journals are allegedly merely ephemeral – their messages ultimately as replaceable as they themselves are, issue after issue. Yet the scholars assembled in this collection claim their value, and both imagine and demonstrate that contemporary readers claimed their value as well. We see these journals as instrumental, reflecting and then also shaping the cultures from which they emerged. We read them in ways that attempt to honor both the writers and the readers in what we might call these "imagined communities."[1] While reading magazines is a pleasurable experience, for the scholar it must also be a technical exercise.[2]

So how do we undertake this exercise and read these journals? And in reading them, how do we account, historically, for the women who wrote for women's journals or who read them, particularly when these publications often lionize the domestic sphere and only teasingly consider alternatives? Do we end up, as we consider the lives of women's journal writers and readers, vacillating somewhere among attributions of opportunism, false consciousness and individual agency?

Readers and writers, we believe, managed to craft relationships with these journals that were at once productive, contested, and significant – to carve out a space of their own. The authors who created this space – among them, in the Chinese case, Fong's poets, Sung's artists, Huang's fiction writers, Hsu's polemicists, and Hu's letter writers – were not always subservient to a larger cultural agenda, and often, in fact, as bell hooks urges, used their writing for women's journals as forms of "talking back."[3]

We must take seriously the notion that both the readers and the writers were engaged in something significant in the first place by putting pen to paper or by reading the journals. One of the critical ways in which women make themselves known to themselves, each other, and the world around them is through their uses of language: by engaging with language through reading

---

[1] Anderson, *Imagined Communities*.
[2] See Hermes, *Reading Women's Magazines*, and McCracken, *Decoding Women's Magazines*.
[3] hooks, *Talking Back*.

the works of others, talking with others about what they read, or writing poetry and prose themselves. "Woman must write her self," feminist theorist Hélène Cixous admonished, and both Jin-Chu Huang and the female authors for *Eyebrow Talk* that she introduces fully concur. Similarly to Cixous, these authors understood that only by engaging with language can women find themselves, discover in a meaningful way their bodies and their minds, and construct their own ideas, their own womanhoods or femininities.[4] Reading, writing, talking about reading and writing – all of these things are modes of breaking silence, a critical step in interrogating the world around us, for as Margaret Atwood writes and as the women writers discussed in, for example, Rachel Hsu's article may have implicitly understood, "Powerlessness and silence go together."[5]

In and outside of women's journals, of course, women struggle with and through language, an entity that simultaneously illuminates and obscures, relates and obfuscates. As Margaret Atwood claims, "language is always both a tool, a medium, and something that limits. It's always both things."[6] So too, are women's journals – tools, or media, and something that limits. Today, as readers with considerable historical and other forms of distance from these publications and their original readers, we ourselves must read with care, finding in the popular or the ephemeral a range of cultural messages, conditionings, and formulations.

Surely women's journals, particularly those designed for women in the domestic sphere such as the early Chinese *The Ladies' Journal*, have provided fairly conservative definitions of womanhood. They offered readers a template for living, one delineated through family and household relationships. They also offered an image of the essential female, a kind of composite woman, in whatever context they emerge from, be it, in the Chinese context, the late nineteenth century reform movement, the May Fourth era, or contemporary life.

But how did magazine readers actually interact with these fairly conservative messages, and with this composite woman? How did they read her? Certainly, the messages to conform, accommodate, and place or accept gendered limitations had an impact. But can we not also imagine women having a range of responses to journal messages? Here we have to imagine the possibilities of reading as empowerment, of reading as a form of resistance, utilizing the mind, letting language liberate as well as constrain. We have to employ, in conjunction with the horizontal, vertical, integrated, and situated approaches emphasized in this volume, reading against the grain.[7] We have to imagine,

---

[4] Cixous, "Laugh of the Medusa," 875.
[5] Atwood in an address to Amnesty International, in Atwood, *Second Words*, 396.
[6] Atwood in an interview with Jan Garden Castro, "Interview with Margaret Atwood," 226.
[7] See, for reading fiction against the grain, Fetterley, *The Resistant Reader;* for reading women's magazines in this way, see Scanlon, *Inarticulate Longings*, and Beetham, *A Magazine of Her Own?*

when we read fiction or editorial materials, that contemporary readers had not one but multiple responses to what they read.

In many women's journals, for example, women are told repeatedly about the rewards of domestic life, particularly if, as in af Sandeberg's chapter, they conform to the new pedagogies the journals promote. Why, we might ask, must women be reminded of this continuously if domestic life is actually as rewarding as promised? Redundancy, which is revealed through careful vertical readings, is one marker for the scholarly reader interested in reading against the grain, as it suggests that contemporary readers may in fact have been behaving in ways that necessitated a kind of reining in.

Another marker for the scholar is the "happy ending." Fiction or even editorial matter in women's journals often follows the pattern of introducing conflict but resolving it in fairly pat ways. As scholars, we ask which element of the piece proved more lasting for the reader: the conflict or its resolution?

As we examine these journals, we can also explore through a horizontal approach the relationship between the visual and the textual elements. When do they support each other and when do they appear impossibly paired? Women's journals often employ visual markers such as reproductions of fine art pieces to communicate class and sophistication, as discussed by Sung. These visual representations may or may not actually provide coherent messages when explored in tandem with the textual elements. Is the artwork meant to elevate the discourse and by extension the reader? Conversely, might artists in the vanguard look to women's journals to expand their audiences and shift definitions of womanhood by visual means?

By giving respect to the actual readers of women's journals, and by employing methodological practices of reading against the grain, scholars learn more about the cultures from which the journals emerge: how often messages have to be repeated in order to become part of the social fabric, how women's journals play with cultural messages in order to keep their readerships, and how women's journal readers negotiate these same messages. We can, as a result, more carefully and profitably interrogate the reaches and the internal dynamics of these imagined communities.

4   Radicalizing Poetics: Poetic Practice in *Women's World*, 1904–1907

Grace Fong

Introduction

This chapter explores the changing status of women and of poetry in the late Qing and the articulation of these two interrelated changes in the discursive space of *Nüzi shijie* (hereafter *Women's World*), the third journal published in the late Qing explicitly targeting a female readership. Similarly to other periodicals of the early twentieth century, *Women's World* constituted a heteroglossic space; that is, the journal included many mixed, hybrid, and even contradictory voices in writings that ranged widely over genres, language registers, content, style, and rhetoric in its diverse columns. The levels of language used ranged from highly ornate parallel prose to simple literary language, to various degrees of mixture of the literary and vernacular, and also of simple spoken colloquial or regional dialects, as found in some transcriptions of public speeches. In rhetoric and content, we find the heroic and revolutionary, the traditional feminine didactic, the modern scientific-hygienic, and the new pedagogical diction. Stylistic and register differences tend to be found between the different columns, whereas thematic and topical issues cross genres and columns.

Within the discursive spaces opened up in this new women's journal, I intend to show how educated women from literati and official families trained in classical poetic genres participated in the broader reformist movement that promoted and produced "new-style" poetry. In *Women's World*, the form and dynamics of women's poetic practice manifest a profound expressive shift to fuse the personal dimension with public concerns in exemplary poems published over the life of the journal from 1904 to 1907. Significantly, the journal also included contributions by male writers who published under female pennames. Together, these literary productions challenge tendencies to make gender assumptions on the basis of language and style. At the same time, I suggest that this emergent poetics in women's poetry published in *Women's World* arose as a short marriage of women's established literary practice in the late imperial period and the late Qing "revolution in the poetic realm" (*shijie geming*), which advocated radically new themes and vocabulary in poetic production.[1] Some of the questions driving the analysis are as follows: Who were the women and men producing these poems? How was poetic discourse implicated in contemporary cultural and social issues? How did this "old" vehicle serve women in their attempts to carve out a "new" voice and public presence at this time? How did gender affect conceptions of the author function? What might be the effect and affect of poetic discourse as an integral part of the journal on women readers as well as male readers interested in changing social and gender relations?

Gender, Genre, and Authorship

Although the chief editor of *Women's World*, Ding Chuwo, was male and the editorial board was controlled by men, as most journals in the late Qing and early Republican period were, the journal actively solicited contributions from women in announcements published in each issue. The women who responded appear to have been new-style educators, students, and readers, and they submitted chiefly poems and essays. Their contributions appear most often in the columns "Public Speeches," "Literary Garden," and "Essays from Women's Schools." However, a trend among male writers in the early twentieth century was to use female pseudonyms, masquerading as women to publish their writings in women's magazines and concealing their true identities. A prominent example is Lu Xun's (1881–1936) younger brother, Zhou Zuoren (1885–1967), who signed variously as Ms. Wu Pingyun (Wu Pingyun nüshi), Ms. Biluo (Biluo nüshi), and Sick Cloud (Bingyun). Zhou was attending the Jiangnan Naval Academy (Jiangnan Shuishi Xuetang) in Nanjing from 1904 to 1905 and his writings began to appear in Issue 5 in the first year of the journal's publication.[2] Zhou was not alone in literary impersonation in *Women's World*. While the young Liu Yazi (1887–1958) usually signed essays using his "male" pennames Yalu and Anru, he published biographies of women using the female pseudonym Ms. Pan Xiaohuang of Songling (Songling nüzi Pan Xiaohuang). I will return to this question of gender and authorship below.

The interrelated question of editor, author, gender, and genre is essential to understanding the evolving discursive space of women's journals in this late Qing moment. To elucidate this issue, I will focus on the contributions by three of the regular "women" contributors to the journal – Du Qingchi and Zhao Aihua, and Zhou Zuoren's feminine persona, Wu Pingyun, all listed in the "Roster of Fragrant Names of Those Who Submitted Manuscripts" (Jigao jia fangming lu) printed on the back cover of Issue 6 (1904), the former two also

---

[1] See Tang, "Poetic Revolution."

[2] See Xia, *Wan Qing nüxing*, 73–74. Michael Hill has written about Zhou Zuoren and other male translators assuming female pseudonyms in their publications; see "No True Men in the State."

identified as "investigators" for the journal (see Table 1). Their writings, when compared, draw attention to the relationship between the gender of the writer and the genre they wrote in. What the reasons or motivations were for the phenomenon of literary cross-dressing by male writers in this period are related to what the author function might signify. The real gender of Wu Pingyun was only disclosed by Zhou himself in his memoir decades later when he wrote a piece on his pennames.[3] He specifically mentioned Ms. Pingyun as one among several pennames he used in that period. He reminisced that he might have used Pingyun (Duckweed Cloud) for its sense of "drifting instability," without associating the image with feminine qualities, but because he was writing for *Women's World*, he decided to add the title "Ms." He explained, "Young men often went through a period when they liked to pretend to be women when corresponding with magazines and submitting manuscripts to them. They didn't necessarily take lightly the fact that editors might prefer women over men. And it was probably a form of first love, an expression of love of feminine beauty."[4] He could not remember how he came to make up the other feminine penname Miss Biluo (Emerald Gauze). In his seventies at the time, Zhou Zuoren thought back to this phenomenon of literary cross-dressing as a passing romantic fad among young men, individually and collectively, and perhaps he was also romanticizing his own youthful female impersonation. But assuming a woman's penname to submit writing could also have been a male writer's opportunistic move to get published. Zhou himself alluded to the fact that editors of women's journals at the time were eager to get contributions from women, as these magazines were aimed at women readers, and showing new possibilities in thinking, writing, and vocation from women would have been an attractive draw.

The second frequent contributor, Du Qingchi, in contrast to Wu Pingyun, whose true identity was unknown at the time, was already an established educator with a public voice and persona. She was a teacher at the Guangdong Women's School in Guangzhou. She had given public speeches that were reported in newspapers and published poems and articles before *Women's World* was founded in 1904. She continued to publish in women's journals in the early Republican period.[5] The third, Zhao Aihua (style name Ms. Yunxi), appears to have been a prolific poet. Sixteen of her poems and poem series were published. However, almost nothing is known about her life except for a skeletal identification given in the aforementioned "Roster of Fragrant

---

[3] See Xia, *Wan Qing nüxing*, 73–74.

[4] Zhou Zuoren, *Zhitang huixiang lu* 1, 141–44. Unless otherwise noted, all translations are my own.

[5] Joan Judge refers to a public speech given by Du that was recorded in the press in 1902; see Judge, *Precious Raft*, 68. For an example of Du's later publications, see her travel record to West Lake, in *Funü zazhi* 1.10 (1915): 3–8.

Names of Those Who Submitted Manuscripts." She was a native of Changzhou (Jiangsu) who "lived at home" (*jujia*) – a term most likely referring to a woman who did not work outside the home.[6] The "Roster" includes the names, age, vocations, and native towns (the latter three categories if known) of twenty-six women. Zhou Zuoren's "Wu Pingyun" heads the list as "Wu Zhuo, [style name] Pingyun of Guiji (Shaoxing)," eighteen years old, with no identified "vocation."[7] Du Qingchi and Lü Yunqing (style name Yichu) are the two teachers identified with their respective women's schools, Guangdong Women's School (Guangdong nüxuetang) and Shimen Wenming Women's School (Shimen wenming nüshu). The names of eight female students are identified with their schools, six among them were students at Du Qingchi's Guangdong Women's School, and six had their age indicated.[8] Zhao Aihua is one among six women in the "vocational" category of "living at home." This roster advertises the active participation of women in the journal and gives authenticity to their gender identity. I provide below an inventory of the contributions by Du Qingchi, Zhao Aihua, and Wu Pingyun (Zhou Zuoren), indicating frequency of publication, to show their different patterns of genre choice:

Du Qingchi's Publications in *Women's World*:

> Issue 4 (1904): 54 – One song lyric to the tune "Jinlü qu," subtitled "Inscribed on the Painting 'Farewell at Li River' by Ju Guquan"
>
> Issue 5 (1904): 63–64 – One series of four seven-character quatrains entitled "Inscribed on the Painting 'Practicing Calligraphy under the Plantain Leaves' by Woman Scholar Deng Zhongrong"
>
> 64 – One series of ten seven-character quatrains entitled "Admonition against Footbinding"
>
> Issue 6 (1904): 13–16 – One public speech entitled "Men and Women Are the Same"
>
> Issue 7 (1904): Front matter – One photograph of herself with the caption "Ms. Du Qingchi" (see Fig. 1)
>
> Issue 9 (1904): 11–15 – One public speech entitled "Slaves of Civilization"
>
> Issue 16–17 (1906): 68 – Three seven-character quatrains entitled respectively "Visiting Guangya Bookstore," "Evening View on

---

[6] In Zhu, *Twentieth-Century Chinese Authors*, Zhao Aihua has Ms. Yunxi as her style name (Zhu, 1765); Wu Pingyun is given as the penname of Zhou Zuoren (1364); and no style name is given for Du Qingchi (237).

[7] Zhou Zuoren was eighteen in 1903. In explaining another penname, Zhou mentioned that the character *zuo* in his personal name is a homonym of the character *zhuo* in his Shaoxing dialect. See Zhou, *Zhitang huixiang lu* 1, 144.

[8] *Nüzi shijie* 6 (1904): back cover. The youngest student was eleven, the oldest forty-one; the others were adolescents. One student was from the Shanghai Patriotic Girls' School (Shanghai aiguo nüxuexiao), and one student from the Shanghai Nurturing Roots Girls' School (Shanghai wuben nüxuetang).

the Pearl River," and "Thoughts during a Return Visit to My Hometown"

118–120 – One essay in the column "Women's School Essays" entitled "On Travel and Reading Newspapers as an Important Responsibility for Women in Establishing Themselves"

Zhao Aihua's Publications in *Women's World*:

Issue 4 (1904): 51 – One series of six seven-character quatrains entitled "Thoughts on Reading *Women's World*"

Issue 6 (1904): 67–68 – One long ancient-style poem entitled "Song of Preserving the Race"

68 – Two seven-character regulated poems entitled "Miscellaneous Thoughts in Late Spring"

Issue 8 (1904): 67 – One series of eight five-character quatrains entitled "Newly Composed Songs of Midnight"

68 – One series of four seven-character quatrains entitled "Composed at Random after Reading Histories"

Issue 9 (1904): 50–51 – Five from a series of ten seven-character regulated poems entitled "Stirred by Events in 1900"

Issue 10 (1904): 50 – One series of eight seven-character quatrains entitled "Deep into the Quiet Night When the Autumn Wind Soughs and the Autumn Moon Shines with Charm, I Happen to Read the *chuanqi* Drama *Fengdong Mountain*. I Am Stirred to Endless Thoughts on the Rise and Fall of Dynasties"

50–51 – One song lyric to the tune "Fenghuangtai shang yi chuixiao," subtitled "Passing by Nanjing in 1903"

Issue 12 (1905): 26 – One seven-character regulated poem entitled "Expressing My Feelings on New Year's Eve, 1904"[9]

26–27 – One series of eight five-character quatrains "New Emotions in 1905"

27 – Two seven-character quatrains "Written to My Two Younger Sisters in Shanghai"

Issue 13 (1905): 61 – One seven-character regulated poem "Celebrating the Second Year of *Women's World*"

Issue 15 (1905): 53 – One five-character regulated poem "By the Frontier"

53 – One seven-character quatrain entitled "Inscribed on the White Orchid"

53 – One seven-character quatrain entitled "Crossing the [Yangzi] River"

53 – One seven-character quatrain entitled "Spring Night"

---

[9] New Year's Eve of the year Jiachen was on February 3, 1905.

Wu Pingyun's (Zhou Zuoren) Publications in *Women's World*:

> Issue 5 (1904): 63 – One set of two seven-character regulated poems entitled "Composed at Random"
>
> 83–85 – Essay entitled "On Life and Death"
>
> 88 – Essay entitled "On How It Is Not Suitable to Use the Character 'Flower' to Be the Substitute Word for Women"
>
> Issue 8 (1904): 43–52 – Translated story "The Heroic Slave Woman" (Part 1)
>
> Issue 9 (1904): 39–48 –Translated story "The Heroic Slave Woman" (Part 2)
>
> Issue 11 (1905): 49–56 – Translated story "The Heroic Slave Woman" (Part 3)
>
> Issue 12 (1905): 45–58 – Translated story "The Heroic Slave Woman" (Part 4)
>
> 59–60 – Under the feminine pseudonym Ms. Biluo of Kuaiji, Zhou Zuoren wrote a series of ten seven-character quatrains on the original story entitled "Inscribed on the Original Text of '*The Heroic Slave Woman*'"
>
> Issue 13 (1905): 67–70 – Short story entitled "Fine Blossoming Branch"
>
> 101–112 – Short story entitled "The Huntress"
>
> Issue 14 (1905): 69–84 – Translated story "The Deserted Jetty" (Part 1)
>
> Issue 15 (Oct. 1905–Jan. 1906): 61–78 – Translated story "The Deserted Jetty" (Part 2)[10]

At a glance, all three "women" continued their submissions till near the end of the journal's life. They clearly engaged in different genres of writing. Except for the set of two poems and two essays published respectively in "Literary Garden" and "Essays from Women's Schools," Zhou Zuoren's female author-persona Wu Pingyun almost exclusively published fiction – two stories, a serialized translation of a long story, and two translated stories. Fiction was decidedly a genre in which scarcely any women wrote until the late nineteenth century,[11] and translations of fiction from Japanese and Western languages were commonly produced by male students who had studied abroad but rarely by women until the early Republican period.[12] On the one hand, contemporary readers might have questioned the female gender of Wu Pingyun

---

[10] In the preface, Wu Pingyun indicates that the story is a translation of "The Man from Archangel" (mistyped as "The Man Orom Archemgle") by Sir Arthur Conan Doyle, identified only by his last name, which was mistyped as "Dayle." *Nüzi shijie* 14 (1905): 69.

[11] On the first known novel by a woman written in the second half of the nineteenth century, see Ellen Widmer, *The Beauty and the Book*, Chapter 6.

[12] For examples of fiction by women in the 1910s, see the essay by Jin-Chu Huang in this volume.

士 女 持 清 杜

Fig. 4.1 "Ms Du Qingchi," *Women's World* 7 (1904)

not only because she wrote fiction, but also because of her even rarer practice of translating fiction. On the other, it is not inconceivable that Wu Pingyun might have been thought of by some readers as a literary woman who was in the vanguard of changing practices in women's writing. Unfortunately, we do not have evidence for either hypothesis.

Woman educator Du Qingchi, who published mostly poetry, also has two transcribed public speeches in the vernacular and one essay in the literary language. Her poems reflect her social life and her concern with women's issues. Du projects clearly the image of an independent, modern, and progressive woman, captured in a photograph showing a young woman of determination, which Du would have submitted to the journal, either on her own initiative or having been solicited by the editor (see Figure 4.1).

In comparison, the poetry of Zhao Aihua seems to present the image of a more "traditional" and mature woman. Her name, Aihua – "Love China" – seems unusual if she belonged to an older generation born in the 1860s or 1870s.[13] Her publications are all classical verse. But her poetry also seems

---

[13] Aihua may also be read as "Love Flowers," which would be more typically "feminine." But it clearly rings with nationalistic overtones in this period. Another possibility is that she adopted this name as an adult.

somewhat atypical in comparison to the poetry by either gentry women or emerging "new" women such as Du Qingchi published in *Women's World*. Some characteristics of her poems suggest the possibility of a male impersonator. For example, her series "Moved by the Events of 1900: Five of Ten Poems" reflects on the destruction of the Boxer Rebellion and its aftermath. Some of the language, allusions, and metaphors suggest strong influence by Du Fu's (712–770) poetry, especially after the An Lushan Rebellion (755–763), and reflect the sentiments of a male poetic persona.[14] For example, consider the well-established topos of climbing to a high place to gaze in line 1 of the first poem, "Alone I ascend the high tower to look at the vast desolation,"[15] in which the male persona contemplates the vast landscape from a height and reflects on the vicissitudes of history and human impermanence. Dated 767 and one of his most anthologized poems, Du Fu's seven-character regulated verse entitled "Climbing on High" (Denggao) articulates his concerns for the devastated Tang empire after the An Lushan Rebellion.[16] In the second poem, Zhao Aihua begins with the line "To live peacefully in my native country – my thoughts run deep."[17] The line not only takes the phrase "To live peacefully in my native country" verbatim from the last line of the fourth poem in Du Fu's famous series "Autumn Meditations: Eight Poems" (*Qiuxing bashou*), which he wrote in 766 after the An Lushan Rebellion, but "my thoughts run deep" (*si zheng chang*) also imitates the ending of Du Fu's line "I have thoughts of" (*you suo si*).[18] The fourth poem alludes to Du Fu's (male) poetic gesture of "scratching the head," a head with thinning hair from worries about the country: "In such years I grieve for my native country/Each time I scratch my head, tears soak my lapels" (lines 7–8).[19]

Yet poetic language is a system of *conventions*; both men and women can manipulate the linguistic signs to construct gendered textual subjectivities that are different from the gender of the historical person. That Zhao Aihua could have been a woman impersonating a male subjectivity by manipulating the poetic repertory is also a possibility. Women poets in the Ming and Qing appropriated masculine poetics to articulate their reflections on history and society.[20] Her poetry complicates any deterministic gender identification based on language and style.

---

[14] This series of poems is "Wenyuan: Yinhua ji," *Nüzi shijie* 9 (1904): 50–51.

[15] *Nüzi shijie* 9 (1904): 50.

[16] Du Fu, "Climbing on High," in Qiu, *Dushi xiangzhu*, j. 20/1766.

[17] *Nüzi shijie* 9 (1904): 50.

[18] Du Fu, "Autumn Meditations," in Qiu, *Dushi xiangzhu*, j. 16/1486.

[19] *Nüzi shijie* 9 (1904): 51. Du Fu's line reads "My white hair becomes even shorter from being scratched" (*Baitou sao geng duan*), in "Chunwang" (Spring prospect), in Qiu, *Dushi xiangzhu*, j. 4/320.

[20] See, for example, the song lyrics in the heroic mode written by women to the tune "Manjianghong" ("River Full of Red") examined by Xiaorong Li in "Engendering Heroism."

The case of Zhao Aihua's poetry only raises again the vexed question of the gender of the writers in women's journals in the late Qing and early Republican period, when so many men published using pennames, and some using *both* masculine and feminine pseudonyms. What were the motivations for and the consequences of male writers who published in women's journals passing themselves off as women? Some recent studies have suggested how this practice might have been linked to the long poetic tradition of Chinese male poets impersonating a female voice and assuming a female persona to articulate their own complaints and frustrations in their subordinate positions vis-à-vis their superiors.[21] In this period it could have been an expression of discontent of the subordinate Han Chinese in relation to the Manchu rulers, of which Zhao Aihua's grief at the destruction wrought by the Boxer Rebellion could have been an example. The feminine trope continued to constitute a site for male articulation. But, as Zhou Zuoren reminisced, young men at the time could just as well have thought that using a female pseudonym might increase the chances of a manuscript being accepted by a women's journal. If literary cross-dressing was so prevalent among men, even though the editors of *Women's World* might not have known the true identity of Wu Pingyun, they might have suspected a male author behind that name. They might have accepted submissions by men posing as women because the presence of the names of women authors would produce an encouraging effect on women readers, the journal's targeted audience. This was in line with the journal's goal of engaging both women and men in a cultural discourse and helping to generate social and educational change.

Radicalized Verse in the "Literary Garden"

At the turn of the twentieth century, as new education for women took shape and spread, women educators and students adopted reformist rhetoric in their writings. Their poetry, too, appeared in the new textual space of the new print media, particularly women's journals and some newspapers. In 1904, *Women's World* published a set of two poems by Kang Tongbi (1883–1969), younger daughter of the famous reformer Kang Youwei, about her travels with her father in India in 1901–1902.[22] Entitled "Traveling in India: Sent to Master Ice Drinker (Yinbingzi)," it was sent to Liang Qichao, who promptly quoted them in full in his "Yinbingshi shihua" ("Remarks on Poetry from the Ice Drinker's Studio") in the literary column of his news publication, the *Xinmin congbao*

---

[21] For example, Hu, *Tales of Translation*, 145–52, and Michael Hill, "No True Men in the State."

[22] *Nüzi shijie* 4 (1904): 54. In a note Kang Tongbi wrote following the poem, she reemphasized her leading role in boundary crossing: "I accompanied my father to visit Jetavana Monastery in Sravati (a Buddhist pilgrimage site), which lay all in ruins. The Dharma has suffered calamities. But as for Chinese women who have come to visit, I am the first one."

(New people's miscellany, 1902–1907),[23] remarking, "Kang Nanhai's (Kang Youwei) second daughter Tongbi has a profound knowledge of historical materials. She is also fluent in English. Last year she went by herself to visit her father in India at the tender age of nineteen, crossing thousands of miles of rough waves and miasma ... Recently I received two poems from her."[24]

Kang Tongbi herself also boldly claims her trailblazing journey to India on the grounds of her gender: "If you talk about a woman scholar traveling to the West (India)/I am the first to do so from China."[25] By having her travel poem reprinted in *Women's World*, Kang Tongbi added her voice to many other women of the time in changing and expanding their physical, spatial, social, and textual horizons.

By the end of the nineteenth century, a critical mass of women from scholar-gentry families had engaged in poetic practice in their everyday lives in a wide variety of personal, family, and social contexts for over three centuries. With some exceptions, the printing of individual women's literary collections was carried out within the contexts of family, lineage, or local community interests.[26] Many of their poems were selected, solicited, or sent for publication in a great number of poetry anthologies. Recent rediscoveries and both known and unknown lost works make the more than 4,000 printed collections of women's poetry of the Ming and Qing periods (1368–1911) recorded in Hu Wenkai's catalogue a conservative estimate.[27] We are in no doubt that writing poetry was a continuing and self-assertive practice among a critical mass of gentry women since at least the end of the sixteenth century.

As poetry was the canonical genre of writing for self-articulation, women negotiated and created textual positions in which to voice their sentiments, thoughts, and concerns. Through interest, practice, and persistence combined with talent, women succeeded in carving a space for themselves in this prestigious genre long dominated in public by male literati. Women's poetry was circumscribed from serving any true public/official function in Confucian patriarchal society. Barred from public roles outside the family, women's engagement with political and social issues remained indirect and peripheral. Nevertheless, their versification had become highly visible in literati culture and society. The strong current of women's literary practice in late imperial China joined with and reinforced the developments in new education for

---

[23] This was the second widely circulated and extremely influential reform-oriented newspaper that Liang edited in Yokohama after *Qingyibao*.

[24] *Xinmin congbao* 4 (1902).   [25] *Nüzi shijie* 4 (1904): 54.

[26] An exceptional woman, Shen Shanbao (1808–1862), arranged and even financed the printing of her first poetry collection in her late twenties before she married. See Fong, "Writing Self and Writing Lives."

[27] See Hu and Zhang, *Lidai funü zhuzuo kao*. For an overview of women's literature, see Idema and Grant, *The Red Brush*.

women promoted and instituted by reform-minded men and women in the waning years of the Qing. Classically trained women born in the 1870s and 1880s stepped out of their homes at the turn of the century, took on the roles of educators in newly established schools for women, and involved themselves in print media and other forms of activism.[28]

The poetry published in the Literary Garden column in *Women's World* demonstrates the participation of both men and women in a rapidly developing revolutionary poetic space. No longer merely enhancing the cultural and social capital of their natal and marital families, the women's verse literally abandoned the old print culture of family publications as they ventured into the public domain of the new periodical press.

Even if women's contributions to *Women's World* were fewer than men's, they were noticeable in the three columns "Public Speeches," "Essays from Women's Schools," and "Literary Garden." The column "Literary Garden," in which classical verse was always published, was one among several columns common to the journals in the late Qing and early Republican period. Except for "Public Speeches," writings in these columns were usually composed in some form of the literary language. Written in the vernacular language are new-style school songs, some fiction, transcriptions of public speeches, and reporting of current events in China and around the world. Among the most prominent and recurring topics treated in this array of journalistic and belles-lettres writings are Western women, anti-footbinding, women's education, women's occupations, women's rights, gender equality, and the state of the Chinese nation. Significantly, the representation and reporting of Western women focus on how they lived, worked, and conducted themselves in their own social and national contexts; they were constructed as new role models for Chinese women.

Wenyuan, the term for the column "Literary Garden," derives from the section "Wenyuan zhuan," which first appeared as a biographical category in the *Hou Hanshu* (Dynastic history of the later Han) in the fifth century. It consists of biographies devoted to subjects known for their literary or refined writing. Therefore, it is the "garden" or "space" where literary writers and their writings are gathered and preserved. Although the "Literary Garden" in *Women's World* published classical poems by both men and women, they were placed in two distinctly named sections according to gender: poems by women were placed in the *Yinhua ji* (Lying on flowers collection); poems by men, who invariably used two-character pennames, in the *Gongyu ji* (Polishing jade collection).[29] Rather than ghettoizing women, this division

---

[28] Those best known for their poetry include Xue Shaohui (1866–1911), Xu Zihua (1873–1935), Qiu Jin (1875–1907), Shi Shuyi (b. 1878), and Lü Bicheng (1883–1943).

[29] In a few issues, only one or the other collection appears.

seems to have been meant to highlight the presence of women as a group of writers. However, as we have seen, their ranks were sometimes "infiltrated" by female impersonators such as Zhou Zuoren's Wu Pingyun and Ms. Biluo.

As classical verse was still the main literary genre in which women wrote in this period when they stepped into the public space of women's schools and journals, reform-minded women who continued the practice of writing poetry provide valuable evidence of their participation as new readers and subjects in transformation. At the same time, the new venue of women's journals functioned as a form of anthologizing that publicized their socially and politically engaged poems. *Women's World* was eager to publish poetry by women teachers and students who were in the vanguard of change.[30]

By submitting their poems to the emerging women's journals for publication, women constructed new personae for themselves. Wang Yuzhen, a reader who was appointed as an "investigator" in Issue 5 (see Table 1), had her first poems published in the "Literary Garden" in Issue 6. In the title of her poem series, "When I Saw the Call for Compositions on the Topic 'Women's China' in *Women's World*, I Felt Ashamed That I Am Not Able to Write Prose, so I Present Poems Instead," Wang candidly admits her lack of training in writing classical prose, but utilizes her training in classical verse to authorize her textual participation in making a different China. Wang's poem series expresses her views on how women nowadays, no longer locked in the inner quarters, could and should come out to participate in building a strong China, even as military women:

> Poem 1
> In the embroidery room, the deep boudoir, idle all day long,
> The nation's fortune or misfortune had no relation to us.
> Now iron locks one after one are opened,
> I hope women will now relieve the world's troubles.
>
> Poem 2
> Summoning and reviving female souls, we forge moral character,
> Chisel the formless mass to create Heaven and Earth.
> Then we will see trees full of peach blooms
> Reflected on the flag of an independent China.
>
> Poem 3
> Rows and rows of strong female soldiers –
> A hundred million emerge like beneficial clouds.

---

[30] See the many poems in the *Yinhua ji* section by female students, identified with the names of their schools. Lü Bicheng and her two sisters are prominent early examples of women teachers whose poems and prose writings were showcased in the "Literary Garden" after chief editor Ding Chuwo came across their 1905 joint collection reported in a newspaper called *Dongbao* (Eastern newspaper). See *Nüzi shijie* 4–5 (1906): 51–64.

> Sending out great compassion, extending the power of their vow
> They all go out to seek happiness for our people.[31]

We see the temporal and spatial movement in Wang Yuzhen's poem series going from the past and the inner chambers (Poem 1) into China's present to work for a bright future (Poems 2 and 3). Her language marries Buddhist and Daoist terminology – formless mass (*hundun*), Heaven and Earth (*qiankun*), compassion (*cibei*), and religious vows (*shiyuan*) – readily with the rhetoric of new patriotism: the nation (*guojia*), the flag of independence (*duli fan*), and female soldiers (*nü junren*). Cloistered women are summoned to transform themselves into upright soldiers who will save their country. In the context of an exploding nationalism among radical intellectuals, fueled by the Qing government's failure to prevent Western imperialist aggression, Chinese women were interpellated as *xin guomin* (new citizens); they were called upon to make themselves into useful members of society and contribute their efforts to rescue the imperiled nation. Many reformers and activists believed the way to achieve this goal and to bring women out of their tradition-ally closeted way of life was through new education. Thus, closely connected to the growing emphasis on women's education outside the home, women's journals opened up a dynamic discursive space for them to express their new ideas and feelings and to participate in nation-building. The circulation of their personal words and sentiments went "public" in a way never imagined before.

The transformed rhetoric, subject matter, and themes of their poetry, as exemplified by Wang Yuzhen's poems above, are evidently a combined effect of women's changing practices and editorial selection. In general, women eschewed an overtly feminine and aestheticized diction, choosing instead a heroic and forthright tone and rhetoric. Social and political concerns regarding gender and nation embed new currencies for ideas and concepts as well as transliterations of Western place and personal names into the poetic language. In the poems on the topic of women's condition and status in *Women's World*, the most frequently used terms include *ziyou* (freedom), *nüquan* (women's rights), *pingdeng* (equality), and *guomin/nü guomin* (citizen/female citizen). Poems related to the nation and political conditions contain terms such as "Zhina" and "Zhongguo" (China), "Dongya/Yadong" (East Asia, referring to China), *gonghe* (republic), *wenming* (civilization), *geming* (revolution), *aiguo* (patriotism), *youguo* (anxiety for the nation), *guochi* (national shame), "Ou-Mei" (Europe and America), "Xi'ou/Dong'ou" (Western/Eastern Europe), *guafen* ([China] cut up like a melon [i.e., dismembered by Western imperialist

---

[31] *Nüzi shijie* 6 (1904): 63. Captured in the project database (with different page numbering) at http://kjc-sv013.kjc.uni-heidelberg.de/frauenzeitschriften/public/magazine/page_content.php?magazin_id=2&year=1904&issue_id=13&issue_number=6&img_issue_page=71.

powers]), and *shijie* (world).[32] Many of these terms are classified by Lydia Liu as "return graphic loans," that is, classical Chinese compounds that were used in Meiji Japan to translate modern European concepts and then later reintroduced into the Chinese language.[33]

There are entire poems and poem series against footbinding and advocating natural feet, which incorporate the new vocabulary in denouncing this pernicious or demonic practice (*duxi/moxi*). A salient example is Du Qingchi's series of ten quatrains on the subject, entitled "Admonition against Footbinding: Ten Poems."[34] In the first poem, Du presents the dark history of the origin of footbinding, presumably started by the dancer Yaoniang at the court of Li Yu (937–978), king of the Southern Tang, to contrast with the liberation of unbound, natural feet experienced in her own day. In some, Du uses the two couplets in a quatrain to structure the transition from past to present and articulate the change from darkness to light and from barbarity to civilization:

> Poem 6
> As long as this demonic practice in China is not eradicated,
> Our whole nation lies sunken, like a sick man.
> Cleansing away the evil air, we escape from the bitter sea,
> Jumping for joy on the stage, our happiness knows no bounds.

Conversely, the two couplets reverse the temporal structure, beginning with the freedom of women's physical movements today and contrasting it to their former restriction and confinement symbolized by the abandoned tiny shoes and stockings, which are still mourned by those who remain benighted. The contrast is also effected in the choice of vocabulary – the modern terms "free bodies" (*ziyou shen*) and "roaming the globe" (*huanqiu*) against the tired clichés, the inert jade hooks (pointy little shoes) and silk stockings:

> Poem 9
> Only now do we leap out into these free bodies,
> With big strides we travel around the globe with friends.
> In the empire there are those who grieve mightily,
> When little jade-hook shoes and silk stockings gather dust in the dark.

If the poem above implies that those who are nostalgic for the eroticized three-inch golden lotus are ignorant men,[35] the last poem in the series declares

---

[32] These terms of course permeate the prose writings in the various columns in this and other periodicals and newspapers of the period.

[33] Liu, *Translingual Practice*, Appendix D, 302–42, passim. For example, *ziyou* had been used to translate "freedom" as early as 1868 in Japan and was later reimported to China.

[34] *Nüzi shijie* 5 (1904): 64. Captured in the project database (with different page numbering) at http://kjc-sv013.kjc.uni-heidelberg.de/frauenzeitschriften/public/magazine/page_content .php&magazin_id=2&year=1904&issue_id=012&issue_number=005&img_issue_page=74.

[35] See Dorothy Ko's observation on the implications of nostalgia in the connoisseurship of bound feet in the late Qing and Republican period, in *Cinderella's Sisters*, 76–79, and passim.

women's total rejection of oppressive traditions by alluding to the artificial gait of Handan and the old ballad "Traveling the Road Is Hard" of the Han dynasty:

> Poem 10
> Who needs to learn the artful steps of Handan anymore?
> "Traveling the Road Is Hard" is newly excised from the *yuefu* songs.
> Announcing with surprise the forward strides made last year,
> On stage everywhere I speak of Madame Roland.

The last turns to new lexicon to herald new women's "advancing steps" (*jinbu*), that is, progress. This new woman sings of a new model, Madame Roland (1741–1793), political activist and supporter of the French Revolution put to the guillotine, who was made famous in China by her biography written by Liang Qichao in 1902.[36]

In the poem "The Natural Feet Society" (*Tianzu hui*), He Chenghui was able to take a comparative global perspective in which to critique this oppressive practice in China, putting it under the same critical lens as European corsets and an African custom of putting stone weights on heads:

> . . .
> Who began binding the feet?
> Make tomb figurines and you will have no descendants.
> In Europe silk bands tighten thin waists,
> In Africa stones press down on heads,
> These old customs become three punishments.
> How extremely vile China is![37]
> . . .

One might suspect that not all the users of these new concepts would have agreed on their intellectual content, and some may not even have had a clear idea of their meaning. It seemed in this contingent moment that new ideas constituted part of the rhetorical force. Noteworthy also is the appearance of poems singing the praise of Western women, many of whose biographies had been published, as discussed in Xia Xiaohong's contribution to this volume. Zhao Aihua submitted a series of six quatrains entitled "Thoughts on Reading *Women's World*" (*Du Nüzi shijie yougan*). Madame Roland appears in the fifth poem:

> Clouds over Europe and rain in Asia are separated by the horizon,
> I know for sure I dreamt of [Madame] Roland last night.

---

[36] See Hu Ying's seminal study of Madame Roland as a late Qing popular icon in *Tales of Translation*, Chapter 4, "Madame Roland and Her Chinese Sister."

[37] *Nüzi shijie* 15 (1905): 53. Captured in the project database (with different page numbering) at   http://kjc-sv013.kjc.uni-heidelberg.de/frauenzeitschriften/public/magazine/page_content .php&magazin_id=2&year=1905&issue_id=22&issue_number=003&img_issue_page=57.

> Waking up from sleep by the green curtain I feel touched,
> Before my eyes I'm ashamed to see the flower of freedom.[38]

This poem subverts the typical boudoir theme by an astonishing yoking together of conventional imagery and sentiment and new concepts and ideas. The images of cloud and rain in the first line – stock metaphors for sexual intercourse, play with the pairing and separation, unity and difference of Europe and Asia. The line also emphasizes the distance of the poet from the one she longs for. But, unlike in a conventional boudoir poem, the poet does not dream of her lover/husband but the exemplary Madame Roland, so familiar to readers then that the poet identifies her by her two-character name Luolan to fit the restrictions of poetic form.[39] Skillfully mastering the evocativeness required of the quatrain, the poet passes over the content of the dream: she does not tell how Madame Roland appeared to her and whether or how they interacted with each other. She wakes up in her boudoir space, signified by the emblematic bed curtain. However, her awakening is also on the intellectual level: she is awakened to new concepts such as "freedom." The poem points to the effective dissemination of knowledge about exemplary Western women in Chinese print. To many Chinese women at the time, Madame Roland has become the "flower" or symbol "of freedom" (*ziyou hua*). The power of the dream encounter seems to suggest a wish to emulate the model but also a sense of inadequacy and shame, implying that the poet, and by extension other women in China, has not yet reached the kind of freedom to act in the waning years of the Qing that Madame Roland had in eighteenth-century France.

Conclusion

Women of the educated scholar-gentry class constituted a unique transitional group whose contributions to social change and women's education in the last decades of the Qing have been largely overlooked in modern historiography.[40] Significantly, their training and accomplishment in classical versification remained important cultural capital, as exemplified by the literary reputation of women such as Qiu Jin and Lü Bicheng. Indeed, Ding Chuwo's presentation of the three Lü sisters' poetry in *Women's World* calls attention to this legacy of women's poetry. *Women's World* was pioneering in introducing the "Literary

---

[38] *Nüzi shijie* 4 (1904): 51. Captured in the project database (with different page numbering) at http://kjc-sv013.kjc.uni-heidelberg.de/frauenzeitschriften/public/magazine/page_content .php&magazin_id=2&year=1904&issue_id=11&issue_number=004&img_issue_page=59.

[39] In the novel *Huang Xiuqiu* (1905), the eponymous protagonist also dreams of meeting Madame Roland, who becomes her mentor and imparts knowledge to and confidence in her. See Hu, *Tales of Translation*, 169–171.

[40] Recent studies on this demographic of women include Hu, *Burying Autumn*; Judge, "The Fate of the Late Imperial 'Talented Woman.'"

Garden" in a journal aimed at educated and educating women readers by publishing their poetry, taking note of many educated women's facility in this genre at this historical moment.

A vertical reading of poetry in women's journals that preceded and followed *Women's World* underlines the particularity of this moment. Neither of *Women's World*'s two predecessors, the *Chinese Girl's Progress* (*Nü xuebao*, 1898–1899) or the *Continued Publication of Women's Journal/Journal of Women's Learning* (*Xuchu nübao/Nü xuebao*, 1902–1903), had this column. Once introduced, the "Literary Garden" would remain a stable feature in women's magazines through the early Republican period. In the last decade of the Qing, for relatively unknown women and the young students of the new women's schools, the publication of their poetry in the "Literary Garden" columns in women's magazines, including the short-lived *Zhongguo xin nüjie zazhi* (Magazine of China's new world of women, 1907) published by radical women students in Japan, attests not only to the prestige of classical verse, but more importantly, to its continuing social and political function as a revolutionary medium in this period. While poetry was still conceived and received as a personal response and expression, it simultaneously became a form of public and progressive expression in the new publishing venue and discursive space of the women's periodical press in the last decade of the Qing. The pioneering appearance of women's classical verse in *Women's World* signaled something different; their new lexicon and rhetoric marked women's incipient political engagement.

This moment of radical poetics seems to have waned with the apparent shift from late Qing social and political activism to a nostalgic aestheticism in the publication of women's poetry in particular and women's magazines in general in the early Republic.[41] The extent to which this strain of "political" and "ideological" poetics of classical verse continued in the Republican period needs further research. But on the whole, the status and function of classical verse became fragmented for both men and women after the fall of the Qing dynasty. Its complex trajectories in the twentieth century are only beginning to be charted.[42]

---

[41] This impression is based on a cursory survey of poetry and remarks on poetry in journals such as the *Funü shibao* (1911–1917), *Funü zazhi*, and a different *Nüzi shijie* (1914–1915), which bears no relation to the one studied in this paper. I have not had access to the early Republican suffragette women's journal *Shenzhou nübao*, which ran from 1912 to1913, to check whether it included a poetry column. Significantly, the poetry of members of the Southern Society also lost its radical political edge after the fall of the Qing. On subtle political critique in women's poetry in *Funü shibao*, see Judge, *Republican Lens*, Chapters 2, 5.

[42] See pioneering studies by Jon Kowallis, Hu Yingjian, Lin Li [Lap Lam], and Wu Shengqing in the bibliography.

5 Redefining Female Talent: *The Women's Eastern Times, The Ladies' Journal*, and the Development of "Women's Art" in China, 1910s–1930s

Doris Sung

Among the many new genres of periodical published at the turn of the twentieth century in China, magazines that targeted female readers played a vital role in valorizing women's rights and showcasing women's cultural production. This chapter uses both horizontal and vertical approaches to explore how these women's magazines created and embodied a new "public discursive space" in which artists and writers – female and male – expressed and shared their opinions on issues related to women's art and women *in* art.[1] They provided a unique space to discuss the function of art in women's lives, women's roles in art education, and the process of professionalization of art over the course of the Republican period.

Two of the most influential gendered journals that served the urban elite were *Funü shibao – The Women's Eastern Times* (1911–17) and *Funü zazhi – The Ladies' Journal* (1915–31). These two journals frequently highlighted the topic of art and echoed the contemporary emphasis on aesthetic education in the curriculum for the new women's public education.[2] At a time when the presence of female artists in the art world was still a new and unfamiliar phenomenon – not only in Chinese society but also in the West – *The Women's Eastern Times*

---

[1] In this chapter, I use the terms "art," "fine arts," and "arts and crafts" to signify *meishu* and *yishu* in the Chinese language. The neologism *meishu*, translated from the Japanese term *bijutsu*, was sometimes used interchangeably with *yishu*. In the context of the Chinese art world of the 1910s to 1930s, these two terms were often used to indicate all kinds of fine arts practices, including painting, calligraphy, drawing, sculpture, architecture, and crafts. This usage is evinced by, for example, the objects included in the *meishuguan* (art pavilion) at the Nanyang Industrial Exposition. The pavilion was divided into four sections – *gongyi* (applied arts), *zhusu* (sculpture), *shougong* (handicrafts), and *diaoke* (carving). Objects on display included painting, calligraphy, drawing, embroidery and other types of handicrafts, ceramics, and stone carving. In the context of women's art production, authors who wrote about women's art practices also used the term *meishu* to connote all types of arts and crafts practices.

[2] For a discussion of the arts and crafts curriculum in women's schools, see Yan, "Buxi de biandong."

and *The Ladies' Journal* served as important historical sources constituting the discourse on "women's art" in China.[3]

Through the prism of the lives and work of a few women artists who were featured in these two magazines, I use horizontal readings to explore the ways in which the notion of female artistic talent was contextualized and redefined in the relatively new genre of women's magazines. By piecing together a little-understood aspect of Chinese women's cultural history of the early Republican period, I also vertically reconstruct a genealogy of women's arts and crafts practices in the reforming Chinese art world of the early twentieth century. The artists I discuss include Shen Shou (1874–1921), Jin Taotao (Jin Zhang 1884–1939), Zhang Mojun (Zhang Zhaohan 1884–1965), Su Benyan (b. circa 1890s), Su Bennan (b. circa 1890s), and Pan Yuliang (1895–1977).

Even though *The Women's Eastern Times* and *The Ladies' Journal* shared the common mandate of advancing female learning and showcasing women's achievements, their representations of women's art diverged. This divergence underlined the shifting circumstances in the development of women's art from the 1910s to the 1930s. From the more conservative painting and calligraphy of the *guixiu* (women of the gentry) in *The Women's Eastern Times* to the more varied works by a diverse group of women artists and students in *The Ladies' Journal*, the two magazines documented distinctive aspects of Chinese women's art practices in the early twentieth century.

Why Gendered Magazines?

I am using gendered magazines as the main source of my analysis for two reasons. First, although the first three decades of the early twentieth century saw a surge in the number of art journals published in China, these publications rarely discussed women's artworks and art practices.[4] Not only were women's works less represented, but also essays written by women also rarely appeared in these journals. Women's magazines therefore filled the void created by the underrepresentation of women's art in art journals published at the time.

The classical language used throughout the entire twenty-one issues of *The Women's Eastern Times* and in the first five volumes (1915–1919) of *The Ladies' Journal* strongly suggests that their target readership was women of the upper social strata, who were well educated and had the opportunity to be tutored in high cultural practices.[5] Although the target readership of *The Women's Eastern Times* was female, the majority of readers and writers in its

---

[3] For a discussion of women artists' struggle for visibility in European art centers in the early twentieth century, see Elliot and Wallace, *Women Artists*, 31–55.

[4] From 1911 to 1937, there were more than 200 kinds of art magazines published in China's metropolises. Xu, *Zhongguo meishu*.

[5] For a discussion of the readership of *The Women's Eastern Times*, see Judge, *Republican Lens*, Chapter 2.

early years of publication were male.[6] These male readers, writers, and editors belonged to the same elite art and cultural circles as the female intellectuals, social activists, and artists represented in the magazines. They were committed to promoting women's social and cultural status and had high esteem for art as a revered practice in women's lives that could also make an important contribution to the nation. In contrast to the underrepresentation of female artists in art journals, gendered magazines highlighted women artists in ways that conformed with their general ethos of intellectual elitism. This elite view of women's art became even more apparent when women artists started to publish essays on their own art-making processes or their own knowledge of art in *The Ladies' Journal*. This process of recognition of women artists as intellectuals and professionals in women's magazines allows us to trace the development of women's art practices in the Republican period.

Artworks by women and photo portraits of artists did frequently appear in many popular early Republican magazines (usually vernacular) and newspapers such as *Shanghai manhua* (Shanghai sketch, 1928–1930) and *Libailiu* (The Saturday, 1914–1916; 1921–1923). However, there was little in-depth discussion of women's art practices in these publications. Images of women artists and their works were often accompanied by simple captions or short paragraphs stating titles of artworks, information such as dates of exhibitions, and brief biographical notes about the artists. Because these portrayals of female artists are generally juxtaposed to photographs of movie stars, socialites, and politicians, they appear more as semi-celebrities than as serious art practitioners. While these publications provide a vivid picture of the art and cultural scene of the period, they lack the intellectual gravitas of the representation of women artists in elite women's magazines. This is the second reason I rely on women's magazines as a unique space for the discourse on women's art practices and art education in the early twentieth century.

While my focus is on the ways women artists were represented in the two magazines, I am mindful, in a horizontal take, of how these portrayals dynamically interacted with other contents of these publications that defined the new Chinese womanhood – essays, verses, photographs, and advertisements on such topics as women and nation, work, family, and daily life. In the pages that follow, I will analyze the representational strategies of specific artists in this broader discursive context.

The Women's Eastern Times, *The Ladies' Journal*, and the Strategy of "Role-Modeling"

The Women's Eastern Times and *The Ladies' Journal* targeted an urban readership that was highly literate and active in the public sphere. One of the key ways

[6] *Ibid.*

the magazines' publishers and editors attempted to engage their female audience was through "role-modeling." This strategy is evident in every issue of *The Women's Eastern Times* and *The Ladies' Journal*. Their pages are filled with photo-portraits of women accompanied by descriptions of their public roles. Through articles and images depicting women engaged in different activities, the two magazines presented their readers with new, exciting, and at times unconventional feminine possibilities. In addition to featuring nationalists, philanthropists, educators, and writers, stories of relatively new professions for women, such as physicians, athletes, musicians, and even hypnotists, are represented.[7]

The ways in which these role models were represented in the magazines, I would argue, was founded on the tradition of biographies of exemplary women that had been used for many centuries to impart moral teachings, as in the canonical *Lienü zhuan* (Arrayed traditions of women's lives).[8] Interpretations of these ancient biographical accounts had never been static; their meanings were repeatedly transformed through the introduction of "parabiographical" elements that reflected the sociopolitical thinking and ethical preoccupations of the time. This practice of "overwriting" intensified at the turn of the twentieth century as compilers and authors used these exemplary stories to advance women's education and national progress.[9] The long tradition of using stories of exemplary women to pedagogical ends thus continued in early-twentieth-century expansions of ancient texts, new-style textbooks for female students, and popular journals and newspapers.[10] Not only did the pool of exemplary women expand, but also the purpose and function of their stories was extended from emulating self-sacrificing women of the past to taking inspiration from "self-constituting subjects of the future."[11] Women's self-creation and embrace of novel experiences and new possibilities were thus highlighted in the representation of elite women in the two magazines.

Among these new feminine possibilities, *The Women's Eastern Times* and *The Ladies' Journal* particularly promoted arts and crafts as a revered cultural practice and a potentially desirable career path for women. This mandate

---

[7] In *The Women's Eastern Times*, there are photo portraits depicting women in their professional roles, such as the physical education specialist Ms. Tang Jianwo, pictured in Western-style clothing in *Funü shibao* 2; the female martial arts master Ms. Teng Xueqin from Baoshan (*Funü shibao* 6); the musician Ms. Teng Zhuo of Hunan (*Funü shibao* 10); and the female hypnotist Ms. Liu Shouhun (*Funü shibao* 21). And in *The Ladies' Journal*, a female doctor named Li Huanqiu wrote a three-part introduction to anatomy (Li, "Jianming jiepouxue").

[8] *Lienü zhuan* (Arrayed traditions of women's lives), compiled by Liu Xiang (79–78 BCE), 34 BCE.

[9] Judge, *Precious Raft*, 11–12.

[10] For a discussion of functions and interpretations of women's biographies in early-twentieth-century texts, see ibid., 12–27; passim.

[11] Ibid., 12.

was evident in the inclusion of a significant number of images of artwork by women – including embroidery, Chinese-style painting, calligraphy, Western-style oil painting, drawing, and watercolor. In addition to images, numerous articles aimed at promoting women's participation in the arts and crafts also appeared in the journals' pages. The editors also focused on how women's artistic practices helped them move across domestic and international boundaries and discussed the importance of education in opening up new feminine possibilities.[12]

Women's Art in *The Women's Eastern Times*

The Women's Eastern Times did not directly promote art as a career option for women as *The Ladies' Journal* would later in the 1920s. The earlier journal did, however, actively promote public recognition of women's artistic talent. In the "inaugural essay" for *The Women's Eastern Times*, the author, who is unnamed but who is most certainly the editor for the journal, Bao Tianxiao (1876–1973), announces that many *guiyuan* (gentry women) were deeply concerned about China's state of chaos and weakness.[13] Bao announces that many of these women were patriotic and worried about current events (*youshi aiguo*). They were also intelligent and knowledgeable (*mingmin tongda*) and capable of discussing issues concerning the nation and society. He asserts, therefore, that his monthly magazine would provide a space for these women to contribute to the nation by publicly expressing their opinions.

Another mandate of the magazine that is laid out in the inaugural essay was to promote women's education. Bao states that education for Chinese women had been lagging behind for the last few thousand years, but that this dark period would finally end if intellectuals worked to promote women's education. *The Women's Eastern Times* advocated women's rights, especially their educational rights, while also focusing on women's family lives and everyday concerns such as health, hygiene, beauty, and home economics.[14] Women who were lauded in the magazine were well-rounded, well-educated, selfless, family-minded, and socially conscious. They were also artistically talented.

Women artists featured in *The Women's Eastern Times* mostly came from elite gentry families. They had been born from the late 1870s to the 1890s and had come of age in the last years of the Qing dynasty. They were exposed to both *jiaxue* (family learning) and the new public education. Their life experience changed rapidly as tensions between traditional ritual teachings and women's

---

[12] For the fine arts components in the new curricula for female schools published in 1907, see excerpts from "Xuebu zouding."

[13] "Fakan ci." On Bao Tianxiao's likely authorship of this "Inaugural essay," see Judge, *Republican Lens*, Introduction.

[14] See, for example, Joan Judge's and Maria af Sandeberg's contributions to this volume.

public roles loomed large in debates on national progress at the turn of the twentieth century. Their modes of cultural practice were often circumscribed by the dichotomy between female talent and virtue that had long characterized women's gender positioning. In terms of artistic styles, these women artists typically followed and continued their predecessors' legacy of female artistry. *The Women's Eastern Times* ultimately represents women's artistic talent as a personal attribute rather than a professional endeavor, however. With very few exceptions, the works featured in the journal were traditional paintings, calligraphy, and *nügong* (women's crafts) – especially embroidery – all of which were closely associated with the artistic production of gentry women in traditional society.

In their effort to showcase the talent of elite women, editors of *The Women's Eastern Times* solicited women's artworks, photo portraits, and literary writings through an open call for submissions.[15] In addition to submitted works, the publisher, Di Baoxian (Chuqing, Pingzi, 1872–1941), and the chief editor, Bao Tianxiao, also actively solicited entries through their personal network in the world of art and culture. Di was a well-known painter and art collector, and Bao a famous writer, and women artists featured in *The Women's Eastern Times* often belonged to the same elite cultural circles. The contributors' personal relationships to the publisher and editor further perpetuated the ethos of elitism in *The Women's Eastern Times*. The representation of the artist Jin Zhang, or Jin Taotao (who was briefly introduced in Julia F. Andrews' chapter in this volume), in the magazine is one telling example of this circuit of connection.

Jin Taotao: A *Guixiu* Artist in a New Era

In the inaugural issue of *The Women's Eastern Times*, there is a cameo photograph of Jin Taotao printed alongside her painting – a painted fan of fish (see Figure 5.1).

The inscription on the photograph reads:

> Visiting Paris at the same time as older brother Gongbo [Jin Cheng]
> For [my brother] to commemorate this happy occasion
> The tenth month of *gengsu* [October 1910]
> Noted by younger sister Zhang

Jin Taotao was the younger sister of the renowned painter Jin Cheng (Jin Shaocheng, Gongbei, 1878–1926), a well-known figure in traditionalist art circles. He was also a high-ranking government official. The inscription on

---

[15] See, for example, "Benbao zhengwenli."

Fig. 5.1 Photo-portrait and a painted fan by Jin Taotao, *The Women's Eastern Times* 1 (June 11, 1911)

the photograph reveals this family relationship, together with Jin Taotao's privileged position and elite social status, which enabled her to travel abroad.[16] Although Jin was an established painter and calligrapher in her own right, she was less well known than her brother, and her connection with him

[16] It would be Jin Taotao's second trip to Europe. This time, she traveled as a married woman accompanying her husband on his diplomatic assignment. Her first trip to Europe took place from 1902 to 1905. At that time, she traveled with Jin Cheng and her two other brothers to England, where she was said to have learned Western painting from a private tutor. Upon his return to China in 1905, following his study in England, Jin Cheng worked as an official in the Department of Justice of the late Qing regime (Yun Xuemei, *Jin Cheng*, 5). In 1907, he was appointed the Justice of the Third Circuit of the High Court of Justice in Beijing. He was sent to attend the International Prison Congress, held in Washington in October 1910. After the congress, Jin Cheng travelled to Europe to survey the prison system there, and it was during this trip that he and Jin Taotao met in Paris.

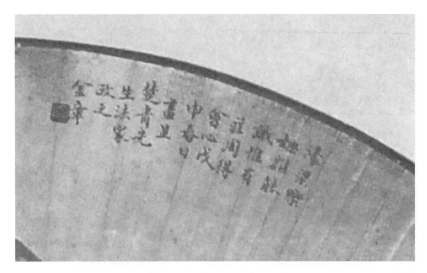

Fig. 5.2 A painted fan by Jin Taotao in *The Women's Eastern Times* 1 (detail)

helped readers position her in the art world. Her cultural position is further manifest in the inscription on the painted fan (see Figure 5.2):

Who would understand the joy of fish?
Only Zhuang Zhou would fully grasp it.
In the spring of the year *mushen* [1908]
Painted for the scrutiny of Mr. Chuqing [Di Baoxian]
Jin Zhang[17]

The inscription reveals that the fan was a gift to Di Baoxian. Reproduced in the front section of the inaugural issue of *The Women's Eastern Times* where monochromatic photographs – produced with the relatively new technology of collotype – were printed, it reflects Di's high regard for her art and the artistic works of gentry women in general.

Besides publishing the newspaper *Shibao – The Eastern Times* and a number of periodicals, including *The Women's Eastern Times*, Di also played a crucial role in promoting Chinese traditional art. His publishing house Youzheng shuju (Youzheng Book Company) published reproductions of ancient paintings, calligraphy, and ink rubbings using collotype printing.[18] Di's commitment to

---

[17] *Funü shibao* 1, image section.
[18] Advertisements for the art books published by Youzheng were printed in *The Women's Eastern Times*. The technology of collotype was first used at the Tushanwan yinshuguan (Tushanwan press) in 1875. Youzheng was said to be the first Chinese publisher to use this new printing technology in China. Zou, "Tushanwan," 199.

promoting and preserving traditional art was also reflected in the editorial direction of *The Women's Eastern Times*. Most of the artworks reproduced in the magazine were Chinese paintings and calligraphy produced by elite women who, like many *guixiu* (gentry women), had been trained to continue the legacy of their talented forebears in these visual arts. Showcasing women's traditional painting and calligraphy was a way for *The Women's Eastern Times* to highlight the cultural erudition and personal merit of well-educated women. At the same time, the journal also reflected the increasing importance of art education in the curriculum for early Republican women's schools and the rising importance of arts and crafts as a viable livelihood for women in this period. The journal provided detailed coverage, for example, of women's achievements in the arts and crafts and in the sphere of art education at the Nanyang quanyehui (Nanyang industrial exposition).

Women's Arts and Crafts at the Nanyang Industrial Exposition

The Nanyang Industrial Exposition, which was held in Nanjing in 1910, was the Qing government's first attempt to host its own industrial exposition fashioned after those held in Japan, Europe, and America. The event was "imagined as both a classroom for national development and as a new kind of spectacle that could accomplish such a pedagogical aim."[19] Among the thirteen pavilions showcasing aspects of China's achievements, including agriculture, machinery, and the military, education was one of the highlights at the exposition. The *jiaoyuguan* (education pavilion) – one of the largest buildings at the exposition – displayed exemplary works produced by teachers and students of different schools and grade levels.[20] The section devoted to women's education (the *nüxuebu*), one of the main sections of the education pavilion, exhibited handicrafts, artwork, and academic work by teachers and students of women's schools.[21] Women's arts and crafts objects were also presented at the *jingjiguan* (capital pavilion), which housed treasures produced at institutions under the *Nonggongshangbu* (Ministry of agriculture, industry and commerce). The *meishuguan* (art pavilion) exhibited Chinese- and Western-style paintings, calligraphy, embroidery, craft objects, and sculptures by

---

[19] Fernsebner, "Objects, Spectacle,"100.

[20] Buildings at the exposition ranged from thirty to three hundred *fangzhang* in area. The education pavilion building was about three hundred *fangzhang*. The large area that the pavilion occupied at the exposition showed that education was an important sector in the project of nation building. Bao Yong'an, ed., *Nanyang quanyehui wenhui*, 134.

[21] Bao Yong'an, ed., *Nanyang quanyehui tushuo*, 109–11.

established artists including some women.[22] Although the presence of women's work at Nanyang was relatively small, women's participation in the event was enthusiastically encouraged.[23] *The Women's Eastern Times*, which was inaugurated a few months after the closing of the exposition, continued the exposition's goal of educating the new citizenry through the visual representation of "material things"[24] by highlighting the works of women who participated in the Nanyang exhibition.

The third issue of *Women's Eastern Times* reproduced two handiworks of *zhaimian huahui* (cotton flowers) made by sisters Su Bennan and Su Benyan (see Figure 5.3).[25] Cameo photographs of the Su sisters, together with the first-class medals they received at Nanyang were photo-collaged onto the images of their handiwork. *Zhaimian* (cotton crafts) was one kind of new-style handicraft that was becoming popular among women in China's metropolises, especially in Shanghai, where, as advertisements in the journal indicated, material for the crafts was widely available.[26] This kind of new-style craft had become a mainstay in the curricula of many women's schools despite the criticism that it lacked practical use and took students' time away from learning more useful skills such as cooking and tailoring.[27] One of the schools that promoted cotton handicrafts was the Minli nüzi zhongxuetang (Minli middle school for women), established by Su Benyan, Su Bennan, and their three sisters.[28] The showcasing of cotton flower works at the education pavilion of Nanyang and the granting of awards to the Su sisters – founders and teachers of an important women's school – were a public endorsement of the role of arts and crafts in women's education. The assemblage of the medals, cameo photographs, and crafts in the photograph in *The Women's Eastern Times* creates a further visual narrative of success that aimed to inspire (more) women to fulfill their artistic potential.

The importance of art in learned women's lives was further endorsed through the representation of Zhang Mojun, a well-known writer, educator, and social

[22] According to Jiang Danshu ("Yishu niannian," 94–96), a well-known art educator in the Republican period, there had been no modern-style art exhibition organized by either the government or private organizations before Nanyang. Despite the fact that the art pavilion only constituted a small part of the exposition, it was the first of its kind in China.

[23] For a discussion of women's participation at Nanyang, see Fernsebner, "Objects, Spectacle," 116–17.

[24] *Ibid.*, 108.   [25] *Funü shibao* 3, image section.

[26] Advertisement for Dong Ya gongsi shuyaoju (East Asia bookstore and pharmacy): "Funü jiyi zaohua cailiao qiju yigai juquan" (Large selection of equipment and supplies for women's craft – paper flower making; *Funü shibao* 4 [November 5, 1911]; 5 [January 23, 1912]; 6 [May 1, 1912]).

[27] Zhuang Yu, Jiang Weigao, "Jiaoyuguan," 51.

[28] The Minli school was established in 1906. A photograph of four Su sisters and students at the school was printed in *Funü shibao* 4, image section: "Xinhai xia Minli Shanghai nüzhongxuetang benkesheng di-yi ci biye sheying" (Picture of the first graduating class of Shanghai Minli middle school for women, Summer 1911).

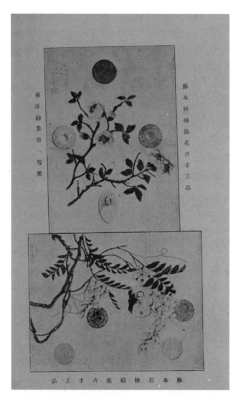

Fig. 5.3 Handicrafts by Su Bennan and Su Benyan, *The Women's Eastern Times* 3 (September 22, 1911)

activist, in *The Women's Eastern Times*.[29] Zhang's oil painting, entitled *Xingshi tu* (Awakened lion), was among the small number of Western-style paintings exhibited in the art pavilion at Nanyang. The painting had garnered high praise from a critic, who stated that Zhang's technique was uncommonly sophisticated and that the lion in the painting looked as if it was alive.[30] This painting, along with two of Zhang's landscape paintings, was reproduced in *The Women's Eastern Times* (see Figure 5.4).[31] Western-style painting was not frequently presented in the journal, which only included a few "*minghua*" (famous paintings) from the West over the course of the magazine's entire run. The inclusion

---

[29] Zhang was a frequent contributor to *The Women's Eastern Times*. Seven poems, letters, and two of her photo portraits were published throughout the twenty-one issues of the magazine. For more on Zhang, see Judge, *Republican Lens*, Chapter 5.

[30] Wu, "Yanjiu tuhua," 173.　　[31] *Funü shibao* 4, image section.

Fig. 5.4 Paintings by Zhang Mojun, *The Women's Eastern Times* 4 (November 5, 1911)

of Zhang's oil paintings – the only Western-style art by a Chinese woman printed in the magazine – was therefore even more distinctive.

The inclusion of Zhang's oil paintings in *The Women's Eastern Times* and the appearance of Western-style art in the journal in general, pushed the boundaries of the usual types of artwork presented in the magazine and provided new visual stimulation to the readers. Zhang's painting, together with her other literary work, demonstrated that she was a learned woman who was deeply immersed in both classical learning and new (Western) knowledge. This portrayal of Zhang was further encapsulated in one of her poems – a colophon she wrote for her oil painting titled "Meiren yima kanjiantu" (A beauty inspecting a sword while standing beside [her] horse). The painting was not reproduced in the magazine, and appears to no longer be extant. We can deduce from the theme of the poem, however, that the subject of the painting was a female knight errant who was concerned about the current national turmoil. In the poem, Zhang announces her wish to journey with this knight-errant to repay the country by carrying out deeds to right injustice. Her patriotic sentiment was personified through the depiction of this imaginative exemplary woman.[32] The poem (and the painting) not only show Zhang's erudition in both classical learning and new knowledge, but also align her with the ideals of an exemplary woman as described by the editor of *The Women's Eastern Times*. Zhang was both "*youshi aiguo*" (patriotic and concerned about current events) and "*mingmin tongda*" (intelligent and knowledgeable).

The Women's Eastern Times further linked women's achievements in arts and crafts to fame and material gain in its representation of Shen Shou. A spectacular embroidered portrait of the Italian Empress Elena of Montenegro, accompanied by a photo portrait of Yu Shen Shou, was printed in the inaugural issue of *The Women's Eastern Times*[33] (see Figure 5.5). The work was the jewel at the capital pavilion of the Nanyang Exposition and attracted high praise from the audience and critics alike. After the portrait was exhibited at Nanyang, it was sent to Italy as one of China's official entries for the International Exposition of Industry and Trade in Turin in 1911.[34] It was granted the highest award at the Turin Exposition and attracted the attention of the empress herself. Empress Elena was said to have sent a letter to the Chinese embassy in Italy to request that the portrait be given to her as a gift.[35] This success reinforced Shen's reputation as a celebrated embroiderer not only in China but on the global stage. The caption to Shen's portrait in *The Women's Eastern Times* states that she was the "Nonggongshangbu nüzi xiugongke zongjiaoxi" (Chief instructor of the Embroidery Program for Women at the Ministry of Agriculture, Industry and Commerce). It further explains that she was bestowed with the honorary name "*Shou*" (longevity) by Empress Dowager

---

[32] Zhang, "Ziti meiren."

[33] Photo-portrait of Shen Shou and her embroidery of the Italian Empress Elena were printed in *Funü shibao* 1. The caption identifies her as Yu-Shen Shou. Yu was the family name of Shen's husband, Yu Jue. Putting their husband's family name before the women's own name was a common way of addressing women in the Republican period. This format is still in use today.

[34] "Jinyao xinwen."   [35] Ibid.

Fig. 5.5 Photo-portrait and embroidery of the Italian empress by Shen Shou,
The Women's Eastern Times 1 (June 11, 1911)

Cixi.[36] Shen was thus one of the first Chinese women artists featured in *The Women's Eastern Times* whose achievement commanded both national and international honors: the royal edict of Empress Cixi and praise from the Italian Empress.[37] During a time when the practice of traditional women's

---

[36] The line "From the imperial decree, the word 'longevity' is bestowed" (*yi zhi jiajiang, yu ci shou zi*) was added to the caption of the photo of the embroidery.

[37] Although there was no mention of Shen's award at Turin or of Empress Elena's praise for Shen's work, the news was widely reported in newspapers in Shanghai at the time. Therefore, readers

crafts was promulgated as a viable occupation for women through school curricula, the portrayal of Shen in *The Women's Eastern Times* would have encouraged young women to enter this field. Possibilities of success in careers in art
were further articulated in *The Ladies' Journal* in the 1920s.

The Ladies' Journal and Women's Art

From the early 1920s to the mid-1930s, the proliferation of specialized art
schools and increased opportunities for overseas studies enabled women artists
to be key figures in the Chinese art world. Similarly to *The Women's Eastern
Times*, *The Ladies' Journal* provided a platform for showcasing women's literary and artistic talent, as well as their new roles in society. Given changes
in the broader historical context, the emphasis on various opportunities made
possible by women's newly defined artistic talent was even stronger in *The
Ladies' Journal*. In one of the journal's inaugural essays, the author states that
women's lives could be greatly enriched by nurturing a variety of talent (*cai
duo wei fu*). Therefore, a *meishu lan* (art column) should be established in *The
Ladies' Journal* to introduce readers to all types of fine arts – including embroidery, epigraphy, painting, and music. The author further asserts that women's
aesthetic sensibility was a "gift from heaven" (*tianji suodan*). *The Ladies' Journal* would help women develop this innate ability so that they could enjoy all
the beautiful things in life.[38]

By the late 1920s, art practice was increasingly considered a laudable occupation for women. In the following, I will examine *The Ladies' Journal*'s contribution to the development of women's artistic practice by focusing on two
special issues on art that were published in 1926 and 1929. Although there
are numerous reproductions of artwork by women and articles related to art
throughout the entire run of *The Ladies' Journal*, these two special issues represent the editors' focused and comprehensive views on women's art. Moreover,
these two issues were published in the late 1920s, when women's participation in the art world reached new heights. Many students had graduated from
specialized art programs and others were returning to China after their studies
overseas to become active participants in the art world. These two issues of
The Ladies' Journal include articles and artworks by a wide range of contributors, including a number of prominent women artists and writers in the art and
culture world.[39]

The strategy of "role-modeling" was still widely used in *The Ladies' Journal*, but the emphasis had shifted. Whereas editors of *The Women's Eastern
Times* generally framed women's artistic talent in terms of self-cultivation and

---

of *The Women's Eastern Times* would most likely have been aware of Shen's achievement in
Italy.

[38] "*Funü zazhi* fakanci," 1–2.

[39] For main contributors to the special issue, see "Bianjishi zhuiyan."

public recognition, the editors of *The Ladies' Journal* put greater emphasis on women artists' professional development, as well as their involvement in social causes and art education. This was reflected in the ways in which artists were represented through images and texts in the two special issues.

The Ladies' Journal's special issue on art published in 1926 was very popular with its audience as evinced by readers' repeated requests to reprint the issue.[40] Although there were a few articles related to art in the "art column" of the first (1915) volume, this special issue was *The Ladies' Journal*'s first attempt to introduce *meishu* (fine art) to its readers with the intention of encouraging women to engage art in various ways in their lives. The issue includes articles on a variety of topics such as the origin and functions of art in society and technical aspects of art, including the basics of oil painting and techniques of seal carving and embroidery. Another main category of articles in this issue focuses on careers in the arts and crafts for women. Authors of these articles introduced to readers possible careers – from more conventional work such as embroidery, seal carving, and Chinese-style painting to newer options such as *tu'an* (pattern) design and photography. Pleas from the authors for women to work in the art field were complemented by articles promulgating the belief that aesthetic sensibility was an innate trait of women and therefore should be nurtured.[41]

The 1926 issue also represented women artists in a new way. One example is an article on the female artist Wang Ruizhu.[42] In previous issues of *The Ladies' Journal*, women artists' works were published in the "picture column" of the magazine. They were not accompanied by introductions to the lives of the artists or discussions of their works. In contrast, a two-page article introduced Wang's life and work in the special issue. The article consists of a photo-portrait of Wang, a piece of her embroidery, and two of her watercolor paintings. The text informs readers that Wang was a graduate of the Joshi Bijutsu Gakkō (School of Art for Women) in Tokyo, and that she was well known for her meticulous skills in dyeing threads to match the "realistic" colors of the objects depicted in her embroidery. The article also tells readers that, among her many other roles – including art educator and mother of five children – Wang was actively engaged in social causes and the promotion of women's rights through her work as an active member of *Nüzi canzheng xiejinhui* (Association for the promotion of women's suffrage). She was also a friend of the artist and revolutionary He Xiangning (1879–1972), with whom she was in the process of establishing an art school for female students. Although the author of the biography still used the strategy of "role-modeling," the information pertaining to Wang's art-works and practice was much more detailed and comprehensive than previous

---

[40] *Meishu zhuanhao* (Special issue on art), *Funü zazhi* 12. 1 (1926). Requests from readers to reprint the issue are seen in "Bianjishi de baogao" and "Bianjishi zhuiyan."

[41] See, for example, Zhu Yin, "Nüzi haomei."   [42] Shao Ying, "Meishujia wang ruizhu."

presentations of women artists in *The Women's Eastern Times* and earlier volumes of *The Ladies' Journal*. The author also contextualized Wang's work in the larger art field and emphasized her career as an artist and educator. This kind of detailed introduction to women artists became more common in later issues of *The Ladies' Journal*, especially in the 1929 special issue on the First National Art Exhibition.[43] The way that the article was written also foreshadowed the frequent appearance of *fangwenji* (interviews) – a genre of writing on notable figures – in the popular press of the late 1920s and 1930s. These interviews involved dialogues between interviewers and interviewees, and hence communicated the "voice" of the person being written about more directly to the readers. There were also more opportunities for artists to publish their thoughts on art in the popular press in the 1920s.[44] Male artists benefited from these new opportunities much more frequently than female artists, however. The 1929 special issue of *The Ladies' Journal* on the First National Art Exhibition was, therefore, a long-awaited platform for women artists to express their thoughts in writing.

Self-Representation of Women Artists in *The Ladies' Journal*

The First Ministry of Education National Art Exhibition (Jiaoyubu quanguo meishu zhanlanhui) was the first large-scale national art event in China organized by the Republican government.[45] *The Ladies' Journal* published a comprehensive report on the exhibition in a special issue devoted to the event (which was already briefly introduced in Julia F. Andrews's contribution to this volume).

A two-part column titled "Zuojia jingyan tan" (Art-makers' experience) includes descriptions by a few women artists – working in both Western and Chinese media – of their personal experiences of learning art and their art-making processes. The first article in the column was written by Pan Yuliang.[46] Pan was one of the few female students who benefited from an overseas education under the Liu Fa qingong jianxue yundong (Work–study program in France, [1919–1921], see Figure 5.6).[47] After receiving an art education in France and then Italy, Pan returned to China in 1928 and produced a large body of paintings on various subjects, including the female nude. Her works were ground-breaking in their audacious depiction of the female body and assertive in their expression of gender consciousness. In the article, Pan announces her

---

[43] *Funü zazhi* 15. 7 (July 1929).

[44] Artists were given space to write about their practices and publish photographs of work in popular magazines such as *Liangyou*, for example. See Tongyun Yin, "From Painter to Artist."

[45] For a description of the scale of the exhibition, see Jiang, "Yishu niannian," 94–6.

[46] Pan Yuliang, "Woxi fenbihua."

[47] A photograph of female students at L'Institut franco-chinois de Lyon, where Chinese students would attend after they first arrived in France, was printed in *Funü zazhi* 8. 7 (1922), image section.

Fig. 5.6 Photo of female students at L'Institut franco-chinois de Lyon, *The Ladies' Journal* 8:7 (1922)

love of pastel and describes her experience using the medium. She also mentions her experience in Europe and her current work after returning to China. The article was accompanied by her pastel painting "Guying" (Looking at one's own reflection) (Figure 5.7), which was mentioned in the article. The painting was printed on the first page of the color plate section, which reflected the importance of Pan's work in the special issue and, by extension, in the larger art world. Li Yuyi, an artist and writer who authored the four reviews of the National Exhibition that appear in the issue, praises the exceptional depth shown in Pan's work. He also asserts that Pan's perseverance during her difficult years as an art student in France and Italy and her international success made her a rare treasure in the bleak environment of the art world in China.[48] In addition to this coverage of Pan and her work, her photograph and short biography were included in the column "Nü qingnian yishujia" (Young women artists) along with twenty-three other women artists. These women included painters, calligraphers, sculptors, and photographers. The composite representation of Pan in the special issue – which includes images and criticism of her work, a photo portrait, a short biography, and her own writing – not only presented to

[48] Li Yuyi, "Jiaoyubu," 1–2.

Fig. 5.7 "Guying" (Looking at one's own reflection) by Pan Yuliang, *The Ladies' Journal* 15:7 (1929)

readers a woman artist who was exceptionally adept in her practice, but also gave a vivid picture of her life and personality. Featuring Pan as a role model, editors of *The Ladies' Journal* further affirmed Chinese women's rising status in both the Chinese and international art worlds.

Conclusion

In this chapter, I have predominantly used a vertical approach to demonstrate the changing strategies of representing women's art in two influential women's magazines. From the more conservative genres of artworks by women of the gentry in *The Women's Eastern Times* to the audacious paintings of the female nude in *The Ladies' Journal*, these women's magazines highlighted various aspects of women's artistic practice in the Republican era. They also provided a platform for women to display their skill in and knowledge of art, thus helping to transform and redefine the notion of female talent. At a time when the institutional system of the Chinese art world and the practices within it were still predominantly male-centered, the two magazines provided a much-needed public discursive space for foregrounding women artists' achievements.

These journals also provided female (and many male) readers with the opportunity to collect relatively high-fidelity reproductions of artwork and photographs. This was made possible by the printing technologies – such as lithography, collotype, and photolithography – that were available in China from the mid-nineteenth century.[49] The practice of collecting printed images is evident in the number of visual materials that have been cut out of the pages of original copies of these magazines housed in libraries in China and around the world. Some of these images may have been excised by library users of later periods. However, I imagine taking photographic reproductions (especially colored ones) from magazines would have been a relatively inexpensive way for early-twentieth-century readers to build their personal collections. Women's magazines with their large number of reproductions of women's artworks thus helped to disseminate and popularize women's art on the quotidian level. The images of artworks excised from their pages could have functioned as standalone artifacts that may have circulated beyond the circle of targeted readers. Not only were the images distributed within national boundaries, but also a whole issue of a particular magazine or clippings of images could have ended up in the hands of individuals or institutions overseas, thus broadening the boundaries of dissemination.[50]

Not only did the two magazines play an important role in disseminating discussions and examples of women's art during their years of publication, but also they now stand as important archives for preserving details about women artists and their works that would have otherwise been lost. Works of art are by nature ephemeral. The preservation of artworks – especially those by women, which were fewer in number than those by male artists – was a difficult task due to political and social turmoil over the course of the twentieth century. *The Women's Eastern Times* and *The Ladies' Journal* served a role, then and now, in keeping the legacy of women artists alive. They are an invaluable resource for reclaiming an accurate picture of women artists' contribution to the development of modern art in China.

---

[49] On the new printing technology in China, see Reed, *Gutenberg in Shanghai*.

[50] For example, copies of *The Ladies' Journal* were found in the collection of the library of L'Institut Franco-Chinois, which is now archived at the Bibliothèque Municipale de Lyon.

6   Constituting the Female Subject: Romantic Fiction by Women Authors in *Eyebrow Talk**

Jin-Chu Huang

Translated by Michel Hockx and Wei-hsin Lin

In the literary landscape of early Republican China, which is glutted with romantic writings, the stories published by women in the short-lived literary journal *Meiyu* (Eyebrow talk, 1914–1916) are so unique and thought-provoking that they should probably be assigned to a different category. Based on a vertical reading of these rarely studied works of fiction, I argue that their plots, themes, and language demonstrate novel ways of constituting female subjectivity beyond the confines of traditional patriarchal structures. Moreover, an integrated reading shows that they do so in ways not found in contemporary fiction by male authors, which so far have received much more scholarly attention.[1] I situate my reading in the wider context of a process of cultivation of women's rights advocacy in the late Qing and the general development of women's education, as well as the sustained efforts during the early Republic to gain political rights for women. Uniquely female forms of self-awareness and subject construction quietly began to burgeon in this period but, as the analysis will show, they also had their lingering limitations.

Before going into the analysis of the works, I provide a brief overview of the work on gender and subjectivity that has inspired my research and that I have found particularly illuminating in the study of early modern Chinese fiction by women.

The Female Subject

The term "female subject" poses complex questions. In this essay I align myself with the Taiwan cultural theorist Liao Chaoyang and adopt his basic definition of female subjectivity as "women determining their own subjectivity."[2] When women who have long been subjected to a patriarchal system start to

* This article represents part of the outcome of a Taiwan National Science Council research project (code NSC99–2410-H-194–118-). A longer Chinese version has appeared in *Zhongguo wenxue xuebao* 3 (2012), 165–87.
[1] Other aspects of the publishing history and eventual banning of *Eyebrow Talk* are discussed in detail in Michel Hockx's contribution to this volume.
[2] Liao Chaoyang, "Pipan yu fenli," 119–20.

explore beyond the boundaries of their conventional roles, it goes without say-ing that activity and passivity, subject position and object position will be deeply entwined.[3] Moreover, owing to social and cultural differences and trans-formations, women writers from different times and places and different gen-erations will express different subjectivities.

Some scholars have argued that even the women writers of the May Fourth generation were not autonomous subjects, but that "they can only count as semi-subjects."[4] This suggests that even less autonomy can be found among the previous generation, active during the 1910s. In reality, the effects of the late Qing women's rights movement had different and unexpected results in differ-ent areas. Fiction by female writers from the late Qing and early Republic does contain elements revealing new forms of subjective awareness. From the late Qing onwards, the discourse of women's rights emerged and women's learning became gradually more popular. Since magazines were flourishing, educated female intellectuals began to use the periodical press as a medium for their own voices. Yet, as has already been well documented in recent scholarship, the initial rise of women's rights was closely linked with political appeals for saving and strengthening the nation.[5] The urgency of the national crisis led to frequent conflicts and a conflation between the *nüti* (female body) and the *guoti* (body politic), with the female subject inevitably reduced to an appendage of the nation-state. The direct appellation of the female subject either suffered dis-regard or was considered inessential. Nevertheless, repeated calls for women's rights in the late Qing opened up opportunities for unraveling traditional forms of patriarchy. The emergence of women writers in the late Qing and early Republic thus constituted one phase in women's quest for new self-definitions and subject constructions.

Through writing, women are able to participate in social activities, while embarking on a journey of self-discovery. Through writing, female subjects are able to "unyoke themselves from their assigned roles," "break free from the constraints of patriarchal order," reveal "hidden female desires," and "express their true selves," in order to "find the strength unique to women."[6] These are the core concepts modern-day feminist theorists use to encourage women to partake in writing. Although the female writers in the late Qing and early Republic may not have had such theoretical support, as the women's rights movement developed, it was through writing that, whether consciously or not,

---

[3] Cf. Weedon, *Nüxingzhuyi shijian*, 39.   [4] Meng Yue and Dai Jinhua, *Fuchu lishi*, 48.

[5] There has been much fruitful research on this topic. For more in-depth discussions, see Liu Ren-peng, *Jindai Zhongguo nüquan lunshu*. See also Mizuyo Sudo, *Zhongguo "nüquan" gainian*.

[6] Li Guiyun, *Menglong, qingming yu liudong*, 20–23. Other theories about women's writing include those put forward by the so-called "French feminists" such as Hélène Cixous, Luce Iri-garay, and Julia Kristeva. See Gu Yanling, ed., *Nüxingzhuyi lilun*, 297–338; Weedon, *Feminist Practice*, 73–86, 163–208; Zhang Yanbing, *Nüquanzhuyi wenlun*, 86–135.

women unveiled their long-repressed subjectivities. Granted, the goal of being one's own master and making one's own decisions could not be achieved immediately. But what could be expected was that the women were empowered through writing, and that writing contributed to their self-awareness and to the construction of new types of female subjectivity. Scholars of modern Chinese fiction, including feminist-inspired scholars, have so far paid very little attention to the specific ways this kind of subjectivity was constructed through fictional texts prior to the "May Fourth" moment. The fictional writings in *Eyebrow Talk* provide us with an excellent opportunity to fill this lacuna.

Love Stories

Eyebrow Talk is one of the very few magazines of the late Qing and early Republican period that featured a large number of female editors and writers. Political instability in the wake of the 1911 Revolution had subdued the literary scene, but by 1914 literary activity was once again flourishing in Shanghai. Urban life, entertainment, and culture all seemed to pick up pace, as if to make up for the stagnation of the previous two years, and there was a flurry of new activity. *Eyebrow Talk* emerged in this lively literary atmosphere. Like other magazines of the same period that used entertainment as their main slogan, *Eyebrow Talk* aimed at *jishi xingle* (seeking instant amusement), *xiaoxian* (leisure), *youxi* (playfulness), and being *hua qian yue xia zhi liangban* (a good companion in romantic settings).[7] Since *Eyebrow Talk* aimed at being a leisure companion, it published large quantities of romantic love stories. Indeed, romance fiction constitutes the main content of the journal.

Although love stories are generally considered to feature rather lowly subject matter and formulaic plot construction, the stories published in *Eyebrow Talk* nevertheless demonstrated both implicitly and explicitly the emerging impact of women's rights and some of the various relevant measures taken in this regard since the late Qing. Besides stories of love and happiness or separation and suffering, this fiction by female authors also displays uniquely female sensibilities. In this essay, I examine the gradual shaping of female subjects, especially in the descriptions of romantic love written by women for *Eyebrow Talk*.

Eyebrow Talk

Each issue of *Eyebrow Talk* was published on the first day of the lunar month, when, according to the journal's manifesto, "the moon is in a crescent shape"[8] and looks like eyebrows; hence the name *Eyebrow Talk*. It was one of the few journals at that time that were edited by women. Though there were two male

---

[7] See "Meiyu xuanyan."   [8] Ibid.

assistant editors, it was the female editors, especially Gao Jianhua, who had the final say and who decided if the journal was ready to come out.

The basic fact that female editors were directing this journal meant that its image was intimately connected to women. The female editors' right to decide which submissions would be included, together with the role of women as writers, meant that *Eyebrow Talk* provided fertile soil to display female subjects. It provided a unique platform not seen in other journals or offered to other female writers at the time. Under the guidance of female editors, works by female writers received tangible and intangible support and encouragement. From these female writers' literary activities, especially their fiction, we can detect the initial formation of female subjectivity.

There were more than twenty people signing their names with the designation *nüshi* (Miss) in *Eyebrow Talk*. For now, ten of these can be confirmed as actually female. In the "Illustrations" section of the first three issues, photos of the editor-in-chief and other female editors and contributors were provided.[9] Therefore, we know that apart from the editor-in-chief Gao Jianhua, other female editors and contributors included Ma Simei, Gu Renchai, Liang Guiqin, Xu Yuhua, Liang Guizhu, Liu Peiyu, Xie Youyun, Yao Shumeng, and Sun Qingwei.[10] Except for Gu Renchai, the other nine all had their works of fiction published in the journal. In addition, a photo of another *Eyebrow Talk* writer, Mrs. Xu-Zhang Huiru, appeared in issue 11, with the caption "A Friend of *Eyebrow Talk*."[11] Assessing this information and taking their photos as evidence, we can be sure that there were ten female writers affiliated with the journal. As for other contributors designated as "Miss," due to lack of evidence and the fact that, as Grace Fong has demonstrated in an earlier chapter, it was not uncommon for male writers to adopt this designation as part of their pen-names in the late Qing and early Republic,[12] we should be careful not to misjudge the

---

[9] In the second issue of the widely available reprint of *Eyebrow Talk*, all the images in the "Illustrations" column are missing. Original copies of the journal were consulted in the Shanghai Library. On the importance of photographs of women writers appearing in the women's press in this period see Judge, *Republican Lens*, Introduction, Chapters 3 and 6.

[10] Each of the photos of Ma Simei, Gu Renchai, and Liang Guiqin published in the first issue of *Eyebrow Talk* carries the caption "editor." In the second and third issues, their titles in these captions are replaced by a more general designation which reads "Female Colleagues in the Editing Department." Gu Renchai, referred to as one of the editors in the first issue, never published any work in the journal. Among the photos of "Female Colleagues in the Editing Department" in the second and third issues, Gu Renchai is also absent. Therefore, we know Gu is indeed an editor, not one of the writers. As for Ma Simei and Liang Guiqin, because their works do appear in the journal, they are both editors and authors. Evidence can be found in the fact that Liang Guiqin's photos are shown both in the photos captioned "Editors" and in "Female Colleagues in the Editing Department."

[11] *Meiyu* 11 (1915), 2322. Page numbers here and below refer to the 2006 reprint.

[12] For example, one of the *Eyebrow Talk* writers, with the pseudonym Meiqian Nüshi (Ms. Meiqian), was proven to be the male writer Gu Mingdao. This is mentioned in the "Publisher's Note" on the first page of the 2006 reprint of *Eyebrow Talk*. For more on male writers writing under feminine pseudonyms in this period, see the chapter by Grace Fong in this volume.

writer's sex and undermine the accuracy and credibility of our argument. Thus, whenever a name indicates a female writer but no evidence can be found to corroborate this, it will be excluded from the discussion here.

Together, these ten female writers published twenty-two short stories and one novel in *Eyebrow Talk*. Gao Jianhua was the most prolific of them, with a total of eight contributions. Xu-Zhang Huiru published four, Liu Peiyu three, and all the others one. The only novel was written by Gao Jianhua, but it was not complete when the journal ceased publication.[13] The storylines feature dramatic twists and turns, but are in general focused on the relationships between men and women. Romance is the common trait of most of these stories.

Both men and women contribute to the development of their love in these stories. Their actions and volition help constitute their subjectivities and they jointly influence the progress of the relationship. However, in a social reality overwhelmingly dominated by traditional institutions, marriage is usually the outcome of amorous relationships. Moreover, the idea that in a relationship the man should play the active role while the woman remains passive was deeply engrained in society at the time. Consequently, female subjectivity was often objectified as a reflection of men's desires. This has been a widespread phenomenon in classical Chinese literature. Yet even while writing in this mainstream tradition, the female writers of *Eyebrow Talk* managed to show surprising sparks of creativity. Examining how these female writers formulated men and women's actions and volition, how they represent the passivity and agency of their female subjects, and how their writings manifest particular gender identities and a consciousness of their own subjectivities will not only help us better understand the impact that the women's rights movement had on China since the late Qing, but also deepen our understanding of the early Republican female writers' self-identification.

In the following sections, I will study how the female writers of *Eyebrow Talk* managed simultaneously to acquiesce to and deviate from the established gender order, and how they were able to display their volition in their fiction. I shall demonstrate that they were empowered by their writings and, through the means of characterization and plot structure, they observed themselves and constructed their subjectivity.

The Female Writers of *Eyebrow Talk:* Self-Identification and the Romantic Subject

As members of the generation growing up during the development of the women's rights movement in the late Qing, the female writers of *Eyebrow Talk* differ markedly from their *guixiu* (gentry women) predecessors when it

---

[13] For the circumstances under which *Eyebrow Talk* ceased publication, see the paper by Michel Hockx in this volume.

comes to self-understanding and individual awareness. Though we have but scant information about the lives of these ten female writers, we can see that they all assumed the roles of either writers or editors, published their works in journals available to everyone, and did not have qualms about displaying their photos in these journals. This speaks to a self-perception and identity attributed to new-style women at the time. The photos of the female editors and contributors included in the first issue of the journal clearly demonstrate their attitude towards their selves and towards writing, which is undeniably in sharp contrast with traditional gentry women authors.

Among these ten writers, Yao Shumeng had two photos published, one featuring herself and the other taken with other people. In the "Illustrations" section in the thirteenth issue of *Eyebrow Talk*, there were photos of two married couples, one of them with the caption "Mr. Zhang Jianyao and Mrs. Yao Shumeng."[14] Hence we know that Yao Shumeng's husband was Zhang Jianyao. Apart from this, the few snippets of biographical information we have are about Xu Yuhua and Gao Jianhua.

Gao Jianhua was Xu Xiaotian's wife. *Eyebrow Talk* contains a relatively large amount of information about her, allowing us to reconstruct part of her biography. In her series of autobiographical articles entitled "Travel Notes from the Lihua Mansion," Gao Jianhua mentions that she was born in Hangzhou and that she began to study at the local Women's Normal College in the spring of 1910.[15] Throughout her "Travel Notes," Gao Jianhua makes a conscious effort to emphasize her physical and mental capacities and her ambition for *zili* (to stand on her own feet) and *zizhu* (to be in control of her own life).

Xu Yuhua was Xu Xiaotian's niece. Her photo in the journal shows her playing the organ. According to a later reminiscence by one of her younger family members she "also attended modern schools" and she "could speak some English."[16] It would seem that she received a modern education and was one of the modern women benefitting from the outcome of the women's rights movement in the late Qing. Since Gao Jianhua was Xu Yuhua's aunt, it is clear that family relations played a role in Xu's contributions to Gao's journal. It was a gesture of support from a niece to her aunt, as well as a gesture of guidance from the older generation to the younger.

According to Xu Xiaotian's own account, he and Gao Jianhua were first cousins.[17] They had a happy married life. Their deep affection toward each other is evident in Xu Xiaotian's series of ten "New Love Letters."[18] In addition,

---

[14] *Meiyu* 13 (1915), 2784.
[15] *Meiyu* 1 (1914), 165. For an overview of Gao Jianhua's life, see Huang Jinzhu [Jin-Chu Huang], *Nüxing shuxie de duoyuan chengxian*, 64–75.
[16] Xu Baowen, "Wo de jiating."
[17] See the second poem in Xu Xiaotian's "Xin qingshu shi shou."
[18] Ibid., 841–43.

in the short story "Talented Scholars and Beautiful Ladies Do Exist," the author Liu Peiyu adopted the perspective of Xu and Gao's pet cat, "Snow Maid," to describe the couple's blissful married life.[19] Liu Peiyu seemed to have some inside knowledge about Gao Jianhua's family life, and must have been either a friend or relative of Gao.

Ma Simei and Liang Guiqin were both writers as well as editors. In the late Qing and early Republican era, those who ran journals together most often knew one another before they became colleagues. Thus, both Ma and Liang could be Gao's relatives or friends as well. In summary, these like-minded female writers worked together and ran a valuable women's literature journal.

We can identify a strand that runs through the works of romantic fiction by these female writers: the development of these romantic narratives invariably revolves around the female protagonists. In other words, whether it is about the pursuit or the fulfillment of love, the plot always centers on the women's needs and wishes. This feature is even more salient if compared with the plots of conventional *caizi jiaren* (scholar–beauty) romances. Scholar–beauty romances often arrange their narratives so that two women, or multiple women, are involved with a single man. Scholars have argued that stories like these serve as solace or compensation for the disappointed or marginalized literati, and that they reflect male writers' collective subconscious.[20] In contrast, in the stories by *Eyebrow Talk* writers, we often see two or more men falling for the same girl. In some cases, they do not even care whether she is married or has once left one man for another. In cases where two people find each other to be the loves of their lives, the man is described such that he will never set his eyes on another woman but remains staunchly loyal to his beloved.

In these romantic love stories, women are not only the subjects of love, but also the center of the world. If we subscribe to the argument that the traditional scholar–beauty romances are the reflections of male writers' collective fantasies about love, then the constantly recurring plots and imaginings of love in the fiction by the female writers of *Eyebrow Talk* can be regarded as demonstrations of the female writers' collective unconscious. Through the creation of these love stories these female writers express the importance they attach to self-reflection beyond male-authored tropes and stereotypes. In these fictional writings about love, they reveal their subconscious needs and desires.

---

[19] *Meiyu* 5 (1915), 931–34.

[20] Arguments related to the function of romance fiction as solace or compensation for marginalized male intellectuals are put forward in the following sources: Hu Wanchuan, *Huaben yu caizi jiaren xiaoshuo*, 217–20; Su Jianxin, *Zhongguo caizi jiaren xiaoshuo*, 260–63; Li Zhihong, *Ming-mo Qing-chu caizi jiaren xiaoshuo*, 102–64. The idea that scholar–beauty romances express the male writers' collective subconscious is discussed in Li, *Ming-mo Qing-chu caizi jiaren xiaoshuo*, 99–128.

Exposing the Female Subject Cloaked in Traditional Gender Consciousness

Early Republican China was still a society bound by traditional conventions and values. Even though the Qing had already advocated the abolition of foot-binding and, during its final decades, the promotion of women's education had achieved some measure of success, early Republican efforts to allow women to assume political rights were continuously thwarted. Women's conduct and their space of activity continued to be highly restricted. Despite the championing of personal freedom and financial autonomy, it proved very difficult to put those ideas in practice. Generally speaking, women were still subservient to men and the vast majority of women still lived their lives within a patriarchal system and with patriarchal values. Even though the romantic writings in *Eyebrow Talk* allude to the female writers' collective unconscious, yet at the conscious level conventional values and gender identities continued to constitute their experiential knowledge and their moral compass. Much of their fictional work also includes a presentation of these values. Nevertheless, there are also women in these works who, given no control of anything, manage to grab any opportunity available to take matters into their own hands, and in this way demonstrate their determination and ability to take action. Xu Yuhua's story "Gone with a Sigh," for example, is a first-person narrative about a girl named Luo Lan.[21] It is apparent to the readers that once the female protagonist has established a good and stable relationship, what matters to her most is education: no sooner does she know whom she is going to marry than she gives up her job in the factory. Not worried too much about her living expenses or her financial independence, Luo Lan cares much more about her own edification. So she asks her lover Lu to tutor her. After she leaves the factory, she feels that she no longer needs to set foot in public places.

Her choice of going back to her boudoir also implies that the female writer embraces the traditional values that prescribe that "the domestic domain is the right place for a woman." To be economically dependent on men was a fate shared by most women in traditional society. Since the late Qing, ideas about "generating" or "dividing" income had surfaced,[22] and calls for women to become financially independent and be able to stand on their own feet and make their own decisions had been heard. Yet in this story, and for this writer, evidently, a woman's intellectual prowess is much more important than her economic independence. The female protagonist, Luo Lan, seizes every opportunity for education, demonstrating her eagerness for the acquisition of knowledge. On the other hand, from an economic perspective, after leaving the factory Luo Lan completely relies on her lover. This new situation thus conforms to the

---

[21] *Meiyu* 1 (1914), 14–16.   [22] Liang Qichao, "Bianfa tongyi: Lun nüxue," 38–39.

traditional gendered division of labor: a man works in the field and a woman cultivates the hearth. This also means that she returns to being or remains a subordinate partner in the relationship.

Xu Yuhua's characterization of women in this story poses a paradox. The female protagonist actively and freely seeks an education, but economically and socially she is completely dependent upon a man. This paradox illustrates the interaction and conflict between a female subject and her social milieu during the early Republican years. It also shows that under certain unique circumstances, activity and assertiveness could co-exist with passivity and submission.

The story concludes with Luo Lan taking the initiative to write a letter and end the relationship with Lu, in order to respect his family's arrangements for a marriage (not to Luo) and to preserve her own moral integrity.[23] Not only does Luo Lan deny herself the opportunity to fight for a marriage with Lu, but she also jettisons this love on her own initiative in order to satisfy his mother's request and in order to conform to the social norms. From the decision she makes to the actions she takes to carry out this decision, it is clear to us that the female writer, deep down, still holds on to traditional values. Luo Lan opposes Lu's suggestion of breaking the engagement but promises him her chastity; she forgoes her love in order to obey both Mrs. Lu's wishes and social morals; and she ultimately deems their love a "private" matter. All this testifies to her acquiescence to the social values and public morals of her time. Once the love between a man and a woman is defined as something private, it is diminished in comparison with the authority of the established social norms and moral values.

This certainly informs the readers of some of the tensions embodied in the modern idea of free (and private) love in early Republican China. Those who pursued free love would have to go through the crisis of being constantly interrogated about their moral standards. Against this social and cultural backdrop, the description of Luo Lan as a moral conformist expresses a certain nobility and elegance: she remains resolute in a dreary situation, and this is exactly the kind of feminine elegance that the story is seeking to depict. However, following this line of argument, we can say the female writer not only consents to the repression of women's need for love but also accepts her assimilation into a conventional patriarchal apparatus. On the other hand, this story also demonstrates the female protagonist's determination and assertiveness, evincing the author's firm belief in subjective agency. Here we have a female subject constructed by the social and cultural factors of her environment and trapped within the confines of a conventionally gendered frame of mind. Yet, on another level, this subject is not entirely passive, as she expresses her wish to be her own master through the spontaneous assessment of her situation and by being conscious of the decisions she makes. What transpires in this story, then, constitutes a

---

[23] Ibid., 17.

complex contrast between the female subject's passivity and assertiveness, involving both self-determined decision-making as well as being the object of others' decisions.

The female writers of *Eyebrow Talk* hardly question women's subordinate economic and social positions. In their stories, there may be differences in the details of how a couple meet and fall in love with each other and how their relationships develop, but when it comes to the realistic dimensions such as daily life, norms of conduct, and morals, their female protagonists are usually ready to assume the weaker role or to accept their inferiority. When it comes to concrete actions to express affection or attain love, the object position of women is especially conspicuous. This shows that, while she has entered a "space of her own" on the pages of the women's magazine, the female author's concept of gender remains quite conservative, shaped both by her social and cultural contexts as well as by her self-awareness and gender consciousness.

Xie Youyun's short story "An Unpredictable Life," published in *Eyebrow Talk* 3 in 1915, narrates the story of the love between a certain Wanxian and a Mr Lu. Again, the emphasis is on Wanxian's adherence to conventional codes of conduct and the dignity she demonstrates in the process. When Wanxian is ensnared and forced to be wed to a gang leader, Chen, she feigns illness by biting her tongue in order not to lose her virginity.[24] What the story tries to illustrate is not so much her resourcefulness as her effort to remain chaste. Towards the end of the story, catching Chen off guard, Wanxian first stabs his eyes out with a pair of scissors, and then plunges the pair of scissors right into his chest repeatedly until she finally kills him.[25]

In the beginning, Wanxian is a fragile and gentle woman who accepts her subordinate place and adheres to traditional values such as keeping one's virginity for one's lover and dying for one's beliefs. In despair, however, she proves capable of extreme actions well beyond expectation. The author tells us twice that she reconsiders her conviction.[26] The outcome of this rethinking is that she turns from a passive to an active person, from a helpless victim to an agent who takes initiative. Her actions derive from her premeditation. In other words, despite being treated as an object, this female protagonist is conscious of her actions and thus endows herself with the power of a subject. Her actions unveil the strong connection between the initiation of her own will and the strength to put it into action. If the formation of a subject has its origin in the inception of self-consciousness, here we observe a woman's mind switching between being passive and active, from being an object to becoming a subject.

What is most intriguing, however, is that after Wanxian commits murder, she turns herself in and is given a death sentence. Before carrying out the sentence, the magistrate inquires about her final wish, to which Wanxian replies

---

[24] *Meiyu* 3 (1915), 412–13.   [25] Ibid., 412–14.   [26] *Meiyu* 3 (1915), 413.

that she wants to be able to put on make-up.[27] She hopes she can embellish her-self before the reunion with her lover in the netherworld. Concepts such as "a woman dresses up to please her lover" and "to be an attractive wife" are the tools used by conventionally gendered power structures to subdue women and give them a gender identity. They are effective ways of exhibiting women's role as different from and subservient to men. At the same time, expressions such as these are conventionally assigned by the linguistic system to signify women. If it is not possible for female writers to break free from the linguistic system, it is difficult for them not to use such clichés. This points not only to real obstacles to getting rid of patriarchal ways of thinking but also to obstacles women will come across in writing. Framed within these dual obstacles is the incongru-ous but salient notion of "liking myself," which is a kind of self-identification. Therefore, to wear make-up can be viewed as how a woman chooses to present her subject.

This story is told in flashback, beginning with the execution of a beauti-ful woman, followed by the description of who she is and what she has been through. This narrative technique helps create her image as a dignified beauty from the beginning, and this image permeates the whole story. From the out-set, Wanxian's role as the Other and her consciousness of her own volition have been intertwined. The obstacles she comes across and the actions she takes only consolidate the mutual infiltration between her dual identity as a female object and a female subject.

When these fictional characters strive for their ideals of love, real pressures related to social status and power often turn out to be the main obstacles to their pursuits. Yet the female protagonists in these stories more often than not have to give up their love out of concern for conventional morality. The relationships between lovers or husbands and wives are usually painted in a flattering light. Words such as "deep, passionate love" or "melancholy attachment" are used to embellish their love. Women are normally the gentle and submissive ones in all forms of interaction with their lovers. However, at the critical moment when they have to make a decision based on the code of ethics, these female pro-tagonists often demonstrate determined initiative and decisiveness, which sees them making decisive choices. The female authors demonstrate a preference for identifying moral concerns as the main motives behind the protagonists' actions, as if only such reasons can ennoble the renunciation of their love. In this way, when these women make decisions, the act itself also informs us of their elevated status in society. It is on that basis that their subjectivities can be further developed and explored.

---

[27] Ibid., 406. This story is narrated in flashback. In the first half of the story, Wanxian is a beautiful prisoner who bears herself with self-respect, while in the second half, the readers finally get to know how she was abducted and why she committed homicide.

Imagining Desire and Presenting the Female Subject

As a whole, fiction by the female writers of *Eyebrow Talk* unsurprisingly features the absence of a desiring subject. Whenever it comes to the depiction of amorous interactions between men and women, the lack of description of women's desires is conspicuous. Yet while it was common practice to dematerialize women's desires, these desires could still be alluded to in a variety of ways.

Gao Jianhua, who published more stories in *Eyebrow Talk* than any other female writer, was not only a confident modern woman. Her works also surprise people with themes that are ahead of their time. In her novel, *The Battle in Spring*, for example, a woman named Lianniang is in love with a man called Nakesi. But as her father, an inveterate gambler, has to clear his debts, he sells her to a wealthy man named Dulü'en.[28] Because Lianniang is filial, she considers it her duty to pay off her father's debts and, thus, writes to Nakesi to end their relationship.[29] Once again, we see the inextricable tangle between a woman as an object and a woman as a subject determined to take action on her own initiative. Though reality forces Lianniang to make a decision that is against her wishes, Gao Jianhua refuses to depict her merely as a silenced and passive victim. Instead, she has Lianniang write to her lover to bid him farewell. With her own hand, she pens the letter and thus breaks off the relationship single-handedly.

Many years later, Lianniang and Nakesi unexpectedly meet again. This reunion rekindles their love for each other and they enter into a sexual relationship.[30] This episode risks violating existing taboos. Romance writings produced in the late Qing and early Republican years almost always illustrate the authors' aesthetics of love as a heartrending romance and never touch upon anything that might be seen as *luan* (illicit sexual behavior).[31] Most female writers in *Eyebrow Talk* adopt this as their bottom line. Not Gao Jianhua, however. Moreover, both Lianniang and Nakesi are consistently painted in a highly positive light. The author seeks to construct the melancholy atmosphere created by their tragic love. It is thus an unexpected twist when they "commit adultery" after getting married to different people and not seeing each other for years. Yet what is even more bemusing is how the author interprets this adultery:

---

[28] [Translator's note] The three texts by Gao Jianhua discussed in this section are all set in Western countries (the US, the UK, and France, respectively). For the Chinese reader, this is obvious from the names of the characters and therefore is not highlighted in the analysis. Our translation reflects the foreignness of the names by transliterating them as a single word, rather than splitting them into a family name and personal name. Gao Jianhua's use of foreign protagonists to address taboo issues is reminiscent of the discussion of foreign stereotypes in Barbara Mittler's contribution to this volume.

[29] *Meiyu* 13 (1915), 2855–60.   [30] Ibid., 2862–65, and *Meiyu* 14 (1915), 3075–76.

[31] One of the most representative examples is Xu Zhenya, *Yuli hun*.

They had been put in an extreme situation and left with no other choice. It was not that they intentionally committed this shameful act. It is natural for lovers to feel more passionate especially when they are forbidden from pursuing their love. When they think there is no future for them, naturally they would choose to consummate their secret love, ignoring accusations of corrupting society and ruining their reputations. This is what an unfulfilled love will lead to.[32]

Obviously, this passage is added to explain the lovers' behavior. Still, the author clearly does not attempt to condemn the traditional code of ethics or to subvert conventional moral teachings. Instead, she aims to intercede for the two lovers who transgress moral boundaries, remind the readers of their misfortunes, and suggest why they bow to the inevitable and, without any premeditation, commit this sin. What merits our attention is the double standard prevalent in society at the time, as it means that, in a case like this, women usually bear harsher blame and punishment. Hence, these intercessory words are but a plea for Lianniang. To mention the accusation of "corrupting society and ruining one's reputation" makes it more apparent that this passage is aimed at women. Showing no intention of defying tradition tells us that this woman author still has in her subconscious the need to meet the moral requests of her society. Nevertheless, to have Lianniang rekindle her secret love and eventually consummate it implies that it is acceptable and understandable for a woman's desires to manifest themselves and to find satisfaction. Because her love is so intense and sincere, the author feels justified in her decision to write about the revelation, transformation, and satisfaction of Lianniang's desires. In the story, a woman's desires are thus released naturally and unwittingly. Even though there is only a short moment of satisfaction, social morality and regulations are sidestepped to allow Lianniang to follow what her heart desires and indulge in a happy and loving relationship. The desiring subject is liberated, thrives, and gets recognition at the critical moment when she deviates from the parameters of the patriarchal order. Brief moments of liberation such as this one are very valuable in the writings of the *Eyebrow Talk* women writers.

In Gao Jianhua's short stories, "Mr Liu Is Better than Mr Ruan" and "A Butterfly's Shadow," we also have women who drift away from traditional morality. Gulunna in "Mr Liu Is Better than Mr Ruan" is described as "flighty, flippant and unfaithful,"[33] not a demure lady in a traditional sense, about which, however, the author shows no misgivings. Gulunna at first elopes with Kangnashi, but later finds out that he is not the one for her. Another male protagonist, Feili, then makes strenuous effort to find Gulunna and these true lovers end up being with each other.[34]

Moli in "A Butterfly's Shadow" originally is under the care of Balishi, who mentors her. Then she gets to know the Vicomte of Bragelonne and runs away

---

[32] *Meiyu* 14 (1915), 3076.　　[33] *Meiyu* 7 (1915), 1435.　　[34] Ibid., 1435–71.

with him. After being abandoned by the Vicomte, she eventually returns to Balishi and marries him.[35] The female protagonists in these two stories each enjoy
the courtship and affections of two men. Both of them fall for the morally flawed
ones before they realize their mistakes and then return to the ones who truly love
them. In comparison with other stories where a woman's chastity is frequently
referred to as her moral bottom line, both stories covertly sidestep issues concerning personal morals and instead emphasize the love triangles. Quietly rip-
pling through the tangled relationships between these protagonists are women's
desires and their satisfaction. The narratives about women's desires discussed
above, whether or not they are put in these stories intentionally, can be taken
as the female author's fantasies or as her unrealistic reveries. Either way, these
inundating desires are described positively and seem aimed at an implied reader
who will understand and accept them. The plots develop in such a way that the
female protagonists' pursuit of love is fulfilled and they are allowed to live
happily ever after.

It is true that when it comes to the portrayal of interactions between men
and women, the authors still conform to specific gender stereotypes and give
men and women active and passive roles to play, respectively. But the development of the plots is also characterized by constant references to women's
desires and their satisfaction. Clearly, women's well-being is the core of these
romance writings. When a woman has command of what she writes, the world
of love in her stories turns into a virtual reality that revolves around women and
exists for the purpose of satisfying women's love and desire. These romantic
stories unexpectedly become a space for the expression of women's desires.
These issues may not be expressed with high-pitched voices in order to attract
attention; however, in the literary landscape of early Republican China they are,
indeed, quite unique.

Another story worth studying is "Favored by His Majesty," by Liang Guiqin.
It deals with the dramatic life of Madame Liu, who is widowed after marry-
ing into the Huang family in the late Ming. In the upheavals of the late Ming,
Madame Liu is taken captive by soldiers who recognize the prize of her beauty
and present her as tribute to a *wang* (prince). After some protracted negotiations, the prince finally wins her consent for marriage by promising her "a gold
bridal crown, a gown granted to the highest-ranking officials," and a wedding
ceremony in the central hall of his mansion. In the following years, she gives
birth to a son and is officially given the title of *wangfei* (princess).[36]

The subtitle of the story reads, "an adaptation of *Notes Taken in A Mountain-
Facing Studio*," referring to the chapter "The Dramatic Life of a Widow" in
a nineteenth-century work by Mao Xianglin.[37] A comparison between Mao's

---

[35] *Meiyu* 10 (1915), 2105–20.
[36] *Meiyu* 1 (1914), 65–74.   [37] Mao Xianglin, *Duishan shuwu.*

text and Liang Guiqin's story reveals that the biggest difference lies in Liang's excision of the section where Madame Liu helps appoint heirs for the Huang family. Liang tells the story in flashback with the emphasis on how Madame Liu carries herself in the Prince's house. In Mao's original version, Madame Liu, after ascending to prominent status, endeavors to appoint heirs for the Huang family, an undertaking that makes salient her image as a venerable and virtuous woman striving for the continuation of her first husband's family line. Liang's adaptation instead focuses on the dramatic anecdotes in her life to manifest her determination to safeguard her image as a decent woman of a certain social standing.

One passage from the story describes how she bursts into tears the first time she serves wine to the Prince. She sobs, "I am a woman of a good social standing. I will never deign to be your servant." Then she "hit her head against a pillar so hard that a loud clang could be heard. An elderly Manchu maid rushed to hold her back. She jumped and wailed frenetically. Her long, knotted hair, black and sleek, loosened and dragged across the floor. The Prince, unable to bear her tormented sorrow, asked the maid to take her back to her room, look after her and not let grief cause her any further pain."[38] Her actions here prove her determination and perseverance not to compromise her chastity, even at the cost of her own life. Under such adverse circumstances, Madame Liu makes it clear that she will still exert herself to defend her self-determined view of her *geren ren'ge* (individual personhood).

At first, she is placed in many situations where she has no control over her life. Whether forced into a marriage or captured and given to the Prince as a tributary gift, she represents a woman perceived as merely an object in society. However, when she is in the Huang family, she shows her talent in business and management and earns herself the position as matriarch with control of the family's fortune. When living in the Prince's mansion, she spares no effort to ensure she is treated with respect. People are often in awe of her adamant and tenacious personality. The Manchu maid is baffled by why Madame Liu is so stubborn and never knows what is best for her.[39] At some point she asks Liu's original maid, Zhang, for an explanation, to which Zhang replies, "Madame Liu has a strong personality. She liked to sit facing south so that all the maids

---

[38] *Meiyu* 1 (1914), 67.

[39] To demonstrate how the Prince never begrudges his consideration and affection toward Madame Liu, the author not only describes how he demands that the maid take good care of her after she hits her head against a pillar, but also how he keeps showering her with valuables: "The Prince bestowed her a box of traditional Manchu costumes and a box of traditional Han Chinese costumes. The next day, ten catties of ginseng and hundreds of Manchu Tana pearls followed, but Madame Liu was oblivious to them. Soon after, he granted her a suitcase of accessories, two circular fans used by court ladies, four purses, four handkerchiefs, one platter of gold ingots and one platter of silver ingots." Yet Madame Liu is not moved by any of this. See *Meiyu* 1 (1914), 68.

and servants in the household would be dutifully at her command."[40] To "sit facing south" alludes to the place designated for a person of authority. This brief character analysis suggests how Madame Liu handles affairs like a queen and thus helps create an image of a strong-minded woman. From this conversation, we can deduce that the author not only intends to write about the dramatic life of a widow, but, more importantly, that she wants to use this protagonist to display a woman's strong sense of self and subjective awareness.

This story demonstrates that the female writers of *Eyebrow Talk* had started to present and promote the actions taken by women to assert their rights. Structural oppression from the established social system still existed and the female protagonists could display their agency and claim their entitlements on condition that they first of all submit to patriarchal relations. What is more important, however, is the fact that no one can avoid tackling the issue of establishing one's identity within the framework of an existing environment. Madame Liu's actions might have amazed readers by showing how women can reverse a difficult situation with their willpower and how the female subject can be full of energy. All the way from the beginning to the end of this story, the authoritative Prince is the one who plays the passive role, catering to the needs of Madame Liu. What the author painstakingly attempts to illustrate is Madame Liu's resolution and actions. In portraying this female protagonist's enormous strength, the author illustrates a woman's self-consciousness and self-identification. The representation of the female subject is hence the most moving aspect of this "old tale retold."[41]

Conclusion

Women in early twentieth-century China lacked self-awareness because they had long been assigned subordinate status in society. This was a real and common phenomenon. The women writers of *Eyebrow Talk* were born in the late Qing and grew up in the early Republic. They received a modern education and were influenced by ideas about women's rights circulating in China at that time. From Gao Jianhua's biography, we can get a glimpse of the bearing of an independent, modern woman dedicated to the pursuit of her aspirations. These female writers did not shun having their photos put in the journal, an action they took to proclaim the existence of their (public) selves. When women writers and editors used the newly opened space of the woman's journal, *Eyebrow Talk*, as the channel for voicing their opinions, this attempt became the catalyst that triggered the formation of new forms of female subjectivity in

---

[40] Ibid., 69.
[41] The term *gushi xinbian* (old tales retold) is borrowed from the title of a famous collection by Lu Xun.

fiction. In narratives that focus on the relationships between men and women, this catalyst, without attracting much notice, started to have an effect and weaved its way through every sentence and every word of the stories. This is a valuable phenomenon emerging in the writings of *Eyebrow Talk*'s women authors and it deserves our careful exploration and understanding, based on the different methods of reading proposed in this volume.

As a whole, because the consciousness of these female writers is still confined within a conventional moral structure and bound to its code of conduct, their stories can generally be interpreted as devoid of women's emotional and sensual desires.[42] Besides, when there are obstacles to their pursuit of love, most female protagonists still choose to stand up for traditional norms and values. However, it is under these conditions that the female protagonists, making the best use of their self-knowledge and volition, can usually reverse their roles from passive to active, take control of the situation, make explicit their self-identification, and become their own masters in the world of love. By portraying these women, the female writers explore the possibility that women can make their own choices and decide their own fates. The silhouette of a female subject thus quietly comes into being.

Writing also empowers these women authors to set free, through the narrow spaces between the lines of their writing, fantasies about love and desire that have long been hidden in the recesses of their consciousness. These spaces harbor a woman's liberated subjectivity and her strength to resist and to defy male control. In summary, in the romance writings by the women authors of *Eyebrow Talk*, a female subject is veiled sometimes, but unveiled at other times. To have a female figure shuttle between being visible and invisible is to reflect both the impact of the women's rights movement ongoing from the late Qing to the early Republic and the tight grip of the patriarchal system that was only haltingly undermined. This is certainly an important chapter in our understanding of the history of Chinese women and their mental and physical development – and magazines such as *Eyebrow Talk* provided the space for it to unfold.

---

[42] It should be noted here that, despite this adherence to moral convention, *Eyebrow Talk* as a whole, by foregrounding public interactions between men and women in the literary and cultural sphere, came under heavy suspicion of moral deficiency and was eventually banned by an exclusively male group of censors. That the censors genuinely took offense is underlined by the fact that, of the hundreds of fiction journals they examined, *Eyebrow Talk* was the only one they banned. See the contribution to this volume by Michel Hockx.

Rebellious Yet Constrained: Dissenting Women's Views on Love and Sexual Morality in *The Ladies' Journal* and *The New Woman*

Rachel Hui-Chi Hsu

Introduction

This paper explores the intriguing interplay between male editorial agency and female authorial subjectivity in Chinese women's journals during the 1920s.[1] In the May Fourth era from the mid-1910s to the mid-1920s, male liberals and radicals upheld cultural iconoclasm and promoted Western ideas to challenge traditional Confucianism. Their opinions gained more authority in academic and cultural circles than did those of female writers who were still fighting for access to higher education. To be sure, some female students abroad had utilized the periodical press as a venue for spreading radical messages against the Qing regime (1644–1912) and oppressive gender norms.[2] These intellectual women's nationalist narratives and their assumption of editorial positions developed in tandem with their emerging feminist consciousness. While nationalism sanctioned their appeal for ideas such as republican motherhood or equal female citizenship, their editorship granted them discursive agency.

In the early 1910s, when the Republican government replaced Qing rule, revolutionary journals gave way to a mass-produced and profit-oriented periodical press. Gone were the late Qing women's journals that female writers both published in and edited. At the time, female-edited journals such as *The Freewoman* (1911–1912) in Britain and *The Woman Rebel* (1914) and *The Forerunner* (1909–1916) in America overtly asserted female rights and were unafraid of opposing male authority. In contrast, there were hardly any

---

[1] I borrow the term "editorial agency" from Liying Sun, who views it as "the key power possessed by editors in the field, which enabled them to select, collect, frame, and integrate materials into their final (trans-)cultural production" (Sun, "Body Un/Dis-covered," 17). The late Qing women editors-and-authors were thus able to express their uncensored viewpoints in their own journals. I also adopt the idea of "subjectivity" from historian Nan Enstad (*Ladies of Labor*, 13), who defines it as "based on the premise that *who one is* is neither essential nor fixed, but is continually shaped and reshaped in human social exchange." In this chapter, I treat "authorial subjectivity" in a journal as a constituting self an author could possess, which was negotiable and changeable in its interaction with editors/publishers.

[2] Nanxiu Qian, "The Mother *Nü Xuebao*"; Xia Xiaohong, "*Tianyi bao* and He Zhen's Views"; Xia Xiaohong, *Wan-Qing nüxing*, 286–325.

Chinese counterparts to be found in the early Republic.[3] Male scholars and writers dominated the editorial positions in the Chinese periodical press, thereby initiating and leading topical discussions. These male editors tended to subsume the "woman question" under the all-inclusive category of "social problems" associated with political and national crises. Given the masculine make-up of their editorial boards, one wonders what would have happened when female writers confronted men in the pages of these journals. What would it have been like when women contributors took issue with men in relation to intimate, and often gendered, matters such as love, sex, and morality? Were they able to freely express opinions that departed from male viewpoints? How did male editors or male writers respond to female writers' critiques?

An integrated reading of two popular women's journals, *Funü zazhi – The Ladies' Journal* and *Xin nüxing* (The new woman), may exemplify how women voiced their dissent in the 1920s' periodical press. Both journals focused on the woman question and targeted female readers. Notably, Zhang Xichen's (1889–1969) editorship of *The Ladies' Journal* from 1921 to 1925 and of *The New Woman* from 1926 to 1929 determined the two journals' outlooks. Zhang was forthright in soliciting articles from women and encouraging them to participate in related discussions in his journals. His editorship and patronage of women throughout the 1920s enabled subtle gender interactions that unfolded in the pages of these male-edited women's journals.

In this article, I identify as "dissenting women" the female authors, contributors, and readers whose female-specific views contradicted those promoted by male editors. I explore gender politics in *The Ladies' Journal* and *The New Woman* by examining the encounters between dissenting women and Zhang Xichen, along with his male comrades, on the subject of love and sexual morality. I first argue that the dissenting women's use of the *lunshuowen* (argumentative essay) to articulate their ideas was itself a rebellion against conventional notions of femininity grounded in such qualities as passivity, docility, and timidity. Unlike literary genres such as fiction and poetry that appealed to sentiment and lyricism, argumentative essays were contentious, critical, aggressive, and logical. The analytic and confrontational traits of the argumentative essay made it a traditionally masculine genre. By expressing their views on love and sex through argumentative essays, these dissenting women positioned themselves as polemicists, but without the legitimacy of nationalism upon which

---

[3] The literary magazine *Meiyu* (Eyebrow talk) was edited by women and had a large female authorship, but its editorial tone concerning the issues of women's rights, gender, and sexuality was more conventional than progressive – even if the fiction it reprinted sometimes opened up new avenues, as Huang's chapter in this volume shows. The more radical *Funü zhoubao* (Women weekly, 1923–1925), edited by Xiang Jingyu (1895–1928), a supplement to the Shanghai daily *Minguo ribao* (Republican daily), was one of the rare exceptions that voiced views similarly radical to those in some of the Western female-edited journals.

their late Qing precursors mostly relied. In this regard, dissenting women challenged traditional expectations of both *genre* and *femininity*, hence helping to create a changing body of female-authored work.

Second, my reading shows that male editors such as Zhang Xichen tended to check and balance those female views that conflicted with male opinions. These male editors, while allowing dissenting women a voice in the journals, often replaced the latter's demand for female emancipation with the call for love and sexual liberation. I suggest that this tendency ignored female-oriented concerns and therefore undermined women's assertion of their gender-specific rights.

Zhang Xichen and His Women's Journals in the 1920s

In its seventeen-year lifespan, *The Ladies' Journal* underwent several thematic changes.[4] Originally, it promoted women's education and knowledge of scientific housekeeping in the service of the ideal of *xianqi liangmu* (virtuous wife and good mother). By 1919, during the height of the culturally iconoclastic and politically nationalistic May Fourth era, the journal shifted its focus towards women's emancipation in response to mounting criticism from progressive liberals.[5] Zhang Xichen took over the editorship in January 1921 and moved the journal into an "innovative" phase (1921–1925) centered on imported ideas of *lian'ai* (romantic love) and *xin xingdaode* (new sexual morality). Zhang had neither a college diploma nor experience abroad, unlike many other contemporary cultural leaders of the May Fourth generation such as Hu Shi (1891–1962) and Lu Xun (1881–1936). His role as editor-in-chief of *The Ladies' Journal* and *The New Woman*, however, made him one of the pivotal figures in the women's periodical press throughout the 1920s.

As soon as Zhang took charge of *The Ladies' Journal*, he sensed the imperative to discuss the "woman question," a heated topic of concern in Chinese society. He first turned to Japanese works for inspiration and soon assembled a cohort of contributors who shared his liberal philosophy of feminism.[6] In early 1922, Zhou Jianren (1888–1984) joined Zhang as assistant editor. Zhou's proficiency in English complemented Zhang's reliance on Japanese sources.[7] Zhang recruited new authors for *The Ladies' Journal* from the Wenxue yanjiuhui (Chinese literary association) and the Funü wenti yanjiuhui (Woman question research association), of which he was a member.[8] These largely male

---

[4] For an overall study of the shifting foci of *The Ladies' Journal* over time, see Jin Jungwon, "*Funü zazhi,*" and Julia F. Andrews's chapter in this volume.

[5] Shen Yanbing, *Wo zouguo de daolu*, 136; Zhang Xichen, "Cong shangren."

[6] Wang Zheng, *Women in the Chinese Enlightenment*, 67–116.

[7] Zhang Xichen, "Cong shangren"; "Bianji yulu" (8:2).

[8] Hockx, *Questions of Style*, 47–85.

contributors collectively embraced the ideas of *lian'ai ziyou* (freedom to love) advocated by the Swedish woman writer Ellen Key (1849–1926). Zhang's editorial prerogative assured that Key's theories of love marriage, free divorce, new sexual morality, and protection of motherhood, which he espoused, were trumpeted in the journal during his tenure.[9]

Ellen Key and her Chinese followers declared that romantic love fostered both the spirit of individual independence and the will to love and give, and therefore should be the only rationale for marriage. For the first time in Chinese history, they posited romantic love as the raison d'être of chastity for both sexes.[10] More importantly, Key and her followers reckoned that love-based sex not only gratified the couple by their mutual commitment of body and soul, but also benefited racial improvement by creating healthy offspring in a loving environment.[11] Such praise of companionate love seriously contravened conventional notions of sexual morality, which demanded women's absolute chastity before marriage, followed by obedience and sexual loyalty after marriage. While criticism of female chastity and calls for mutual conjugal loyalty based on love emerged in the late Qing period, it was not until the early 1920s that a discursive turn from *zhencao* (chastity) to a new sexual morality took place.[12] Borrowing the neologism of romantic love and new sexual morality from the Japanese, Zhang and his friends introduced a new concept of chastity bound to love, rather than marriage; the mutual affection between (heterosexual) lovers necessitated their sexual loyalty to each other.[13] Zhang Xichen dubbed this *lian'ai daode* (love morality), and with the ideal of *lingrou yizhi* (flesh-and-soul as one), underscored the inseparability of love and sex.[14] Unless the woman became pregnant or one of the partners got hurt, Zhang indicated, premarital and extramarital sexual behavior (including even polyamorous relationships) should be allowed.[15] As radical as such notions seemed to be, Zhang and Zhou had no intention of abolishing the institution of

[9] Chiang, "Womanhood"; Honma, "Xing de daode de xin qingxiang."

[10] For a comprehensive understanding of the genealogy of romantic love in modern China, see Haiyan Lee, *Revolution of the Heart*, 140–85.

[11] Wu Juenong, "Jindai de zhencaoguan." Zhang once asserted his wish to "solve the Woman Question by way of [advocating] romantic love." Hence, he devoted most of *The Ladies' Journal*'s space to elaborating and promoting the significance of freedom to love. Wang Pingling and Zhang Xichen, "Tongxin: Lian'ai wenti de taolun." Also see "Bianji yulu" (8:7).

[12] Zhou Zuoren, Hu Shi, and Lu Xun had opened a discussion criticizing conventional female chastity and the double standard of sexual morality in 1918 in *New Youth* (Xin qingnian). Yosano, "Zhencao lun"; Hu Shi, "Zhencao wenti"; Tang Si [Lu Xun], "Wo zhi jielieguan."

[13] See Gao Shan [Zhou Jianren], "Zhencao guannian de gaizao."

[14] Selu, "Ailunkai nüshi yu qi sixiang."

[15] Ibid. Also see Zhou Jianren, "Xingdaode zhi kexue de biaozhun"; Zhang Xichen, "Xin xingdaode shi shenme."

marriage.[16] Integrating eugenics into their discourse of romantic love and sex as Key did, Zhang and Zhou maintained that one should coordinate individual choice with social welfare when enjoying sexual freedom so as to fulfill the true spirit of the new sexual morality.[17]

The "innovative" editorial scheme proved effective: Zhang Xichen soon tripled sales of *The Ladies' Journal*.[18] To further boost readership, Zhang lowered the original price by a third, from three *jiao* to two *jiao*, in January 1921.[19] The rise in sales, however, did not solve what he observed as the "odd phenomenon" of having a wide female readership yet few female contributors. In an editorial in *The Ladies' Journal* in May 1921, Zhang encouraged educated women to "offer their opinions boldly" as role models for the younger female generation. "Our journal," he stated, "really wants to provide a discursive space for women with lofty ideals."[20] Two months later, Zhang reiterated his regret that the cry for women's emancipation from women themselves was far weaker than that from men.[21] Zhang's encouragement of female contributors continued after he moved from *The Ladies' Journal* to *The New Woman*.

The New Woman's contributors consisted of veteran writers and a new array of young intellectuals from various ideological backgrounds, evidence of Zhang's extensive cultural and publishing network. While Zhang welcomed diverse voices in his journal, his belief in romantic love as the cornerstone of modern sexual morality prevailed.[22] The series of debates over the topic of romantic love in *The New Woman* from 1927 to 1929 attested to Zhang's liberal attitude towards dissenting opinions *and* his editorial agency in outweighing his opponents.[23]

Notwithstanding the challenges from both the conservative right and the radical left, Zhang's editorship of *The Ladies' Journal* and *The New Woman* enabled him to propagate notions of romantic love, new sexual morality, and their eugenic significance. His editorial career through the 1920s embodied the objective of Chinese male liberals of reformulating modern individuality and women's rights through discourses of romantic love. On the other hand, as we shall see, men's perceptions of the emancipatory possibilities of free love and sex did not necessarily reflect those of all members of the fair sex.

---

[16] Wang Zheng, *Women in the Chinese Enlightenment*, 116; Zhang Xichen, "Xin xingdaode"; Chiang, "Womanhood."

[17] Sakamoto, "The Cult of 'Love and Eugenics.'"

[18] The sales volume of *The Ladies' Journal* was raised from three thousand to more than ten thousand per issue. Zhang Xichen, "Cong shangren."

[19] The journal was priced in a monetary unit of *yuan*; 1 *yuan* equals 10 *jiao*, or 100 *fen* (cf. "Guanggao"). In the 1920s, 3 *jiao* could buy about a kilogram of pork in Shanghai. See *Shanghai jiefang qianhou*, 343–45.

[20] "Bianji yulu" (7:5, 108).

[21] "Bianji yulu" (7:7, 116).   [22] Lee, *Revolution of the Heart*, 178–85.

[23] The debates were branded *fei lian'ai yu fei fei lian'ai lunzhan* (Debates between anti-love and anti-anti-love). Cf. Xu Huiqi [Rachel Hsu], "1920 niandai de lian'ai yu xin xingdaode lunshu."

Independent from Men: Women Who Spoke for Themselves

In Yung-chen Chiang's revisionist article on the first two phases of *The Ladies' Journal* between 1915 and 1925, he underscores female writers' nonconformity to the male-dominated motif of "good wives and virtuous mothers." "[W]omen writers," he argues, "made the first phase of the magazine the most cacophonous period in its history." This cacophony, Chiang states, vanished after the 1920s.[24] Chiang's assertion challenges most previous scholars' analysis of *The Ladies' Journal* as being conservative in its first phase and progressive in its second phase.[25] Chiang's reexamination of the journal's early history, albeit insightful, omits the dissension between male and female writers in the second phase. Thus, he oversimplifies the complexity of the journal's discourses in the first half of the 1920s. While female writers in the first phase challenged the editorial espousal of domesticity as Chiang claims, those in the second phase problematized the male editorial cult of romantic love and new sexual morality with their distinctive female points of view.

The female writers who contributed to *The Ladies' Journal* during Zhang Xichen's editorship were college or high school students who were more susceptible to modern ideas such as freedom of love, marriage, and divorce. Zhang's establishment of several new interactive forums in the journal enabled these female writers to express their personal experiences or thoughts in nonliterary genres.[26] Significantly, Zhang's promotion of editor–reader interactions created an unprecedented dialogue between readers/writers of both sexes and the (male) editor.

I argue that it was under Zhang Xichen's leadership in the first half of the 1920s that contention between the two sexes over intimate matters emerged. Moreover, the cacophonous voices from female writers continued throughout the lifespan of *The New Woman*. In the following section, I will analyze five women contributors' confrontations with men on the topics of love, sex, and marriage.

Asserting Female Sexual Autonomy and Freedom: Jiang Fengzi

Scholars who study *The Ladies' Journal* tend to characterize its discussions of love, sex, marriage, and divorce under Zhang Xichen's leadership as coherent and homogeneous.[27] Nevertheless, a few female writers in this phase successfully voiced female-specific opinions that conflicted with men's. The case of

---

[24] Chiang, "Womanhood."   [25] Ibid.

[26] These forums included *Tongxun* (Correspondence), *Ziyou luntan* (Free forum for discussion), *Duzhe julebu* (Readers' club), *Tanhua hui* (Conversation exchange), and *Du qianhao* (Review of the previous issue).

[27] Wang Zheng, *Women in the Chinese Enlightenment*; Chiang, "Womanhood."

Jiang Fengzi (fl. 1920) typified women's capacity to elucidate and defend their own views despite male objections.

Jiang Fengzi was one of the most prolific female writers in the second phase of *The Ladies' Journal*. She contributed epistolary essays, reportage, prose poetry, fiction, and analytical essays that touched upon various aspects of the woman question.[28] A member of the Woman's Question Research Association, Jiang actively advocated women's rights and gender equality. Not only did she put her ideas of free love into practice by running away with a married man, but also she engaged in disagreements with her senior male colleagues. In 1920, Jiang managed to dissolve her marriage contract, which had been prearranged by her parents. She described the process of breaking off the engagement in an article in *The Ladies' Journal*, entitled "My Divorce" (April 1922).[29] Later, Jiang left home to study at Taizhou Girls' Normal School in Zhejiang Province, where she fell in love with Zhang Rentian (1887–1995), a married intellectual who helped her file the earlier disengagement lawsuit. When Zhang Rentian went to Shanghai in the fall of 1922, Jiang followed him there and worked in a cotton mill.[30] At some point before the end of 1924, Jiang took a teaching position at the Zhejiang Yude Girls School. By the time her article appeared in the first issue of *The New Woman* in January 1926 – also the last time she contributed to one of Zhang Xichen's journals – she had settled in Pandang Serai, Penang, Malaysia.[31]

Rather than mimicking men's cult of *lian'ai shensheng* (sanctity of romantic love), Jiang delved into the concepts of "romantic love" and "freedom." The August 1922 issue of *The Ladies' Journal* carried three argumentative essays by Jiang, entitled "Lian'ai ziyou jieda kewen" (Q & A on freedom to love). She explained at the onset that the essays were her joint response to some teachers and friends, with whom she exchanged views on the topic of love. She then differentiated the ideas of *ziyou lian'ai* (free love) from "love's freedom." To her, free love implied free (sexual) indulgence in love; its point was to be able to love (and have sex) completely at will. Love's freedom, in contrast, indicated the freedom to love (*lian'ai ziyou*), in which spiritual affection came before physical union.

Writing in an analytical, theoretical, and impersonal manner, Jiang Fengzi's essays displayed a rational argument in the face of male writers' disagreement. Rarely had other Chinese female writers at the time engaged in a semantic discussion of romantic love and freedom as Jiang did. From the point of view of exercising one's freedom, Jiang classified free love as "passive," while freedom

---

[28] For examples, see Fengzi, "Nüzi jiefang yu nüzi jiaoyu"; "Songxing"; "Yi xu jie ge fengzi."
[29] Fengzi, "Wo de lihun."
[30] "Xu Jie Zizhuan" (Autobiography of Xu Jie), accessed July 30, 2017, http://www.tt.zj.cn/Html/Article/wenhua/zuojia/78.html.
[31] Fengzi, "Nanyang tongxin."

to love was "active." That is, one who embraced free love could only be free *within* the realm of love, whereas the believer of love's freedom had the liberty to love or *not* to love. Jiang's unorthodox interpretation of love and freedom led her to include singlehood within her definition of freedom to love as an option as desirable as romantic love. "It is my freedom to favor singlehood; it could also be my freedom to prefer romantic love. I will be celibate when I choose the former; I will be in love when I go for the latter. It should all happen freely, and I see no contradictions in such an arrangement," claimed Jiang.[32] She further argued that "From the individualist perspective, singlehood is extremely happy and free; it [therefore] serves the social welfare to strive for one's own happiness."[33] Likewise, Jiang insisted that the logical result of love's freedom was the total rejection of the marriage system, which subordinated women to men as their private property.[34] She viewed marriage as inseparable from familial control and as legally beneficial only to men. It was therefore detrimental to a true love union between the sexes.[35]

Jiang's adoption of the argumentative essay to clarify her opinions on love and freedom is telling, since most of the other women contributors in *The Ladies' Journal* still relied on literary genres to talk about issues of love and sex. Ultimately, Jiang's philosophical analysis of freedom to love may be summed up by her own exclamation: "One does not live exclusively for romantic love!"[36] "Marriage is indeed the root of all evil!"[37] Despite characterizing and valuing the essence of love's freedom as *zhen, shan, mei* (true, good, and beautiful), she refused to exalt romantic love as the only key to women's emancipation as had Zhang Xichen and his male comrades.[38] Her proposal of singlehood as a legitimate choice afforded by love's freedom defied male liberals, including Zhang Xichen, whose reaction will be examined in the next section.[39]

Contesting Male Divorce: Xu Hemei and Lian Shi

Jiang Fengzi was not the only woman who dared to clash with male mainstream ideas in *The Ladies' Journal* and *The New Woman*. Two women contributors' criticism of a male intellectual's account of his divorce revealed similar female dissonance. Free divorce was one of the three credos – along with freedom to love and free marriage – championed by Zhang Xichen. In February

---

[32] Fengzi, "Lian'ai ziyou jieda kewen di-yi."
[33] Fengzi, "Lian'ai ziyou jieda kewen di-er."   [34] Ibid.
[35] Ibid; Fengzi, "Lian'ai ziyou jieda kewen di-si."
[36] Fengzi, "Lian'ai ziyou jieda kewen di-san."
[37] Fengzi, "Lian'ai ziyou jieda kewen di-er."   [38] Fengzi, "Lian'ai ziyou jieda kewen di-san."
[39] For discussions about singlehood in modern China, see You Jianming [Yu Chien-ming], "Qianshan wo duxing?"

1923, *The Ladies' Journal* published male university professor Zheng Zhenxuan's eighteen-page personal account of his divorce, which prompted intense reactions from readers. Using the pen-name Kuangfu, Zheng detailed how he was forced into a parent-arranged marriage. He then used his failure to reform his old-fashioned wife to rationalize his decision to divorce her.[40] Two months later, Zhang Xichen set up an open forum for *The Ladies' Journal*'s readers to comment on Zheng's tale of divorce. Some male readers who had had a similar experience expressed understanding, whereas others who were attentive to women's plight sympathized with Zheng's deserted wife.[41] None of the male readers' responses, however, were as critical as those of two female contributors: Lian Shi and Xu Hemei.

Lian and Xu's feminist tendency was explicit in the titles of their articles, "The Age Where Women Are Not Human: Urging Men All over the World to Reflect on Themselves" by Lian and "The Bias of Biased Men – Criticism of Mr. Kuangfu" by Xu. They both demonstrated an awareness of female subordination in a gendered hierarchy that led to their fierce protest against Kuangfu's condescending attitude towards his wife. Lian Shi found this case proof of male mistreatment of women in China. She questioned Zheng's right to demand his wife's unconditional submission and his willful decision to transform her. Lian ended in a mournful tone, bemoaning Chinese women's unchanged misery in an inhuman age, full of sacrifices and suffering.[42]

While Lian Shi expressed her grievances in a relatively sorrowful manner, Xu Hemei penned angry polemics against male prejudice. She listed Kuangfu's biases – presuming he was always right and that his wife should have unconditionally obeyed him and showed him her affection, to name a few – and accused him of arrogance and thoughtlessness. Instead of lamenting his divorce from his wife, Xu sarcastically celebrated it, for his wife finally got to leave this authoritarian husband. Xu concluded by advising Kuangfu to forgo his male prejudice, lest he encounter similar misfortune in a second marriage.[43]

Lian and Xu's essays highlighted the substantial gender gap governing the practice of free divorce in early twentieth-century Chinese society.[44] The misery that many illiterate Chinese women faced when their betrothed abandoned them for new, better-educated lovers inspired the complaints of Lian and Xu. Speaking from a position of female experience and same-sex empathy, Lian and Xu voiced thoughts that were foreign to the other sex.

---

[40] Kuangfu,"Wu ziji de hunyinshi."

[41] For examples of the former, see Ke Shi [Zhou Jianren], "Aiqing de biaoxian yu jiehun shenghuo." Y. D., "Wo de lihun qianhou." As for the latter, see Dai Qiu, "Xin jiu de chongtu." Weishisheng, "Tai fuyu kexuejia zecai de Zheng xiansheng."

[42] Lian Shi, "Funü de feiren shidai: cu putianxia nanxing fanxing."

[43] Xu Hemei, "Pianjian de nanxing zhi pianjian."

[44] Xu Huiqi [Rachel Hsu], "*Funü zazhi* suo fanying de ziyou lihun sixiang jiqi shijian."

"For Men": Chen Xuezhao

Chen Xuezhao (1906–1991) was one of the junior female writers whom Zhang Xichen rallied to contribute to his journals. Before setting off for France in 1927 to pursue her Ph.D. in literature, Chen completed her studies at the Shanghai Patriotic Girls' School and ventured to start her literary career in the periodical press.[45] She corresponded with Zhang Xichen and Zhou Jianren and published articles in *The Ladies' Journal*. Later, she helped found *The New Woman* and became its special correspondent. When she traveled to France for study in May 1927, she continued to contribute articles to both *The Ladies' Journal* and *The New Woman*.

Notably, unlike the prose and lyric writings she sent to *The Ladies' Journal* from 1924 to 1927, Chen's essays in *The New Woman* featured blunt criticism of men. The first and most representative essay was *"Gei nanxing"* (For men), published in December 1926. Zhang Xichen's editorial note remarked that, "despite a certain unavoidable extreme tinge, it ['For Men'] was by far the boldest recent writing."[46] Presumably, for Zhang, the boldest arguments in "For Men" were Chen's indictment of remnant masculine *nuxing* (servility) encouraged by feudal ethics, her opinion that the two sexes were not cooperating to solve the woman question, and her declaration of war against men. At the outset of the essay, Chen explained that the failure of *The New Woman*'s previous issues in presenting a proper discourse on the New Woman drove her to write this piece. She began by distinguishing her denunciation of male misconduct from her respect for some senior male friends. She proceeded to give several examples of the ways that even educated men capriciously treated and despised (educated) women. Above all, she accused Chinese men of looking up to Western women while looking down on Chinese women. These personal observations and experiences led her to sum up that Chinese men neither understood women nor were concerned about women's plight. "We [women] cannot but form a battle line and declare war on men," Chen concluded, "if men still won't try to understand women!"[47]

Zhang Xichen's characterization of the radicalism of "For Men," evidenced in terms such as "extreme" and "boldest," anticipated the reaction from male authors. Chen's essay intrigued, or annoyed, Zhang Xichen and his male colleagues. Their direct response was an editorial call for essays that appeared in *The New Woman* in January 1927. Entitled *"Xiandai nüzi de kumen wenti"* (The dilemma of modern women), the series of essays consisted of twenty-two articles – nineteen by men and three by women (including Chen Xuezhao). These essays discussed women's "dilemma" as to whether they should devote

---

[45] Kinkley, "Introduction."   [46] "Paiwan yihou."
[47] Chen Xuezhao, "Gei nanxing."

themselves to domesticity or society.[48] While some male contributors showed respect for women's preferences, most of the articles argued that it was a woman's natural and vital calling to be a wife and mother.

Chen Xuezhao was the only contributor to this discussion who questioned why women alone faced such a dilemma. Using the same frank tone as in "For Men," she challenged the theme of this essay solicitation, which posited being a wife and mother as the duty of a woman. In contrast, she defined this so-called duty as a *human right*, just as men had the right to be husbands and fathers. She highlighted the gender inequalities dictating marital roles and career choices even within the nuclear family. Even though men might show chivalry to women during courtship, it was women who had to sacrifice their previous careers (if they had one) for the family once they were married. Housewives, Chen argued, involuntarily became economically dependent – hence inferior – to their husbands. Reasserting her position in "For Men," Chen denounced the educated *xin nanxing* (new man), who devalued educated women as they did illiterate women. For her, uncivilized and misogynist attitudes towards women exposed deep-rooted inequities engrained through patriarchal ethics.[49] At the end of the essay, Chen called for women to struggle for economic independence through education, and for an end to male expectations of female submissiveness.

In both essays, Chen Xuezhao opposed gender philosophies that equated female domestic duty with biology in order to serve the interests of men. She believed that the key to women's emancipation was autonomy and economic independence. In her view, the new family still frustrated women when they had to relinquish their careers for marriage and children. By acutely attributing women's subjection and suffering to men's misbehavior, Chen Xuezhao's argumentative essays were the most militant among female contributions in *The New Woman*.

Critiques of Marriage and Ellen Key: Deng Tianyu

Deng Tianyu, a young anarchist from inland China, was another woman writer who trumpeted women's rights as a radical feminist in *The New Woman*. Deng and her comrade lover Lu Jianbo studied and worked in Chinese coastal cities while dedicating themselves to social revolution and women's emancipation.[50] Her first two articles for *The New Woman* introduced readers to local marriage customs and folksongs of her hometown.[51] In January 1927, she wrote

---

[48] Bianzhe, "Xiandai nüzi de kumen wenti."
[49] Chen Xuezhao, "Xiandai nüzi de kumen wenti: shi."
[50] Lu Jianbo and Deng Tianyu, "Xieci: Zhi Huang Zhong, Du Keming da yishi"; Tianyu, "Shidai xia xisheng de xin nüzi."
[51] Deng Tianyu, "Wo xiang de hunzu"; Tianyu, ed., "Nanchong jiage."

an open letter in *The New Woman*, defending her highly criticized free union with Lu Jianbo as a declaration of free love and a denunciation of the marriage system.[52] "Both conventional and new marriages," Deng claimed, "are contracts to sell one's body and soul." She continued, "Neither liberated human beings nor noble romantic love have anything to do with the custom of marriage. Why bother keeping it?"[53] Like Jiang Fenzi, Deng considered marriage as the root of all evil and the enemy of autonomous (free from family) and genuine (without material considerations) union between the two sexes, which the new sexual morality promoted. In the mid-1920s, the fervent call for Chinese national and social revolution clashed with discourses on personal romantic love. Many young people were torn between love and revolution.[54] Deng drew from her own experiences and the free union of two leading Russian-American anarchists, Emma Goldman (1869–1939) and Alexander Berkman (1870–1936), to affirm the compatibility between personal love and social well-being.

Unlike Chen Xuezhao, Deng Tianyu did not focus on the wrongs perpetrated by men. Nevertheless, she challenged Ellen Key's maternalist discourse, the doctrine espoused by Zhang Xichen and his male colleagues. Deng's feminist ideas concerning children's public education and gender equality at work conflicted with Key's eugenic scheme, which valorized the role of the mother in educating her child in the home.[55] Deng did not object to maternity *per se*, but she resisted the maternal imperative espoused by Key and her Chinese male followers.[56] Her essay "Tangshi wo youle xiaohai" (If I had children) in response to *The New Woman*'s solicitation in January 1928 exemplified her disapproval of Key's affirmation of maternity as women's exclusive duty.[57] In "Women and Housework," another article in *The New Woman*, Deng further criticized Key's contempt for the significance of women's social roles. "While she [Key] exalted women's maternity from hell to heaven," Deng complained, "she repositioned and locked women in the dungeon of heaven. Men can so easily utilize this fresh excuse to shut women out of every social and academic activity."[58]

Ideologically, Deng tried to use the ideals of free love to liberate women from the marriage system that was controlled by familial authority and that hindered women's efforts to do *zhandou* (combat) for social revolution. In short, she emphasized the importance of women's autonomy in both their actions and thoughts.

---

[52] Tianyu, "Women de jiehe."   [53] Ibid.
[54] Liu Jianmei, *Revolution plus Love*; Lü Fangshang, "1920 niandai Zhongguo zhishifenzi youguan qing'ai wenti de jueze yu taolun."
[55] Key, *The Century of the Child*.   [56] Tianyu, "Tangshi wo youle xiaohai: yi."
[57] Ibid.   [58] Tianyu, "Funü yu jiashi."

Male Editorial Agency vs. Female Authorial Subjectivity

Most male contributors to *The Ladies' Journal* and *The New Woman* recognized that women ought to emancipate themselves. These men were, nonetheless, anxious to theorize the "woman question" themselves in order to guide women in this endeavor, a trend demonstrated by Zhang Xichen's editorial agency. In doing so, they discursively endorsed "collaboration" instead of "competition" between men and women in advancing their version of gender equality. Views that did not conform to this narrative of harmony were often treated as heresy that needed to be condemned. The fact that Zhang encouraged women's contributions to his journals did not necessarily signal his acceptance of their feminist contentions. For every article that revealed women's discontent in *The Ladies' Journal* and *The New Woman*, he regularly published male responses as counterpoint or even counterattacks. Typically, Zhang Xichen commented on female writers' complaints with reservations; yet he never restrained male contributors from opposing dissenting women's opinions.

The following section argues that the interplay between dissenting women, male writers, and Zhang Xichen reveals that the editor had an obvious advantage in checking, if not discouraging, female authorial subjectivity from reaching its full potential. Without directly targeting the fair sex, the superiority of male editorial privilege prevailed over female authorial dissonance. Moreover, I suggest that by participating in these cross-gender dialogues or disputes, these dissenting women rebelled against conventional femininity. The contents of their argumentative essays displayed rationality, lucidity, analytical depth, and even forcefulness. Their narratives differed not only from those of their female predecessors as described by Yung-chen Chiang, but also from the gender philosophy of male liberals as represented by Zhang Xichen.

Throughout Zhang Xichen's tenure at women's journals of the 1920s, male writers appeared as gatekeepers of the publication whenever there were arguments put forth by dissenting women. This was evident in men's reactions to Jiang Fengzi's essays and in Lian Shi and Xu Hemei's criticism in *The Ladies' Journal*. It is also manifest in the male response to Chen Xuezhao's declaration of gender war in *The New Woman*.

Jiang Fengzi's non-normative view on love's freedom, in which singlehood could serve as an alternative practice, received two kinds of male responses in *The Ladies' Journal*. The first one was a "Study on the Singlehood Issue" in October 1922. With the absence of women contributors, the four male participants talked about singlehood in an authoritative manner supported by Western theories. The first article by Zhang Xichen considered the increase in singlehood as "a sick phenomenon in a civilized society."[59] Zhou Jianren followed by

---

[59] Selu, "Wenming yu dushen."

deprecating singlehood as a means for female self-reliance.[60] They both preferred a "constructive" solution to gender conflict, meaning love-based marriage, rather than the passive compromise of singlehood. Kong Xiangwo, the third participant in the Singlehood Issue, echoed the editors' dislike for singlehood by listing the negative consequences of singlehood for individuals and society.[61] Intriguingly, the fourth article tried to defend Ellen Key's celibate life, explaining that she was too good to find a compatible love match.[62] Altogether, the "Study on the Singlehood Issue" conveyed an editor-sanctioned, male-oriented message of favoring romantic love over the more problematic singlehood.

Zhang Xichen carried his cult of love through in the forum "Lian'ai ziyou yu ziyou lian'ai de taolun" (Discussion of freedom to love and free love) in February 1923. Being the only female participant, Jiang Fengzi stood alone on one side, contending that freedom to love implied the choice both to love and not to love. She insisted that her interpretation was a synthesis of thesis (to love) and antithesis (not to love).[63] Upon Zhang Xichen's request, Wu Juenong (1897–1939) responded to Jiang's essays by pointing out her logical fallacy of incorporating singlehood into love's freedom. To him, romantic love entailed love, sex, and eventually marriage; singlehood had nothing to do with romantic love.[64] Zhang Xichen concluded this discussion, posing as a just conciliator. He judged that the (male-)established notion of love's freedom, which excluded singlehood, should be maintained.[65] Jiang Fengzi's heterodox characterization was thus vetoed by an editorial and male version of love's freedom.

Lian Shi and Xu Hemei's indictments of Kuangfu's (Zheng Zhenxuan) treatment of his divorced wife similarly provoked some male readers' antipathy, as expressed in the column "Reviewing the Previous Issue" in June 1923. One disgruntled reader, Dongyuan, thought that although Lian and Xu made their points, they were inevitably biased.[66] Chen Moruo, another reader, denounced Lian and Xu for what he viewed as an exacerbation of the struggle between the two sexes. Chen's retort expressed men's general belief that women's emancipation should only be carried out as part of a broad social revolution and through cooperation between men and women. For these men, female-specific views such as those of Lian and Xu served nothing positive and destroyed gender harmony. The fact that no rejoinder from Lian and Xu appeared in the journal suggests that the editor intended to close the case with the comments from men.

---

[60] Zhou, "Zhongguo nüzi de juexing yu dushen."
[61] Kong Xiangwo, "Dushen de wojian."
[62] Harada, "Chang muxing zunzhong lun de Ailunkai nüshi weishenme dushen."
[63] Fengzi, "Lian'ai ziyou ji xupian."   [64] Y. D., "Ziyou lian'ai yu lian'ai ziyou xupian."
[65] Zhang Xichen, "Du Fengzi nüshi he YD xiansheng de taolun."
[66] Dongyuan, "Du qianhao."

In contrast to the straightforward disputes between men and female writers in *The Ladies' Journal*, the gender interactions in *The New Woman* were indirect and backhanded. Chen Xuezhao's defiant essay triggered the first male reaction from a reader named Mo Xinghan. Addressed to Zhang Xichen (instead of Chen) in the journal's correspondence column in January 1927, Mo criticized Chen's indictment of men in her "For Men." Posing as a rebuttal to Chen's feminism, Mo's open letter sarcastically articulated his opinion of women. He provided several examples of female misconduct, such as tricking men out of money and love, as evidence that women were responsible for their own misery.[67]

Chen Xuezhao's indirect reply to Mo's satire appeared in the form of a wrap-up essay for the discussion of "The Dilemma of Modern Women" in March 1927. After summarizing the points made by the invited contributors, she expressed her reproof of those people, mostly men, who favored wifely and motherly roles as the means for women to realize themselves and serve society. Departing from her exclusive criticism of men in "For Men," Chen also pointed her finger at some educated new women who maintained a male-centered patriarchal mindset.[68] She reproached these women as self-demeaning and admitted that women too could be at fault. In the end, she called for women to "rise up and be real human beings!" a typical male intellectual slogan first articulated during the May Fourth era.[69]

Given Chen Xuezhao's severe criticism of the opposite sex in "For Men," her final essay in *The New Woman* was anticlimactic. Her theory of "men's fault," was replaced by "the fault of both sexes" in explaining women's subjugation and gender injustice. The essay read as if she was shifting from female-oriented feminism to male-centered individualism and humanism. Yet, in her later reportage as a foreign correspondent to France for *The New Woman*, she deplored the misconduct of male Chinese overseas students.[70] Chen's genre change from argumentative essay to reportage of writings could be understood as a compromise between authorial subjectivity and editorial agency. While her last essay implies her alignment with *The New Woman*'s male-oriented gender philosophy, she retained a critical attitude in her reports on foreign lives.

As for Deng Tianyu, her silence in *The New Woman*'s debates about romantic love, in which her lover and anarchist comrades participated, disclosed another type of gender confrontation. On the one hand, her male anarchist comrades were indeed invested in attaining total sexual freedom. Yet their insensitivity to gender difference and objection to romantic love collided with Deng's

---

[67] Mo Xinghan, "'Gei Nanxing' de fanying."

[68] Chen Xuezhao especially mentioned Zhou Jun, one of the women contributors to the solicitation, who had studied in Germany and still clung to the "virtuous wife and good mother" ideology. Chen, "Xiandai nüzi."

[69] Chen Xuezhao, "Xiandai nüzi."   [70] Chen Xuezhao, "Lü Fa tongxin."

beliefs and prevented her from siding with them in the debates. On the other hand, her denial of marriage also kept her from favoring the side of Zhang Xichen. As Zhang and his male adherents were fighting against male anarchists' denunciation of romantic love, Deng's less provocative articles, which appeared simultaneously in *The New Woman*, were left unchallenged.[71] Presumably, Deng's anarchist denial of marriage was tolerated in the journal for her pro-love and pro-procreative stance, which fit Zhang's gender philosophy. To a certain extent, Deng's authorial subjectivity benefitted from the quarrels between Zhang Xichen and her male comrades. It was undoubtedly Zhang, the guardian of his journals, however, who dominated the discourse.

It was unclear why Zhang Xichen stopped publishing articles in the last year of *The New Woman*; gone as well were the debates, article invitations, and correspondence about intimate matters. Instead, a new column, "Feihua" (Moonshine), appeared frequently from January to August 1929. "Moonshine" carried short vignettes, written exclusively by men, on topics such as love, sex, women, and gender relationships. Notably, several of these short pieces tended to make fun of women and mocked their powerlessness and vanity, which provoked no protests from female writers.[72] Interestingly enough, in March 1929, an essay by a woman writer, Xinjun, targeting men's condescending tone appeared in the first issue of *Funü gongming* (The woman's resonance), a new women's journal edited by women. Titled "Nanzimen shuo" (Men said), it appealed to men to refrain from ridiculing women and instead to encourage women's self-improvement.[73] Xinjun's essay provoked a retort from a male author, Jiezi, who published "Nüzimen shuo" (Women said) in *The New Woman*. "If I were a woman," Jiezi scorned, "I would hope that men would constantly supervise and criticize women in order to keep stimulating a response, so that we can break the invisible chains of patriarchy and put men in their place. But new women nowadays do not think along these lines. What more can be done?"[74] Yuren, another female author, responded to Jiezi's "Women Said" in *The Woman's Resonance*. Yuren tried to reason with Jiezi and called a truce to end the paper battle.[75] The cross-journal dispute ended in Jiezi's insistence that women shifted the blame onto men for women's wrongs.[76] His male perspective met no further challenge through the end of *The New Woman*.

Conclusion

The encounter between male editors and women authors in the pages of Chinese women's journals during the 1920s epitomized the intricate gendered reasoning

---

[71] Tianyu, "Shidai xia"; "Funü yu wuyue."
[72] Changwen, "Duan bitou"; Hong Jun, "Duan bitou zhi xu."
[73] Xinjun, "Nanzimen shuo."   [74] Jiezi, "Nüzimen shuo."
[75] Yuren, "Dule 'Nüzimen shuo' yihou."   [76] Jiezi, "'Nanzimen shuo' yu 'Nüzi men shuo'."

and prioritizing of individual rights, social activism, and national salvation. At the time when what Haiyan Lee has called an "enlightened structure of feeling" dominated the sentiments of May Fourth liberals, it prevailed among both men and women.[77] Many educated women joined the male-led project of modernity, in which general calls for individual freedom, self-awakening, and autonomy also offered a solution to the woman question. Women's magazines were the space where these solutions could be debated, if not tested, and integrated reading across magazines and related print publications helps us to reconstruct those debates. By the 1920s, when national and social crises summoned individual dedication, male intellectuals highlighted the imperative of awakening women to work with them, rather than fight against them. The rhetoric of "gender collaboration" dictated the mainstream discourse on gender and women's issues. Male editors of women's journals, such as Zhang Xichen, embodied a paternalistic mindset of patronizing female contributions as well as guiding them along the right track. His editorial agency was buttressed by his thematic initiative, the rhetoric of "collaboration" between the two sexes, and the contributors' authorial cooperation. In the nationalistic and revolutionary social milieu, most female writers emphasized what they could contribute, rather than what they were entitled to receive, by asserting gender equality and women's rights.[78] Their sense of duty to collective well-being drove them to believe that cross-gender social and national revolution should precede and also lead to women's emancipation.

If female authorial subjectivity was curbed in male-edited journals, it was not because of the authors' status as women, but because they held dissenting views. In the space that women's journals provided, these dissenting women daringly pointed to the pitfalls of male-dominated discourses, which promoted freedom of love, marriage, and divorce, allegedly in a gender-neutral fashion, but ultimately in a way that could potentially harm women's autonomy and agency. Rather than clinging to literary styles of writing, these dissenting women consciously appropriated male argumentative writing. They risked articulating female-specific problems and heterodox notions that were often targeted by men as sabotaging gender harmony. In this way, these Chinese dissenting women echoed some of their Western sisters in combating male-centered, mostly heterosexual sexual liberation by demanding their own versions of emancipation.[79] Admittedly, the dissenting women portrayed in this article did not assert female same-sex love or homosexuality to counterbalance the principle of heterosexual normativity that reigned in *The Ladies' Journal*

[77] Lee Haiyan, *Revolution of the Heart*, 95–217.

[78] He Xiangning, "Guomin geming shi funü weiyi de shenglu." Also see Gilmartin, *Engendering*; Ke Huiling, "Xingbie yu zhengzhi."

[79] Bland, *Banishing the Beasts*; Jeffreys, *The Spinster and Her Enemies*.

and *The New Woman*.[80] Nevertheless, having emphasized women's particular interests and concerns, they made claims for sexual autonomy and the free choice of love from a female perspective.

Moreover, these dissenting women usually matched their words with deeds, which sharply contrasted with many male liberals, who preached progressive ideas of love and sexual morality on paper while obeying their parents' arranged marriages in real life. Jiang Fengzi and Deng Tianyu were brave enough to choose a thorny road to freedom by eschewing a family-arranged engagement and rejecting conventional marriage. In the face of their male senior literary patrons, these dissenting women were daring in words and true to themselves in action. Importantly, they transgressed conventional femininity and therefore changed the "body" of their lives in three senses: in form, in content, and in action.

The discursive endeavors of dissenting women as evidenced in my integrated reading of *The Ladies' Journal* and *The New Woman*, were significant even if their rebellious texts always met with male resistance and containment. Their challenge to male privilege in both theory and practice exposed an asymmetrical power relationship between the sexes under the disguise of cross-gender teamwork. Exercising his editorial agency, Zhang Xichen may have been able to limit contributors' authorial subjectivity whenever deviant notions were asserted. Nevertheless, the fact that women were encouraged to contribute writings to the "women's journals," edited and published by men, inevitably led to some divergence from Zhang's editorial vision. Reading more closely and understanding the cacophony of voices of dissenting women, we can no longer treat 1920s discourses on love and sexual morality in *The Ladies' Journal* and *The New Woman* as homogeneous. The inclusion of these female dissenting voices meant that the grand narrative of the journals was undeniably disrupted, even if it was not fundamentally changed.

---

[80] For the study of modern Chinese female same-sex relations in fictional or autobiographical writings, see Sang, *The Emerging Lesbian*.

8   Voices of Female Educators in Early-Twentieth-Century Women's Magazines

Siao-chen Hu

In the preface to a recently published compilation of turn-of-the-twentieth-century Chinese women's journals, the editor-in-chief explained that his interest in women's magazines started with a letter in his personal collection. The letter was written by a woman named Yi Yu (style name Zhonghou) and addressed to her brother Yi Shunding (1858–1920), a renowned poet and scholar of the late Qing and early Republican era. In the letter, Yi Yu mentioned that her autobiographical story, entitled "Tiaonian mengying" (Recollections of my girlhood), was published in *Funü zazhi – The Ladies' Journal*.[1] Yi Yu is not a prominent figure in modern history, but I remembered reading many poems by a woman author named Yi Yu or Huang Yi Yu when I did research on the early stage of *The Ladies' Journal*, and I clearly remembered identifying her as a school teacher. I also remembered seeing her name in another women's magazine, *Zhonghua funüjie – The Chung Hwa Women's Magazine*, a periodical I relied on as a source for female teachers' statements on women's education.[2] The repeated appearance of this particular woman author's name became a link, making me realize some of the shared ground for these two competing women's magazines, as well as the dominance of the educator's voice, especially in the case of *The Chung Hwa Women's Magazine*. After all, in the 1910s, notwithstanding the predominance of the *xianqi liangmu* – "virtuous wife, good mother" discourse, the Chinese Beiyang government continued the policy of promoting women's education. In 1915, the year when both *The Ladies' Journal* and *The Chung Hwa Women's Magazine* started, President Yuan Shikai appointed four women educators – Zhu Zonglian, Ji Zonglan, Qian Weizhen, and Lü Huiru – as educational inspectors and sent them to investigate the current situation of women's education in all provinces of China.[3] All four of these women were active contributors to women's magazines of the time.

In this article, however, instead of focusing on educators' discourse on particular issues, I will look at the social networking function of the women's

[1] Chu Guoqing, "Zhongguo jinxiandai nüxing qikan shulüe."
[2] Hu Xiaozhen [Siao-chen Hu], "Xingtan yu wentan."
[3] Feng Yuehua, *Jiangsu funü yundong shi*, 43–47.

magazines for female educators and their implied pupils. Through an integrated and situated reading of the journals and related materials, I will argue that both *The Ladies' Journal* and *The Chung Hwa Women's Magazine* served as fora for educators and students, and that in the case of the latter, the magazine served as a space of friendship and social networking for a specific and half-closed community of female educators. Early Republican women's journals did not exist only to provide knowledge, information, and entertainment. They also provided a textualized space for interrelationships.

The Case of *The Ladies' Journal*

The Ladies' Journal has become one of the most fully studied women's magazines of the Republican era.[4] In my previous studies I paid more attention to the early stage of the magazine (1915–1919), when Wang Yunzhang (1884–1942) served as the editor-in-chief. Wang is often categorized as a writer of the *jiupai* (traditional) school, and the magazine has been considered ideologically conservative under his editorship. Generally speaking, the magazine in its early stage spoke for women's education under the premise of the "virtuous wife, good mother" theory. It also promoted the idea of women's career choices and economic independence, but often argued against women's suffrage. In short, it was a public space for contested questions.[5]

The magazine's contributors included writers of the "traditional school," scholars, and high school/college teachers and students. The concept of education was emphasized, and the magazine customarily specified the educational institution with which a particular contributor was affiliated. This was most prominent in the cases of women teachers and students. For example, in the illustrations at the front of the first issue, there are portraits of three principals of women's schools. Other pictures are also attributed to women teachers or students. There are four congratulatory essays for the founding of the magazine, and three of them are by school teachers. Especially in the "Lunshuo" (Essay) column, there are nine essays by women, of whom three were graduates of the First Girls' School of Jiangsu. The column "Wenyuan" (Literary garden) consists of poetry and prose, and the prose section features compositions by girl students.[6] On the other hand, the "Xiaoshuo" (Fiction), "Yihai" (Translation), and "Zazu" (Miscellany) columns are largely dominated by male authors. A simple overview of the first issue demonstrates what an essential part women teachers and students played in the journal, and which social groups the magazine initially targeted.

---

[4] See, for example, Murata, *Fujo zashi*.   [5] See Hu, "The Construction of Gender."
[6] For an analysis of the poetry section, see Hu, "The Construction of Gender."

In the second year of *The Ladies' Journal*, when the magazine was temporarily under a woman editor-in-chief, it underwent small yet not insignificant changes. For example, the "Essay" column was renamed "Sheshuo" (Editorials), and the translation column was cancelled. Two new columns were added – "Zhongwai dashiji" (Reports of national and international events) and "Guowen fanzuo" (Composition examples). In the "Reports" column, the readers could learn about both national and international issues, information that went beyond the norm of literary pursuits and good motherhood. The new editor-in-chief, who some suggest was merely nominal, must have played a role in establishing the parameters of these two new columns. The changes indicate two concerns, both related to the idea of the magazine as a medium for women's education. The first concern is evident: what could and should be taught to a female audience was no longer limited to feminine virtues and household duties. The second is more intriguing and difficult to fathom: why did the new editor-in-chief find it necessary to set up a new column for girl students to publish their essay compositions?

We must first try to understand the editor-in-chief's role. On the opening page of the last issue of the first year, an "announcement of grand-scale innovation" was made in *The Ladies' Journal* (1:12, 1915). Readers were notified that starting from the second year, a Mrs. Zhu Hu Binxia (1888–1931) was invited to be the magazine's new editor-in-chief. A brief curriculum vitae of the new editor was then given: she was a native of Wuxi county and had gone to Tokyo to study at the Jissen Girls' School under the guidance of Shimoda Utako, the famous woman educator. She later had gone to the United States to study first at Walnut Hill School and then at Wellesley College, majoring in literature, history, and philosophy. After seven years of study she had graduated with a bachelor's degree.[7] She then visited Cornell University for several months, consulting materials related to women's education. She was also appointed by the Ministry of Education as a delegate and participated in the meeting of the international association for children's happiness in Washington, DC. Returning to China, she first taught at the Lize Girls' School in Tongli, Wujiang, in Jiangsu province, and then at Pudong High School in Shanghai. This information highlights Hu Binxia's status as a leading woman teacher. As the announcement claimed, "she will yield extraordinary brilliance in the field

---

[7] Professor Ellen Widmer told me in a personal email that Hu Binxia was one of the first two Chinese students admitted to Wellesley College, and that her picture could be found in the 1913 yearbook. In another email she informed me that, according to a thesis she consulted at the Wellesley library, Hu attended Laura Haygood, a missionary high school in Suzhou, before she went to Walnut Hill. I have not yet had the opportunity to look at these materials at Wellesley. My gratitude goes to Professor Widmer. Hu Binxia was the sister of Hu Dunfu, Hu Mingfu, and Hu Gangfu; all three were among the earliest Chinese students who went to study in the United States, and later became famous scientists.

of the media as a star among women." Under her editorship, "our magazine will be even more agreeable for women to read."[8] In other words, Hu was chosen first for her sex, and second for her accomplishment in the field of education, as the magazine was originally designed to serve the needs of women teachers and students. Hu's affiliation with Japanese and American educational institutions was also emphasized, pointing to a desire to place the magazine in its international context. Given these insights into the new editor-in-chief's background, it is understandable why new columns on sociopolitical topics and international affairs were added to *The Ladies' Journal* under her editorship. But again, how do we explain the column for students' compositions?

The column started with a scholar's experiment in the teaching of the Chinese language. In August 1915, Qian Jibo (1887–1957),[9] whose wife was the sister of the magazine's first editor, Wang Yunzhang, was invited to teach at the Lize Girls' School in Wujiang, Jiangsu province. At that time, Qian was already a highly recognized scholar. As a teacher of Chinese, Qian was convinced that in modern educational institutions, learning Chinese, the national language and symbol of the national spirit, should be the core of education. It was, however, often neglected or not properly taught. To correct this, Qian proposed a plan for teaching essay writing, and *The Ladies' Journal* was chosen as his laboratory. He wrote an article entitled "Manifesto for teaching Chinese at the Lize Girls' School in Wujiang," which was published in the "Essay" column in *The Ladies' Journal*.[10] Qian says in the article,

I believe that the written language of a nation is the core of its citizens' spirit. If the citizens of a nation lack the ability to use its written language for the purpose of transmitting ideas, then "the citizens cannot fully be part of the nation" and "the nation cannot fully rely on its citizens." ... Nowadays those who claim themselves to be students of China's teachers' schools are not capable of wielding pens to write properly in China's written language. This is what I used to call "the nation not being for the citizens" and "the citizens not being for the nation."[11]

He then explained his method of teaching essay writing. As he proposed, he would routinely pick a topic and ask his students to write essays. After the students finished writing their essays, he would show them a demonstration essay that he had written. Then he would correct the students' essays, make them

---

[8] "*Funü zazhi* da gaizao," *Funü zazhi*, 1:12, first page after table of contents, no page number. This page can be found in the accompanying database, http://kjc-sv013.kjc.uni-heidelberg .de/frauenzeitschriften/public/magazine/page_content.php?magazin_id=4&year=1915&issue_ id=74&issue_number=012&img_issue_page=005

[9] Most people know little about Qian Jibo except that he was Qian Zhongshu's father. He was actually an outstandingly accomplished scholar, covering a wide range of disciplines. See Liu Guiqiu, *Wuxi shiqi.*

[10] Qian Jibo, "Wujiang Lize" 1–5.   [11] Ibid.

study the revisions, and submit the polished versions, together with his demonstration essay, to *The Ladies' Journal*. In so doing, he tried to transform the magazine into a pedagogical space, not only for his students at Lize, but also for any students among readers who desired to learn, or any teachers who searched for effective teaching methods. It should be pointed out that Qian preferred topics that were related to contemporary sociopolitical issues. In that issue of *The Ladies' Journal*, for example, four of Qian's students published their essays and Qian himself sent in two demonstration essays. All were on the topic of "Inscription on the back of Lize Girls' School monument for national humiliation" and "Drafting a letter to Madam Wu Zhiying of Tongcheng, asking for her calligraphy for the inscription on the back of our school's monument for national humiliation."[12] Using the same formula, Qian kept sending his students' and his own essays in to *The Ladies' Journal*.[13]

Qian also encouraged translation. He proposed that, by practicing translation, students could learn Chinese and foreign languages, and acquire new knowledge at the same time. He put his theory into practice and submitted translation experiments to *The Ladies' Journal* to publish. Probably because Qian's teaching experiment won the approval of the editorial board, when Hu became the new editor-in-chief, she decided to set up a separate column for sample writings. It is also relevant that Hu Binxia used to teach at the Lize Girls' School. In any case, Qian's experiment evidently attracted attention as well as followers. In *The Ladies' Journal* 2:2, apart from seven essays by Qian's students, there are also six essays on three different topics by students from Hanzhang Girls' School of Liuyang.

The practice seemed to be well received, with the number of essays submitted to the magazine growing steadily. But as it developed, it also aroused criticism. In the *Benshe tongxin* (Correspondence) section in *The Ladies' Journal* 2:6, there is a response from the editor to a reader who sent in a letter speaking against publishing essays by a group of students. The editor penned the following response:

To Ms. Zhibai:

In your letter, you pointed out that, upon opening of our humble magazine, one always sees such words as "Private Lize School of Wujiang" and you criticize us for this. You also said that the essays submitted by Lize School students are not qualified to represent Chinese women's literary talent. Your criticism stands indeed. However, writing is for the public to use. What counts is not quantity, but quality. Our humble magazine includes essays sent by Lize School in the column of composition examples. What we mean by

---

[12] Qian Jibo, "Lize nüxue." The national humiliation refers to the Treaty for the Twenty-One Demands that Yuan Shikai signed with Japan in May 1915.
[13] For a brief discussion of Qian's experiment in teaching essay writing, see Liu Guiqiu, "Bashi nian."

"example" is to show students some principles of writing, and no more. Furthermore, we have more than once published essays submitted by Hanzhang Girls' School of Liuyang, Women Teachers' School of Henan province, and Women Teachers' School of Wuxi county. Since the column is not reserved for essays from Lize, it is evident that we never take essays from Lize to represent Chinese women's literary talent. Your advice is sincere and earnest, so we are convinced that you value our humble magazine. How could we not appreciate your great kindness? If you could endow us with wonderful writings of yours, or recommend to us good works, so that our humble magazine has the opportunity to explore and expand, we would be boundlessly grateful.

By Shouheizi[14]

It is an intriguing case. *Zhibai* (literally, knowing the white) and *shouhei* (keeping the black) are a pair of complementary concepts from the Daoist classic *Daodejing*. Two hypotheses can be put forward. The first is that the reader who sent the letter called herself Ms. Zhibai and the editor teasingly called herself Shouhei in response. The second is that both the criticism and the response were purposefully made up by the editor to provoke discussions. In either case, it was not the teaching of essay writing that was being opposed, but the appropriation and manipulation of the magazine as a space for public opinion. After objections were raised, the magazine continued to publish essays sent by a group of students for some time, but Qian's experiment of teaching essay writing was short-lived, as he soon took up a college position elsewhere. This is one example of how teachers and students viewed the magazine as a vehicle for education, or a pedagogical space. And in this case, it was a male scholar teaching a group of girl students and trying to reach a broader female audience.

While Qian Jibo's tone and attitude were impersonal, women preferred a more intimate and personal relationship with fellow contributors as well as readers. Even the correspondence cited above between the woman editor and a woman reader suggests a sense of closeness. Yi Yu is a prime example of a woman who used the magazine to interpersonal ends.

As noted above, Yi Yu published an autobiographical story called "Recollections of My Girlhood" in *The Ladies' Journal* (1:6, 1:7, 1:8, 1:9, 1:10). Though it was classified in the "Fiction" column, Yi Yu claimed it was a truthful account of what she heard, saw, and experienced as a girl. She jotted down what came to her mind, she said in the preface, to record the ideas current in society, the situation of education, the words and deeds of her parents, and the joys and sorrows of her family. By so doing, she hoped to convey to all women what she thought about history, politics, and morality. Compared with other fictional

---

[14] The letter appears in the original as a notice from the journal, which can be consulted in the project database at http://kjc-sv013.kjc.uni-heidelberg.de/frauenzeitschriften/public/magazine/page_content.php?magazin_id=4&year=1916&issue_id=315&issue_number=6&img_issue_page=144.

stories published in *The Ladies' Journal*, either in literary or vernacular Chinese, "Recollections of My Girlhood" has more appeal, as it retrospectively recounts intimate scenes from the personal life of a little girl. In many ways, it is a forerunner of Pu-wei Yang Chao's (1889–1981) *Autobiography of a Chinese Woman*, though Yang's was written in modern vernacular Chinese (and also in English), whereas Yi was still writing in literary Chinese.[15]

The story does not follow a particular chronological order; instead, it focuses on several important aspects of the author's life. The first is education. Yi tells funny stories about how she and her brother studied with private tutors, skipped classes, and were punished by stern teachers. When she was studying under the guidance of private tutors, she was made to memorize classic texts without understanding them. In reflection, she says that the texts did not meet the psychological demands of children, and memorizing all day was as boring and tasteless as chewing wax. She complained that traditional tutors, no matter how kind or stern, knew little about children. Their ways of teaching were, therefore, inappropriate and even damaging to pupils. Modern schools appear to her a much better choice. However, Yi Yu also criticized teachers in modern schools who spent all of their time lecturing in class, giving students no time to recite and think. She concluded by saying that she was determined to pursue what Confucius said to be the second best happiness in life, teaching talented students from around the world. Yi Yu reveals her self-identity by beginning with her memory of studying with tutors and ending with her commitment to the career of an educator.

The second aspect of Yi's life that her account focuses on is her first-hand experience of foot-binding. Although her open-minded father was against ear-piercing and foot-binding, Yi Yu was afraid of being different, and voluntarily chose to have her feet bound. She details the sufferings she underwent during the process, explaining that young women of the day must learn about the past in order to value what they enjoy now. The third topic in her recollection is her father's political career and her mother's nourishing family teaching. The fourth and final topic is her mother's account of what the family encountered during the Taiping Rebellion, a tale of violence, cruelty, irrationality, and miraculous redemption. This part of the "Recollection" deserves particular attention because it is told from her mother's perspective, whereas most narrative accounts of the Taiping Rebellion that have come down to us are by men.

---

[15] Yang Buwei (Pu-wei Yang Chao) was born to a distinguished family in Nanjing. She worked as the principal of Chongshi Girls' School in 1912, when she was only twenty-two. Later she went to Japan and studied medicine at the Tokyo Imperial University. After returning to China, she ran a private hospital in Beijing. She married Zhao Yuanren (Chao Yuen-ren), a renowned Chinese linguist. In *Autobiography of a Chinese Woman*, Yang told personal stories of her girlhood that were closely intertwined with historical events of modern China.

Yi Yu published the recollection in *The Ladies' Journal* with the intention of educating by sharing her personal experiences. She discussed teaching and learning, not as theory, but as the product of what she had lived through and perceived with her own eyes and body. By telling the life story of a growing girl, she established a psychological bond with her (women) readers. This sense of intimacy and community is particular to women authors and readers in the context of magazine publication. Modern media, especially the journals targeting women, opened a channel for women to express their autobiographical desire, that is, the urge to talk about oneself directly to readers who are expected to understand. These magazines thus replaced the letters and poems late imperial Chinese women had used to perform this same subjective function in the past.

Poetry continued to be published in women's journals,[16] however, and it continued to serve as a medium for building, transmitting, and publicizing friendship as it had for both men and women for centuries. Yi Yu published a poem addressed to a friend in *The Ladies' Journal* 1:9. The poem is entitled "To Fan Yunsu, I received her letter when I was in Tongzhou."[17] It runs as follows:

> . . .
> Spring splendors hit my eyes, yet I seem not to see them, because
> Thinking of you day and night, my worrying heart is anxious.
> When your letter arrived, I read it hundreds of times without getting tired,
> While warm tears shed on my chest, stopped, but started again.
> Like shrikes and swallows, we fly in different directions.
> Things of the past are unbearable to think, but melancholy is for us to share.
> . . .
> My life has been in dejection, and I often lack happiness.
> My heart never opened, and my face never brightened, until I met you.
> Our minds are solitary, our dispositions aloof, we share the same eccentricity,
> And our tastes for sourness and saltiness are not concurrent with the world.
> . . .
> As long as I am alive, I will meet you again,
> But before that, to respond to you, I can only rely on this sheet of letter.

The poem refers to Yi's friendship with a Madam Fan Yunsu. Yunsu was the style name of Yao Yiyun, who also published works in *The Ladies' Journal*, including poems from her poetry collection *Yunsu xuan shigao*, and an essay on how to be a good stepmother. Who was Yao Yiyun? What was her relationship with Yi Yu? And furthermore, how are we to understand the representation of their friendship in the context of magazine publication? What does this poem suggest about the purposes to which women could put these magazines? To explore these questions, I will turn to *The Chung Hwa Women's Magazine*,

---

[16] See Grace Fong's contribution to this volume.
[17] Huang Yi Yu, "Ji Fan Yunsu." "Tongzhou" refers to the city of Nantong, Jiangsu province.

which reveals a discursive field that was at the same time more professional and more intimate than *The Ladies' Journal*.

The Case of *The Chung Hwa Women's Magazine*

The Chung Hwa Women's Magazine and *The Ladies' Journal* shared the same starting date and place of publication and directly competed for women's attention. While *The Ladies' Journal* was the longest-lasting women's magazine in the Republican era, *The Chung Hwa Women's Magazine* was short-lived – running for only eighteen issues. *The Chung Hwa Women's Magazine* claimed to "honor theories of scholars and good deeds of women," and "strive to bring together proper codes of behavior, methods of tailoring and cooking, approaches to educating children, and new crafts, skills and careers of Chinese and foreign women." It aimed at "the enrichment of knowledge and the cultivation of spirit for female students and housewives."[18] Similarly to the general tone of *The Ladies' Journal*, *The Chung Hwa Women's Magazine* stood by the "dutiful wife, good mother" principle, and had reservations about women's participation in political activities.

What distinguishes *The Chung Hwa Women's Magazine* from *The Ladies' Journal*, however, is a more vigorous concern for education. Although education was a topic of concern in *The Ladies' Journal*, as it was for both the Sun Yatsen and Yuan Shikai governments, the community of educators with a stake in *The Chung Hwa Women's Magazine* was much stronger.[19] *The Ladies' Journal*, though supported by women, was still largely dominated by male scholars and writers. In this respect, *The Chung Hwa Women's Magazine* served as a better field of communication for female educators and students.

Starting from the first issue, *The Chung Hwa Women's Magazine* included the following columns: "Tuhua" (Paintings), "Wenzhong" (Essays), "Wenyi" (Literature), "Chengji" (Students' works), and "Tebie jishi" (Reports on special school events). A comparison of matching columns in the two magazines reveals that the "Lunshuo" (Essays), "Xueyi" (Knowledge and skills), and "Jiazheng" (Family management) columns in *The Ladies' Journal* are similar in nature to the "Wenzhong" (Essays) column in *The Chung Hwa Women's Magazine*, and cover topics such as women's education, equality between the sexes, marriage, women's careers, social issues, and guidance on practical techniques.

---

[18] See the self-advertisement in *The Chung Hwa Women's Magazine* 1:3.

[19] Studies have been done on the construction of knowledge about housekeeping, popular science, medicine, etc., in *The Ladies' Journal*. See, for example, articles in Murata, *Fujo zasshi*. Women's education was a major achievement of both the Sun Yatsen and Yuan Shikai governments. Girls' schools, especially schools for training female teachers, were set up in all provinces in a short period of time, and stimulated a strong sense of community among female teachers. See Shu Xincheng, *Zhongguo jindai jiaoyushi*.

Concerning the contributors, there is some overlap. For example, Mei Meng was the major author of articles on popular science in both magazines. But generally, there seems to be two camps of authors who wrote for the two journals. Many of the article contributors to *The Ladies' Journal* in its early years were women students, while many of those who wrote for the literary columns were so-called Mandarin-Duck-and-Butterfly writers. Those who wrote for *The Chung Hwa Women's Magazine*, on the other hand, were often professionals. In the first issue alone, several scholars contributed articles. They include Lu Shouqian, who wrote "Furen dushen shenghuo wenti" (On the livelihood of women who stay single), which promoted career training for single women. Lu's book on the problem of marriage – *Hunyin xun* (Lessons on marriage) – was later published by Chung Hwa Bookstore in 1917. Ouyang Pucun, the editor of *Zhonghua da zidian* (Chung Hwa encyclopedia dictionary, 1915), contributed "Jiehun wenti zhi yanjiu" (Studies on the problem of marriage), which proposed a marriage system that was a compromise between traditional and modern ideas, and opposed the idea of women's celibacy. Yu Qing'en (1884–1930), who contributed an essay entitled "Ying'er baoyu fa" (Methods of childcare), received a doctorate in public health from the University of Pennsylvania. He was one of the founders of the Chinese Medical Association, editor of the journal *Zhonghua yixue* (Chung Hwa medicine), and also a literary writer. Wu Dingchang (1884–1950), a late Qing official who became a prominent figure in finance in the early Republican era, translated "Deguo xiaoxuexiao jiashike zhong tiaoshi fa" (Culinary instruction in German elementary schools) from Japanese for the journal. In 1926, he became the director for the influential newspaper *Dagongbao*. Finally, Wang Changlu, whose article "Fude" (On female virtue) opens the pages of the founding issue, was a Buddhist scholar who was perhaps better known for having challenged Hu Shi on his notion of filial piety. This list of authors is indeed impressive. What is noteworthy is that many of the authors we see in *The Chung Hwa Women's Magazine* also wrote for other magazines issued by the Chung Hwa Bookstore, but they seldom contributed to other women's magazines.[20]

The male authors of *The Chung Hwa Women's Magazine* were thus mostly scholars and experts. What about women authors? In the first issue, Liang Lingxian, Liang Qichao's daughter, shared her expectations for Chinese women. Gao Junyin, a graduate from the Aiguo Girls' School (Aiguo nüxiao), which was founded by Cai Yuanpei, also contributed an article. She was the niece of Gao Mengdan (1870–1941), who took charge of the publication of textbooks for the Commercial Press, and the wife of Lu Feikui (1886–1941),

---

[20] None of the authors discussed in this passage contributed to *The Ladies' Journal*. The project database (http://womag.uni-hd.de) also shows that they are not authors in any of the four chosen women's magazines (*Nüzi shijie*, *Funü shibao*, *Funü zazhi*, and *Linglong*).

the founder of the Chung Hwa Bookstore. A number of other women authors who were knowledgeable on topics such as international affairs (e.g., the Great War), but whose backgrounds I have not yet been able to trace, also contributed to the journal regularly.[21] What is clear about many of these authors – men or women – is that they came from the same social circle, one that revolved around the Chung Hwa Bookstore.

The magazine highlights the intimacy of relations between women within this Chung Hwa circle. One important example is Yao Yiyun, the addressee of Yi Yu's poem. The late Qing scholar Ye Changchi (1849–1917) once recorded in his diary that someone showed him an epigraph prepared for a Madame Fei. He said,

(The epigraph) was composed by Lü Bicheng of Jingde, handwritten by Yao Yunsu of Tongcheng, and with a seal carved by Wu Zhiying, also of Tongcheng. All three are women . . . Yao's calligraphy is powerful.[22]

In this record, Yao Yunsu is mentioned with two other literary women from Anhui province. All three women were celebrities of their time. However, while Lü and Wu continue to be discussed by scholars of modern Chinese history, Yao is no longer mentioned except in studies on her husband.[23]

From a prominent family, Yao Yunsu was the granddaughter of Yao Ying, one of the central figures in the Tongcheng school of prose writing. She married Fan Dangshi (1854–1905, style name Kentang and Bozi), a famous late Qing poet and scholar from Tongzhou (Nantong, Jiangsu province).[24] Fan associated with Wu Rulun (Wu Zhiying's uncle) of Tongcheng and Chen Sanli (1853–1937), and was highly acknowledged for his achievements in poetry. It was through Wu Rulun's introduction that Fan married Yao Yunsu. Chen Sanli described Fan as a literary man who was interested in national affairs. Having experienced the disastrous events in the late Qing, he grew impatient with traditional scholarship and promoted Western learning.[25] In his last years, he was enthusiastic about the modernization of education, and in 1902, he collaborated with Zhang Jian (1853–1926, late Qing *zhuangyuan*, Republican industrialist and educator) to establish a modern school in their hometown, Nantong. He died with the mission unrealized.

After Fan's death, his widow, Yao Yunsu, was determined to uphold her husband's commitment to modern education. She refused to use the money donated

---

[21] The women authors mentioned here are not to be found in the project database.

[22] Ye Changchi, *Yuandu lu riji chao.*

[23] Lü Bicheng was one of the most famous woman writers of traditional *ci* lyrics in the early twentieth century (see Grace Fong's work and her chapter in this volume). Wu Zhiying was Qiu Jin's friend. With the collaboration of Xu Zihua, she took great risk to bury Qiu's remains beside the West Lake.

[24] For detailed studies on Fan Dangshi, see Wang Yamin, *Nantong Fan shi shiwen shijia*; Wang Chengbin, "Fan Bozi"; Gong Min, "Fan Dangshi."

[25] Chen Sanli, *Sanyuan jingshe.*

to her after she was widowed for personal purposes, and proposed to use it instead to establish a girls' school.[26] She collaborated with Zhang Jian and established China's first school for training women teachers, Nantong Women Teachers' School, in 1905. The school opened in 1906 with Yao as the first principal. She served at that post for fifteen years. In 1919, she was invited to make a contribution to her hometown in Anhui. In 1924, Zhang Jian asked her to return to teaching at the Nantong Women Teachers' School.[27]

Yao's guidelines for women's education are rather conservative by today's standards. In a review of the school's ten years of history, Yao reaffirmed that the goal of the school was to "recover the grandeur of women's education in the ancient Three Dynasties." She encouraged students to "understand the new yet to be cautious about what they chose" and "more importantly, to understand the old and know what to keep." Furthermore, she expected the students who would become teachers to "abide by women's virtue, have no regard for extreme views," "stay away from arrogance, and be chaste, diligent and frugal."[28] She was like many contemporary women of similar background – aggressive and firm in action, and conservative and equally firm in thought.

As this brief review shows, Yao Yunsu was raised in a literary family, influenced by her husband's enthusiasm for education, and dedicated her own life to women's education. As she said about herself, "My late husband always hoped to educate people of his hometown. Heaven cut short his life and he did not live to realize his ideals. Through my determination to do the best that I could to make up for the regrets he left behind, my heart, which was like extinguished ashes after his death, was revived."[29] Yao was greatly respected and loved by students. Several hundred students of the Women Teachers' School and its affiliated elementary school gathered to dance for the celebration of her sixtieth birthday. In a personal letter to the historian Zhang Cixi (1909–1968), Yao reviewed her career as a woman educator, and concluded by saying "all my life, what has delighted me is my students and girlfriends. Students are as good as my own children."[30]

As Yao's remark shows, after losing her husband, she considered friendship to be the most important thing in life. She was a recognized poet herself and often used the conventional function of poetry exchange to express friendship.[31] The publication of poems and letters such as Yao's in journals such as *The Chung Hwa Women's Magazine* made personal friendship public and shareable. While Yao did publish an article on the importance of prenatal

[26] See Xu Ang, "Fan Yao Taifuren"; "Yao Yiyun shiwen."

[27] For a review of the school's history, see Fan Beiqiang, "Nantong nüzi."

[28] Quoted from Chen Xiaofeng, "Yao Yiyun."   [29] Chen Xiaofeng, "Yao Yiyun."

[30] Zhu Deshang, *Sanshi nian*, 141–42; Xu Yishi, *Lingxiao yishi suibi.*

[31] Yao was listed in Wang Yunzhang's record of women poets: "Yao Yiyun of Tongcheng is the wife of Fan Dangshi of Tongzhou. She has a collection entitled *Yunsu xuan shigao*. Famous works of hers are too many to cite here." Wang Yunzhang, *Ranzhi yuyun, juan* 5.

training in the journal, most of her work in the magazine is poetry, especially poems addressing other women.[32] Wu Zhiying was the recipient of one of these poems, which was published in *The Chung Hwa Women's Magazine*.[33] In the piece, Yao stressed the disappointment she and Wu shared concerning the extent of corruption in China. Yao also addressed several poems to Lü Huiru (1875–1925), the principal of the First Women Teachers' School of Jiangsu, who was also originally from Anhui province.[34] Lü was in Nanjing when Yao was in Nantong and the proximity of their schools gave them opportunities for social intercourse.[35] While Yao was a mother-like figure for her students, Huiru, the elder sister of the famous lyric writer Lü Bicheng, was nicknamed "Tiger Lü," and described by her "progressive" students as a stubborn, strict, self-centered, and anti-revolutionary woman. Despite this alleged difference in personality, Yao and Lü evidently belonged to the same community of women educators and shared certain sentiments.

Among those who received poems from Yao Yunsu that were published in *The Chung Hwa Women's Magazine*, Wu Zhiying and Lü Huiru were the most famous. The others were mostly Yao's colleagues at school.[36] The person who received Yao's most passionate friendship was Yi Yu, whose "Recollections of My Girlhood" was discussed above, and who came to teach in the Nantong Women Teachers' School in 1907. Within one year, *The Chung Hwa Women's Magazine* published four of Yao's works that are related to Yi Yu. Issue 1:6 includes a poem entitled "Seeing off Yi Zhonghou who is returning to Longyang."[37] In the preface to the poem, Yao described her friendship with Yi in detail. She says,

I therefore said to Zhonghou, sighing, "I regret very much that I wrote a letter to invite you to travel here to the East, yet you are deserting me before a year's end." Is it your own will to leave? No, it is against your will. Your brother Shifu [Yi Shunding's style name] and my late husband were friends for years, it is a pity that I did not know you then. It is because you have come here to teach that I finally met you. What we value in friendship is to know each other's heart. People gather to talk and drink at parties, but in many cases their interests and tastes do not match. If one is not prosperous in life but finds a true friend who understands without words, it is what we call the true communication

---

[32] Fan Yao Yunsu, "Taijiao."   [33] Fan Yao Yunsu, "Zeng Wu Zhiying nushi."

[34] Fan Yao Yunsu, "Chou Lü Huiru nü xiaozhang"; "He Lü Huiru."

[35] For example, one of Yao's poems indicates that they sojourned together to the Qingliang Mountain and composed poems there. See Fan Yao Yunsu, "Lü Huiru xiaozhang."

[36] For example, there is a poem to Chunqi, who was also teaching at the Nantong Women Teachers' School: Fan Yao Yunsu, "Bu Chunqi." Yao also had a personal relationship with Chunqi, whose husband was Chen Hengke (1876–1923, style name Shizeng). Chen Hengke was Chen Sanli's son, Chen Yinke's brother. At nineteen, he married Fan Xiaochang, Fan Dangshi's daughter with his first wife. In other words, Yao was Chen Hengke's mother-in-law. Another poem was written after the rhyme of Ye Mengqing's poem, while Ye was also a teacher at Yao's school. Fan Yao Yunsu, "Yong bai hehua."

[37] Fan Yao Yunsu, "Zeng Yi Zhonghou."

of feelings. It is a gift from Heaven that cannot be obtained by human force. My mother died when I was young, and I accompanied my father on his official journeys to the west of the Yangzi river. Later I traveled with my husband to the north. I met many *guixiu* (gentry women) of so-called famous families. Some were handsome in talent and honest in disposition, but in terms of what they wrote, said, and did, none of them truly broke the conventional limitations of the female sex. It is impossible to find among them someone like you, my friend, who is generous and unrestrained in mind, kind and honest in words and deeds, able to write beautifully, and well-trained in scholarship, but never conceited. Your nature is that of a true *junzi* (Confucian gentleman). After my husband died, my vitality was almost exhausted. But then I met you. With your generous love, you rid me of the deep sorrows that had surrounded me. Ours is such a wonderful friendship! If we had never met, then nothing could have been done. Now we have met, but have to part in the end! I'd rather that we had never met in the first place! This is why I regret deeply that I have invited you. At this moment the day of your departure is decided, and the north wind is cold and gusty, doubling the sadness of parting. Now off you go! Please take good care. But with my deep sorrows and poor health, I know not about the future. Here's just a few words to express my feelings, and a song to give you.

The preface is narrative in nature, detailing their relationship, and also revealing information about their backgrounds. As both Yao and Yi were from distinguished families, readers could easily identify them. The publication of Yao's parting poem to Yi, especially the preface, was meant to draw readers into their friendship.

Yao Yunsu continued to publish her poems to Yi Yu.[38] In each poem she reemphasized the depth and uniqueness of their friendship, and how it made up for her great loss in life. She suggested that the friendship with Yi was a good, if not better, substitute for conjugal love. For example, she said in one of the poems, "Since I lost my husband, I cut off all attachments with the world. But then suddenly I met you, and my lonely heart was touched."[39] Yao further extended her friendship with Yi Yu to her niece Yi Mengwei. The magazine published four poems by Yao to Mengwei.[40] In these poems Yao not only expressed her admiration for the young talented friend, but also repeatedly stressed her relationship with Mengwei's aunt Yi Yu.

Besides these poems to friends and colleagues, Yao Yunsu also published poems addressing all the teachers and students in her school. In these poems, she wrote in a different tone, as if she was giving a public speech. In her farewell poem to students before she retired from the Nantong Women Teachers' School, she reviewed her career as a principal, stating her views on the triangular model of women, family, and nation, and encouraging students to

---

[38] Fan Yao Yunsu, "Yong Liangdang," "Die yun," "Jihuai."
[39] Fan Yao Yunsu, "Yong Liangdang."
[40] Fan Yao Yunsu, "Wen Zhonghou," "He Yi Mengwei," "Zengbie Yi Mengwei," "He Mengwei."

concentrate on learning.[41] From friends to students and colleagues, and by way of the women's journal, Yao Yunsu managed to build and expand an intimate female community.

The case of Yao Yunsu and Yi Yu is not a singular example. Many of the frequent female contributors to women's magazines, such as Liu Sheng, Zhu Zongliang, Shi Shuyi, Guo Jianren (1869–1940), and Jiang Yingqing, were also professional teachers. Like Yao Yunsu, they published works in women's magazines, not only to declare their views on public affairs, but also to express personal feelings that were particular to them as educators. As educators, they were able to transcend the family boundary of relationships, build a community with students and colleagues, and expand this community to include readers of the magazines. In this way, the public space of women's magazines could also serve as a field for the voicing of personal, intimate feelings.

It is not easy to explain why *The Chung Hwa Women's Magazine* was outlived by *The Ladies' Journal*. Although the two magazines were published by the two most influential publishers at the time, and seemed to address similar questions and appeal to the same readership, they were subtly and significantly different. As I have tried to demonstrate in my readings, not only was the question of education emphasized in *The Chung Hwa Women's Magazine*, but also the personal lives of female educators were exposed through the publication of personal letters and exchanges of poems, and a sense of women's community and intimate personal feelings emerges from its pages. This does not, I would argue, reflect a conscious editorial strategy deliberately employed to attract more women readers. Rather, it was the result of a small group of women authors trying to reach for each other in the imaginary space created by the women's magazine. In the late imperial period, women's space was confined, but writing women still remained in contact with one another by sending family members and friends poems and letters. These works were supposed to be personal and private, but often became aesthetic objects for general appreciation, as they were integrated into a print culture context and situated within a wider context of social change. Women authors who exchanged poems and letters in the pages of the magazines were, to a certain extent, continuing this late imperial tradition. The difference between earlier and later practices is that they found what they thought to be a better vehicle and a more open space for sharing their intimate feelings not just among themselves but also with others. Evidently, these women authors wished to expand, at least on the psychological level, the sense of intimacy they shared with close colleagues to other female educators and students who composed the readership. Judging from the relatively short publication span of *The Chung Hwa Women's Magazine*, however, the imaginary community did not grow as they had probably wished.

---

[41] Fan Yao Yunsu, "Zhiyan."

As a textual space, I would argue, *The Chung Hwa Women's Magazine* might have suggested a closed circle of women writers, too closed to be able to offer interpersonal intimacy to real but anonymous readers. This does not undercut the important and unique role that *The Chung Hwa Women's Magazine* played in fostering close ties among women within its community. *The Ladies' Journal*, on the other hand, seemed to be a more open space, which enabled it to engage a broader community of (women) readers.

Room for Improvement: The Ideal of the
       Educational Home in *The Ladies' Journal*

Maria af Sandeberg

> Evidence shows that the quality of the material home environment directly
> influences children's lives. At the time, I therefore attempted, to the best of
> my ability, to change those aspects of the material environment which might
> influence their lives, in the direction of beauty. I added beautiful equipment
> everywhere, in order for them to receive beneficial education in this beautiful
> environment, and through an imperceptible influence shape their noble
> and exquisite feelings and character. I think all home teachers need to pay
> particular consideration to this matter.
>
> Liu Heng, "Yi ge shujiaqi zhong jiating jiaxue sheshi de jingguo" (My
experience of arrangements for home teaching during the summer holidays)

When Miss Liu Heng wrote in *Funü zazhi – The Ladies' Journal* in 1931 about
her methods for teaching her younger sister and nephew, her assumptions
were that the home was a crucial site for education, and that the physical
environment impacted the formation of intellect and character. These beliefs,
which had been developed in *The Ladies' Journal* (1915–1931) over several
years, were characteristic of two themes of Republican Chinese women's
magazines: the theme of *jiating jiaoyu* (home education), which was about the
significance and methods of education imparted to children in the home, and
the theme of the *meili de zhuzhai* (beautiful house/home), which concerned
the material aspects of home improvement.

Texts that participated in these discourses on child development and on
home improvement in *The Ladies' Journal* combine to make up what I call the
"educational home," a domestic ideal characterized by nationalism, a psychological conceptualization of human nature, and middle-class consumerism. It
can be seen as part of what Helen Schneider calls the "happy family ideology"
formulated by the Chinese women's press in the first half of the twentieth
century. Descriptions of the educational home stressed the role of the bourgeois
housewife in the transmission and implementation of modern knowledge. It
also closely linked family life to the health of the nation, always assuming the
domestic space to be of public interest and political significance.[1]

---

[1] Schneider, *Keeping the Nation's House*, 20–56.

The fact that the ideal of the educational home was articulated in a women's magazine does not indicate that it was of concern to women only. In China's Republican period the women's magazine was not so much defined by "explicitly positioning its readers as 'women,'" as had been the case in nineteenth-century Britain,[2] as by its use of "woman" as a rubric under which various concerns about the gendered aspects of modern life could be voiced. The way editorials address both men and women, and the fact that a great number of letters and essays from readers were sent to the magazine by male contributors, indicate that its readership included, and was meant to include, men as well as women.

It is through horizontal readings of *The Ladies' Journal* as one multi-authored text that the educational home becomes visible, as this ideal was never explicitly theorized by any one writer at any one time. Materials in a variety of genres – prescriptive articles, advertisements, images, and essays sent in by readers – combine to create a rich and nuanced picture of the home as a pedagogical and aesthetic space. Horizontal readings of, say, texts about home decorating and articles on children's psychology appearing in one and the same issue reveal the complex domestic ideal with which a reader of the magazine would have been confronted.

In this essay, I will put these horizontal readings in perspective, by also engaging in a vertical reading of the magazine, paying close attention to changes over time. Such a reading allows me to chart how the themes of home education, the beautiful house, and the educational home developed and interacted throughout the history of *The Ladies' Journal*.

Home education had long been a central concern of the Chinese women's press. Late Qing and early Republican women's magazines promoted the idea that educated mothers excelled at molding their children into good citizens and used this to bolster their argument for the education of women.[3] In *Funü shibao* (The women's Eastern times), writers made this argument by stressing the importance of early education[4] and the decisive influence of mothers on their children.[5] The theme of home education runs through the entirety of *The Ladies' Journal*. The Montessori method, for example, was introduced to the readers of *The Ladies' Journal* as early as 1915.[6] By the second phase of the magazine (1919–1925), such modern approaches to education were passionately endorsed by a large number of *The Ladies' Journal* contributors.

---

[2] Beetham, *A Magazine of Her Own?*, ix.
[3] Judge, *Precious Raft*; Schneider, *Keeping the Nation's House*.
[4] Zhao Yuan, "Jiating jiaoyu lun," 24.
[5] Chu Qizhen, "Jiating jiaoyu"; Ye Tao, "Ertong zhi guannian"; Zhao Yuan, "Jiating jiaoyu lun."
[6] Fei Zhi, "Mengtaisuoli jiaoyu fa."

The beautiful house, on the other hand, was a later interest of the Chinese women's press. Although there was plenty of discussion in *The Women's Eastern Times* and the early *Ladies' Journal* of what activities women should undertake in their homes, the shape and form of the home environment itself were seldom explored, and there were no images of decorative household objects, interiors, or residential houses. From 1925, articles on architecture and on interior and garden design began to find their way into *The Ladies' Journal*. After the change in editorship in 1926, art became a favorite topic of the magazine, and in the second half of the 1920s, *The Ladies' Journal's* ideal housewife was expected to transform the home into an "artistic paradise" where good taste was evident in every detail of the interior.[7]

The increased importance of aesthetic aspects of the home continued in the Chinese women's press, into the 1930s and long after the demise of *The Ladies' Journal*. In the 1930s, the women's magazine *Linglong – Linloon Magazine* featured photographs of interiors in the latest art deco designs. Magazines on home life such as *Jiating xingqi* (Home weekly) and *Jiating zazhi – Happy Home* advised readers on how to tastefully decorate their homes,[8] and the art magazine *Meishu shenghuo* (Art and life, 1934–1937) targeted the middle-class female consumer in its promotion of Chinese design and technology.[9]

The Impressionable Child

The theme of home education in *The Ladies' Journal* resonated with the "unprecedented explosion in discourse about children, childhood and child-development"[10] taking place in China between 1917 and 1937. During its second or New Culture phase, in particular, many contributors to *The Ladies' Journal* advocated a child-centered approach to education, directly influenced by foreign educators, psychologists, and philosophers such as Maria Montessori, Edward Thorndike, Ellen Key, and John Dewey, and inspired by the educational pioneers of the Romantic period in Europe: Jean-Jacques Rousseau, Johan Heinrich Pestalozzi, and Friedrich Wilhelm August Fröbel.

Adopting a child-centered approach meant respecting the child's unique characteristics, and adapting pedagogical methods accordingly, a stance presented as a departure from a traditional view of children as inferior versions of adults. Traditional family hierarchy was challenged from the evolutionist position that children, as the future of the species, actually mattered more than their parents. This idea was represented in *The Ladies' Journal* through references to or translations of the work of the Swedish educator Ellen Key

---

[7] Jiang Xingde, "Wei xin zhufu."   [8] Dikötter. *Things Modern.*
[9] Waara, "Invention, Industry, Art," 75.   [10] Jones, "The Child as History," 700.

and the Japanese politician Abe Isoo, for example.[11] In *The Ladies' Journal*, this transnational modernizing discourse was adapted to target the Chinese "traditional" family in particular.

The child-centered approach to education demanded that the nature of the child be explored. Educational advice was underpinned by knowledge of the child through the modern disciplines of biology and psychology. In *The Ladies' Journal*, parents were encouraged to pay attention to psychological and physiological traits of children such as various instincts, curiosity, love of play, and need for physical activity. These characteristics were natural and physically present in the brain and body, and as they could not be eradicated, they should instead be put to educational use.

One instinct, the propensity for imitation, received particular attention.[12] This characteristic tied in with traditional notions of education through the emulation of exemplars, but was reimagined in scientific terms. Bai Ben, in 1926, defined imitation as "the child's reaction to an external stimulus, where the reaction resembles the stimulus in form and quality." If parents are aware of the nature of imitation, Bai Ben argued, they may put this natural disposition of children to use in their education, and follow the example of Mencius' mother, who repeatedly moved in order to avoid negative influences on her son.[13] If the outside stimulus was repeated, the action in question was likely to turn into a habit, another cornerstone in the psychological conception of children. In 1922, Wang Yigang had explained habits in terms of reflex paths in the brain.[14] If a habit was to be changed, a new neural pathway had to be laid down, and it was the parents' job to provide the stimuli that would effect the change.

Writers showed most interest in those characteristics of the child that allowed education. Despite the importance granted to the child's personality and imagination and the charms of childhood, contributors to *The Ladies' Journal* dwelled less on the appreciation of the child in itself, and more on the opportunities for education that its special characteristics afforded. Activity, curiosity, and imitativeness were translated into "educability" and "plasticity."[15] The child as psychological being was above all impressionable.

This meant that children were susceptible to teaching not only through direct moral and intellectual instruction, but also through subtle emotional and physical influences. Such influences could be exerted with the help of educational commodities suited to children's special characteristics: children's literature and toys. The novel idea that children required specially designed reading materials was an important ingredient in a child-centered education.[16] The

---

[11] Selu, "Ailun Kai"; Jiang Yan, "Ertong benwei yu minben zhuyi." For a discussion of translations of Abe Isoo's work in *Funü shibao*, see Judge in this volume.

[12] Qian Yusun, "Guanyu ertong benneng"; Zhu Zhidao, "Wo jiang zenmeyang zuo fumuqin."

[13] Bai Ben, "He wei mofang?"   [14] Wang Yigang, "Ertong e xiguan jiaozhengfa."

[15] Xie Yinian, "Ertong shiqi de zhongyao."   [16] Farquhar, *Children's Literature in China.*

fairy tale, for example, was considered ideal for younger children, because it spoke to the child's "psychology" at a specific developmental stage. Toys, like fairy tales, contributed to the pedagogical influence of the home environment, as long as they were made to suit the child's psychology and biology. Articles in *The Ladies' Journal* between the 1920s and the 1930s advised parents on how to choose toys, recommending those that were attractive, hygienic, and educational.[17]

The task of choosing toys and story books for children was not to be under-taken lightly. Susan Fernsebner has described how toys, as objects capable of shaping the future citizenry of China, "were invested with a salvational power by educators and entrepreneurs alike."[18] Parents were told not only to be on guard against dirt and poisonous materials, but also that grotesque, supersti-tious tales of ghosts and goblins would damage children's fragile psyches, and that "immoral" objects such as mahjong tiles (linked to gambling) would corrupt them. Contributors to *The Ladies' Journal* who supported the goals of the National Products Movement expressed their unease over the influx of foreign toys.[19] Xu Yasheng, in 1929, suggested that the very foreignness of imported goods might imperceptibly corrupt the impressionable youth of China, thereby damaging more than the national economy: "children's toys afford children opportunities to gain knowledge, however, if foreigners were to put a lot of harmful knowledge into the toys, then will not many children, who have bearing upon the destiny of China, be used by another country?"[20]

When it came to the pedagogical equipment of the educational home, *The Ladies' Journal* offered more than just advice. In the early 1920s it provided examples of children's literature, such as translations of H.C. Andersen's fairy tales, and served as an advertising platform for the Commercial Press's many periodicals for children and young people. For parents in need of ideas for outdoor and indoor games, The Commercial Press apparently provided a series of 15 booklets called *Ertong youxi yongshu* (Children's games how-to), as advertised in *The Ladies' Journal* 4, 1926.[21] The magazine also advertised the line of "educational" toys that The Commercial Press itself produced and that could be bought through a catalogue from 1918.[22] These toys included building blocks and other construction toys, numerical games, cube puzzles, tin toys, chess games, sports equipment, and handicraft materials, and were

---

[17] Chaoran, "Jiaoyu zinü de liyu;" Xie Yinian, "Ertong shiqi."

[18] Fernsebner, "A People's Playthings," 270.

[19] Ding Xilun, "Dui ertong wanju de yijian;" For an in-depth study of the National Products Move-ment, see Gerth, *China Made*.

[20] Xu Yasheng, "Ertong wanju," 16.

[21] The page with this advertisement can be found in the "Chinese Women's Magazines" database at http://kjc-sv013.kjc.uni-heidelberg.de/frauenzeitschriften/public/magazine/page_content .php?magazin_id=4&year=1926&issue_id=492&issue_number=004&img_issue_page=95.

[22] Jones, *Developmental Fairy Tales*, 122–24.

advertised as "educational," suited to children's "psychology," and, crucially, as domestic products[23] (Figure 9.1).

The Father or Mother I Aim to Become

"Imitation is the natural tendency of the child, but how to make the child, through imitation, turn into a citizen sound in body and mind, is nonetheless the responsibility of its parents," wrote Bai Ben in 1926.[24] Considering the centrality of the child to the future of the nation, bringing up and educating children was not simply a private matter. Throughout the 1920s, self-styled experts wrote authoritative pieces in *The Ladies' Journal* impressing upon parents the great responsibility that child-rearing entailed. Essays solicited from readers echoed this sentiment. In a collection of reader's essays entitled "The Father/Mother I Aim to Become" from November 1925, at the beginning of *The Ladies' Journal's* third phase, twelve parents and prospective parents agreed that having children meant creating persons for humankind and citizens for the nation, and was not to be attempted for selfish reasons. Previous generations had wrongly believed that having children required no specialized knowledge, but modern parents needed to be well-versed in educational methods, children's psychology, and hygiene.[25] It was therefore advisable to read a number of parenting manuals before the birth of one's first child, wrote Liu Xiaobo, who recommended *The Training of the Child* from 1912 by the English educator Gustav Spiller.[26]

The writers of these articles appeared to consider themselves and their spouses entirely responsible for their children, rather than sharing this burden with other relatives. Their attitude accords with the New Culturalist project of family reform.[27] It is also consistent with most prescriptive articles on child-rearing in *The Ladies' Journal*, which assumed the ideal family to be a "small" or conjugal family (*xiao jiating*). Although most of *The Ladies' Journal's* articles on child-rearing address parents jointly, they usually accord women the larger share of the responsibility. A 1921 article that outlined the organization of the modern "small" family represented the different tasks of family members in the form of a diagram. Whereas the father provided financial support and represented family interests, the mother was responsible for all aspects of housework, including managing the household economy and

---

[23] See for example an advertisement in 1, 1926 for The Commercial Press's toys in our database: http://kjc-sv013.kjc.uni-heidelberg.de/frauenzeitschriften/public/magazine/page_content.php?magazin_id=4&year=1926&issue_id=489&issue_number=001&img_issue_page=1.

[24] Bai Ben, "He wei mofang?"   [25] Xu Xuewen, "Wo jiang zenmeyang zuo fumuqin?"

[26] Liu Xiaobo, "Wo jiang zenmeyang zuo fumuqin?"; Spiller, *The Training of the Child*

[27] For an analysis of the ideal of the small family see Glosser, *Chinese Visions*.

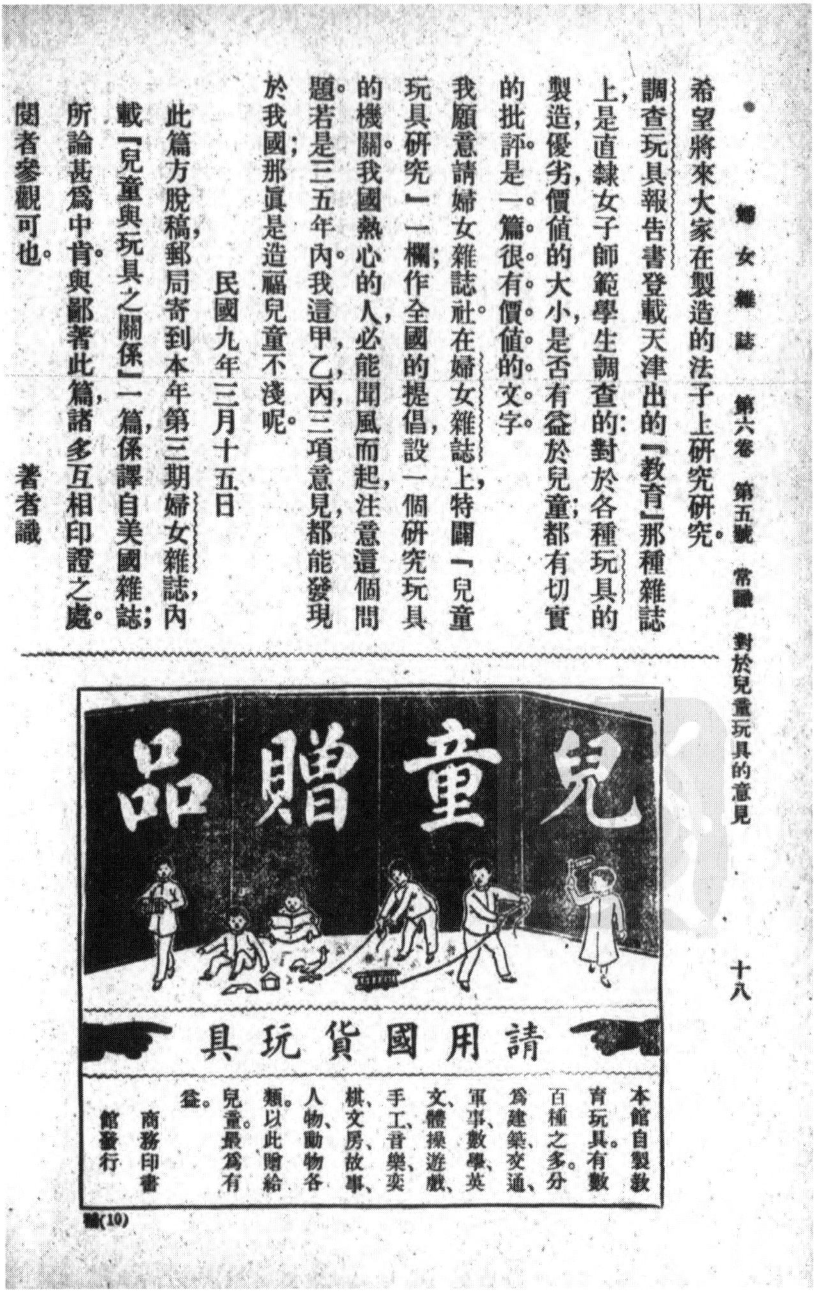

婦女雜誌　第六卷　第五號　常識　對於兒童玩具的意見

希望將來大家在製造的法子上研究研究。

調查玩具報告書登載天津出的『教育』那種雜誌上,是直隸女子師範學生調查的:對於各種玩具的製造優劣價值的大小是否有益於兒童都有切實的批評。是一篇很有價值的文字

我願意請婦女雜誌社在婦女雜誌上特闢『兒童玩具研究』一欄作全國的提倡設一個研究玩具的機關我國熱心的人必能聞風而起,注意這個問題若是三五年內我這甲乙丙三項意見都能發現於我國那眞是造福兒童不淺呢。

民國九年三月十五日

此篇方脫稿郵局寄到本年第三期婦女雜誌,內載『兒童與玩具之關係』一篇係譯自美國雜誌,所論甚爲中肯與鄙著此篇諸多互相印證之處。閱者參觀可也。

著者識

十八

Fig. 9.1 Advertisement for educational toys, *The Ladies' Journal* 6:5 (1920), 67

the children's education.[28] Many later articles in *The Ladies' Journal* continued to depict mothers as the major influence on their offspring.[29] Among the twelve contributors to "The Father/Mother I Aim to Become," two writers, one of whom presents herself as female, argued that mothers carry the greater responsibility for children's upbringing. Motherhood is a woman's duty, and this duty makes her important, claimed Yiwen.[30] Miaoyi defended the ideal of *xianqi liangmu* (virtuous wife, good mother) and argued that the good mother (*liangmu*) was uniquely valuable and could not be replaced with a "good father" (*liangfu*).[31] Several of the male contributors, however, either discussed joint parental responsibilities or foregrounded the responsibilities of fathers.[32] Contributor Ouling and his wife had together decided on a gendered division of responsibilities: he was in charge of the children's education, she of feeding and clothing them, while both shared responsibility for the formation of the children's moral character.[33]

Mothers and fathers alike were faced with the difficult task of navigating between indulgence and strictness. Joan Judge has analyzed how in late Qing biographies of women an earlier ideal of the *cimu*, the "loving" or "kind mother," was often caricatured as the ignorant mother who spoiled her children, unlike the modern ideal of the knowledgeable "good wife and virtuous mother" (*liangqi xianmu*) and the responsible "mother of citizens" (*guomin zhi mu*).[34] Most of the essays on "The Father/Mother I Aim to Become" warned against spoiling one's child. Ruiyun's contribution to the call for papers, a short story entitled "It Is Too Late for Me to Repent," warned of the consequences of *ni'ai* or "overindulgent love" through the fictional depiction of an indulgent mother whose son squanders the family fortune.[35]

Strictness, however, was seen as the hallmark of a traditional Chinese educational method ill suited to children's' psychology. Children who acted in the correct way out of fear of punishment failed to internalize the moral codes behind their actions. Furthermore, the fear and hatred felt by the punished child drove a wedge between child and parent, undermining the psychological processes of imitation, assimilation, and identification through which children learned. Several of the essays came close to the child-centered approach in their solutions to the dilemma. They called for fewer punishments, and advocated formulating instructions to children as positive encouragement rather than

---

[28] Bao Zhen and Tai Guangdian, "Xin jiating."   [29] Dan Yuan, "Mujiao de shili."
[30] Yiwen, "Wo jiang zenmeyang zuo fumuqin."
[31] Miaoyi, "Wo jiang zenmeyang zuo fumuqin."
[32] Wu Zuxiang, "Wo jiang zenmeyang zuo fumuqin"; Zhu Zhidao, "Wo jiang zenmeyang zuo fumuqin"; Lin Wenfang, "Wo jiang zenmeyang zuo fumuqin."
[33] Ouling, "Wo jiang zenmeyang zuo fumuqin."   [34] Judge, *Precious Raft*, 108.
[35] Ruiyun, "Wo jiang zenmeyang zuo fumuqin." The same theme was developed two years later in another short story; see Chen Bochui, "Ta de binggen."

negative bans or threats. The child was to be shown respect, and teaching through example was considered much more efficient than lecturing.[36] In the period from 1920 to 1925 "love" had been a favorite topic of *The Ladies' Journal*, and Ellen Key's idealized perception of it had provided discussions about love with an air of theoretical authority.[37] In the third phase of the magazine, love was less theorized but remained a major theme, with a special issue on the topic published in 1926.[38] To some of the contributors, familial ties were no longer maintained by a sense of duty or gratitude but by emotional affinity, and the psychological processes of assimilation and suggestion through which children learned were powered by love, which, according to the female teacher Hong Jingfang, was "a great force without which nothing can be accomplished."[39] In spite of the dangers of indulgence, not only the "kind mother" (*cimu*) but also the "kind father" (*cifu*) was depicted as a positive role model by Wu Zuxiang.[40]

The contributors to the collection of articles entitled "The Father/Mother I Aim to Become" did not portray themselves as consumers. To the contrary: most of them presented the modern parent as an idealist prepared to forego material wealth for the sake of his or her children, and by extension, for the sake of the nation's future. They wrote about frugality, thrift, and self-sacrifice. However, in their accounts we find hints that parents had to carry out their responsibilities not only as providers, teachers, and moral exemplars, but also through consumer choice. Parents were faced with a series of consumer decisions to make on behalf of their children, and some of the contributors volunteered their advice on the choice of parenting manuals, on what color of children's clothing to buy, on whether to feed cow's milk or breast milk substitute to one's baby,[41] and on the importance of buying toys and children's literature.[42] Mothers were asked to create a stimulating home environment where the child's moral, emotional, intellectual, and aesthetic faculties may develop and told how to beautify their homes in order to improve their children's love of beauty.[43]

[36] Liu Xiaobo, "Wo jiang zenmeyang zuo fumuqin"; Hong Jingfang, "Wo jiang zenmeyang zuo fumuqin"; Yiwen, "Wo jiang zenmeyang zuo fumuqin"; Zhu Zhidao, "Wo jiang zenmeyang zuo fumuqin."

[37] For the reception of Ellen Key in *The Ladies' Journal*, see Chiang, "Womanhood." See also Hsu in this volume.

[38] For a discussion of the special issue on "Love," see Haiyan Lee, *Revolution of the Heart*, 158–62.

[39] Hong Jingfang, "Wo jiang zenmeyang zuo fumuqin"; Zhu Zhidao, "Wo jiang zenmeyang zuo fumuqin."

[40] Wu Zuxiang, "Wo jiang zenmeyang zuo fumuqin." Wu may have been identical to the differently spelled fiction writer Wu Zuxiang (1908–1994), in which case he was only seventeen years old when discussing his plans for fatherhood.

[41] Liu Xiaobo, "Wo jiang zenmeyang zuo fumuqin"; Zhu Zhidao, "Wo jiang zenmeyang zuo fumuqin."

[42] Wu Zuxiang, "Wo jiang zenmeyang zuo fumuqin."

[43] Miaoyi, "Wo jiang zenmeyang zuo fumuqin"; Yiwen, "Wo jiang zenmeyang zuo fumuqin."

The almost miraculous influence of one educational commodity, the educational poster, was described by one Ouling.[44] He and his wife wished their two daughters and three sons to achieve a middle school education, and they believed that they as parents were ultimately responsible for the success of their children. Once all five children were in school, however, it turned out that although the two eldest were quiet and studious, the youngest two were lazy and the middle one, a boy, so disruptive he came close to getting expelled from school. Admonitions and reprimands had no effect. The parents did not, however, abandon their belief that every child can be educated. Consequently, they implemented two new pedagogical methods: first, they stopped scolding the offending children and used the strategy of positive reinforcement. Second, they hung a number of educational posters around the house. Soon the lazy kids were working harder, and the unruly son calmed down. At the time of writing, Ouling's older children had entered university, while the three younger ones, who had been failing previously, were getting good grades in middle school.

The Beautiful House

Beginning in 1925 with Zou Shengwen's garden design series, which ran intermittently from the fifth issue of 1925 to the fourth issue of 1927, *The Ladies' Journal* turned to a more spatial imagination and a more aesthetic approach to domesticity. The relevance of art to the housewife reader was demonstrated by articles that linked the artistic with the feminine,[45] and articles on artistic approaches to interior design and household objects. Interior and garden design were presented as means of expressing one's own character or artistic sensibilities[46] and of establishing a style that distinguished the educated, urban middle class from other strata of society through its modernity, individuality, and restraint. Li Yuyi, a frequent contributor to *The Ladies' Journal* on topics such as art and architecture, advocated in 1928 a "painterly" (*tuhuahua*) style of decorating, which avoided both the crudeness of traditional rustic styles and the ostentation of the urban rich.[47]

Occasionally, advocates of home improvement found support in biological and psychological discourses. In 1926, Li Songyao argued that the urge to beautify one's home was a hallmark of evolution: the more advanced the animal, the more concern it showed for its nest.[48] The home environment, and particularly its color scheme, had a direct impact on the psychology of its inhabitants. The comical belief that Chinese married couples quarreled a

---

[44] Ouling, "Wo jiang zenmeyang zuo fumuqin."   [45] Zhu Yin, "Nüzi aimei."

[46] Zou Shengwen, "Xiyang zaoyuan fa," 170–71; Li Yuyi, "Congsu."

[47] Li Yuyi, "Congsu." (Li Yuyi is also mentioned by Doris Sung in this volume.)

[48] Li Songyao, "Jia nei meizhuang."

宅　住　的　麗　美

「題周的住」刊月本召巻

Fig. 9.2 "A beautiful dwelling," *The Ladies' Journal* 13:1 (1927), 1

lot because the reds and purples of Chinese interior decorating impacted their mood apparently contained a kernel of truth. This prompted Li Songyao to recommend whites, greens, and pastels for their calming effect. In his later article, Li Yuyi agreed with his view that colors influence our mood and behavior, and added that depression, marital disharmony, or unruliness in children may originate with bad home decorating.

Domestic space was reimagined as quantifiable and transformable through the use of photographs, plans, and maps. Shaoying's 1927 description of an ideal house for a nuclear family of "the ordinary middle class" was heralded by a full-page color picture entitled "beautiful house," published in the previous issue (see Figure 9.2), and complemented by maps of the layout of the garden and interior of the same house (see Figure 9.3).[49] These images were originally from an American house plan catalog, where the house in question was described as designed in the Spanish style popular in the western United States.[50] It may, however, have been obtained by Shaoying via an American women's magazine, as these had frequently featured such plans since the turn of the century.[51]

In the eleventh issue of 1926, the magazine published a collection of articles solicited from the readership on the topic of "The ideal dwelling," in which eight readers described their ideal living arrangements, focusing on the material aspects of the home. If we compare their visions with those of the winners of a 1922 readers' architecture competition in the American women's

[49] Shaoying, "Zhu de wenti."   [50] Carr & Johnston Co., *Practical Homes.*
[51] Dethier, "The Spirit of Progressive Reform."

—第十三卷第二號—　（二）

北極天氣寒冷，終年聚冰，人民藉冰堆成房屋，以爲住宅。熱帶氣候炎熱茂林稠木叢生，人民卽樹蔭爲室，這種因地不同以致大生差異的住宅本篇不爲詳及了。此外最影響住宅的，就如個人的經濟。經濟富裕的自然可以造高樓大廈盡建築的能事。反之如江濱草棚亦有無數人在內消磨個人的人生。

有上各點的不同，那麼對於住宅這個問題，不能一槪而論是無容細述的了。此刻我們不去將各地各處各式的住宅來加評點，但就通常中產階級的人最低限度容許的房子來建議一種。好在現在組織新式小家庭的日多，所以對於小家庭夫婦及子女數人能住的屋子略說一二。

住宅不僅是逃避風雨，還是家人親屬敍天倫樂事之所，所以選擇住宅，當適乎衛生，簡便應用，以及能使人感覺美滿愉快啓發人生的樂趣。這是我們對於住宅最緊要的要求。

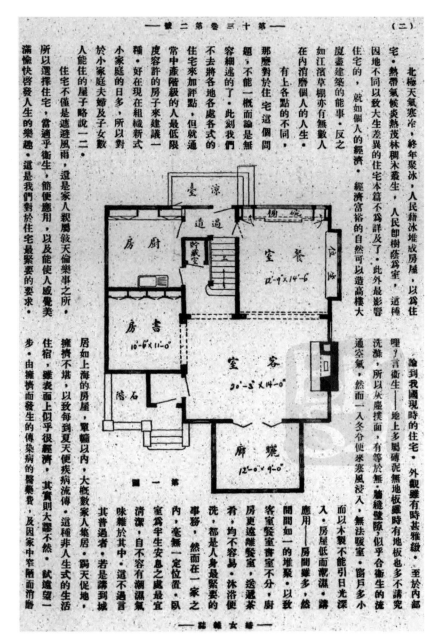

論到我國現時的住宅，外觀雖有時甚雅緻，至於內部哩？言衛生——地上多鋪磚泥無地板簷時有地板也多不講究洗滌，所以灰塵撲面，有等於無，牆縫壁隙似乎合衛生的流通空氣，然而一人冬令便來塞風浸入，無法暖室，窗戶多小而以木製不能引日光深入。房屋低而載濕，諸應用——房間雖多，然間間如一的堆聚，以致客室餐室書室不分，廚房間遠離雜餐室，送選茶看，均不容易，沐浴便洗，都是人身最緊要的事務，然而在一家之內，毫無一定位置。臥室爲半生安息之處最宜清潔，自不容有潮濕氣味難於其中，這不過言其普過者，若是講到城

居如上海的房屋，羣驅以內，大概數家人集居，鬮天促地，擁擠不堪，以致每到夏天便疾病流傳，這種非人生式的生活住宿，雖表面上似乎很經濟，其實則大謬不然，試遠望一步。由簇擁而發生的傳染病的醫藥費，及因家中窄隘而消磨

婦女雜誌

Fig. 9.3 Map of the first floor of the "beautiful dwelling," *The Ladies' Journal* 13:2 (1927), 41

magazine *The Ladies' Home Journal*, we find that whereas the American contributors are making realistic and practical plans, and in some cases send in the plans of houses they have already built,[52] the Chinese plans are more utopian, and include collective villages and extravagant "artistic paradises." The Chinese readers pay less attention to practical matters such as building materials, plumbing, and cleaning. Although one contributor is lucky enough to own a plot of land on which to build, for the most part, their plans are nothing more than "castles in the air," as one contributor puts it.[53] Most of them share, with the American would-be architects, the ideal of a Western-style suburban single-family home, a self-contained unit surrounded by gardens, and with clearly demarcated rooms labeled according to their function. However, the contextualization of this ideal house is different in each case. The Chinese accounts contrast the functionality and hygiene of the modern Westernized house with the shortcomings of the sprawling complexes of "traditional" Chinese houses. These are so dark and damp that entering a bedroom is like going into "Hell,"[54] the courtyards and empty spaces attract snakes, scorpions, and millipedes,[55] and if, like contributor Wanfang, you are unlucky enough to share your family compound with twelve other households within the extended family, you will find yourselves living amidst excrement from some five dozen chickens.[56] Chinese houses, these writers complain, are wasteful in their use of space, rooms have fancy names but no specific functions, and indoor and garden space are confused.[57]

In the American house plans, the most important room is the kitchen, but in the Chinese ones this is not the case. Indeed, two contributors altogether neglected to equip their houses with kitchens or dining rooms.[58] Instead, the contributors dwell on the physical exercises taking place outside and the cultural pursuits going on indoors. The gardens are equipped with everything needed for a healthy life: bicycles, areas for ballgames, and in one case, even a pond used as a swimming pool. Inside, whole rooms are devoted to art or cultural activities: there are music rooms, with collections of Western and Chinese musical instruments, there are picture rooms where paintings and posters are displayed, and there are reading rooms full of books. In one house, such a reading room doubles as a scientific laboratory.[59] The *huikeshi* (reception room), which is an important room in almost all the house designs, is sometimes also equipped with musical instruments and reading materials.

---

[52] Brinckloe, "The Home I'd Like to Have."
[53] Junyue, "Lixiang de zhuzhai."   [54] Meng Ping, "Lixiang de zhuzhai."
[55] Ke San, "Lixiang de zhuzhai."   [56] Wanfang, "Lixiang de zhuzhai."
[57] Ke San, "Lixiang de zhuzhai;" Meng Ping, "Lixiang de zhuzhai"; Yicheng, "Lixiang de zhuzhai."
[58] Helin, "Lixiang de zhuzhai;" Baosun, "Lixiang de zhuzhai."
[59] Junyue, "Lixiang de zhuzhai."

Some contributors clearly designate spaces belonging to children: there are children's bedrooms, sandpits, and spaces in the garden where children can play with bikes and hoops. Others have educational activities take place in other parts of the house, often in what could be considered the women's space. Meng Ping's "work room" is primarily intended for his wife's use, but will be decorated with educational posters for the sake of the children, who "in accordance with their psychology" will want to keep close to their mother.[60] Regardless of whether separate spaces are set aside for them, children are to receive a beneficial influence from the ideal dwelling. Helin writes, "I am convinced that children raised in this Paradise would most certainly acquire good habits such as the love of cleanliness, the love of exercise, the love of work, the love of art and so on."[61] "How strong and lively the children are, who live in this house!" Junyue exclaims. "Those innocent souls, when they are looking at the flowers, they feel as if they themselves have turned into flowers!"[62]

Unlike the kitchen-centered houses in the American competition, the Chinese ideal dwellings, with their emphasis on cultural activities and healthy influences, were educational homes. Here, personal fantasies of material comfort and aesthetic pleasures were justified through the ennobling influence of the ideal dwelling upon its inhabitants, young and old. All the activities of the ideal dwelling were purposeful and served to strengthen the body and sharpen the intellect. In the words of one of these articles, "with so many things to do there will be no need for useless pleasures."[63]

The Home Library

The seventh issue of 1927 was the issue of *The Ladies' Journal* where the educational home truly came into its own. The issue was themed to fit in with the season, focusing on the pastimes and dangers of summer. In eight solicited articles on the theme of summer studies, students tell of their experiences of, and plans for, the summer holidays. In these short pieces the ideal learning environment emerges as a place that is spacious, airy, well lit, close to nature, and equipped with library, playroom, and toys.[64]

Two different articles in the same issue elaborated on the idea of a "home library," a strictly organized space modeled upon school and public libraries. In the first article, Chu Hui planned out this space in minute detail (see Figure 9.4).[65] The home library, he explains, should be housed in a relatively large room in the part of the house that is furthest away from the bedrooms, to avoid the noise of crying babies, and the kitchen, to avoid cooking smells. A

---

[60] Meng Ping, "Lixiang de zhuzhai."   [61] Helin, "Lixiang de zhuzhai."
[62] Junyue, "Lixiang de zhuzhai."   [63] Baosun, "Lixiang de zhuzhai."
[64] Li Rongzhang, "Shujia nei"; Yu Jing, "Shujia nei."   [65] Chu Hui, "Jiating tushushi wenti."

（五九）　　　　—家庭圖書室問題—

然他不可缺少的。如房屋過大就太寬，房屋過小就太窄，從個人的經驗，一間大些的屋，恰是不寬不窄。

（如藏書不敷，可以改為兩間或三間。）至於方向，則以南向為上，多溫而夏涼，光線充足；若不能南向，則以坐西北而向東南者為佳。

（C）設備和佈置　圖書室的設備和佈置，本是很費經濟的事。今從最經濟的辦法把各種設備和佈置法分述如下。

（1）窗戶　書室的窗戶，宜開於室之南北兩面，門宜用半截大玻璃式，窗亦須用大玻璃製造，宜高宜闊，務使室內全體光明。窗戶之面積，須佔全地板五分之二。窗外不可有障礙之物，如直射之光，須設窗幛以避之。

（2）書廚和閱報架　書廚的大小，常以書室的大小藏書的多少為比例。創辦時最好先做四具，（佈置法如下圖）式樣為長方形，

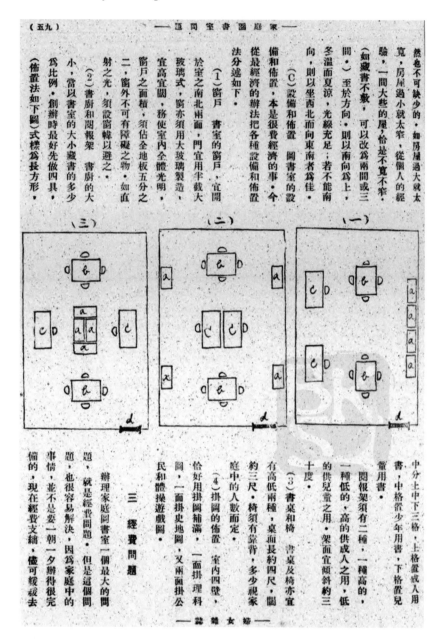

中分上中下三格，上格置成人用書，中格置少年用書，下格置兒童用書。閱報架須有二種，一種高的，一種低的。高的供成人之用，低的供兒童之用。架面宜傾斜約三十度。

（3）書桌和椅　書桌及椅亦宜有高低兩種，桌面長約四尺，闊約三尺。椅須有靠背，多少視家庭中的人數而定。

（4）掛圖的佈置　室內四壁，恰好用掛圖補滿。一面掛理科圖，一面掛史地圖，又兩面掛公民和體操遊戲圖。

三　經費問題

辦理家庭圖書室一個最大的問題，就是經費問題。但是這個問題，他很容易解決，因為家庭中的事情，並不是要一朝一夕辦得很完備的，現在經費支絀，儘可稍稍從緩

—婦女雜誌—

Fig. 9.4 Three alternative floor plans for Chu Hui's home library, *The Ladies' Journal* 13:7 (1927), 119

location next to the garden is preferable. The lighting of the room is important, and Chu Hui explains how large the windows must be and how to block out sunlight with curtains. The room is furnished with four book cupboards, two tables, two pulpits for newspaper reading, the surfaces of which are to incline thirty degrees, and a number of chairs corresponding to the number of family members, eight chairs in Chu Hui's example. Chu Hui advises that tables and pulpits be of varying heights, to suit adults and children. The book cupboards each consist of three parts, a top section where books for adults are stored, a middle section containing books for *shaonian* (adolescents), and a lower section for children's books. The walls should be covered with pictures and educational posters.

Of an overall budget of 300 yuan for initial outlays on books, furniture, and decorating, 81 yuan was to be spent on reading materials for grown-ups, and 36 yuan each on reading materials for children and adolescents. Chu Hui gives precise recommendations as to what books and periodicals to buy in the form of a list extending over a page and a half of the magazine. More than half of the recommended publications, or types of publications, are recorded by the author as being available from the Commercial Press, but enough publications from rival publishers are mentioned so that an air of neutrality is maintained. Among the recommended readings for adults we find, not surprisingly, *The Ladies' Journal* itself. It is possible that Chu Hui as an occasional contributor to the magazine may have used this kind of advertising of the Commercial Press's products to increase his chances of getting the article accepted.

The second article on the subject was by Xu Shangmu (Xu Yitang 1896–1953), who worked as editor at *The Ladies' Journal* between 1926 and 1928 before leaving for Paris, where he was to complete his PhD thesis in anthropology in 1932. Inspired by Chu Hui's contribution, he elaborates on the idea of the home library, creating a version of it that is both more realistic in that it is adaptable to different circumstances, and more idealistic in its vision of children's education. "Parents with an understanding of education," he writes, agree that every home needs three facilities: a combined gym and bathroom, a playroom equipped with toys, and a home library.[66] Exercise, play, and study should combine to form a complete education. Xu prefers to begin by using a smaller room for the library, because in a big room the book collection would appear small to children. If the library collection eventually outgrows its original room, so much the better. He equips the library entirely with child-sized furniture. His library not only is designed for the children's use, but will be managed by the children themselves. They label the books, categorize them, place them on designated shelves, lend the books to other users, and keep a register of the books borrowed. Each month they put together statistics

[66] Shangmu, "Ertong yu jiating tushushi."

based on the register and present these in the form of a wall-chart. They busy themselves with the beautification of the library room, and their works of art ornament the walls. Although their parents retain economic control of the home library, involving the children in the purchase of books has educational value: browsing book catalogs improves reading skills, by adding together the prices children practice numeracy, and so on. Once the children have experienced the joy of opening a packet of books they themselves have ordered, they are much more likely to save their pocket money for books. The library is a training ground for a number of life skills, and a place where good habits are formed: orderliness, responsibility, frugality, hard work, and love of learning.

Xu Shangmu argued that if some youngsters found it difficult to muster enthusiasm for reading even in the home library, it was up to the parents to devise activities such as reading clubs or storytelling in order to awaken their interest. Public libraries in America, he tells us, often organize "story hours," and this has proved an efficient way of attracting children to reading. Chinese mothers may copy this idea in the home library.

In a separate article in the same issue of the magazine, Xu Shangmu provides us with a vivid description of a storytelling session in the home.[67] This time, it does not take place in a library but in the courtyard of the home on a summer afternoon, where a crowd of children (siblings, cousins, and neighbors) on tiny chairs are eagerly waiting for Mother to come and sit in the rattan chair they have arranged for her. When she appears, Mother asks the children what they have been doing earlier that day, and then ingeniously turns the conversation to a fairy tale on a related topic. She speaks clearly and with dramatic flair, raising and lowering the tone of her voice, and illustrating the story with expressive gestures. There are no problems with discipline, because listening to the story is entirely voluntary, and Mother's inspired performance holds her audience captive. Little helpers take turns fanning Mother, and in the end her hard work is rewarded by a cup or two of cooling tea. This charming vignette is first of all meant to promote a joyful pastime that gives happiness to families, Xu explains, but many educators agree that storytelling is a powerful educational tool, too. The joy it provides children and parents strengthens the emotional bond between them, encourages children's imagination, and provides a starting point for their studies of language and literature.

The ideal of the educational home was eventually challenged in *The Ladies' Journal*. In the fourth, "New Culture revival," phase of the magazine, the idea of the educational home as a recipe for ideal citizens was disputed by Lin Zhongda in a long, authoritative article where he lamented the disastrous state of Chinese childcare, characterized by suffering, neglect, and high infant mortality.[68] Like so many other writers before him, he thought ignorant

---

[67] Shangmu, "Gushi de jiangfa."   [68] Lin Zhongda, "Dui xin Zhongguo qingnian funü."

mothers and faulty methods of home education had contributed to this crisis. However, to him, the main problem was a different one, namely that women – and especially peasants and working-class women – were forced to work and take care of their children at the same time. To solve this problem, Lin argued, it was necessary to look beyond the liberated, enlightened middle-class housewife, because her success as educator depended on the labor of other women who, in turn, were made to neglect their children. Young women ought to work together to found a system for communal child care that would suit all classes of society. Thus, the educational home appeared to Lin only a partial and temporary solution to the problem of improving China's youth.

However, the educational home and its home library did not disappear from the pages of *The Ladies' Journal*. Numerous articles continued to advocate child-centered ideals for upbringing, and provided advice on pedagogical equipment. In 1931, the last year of the magazine, Miss Liu Heng contributed the article on home education cited at the beginning of this chapter.[69] Here, she reported on her implementation of the educational home ideals in real life. While teaching her little sister and nephew in her relatives' house in Jigongshan one summer holiday, she was given the opportunity to organize the rooms used by the children. Her efforts resulted in two simple, tidy, and elegant bedrooms where regular sleeping habits were instilled, a home library similar to those described by Xu Shangmu and Chu Hui, and a *zuoyeshi* (homework room) where children would write their diaries, practice mathematics, and house their vast collections of insects, leaves, and minerals brought back from expeditions into the forest.

Liu Heng's library contained books, magazines, toys, and musical instruments, all organized into different categories, with fairy tales, songbooks, and an impressive collection of children's magazines neatly sorted into different stacks. Like Chu Hui, Miss Liu attached a map of the layout of her pedagogical space. Although the maps show furniture in fixed positions, Miss Liu stressed the importance of changing the furnishings of the rooms as often as possible, in order to stimulate the children's minds. In addition to hanging landscape paintings and portraits of prominent historical figures on the walls, Liu Heng put up a new educational card outside the schoolroom door every morning. The curiosity this arrangement provoked helped the children remember the messages on the cards, such as "rise early and breathe the fresh air" (see Figure 9.5).[70] For all its sensible opinions and practical advice, Liu Heng's account retained an element of fantasy or escapism, at least for the readers, most of whom would not have had access to the exclusive Jigongshan area.

[69] Liu Heng, "Yi ge shujiaqi."   [70] Liu Heng, "Yi ge shujiaqi," 87–88.

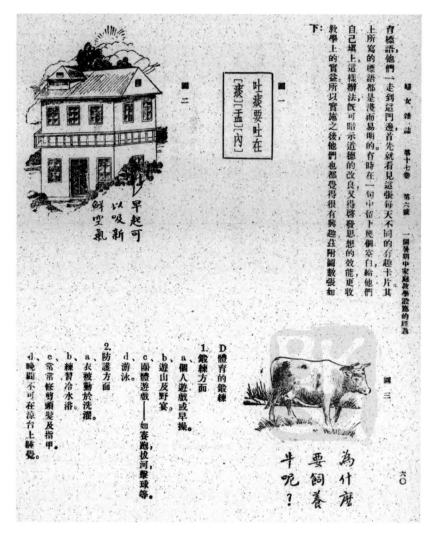

Fig. 9.5 Liu Heng's educational cards, *The Ladies' Journal* 17:6 (1927), 69

Conclusion

In Republican period China, magazines such as *The Ladies' Journal* were
perfectly suited to the construction and promotion of life-style ideals. They
were able to provide, at one and the same time, the theoretical justification for
such ideals in the form of serious articles and editorials, advertisements for
the consumer goods needed to perform the life-style in question, and reader
responses that negotiated and adapted the ideals to their respective realities.

In this article, I have explored one such life-style ideal: the educational home. By reading the magazine vertically, over time, I have established that the theme of home education was a prominent feature of the magazine from its beginnings in 1915 and onward, and that another, more spatially and aesthetically oriented discourse of home improvement – the theme of the beautiful home – entered from around 1925. These two themes, I argue, both contributed to the ideal of the educational home, which combined the notion of a child-centered education with the idea of the importance of physical domestic space.

In *The Ladies' Journal*, editors and readers alike invariably stressed the heavy responsibilities of parents, often linking their task to the project of creating a new and better citizenry for China. The ideal of the educational home was a way of meeting these demands, promising any middle-class reader with a sense of national pride and some knowledge of modern psychology and hygiene the opportunity to contribute to the national good by transforming his or her home into a perfect environment for child rearing.

The legend of Mencius' mother had long reminded people of parents' duty to provide their children with a beneficial environment. However, it was the modern idea of a psychologically and physiologically correct upbringing that made the home *as a physical space* of interest to the educator. The psychological approach to education entailed that it was the sum total of impressions on the child that shaped its intellect and character. Education happened not only through instruction and the influence of moral exemplars, but also through the provision of a stimulating physical environment. The space of the home, down to the tiniest detail of its organization and decoration, influenced the formation of the next generation of Chinese citizens.

Although the perfect house remained out of reach for most readers of *The Ladies' Journal*, there were other, more affordable commodities that could improve the educational qualities of the home environment. Books, magazines, pictures, and toys all helped create a totality of beneficial influence. If many other types of consumption would have been deemed wasteful, frivolous, or tasteless by those writing for *The Ladies' Journal*, consumption for creating the educational home was not. In the ideal of the educational home, political idealism and consumerism came together to create seemingly perfect combinations of culture and commercialism, responsibility and enjoyment. Just as for the child, play was both enjoyment and preparation for future duties. The aestheticism and comfort of the educational home were enjoyable and purposeful at the same time.

Part III

Gendered Space and Global Context: Foreign Models, Circulating Concepts, and the Constitution of Female Subjectivities

The discursive space of the early-twentieth-century Chinese print media was constituted within a global context – it was part and parcel of global modernity. Upright Japanese educators, intrepid French heroines, and hygiene-savvy German doctors, but also Indian, African, and Southeast Asian counterfoils, served as the multicultural backdrop to the imaginative space that made up these journals. Authors in this section follow women's magazines from their very beginnings with the first Chinese woman's journal, *Nü xuebao – Chinese Girl's Progress*, published in 1898 and its radical 1902–1903 successor, *Xuchu nübao/Nü xuebao* (Continued publication of women's journal/Journal of women's learning), to contemporary magazines. In all of the chapters assembled here, the relationship between local and global, self and Other, plays a dominant role, thus expanding the space and reach of the Chinese women's journal and, by extension, the imaginary of its readers.

Qian tackles the idea of *guo* (country, state, nation) in a conflicting setup of more conventional and more radical but continuously intersecting worldviews. Xia Xiaohong, whose focus is on Western heroines, and Joan Judge, who examines medical knowledge, both trace triangulating discourses about women generated in Europe, mediated by Japan, and rearticulated in the Chinese women's press. Paul Bailey, in contrast, examines how non-Western (particularly Asian) women were discursively represented on the pages of the women's press and to what ends. He and Mittler, in her contribution, question how the image and status of foreigners changed over time and what this change can tell us about evolving perceptions of (wo)manhood in China. In their opening reflection, Nathalie Cooke and Jennifer Garland, experts on the Canadian women's journal *Châtelaine*, for which they have created a database of advertisements,[1] emphasize that the idealized self as projected in women's journals can only be constructed in relation to an Other.

---

[1] http://chatelaineads.mcgill.ca/browse.php. See also Cooke and Garland, "Putting Questions to Images."

Reflection
Lived and Idealized Self and Other in
Women's Journals

Nathalie Cooke and Jennifer Garland

Women's magazines serve as sites of negotiation between prescriptive and descriptive practice – what women are told to do (in advertising, feature articles, and editorial copy, for example) and what they describe themselves as doing (in testimonials, interviews, columns, and letters to the editor). As such, they reinforce existing stereotypes of women's roles through their editorials and advertising while also providing an outlet for women's creative and life writing, opening avenues for lived and idealized selves and others. While this paradigm can account for the popularity of women's magazines for both readers and advertisers, it fails to capture the dynamic and "contestatory" space that studies in this section of the book on "Gendered Space and Global Context" describe as constituting the genre. Consequently, we propose here a more nuanced paradigm, one foregrounding interplay and exchange of opinions – multidirectional rather than unidirectional – where the act of reading brings individual readers into contestatory negotiation with gender and body ideals, as well as with sociocultural norms from many parts of the world, not just China.[1]

Our own scrutiny of women's magazines began with *Châtelaine*,[2] which dominated the genre in Canada since its founding in 1928.[3] Through the 1950s, *Châtelaine's* "exemplar" was the American women's magazine *Ladies' Home Journal*,[4] which served as the template for many of the Chinese women's journals as well, notably *Funü shibao* (The women's Eastern times) and *Funü zazhi – The Ladies' Journal*, discussed by Judge and Bailey in this section. *Châtelaine's* Canadian focus and respect for regional diversity within the country aided in building a loyal fan base for the magazine.[5] It also engaged readers through its coverage of social change and the women's movement. Even under

---

[1] Levine, *The Myth of the 1950s*, 61–70 provides a helpful context to the contestatory paradigm. What he calls the "myth of the 50s" disrupts a number of the tidy historical assumptions about the mid twentieth-century United States. See particularly the chapter on "Men and Women."
[2] Cooke and Garland, "Putting Questions to Images."
[3] Light and Pierson, *No Easy Road*, 18. *Châtelaine* enjoyed a "large readership" even a year after its launch, thereby eclipsing the *Canadian Home Journal* and taking market share from the *Ladies' Home Journal*.
[4] Anderson, *Rebel Daughter*, 119.   [5] Korinek, *Roughing It in Suburbia*, 2.

male editorship, which, it should be said, was not unusual for women's magazines of the mid-twentieth century in North America (or earlier in China), it showed editorial courage through forthright coverage of women's issues.

That *Châtelaine* continued to be funded largely by advertising dollars,[6] as well as by subscriptions, put into play a practical reality of a genre at the intersection of prescriptive and descriptive practice. The rhetorical politics of advertising copy explicitly casts readers into the role of Mrs. Consumer, but implicitly invites them to observe and align themselves with some version of women's bodies or lived experience. This rhetorical dynamic can be applied to Chinese women's magazines: in the advertisements discussed in Judge's study, but also underlying the genre more broadly, with a marked discrepancy between an increasingly modernized reality (including a new sense of state, race, and territory, as Qian notes) in the world of the magazine and a far more conservative lived reality both assumed by it and indeed conjured into existence within its pages, as Qian discusses very clearly. Consequently, while some women's magazines remained conservative, others offered glimpses into recent innovation and future thinking, particularly about women's roles. Significantly, by pointing to the world beyond the magazine as one that was not consistently forward thinking, women's magazines signposted their ability to be a significant source of information about pathways to the future.

Given such a consistent formula, whereby magazines serve a largely informational and even didactic function, what then is the endless fascination of women's magazines that fuels the industry and brings readers back time and again? Most obviously, it hinges on the ever-changing and elusive nature of the gendered ideal presented on its pages. In this didactic paradigm, the reader comes to the magazine to discover and understand the gendered ideal in order to emulate it. However, in our alternative contestatory paradigm, which acknowledges elements of both prescriptive and descriptive practice, arguments for and against change are seen to coexist, providing tension and energy that fuel the genre and engage readers in issue after issue.

The contestatory paradigm acknowledges that readers may disagree with arguments published in the magazine, may view and reject the aesthetic ideals on offer, and may resist the invitation to move towards modernity as configured within the pages of the magazine. The act of reading in this

---

[6] Young and Young, *The 1950s*, 147. "In 1950, magazines remained a leading mass medium in terms of advertising revenue. Collectively, they commanded 9 percent of all the advertising dollars in the United States. Television, however, whittled away at this figure, just as it would do with all print media. By 1960 the number had fallen to 7.7 percent." As well, some critics have noted that print advertising's influence may have dwindled due to the increasing sophistication of readers and viewers with regard to its methods, as well as the constraints on advertising due to the growth of a consumer rights movement during the 1960s and 1970s; see, for example, the chapter on "A New Consumerism" in Cross, *All-Consuming Century*, 145–91.

contestatory paradigm is a dynamic process, one of negotiation and active engagement. Mittler, in her chapter, illustrates this negotiation when she discusses the presence of foreigners in Chinese women's magazines and the way difference may sometimes be read as providing a moral lesson, yet other times simply naturalized, reinforcing the Chinese sense of Self. One advantage of the "contestatory" paradigm over the "didactic" paradigm is that it accounts for the existence, and even the success, of women's magazines that are not wholly aligned with the predominant sentiments or practices of their contemporary moments. Such is the case with the magazines under scrutiny in the studies that follow.

10 Competing Conceptualizations of *Guo* (Country, State, and/or Nation-State) in Late Qing Women's Journals

Nanxiu Qian

The 1898 *Nü xuebao – Chinese Girl's Progress* initiated Chinese women's journalism and was followed by the 1902–1903 *Xuchu nübao/Nü xuebao* (Continued publication of women's journal/Journal of women's learning). Each of them, however, embodied in a different way "one particular paradox" of the time: "while the figure of Woman [served] as a powerful symbol of the modern nation-state, actual women [had] to struggle for the right to participate in national political life."[1] Whereas the 1898 journal focused on women's equal sociopolitical and educational rights, its 1902–1903 successor conformed more to men's nationalistic discourse. Due to the rising prominence of nationalist discourse in the early twentieth century, and in the process of "canonizing" Chinese women's journals, however, the memory of the former was excised, while the "birth" of women's journalism in China was attributed to the latter. A vertical and integrated reading of concepts of *guo* (country, state, nation-state) in these two journals in modern Chinese historiography may help us understand the complex ways women's emancipation was entangled with nationalism in a period when – as part of the discourse on how best to become modern – "the national question" and "the women's question" were confronted simultaneously, and this may further explain why canonization took the path it did.[2]

The historical backdrop to the rise of the late Qing nationalist discourse has been described by Richard J. Smith as follows:

Naturally enough, the lingering sense of the Qing as a universal empire hindered the rise of modern nationalism – the identification of the individual with the nation-state and the general acceptance of a multi-state system of other sovereign (and competing) national entities. The Sino-Japanese War of 1894–1895, however, shattered the dynasty's outmoded self-image at a single blow ... A surge of Chinese nationalism ensued, and with it a burst of reform sentiment. New print media and new forms of political and social activity helped to spread reformist ideas.[3]

I am deeply grateful to the three volume editors for their help with revision and editing, and to the two anonymous readers for their enthusiastic criticism. Unless otherwise stated, all translations are mine.

[1] Judge, "Talent, Virtue, and the Nation," 765.
[2] Ibid., 767.   [3] Smith, *The Qing Dynasty and Traditional Chinese Culture*, 391.

In these changing sociopolitical circumstances, the already complex and ambiguous connotations of *guo* evolved into more imbricated territories of signification. As women reformers had demanded an end to the longstanding demarcation between the inner and the outer domains so that women could share equal rights with men, the question of how women should function once they walked out of the inner quarters had not been resolved. It was entirely unclear what the relationship should be between women's changing selves and the evolving concept of *guo* that synthesized the major concerns of the reform era. The term *guo* hence entered late Qing women's journalism as a central and contested concept from its inception. Indeed, the *Chinese Girl's Progress*, published in the heyday of the late Qing reforms, expressed women reformers' "struggle for the right to participate in national [the *guo*'s] political life."[4]

Accordingly, leading contributors of the journal reinterpreted *guo* – conventionally the Confucian patriarchal state/empire – as a country ideally co-governed by men and women. The *Continued Publication of Women's Journal/Journal of Women's Learning* claimed to follow its 1898 predecessor, but soon veered towards a much more ardently nationalistic approach amid increasing anti-Manchu sentiment, an approach that a number of later women's journals also followed. Adhering to what has been described as the "contestatory paradigm" typical of journalistic writing in the reflection by Nathalie Cooke and Jennifer Garland above, the definition of *guo* in these first two women's journals thus took on different meanings that were more or less compatible with these differing political agendas. Three basic meanings of *guo* are apparent in their pages: (1) *guo* as the "state" or sovereign political entity; (2) *guo* as the "country," combining its geographic region, sovereign territory, and its people with shared cultural traditions; (3) *guo* as the "nation-state," with its political sovereignty closely aligned to race, a notion influenced by Western ideas.

This chapter examines these competing conceptualizations of *guo* as they developed in these two women's journals, each of which emerged against a specific temporal, spatial, and intellectual backdrop. In a close reading of their multigenre writings, which reflect multiple levels of concern, from sociopolitical, cultural, and moral to psychological and emotional, this paper addresses the following questions: Which intellectual resources informed different understandings of *guo*? What kinds of sociopolitical circumstances enabled each process of conceptualization, as an inflection to a global grammar of modernity? How did each vision and version of *guo* inspire the social repositioning of women with and within the *guo*, and in turn reassign their responsibilities for the *guo*? And finally, but most importantly: what role did the genre of women's journal hosting this discourse play in these processes?

---

[4] As phrased by Judge, "Talent, Virtue, and the Nation," 765.

To Cultivate the Self, to Regulate the Family, to Order the Country: Gendering *Guo* in the *Chinese Girl's Progress*

The *Chinese Girl's Progress* was published in Shanghai as the think tank of the 1897–1898 Shanghai reform campaign for women's education.[5] This campaign was headed by the *Nü xuehui* (Women's study association) and committed to establishing the first Chinese *nü xuetang* (girls' school). The all-female members of the Association immediately seized upon the news media to disseminate their reform ideas, for they saw in this new genre the capacity to "spread news about the female Way and distribute women's universal love," as they wrote in their May 17, 1898 announcement of the publication of *Chinese Girl's Progress*.[6] Women contributors to the publication, typified by Pan Xuan in her "Foreword to the *Chinese Girl's Progress*," elaborated on this understanding of the function of women's journals. Pan argues that, on the one hand, the journal would serve as the "leaves and blossoms" of the educational campaign for women. It would promote the objectives of the campaign and display its achievements to the public.[7] On the other hand, the journal would open women's minds to fresh ideas. It would therefore serve as "the starting point for us 200 million Chinese women to demand equal rights." In this sense, the *Chinese Girl's Progress* was comparable to a baton in a commander's hand: "Whenever the commander raises her baton," Pan wrote, "the soldiers will cry in one voice, and the enemies will all flee!"[8]

Women reformers encouraged the submission of creative and original ideas from Chinese and Western *xianshu mingyuan* (virtuous and talented ladies) and made clear that they would publish whatever women could contribute without confining themselves to *chengjian* (conventional viewpoints).[9] The journal lasted from July 24 to late October, 1898.[10] Two months after its inauguration, its circulation had reportedly risen from a handful to several thousand copies.[11] All the articles were written by women, mostly by the journal's all-female editorial board of more than twenty members. The entire run of the journal hence offers a forum of multiple female voices.

---

[5] Articles about this first Chinese women's journal include Pan Tianzhen, "Tan Zhongguo jindai di-yi fen nübao"; Du Jikun, "Zai tan *Nü xuebao*"; and Yu Fuyuan, "Guanyu *Nü xuebao*." Twelve issues of *Chinese Girl's Progress* seem to have been published, all extant as late as 1963 (Du, "Zai tan *Nü xuebao*," 55; Yu Fuyuan, "Guanyu *Nü xuebao*," 52–53). Now only the first eight issues can be found in the Wuxi Library, Jiangsu province. I also acquired a photocopy of the ninth issue thanks to Professor Xia Xiaohong.

[6] Shen, Lai, and the women trustees of the Shanghai guishuli nüxue hui shushu, "Zhongguo Nüxue."

[7] Pan Xuan, "Shanghai *Nü xuebao* yuanqi," 2b.

[8] "Lun *Nü xuebao* nanchu," 2b.   [9] Shen et al., "Zhongguo Nüxue."

[10] See Du Jikun, "Zai tan Nü xuebao," 55; Yu Fuyuan, "Guanyu Nü," 52–53.

[11] See *Nü xuebao* 8 (Sept. 1898): 1a.

In its inaugural editorial, "Preface to the *Chinese Girl's Progress*," the leading contributor, Xue Shaohui (1866–1911), pointedly addresses the connection between women's education and their political roles, which hinged on their relationship with the *guo*. For this purpose, Xue takes up the famous eight-step "classic account" from the "Daxue" (Great Learning) but provides a gendered reading of it. She explains that the social order was derived from the family and the family was grounded in the self-cultivation of individuals, and then argues, "Since regulating families necessitates cooperative efforts of both men and women, self-cultivation refers to both men and women."[12] She continues,

The "Zhongyong" (Doctrine of the mean) states: "The Way of the superior person begins with common men and women...As ignorant as common men and women are, they could still get to know [the Way]; as unworthy as common men and women are, they could still act [according to the Way]."[13] This shows that the Sage expects men and women to engage in learning without any discrimination. We inner-chamber women may not know all the things under Heaven, and we may not be skilled in all the crafts necessary to put states in order and ensure peace in the world. Yet to put states in order and ensure peace in the world we should first regulate families, and to regulate families we should first investigate things and perfect our knowledge. The Way, broad and grand, is for men and women to walk together.[14]

Referring to the "Doctrine of the Mean," Xue claims that the *junzi zhi dao* (way of the superior person) must be co-created by men and women. Both the "Great Learning" and the "Doctrine of the Mean" are core Confucian classics from the *Liji* (*Book of Rites*) and both were later included in the "Four Books" (*Sishu*). The *guo* invoked in the eight-step "classic account" should therefore refer to the conventional Confucian state. Although this state places women in a "cloistered position in the home," the home is, as Susan Mann argues, "the place where filial respect and collegial relations begin, extending outward through those who rule."[15] Women, especially writing women who can make their voices heard in public through their publications, are "at the center of

---

[12] Xue Shaohui, "*Nü xuebao xu*," 3a. The eight steps "classic account" is detailed in the *Liji* [*zhengyi*] ([Orthodox commentary on the] *Book of Rites*), "Daxue," in Ruan Yuan (1764–1849), ed., *Shisanjing zhushu* (Commentaries on the thirteen Chinese classics), 2 vols. (1826; rprt. Beijing: Zhonghua Shuju, 1979), *juan* 60: 2, 1673: "Those of old who wished to illumine luminous Potency to the world first ordered their own states, for which they first regulated their own families, for which they first cultivated their own persons, for which they first rectified their own minds, for which they first integrated their own intentions, for which they first perfected their own knowledge. The perfecting of knowledge depends on investigating at the things. Only after the things have been investigated is knowledge perfect, and only then is there integrity of intention, and only then are minds rectified, and only then are persons cultivated, and only then are families regulated, and only then are states in order, and only then is the world at peace" (trans. Graham, *Disputers of the Tao*, 132–33, modified).
[13] *Liji* [*zhengyi*], "Zhongyong," *Shisanjing zhushu*, *juan* 53:2, 1626.
[14] Xue Shaohui, "*Nü xuebao* xu," 3a.   [15] Mann, *Precious Records*, 204–05.

political discourse and at the heart of aesthetic expression."[16] Women's political position and function in the Confucian state requires them, Xue argues, to engage in equal learning with men. They would walk side by side with men through the eight steps of the Way, from self-cultivation to family and state management and eventually to world harmony.

Yet China and the world are undergoing rapid changes, Xue continues. Women should therefore respond to the situation accordingly:

Today New Learning from all the countries has been glamorously and beautifully developed, going beyond the scope of our ancient philosophers and the one hundred schools of thought. If we women, staying in the inner chambers all day long, still maintain the division between the inner domain and the outer domain and limit our learning [within a narrow field], how can we talk about gaining knowledge so as to conform to the principle of the "new people"?[17]

Vis-à-vis the nationalistic divide between *Xixue* (Western learning) and *Zhongxue* (Chinese learning) that was a central epistemological tenet of the late Qing reform era and that often positioned the two in a clear and hierarchical binary, Xue offers a temporal concept, *Xinxue* (New learning). She views the rise of New learning as a worldwide and common intellectual response to current changes, in which China stands on an equal footing with other countries in expanding traditional learning to a much broader spectrum of knowledge.[18] To acquire New learning, women have to break the long-standing segregation between the *waiyan* (outer domain, literally, outer words) and the *neiyan* (inner domain, literally, inner words), expanding their horizons to include all sorts of useful knowledge regardless of its origin.[19]

This call for bridging the inner and the outer domains signals an unprecedented breakthrough in women's social positioning in China. Previously, although the husband–wife relationship stood as the basis of the conventional social structure, a wife "remained an *inner* helpmate and was never called upon to partake in his [the husband's] world in a public capacity."[20] In other words,

---

[16] Ibid., 205.   [17] Xue Shaohui, "*Nü xuebao xu*," 3a.

[18] See Lackner and Vittinghoff, eds., *Mapping Meanings*, for a discussion of the ways in which the "New learning" was a "disunified occupation," marked by encounters between Chinese and Western thinkers that were reciprocal and transcultural, blurring the distinction between what was "indigenous" and what was "foreign." See also the insightful review of this volume by Mann in *China Review International* 12:1 (2005), 147–51.

[19] The earliest and most authoritative demarcation between the *nei*, inner domain, and the *wai*, outer domain, was delineated in the "Neize" (Inner principles) of the *Book of Rites*: *nan bu yan nei, nü bu yan wai* (Men should not speak of domestic affairs, and women should not speak of public affairs), and again *neiyan bu chu, waiyan buru* (inner words should not go out, and outer words should not go in) (*Liji* [*Zhengyi*], in *Shisanjing zhushu, juan* 27, 2:1462). Zheng Xuan (127–200) commented that this demarcation indicates *shiye zhi cixu* (the allotment of responsibilities [for men and women]) (ibid.).

[20] Ko, *Teachers of the Inner Chambers*, 183.

women participated in political affairs only through the agency of the family and marriage. Now walking out of the inner chambers, women could, as Xue has argued earlier, become their own agents in direct contact with the *guo*. They could "present their scholarly and literary *cai* (talents) and *yi* (artistic accomplishments) to be selected for the use of the state."[21]

In another essay, "On the Connection of Women's Education to the Way of Governing," published consecutively in the third and fourth issues of the *Chinese Girl's Progress*, Xue details how historically women have provided major political services to the *guo* with their *cai* and *yi* acquired through learning. These contributions include *ren shicai* (assuming the position of a diplomatic envoy), *bao jiangtu* (protecting the territory), *zi lizhi* (assisting governing), *bei shiguan* (completing historical records), *biao shifan* (standing as a teacher and a role model), *zhang wenheng* (evaluating [male] literary talents), *lie wenyuan* (being listed [with men] in the garden of literature), *lu wugong* (establishing military merits), *cheng yixia* (braving righteous gallantry), and *kua jiyi* (boasting technical and artistic accomplishments). Women have literally contributed to every aspect of China's "great achievements in managing the state and transforming the people" (*zhihua zhi gong*).[22] New learning would certainly increase their capabilities to serve the *guo* in all these respects.

Only by breaking the inner/outer barricade and absorbing "New learning" could women align themselves with the new womanhood and the *xinmin zhi zhi* (principle of the new people) that had also been encoded in the Great Learning: *gou ri xin, riri xin, you ri xin* (If you can one day renovate yourself, then do so from day to day! Always keep renovating yourself!).[23] This new womanhood, Xue concludes in her "Preface to the *Chinese Girl's Progress*," possesses the overarching capacity to manage the household, govern the state, and harmonize all under Heaven. For, Xue argues, "Laozi says: 'The *Dao* [Way] is the mother of all things.' Mothering is precisely women's business. Who says that the *kundao* [female *Dao*] cannot achieve anything?"[24] From a Daoist point of view, women and their *Dao* give birth to all things and will therefore take best care of the world.

Xue's understanding of *guo* is rooted in but has surpassed the conventional political state, coming to represent a much broader entity that comprises

---

[21] Xue Shaohui, "Chuangshe Nü xuetang," 6a–6b.   [22] Xue Shaohui, "Nüjiao yu zhidao," 2a.

[23] The "Great Learning" in the *Book of Rites* reads as follows: "On Tang's bath tub were engraved the following words: 'If you can one day renovate yourself, then do so from day to day! Always keep renovating yourself!' The 'Decree of Kang' instructs: 'Encourage people to renovate themselves!' The *Shijing* (*Book of Songs*) has the following lines: 'Although Zhou is an old state, it is destined for self-renewal.' Therefore, the *junzi* (superior man) tries his utmost to do everything he can [for renovating himself]" (*Liji* [*Zhengyi*], "Daxue," in *Shisanjing zhushu, juan* 60, 2: 1673–74; cf. James Legge, trans., *The Great Learning*, in Legge, *Chinese Classics* 1, 361–62).

[24] Xue Shaohui, "*Nü xuebao* xu," 3a.

the people, the land, the culture, and all that women can mother. Correspondingly, Xue's account of women's political functions also includes their cultural achievements. In this sense, Xue's *guo* probably should be rendered as "(mother) country."

To be sure, the concept of the nation-state had already been introduced to women by this time. Liang Qichao, in his essay "Lun nüxue" (On education for women), which inspired the Shanghai 1898 reform campaign for women's education, argues that the purpose of educating women was *baoguo, baozhong, baojiao* (to protect the state, the race, and the religion).[25] This equation of state, race, and religion – which refers to Confucianism and therefore a shared culture – indicates that, when writing "On Education for Women," Liang incorporated nationalism into his understanding of the *guo* as the nation-state.[26] In the first nine issues of the *Chinese Girl's Progress* that I have examined, however, only two essays explicitly echo Liang's nationalistic justification for women's education.[27] The other women contributors seem more inclined to share Xue's vision of *guo* – the vision that foresaw that women would participate in a range of state affairs on the same political and intellectual footing as men by their partaking in New Learning.[28]

Along with this understanding of *guo* arose the concept of *aiguo*, "loving the *guo*" or "love for the *guo*." *Aiguo* as a term had appeared as early as the *Zhanguo ce* (Intrigues of the warring states), in which it indicated a ruler's love for his state.[29] Women contributors to the *Chinese Girl's Progress* reconceptualized *aiguo* to promote their reform agendas. Lu Cui, for instance, published "Nüzi aiguo shuo" (On women's *aiguo*), defining *aiguo* as women's equal rights in voicing their opinions on state affairs and enjoying the same political and educational privileges as men. She argues,

---

[25] See Liang Qichao, "Lun nüxue," 1a–3b. "Religion" here refers to Confucianism, which Kang Youwei and his fellow male reformers intended to transform into a Chinese state religion, comparable in certain ways to Christianity in the West; see Nanxiu Qian, "Revitalizing the *Xianyuan* (Worthy Ladies) Tradition," 429.

[26] Cf. the definition of the nation-state: "A political unit consisting of an autonomous state inhabited predominantly by a people sharing a common culture, history, and language," in *The American Heritage Dictionary of the English Language*, 4th edn., s.v. "nation-state." For a thorough discussion of the definition of the nation-state and nationalism see the entry *Nationalism* from the summer 2010 edn. of the *Stanford Encyclopedia of Philosophy* (http://plato.stanford.edu/archives/sum2010/entries/nationalism/, accessed 7 Jan. 2015).

[27] See Xu Fu, "Chaozhou," 3b, and Kang Tongwei, "Nüxue libi shuo"; for an analysis of Kang's nationalistic argument, see Judge, *Precious Raft*, 93.

[28] Xue herself has clearly noticed the intense competition between nations all over the world, but, bearing a strong belief in Daoist naturalness and the Confucian ideal of world harmonization, Xue and her fellow women reformers seem not to want to join the rising nationalistic fervor. For a detailed discussion, see Nanxiu Qian, *Politics, Poetics, and Gender*, especially 115–16, 123–58, 261–66.

[29] See Liu Xiang, ed. *Zhanguo ce*, "Qin ce," *juan* 2, 1:50; "Zhongshan ce," *juan* 33:3, 1191.

Our country is now increasingly endangered by imperial invasions. Whoever has a voice should heave a sigh! Last month His Majesty decreed that each of His people might present their opinions. Since "people" should include both male and female, we women should also present a collectively signed memorial to the emperor with our candid views. This way we will not regret being Chinese women who stand [equally with men] under Heaven.[30]

Lu Cui then makes a systematic list of requests to the emperor. She asks him to open girls' schools, publish women's journals, build libraries and reading clubs for female readers, become a patron of art exhibitions for female artists, run gynecological and obstetrical hospitals, and even organize beauty pageants. The most solemn request that Lu Cui puts forward is to establish an educational bureau for women, to hold female civil service examinations, and to select members for a female parliament. Lu Cui's demands resonate with Xue's historical account of women's broad range of political service to the state, built upon their versatile talents and erudite learning.[31] In brief, women reformers believe that only by achieving equal educational and political rights can they better serve the endangered country. In protecting the safety of the country and developing its civilization, they will reach the goal of *aiguo*.

Some historians credit Liang Qichao with minting the term *aiguo* in his essay "On *Aiguo*," published in February 1899,[32] which is obviously not the case. How the concept *aiguo* evolved into its modern sense during the reform era merits a separate study. What I want to emphasize here is the different meanings of *aiguo* in Liang's writings and the *Chinese Girl's Progress* in terms of how it is conceived. Liang's nationalistic version places sovereignty before people's well-being and can best be rendered as love for the nation-state.[33] In contrast, the women contributors' version of *aiguo* is more culturally and socially oriented – to nurture and protect the country as a whole, including its families, people, and traditions. To some extent, women reformers continued to reconceptualize *aiguo* within the discursive frame of China's imperial system. This is evident in Lu Cui's appeal to the Guangxu Emperor and Xue's demand that women be "selected for the use of the state" – the same privilege that men had enjoyed through the civil service examination regime. This imperial momentum later made women reformers turn to constitutional monarchy as a smooth transition to republicanism.[34]

---

[30] Lu Cui, "Nüzi aiguo shuo," 2b.   [31] See ibid., 2b–3a.
[32] See Zheng Shiqu, "Liang Qichao de aiguo lun," 175.
[33] Hao Chang, in discussing Liang's earlier essay "Shuo qun" (On grouping) (published in 1897), believes that Liang's concept of *qun* signifies, among other things, "an implicit but ambivalent acceptance of the ideal of the nation-state." See Hao Chang, *Liang Ch'i-ch'ao*, 111.
[34] See Nanxiu Qian, *Politics, Poetics, and Gender*, 93–94, 117–18, 254–59.

In addition to building on Chinese ideas, the 1898 women reformers also drew upon Western intellectual resources in conceptualizing *guo* and women's role within it. The broad influence of Western ideas shown in the *Chinese Girl's Progress* resulted first from the broad networks of individuals involved in the 1897–98 Shanghai campaign for women's education. The initiators of this campaign included prominent diplomats to the West, such as Xue Shaohui's brother-in-law Chen Jitong (1852–1907), who received systematic Western education during his early studies in the Fuzhou Naval Academy and his sixteen-year diplomatic career in Europe. The campaign also received strong support from Western diplomats, missionaries, and journalists in Shanghai, both men and women. Second, the 1898 Reform Movement was triggered by China's defeat in the 1894–95 Sino-Japanese War, which naturally pushed the demoralized Chinese gentry to seek reform models from the West. Consequently, the *Chinese Girl's Progress* registered women's overwhelming desire to imitate the West in achieving their reform goals, including their particular approach to *guo* and *aiguo*.[35]

Xue would further elaborate this approach in her interpretation of foreign women's lives in the *Waiguo lienü zhuan* (Biographies of foreign women), which she compiled with her husband Chen Shoupeng (1857–1928?) in the aftermath of the 1898 Reform Movement. Using foreign women's lives as a point of reference, the couple continued their reform design of repositioning the ideal "woman" in an ideal space, at home and in society, within the intersecting frameworks of family, state, and world. Xue defines, for instance, a successful female ruler as one who rules with *ci* (motherly love) and *xue* (learning) to nurture both the people and their culture. She imagines the world of the Greco-Roman goddesses as a matriarchal women's country ruled as a republic. Ultimately, Xue hoped that the *Biographies of Foreign Women* would help cultivate Chinese women and increase their understanding of and communication with foreign women. So women would work together to achieve world harmony, the last of the conventional eight steps prescribed in the "Great Learning," which men had never been able to accomplish on their own.[36] Bringing to the fore multiple intellectual resources from both inside and outside of China in understanding *guo* as part of the formation of modern China, the message of the earliest Chinese women's journals was distinctly gendered: in their conception of *guo* they were opening a space for women to act and be the creative agents in determining their country/state/nation's fate.

---

[35] See Nanxiu Qian, "Revitalizing the *Xianyuan*."
[36] See Nanxiu Qian, "Borrowing Foreign Mirrors," and "Qing-mo nüxing."

Guo as Nation-State in the *Continued Publication of Women's Journal/Journal of Women's Learning*

Literally and metaphorically, the *Chinese Girl's Progress* and its 1902–1903 successor edited by Chen Xiefen (1883–1923) followed each other like "mother" and "daughter."[37] Not only did Chen claim the inheritance of the 1898 Shanghai campaign for women's education but also several daughters of the contributors to and supporters of the *Chinese Girl's Progress* wrote for Chen's journal.[38] Yet the focal concerns in this "daughter" journal soon diverged from those of its founding "mother." Among them was the understanding of *guo*, which came to denote primarily the nation-state. This change already began with the first issue of the new journal (May 8, 1902): in her essay "Nannü yiyang" (Men and women are the same), Chen Xiefen argues that the recognition of gender equality is "the prerequisite for empowering the *guo* and the *zhong* (race)."[39] Here *guo* is directly tied to race, and together they come to stand for the nation-state. Chen received strong support from male

---

[37] Chen Xiefen initiated the *Women's Journal* in late 1899 with four issues. She republished it as a monthly in 1902 under the title *Continued Publication of Women's Journal* and renamed it *Journal of Women's Learning* in 1903; see Shanghai tushuguan, ed. (1965, 1980), s.v. *Nübao*, *Nü xuebao*, footnote to the entry. See also Xia Xiaohong, "Wan-Qing liangfen *Nü xuebao*," 25–33. Since the 1899 *Women's Journal* has long been lost, this chapter focuses on the nine issues of the 1902 *Continued Publication of Women's Journal* and the four issues of the 1903 *Journal of Women's Learning* (Shanghai Library collection). For the connection and difference between the 1898 and the 1902–1903 journals, see Nanxiu Qian, "The Mother *Nü Xuebao*."

[38] In *Continued Publication of Women's Journal* 1, Chen recollected the Girls' school established in the 1898 campaign for women's education; see her "Nüshu shenshao." In *Continued Publication of Women's Journal* 2, Chen reported two continual operations following on the 1898 campaign: to reopen the 1898 Nü xuetang (Girls' school) under the original superintendent, Shen Ying, and to reestablish the Nü xuehui (Women's study society) with the original members as its nucleus. The first meeting of the resumed Women's study Society was held on 7 May 1902. Twenty women, most of them on the editorial board of the *Chinese Girl's Progress* and the faculty of the 1898 Girls' school, attended the meeting, along with several daughters of the 1898 reformers. See Chen Xiefen, "Jiang kai nü xuetang" and "Nü xuehui timing lu." Daughters of the 1898 reformers who later wrote for Chen's journal included Xue Shaohui's two nieces Chen Qian (b. 1884?) and Chen Chao (b. 1885?), and the daughters Wu Ruonan (1886–1973) and Wu Yanan of a male reformer, Wu Baochu (1869–1913). Chen Chao alone published four articles and a long poem to express admiration for Chen Xiefen's reform determination.

[39] *Xuchu nübao* 1, Column "Nübao yanshuo" (Vernacular speeches in the *Women's Journal*), 3a. The major essays in the 1902–1903 *Continued Publication of Women's Journal/Journal of Women's Learning* include twenty-three *lunshuo* (essays) in classical Chinese, and thirty-six *yanshuo* (vernacular speeches). Chen Xiefen alone published eleven *lunshuo* and twenty-nine *yanshuo*, eight other women contributed four *lunshuo* and seven *yanshuo*, and the remaining eight *lunshuo* were by men. Chen also reprinted a great number of men's writings from other periodicals. Thus, although the 1902–1903 publication had much more space (fifty to sixty pages in each issue, compared with eight pages each issue of the 1898 *Chinese Girl's Progress*), it did not offer enough opportunities for diversified voices of women. See Nanxiu Qian, "The Mother *Nü xuebao*."

reformers on this point. Jing Yuanshan (1842–1903), one of the initiators of the 1898 Shanghai campaign for women's education, for one, was invited to give a speech at the first meeting of Chen Xiefen's Women's Study Society on May 7, 1902, and he too argued for "empowering the nation-state and the race."[40] When asked how to achieve this aim, many of the male reformers would continue to hold up the eight-step "classic account," which women authors in the earlier journal had creatively linked to the need for women's education. Jing Yuanshan contended that "once the family is regulated, the state will be ordered."[41] And Jiang Zhiyou (style name Guanyun) (1865–1929), another invited speaker, argued that "only after the establishment of women's education may there be the perfect people, the perfect family, and the perfect state."[42]

Yet here, as in Chen's own argumentation, the "perfect state" was now considered in distinctively nationalistic terms. In an article for the third issue of *Continued Publication of Women's Journal*, "Yao you aiguo de xin" (We must embrace patriotism), Chen explains that "*Guo* is a collective entity of all the people."[43] She continues the argument in her vernacular essay in issue 6, "Curriculum is most important for girls' Schools," saying: "What is most crucial for these young women [at girls' schools] is that they have the idea of loving the *guo* and the will to empower the race."[44] Once "*aiguo*" (loving the *guo*) is connected with "*qiangzhong*" (empowering the race), *guo* becomes the institutional mechanism by which the political, social, and economic interest of the Han Chinese people can be fully satisfied – in other words, a nation-state capable of correcting "*guoshi ruo*" (national weakness) and "*renzhong lie*" (racial flaws).[45] Accompanying this definition of *guo*, Chen Xiefen published in the same issue the woman revolutionary Du Qingchi's "Preface to the Guangdong Transformation Girl's School," in which Du declares, "Men and women are equal to the *guo*. In this sense, assisting the husband and teaching the children are trifling matters, whereas loving the *guo* is a grand matter."[46] Thus, in the name of nationalism, the Confucian social order is subverted and women are repositioned. Conventionally women had their responsibility for the family and thus, if indirectly, to the state. Now the state would be put ahead of the family, and women's primary responsibilities shifted from their families to their state.

To enhance the journal's redefinition of *guo* and repositioning of women within the *guo*, Chen Xiefen would publish a number of historical records, literary works, and essays, either composed by Chinese authors or translated

---

[40] See "Nü xuehui timing lu," 6a; and the speech by Jing Yuanshan, under Shan Xi longsou (The deaf old man from the Shan stream), "Di yici Nü xuehui yanshuo," 1b.

[41] Ibid., 1a.

[42] Speech by Jiang Zhiyou, under Jiang Guancha Guanyun (Censor Jiang Guanyun), ibid., 3b.

[43] Chen Xiefen, "Yaoyou aiguo de xin," 1a–2b.

[44] Chen Xiefen, "Nü xuetang di-yi kecheng yaojin," 2b.   [45] See ibid., 2a.

[46] Du Qingchi, "Guangdong Yifeng Nü xuexiao xuyuan," 2a.

from foreign languages. Each piece would mobilize certain intellectual resources in defining the *guo* and the ensuing reassignment of women's responsibilities in the *guo*. Right after Du Qingchi's aforementioned essay in *Continued Publication of Women's Journal* 6, Chen published a piece about the women of Sparta. She recounts,

Sparta (tenth century BCE–146 BCE) established its educational system not only for men but, more importantly, also for women. The Spartans saw women not as a part of the family but as a part of the *guojia* [state]. Therefore, no men of other countries could compete with the Spartan men with respect for their women ... The Spartan women considered the purpose of self-cultivation to be to give birth to courageous and healthy citizens on behalf of the state. They would not, however, pay attention to things such as sewing and cooking.[47]

Using the ancient European story as an intellectual resource, Chen Xiefen and her colleagues advocated dissolving women's bondage to the family. They pushed women to face the nation-state directly, not as talented individuals as the *Chinese Girl's Progress* proposed but as birth machines empowering the race. Women were thus asked to serve the *guo* with their fertile wombs rather than their creative minds. They would be deprived of their traditional position as educators of their children – sons and daughters – and assistants to their husbands, and thus also of the ability to expand their influence to the state through those relations. Furthermore, in order for them to breed strong children, their education is redirected from knowledge acquisition to physical exercise, as the article argues: "All women should take rigorous education equally with men, focusing specifically on soccer, wrestling, boxing, and all sorts of gymnastics. They should compete with one another."[48]

   This repositioning of women within the *guo* also redefined the connotation of "loving the *guo*." And thus the story of the Spartan women continues:

The [Spartan] women possessed such noble and pure personalities that no women in the other Greek city-states could measure up to them. [Among all their virtues] the Spartan women most valued their heart/mind of loving the *guo*. There was a woman who had eight sons. All of the eight died for the state in the Messenian War, and Sparta thereupon won a great victory. As the army returned and the ritual was held for mourning the fallen soldiers, the mother did not shed a single tear. She prayed in a loud voice, saying: "O Sparta, I gave birth to these eight men because of my love for you!" Her words were broadly circulated in contemporary eulogies. From this story, we can see that the Spartan women encouraged their men with the heart/mind of loving the *guo*. From this story, we can also see the spirit with which the Spartans established their *guo*.[49]

It is unclear which Messinian War is referred to in this episode, the first (ca. 743–ca. 724 BCE) or the second (685–668 BCE). Both were fought when

---

[47] Chen Xiefen, "Sibada nüzi," 1a.   [48] Ibid.   [49] Ibid., 1b.

the militarily stronger Sparta invaded Messinia and enslaved its people. The translator celebrates the mother's devotion to the empowerment of the *guo* regardless of whether the war itself was justified.

Chen Xiefen also published a one-act drama entitled "Aiguo nü'er chuanqi" (Romance of patriotic girls) in the sixth issue of *Continued Publication of Women's Journal*. The five characters in this piece are all modeled on reformers of the time. The leading female role, Xie Jinqin, is modeled on Xue Jinqin (1883–1960), and the supporting female role, Yu Mengban, on Wu Mengban (1883–1902).[50] The drama starts with Xie Jingqin's *youguo zhi cheng* (sincere concern about the *guo*) as China faces increasing imperial aggression amidst international competition. Xie therefore contends that Chinese women should abandon their conventional family duties and their literary and artistic interests:

> Why talk about Girl Xie, Lady Ban, and women's education?
> I know long ago that having no talent is a woman's virtue!
> I only fear some poetic sprite,
> To claim herself a heroine, by composing eight pentasyllabic lines,
> She can easily fall for love-bird [literally, Mandarin ducks] tales,
> Autumn thoughts in the painted pavilion,
> Flying flakes of snow in the frontier,
> Spring longing on the copper path,
> And jade flute on the tower.
> Even with one thousand kinds of such talents,
> She is only capable of sticking to the kitchen.[51]

Invoking the saying popular in late imperial China, that *nüzi wu cai bian shi de* (having no talent is a woman's virtue),[52] Xie Jingqin condemns traditional Chinese women's education for having confined them to narrow, trivial personal feelings. This aria hence delivers a harsh backlash against the 1897–1898 Shanghai campaign for women's education, during which women defended their rights to education and contended that "obtaining talent through learning is itself a virtue."[53] The aria dismisses Girl Xie (Xie Daoyun, ca. 335–after 405) as a mere "poetic sprite," despite her prominent place among the 1898 women reformers as the most eminent woman of talent.[54] Instead, the drama celebrates Queen Victoria as a role model for her achievements in empowering the British nation. In nationalistic fervor, the drama ends with a chorus in

---

[50] See Xia Xiaohong, "Wu Mengban," 93. According to Xia, the drama was written by a Chinese student and originally published in Japan in the *Xinmin congbao* (New people's miscellany), edited by Liang Qichao (ibid.).

[51] *Xuchu nübao* 6 (1902), Column "Nübao fujian" (Appendix), 2b.

[52] Mann, *Talented Women*, xv. For a discussion of the origin and development of the famous phrase "having no talent is a woman's virtue" in the Ming–Qing period, see Liu Yongcong, *De, cai, se, quan*, 165–252.

[53] Nanxiu Qian, "Borrowing Foreign Mirrors," 69.

[54] See Nanxiu Qian, "Revitalizing the *Xianyuan*," 424.

favor of women's martial vigor: "The Jingwei bird, dashing between Ocean and Heaven, was actually female./We should make every Chinese household worship heroines./With slim white hands, we shall restore the beauty of our mountains and rivers."[55] And accordingly, the author suggests a new job for women – to become women warriors guarding the *guo*. Here *guo* means specifically China's territorial integrity in light of Western colonialism, which had swallowed up old countries such as India, not cultural homogeneity, which the mother generation had considered to be the basis of strengthening themselves as well as the country.

In an essay published in the eight issue of *Continued Publication of Women's Journal*, Chen Xiefen privileged racial conflict over gender conflict, thus detaching Chinese women further from their traditional engagements. She asserts that Chinese women would not mind being Chinese men's slaves "had there not been other races coming to compete with ours."[56] Nonetheless,

today the white race has become so powerful that they have gradually adopted the way yellow men restrained their women, and used it to rule the two hundred million [Chinese] men. Therefore, some men love our *guo* so much that they have changed their tactics from enslaving women to promoting education for women... Should we two hundred million Chinese women follow the old custom and be happy to be slaves' slaves? Or should we invigorate ourselves and seize upon this opportunity as men are promoting women's education? If we unite with these hot-blooded men, we can take on the responsibility to *jiuguo jiuzhong* [rescue our *guo* and our race].[57]

This self-positioning as slaves' slaves totally changed the tone from that in the *Chinese Girl's Progress*, which had identified women as equal co-managers of the family and the state in China's long history. For the first time, radical Chinese women willingly reduced their elite social status, revealing their anxiety about China's failure in global competition. This anxiety intensifies the discourse of "loving the *guo*" from *bao* (protecting) to *qiang* (empowering) and then *jiu* (rescuing) the race and the nation-state.

The inclusion of the Japanese feminist Shimoda Utako's (1854–1936) "Lun Zhongguo nüxue shi" (On education for Chinese women) in the *Continued Publication of Women's Journal*, issue 9 completes the nationalistic discourse of "loving the *guo*." Making references to social Darwinism, Shimoda accuses footbinding of making Chinese women "useless" and causing them to produce unhealthy children and thus weaken the Chinese race. Shimoda warns the Chinese people, "Today's world is a world of racial competition. The superior wins and the inferior loses; the strong survives and the weak disappears. The

---

[55] Chen Xiefen, "Aiguo nü'er chuanqi," 2b–3a. For a discussion on the valorization of *nühao* (heroine) in the *Continued Publication of Women's Journal/Journal of Women's Learning*, see Xia's chapter in this volume.

[56] Chen Xiefen, "Nannü dou yao kan," 2a.   [57] Ibid., 2a–2b.

five continents, as large as they are, cannot tolerate such a weak and inferior nation on earth!"[58]

Shimoda, however, sees hope in Chinese women. She recalls that when Chinese men waved Japanese flags to welcome the Eight-Power Allied Forces into Beijing, women who were assaulted by the foreign invaders killed themselves:

This is the most beautiful characteristic of your women. While those who commit suicide knew only to love their bodies, education will enlighten them to loving the nation. We should educate women to love their nation as they love their bodies. They should seek ways to protect the nation and themselves and to make the nation and themselves independent. Any foreigners who dare damage even one small bit of their nation are insulting their nation. What they have done is no different from insulting these women's bodies, and women would take this as unbearable humiliation. Even with their bodies violated, they would avenge this resentment and protect the nation until their last breath![59]

Shimoda appeals to the late imperial cult of chastity, which had been overturned by the *Chinese Girl's Progress*, and assigns Chinese women the difficult responsibility of protecting the nation with their lives and chastity. Pushing women's position closer to the *guo*, she identifies a woman's sexual body with the nation's geo-body, and thus politicizes the former and genders the latter.[60]

Shimoda's proposition was echoed by Chinese male nationalists, such as Jiang Zhiyou in his speech at the opening ceremony of the Aiguo nüxuexiao (Patriotic girls' school), which is published in *Continued Publication of Women's Journal*, issue 9. Jiang divides human communities into three types – outdated *shenjia zhuyi* (family-ism), future *shijie zhuyi* (cosmopolitanism), and *guojia zhuyi* (nationalism), which "we should endeavor to work on in the present." Although family-ism had been China's social focus, it was now obsolete. "Its *zhen* (chaste), *jie* (virtuous), *xiao* (filial), and *lie* (martyred) daughters, with their integrity, disposition, and fine qualities, are worthy of emulation today," but only if these girls are attuned in their actions and minds to nationalism. Appropriating the late imperial cult of chastity to nationalistic ends, Jiang modernizes traditional women who sacrificed their bodies to protect Confucian morality into *yingxiong haojie zhi nüzi* (heroines) who would sacrifice their bodies to rescue the nation-state. Jiang elevates these heroines as *shangpin zhi nüzi* (women of high quality), and sees them as models for the *xinfa* (new method) in girls' schools. In sharp contrast, he denigrates *cainü*

---

[58] Shimoda, "Lun Zhongguo nüxue shi," 2a. Judge points out that Shimoda "took a meliorist stance" in reading this incident, merging "Confucian principles with new nationalist concerns" (Judge, *Precious Raft*, 184).

[59] Shimoda, "Lun Zhongguo nüxue shi," 3b–4a.

[60] I borrowed the concept "geo-body" from Winichakul, *Siam Mapped*, 16. It "describes the operations of the technology of territoriality which created nationhood spatially."

(women of talent), favored in the earlier journal, as *xiapin zhi nüzi* (low-quality women), for they were trained by the *jiufa* (old method).[61]

Chen Xiefen, too, in her design of the *Zhongguo nüzi zhi qiantu* (Future of Chinese women), leverages what she assumes to be the *te mei xing* (most beautiful quality) that Chinese women possess to nationalistic ends:

> According to a slanderous comment on Chinese women: *zui du furen xin!* (A woman's mind is most malicious). I know, however, that this malicious nature is actually the most beautiful quality our women possess...Once we women understand that the Manchus are aliens who brutalize our compatriots and cede our territory [to foreign invaders], strong hatred will grow in us. We'll use all of our ability to fight against them regardless of our personal safety. What we call the "malice of a woman's mind" means this: As soon as we know who is not [our own], we shall fight him to the last minute.

This essay, published in the last issue (the fourth) of the *Journal of Women's Learning* in November 1903, signals the final separation of the "daughter" from its founding "mother." Blaming China's sad situation on the alien "Manchus," Chen Xiefen advocates establishing a pure "Chinese" nation-state. To reach this goal, Chen invokes Chinese women's *duxing* (malicious nature) and praises it as their "most beautiful quality." For this malicious nature nurtures women's *baofu xin* (spirit of vengeance) and so enables them to overthrow the Manchu regime. Chen thus replaces *cainü* who serve the *guo* with their talents with *nühao* (heroines) who purify the race by killing aliens. The nurturers of life are transformed into life's destroyers to avenge the suffering and humiliation of their own race.

Similarly to its 1898 "mother" journal, the 1902–1903 "daughter" journal linked its conceptualization of *guo* to the idea of a global imaginary. The occupation of the capital Beijing by the Eight-Power Allied Forces stirred up resentment against the West among the Chinese intellectual elite, which resulted in the journal's social Darwinist stance on the conflict between the white and the yellow races.[62] Furthermore, after the Qing court's heavy-handed persecution of the revolutionary *Subao* (Jiangsu journal), which had been published by Chen Xiefen's father, Chen Fan (1860–1913), in June 1903, Chen Xiefen escaped to Japan and received strong revolutionary/nationalistic influence from Japanese feminists. The last issue of the 1903 *Journal of Women's Learning*, which Chen Xiefen published in Tokyo, clearly reveals this orientation.[63]

Evidently, these particular sociopolitical circumstances determined the reconceptualization of *guo* and thus informed these particular inflections of the "nation-state" within the global grammar of modernity.

---

[61] Jiang Zhiyou, "Aiguo nü xuexiao," 1b–2b.
[62] See Nanxiu Qian, "The mother *Nü Xuebao*," 286–89.   [63] See ibid., 257 n3, 280.

Conclusion

As mentioned at the outset of this essay, the *Chinese Girl's Progress* has been eliminated from the genealogy and canon of Chinese women's journals, whereas the *Continued Publication of Women's Journal/Journal of Women's Learning* has been celebrated. We may explain this historical choice by drawing upon Benedict Anderson's theory of the formation of nations, and in particular the new temporal consciousness that helps to formulate the sense of a new community in historical lineage and gives new communities a sense of homogeneous time in reading the news media.[64] From the two women's journals examined in this chapter, we can see that each formulated its version of *guo* under the sway of a "new temporal consciousness" that interacted with certain aspects of China's "historical lineage." The *Chinese Girl's Progress* stood firmly on its Confucian and Daoist roots and understood changes in the world primarily in terms of knowledge expansion. The women reformers subsequently conceptualized *guo* as a special culturally bound entity that provided the best opportunity for women to "mother" all under Heaven in their own terms. The *Continued Publication of Women's Journal/Journal of Women's Learning* was published in the wake of the 1900 Boxer Rebellion and the ensuing invasion of the Eight-Power Allied Forces. In the view of the revolutionaries, both of these events were the product of the Manchu nobles' mishandling of the situation, which fueled nationalistic sentiments.[65] Under these circumstances, the *Continued Publication of Women's Journal/Journal of Women's Learning* refuted the more autonomous themes of the *Chinese Girl's Progress* and invoked a new nationalistic patriarchy.

The deletion of the *Chinese Girl's Progress* from modern Chinese historiography typifies the extent to which women's emancipation has long since been entangled with nationalism. The elimination of its memory started as early as 1907, barely a decade after its publication, in the event of registering a more "revolutionary" beginning of Chinese women's journalism. In the inaugural issue of the *Shenzhou nübao* (China women's journal/Women's journal of the divine continent) (December 1907), a periodical that claimed to have continued republican martyr Qiu Jin's (1875–1907) *Zhongguo nübao* (Chinese women's journal), the editor Chen Yiyi (a.k.a. Chen Zhiqun, 1889–1962), a central figure in late Qing journalism for women, attributed *mengnie chuxing* (the first sprout) of women's journals to the 1902–1903 *Continued Publication*

---

[64] For Anderson's discussion on "temporal consciousness" and "homogeneous time," see his *Imagined Communities*, 22–24. See also Winichakul, *Siam Mapped*, 16.

[65] See Nanxiu Qian, "The mother *Nü Xuebao*," for a detailed discussion on how the 1900 incident influenced the formation of the nationalistic discourse in the *Continued Publication of Women's Journal/Journal of Women's Learning*.

of Women's Journal/Journal of Women's Learning.[66] Chen Yiyi reiterated this assertion in his investigation of women's periodicals published in the third issue of *China Women's Journal* (February 1908),[67] and again in the first issue of his *Nübao* (Women's journal) in 1909.[68]

The *Continued Publication of Women's Journal/Journal of Women's Learning*'s radical conceptualization of *guo* and the reassignment of women's responsibilities in the *guo* suited the revolutionary mood of the time. They were also in sync with the momentum of nationalistic patriarchy, which succeeded Confucian patriarchy. In contrast, the 1898 *Chinese Girl's Progress*'s version of *guo* and of women's role within it may have made nationalistic men uneasy. Its strong sense of subjectivity and sweeping demands to become the intelligent "mother" of the world must have sounded shockingly unfamiliar to patriarchal ears. It is significant in the writing of a history of women's journals as a genre that canonization only allows some of them a room of their own, while eliminating the recollection of others. Yet these others may have lingered in the personal memories of, perhaps, not just a few readers.

[66] Chen Yiyi, "*Shenzhou nübao* fakanci," 9. For Chen Yiyi's life, his connections with Qiu Jin, and his contribution to late Qing women journalism, see Xia Xiaohong, "Wan-Qing nüxing."

[67] Originally in *Shenzhou Nübao* 3 (1908); included in *Nülun*, 11–12. This investigation listed eleven journals, plus the *Huixing nü xuebao* (Huixing journal of women's learning) that Chen mentioned in the *Nülun*, p. 13, and his own *Women's Journal*, Chen recorded thirteen women's journals published by 1909.

[68] Chen Yiyi, "Fakan ci": 1. Because of the lack of the 1899 issues of Chen Xiefen's *Women's Journal* and misguided by Chen Yiyi's account, I had hastily concluded that Chen Xiefen's 1902 *Xuchu nübao* continued the 1898 *Nü xuebao*; see Qian, "The Mother *Nü Xuebao*," 257–65. Xia Xiaohong's recent research confirmed that Chen Xiefen indeed published four biweekly issues of the *Nübao* in late 1899, and hence her *Xuchu nübao* continued her own journal; see Xia, "Wan-Qing liangfen *Nü xuebao*," 6–8.

11　Western Heroines in Late Qing Women's Journals: Meiji-Era Writings on "Women's Self-Help" in China

Xia Xiaohong
Translated by Joshua A. Fogel[1]

Biographies of Western exemplars first published in Meiji Japan left a profound imprint on the late Qing period. They were particularly successful because they appeared in "women's self-help" writings, which were sold in immense quantities at the time in Japan. Not only were individual volumes translated in a timely fashion, but also copious materials from these sources were published in the biography columns in Chinese women's journals.[2] This essay examines, in a vertical reading, three consecutively published and influential late Qing women's journals: *Nübao* (Women's journal, later continued as *Xuchu nübao* [Continued publication of women's journal], and later again renamed *Nü xuebao* [Journal of women's learning]), *Nüzi shijie* (Women's world), and *Zhongguo xin nüjie zazhi* (Magazine of China's new world of women). I explore the ideas inherent in the biographies of Western heroines in these journals by locating them within their respective Chinese and Japanese contexts and intertexts. In an integrated reading, I look for connections between these translations and the objectives of women's journals of the time. At the same time, I provide a deeply situated reading of late Qing Chinese women's journals, scrutinizing their particular invention of womankind within a view of the broader global milieu.

"Women's Self-Help" in the Meiji Era

Following the Meiji Restoration, Western civilization was introduced into Japanese society at an accelerated pace. Amid the waves of enlightenment in the world of thought, July 1871 (the fourth year of the Meiji period) witnessed

---

[1] The translator would like to thank Nanxiu Qian for reading through an earlier and rougher version of this translation and helping to correct particularly problematic areas. The only emendation that I have made to Xia's manuscript is to add the dates of the people mentioned where that information was available – JAF.

[2] Individual volumes include Iwasaki and Mikami, *Sekai jūni joketsu*; the following year in February, it was published in a Chinese translation with the same title in Shanghai.

the publication of the translation by Nakamura Masanao (1832–1891) of Samuel Smiles's (1812–1904) *Self-Help* into Japanese under the title *Saigoku risshi hen*. This translation, intended for the fashioning of "independent and autonomous" character among the Japanese people, was highly appealing to young readers because the writing style of the original text dotted storytelling with didactic maxims.[3] Together with another work translated by Nakamura and published in the same year – *On Liberty* by John Stuart Mill (1806–1873), *Jiyūron* in Japanese – these two volumes formed "the most widely distributed works of enlightenment in the early Meiji era."[4]

Along with the popularity of *Self-Help*, a succession of imitations began to appear. Among them were similar works about women, compiled by different authors and driven by different modes of thought, but all consistent in their orientation toward "encouraging the ambitions of women and girls."[5] Over time, the mode of compilation was gradually transformed from slavish imitation of Nakamura's text to works that contained biographies only and reduced the number of maxims. Although there were volumes that mixed Japanese with Westerners, most works tended to separate the two.

The great success and popularity of "women's self-help" books in the Meiji period, which undertook the mission of refashioning the very character of Japanese women, soon spread to China. Because these books were relatively accessible to the Chinese, those who translated the biographies of Western heroines in the "biography" columns of late Qing women's journals generally used these new collections as their sources. In this way, the late Qing process of transplanting Western female paragons was similar to the Meiji Japanese experience.

"Western Beauties" in *Chinese Girl's Progress/Journal of Women's Learning*

Women's Journal, Continued Publication of Women's Journal, and *Journal of Women's Learning* (1899–1903) were edited by Chen Xiefen (1883–1923), daughter of Chen Fan (1860–1913), who owned the Shanghai newspaper *Subao* (Jiangsu journal). Initially, Chen Xiefen edited the journal as an extracurricular activity while she was a student. When the journal changed its name to *Journal of Women's Learning* after 1902, she became a professional journalist. Chen's single-handed management of the journal marks the beginning of a new phase in Chinese press history.[6] As the journal was initially included gratis

---

[3] Nakamura, "Sōron"; original in Kanbun. Nakamura had served as supervisor of Japanese students in Britain.

[4] Kindai Nihon shisō shi kenkyūkai, *Jindai Riben sixiang*, 41.

[5] Shirose, *"Taisei retsujoden* shogen" (Introduction to *Biographies of Western Women*), in *Taisei retsujoden*.

[6] China's first women's paper, *Nü xuebao – Chinese Girl's Progress*, discussed in Qian's chapter in this volume, began publication on July 24, 1898; writing and editorial work was primarily the

in the newspaper, male readers of *Jiangsu Journal* were among its expected readers. It is, however, clear that the journal was also aimed at women, with a particular focus on female students. Despite the fact that Chinese education for girls had only recently begun to emerge and girls' schools run by Western missionaries were few in number at the time, teachers and students in these few girls' schools did indeed demonstrate considerable interest in this one and only women's journal.[7]

Throughout its existence, *Women's Journal* (and later *Journal of Women's Learning*) was primarily concerned with promoting female education and "extending the general principles of women's rights."[8] Chen Xiefen devoted considerable energy to the collection of women's biographies. She explained in one of her essays,

In every region of every land, if a woman, live or dead, possesses special talents and erudite learning, and carries lofty ambitions and has accomplished extraordinary things, her relatives and friends should valorize her by writing her a biography, a eulogy, or a poem. Or, they can simply describe her deeds and this journal will help polish them. Either way is fine.[9]

To be sure, the object of this appeal for submissions to the journal was confined to "relatives and friends," and included poetry. This was not fully consistent with what was actually published later. The proposed standards of selection were also general and vague. Even so, this first solicitation for articles on the theme of women's accomplishments is of immense significance. Only a few biographies of Chinese women ultimately met the editor's standards, and stories of Western heroines had to be translated. Therefore, it was not yet possible to include an independent column for "biographies" in the journal.

Aside from the last issue, the biographies Chen published were all essays submitted to the journal or transcribed from other sources. As a result, her editorial disposition is only manifest in the choice of selections published. Among them were four translated biographies of Western women that appeared in differently titled columns: "Picha nüren zhuan" (Biography of [Harriet]

responsibility of the women board members and teachers at women's schools in China. When Chen Xiefen founded her own women's journal in 1899 she first used the title *Nübao* (Women's journal), then, as Qian explains in her chapter, changed it to *Xuchu nübao* (Continued publication of women's journal), and then in 1902 to *Nü xuebao* (Journal of women's learning). When Chen initially founded *Nübao* in 1899 she was studying at the McTyeire Home and School for Girls founded by American missionaries.
[7] See under the collective title "Wuben nüxuetang keyi" – where there appears a seven-point editorial of female students concerning *Women's Journal*.
[8] (Huang) Shouqu, "Wuben nüxuetang keyi." For this essay, I am using a reprint of the *Journal of Women's Learning* obtained from Professor Nanxiu Qian; special thanks go to her.
[9] Chen Xiefen, "Xuban *Nübao* shili."

Beecher [Stowe]) in the editorial column;[10] "Luolan furen zhuan" (Biography of Madame Roland) as an appendix; and both "Bishimaike furen zhuan" (Biography of the wife of Bismarck) and "Yingguo nüjie Niejike'er zhuan" (Biography of [Florence] Nightingale of England) as "translated items." When the journal moved to Tokyo, Chen had the opportunity to personally access "women's self-help" writings of the Meiji period, and she had greater autonomy in selecting and editing translated items. Both the original "Biography of [Florence] Nightingale of England,"[11] signed with the translators' names, and Chen's own vernacular rewriting of the serial "Shijie shi nüjie yanyi" (Tales of ten world heroines) appeared in the final issue of the *Journal of Women's Learning*.[12] Unfortunately, this issue also marked the premature death of the journal.

The biographies carried in the pages of Chen's journal were mostly transcribed from elsewhere, and Chen had studied English, not Japanese; thus, Chen may actually have been unaware that the "original pieces" she selected had been translated from Japanese. Many of the biographies of Western heroines that she published bore the imprint of Meiji-period writings on "women's self-help." Once we track down the originals, it is evident that most of them come from *Sekai kokon meifu kagami* (A mirror of famous women of the world, past and present).[13]

The biographies of Madame Roland and Bismarck's wife are good examples. The immediate source for the former is Liang Qichao's (1873–1929) biography of Madame Roland, which he published in the journal he was editing in Yokohama, *Xinmin congbao* (New people's miscellany).[14] The immediate source for the biography of Bismarck's wife, on the other hand, was the Shanghai periodical *Dalu bao* (The continent), and it then appeared, just a few months later, in the *Journal of Women's Learning*.[15] The Japanese originals are, respectively, "Fukkoku kakumei no hana (Rōran fujin no den)" (Flower of the French Revolution, a biography of Madame Roland) and "Bisumaruku fujin" (Bismarck's wife) from the chapter entitled "Seijika no tsuma" (Wife of a politician), both from *A Mirror of Famous Women*.

Madame Roland (Marie-Jeanne Roland de la Platière, 1754–1793) was one of the first Western heroines introduced to Japan. Her name appears as early as 1876 in Shirose's *Taisei retsujoden* (Biographies of Western women), and she later appears frequently in many "women's self-help" writings.[16] The

---

[10] This essay originally appeared in 1902 in *Xuanbao* 選報 (Election reports), a journal edited and printed in Shanghai.

[11] Qianhui and Zhidu, transl., "Yingguo nüjie."

[12] Chunan nüzi, "Shijie shi nüjie."   [13] Tokutomi, *Sekai kokon meifu kagami.*

[14] Liang Qichao, "Luolan furen zhuan."   [15] "Bishimaike Furen zhuan."

[16] Shirose's *Taisei retsujoden* (Biographies of Western women), published in 1876, may be considered the first Japanese work to introduce the achievements of Western heroines.

biography of Madame Roland edited by Tokutomi Roka under the title "Flower of the French Revolution" established a close relationship between the subject of the biography and the French Revolution, the high tide of Madame Roland's life and activities. The Japanese scholar Matsuo Yōji meticulously went through the text comparing and examining it in its entirety and thus establishing that Liang Qichao's "Biography of Madame Roland" (aside from the beginning and the tail end) was a translation fundamentally based on Tokutomi's piece. Liang's deletions and emendations, which watered down the original's description of Madame Roland's radical ideas and actions, corresponded to Liang's retreat from revolution to reform at the time.[17] It remains evident, however, that Madame Roland was a political figure and that Liang Qichao's objective in translating her biography was to convey her political ideals.

Chen Xiefen's transcription of the text in *Journal of Women's Learning* again subtly changed the essay. By calling Roland "the first heroine of the modern age," Chen emphasized Madame Roland's patriotic enthusiasm. This is the thrust as well of the opening lines of Liang's "Madame Roland," a landmark at the time:

Who was Madame Roland? She was the mother of Napoleon, the mother of Metternich, the mother of Mazzini, the mother of Kossuth, the mother of Bismarck, and the mother of Cavour. In short, all men of the nineteenth-century European continent could not but regard her as mother; all civilizations of the nineteenth-century European continent could not but regard her as mother. Why? Because the French Revolution was the mother of nineteenth-century Europe, and Madame Roland was the mother of the French Revolution.

This passage uses Madame Roland's gender as a metaphor and extends her status as a woman to that of the mother of great men and of civilization. It thus promotes the popular late Qing notion that women were *guomin zhi mu* (mothers of citizens) and detaches Roland from the political message Liang had wished to convey.[18] The version of the biography in *Continued Publication of Women's Journal* ends just as Madame Roland is about to appear on the stage of the French Revolution, making this section, which had been specifically added by Liang Qichao, all the more eye-opening.

Unlike this biography, which emphasized Madame Roland's identity as a politician, the biography of Bismarck's wife emphasizes the status of its subject as the "wife of a politician." This biography focuses on the profound familial joy that Johanna von Puttkamer (1824–1894) shared with her husband, the famous German "prime minister of blood and iron" (Otto von Bismarck, 1815–1898). When the *Journal of Women's Learning* transcribed the essay, however, it deleted the opening lines of the original from *The Continent*, which recorded the mourning for Mrs Bismarck in many countries after her death in

---

[17] Matsuo, "Ryō Keichō to shiden."

[18] See my essay, Xia Xiaohong, "Shijie gujin mingfu jian."

1894 and her husband's great sadness. Also deleted were the following lines added by the translator from *The Continent* in order to elevate her importance: "The story of the life of [Bismarck's] wife is the story of the life of Count Bismarck; the story of the life of Count Bismarck is the story of Germany's recent history." Thus, it is emphasized that from the time she recognized Bismarck as a hero and accepted his marriage proposal, until the couple reached old age together, Mrs Bismarck's life was always centered on her husband.

It was not that Mrs Bismarck lacked all political aspirations. The original Japanese text notes that "she was truly a woman with honorable intentions." Yet, in a letter she wrote to an English woman, she regretted that "my country has no room for a movement devoted to women's freedom." In tracing the reasons for this, Tokutomi Roka concluded that Bismarck feared the consequences of an "Empress Dowager" becoming involved in politics, and thus, according to him, "Mrs [Bismarck] lacked a clear opportunity to satisfy her honorable intentions."[19] In the Chinese translation, this was changed to actually draw an analogy with the Empress Dowager's *juzhi* (obstruction) of the political reform movement.

In any event, Mrs Bismarck accepted this limitation. Thus, the Chinese translator changed the text from what it had been in the Japanese original, and added material before coming to the conclusion: "Now, Mrs [Bismarck] made her family the nation and her family politics national politics. With her electric mind, she assisted Bismarck in accomplishing his life-long enterprise and so touched numerous political figures of the time. She was truly a technician of the political machine, a 'political wife.'" The original Japanese text used the term political "woman" (*fùren*) but the translator rendered it as political "wife" (*fūren*). Whether or not this was a slip of the pen, "wife" and not female politician was without a doubt the core notion of this biography, which emphasizes that, without engaging directly in politics, women might still gain political fame in assisting their husbands.

After Chen Xiefen fled to Japan, she included a section in *Journal of Women's Learning* entitled "Shijie shi nüjie yanyi" (Tales of ten world heroines), which was written in the vernacular.[20] This work was based on the anonymous *Shijie shi nüjie* (Ten world heroines), published in March 1903.[21] *Ten World Heroines* was in turn based on two Japanese texts: *Sekai jūni joketsu* (Twelve world heroines) by Iwasaki and Mikami and Tokumi's *Sekai kokon meifu kagami* (Past and present world-famous women exemplars). Material derived from the

[19] "Bisumaruku fujin," in the chapter entitled "Seijika no tsuma" in Tokutomi, *Sekai kokon meifu kagami*, 114–15.

[20] Chunan nüzi, "Shijie shi nüjie."

[21] Cf. *Shijie shi nüjie*. According to the diary of Zhou Zuoren (1885–1967), in an entry dated April 9, 1903: "On that day received from Lu Xun 'a letter dated the fifth from Japan.' Says he's asked someone to bring *Shijie shi nüjie* from the booklist." See Lu Xun Bowuguan, ed., *Zhou Zuoren riji*, 383–84.

latter constitutes no less than half of the Chinese work. The anonymous "editor" also added much to the translation concerning "revolution" and "women's rights," and thus he could boast of *Ten World Heroines* that "although it was a compilation of translations, it really was closer to an [original] work."[22]

We can see in Chen's addition of *yanyi* (tales) to the title that her original plan was to use an anecdotal tone to recast the stories of these "ten extraordinary heroines." Aside from amusement ("to extinguish all of our sisters' melancholy"), Chen considered it most important to appreciate and emulate Western heroines so that "one can learn how to make herself a heroine. Would this not be something of real value?"[23] Immediately beneath the title, there was a decorative frame with four Chinese characters meaning "Western beauties." This subtitle not only demarcated the scope of "world heroines"; it also clearly followed the lead from Liang Qichao's idea that the twentieth century would be "an age in which the two civilizations" of East and West "would marry"; thus "Western beauties would be able to breed ideal babies for us to invigorate our race."[24] This encompassed the higher aspiration of introducing these Western heroines in order to reform the character of the Chinese people.

The tale of "Meishi'er" (Louise Michel, 1830–1905) appeared in the final issue of Chen Xiefen's *Journal of Women's Learning*. Michel's biography in *Ten World Heroines* is based on the chapter "Rui Miseeru joshi" (Ms Louise Michel) from Iwasaki and Mikami's *Twelve World Heroines* and material from "Yashamen no jobosatsu (Rui Miseeru)" (Louise Michel, a female bodhisattva with a she-devil face), a chapter in Tokumi's *Past and Present World-Famous Women Exemplars*. The anonymous "editor" also added a number of details to render it a more revolutionary piece. In the text proper of these two Japanese biographies, there is a reference to Michel as "a female general of the anarchist party," and this was used as the title of her biography in the *Ten World Heroines*, clearly demonstrating the intentions of the editor-translator.

When Chen Xiefen was revising the piece again, for publication in her journal, she was obviously concerned that her readers included young girls. Considering the need for entertainment as well, she cut out the first full two pages, which advocated "give me *liberty* or give me *death*" and the anarchists' advocacy of violent revolution, and directly recounted Michel's life from birth. Although this vernacular tale only tells Louise Michel's life as a girl prior to the age of fourteen when her political career had yet to begin, her revolutionary temperament was already in evidence.

Compared to the version to be found in *Ten World Heroines*, Chen Xiefen's rewrite was moderate in many areas. Not only was the title simplified to

---

[22] "Liyan" (Introductory remarks), in Shijie shi nüjie, 1–2. For related matters, see my essay, Xia Xiaohong, "Shijie gujin mingfu jian." See also Judge, *Precious Raft*, 25–27, Chapter 5, passim.
[23] Chunan nüzi, "Shijie shi nüjie yanyi."   [24] Liang Qichao, "Lun Zhongguo xueshu sixiang."

"Meishi'er," but also, while the earlier text had Michel state in her youth, "I stand for justice and righteousness – even if we must use violence, I shall not retreat,"[25] in Chen's hand this changed to "I stand for the public and for justice and righteousness – if I thus offend someone, so be it!" Nonetheless, Chen Xiefen quoted in detail the earliest sprouts of Michel's ideas of women's rights and revolutionary thought from the *Ten World Heroines*, which in turn borrowed the passage from *Past and Present World-Famous Women Exemplars*. It reads: "At leisure she would ask her male cousin to sing the 'Song of Women's Rights,' and she would accompany with a flute. She would make a stage in an overgrown field and direct a group of children to enact the French Revolution. Grasping a short sword, spirits invigorated, she assigned herself to be in charge of the guillotine (*kouleqin*), shouting 'Long live liberty!!! Long live [liberty].'"[26] As she did not understand the word *kouleqin*, which was the phonetic rendering of "guillotine," she translated it as "broke down the jail." Furthermore, in her narrative, Chen also adjusted the topic to the current situation in China. For instance, she explained the word "liberty" after "long live liberty" as follows:

The two-character expression *ziyou* (liberty, freedom) has numerous fine points to it, so that it would be impossible to name them all in a short period of time. Its general meaning is that each person has his own right to freedom as long as he uses it appropriately. The rich may not control the poor, and the strong may not control the weak. Nonetheless, if someone does do something wrong, even if it is the high and mighty emperor of China, he must be placed under the control of ordinary people.

With this explanation, the text about a Western heroine's activities transmitted new ideas and new knowledge as well as fostering a new morality. It thus put into practice the primary intention of *Women's Journal* and *Journal of Women's Learning*, that of promoting women's education – for the sake of the Chinese nation.

The introduction of Western women by these two journals clearly transcended the traditional *lienü zhuan* (biographies of exemplary women). Instead it aligned itself with the Meiji-era "women's self-help" materials in moving from celebrating "famous women" to honoring "heroines." At the very least one-half of the biographies came from Japanese sources. Most of them bore the expression *nüjie* (heroine, Japanese *joketsu*) in their titles. The trajectories of these "Western beauties" were numerous and confused. Western learning still carried within it notions of patriotism, wise wives, revolution, women's rights, and the like. The biographies of Harriet Beecher Stowe and Florence Nightingale both affirmed a sense of national salvation and were consonant with the journal's principles of promoting women's education and women's rights. They

---

[25] *Shijie shi nüjie*, 3.
[26] *Shijie shi nüjie*, 4. On the circumstances, see Tokutomi, *Sekai kokon meifu kagami*, 241–42.

also echoed the manifold expectations of women scattered through many other articles. Most worthy of our attention is Chen Xiefen's intention to introduce these "Western beauties" in order to reform the character of Chinese women and give birth to robust new Chinese citizens. In importing diverse images from the West via Japan, the biography column in *Journal of Women's Learning* thus provided late Qing women in this transitional era with fresh models of women.

Western "Love of the Race" in *Women's World*

When *Women's World* initially appeared in 1904, women's education had gradually begun to develop in various parts of China. Ding Zuyin, Xu Nianci (1875–1908), and others took advantage of the favorable situation and founded a girls' school in Changshu in December of that year. The journal's intended readership was primarily teachers and students at girls' schools. This is evident in a special column, "Nüxue wencong" (Female learning series), and other columns such as "Shiye" (Industry), "Kexue" (Science), and "Weisheng" (Hygiene), which functioned as school texts and were added after the journal's "major reform" with the fifth issue.

It was with the publication of *Women's World* that "biographies" (historical biographies [*shizhuan*]) were assigned a regular column for the first time in the history of Chinese women's journals. Considering that Zhao Bizhen's translation of *Twelve World Heroines*, the anonymous *Ten World Heroines*, and Ding Zuyin's own translation of Muramatsu's *The Wives of Great Heroes [in the Modern West]*[27] all appeared one year prior to this, translated introductions of Western heroines were clearly extremely popular at this time. Launched in early 1904, *Women's World* aimed to go in a different direction. In the inaugural issue, the editor repeatedly stated that "we shall not display European fashions, but we shall offer our national essence." The editors went to great pains to commend outstanding ancient Chinese women of "valor," "knights-errant," and those accomplished in "literature and the arts." They expressed the hope that "our most beloved and intimate 200,000,000 female compatriots" would continue and enhance the glories of the tradition. "Together we must cultivate ourselves to become female generals, female knights-errant, and female scholars, struggling for existence in the twentieth century."[28] Evidently, the rediscovery of *nüjie weiren* (great women figures) in China became a new approach in *Women's World* as it sought models for women to emulate.[29]

A close examination of the content of the journal demonstrates that while it was generally consistent with this Chinese orientation, the "Biographies"

---

[27] Iwasaki and Mikami, *Shijie shi'er nüjie*; Anonymous, *Shijie shi nüjie*; Muramatsu Rakusui, *(Jinshi Ou-Mei) haojie zhi xijun.*

[28] (Ding) Chuwo, "Nüzi shijie songci." See also in the same issue Jin Yi, "*Nüzi shijie* fakanci."

[29] This formulation was first used in Yalu, "Zhongguo di-yi nü haojie"; in 1906 the Xinminshe in Yokohama also published Xu Dingyi's *Zuguo nüjie weiren zhuan*.

column ultimately revealed a move from China to the West. Every biography that appeared in the first four issues of *Women's World* was of an ancient Chinese female soldier or female knight-errant.[30] These texts loyally carried out the editor's initial aim of commending China's national essence. They thus offered a model for those desiring the immediate cultivation of "female soldiers" and "female knights-errant." The fifth issue of the journal published a lead article entitled "Nüquan shuo" (On women's rights) by Ding's classmate and close friend Jiang Weiqiao (1873–1958), who also figures in Paul Bailey's chapter in this volume. Jiang criticized "wild chatter about women's rights" and "wild chatter about liberty," and launched a debate between "women's rights" and "women's education." The "Biographies" column then began publishing essays about the activities of Western heroines for the first time in the fifth issue, and thereafter Western trends gradually overcame Eastern trends, creating roughly an even split between the two.

Aside from two articles concerning contemporary Russian figures, the other five Western women's biographies that appeared in *Women's World* again clearly had their origin in Meiji-era "women's self-help" materials. Each of the authors was really a translator.[31] The only essay whose original I have not yet been able to track down is an essay on the English humanitarian Mary Carpenter.[32] Of the Japanese originals, the earliest published were Takekoshi's *Fujin risshi hen* (On women's self-help) and Shibusawa's *Taisei fujo kikan* (Western female paragons), both 1892, and the latest was Katō's *Joshi risshi hen* (On women's self-help), 1903.[33] It is clear that the Chinese drew on many and varied Japanese materials.

The models of Western heroines as they appeared in the Japanese originals were similarly of many and varied sorts. Florence Nightingale (1820–1910), who administered first aid on the battlefield and was a well-known founder of the Red Cross, was much admired for her "humanitarian" and compassionate temperament. Margaret Roper (1505–1544), eldest daughter of Thomas More

---

[30] See, for example, Shen Tongwu, "Nü junren zhuan"; Yalu, "Zhongguo di-yi nü haojie"; and Liu Yazi, "Zhongguo nü jianxia."

[31] The following lists the articles and their Japanese originals: "Jundui kanhufu Nandige'er zhuan" (Biography of the army nurse, Nightingale) was taken from "Kangofu, Furorensu Naichingeeru" (Florence Nightingale, nurse), a section in Takekoshi, *Fujin risshi hen*; "Xingchang zhi baijin" (White clay on the execution ground), a section in "Furenjie zhi shuangbi" (Double jade piece in the world of women), was taken from "Rōbaa fujin" (Mrs. Roper), a section in Shibusawa, *Taisei fujo kikan*; "Heiye zhi mingxing" (Star in the night) was taken from "Shakai kairyō undō no haha, Uiruraado fujin" (Mrs. Willard, mother of the social reform movement), a section in *Past and Present World Famous Women Exemplars*; "Nü wenhao Haili'aide Feiqushi zhuan" (Biography of Harriet Beecher, great female writer) was taken from "Bungakusha Biichaa Sutō fujin" (Mrs. Beecher Stowe, author of literature), a section in Katō, *Joshi risshi hen*; and "Nü cike Shalutu Geerdie zhuan" (Biography of Charlotte Corday, assassin) was taken from "Shaarotto Korudei jō" (Ms. Charlotte Corday), a chapter in *Twelve World Heroines*.

[32] Juewo, "Yingguo da cishanjia."   [33] Takekoshi, *Fujin risshi hen*; Katō, *Joshi risshi hen*.

(1478–1535, author of *Utopia*), was designated a "filial daughter" in Shibusawa's *Western Female Paragons*. Frances Willard (1839–1898) was a founder of the International Women's Christian Temperance Union (dubbed in the Japanese text the *Bankoku fujin kyōfukai*, or International Women's Society for Moral Reform), whom some referred to as the "mother of the social reform movement." Harriet Beecher Stowe (1811–1896), author of *Uncle Tom's Cabin*, is always listed as a literary author. Tokutomi Sohō (1863–1957), in his dedication for *On Women's Self-Help*, made a special point of praising how "in her one work, *Uncle Tom's Cabin*, she made several million slaves look toward the sunny day of freedom."[34] Charlotte Corday (1768–1793), whose name became associated with the history of the French Revolution, was described as unswervingly determined and courageous in Iwasaki and Mikami's *Twelve World Heroines*, "brandishing the bare sword in her delicate hand, she killed the terrorist Jean-Paul Marat with one strike, and she then calmly went to meet her own death."[35]

These Western women featured in the Meiji "women's self-help" series, whether nurses, filial daughters, social activists, authors, or assassins, shared their "concentration on a particular goal and steadfastness irrespective of the consequences," as Nakamura Masanao noted in his introduction.[36] Ding Zuyin, however, had a different understanding, which he derived from Shibusawa Tamotsu, compiler and translator of *Western Female Paragons*. Shibusawa had written

For the purpose of discussion, we have only considered the weaknesses of Japanese women and the strengths of Western women. We have found Japanese women to have narrow minds while Western women are broad-minded. Because of our narrow-mindedness [and subjugation to our own feelings], we focus our love on one specific person and ignore the suffering of most people. Because of Western women's broad-mindedness, they can love one person while loving many others at the same time. Even in uncertain and difficult times, they do not forget their duty to devote themselves sincerely to the collective.[37]

The influence that these views exerted on Ding Zuyin accounts for his presentation in *Women's World* of the collective ethos of Western heroines. His "Lament for Womankind" was published in the "Editorial" column in the sixth issue of *Women's World* (June 1906).[38] He identified three causes of Chinese women's weaknesses: They "do not love their own kind," they "are not warrior-like," and they "are not soldierly." The latter two points are clearly in agreement with the discussion above about the desire to make "female knights-errant" and "female soldiers." In Ding's argument, the "love" in the

---

[34] Sohō sei, "Fujin risshi hen ni daisu."   [35] Iwasaki and Mikami, "Shaarotto Korudei jō."
[36] Nakamura, "*Saigoku risshi hen* daijūichi hen jo"; original in Kanbun.
[37] Shibusawa, *Taisei fujo kikan*, 2.   [38] (Ding) Chuwo, "Ai nüzhong."

expression "not loving the race or kind" replaced "private," "carnal love" "between men and women" with a much broader spirituality: "Those who love their roots extend themselves to protect every individual and the whole nation: they are the instruments for absorbing the masses and the substance that makes a nation cohere." If we read this together with the following statement from his essay on the "She-devil," we can see that Ding wanted women to expand their personal relations to love of nation and race. His critique of Chinese women's weaknesses was derived from a comparison of China with the West. "These three positive female traits all exist in Western countries and all are absent in our country; they are nurtured daily in the Western countries and ravaged daily in our country. How can our nation not perish? How can our race not disappear?"[39] The conclusion is not difficult to foresee: to eliminate the diseased roots of the ills afflicting Chinese women, he had no choice but to recommend the "good female traits" of the West. Western heroines' biographies thus appeared in timely fashion in the pages of *Women's World*.

The achievements of Western women featured in *Women's World* had generally coincided with Ding Zuyin's specific editorial concerns. These include two essays by Xu Nianci, the biographies of Nightingale and Carpenter.[40] The former recounted Florence Nightingale's ministering to the dying and healing the injured, and related them to the contemporary Russo-Japanese War. He hoped her biography would serve as "a source of reflection" and encouragement to Chinese women. The latter piece discussed the lifetime of philanthropic work performed by Mary Carpenter (1807–1877), a founder of a free school for poor children. It emphasized that "women have a wealth of love, especially for children. This distinctive virtue is consistent, past and present, East and West." This latter biography resonated with Ding Zuyin's "Lament for Womankind," which appeared in the same issue.

Unlike Xu Nianci's introduction to Florence Nightingale, which was generally faithful to the original, Ding's own translations were freer.[41] His essay about Margaret Roper deletes the introduction about her father, Thomas More, which was included in the first half of the original, which was itself excerpted from a volume entitled *Eikoku bungaku shi* (History of British literature). Instead it focuses on the moving circumstances surrounding the persecution of Thomas More and his daughter's willingness to take risks, visit her father in prison, and secure and bury her father's remains. His discussion of Frances Willard similarly excised a large portion of her life story before she turned twenty years of age and foregrounded her major achievements in reforming numerous social ills.[42] At the end of another piece, he added his own

[39] (Ding) Chuwo, "Shuo nümo."
[40] Gu'an, "Jundui kanhufu," and Juewo, "Yingguo da cishanjia."
[41] This is especially true of his "Furenjie zhi shuangbi."   [42] Daxia, "Nü cike."

commentary, which emphasized the importance of affection: "Alas! Many in the world, particularly women, love the race. Although sacrifice for the family is different from sacrifice for the entire nation, there is no reason to dismiss love of family."[43] Ding Zuyin even recognized women willing to die for the family alone. His esteem for love reached a high tide in his "Biography of Harriet Beecher, great female writer." This essay spared no effort in singing the praises of Harriet Beecher Stowe as an "extraordinary woman in the literary world . . . at the time of the American Civil War":

We endeavor to expose her good deeds to the world, and to instill the power of her love in people's minds. Was there any ancient hero who could move people as she did? Is there any other such literary figure in the world? Is there any such female literary figure who could transform people as she could, and whose deeds merit our eulogies and tears?

The author of *Uncle Tom's Cabin* thus earned a string of glorious appellations: "loving flower of the world," "goddess of liberty," and "vanguard of the literary revolutionary army."[44] It is evident that in Ding Zuyin's mind "women writers" needed to be "figures of great affect" whose loftiest ideal was to expand their "power of love" to the world.

This view is echoed in a biography of Charlotte Corday, who agitated for national revolution and used violence and assassination. The translator indicates that in this case, when violence was used to control violence, it derived from the heart. Thus, Charlotte Corday proclaimed after assassinating Marat (1743–1793), "I could not bear to witness the destructive actions of these thugs who compelled my sacred fellow citizens to give up their lives. I thus vow to sacrifice my life in the interest of peace and happiness."[45] No such words exist in the source from which this biography was taken, Iwasaki and Mikami's *Twelve World Heroines*. Instead the biography simply noted: "I have completed what I intended to do today, and now I am at your disposal."[46] That she "could not bear" to stand by as violence was being perpetrated was thus understood as great love for the people of the world.

The best summary of the general tenor of these selections from the Meiji-era "women's self-help" books that served as the sources for *Women's World* is the argument mentioned in an "editorial" in issue 7 entitled "On forging mothers of citizens":

Motherly love and kind-heartedness are distinct character traits of woman. If we examine the civilized nations of the world, among royal parties, political parties, or moderate parties, progressive parties, revolutionary parties, anarchist parties, or in any society, we will always find heroines who can astonish Heaven and move Earth. The enterprises they undertake include founding soup kitchens, clinics, shelters for paupers

[43] (Ding) Chuwo, "Furenjie zhi shuangbi."   [44] (Ding) Chuwo, "Nü wenhao."
[45] Daxia, "Nü cike."   [46] Iwasaki and Mikami, "Shaarotto Korudei jō."

and outlaws, an International Society for Moral Reform, and Red Cross stations . . . We can see that women are only too happy to sacrifice the present and themselves to provide services to the masses.[47]

According to the editorial board of the journal, as represented by Ding Zuyin, women's distinctive character of "motherly love and kind-heartedness" that transcends politics was the highest ethical standard but at the same time also a deficiency in Chinese women. Determined to forge "mothers of citizens," *Women's World* concluded that the meaning of all of the biographies of Western women translated and introduced in the journal could be summed up as humanitarianism, especially a kind of universal love.[48] As Ding Zuyin praises "the power of the flower of love," he uses this philosophy of love to offer the following criticisms as well: "Some great activists of the world often appropriate the good names of liberty and equality and use them to destroy the family and extinguish social morality. Would they not feel ashamed facing these female heroes [who have done so much with love]?"[49] Such a perspective reflects a change in the position of the journal, which from the fifth issue was more reluctant to foreground notions of liberty and women's rights for "women who [lacked] erudition and morality."[50] It reveals the extent to which *Women's World*'s perspective on Western heroines was born of, and in agreement with, circumstances specific to the late Qing – in grappling with gender, they addressed important issues of a global modernity-in-common, but did so in a Chinese idiom.

"Female Citizens" of the West in the *Magazine of China's New World of Women*

The *Magazine of China's New World of Women* was founded in Tokyo by the overseas medical student and secretary for foreign affairs of the Chinese women's student association in Japan, Yan Bin. It is thus not surprising that most of the authors who wrote for this journal were overseas students, and that no small number of them were women. Their knowledge of the Japanese language and of Meiji publications would have been superior to Ding Zuyin's.[51]

---

[47] Yate, "Lun zhuzao guominmu."

[48] Jin Yi, "*Nüzi shijie* fakanci": "Women are the mothers of citizens. If we want a new China, we must have new women; if we want a strong China, we must have strong women; if we want a civilized China, our women must first be civilized; if we wish to deliver China from suffering, we must first deliver our women from suffering. About this there can be no doubt."

[49] (Ding) Chuwo, "Furenjie zhi shuangbi."   [50] (Ding) Chuwo, "Nüquan shuo."

[51] "Benshe tebie guanggao," published in the *Magazine of China's New World of Women* 5, which was supposed to "come out in August of the Western calendar"; but preparation for the printer "took seventy or more days before it would be ready." It went on to state that the issues for the remainder of the year "are estimated to appear within the two months of November and December."

In her "Inaugural statement," Yan Bin paid close attention to the spiritual education of "female citizens." From the negative point of view, she noted that "although China has the appearance of many female citizens, it lacks the spirit of a female citizenry, and this is like a people without a people." From the positive angle she stated, "we must develop our new morality and enliven our new thinking: to educate one woman is to gain one more Chinese female citizen."[52] It is not difficult to see that female students in Japan such as Yan Bin were themselves committed to the "newest theories of education," and were, thus, in close concert with the nationalist mode of thought prevalent in Japan at this point in time. They therefore published a journal that aspired, first and foremost, to create a "female citizenry."

In the view of Yan Bin and others, Western heroines would bear the weight of "women's new civilization" and serve as spiritual teachers of China's "female citizens." This was apparent in the biographies column in the new journal.[53] From its inaugural issue, it published a continuous string of biographies of women. Of the eleven biographies, only one was of a Japanese and one of a Chinese woman.[54] All the others were Western.

For the most part, these biographies stemmed from a 1906 volume by Nemoto Tadashi entitled *Biographies of Successful European and American Women*.[55] An advertisement announcing this book also appeared on the pages of the journal.[56] Moreover, a "translator's note" appended to one of the foreign biographies, that of "British novelist Ms. Eliot," directly stated, "I read the *Biographies of Successful European and American women*."[57] Of the nine biographies of Western women published in the journal, six in fact derived from this source. Among these six biographies, two were of British women and four of Americans. The original text had fifteen biographies, ten of women from the United States, reflecting the same balance. This clearly demonstrates the importance of the Japanese volume for those involved in the making of this Chinese journal.

The same advertisement that announced the publication of *Biographies of Successful European and American Women* also announced a "Biography of Joan [of Arc], Heroine Who Saved France" (issue 3).[58] The original source

---

[52] Lian Shi, "Fakanci."

[53] There were numerous changes made to the biographies column in the *Magazine of China's New World of Women*. At first placed in the "Yishu" (Translation) column, in the second issue it was accorded a separate entry as a "Shizhuan" (Historical biography) column, and this continued until the fourth issue; from the fourth issue the two columns "Yishu" and "Jizai" (Records) were combined with "Shizhuan" and renamed "Zhuanji" (Biographies).

[54] Issue five carried Lian, "Luo Ying nüshi zhuan," and issue six carried Zhuo, "Houteng Qingzi xiaozhuan."

[55] Nemoto, *Ō-Bei joshi risshin den*.   [56] "Benshe chuban shuji yugao."

[57] Qi Zhan, "Yingguo xiaoshuojia Ailiatuo nüshi zhuan."   [58] Mei Zhu, "Faguo jiuwang nüjie."

for this biography was a Japanese work, *Jannu daruku* (Jeanne d'Arc), by novelist Nakauchi Giichi (1875–1937).[59] Additionally, two articles in issue 6 of the journal – "Ms Novikoff, Russian Female Diplomat and Unofficial Plenipotentiary" and "Ms Adam, Queen of the World of French Journalism" – were both taken from Tokutomi's *Past and Present World Famous Women Exemplars*.[60] These texts were signed but not by translators, a practice that followed one already seen in *Women's World*.

Evidently, the *Magazine of China's New World of Women* and the original source coincided in their ultimate aim. To borrow Nemoto Tadashi's language:

What is most essential in establishing oneself is to show restraint and remain hardworking...From what I have observed, however, in addition to restraint and assiduousness, women and girls who have succeeded in establishing themselves have another quality as well. What is that? It is the moral behavior of benevolence, wisdom, motherly love, and kindness. Moreover, no matter how full of ability and wisdom and refined in learning a girl is, if she lacks a benevolent mind, then her learning, talent, and wisdom will not only be of little help to others or herself, but they will in fact prove injurious to her and harmful to others.

Thus, the strength of those women whose stories were included in the *Biographies of Successful European and American Women* was "to be restrained and remain hardworking while demonstrating the moral qualities of benevolence and motherly love. They were, thus, able to establish themselves, and achieved great merit and world fame."[61] We can see that, although Nemoto selected Western women from many different countries, he continued the "self-help" tradition.

Yan Bin presented what Nemoto commended as "benevolence, wisdom, motherly love, and kindness" as "the new international female morality," which she defined as "motherly love, wisdom, and universal love." She related these qualities to the status of "female citizens" and to "patriotic thought." These women's goals would be to "enrich the country and benefit the people, and make up for the deficiencies in the world."[62] The leading role of the biographies in her journal was to model this "new morality." Needless to say, Florence Nightingale was such a model. Even the American journalist, commentator, and reporter Margaret Fuller Ossoli (1810–1850) was praised for her "benevolent heart and realization of the Christian doctrine of universal

[59] Nakauchi, *Jannu daruku*.
[60] The Japanese titles were respectively "Mukan no Rokoku zenken taishi (Novikofu fujin)" from the chapter entitled "Ōshū seikai no san joketsu" (Three heroines from the world of European politics) and "Fukkoku shinbunkai no joō (Adamu fujin)."
[61] Nemoto, "Shogen" (Preface), in *Ō-Bei joshi risshin den*.
[62] Lian Shi, "Benshe wu da zhuyi yanshuo."

love," which were seen as displayed in her enthusiastic support for the Italian unification movement when she was living in Italy.[63]

To encourage Chinese women to be responsible to society, Yan Bin and others gave prominence to Western women's capacity for action.[64] As the "leader of the Female Anti-Slavery Society," Lucretia Mott (1793–1880), for example, "advocated the principles of liberty and equality, not just as empty speech but also in action." The translator of her biography praised her as an "activist on behalf of universal love" and used this appellation in the revised title to the biography. At the beginning of the biography, the translator went to great pains to emphasize Mott's contribution to the abolition of slavery in America: "America freed the slaves and everyone said this was due to the power of President Lincoln. They do not know that the prime mover in abolishing slavery was not a man but a woman."[65] The journal also featured a biography of Mary Ashton Rice Livermore (1820–1905), who made outstanding contributions during the American Civil War. The biography described her achievements as "a great speaker, celebrated reporter, and a leader of the United States Sanitary Commission," which provided the Northern army with vigorous support.[66] Yan Bin, in an article summarizing the "great deeds of American women in wartime" which appeared in the same issue of the journal, quoted extensively from Livermore's speeches. Yan Bin opened her essay with praise: "American women are by nature extremely vivacious and promising. With patriotic minds and deep sincerity, they are far more capable than women from other countries."[67] This language echoed that of the biography and would have made a profound impression on the reader.

The connection between this celebration of women's activism and the late Qing context is amply reflected in the magazine's admiration for heroines who saved their nations. The title of Mei Zhu's biography of Joan of Arc (1412–1431) is "A French Heroine Who Saved the Nation." It was the longest article in that issue of the journal.[68] Even Mary Livermore, who took part in her nation's war effort, was praised by translator Zhuo Hua for her "sacrifice for the nation." Zhuo Hua revealed the motivation for translating this biography: "my motherland's desperate situation seems like America in 1861."[69]

---

[63] Lingxi, "Meiguo da xinwenjia." At the front of the same issue of the journal is a listing of names of supporters of it. "Wang Lingxi from Hubei, a man," would have been the translator of this piece.

[64] Lian Shi, "Mingyuxin yu zerenxin."

[65] "Bo'aizhuyi shixingjia."   [66] Zhuo Hua, "Da yanshuojia."

[67] Lian Shi, "Ji Meiguo furen zhanshi zhi weiye." Here, Livermore's name is rendered as "Libamao."

[68] Mei Zhu, "Faguo jiuwang nüjie Ruo'an zhuan." This biography took up thirty pages in the journal; the next longest biography, "Chuangshe wanguo hongshizi kanhufu duizhe Naitingge'er furen zhuan," was only ten pages, split between issues 1 and 2. On this biography, see also Judge, *Precious Raft*.

[69] Zhuo Hua, "Da yanshuojia."

Impassioned calls for women to be patriotic and save the nation are also evident in the objective of women's education. In her translation of and introduction to Mary Lyon's (1797–1849) efforts to promote women's higher education in the United States, Lingxi frequently deleted references in the original to "good wives and virtuous mothers" as "the motive force for social advancement" and the "greatest basis for genuine civilization."[70] Clearly, Lingxi did not accept this basic tenet of the Meiji-era principle of women's education. Instead she rendered Lyon's educational ideal of developing women's education as a basic element of national civilization. She stated that Lyon received the highest praise because she "sacrificed her own life for the happiness of citizens."[71] Ultimately, here, the nation is placed above the family.[72]

The same ideas are evident in two biographies from the expanded edition of Tokutomi's *Past and Present World-Famous Women Exemplars*: the Russian Olga Novikoff (1840–1925) and the Frenchwoman Juliette Adam (1836–1936). In 1877–1878, during the Russo-Turkish Wars, Ms. Novikoff shuttled back and forth in an effort to reconcile the differences between England and Russia, and used her diplomatic skills to help Russia prevail. Juliette Adam, a political analyst for the press who had been the secretary to Léon Gambetta (1838–1882) in the French Cabinet, maintained throughout her life "the sentiment of patriotism and the ideal of revenge." This sentiment was first aroused at the time of the Franco-Prussian War, when she facilitated a Russo-French alliance to resist Germany. The translator chooses these two European political heroines – one dubbed a "female secret emissary of the Tsar" and one a "defender of France" – precisely because "among the many millions of Western women, they were the only ones who stood out among the stately politicians, assisted society, and benefited the nation."[73] While the original texts only praised these two women's eloquence, this emphasis reveals the concern of the editors of the Chinese women's journal.

One can see then that, in contrast to the earlier women's journals we examined, the Western women introduced through translation in the *Magazine of China's New World of Women* had dispensed with the familial model of prudent wives and filial daughters and even consciously rejected the ideology of "good wives and virtuous mothers" current in Meiji Japan. This third journal, which sought to cultivate the spirit of "female citizens," focused on patriotic heroines and even female politicians. At the same time, this meant that, by shifting the emphasis from "benevolence" to "patriotic thought," Yan Bin and her colleagues had clearly advanced a step beyond *Women's World*.

---

[70] Cf. Nemoto, *Ō-Bei joshi risshin den*, 75, 82, and Lingxi, "Meiguo da jiaoyujia."

[71] Lingxi, "Meiguo da jiaoyujia." See also Judge, *Precious Raft*.

[72] On this biography of Lyon, see also Judge, *Precious Raft*, 68–69.

[73] Zhenguo, "Eguo nü waijiaojia" and "Faguo xinwenjie zhi nüwang."

Conclusion

Our discussion of three women's magazines, the *Women's Journal/Continued Publication of Women's Journal/Journal of Women's Learning*, *Women's World*, and the *Magazine of China's New World of Women*, enables us to see clearly the immense impact of Meiji-era "women's self-help" writings on late Qing women's journals. The continuous references to various sorts of Western heroines enriched the models from which Chinese women could draw and played a direct role in reforming Chinese moralities – old and new. The impact of this restructuring of the spirit of modern Chinese women was far-reaching. In translations and transplantations, the Chinese translators added their own commentaries at the beginning and end of their essays, as insertions within the essays, or even in rewriting the originals. In this way, they used the pages of late Qing women's journals to reinterpret and revise the biographies that had been expounded in the Japanese originals to suit the circumstances of the late Qing. This allowed new conceptions of womanhood to take root among Chinese women. The biographies columns in China's women's journals were thus instrumental in extending the global imaginaries of readers in the late Qing. By creating a new ethos in the discursive field carved out and created by women's journals of the late Qing period, these media had an important impact on the formation of Chinese modernity.

12 Foreign Knowledge of Bodies: Japanese Sources, Western Science, and China's Republican Lady

Joan Judge

A photograph of a Japanese woman in Chinese dress appeared in *Funü shibao* (The women's Eastern times) in May 1912, some three months after the abdication of China's last emperor and the swearing in of its first Republican president (Figure 12.1). In a letter printed in the same issue of the journal, the woman Chen Yiying tied this portrait to global hierarchies of knowledge and power in the early Republic. She protested the current trend among her compatriots of embracing the new political regime by adopting a new, Western sartorial regime. Western clothing, she argued, was inferior to Chinese in terms of *weisheng* (health), convenience, aesthetics, and cultural appropriateness. Chen appealed to the foreign authority of the woman in the photograph, her Japanese friend, Kinbara Murako, to support her claim. Both Murako, who taught at the *Jingzhi nüxuexiao* (Jingzhi girls' school) in Wuxi, Chen explained, and her sister Tomiko, who worked for the Red Cross, preferred Chinese over Japanese or Western clothing. If the likes of the respectable and evolved Kinbara sisters imitate our strengths, Chen asked, why should we imitate others' weaknesses?[1]

Chen Yiying's concern in her letter was how best to clothe the body of the Republican Lady – a demographic of upright, educated, and newly public Chinese women.[2] She was not preoccupied only with style and fashion, or even with comfort, however. She also focused on *weisheng*, an ancient Chinese concept that had acquired new valences of meaning from the turn of the twentieth century, when it was used to translate the Western notion of "hygiene." Clearly aware of the term's new cachet, Chen nonetheless used it in ways resonant with earlier Chinese discourse: as a verb connoting guarding health through a range of physical and mental practices rather than merely as a noun describing a sanitary state.[3] Chen also emphasized cultural

---

[1] Chen Yiying, "Shuhan wen."

[2] On the notion of "Republican Ladies" and the demographics of women it includes, see Judge, *Republican Lens*, particularly Chapter 2.

[3] On the complex uses of *weisheng* in this period, see Lei, "Moral Community," particularly 480–81, 496. On the concept in *The Women's Eastern Times*, see Judge, *Republican Lens*, Chapters 2, 4. For an excellent treatment of the concept of *weisheng* in late Qing print culture

君原金人本日習教女國中

Fig. 12.1 Ms. Kinbara, Japanese teacher in China, *The Women's Eastern Times* 6 (May 1912)

appropriateness, joining ongoing efforts to redeem China's cultural stature in the face of over half a century of successive military defeats and domestic policy failures.

As respectable women's bodies emerged into the public field in the early Republic, they became, as did Kinbara's, loci of triangulating Chinese, Japanese, and Western discourses about China's viability in the new geopolitical order. Women's journals were central to this process, serving as prime sites for the circulation both of female photographic portraits and of the global discourses that surrounded them. Platforms where the once sequestered female figure could become an object of public discussion, public spectacle, and public scrutiny, the journals were laboratories for the exploration of gender ideas, including ideas related to the physical female body.

The women's periodical press differs from other materials concerned with women's health that were published in the early twentieth century. While

see Zhang Zhongmin, *Chuban yu wenhua zhengzhi*. See also Rogaski, *Hygienic Modernity*, on the ways the term *weisheng* came to encompass such ideas as national sovereignty.

political, pedagogical, or medical texts advanced systematic ideological or scientific claims about the female body, women's journals provided their audiences with an aporetic cacophony of often foreign-derived illustrations and information. Loosely disciplined by one editorial voice, the journals were multivocal, multigeneric, and multiregistered. Images talk back to texts across their pages, advertisements absorb dichotomies posited in topical articles, and cover art elides geographic divisions that mark the sources of the journal's content as either local or global.

Despite this chaotic richness, these sources do not merely convey an anarchy of perspectives on women's physicality. Serving as an invaluable perspective on the range of possibilities that emerged in this period, they offer a wealth of rare materials. These include photographs such as Kinbara's that would have otherwise been lost to history and writings by women such as Chen who left no other public record.[4] The journals also published surveys that document forgotten social practices, promoted essay contests on themes that highlight contemporary preoccupations, and featured poetry that tied personal feelings to fast-changing political events.

These richly varied materials require a methodology that is both flexible enough to accommodate their diversity and rigorous enough to make sense of it. This chapter combines two approaches that seek to achieve this aim. The first, a horizontal reading, examines the full range of materials directly related to the female body in these publications against one another – essays, images, surveys, essay contest themes, and advertisements.[5] The second, a situated reading, positions illustrations, articles, and individuals in their broader social and global contexts. Rather than uncovering a singular prescriptive narrative on Chinese women in the early Republic, such a reading reveals the unevenness of the social field that *The Women's Eastern Times* sought to both shape and capture.

In the pages that follow, I first outline the journal's objective of calling a new kind of Republican Lady into being and promoting a new level of transparency on issues related to women's reproductive health. I then introduce the triangulating global forces present in the early Republican period and manifest in the pages of *The Women's Eastern Times*. Finally, I offer a horizontal and situated reading of two prominent topics of concern in the journal that were central to women's health and informed by these triangulating circuits of knowledge: menstruation and childbirth.

---

[4] Chen did write at least two other articles, which appeared in the women's journal *Nüzi shijie* (Women's world).

[5] Although the poetry and fiction published in *The Women's Eastern Times* include relevant material on the female body – poems on illness, stories about prostitution, for example – they did not directly address the themes of this chapter – global influences on the Chinese discourse on women's reproductive health – and will not be a focus of the chapter.

The Women's Eastern Times **and the Republican Lady**

The Women's Eastern Times was visually and discursively innovative. The first journal to be adorned with cover girls vividly rendered in color lithography, it also featured as many as sixteen pages of striking photographs at the opening of each issue. Reproduced using the latest colored copperplate and collotype printing technology, most of these 425 photographs were of Chinese and foreign women.[6]

The lead editor, Bao Tianxiao, was committed to simultaneously engaging and transforming the *guixiu* (genteel, literate women) who constituted the journal's primary female audience.[7] The new Republican Lady he was determined to call into being would retain the *guixiu*'s moral dignity while losing what Bao considered to be her misplaced modesty. She would expand her global and intellectual horizons by moving beyond the ethereal realms of the literary and fine arts. Attuned to foreign scientific theories and practices, she would contribute her own *shiyantan* (accounts of real life and death experience) to the journal.[8] Bao repeatedly beseeched the journal's contributors to send in such accounts, together with personal diaries and photographs. He also announced that *The Women's Eastern Times* would serve as a platform for the discussion of women's mental, physical, and reproductive health. "Every year," he declared, countless "female compatriots die mistakenly at the hands of ignorant female quacks (*yongyi yufu*)." The journal would help remedy this situation by enlightening its readers about medicine and hygiene.[9]

Bao's editorial preoccupations are further mirrored in the topics he set for the essay contests advertised in sixteen of the journal's twenty-one issues, and in the winning entries, of which three or four were often published. Jiaoxin, winner of the contest theme announced in issues 13 and 14, "Nüzi dang you putong yixue zhishi" (Women should have basic medical knowledge), echoed Bao's concerns. He implored his readers not to lose themselves in poetic ruminations on the wind and the moon, as *guixiu* were wont to do. Rather they should follow young women "in all Eastern and Western countries" who studied obstetrics (*chanyu*) in school and were able to effectively minister to their families' everyday medical needs.[10]

The Women's Eastern Times not only anticipated women such as Jiaoxin's would-be obstetrical experts who were not yet but also celebrated women who were: it simultaneously published the *shi* and *ci* poems of *guixiu* authors, for

---

[6] On the photographs in *The Women's Eastern Times* see Judge, "Portraits."

[7] Bao articulated his vision of the Republican Lady and his ambitions for the journal in his editorial column. The column was entitled *Bianji shi* in issues 1 to 17, and *Bianji shi zhi tanhua* from issue 18.

[8] Bao Tianxiao, "Bianji shi," *Funü shibao* 2 (1911).

[9] Bao Tianxiao, "Bianji shi" (From the office of the editor), *Funü shibao* 6 (1912).

[10] Jiaoxin, "Nüzi dang you putong yixue zhishi," 5.

example, while encouraging them to abandon the literary arts and take on new practical professions. This dual mandate yielded productive disjunctions in the pages of the journal in ways that more theoretically bounded texts could not. Male-authored screeds about the collective inadequacies of "Chinese women" abut visual and discursive evidence of cosmopolitan, accomplished Chinese women. One such disjunction appears in the second issue of the journal. In one of several essays published in *The Women's Eastern Times* related to the United States, an author using the pseudonym Xingyi set up a series of dichotomies unfavorably comparing Chinese and American women.[11] He claimed that Chinese women were *ruo bu shengyi* (so weak they could hardly bear the weight of their own clothing) while American women were vital (*xianyan*) and brave and sturdy (*yongjian*). His assertion was challenged in the very same issue of the journal, however, by a photograph of and an article by the (vital and sturdy) Japanese-trained physical education specialist Tang Jianwo (see Figure 12.2).[12]

Triangulating Global Forces

This example highlights the triangulating global forces omnipresent both in the period and in the journal. Tang Jianwo's Japanese education enabled her to fulfill the ideal of American womanhood put forward by Xingyi: while Japanese-trained, she chose to represent herself in Western dress. Chinese authors, including Tang Jianwo and Xingyi, together with publishers, editors, and translators, had several overlapping motivations in highlighting Western models and actively seeking foreign expertise. Imported visual and textual sources served as new resources for imagining Chinese womanhood. They also expanded the parameters of what could be seen and discussed in the pages of a respectable Chinese journal. Foreign sources sanctioned the introduction of topics not normally broached in public, such as women's reproductive health, and they helped deter local critiques of such discussions.[13] They also helped to close a perceived knowledge gap that many feared was the source of China's weakness vis-à-vis both Japan and the West, a gap that extended from technological expertise to physiological understandings of the female body.

All foreign sources operative in *The Women's Eastern Times* and other Chinese periodicals were not equal, however. While Japan was the primary source of new knowledge, "the West" dominated the local imaginary. Japan's

---

[11] Xingyi, "Meiguo funü," 52. Also by Xingyi, "Meiguo Bolingma'er"; "Meiguo huade"; "Meiguo hunjia."

[12] Xingyi, "Meiguo funü," 52. In Tang's article she sought to contribute to the strengthening of Chinese women by publishing an illustrated guide to exercises for the family using a rope. Tang Jianwo, "Sheng ticao."

[13] One such critique of an article on the perils of childbirth was voiced in a letter to Bao Tianxiao ("Bianji shi," *Funü shibao* 2 (1911), 56).

Fig. 12.2 Physical education specialist *(tiyu jia)* Tang Jianwo in Western dress, *The Women's Eastern Times* 2 (July 1911)

role in the journal – and the period – was predominately textual and mediating, while the "West's" was visual and mediated.

Textual Flows

Japan's textual prominence in *The Women's Eastern Times* both conforms to and diverges from broader translation patterns in early-twentieth-century China.[14] Sixty-three percent of the foreign books rendered into Chinese in 1911, the year *The Women's Eastern Times* was founded, were translated from Japanese. While this number dropped to forty-five percent in 1913 and nineteen percent in the journal's last year of publication, 1917, the pervasiveness of Japanese translations in the journal continued. This suggests a heretofore unacknowledged deviation in translation practices between the periodical

---

[14] See Judge, "Mediated Imaginings," and Judge, *Precious Raft*, as well as Xia Xiaohong's contribution to this volume, for discussions of Chinese translations of women's biographies from the Japanese.

press and books, a deviation that demands further investigation, as periodicals were a primary source of information in the early Republic.[15] The reasons for Japan's role as China's gateway to the West have been well documented. From the 1870s, Japanese scholars and publicists had themselves translated an enormous number of Western works in a range of fields including politics, law, and social and educational theory.[16] These Japanese translations in turn became the source of Chinese translations by overseas students, publicists, and scholars.[17]

The Japanese sources for Chinese articles on the body were generically diverse. Although it was not common practice for authors to name their sources in this period, *The Women's Eastern Times* translators occasionally provided attributions for their translations. Most of the cited sources were periodicals, the majority of them women's journals. They include an early Meiji journal, *Nihon shin fujin* (The new woman), founded in 1884, *Shin fujin* (New women's magazine), established in 1911, and *Jogaku sekai* (World of women's education), published from January 1901 to June 1925. The weekly *Fujo shinbun* (Women's and girls' newspaper, 1900–1923), which like *The Women's Eastern Times* emphasized readerly engagement and targeted educated, middle-class readers, was most likely another source.[18]

Cited Japanese materials also include general interest magazines such as *Shin Nihon* (New Japan) launched in April of 1911, newspapers such as the *Ōsaka mainichi shinbun* (The Osaka daily news), and serials including *Ōshū senso jikki* (Veritable account of the European war). *The Women's Eastern Times* published translations of full texts of or excerpts from book-length treatises such as Miyamoto Keisen's *Seiyō danjo kōsaihō* (Social interactions between men and women in the West, 1906) and Aoyagi Yûbi's *Jissen mutsūan sanpō, fuku: Ijutsu no shinpo* (The practice of painless childbirth: Supplement on medical progress, 1915).

In some cases, Japanese material was translated almost immediately, suggesting that Chinese writers were immersed in the current Japanese

---

[15] In the period from 1911 to 1927, approximately twenty-four percent of translated books were first published in Japan, twenty-three percent in England, twenty-one percent in the United States, seven percent in France, four percent in Germany, and close to six percent in Russia. Wang Qisheng, "Minguo shiqi de Rishu Hanyi," 47.

[16] On this process see Howland, *Translating the West*.

[17] The phenomenon of overseas study in Japan which spearheaded many of these translations has already been well studied, particularly for the period up to the 1911 Revolution. See Sanetô, *Chūgokujin Nihon ryūgaku shi zōho*; Huang Fuqing [Huang Fu-ch'ing], *Qing-mo liu-Ri xuesheng* (translated by Whitaker as *Chinese Students in Japan in the Late Qing Period*); Harrell, *Sowing the Seeds of Change*. On female students, see Judge, "Between *Nei* and *Wai*," and Judge, "Beyond Nationalism."

[18] On *Fujo shinbun* see Fujo shinbun, "'Fujo shinbun' to josei no kindai." The journal covered many topics central to *The Women's Eastern Times*, such as women's education, daily life, suffrage, the protection of mothers, and the elimination of prostitution.

discourse and always attentive to material they could potentially share with their readers.[19] In other instances, the time lag was significant.[20] The Japanese themselves occasionally made translated material on women's health available to readers of *The Women's Eastern Times*. The pharmaceutical giant Tsumura Juntendô, which produced Chūjōtō (Zhongjiangtang), an herbal treatment for women's disorders, offered Chinese consumers a free Chinese translation of "Women's Health" (*Fujin eisei*, Chinese: *Furen weisheng shu*) that was written by one of the medicine's developers, the German-trained doctor Ogata Masakiyo (1864–1919).[21]

Just as the Japanese expert Ogata was European-trained, the material translated or derived from Japanese texts in *The Women's Eastern Times* generally referenced, was inspired by, or was a direct translation of Western material. These doubly mediated texts made it possible for Chinese authors/translators to broach sensitive topics such as prostitution, female same-sex love, and gender discrimination.

In one of the rare instances where a Chinese author cites a specific Japanese source, Shao Yi notes in an article on the evils of prostitution that she had recently read an article in the Japanese journal *World of Women's Education* on the abolition of prostitution in Europe and America.[22] In other instances, Japan's mediating role is indirectly evident. One example is the 1912 *Women's Eastern Times* article "Funü tongxing zhi aiqing" (Same-sex love among women). Although the author, Shanzai, did not cite Japanese sources in this article, he published two other articles in the same issue of *The Women's Eastern Times* that had clear Japanese referents. He also invoked Western theories of sexology that were widely discussed in Japanese periodicals of the time, such as Havelock Ellis's *Studies in the Psychology of Sex*.[23] In a

---

[19] An article on the history of the women's suffrage movement by Waseda University Professor and Christian socialist Abe Isoo (1865–1949), for example, appeared in *Shin Nihon* in July of 1915 and was translated in *The Women's Eastern Times* four months later. Abe, "Fujin yundô jyûgonen shi"; Hui, "Nüzi canzheng yundong."

[20] Miyamoto Keisen's *Social Interactions between Men and Women in the West* was published in Tokyo in 1906 but not translated in *The Women's Eastern Times* until 1915. Miyamoto, *Seiyo danjo kōsaihō*; Miyamoto, Hui trans., "Xiyang nannü jiaoji fa."

[21] "Zigong bingxue." The Tsumura juntendô was established in 1893. The name Chūjōtō allegedly comes from the Princess Chūjō, who lived at the time of the Empress Koken (r. 749–758) and Emperor Junnin (r. 759–764). See also "Japanese Folk Medicines."

[22] Shao Yi gave the date for the article and I was able to trace it: Vurideeru, "Kyō no haishō mondai."

[23] Shanzai's two other essays in the same issue of *The Women's Eastern Times* include one on children's toys that was translated from a Japanese newspaper, and one on women's facial hair that made reference to the research of the Japanese Terada Shirô. Shanzai, "Funü"; "Xuanze"; "Xuran." Sang (*Emerging Lesbian*, 107) also hypothesized that Shanzai knew Japanese, but she suggested he consulted German texts, which I think is unlikely. On female same-sex love in Japan, see Pflugfelder. In China, see Sang, *Emerging Lesbian*, 106–09, on this particular article by Shanzai, which Sang misdates. See also Judge, *The Precious Raft*, 80–82.

number of cases, the original Japanese authors of texts translated into Chinese announced their indebtedness to Western inspiration. In what was one of the most powerful feminist statements to appear in *The Women's Eastern Times*, the original author of the translated article who wrote under the name "Xin nüzi zhi yi ren" (A new woman), and who was claimed to be Japanese, announces that Western new women were her primary source of inspiration. While she conceded that a handful of East Asian women had resisted male domination in the past, true female resistance only began with Western new women, such as courageous British suffragists.[24]

Similar patterns of triangulation are apparent in advertisements produced by Japanese companies for the Chinese print market. Although Tsumara's medicine Chūjōtō was based on principles of Chinese medicine, and although the illnesses it targeted were described in these terms – deficiency of *qi* and blood (*qixue kuisun*), for example – the pharmaceutical company's authority was Western-derived. The German-trained Ogata Masakiyo used European and American scientific principles in updating the allegedly ancient Chūjōtō cure for women's ailments.[25]

Visual Flows

A hierarchy of global influences is evident in the Chūjōtō advertisement for a Japanese product based on Western scientific expertise and in the countless Japanese articles that served the translators for *The Women's Eastern Times* as conduits for Western knowledge. This triangular pattern with "the West" at its apex is further evident in the visual contents of the journal. These include photographs of Chinese women, portraits of foreign women, cover art, and illustrated medical advertisements.

Japanese fashion was not completely absent from *The Women's Eastern Times*, but it often bore a Western imprint.[26] The first issue of the journal featured "Hanko style" reformed clothing. Designed by Kajita Hanko, this style of dress merged elements of Japanese old-style clothing with elements

---

[24] "(Riben) Xin nüzi." East Asian women who resisted male oppression included China's powerful and much maligned Empress Wu (624–705), who briefly ruled as emperor during the Tang dynasty, and the "She-devil" Takahashi Oden (d. 1879), who was executed for murdering her lover and poisoning her husband, together with daring female knights-errant and courtesans who toyed with the affections of powerful men.

[25] "Zigong bingxue." Ogata had studied in Germany from 1889.

[26] For examples of images of Japanese fashion featured in the journal, see "Riben xinshiji," *Funü shibao* 9 (1913), captured in the project database at http://kjc-sv013.kjc.uni-heidelberg .de/frauenzeitschriften/public/magazine/page_content.php?magazin_id=1&year=1913&issue_ id=33&issue_number=009&img_issue_page=17. See also "Riben funü zhi xin zhuangshu" (The new fashion styles of Japanese women), *Funü shibao* 10 (1913), in the database at http://kjc-sv013.kjc.uni-heidelberg.de/frauenzeitschriften/public/magazine/page_content.php? magazin_id=1&year=1913&issue_id=34&issue_number=010&img_issue_page=8.

Fig. 12.3 Younger sister of the wife of Kajita] Hanko wearing Kajita-style reformed clothing, *The Women's Eastern Times* 1 (June 1911)

of Western clothing (Figure 12.3).[27] *The Women's Eastern Times* also featured several portraits of Chinese women – usually overseas students in Japan – photographed in Japanese attire.[28]

Western dress was nevertheless the more pervasive choice. This is evident in photographs of Chinese activists, educators, and publishers, whether posing for individual portraits (Figure 12.4), engaged in volunteer activities (Figure 12.5), or casually observed in public.[29]

---

[27] Kajita's clothing reform ideas were featured in special supplements to the Japanese *Yomiuru shimbun* eight to eleven years before they appeared in *The Women's Eastern Times* (January 1900 to the summer of 1903) and were promoted by the Japanese Women's Association (Nihon funjo kai). The garments Kajita designed for women were often modeled by the younger sister of his deceased wife, Toriko, as in the *Funü shibao* image. Yamada, *Woodblock Kuchi-e Prints*, 160.

[28] See for example "Revolutionary Army Woman Warrior Lin Yuan Gaozi in Japanese Dress," *Funü shibao* 5 (1912); and the Teng sisters from Hunan, musician Ms. Teng Zhuo of Hunan, *Funü shibao* 10 (1913), and physical education specialist Teng Chao of Hunan, *Funü shibao* 12 (1914).

[29] See, for example, a Chinese woman in Western clothing in front of the Arcadia Building (Ankaidi) in Zhang Garden, *Funü shibao* 9 (1913).

Fig. 12.4 Ye Jingzi, *Zhongguo nüxia* (Chinese female knight-errant) in Western dress, *The Women's Eastern Times* 5 (January 1912)

Fig. 12.5 Female volunteers at a *saizhenhui* (exhibition) teashop, *The Women's Eastern Times* 8 (September 1912)

Fig. 12.6 Cover for *Jogaku sekai* (World of women's education)

The iconic status of the "Western woman" in the Chinese imaginary of the period is further emphasized by the preponderance of photographs of Western women published in *The Women's Eastern Times*. Among the foreign portraits printed in the journal, there were more than three times as many portraits of Western women (eighty-one) as there were of Japanese women (twenty-five). They include wives and daughters of American politicians including W. H. Taft (1857–1930); British suffragists such as Ms. Christabel Pankhurst (1880–1958); and the Polish-French scientist Madame Curie (1867–1934), together with Greek, Russian, and Italian princesses.

Western elements are also prominent in the journal's cover art. While Chinese authors and editors mined Japanese women's magazines for their discursive content and photographs, Chinese artists did not take their cues from the covers of these same Japanese magazines. Many of these Japanese journals featured typographic designs on their front covers (Figure 12.6). Others featured sedate women in (albeit new-style) kimono (Figure 12.7). The cover girls in *The Women's Eastern Times*, in contrast, were often engaged in some form of new, Western-inspired leisure activity – playing tennis, strolling on an afternoon hunt, photographing nature – or in new urban practices that originated in the foreign concessions of Shanghai – mailing a letter, using a faucet for running water (Figure 12.8).

Fig. 12.7 Cover for *Jogaku gahō* (Illustrated journal for female students) with woman in kimono

Fig. 12.8 Cover for *The Women's Eastern Times* 18 (June 1916)

The American *Ladies' Home Journal*, which some *Women's Eastern Times* authors explicitly referenced in their essays, served as the inspiration for a number of the journal's covers.[30] According to the memoirs of an early twentieth-century Chinese journalist, one of the two artists responsible for the covers of *The Women's Eastern Times*, Xu Yongqing (1880–1953), compiled a copybook for his illustrations out of pictures he tore from foreign magazines purchased in a secondhand store in Shanghai.[31] It is highly likely that members of the expatriate American community in Shanghai subscribed to or had family members send them the *Ladies' Home Journal* and that discarded issues of the magazine would have ended up in these secondhand bookshops. There is a marked similarity between at least one of Xu's covers (issue 12), and a *Ladies' Home Journal* cover from 1899 (Figures 12.9, 12.10). In other cases, the subject matter of an American cover has been transposed to a hybrid Chinese context (Figures 12.11, 12.12).

The prevalence of things Western is also apparent in the illustrated medical advertisements in *The Women's Eastern Times*. While advertisements for the Japanese Chūjōtō appear frequently in the journal (in ten out of the twenty-one issues), they are not as diversely illustrated as advertisements for Western patent medicines, in particular Dr. Williams' Pink Pills for Pale People (Weilianshi dayisheng hongse buwan). Featured in eleven of *The Women's Eastern Times'* issues, Dr. Williams' advertisements included lengthy narratives highlighting the experience of a "real" Chinese woman (or man) who was represented in the ad by a photograph or drawing, as in the example of a Tianjin woman in Figure 12.13.

Advertisements for local Chinese pharmaceutical companies also boast a Western rather than a Japanese cachet. All of these pharmacies are identified as *yaofang*, a new term for a Western-style pharmacy as distinct from old-style Chinese drugstores or *tang*. A number of these new-style pharmacies further posited global connections in their names: the Wuzhou Dayaofang (Great world pharmacy), the Zhong-Fa Lao Yaofang (Old Sino-French pharmacy), and the Zhong-Xi Dayaofang (Great Sino-Western pharmacy). The Great World Pharmacy, which had more advertisements (thirteen) in the journal than any other drug company, Chinese or foreign, produced a number of medicines for women, including Nüjiebao (Women's treasure). Great World promoted this medicine with a Westernized woman's face. While the Luo Wei Yaofang (Luo Wei pharmacy) did not invoke a foreign connection in its name,

---

[30] A frequent contributor, Zhou Shoujuan (1895–1968), claimed he translated a short piece entitled "Women's Nature" from the *Funü jiating bao* (Ladies' home journal) in 1912, [Zhou] Shoujuan, trans. "Funü zhi yuanzhi." Another article on American women noted two famous women's magazines in the United States: *Funü jiating bao* and *Funü jiating zhi ban* (Ladies' home companion), Xingyi, "Meiguo funü," 53.

[31] Zheng Yimei, *Yihai yishao xubian*, 43.

Fig. 12.9 *The Women's Eastern Times* 12 (January 1914)

Fig. 12.10 *Ladies' Home Journal* (February 1899)

Fig. 12.11 *The Women's Eastern Times* 5 (January 1912)

Fig. 12.12 *Ladies' Home Journal* (July 1902)

Fig. 12.13 "A woman from Tianjin had been suffering from stomach-ache" (Tianjin mingfu ceng huan weiji), *The Women's Eastern Times* 4 (November 1911)

advertisements proclaimed that its Hongxue lun buyao (Red blood wheel tonic) was custom-made in England's most famous pharmaceutical factories (see Figure 12.14).[32]

Despite claims for the foreign provenance of these various medicines, the narratives describing their efficacy were rooted in Chinese medical discourse.

All medicines that targeted women focused on blood as the defining essence of female health. Addressing the dangers of Blood fatigue and Blood depletion, the need for Blood-nourishing remedies, and the perils of irregular menstruation, these advertisements represent a continuum with late imperial Blood-centered *fuke* (obstetrical and gynecological) texts.[33]

---

[32] "Wo rufa"

[33] I follow Charlotte Furth in capitalizing the word Blood when it refers specifically to women's reproductive health. The female body had been understood as ruled by Blood from the time of the *Yellow Emperor's Inner Classic*, while the male body was ruled by *qi*. Blood remained the central principle of women's medicine in the Song Dynasty, when *fuke* (obstetrics and gynecology) became a discrete field, and continued to be of paramount importance through the Ming and Qing dynasties, even as the universal rather than gendered dynamics of bodily function were increasingly emphasized. See Furth, *A Flourishing Yin*, and Wu, *Reproducing Women*.

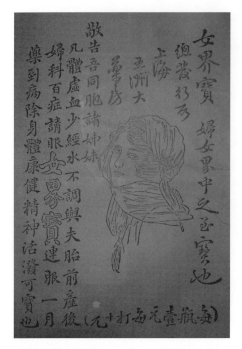

Fig. 12.14 "Nüjiebao – [it is] the most precious thing for women indeed" (Nüjiebao-funüjie zhong zhi zhibo ye), *The Women's Eastern Times* 10 (May 1913), 11 (October 1913)

Foreign Knowledge of Bodies: Menstruation and Childbirth

Menstruation

Despite this enduring evocation of longstanding Chinese medical principles, advertisements also marked a radical departure from the late imperial period in catapulting the discussion of women's reproductive health into the public realm. Although menstruation had long been recognized in Chinese medical discourse as a key source of women's illness, it had not been a topic of broad public discussion.[34] Qu Jun (Shaoheng, 1888–1960), an overseas medical student in Japan and future leading gynecologist in China, offered an explanation for this. He stated that menstrual blood was universally considered to be

---

[34] Since at least the second century, doctors had included an ensemble of gynecological disorders associated with impaired menstrual flow among the "thirty-six diseases of women." Even when Zhang Jiebin (1563–1640) de-emphasized the gender specificity of women's illnesses in the late Ming dynasty and reduced this number of diseases to nine, menses was still first among them. Wu, *Reproducing Women*, 48.

filthy and impure (*huizhuo*). The aversion to openly discussing menstruation was, however, particularly strong in China. According to Qu, Chinese women refused to disclose the details of their menstrual ailments not only to men, but also to other women, and even to their doctors.[35]

In keeping with this widely held assumption that Chinese women refused to openly discuss menstruation, advertisements that broached the topic did so using men's voices. In narratives commissioned by foreign patent medicine companies, including Dr. Williams' Pink Pills for Pale People, Japan's Chûjôtô, Doan's Kidney Pills, and Chinese pharmaceutical companies that mimicked their foreign counterparts, it was husbands and fathers who described the female suffering that resulted from blocked and irregular menses, the miraculous curative powers of the advertised medicine, and, in several cases, the joyful birth of a child that quickly followed treatment.

Among the many ailments Doan's Kidney Pills could allegedly cure was so-called blocked menses (*jingbi*), a potentially debilitating and even fatal malady that was paired with dried blood in an advertisement printed in the seventh issue of *The Women's Eastern Times*.[36] The Japanese Chûjôtô treated menstrual irregularity (*jingshui butiao*), cramps, and other ailments with its "magical elixir for gynecological problems."[37] The Chinese Great Sino-Western Pharmacy and the Great World Pharmacy also boasted the efficacy of their respective medicines – Fumei'er nü jindan (Fumei'er pills for women) and Haibo yao (Haibo medicine) – in regulating menstruation.[38] It was Dr. Williams' Pink Pills that made the most sustained claims, however, for curing irregular menstruation and thus expediting the birth of sons.[39]

Medical experts also wrote informative articles on menstruation for *The Women's Eastern Times*. While studying in Osaka, Qu Jun published detailed discussions of menstruation in articles on women's hygiene, together with a survey on the onset of menstruation.[40] These articles foreshadowed Qu's long career as a gynecologist committed to both improving medical practice and popularizing medical knowledge in China.[41] Over the course of his career,

---

[35] Qu Jun, "Funü zhi weisheng," 25.

[36] "Dou'an shi." On blocked menses see Wu, *Reproducing Women*, 85.

[37] "Jia you juwan." See also "Zigong."   [38] "Fumei'er;" "Bi weixian."

[39] See, for example, "Nongzhang"; "Zheng tongling."

[40] Qu Jun, "Funü zhi weisheng"; "Furen zhi weisheng"; "Diaocha." After graduating from the Osaka Higher Medical School (Ôsaka Kôtô Igakkô) in 1916, Qu founded a number of hospitals in China and went on to study further in Germany from 1923.

[41] Together with his wife Yao Yingnai, who also studied in Japan, Qu Jun founded the Qu Shi Fufu Yiyuan (the Dr. and Mrs. Qu Hospital) in 1922. He was also involved in the founding and running of the Nüzi Chanke Xuexiao (Women's School of Obstetrics) and the Shengsheng Gaoji Zhuchan Xuexiao (Advanced School for Obstetrics), established in 1923. That same year he was sent by the Ministry of Education to study in Germany. He continued to write and be active in this field through at least the 1930s. Yao Yi, *Kindai Chūgoku no shussan to kokka shakai*, 115, 124, 129.

he not only wrote articles in specialized journals and teaching materials for use in training hospitals, but also composed a popular songbook on *fuke*, *Tongsu chanke sanbai yong* (Three hundred popular songs on gynecology), and co-authored a play, *Shengsi guantou juben* (Script for a life-and-death crisis), that promoted modern midwifery.[42]

Similarly to Bao Tianxiao, Qu was deeply concerned that Chinese women were not only suffering but dying as a result of what he described as benighted taboos against the open discussion of issues related to female reproductive health. In his writing, Qu followed *fuke* principles in, for example, describing the menstruating woman as particularly susceptible to wind and to blood stagnation.[43] He departed from received Chinese discourses, however, in his attentiveness to global methods for attenuating these vulnerabilities.[44] While he criticized Japanese women for not wearing pants, which exposed them to the invasion of cold wind, he commended them for being increasingly assiduous about hygiene at the time of their periods. He specifically lauded them for inserting either absorbent cotton (*tuozhimian*) or sterilized cotton (*xiaodumian*) into the vulva to prevent the flow of blood. He noted, however, that these Japanese methods had been superseded by even more advanced Western products. Because there was a risk of the cotton Japanese women used getting lodged in the cervix, they were increasingly following *Ou-Xi furen* (women in Europe and the West) in using menstrual pads (*yuejing dai*).[45] Some fifteen years after the very first – and not highly successful – disposable napkins were commercially available in the United States, nine to ten years *before* Kotex pads were manufactured and widely advertised, and some twenty-seven years before advertisements for menstrual pads appeared in Chinese women's journals, Qu Jun advocated the use of such products in *The Women's Eastern Times*.[46]

In early 1915, Qu continued his efforts to demystify, scientize, and globalize Chinese notions of menstruation by designing the Zhonghua Minguo funü yuejing diaocha biao (Republican Chinese survey of women's menstruation) – see Figure 12.15. In his introduction to the survey, Qu notes that unlike China, which lacked a unified system of medical knowledge, all civilized (*wenming*) nations kept statistics on menstruation. Such statistics were, he argues, critical for predicting a woman's fertility and managing her health. His concern with the future happiness of the 200 million women of China inspired his effort to integrate the most intimate details of their lives into global circuits of knowledge. He provided his readers with a table that recorded the average age at the onset of menstruation in countries all over the world, including Russia, Sweden, Denmark, Norway, Italy, Spain, Japan, India, and the Netherlands.

[42] Wang Yugang and Qu Shaoheng, "Shengsi guantou juben."

[43] On wind as a pathogenic agent in Chinese medicine, see Unschuld, *Medicine in China*, 70–73.

[44] Qu Jun, "Funü zhi weisheng," 25–26.   [45] Qu Jun, "Funü zhi weisheng," 26–27.

[46] On the development of sanitary pads in the West and advertisements for them in *Funü zazhi* from 1928, see Zhou Chunyan, *Nüti yu guozu*, 115.

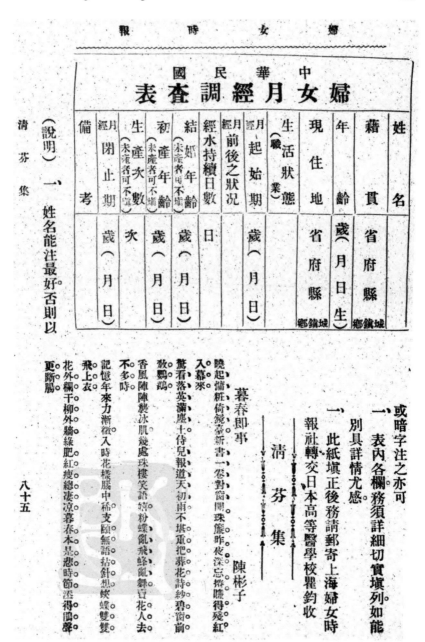

Fig. 12.15 Republican Chinese survey of women's menstruation, *The Women's Eastern Times* 16 (February 1915), 85

He then encouraged his *Women's Eastern Times* audience to fill out his own survey, which was printed in the journal.[47]

The survey requested information on the women's personal and medical histories: their last name (in recognition of the potential reluctance of some women to fill out the survey, Qu noted that they could use a pseudonym), native place, age, and current place of residence, together with age at onset of menstruation, characteristics of periods from beginning to end, duration of periods, age at marriage, age at birth of first child, number of births, and age when periods ended. Similarly to patent medicine advertisements, which were premised on male involvement in women's gynecological difficulties, Qu assumed that male assistance would be necessary if his project was to succeed. He asked for men's cooperation in overseeing the completion of the surveys and in mailing them to the Shanghai *Women's Eastern Times* society. The office of *The Women's Eastern Times* would then send all completed surveys to Qu in Japan.[48]

Childbirth

The process of childbirth was similarly scientized through the influence of triangulating global forces in the pages of *The Women's Eastern Times*. As with menstruation, Chinese theoretical and practical methods of approaching this most mysterious, dangerous, and essential physical process were deemed inadequate by contributors to *The Women's Eastern Times*. According to Jiaoxin, author of the winning essay on the need for women to have basic medical knowledge, revered sagely texts such as *Dasheng bian* (Treatise on easy childbirth, 1715) offered little useful instruction. At the same time, Chinese old-style midwives (*wenpo*) were stupid, vulgar, and completely lacking in the requisite medical knowledge.[49]

Authors in *The Women's Eastern Times* attempted to overcome these deficiencies by introducing new methods for managing childbirth in a range of essays that appeared in the journal from its first to its last issue. These articles, which were written by both women and men, included reflections on personal experience and introductions to various forms of foreign expertise.

---

[47] Qu Jun, "Diaocha."

[48] Qu Jun, "Diaocha." There is no follow-up on the survey in *The Women's Eastern Times* or in any of the archival or secondary material I have found on Qu to date. This may suggest that few women were willing to fill out the survey, even with the assistance of their husbands.

[49] Jiaoxin, "Nüzi dang you putong yixue zhishi," 4. The *Treatise on Easy Childbirth* was a two-chapter text written by an anonymous lower-level literatus who signed his preface with the sobriquet "Lay Buddhist Jizhai," and whom Yi-li Wu has identified as Ye Feng (fl. 1715). Ye argued that childbirth was an innately trouble-free process that only became difficult through unnecessary human intervention. Childbirth should not be expedited through drugs, rituals, or manipulations on the part of doctors, midwives, or family members. Wu, *Reproducing Women*, 67–70.

While men authored most of the articles on menstruation that appeared in the journal, a number of women wrote or translated essays on topics related to childbirth.[50] Outstanding among them is Qiu Ping's "Chanfu zhi xinde ji shiyan tan" (Acquired knowledge and experience of women in childbirth). Personal experience drove Qiu to write her article: Two of her fellow students and friends had died from complications of childbirth (*channan*). Her account is an unsystematic reflection on various aspects of childbirth: how the experience differs according to the age of the birth mother (from fifteen to forty-two), how to manage infections when breastfeeding (clean the nipples with soft, sterilized cloth), the various instruments a wealthy Japanese man used in facilitating his wife's fifth healthy birth (including various kinds of lamps), measures to take in the case of early labor (including calling a doctor), and the swelling of the uterus in pregnancy.[51]

The key point Qiu made was that ignorant Chinese midwives – old women with no knowledge of physiology (*shengli*) or medicine – were the source of China's high maternal and infant mortality rates. The solution to this problem was to follow Japan in replacing these untutored old women with young women trained in midwifery or nursing and knowledgeable about scientific biomedicine.

Qiu used Japanese midwifery schools as a model for the development of midwifery education in China. Her account includes a general description of Japanese classrooms equipped with specimens, skeletons, visuals, and wax models of fetuses and the reproductive organs. It also includes details from an investigation of a midwifery school (*chanpo xuexiao*) in Tokyo recorded in the travel diary of a certain Cheng Bojia. Mizuhara Zen, a Japanese authority on obstetrics, taught at the school Cheng visited.[52] His classroom included a skeleton in a glass case, a model of a birthing bed, and visual representations of the physiology of the body. His curriculum comprised courses in anatomy (*jiepouxue*), physiology (*shenglixue*), and midwifery (*chanpoxue*).[53]

Qiu Ping considered Japan to be a model for the development of Chinese midwifery because Japanese obstetrics was grounded in Western scientific expertise. Mizuhara, for example, was trained in German methods and had translated the work of the German gynecologist Max Runge (1849–1909).[54] A parallel triangulating pattern is evident in a solution to the dangers of childbirth that Bao Tianxiao enthusiastically introduced to his readers in issue 19 of the

---

[50] In addition to Qiu Ping's article discussed at length below, these include Tang Jianwo, "Furen bing," and Tsugawa, "Cuimian shousheng fa."

[51] Qiu Ping, "Chanfu zhi xinde ji shiyan tan," 17.

[52] Mizuhara was the co-author, with Kobayashi Haru, of a 1907 text on childbirth, *Anzan tebiki: Gokai kyōsei* (Guide to easy childbirth: Correcting misunderstandings).

[53] Qiu Ping, "Chanfu zhi xinde ji shiyan tan," 19–20.   [54] Runge et al., *Sankagaku.*

journal.[55] While the science of this method had been developed in Germany, the article that explained it in issues 20 and 21 of *The Women's Eastern Times* was translated from Japanese. The author of the original Japanese text, Aoyagi Yūbi, was a Christian convert who had studied English.[56]

Aoyagi's text, *The Practice of Painless Childbirth*, does not appear to be a direct translation. He makes no mention of his sources in his preface, and the backmatter lists him as author rather than translator.[57] Since he allegedly knew English, he could have read a number of books or articles on the topic written in 1914 and 1915.[58] While he may have consulted these works, however, none of them appear to have served as a direct source for his treatise.

In his preface, Aoyagi explains that a painless method of childbirth had been discovered by Drs. Bernhardt Kronig and Karl Gauss at the Women's Clinic of the State University of Baden twelve years prior to his writing. The discovery involved the use of scopolamine (*sikepoluomeng*) or "twilight sleep" to lessen the difficulty of childbirth.[59] His proclaimed purpose in writing *The Practice of Painless Childbirth* was to explain Kronig and Gauss's method (Figures 12.16 and 12.17).

Bao Tianxiao declared that the translation on the painless method in *The Women's Eastern Times* would not only mark a new era in medicine but also serve as a new gospel (*fuyin*) for women.[60] The first of two parts explains Kronig and Gauss's method, introduces the wonder drug scopolamine, and describes the pain of childbirth, which the method sought to alleviate. The second part discusses the effect of the treatment on women's health, addresses opposition to it, and describes a number of practical aspects of the method, including the cost, the dose of the injection, and the equipment needed in the birthing room. It concludes with a discussion of the experience of some women who had undergone Kronig and Gauss's treatment.[61]

---

[55] Bao Tianxiao, "Bianji shi zhi tanhua," *Funü shibao* 19.

[56] Aoyagi wrote frequently on issues such as love and sex in Japanese women's periodicals. He contributed to *Jogaku zasshi* (Journal of women's education) from 1893 and served as editor of the journal from 1903. He later published another women's journal, *Onna no sekai* (Woman's world). According to an advertisement in *Funü Shibao*, the publisher of *The Women's Eastern Times* published a translation of another of Aoyagi's works on marriage, *Saishin kekkongaku*; Chen Shiwu trans., *Zui xin jiehunxue* (Shanghai: Youzheng Shuju, 1915).

[57] Aoyagi Yūbi, *Jissen mutsū ansan pō*, 1–2, backmatter.

[58] These include Williams, *Twilight Sleep*, and Boyd and Tracy, *Painless Childbirth*, together with an article by Marguerite Tracy and Constance Leupp that appeared in *McClure's Magazine* in New York in 1914.

[59] Qin and Zhi; Zhi and Qin.

[60] Bao Tianxiao, "Bianji shi zhi tanhua," *Funü shibao* 19, 114.

[61] Qin and Zhi, "Wutong anchan fa"; Zhi and Qin, "Wutong anchan fa xu." Ironically, by 1916, when *The Women's Eastern Times* articles appeared, the treatment had already been discredited in both Germany and the United States (Sloan, *Birth Day*, 108ff.).

Fig. 12.16 Photographs of doctors as featured in Aoyagi's *The Practice of Painless Childbirth*, front matter

Conclusion

The two-part article on painless childbirth, a Chinese translation of a Japanese text outlining German medical practice, exemplifies the triangular flow of textual information on the female body typically featured in *The Women's Eastern Times*. The multiplicity of sources available at each node of this knowledge circuit did not yield a coherent set of facts or a consistent line of argument either within one issue of the journal or over its entire run. Chinese editors, authors, and translators, who were driven by their own social and commercial agendas and constrained by their own linguistic and professional limitations, often serendipitously encountered and selected particular Japanese texts for translation or inspiration. These Japanese materials were themselves often drawn through similarly serendipitous processes from a diverse pool of European and American sources.

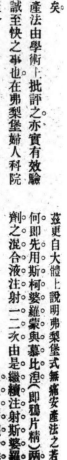

可恐之苦事矣。

且此無痛安產法由學術上批評之亦實有效驗

而毫無危險誠至快之事也在弗梨堡婦人科院

分娩之產婦至今（無）

約有五萬人其中（無）

三萬六千人之成（殖）安（產）

續之得大量統計

據之得詳細調查安

而證明左之二事

法之成產

第一　弗梨堡大（德國巴丁大學

婦人科院所成　　醫科教授古士

行之安產法　　者（氏（下）

第二　此安產法非但不遺害產兒且能預防

迫為外科分娩之危險

增進其幸福之力

於母體且有

不特毫無害

無痛安產法

四十七

最宜注意者即弗使過於深睡祇令喪失記憶近

事之能力及感覺而對於暗示之感應力及筋肉

作用則仍使繼續存在睡眠中焉欲此輕淺睡眠

德國巴丁大學

附屬弗梨堡婦

人科院長克妻

垤氏（上）

蒙使產婦趨於睡

眠狀態此睡態

極輕淺而其周

稍加刺戟即恐驚

醒凡預防此故產

宇內維持絕對之

靜肅且使光綫黯

淡呈暮色蒼茫之

觀焉

而催眠安產時有

實行無痛安產法

茲更自大體上說明弗梨堡式無痛安產法之若

何即先用斯柯婆羅蒙與慕比涅（即鴉片精）兩

劑之混合液注射一二次由是繼續注射斯婆羅

Fig. 12.17 Photographs of doctors as featured in a translation of Aoyagi's work in Qin Zhong, *The Women's Eastern Times* 20 (November 1916), 47, (identical to those in Fig. 12.16)

The heterogeneity of the messages conveyed in these articles was further compounded by the journal's visual texts, including its cover art, photographs, and illustrated advertisements. These images could reinforce particular textual claims such as Chen Yiying's assertion that Chinese clothing (and culture) were superior to Western alternatives. They could also undermine such claims and highlight aporias both within the journal and in the period, just as Tang Jianwo's photograph subverted Xingyi's contention that Chinese women were weaker and willowier than their American counterparts. Visuals could also help to pry open new discursive terrain. As foreign-inspired cover girls and portraits of Western and Chinese women projected the female figure into public space, they also heralded the public discussion of women's intimate bodily processes. These discussions of such topics as menstruation and childbirth, in turn, implicitly acknowledged the complexity of women as physical and sexual beings.

The value of journals such as *The Women's Eastern Times* lies in what they reveal about the multiregistered local and global knowledge of the female body circulating in the early Republic. Clearinghouses of rich stores of information, these materials are productively analyzed through the methods of horizontal and situated reading. Such readings yield a fine-grained sense of historical processes and of the habits of mind that shaped everyday knowledge of the body in this period.

The periodical press also had a profound impact on the women it interpellated as Republican Ladies. This includes women such as Tang Jianwo and Qiu Ping, who responded to Bao Tianxiao's call for social transparency and readerly engagement by contributing their photographic portraits and/or reflections on topics related to female reproductive health. It also includes more passive female readers of the journal. These women had formerly been exposed to portraits of exemplary women and didactic and literary texts that reproduced a largely coherent universe of moral knowledge. As readers of *The Women's Eastern Times*, they confronted new, foreign-derived images of womanhood, together with newly empowering bodies of knowledge and triangulating translations of knowledge about bodies. Reading the journal, they acquired a deeper understanding both of the female body and of the complex global knowledge circuits in which it was embedded.

13 "Othering" the Foreign Other in Early-Twentieth-Century Chinese Women's Magazines

Paul J. Bailey

Introduction

In 1891, the scholar-reformer Song Shu (1862–1910), writing about the pressing need for female education in China, sought to buttress his argument by emphasizing that illiteracy amongst Chinese women was *even* higher than amongst women in India or Japan.[1] Song's observation was significant in two ways. First, it reflected the unravelling of prior confidence in the global superiority of Chinese women. Liu Xihong, a member of China's first permanent diplomatic mission to Britain in 1876 (and later China's first Minister to Germany), for example, critiqued the "perverse" gender customs he witnessed in Britain – women selecting their own marriage partners, or married women not appreciating the virtue of being an obedient daughter-in-law. Liu also exuded self-satisfied confidence that the "traditional" Chinese woman represented the best of Chinese civilization.[2] Song Shu's views, in contrast, reflect an increasing tendency during the 1890s to scapegoat Chinese women as the root cause of the country's economic and political weakness. More interestingly, however, Song – with his reference to India and Japan – had situated Chinese women within a *global* context, a global context in which Chinese intellectuals were increasingly compelled after the turn of the twentieth century to interrogate the raison d'être of their own cultural and social values in the wake of growing Western (especially Anglo-American) military and economic world hegemony.

While Song Shu hinted at a condescending approach to (and a lack of identification with) women in the non-Western (especially Asian) world, quite a different and novel outlook characterized a group of Chinese activists and revolutionaries in Japan during the early years of the twentieth century. Inspired by, and seeking common cause with, anti-colonial and nationalist

[1] Zhu Youhuan, *Zhongguo jindai xuezhi*, 865.
[2] Ying Hu, "Reconfiguring *Nei/Wai*," 73. In Liu's view, gender roles were an illustration of the incorrigible *waiyi* (Other), in this case referring specifically to the West. Excerpts from Liu's journal are translated in Frodsham, *The First Chinese Embassy*.

movements in the Philippines, India, and Vietnam (as well as in South Africa and Cuba), they began to "imagine" a different kind of "Asia" that was not rooted in state-centered practices or "national-chauvinist culturalism" but on the shared experiences and activities of peoples confronting *wangguo* (literally, "loss of state or country"). Originally denoting an internal change of dynasty, *wangguo* now referred to a loss of the "civilization" or "nation."[3] By the same token, the expression *tongzhong* (same kind/race), originally used by the Chinese official Zhang Zhidong in the 1890s to emphasize China's affinities with Japan, took on a wider meaning at the turn of the twentieth century. It came to encompass the Chinese people's links with Filipinos, Vietnamese, Koreans, and Indians (and even Poles, Afrikaners, and Hawaiians).

In 1903, a remarkable essay by Tang Tiaonai (Erhe) highlighted the West's manipulation of the labels *wenming* (civilized) and *yeman* (primitive) in both legitimizing its colonial conquests and producing a Eurocentric world history that positioned non-Europeans in a position of inferiority:[4]

I read white people's histories. When writing of the colonies they built up, they always decorate [their histories] with glamorous rhetoric exaggerating their orderly rule of law. They provide plenty of indisputable evidence of the extent of the primitive customs and ignorance of the native people, as proof of why these peoples deserve to be conquered.[5]

In Japan, Chinese activists personally met Filipino, Vietnamese, and Indian nationalists. With the aim of promoting mutual assistance among peoples engaged in the struggle for national and cultural independence in Asia, Chinese and Indian activists founded the short-lived Yazhou heqin hui (Asian

---

[3] This discussion draws on Karl, "Creating Asia." See also Karl, *Staging the World*, 3, which argues that nationalist discourse in the last decade or so of the Qing underwent a transformation from an initially "expansive global or internationalist (particularly referring to the non-Euro/American world) moment of identification" in the years 1895–1905 to a conceptualization of "racial-ethnic revolution" in pursuit of state power in 1905–1911. See also Duara, "Asia Redux," which discusses the role of Asian intellectuals at this time – the Japanese Okakura Tenshin (1862–1913), the Chinese Zhang Binglin (1868–1936), and the Indian Rabindranath Tagore (1861–1941) – in the promotion of a "cultural" Asia that evoked earlier (precolonial) trading and maritime links but now enabled by contemporary imperialist technologies and modes of regional integration. For a wide-ranging study of how East Asian, South Asian, Arab, Turkish, and Persian thinkers and activists responded to Western hegemony during the course of the twentieth century, and their significant impact on processes of intellectual, as much as political, decolonization, see Mishra, *From the Ruins of Empire*.

[4] Tang Erhe (Tang Tiaonai) (1871–1940) studied medicine in Japan before 1911; after 1912, he became the chancellor of Beijing Medical College. He ended up as an official of the Japanese-sponsored Beijing government in 1937.

[5] Tang Tiaonai (mistakenly referred to as Tang Tiaoding) is cited in Karl, "Creating Asia," 1108. Tang was much influenced by the *History of the War for Philippine Independence* written by the Filipino patriot Mariano Ponce. Originally published in Spanish in 1900, it was soon translated into Japanese (1901) and Chinese (1902). Ponce drew attention in his book to the ways in which Filipinos had regularly been represented in the West as "primitives" and "relics of the stone age." Karl, *Staging the World*, 102–4.

solidarity society) in 1907.[6] Intending to enlarge its membership to include Koreans, Vietnamese, Filipinos, Burmese, and Malays, the Society recognized that they represented a diversity of cultural and religious traditions, but that they could be joined together (under the banner of their imagined "Asia") on the basis of their common experience of imperialism and *wangguo*.[7]

The anarchists Liu Shipei and He Zhen, co-editors of the journal *Tianyi bao* (Journal of natural justice), published in Japan (1907–1908) were Chinese members of the Asian Solidarity Society. In a 1907 article published in the *Journal of Natural Justice* Liu Shipei condemned what he perceived to be the fraudulent nature of Western civilizing discourse. This discourse, he claimed, simply masked the barbarous treatment of indigenous peoples by the Western imperial powers (e.g., in India and Vietnam), as well as of native Americans, blacks, and Chinese in the United States.[8] In another 1907 article co-authored by Liu Shipei and He Zhen, a future scenario was imagined in which a successful anarchist revolution in China would lead to an alliance with weaker Asian countries and European anarchist parties to destroy white hegemony.[9] He Zhen herself was not only one of a group of Chinese female radicals at this time who critiqued the "patriarchal" nature of Confucian ideology, but also one of the first Chinese thinkers to argue (in a 1907 article on the question of women's labor) that the introduction of Western capitalism and industrial wage labor in China would have a dire impact, especially in its exploitation of lower-class women.[10] In a series of essays published in 1908, Lu Xun cautioned against the simplistic conflation of the "modern" with the "civilized" West, critiquing teleological notions of history and the assumption that the Western experience represented a universal model for modernity.[11]

---

[6] The Society's official English title was the Asiatic Humanitarian Brotherhood. Chinese founders included the anti-Manchu revolutionary Zhang Binglin.

[7] In some cases, *wangguo* could *precede* the coming of the West. Thus India was said to have been "lost" to the Mughals, while China had been "lost" to the Manchus. It might also be noted that the Middle East and Central Asia were not included in this particular imagined "Asia." For a discussion of the different ways Asia has been "imagined" throughout the twentieth century (imperialist Asia, nationalist Asia, universalist Asia, regionalist Asia), see Acharya, "Asia is Not One."

[8] Liu Shipei, "Wuzhengfuzhuyi."

[9] He Zhen and Liu Shipei, "Lun zhongzu geming."

[10] On this, see Karl, "On Women's Labor." Karl argues that for He Zhen, Euro-American countries (and Japan) – rather than being viable models for China – represented merely "more advanced ways in which newly-emerged and now-globalizing forms of oppression – industrial waged labor, democratic polities, enlightenment knowledge – could attach themselves to native forms of subjection, to reconfigure and deepen these extant forms on a larger, more thorough, and more disguised scale."

[11] Eileen Cheng, "In Search of New Voices from Alien Lands." Cheng further observes that in his vernacular stories after 1918 Lu Xun often implied that discourses appropriated from the West (for example, pertaining to science, hygiene, and individualism) were no more than tactics of "civilizing" oppression.

This chapter explores this theme of China's varied self-positioning in the global order through an examination of the emerging Chinese women's press during the transitional period between the last years of the Qing monarchy and the early years of the Chinese Republic. It seeks to investigate how both Western and non-Western women were discursively represented. It questions, for example, whether these representations might have echoed this particular early-twentieth-century Chinese revolutionary identification with Asia, as well as its concomitant questioning of "Euro-American centrality" and deconstruction of Western notions of "civilization" and "progress."[12]

Multiple Western Others in the Chinese Women's Press

We have seen in the preceding chapters that from its beginnings the Chinese women's press predominantly focused on comparisons with the West. Articles cited Western practice and attitudes as the *benchmark* against which to evaluate the situation and status of Chinese women. This might mean, for example, contrasting Chinese women unfavorably with their Western counterparts, such as a 1904 article in *Nüzi shijie* (Women's world) describing Western women as *xianshen* (immortals) with their healthy bodies and love of the outdoors in comparison to listless and emaciated Chinese women.[13] The "biography" sections of these journals also tended to focus on Western women.[14] The second issue of *Zhongguo xin nüjie zazhi* (Magazine of China's new world of women) in 1907, for example, featured an illustration and biography of the American educator Mary Lyon (1797–1849), who would regularly appear in the biographical columns of women's journals throughout the 1910s. In 1917, *The Ladies' Journal* published translated excerpts from Sarah Knowles Bolton's 1886 book *Girls Who Became Famous* (*Taixi lienü zhuan*), which, along with Mary Lyon, featured portraits of the writer and abolitionist Harriet Beecher Stowe (1811–1896), writer and champion of native Americans Helen Hunt Jackson (1830–1885), and English prison reformer Elizabeth Fry

---

[12] I borrow the phrase "Euro-American centrality" from Karl, *Staging the World*, 83. Some of the contributors to this women's press, having also studied in Japan before 1911, would most likely have been aware of this train of thought. For example, it is quite possible that Chinese students and activists in Japan at this time would have at least been acquainted with the ideas of Liu Shipei and He Zhen; furthermore, as noted in note 5, Mariano Ponce's study of Philippine independence and its critique of Western civilizing discourse was translated into Chinese in 1902.

[13] "Nüzi jianyi de tiyu."

[14] As Xia Xiaohong notes in this volume, the first biographies of Western women drew on Japanese works on Western "female heroines," such as Tokutomi Roka, *Sekai kokon meifu kagami* (A mirror of the world's famous women), published in 1898.

(1780–1845).[15] As late as 1942, a collection of Chinese and foreign women's biographies primarily featured Western women (including Mary Lyon). The sole non-Western woman included in the collection was the Indian poet and political activist Sarojini Naidu (1879–1949).[16]

The early Republican women's press also appropriated Western models as a way of *valorizing* conventional Chinese notions of womanhood, a rhetorical strategy that was already apparent in the first readers for girls' schools in the last years of the Qing and the first detailed collective biography of Western women published in 1906 by the female poet and educator Xue Shaohui (1855–1911). These texts had often assimilated foreign models such as Joan of Arc or Florence Nightingale to traditional Chinese notions of feminine virtue.[17] Similarly, *Funü zazhi – The Ladies' Journal* featured articles on the mothers of George Washington and Napoleon Bonaparte as exemplary *xianmu* (virtuous mothers) who embodied the virtues of modesty, self-sacrifice, and frugality.[18]

Following this practice of appropriating Western models to conservative ends, Western practice was occasionally cited to justify condemnation of gender radicalism in China. This was apparent in the wake of a vociferous Chinese suffragist campaign (1911–1913) for equal political and educational rights in the early Republic. In the first issue of *The Ladies' Journal* in 1915, a Shanghai teacher, Yu Tiansui, rebuked "unrestrained" young Chinese women whose demands for equality with men he felt had gone too far and provocatively described them as *fanjia zhi ma* (unharnessed fillies). In contrast, he pointed to the example of "responsible" American women, who took their household and marital duties seriously.[19] Contributors to *The Chung Hwa Women's Magazine* likewise wistfully looked to the West, where – in the view of one such contributor – a more "cautious" and "sensible" approach to women's rights was beginning to prevail (at a time, he noted, when Chinese women perversely were demanding *more* equality).[20] Liang Lingxian, another contributor to *The Chung Hwa Women's Magazine*, whom we have already encountered in

---

[15] "Taixi lienüzhuan." Sarah Knowles Bolton (1841–1916) was a writer and leading member of the Women's Christian Temperance Union. It is significant that the Chinese translation of Bolton's book reads as "Biographies of Western Women."

[16] Lu Manyan, *Zhongwai nüjie zhuan*. The Western women discussed in the collection included the educator and suffragist Ellen Key (1849–1926), the philosopher and women's suffrage pioneer Jane Addams (1860–1935), the social activist and leader of the early women's movement Elizabeth Stanton (1815–1902), and the birth control advocate Margaret Sanger (1879–1966). Sarojini Naidu was the first woman to preside over the Indian National Congress (in 1925); after independence in 1947 she became governor of Uttar Pradesh state.

[17] Judge, "Blended Wish Images"; Nanxiu Qian, "Borrowing Foreign Mirrors."

[18] "Yingxiong taidu zhi Huashengdun mu"; Xu Chan, "Napolun zhi mu."

[19] Yu Tiansui, "Yu zhi nüzi jiaoyuguan."

[20] Wu Chongmin, "Nannü ziyou pingdeng zhenjie." On the critical discourse in both the women's and periodical press pertaining to Chinese female students' attitudes and behaviour during the early Republic, see Bailey, "Unharnessed Fillies," and Bailey, *Gender and Education in China*.

Siao-chen Hu's chapter, insisted that it was right and proper for women to provide help and support for their menfolk and not to engage in a "foolish" struggle with men over equal rights. She similarly drew attention to "civilized" practice in the West, where apparently women's devoted service to husbands and households was highly valorized.[21] Translations from American and British middle-class magazines on domestic management, as well as on orderly and skilled American housewives, filled the pages of the Chinese women's press in the 1910s.[22]

Examples of those who used the West to buttress conservative views are abundant. In the wake of the 1911 Revolution, for example, the military governor of Jiangsu and Zhejiang rejected a petition submitted by a Ms. Lu Jiangzhen in January 1912, proposing the creation of a women's military training institute. The governor observed that *even* in the West there were no such military schools for girls.[23] Other commentators, such as the school textbook compiler and educational official Jiang Weiqiao (1873–1953), referred admiringly to the West (and especially the United States), where the teaching of domestic science was considered an essential component of female education, and "housewifery" was valorized by society as a professional vocation.[24] This served as an important counterexample to Jiang's description of Chinese female students' "arrogant" refusal to take the learning of household skills seriously, a dangerous trend, he claimed, for the future of the country.[25]

Yet commentators in the early Republican women's press who were fiercely critical of the direction in which they perceived women's education in China to be heading and who favored a moderate approach to the "woman question" also drew attention to the dangers of taking the West as a model. A contributor to *The Women's Eastern Times* in 1911 warned that *Oufeng* (Europeanization) was gradually *ran* (infecting or contaminating) China's women. They should be careful not to blindly emulate inappropriate Western customs such as holding hands and kissing in public, or free marriage and divorce.[26] Several years later a contributor to *The Ladies' Journal* insisted that what China needed at the present time was *not* a *xiyangpai xin nüzi* (Western-style new woman), but

[21] Liang Lingxian, "Suo wang yu wuguo nüzi zhe."

[22] See, for example, "Meiguo yibai xianqi zhi zishu," a translation from an American housewives' magazine on the competition to discover the superior housewife in each state; and Hu Binxia, "Meiguo jiating." As Joan Judge notes in this volume, translations of Western works (books, periodical literature, etc.) in the early twentieth century were based primarily on initial Japanese translations. By the late 1910s, however, articles from British or American women's magazines and periodicals were being translated directly into Chinese. For example, a 1918 article in *The Ladies' Journal* on the "scientific" way of washing dishes and thereby extinguishing dangerous bacteria was translated directly from *The Mother's Magazine* (1905–1936), referred to in Chinese as *Mufan zazhi* (literally "Magazine of the model mother").

[23] *Minli bao* (Independent people's newspaper), January 2, 1912.

[24] Jiang Weiqiao, "Lun nüxuexiao." See also Gao Junyin, "Lun nüxuexiao."

[25] Ibid.   [26] Jiang Renlan, "Lun funü zuixin Xifa."

rather a *jinshen* (circumspect) and *limao* (courteous) domestic manager who could ensure the smooth running of the household.[27] In magazines such as *The Women's Eastern Times* and *Zhonghua funüjie – The Chung Hwa Women's Magazine*, women's lifestyles and attitudes in France, in particular, were held up as a negative example, portrayed as the very epitome of hedonism and deca-dence and the source of the break-up of families, increasing divorce, and a declining birth rate. German women, by way of contrast, were often referred to as authentic "good wives and virtuous mothers" because they were obedi-ent and *wenrou* (soft and gentle). Prudent household managers, they were also deemed less arrogant and domineering than French women.[28] Even in the pages of the radical May Fourth journal, *Xin qingnian* (New youth), a certain Liang Hualan regretted in 1917 that diligent and hard-working American housewives were being "corrupted" by the "French disease" (code word for a society in which women behaved in an "unrestrained" and "irresponsible" manner).[29]

Such was the extraordinarily cacophonous nature of gender discourse in the women's press during the early Republic that at the same time as contributors were warning of the "dangerous" influence of the West in undermining social mores, female authors continued to join male contributors to the women's press in using Western women as a benchmark. Women writers who strongly supported women's political, educational, and economic rights often framed their discourse with references to Western women, in the sense that they believed that, given the right opportunities, Chinese women would surpass their Western counterparts in impact and achievement. As early as 1903, Chen Xiefen (1883–1923), the pioneer of the Chinese women's press discussed in Nanxiu Qian's chapter, had insisted in her journal *Nü xuebao* (Journal of women's learning) that characteristics such as perseverance and a seething hatred of social injustice, which Chinese women possessed as a result of their long history of oppression, would equip them in the future to achieve far more than their Western "sisters."[30] Such confidence increased in the aftermath of the 1911 Revolution. In 1912, a Ms. Zhao Fengru confidently predicted in *Shenzhou nübao* (China women's news)[31] that the potential of Chinese women to contribute to national reconstruction was unlimited. She proposed the creation of a *nüzi guomin yinhang* (female citizens' bank) in which women would pool their resources (e.g., through donations of jewelry, hairpins, rings, and bracelets) and assume the role of the nation's creditors. In a burst of almost Maoist-like voluntarism, Zhang declared that Chinese women with

---

[27] Wang Jiting, "Funü yingyou zhi zhishi."
[28] Wang Changlu, "Fu de." See also Liu Sheng, "Zhongguo nüxue shifan lun"; Li Foru, "Nüjie zhenyan"; Xu Chan, "Ou-mei geguo furen yuedan"; and Zhiyuan, "Deyizhi zhi nü."
[29] Liang Hualan, "Nüzi wenti."   [30] Chen Xiefen, "Zhongguo nüzi zhi qiantu."
[31] The expression *Shenzhou* (literally, "the Divine Continent/Land") was often used at this time to denote China. See the entry on this journal in the Appendix.

their growing economic influence and enhanced educational opportunities, would be able to "surpass" Western women within ten years. She continued, *yi zu er dengfeng zaoquan* (In one leap, they [Chinese women] will reach the peak of perfection).[32] A 1912 article in *The Women's Eastern Times* further declared that the advent of the Republic provided the perfect opportunity for China "to move ahead of the West" by immediately implementing women's suffrage. This view was shared by a female contributor to the major newspaper *Minli bao* (Independent people's newspaper), who noted that such a measure was "a dream yearned for in the West" but not yet actualized.[33]

This vertical and integrated overview of late Qing and early Republican Chinese women's magazines illuminates the presence of a particular discourse that often favorably contrasted a "conservative" West with a "radical" China. This intriguingly inverts the approach adopted by radical May Fourth intellectuals such as Chen Duxiu, who cited a "progressive" West to condemn China's "feudal" gender practices. At the same time, it provides evidence of multiple and contradictory voices in these early women's journals and complicates our understanding of how the West was perceived in early-twentieth-century China. The fact that contributors to the Chinese women's press might enlist Western practices and attitudes to buttress their conservative (as well as more radical) stance on gender issues (as we have already seen in Qian's, Xia's, and Judge's contributions) demonstrates that there were in fact multiple perceived "Wests" from which Chinese commentators could and would draw very different lessons in accordance with their own agendas.[34]

Source of Cultural Authenticity or Symbol of Civilizational "Backwardness"?

The Non-Western Female Other

No matter how contradictory the many discourses that involved Western women – positive or negative – may have sounded, the ideal of rational

---

[32] Zhang Fengru, "Faqi nüzi guomin."

[33] Jiang Renlan, "Shuo nüzi canzheng zhi liyou"; Ou Peifen, "Jinggao zheng xuanjuquan." Male commentators in the newspaper press at this time were generally hostile to the idea of women's political rights. On the women's suffrage debate in 1911–1913, see Bailey, *Gender and Education in China*, 75–78.

[34] An intriguing 1919 news report in *The Ladies' Journal* on the United States, for example, noted that appropriate discipline was imposed on young women, to the extent that if they paraded through the streets with their faces daubed with makeup they would be hauled off by female police officers to have their faces washed ("Nüjie yaowen," 4). An earlier article on women and smoking in *The Women's Eastern Times* bewailed the "unseemly" habit of young Shanghai women openly smoking in public, in contrast to practice in the West where men and women did not smoke openly in each other's company ("Funü yu zhiyan.")

and scientific domesticity promoted by *The Women's Eastern Times, The Ladies' Journal*, and *The Chung Hwa Women's Magazine* in the early years of the Republic drew on Western practice and knowledge.[35] Catering to an emerging urban middle class (male and female) fascinated with material and consumer modernity, specialized articles in these magazines expounded on science, nutrition, hygiene and medicine, and child psychology. The first issues of *The Ladies' Journal*, for example, published a regular column "Jiating xin zhishi" (New household knowledge) that informed its readers of the latest and most scientific ways to wash clothes (using "Fuller's Earth," an absorbent powdery clay, for example) or preserve woolen garments with the judicious application of "Keating's Insect Powder," a product much in demand in late Victorian Britain. Early issues of *The Women's Eastern Times* also featured advertisements for Hazeline Snow, a facial moisturizing cream first manufactured in the United States in 1892.[36]

Much of this knowledge – at least during the first two decades of the twentieth century – was mediated by Japan, as Joan Judge and Xia Xiaohong note. How, though, did the Chinese women's press represent Japanese women? In many ways, Chinese women's journals and magazines during this period exhibited near-schizophrenic attitudes. In the journals published by Chinese students and activists in Japan during the early years of the twentieth century, Japanese womanhood was alternatively held up as a model worthy of emulation or as a negative example of "backward" submissiveness. In 1909, Chen Yiyi, who, as Nanxiu Qian notes in her chapter, canonized the genealogy of radical women's journals, described Japanese women in his journal *Nübao* (Women's journal) as nothing more than *gaodeng nuli* (high-class slaves) due

---

[35] On domesticity discourses and women's education in early-twentieth-century China, see Bailey, "Active Citizen or Efficient Housewife?" and Bailey, *Gender and Education in China*. On the discourse and practice of domestic management and its identification with nation-building during the Republican period, see Schneider, *Keeping the Nation's House*. Early Republican women's magazines consulted for this chapter, in addition to *The Women's Eastern Times* and *The Ladies' Journal* (issues of which were located in Nanjing University Library and the Library of Congress, Washington DC), include *Shenzhou nübao* (China women's news, 1912–1913), located in the library of the Institute of Modern History, Academia Sinica, Taibei, and *Nüzi shijie* (Women's world, 1914–1915), *Nüzi zazhi* (Women's magazine, 1915), and *Zhonghua funüjie – The Chung Hwa Women's Magazine* (1915–1916), all located in the library of the Modern History Research Institute, Chinese Academy of Social Sciences, Beijing. There are also a few issues of *The Ladies' Journal* in the Bibliothèque Nationale in Paris, which I discovered while doing research there in the early 1980s. The library of SOAS, University of London, has a complete original set of *The Ladies' Journal*. It is worth noting that as late as the 1990s, when I was conducting research on early-twentieth-century women's education in China and consulting these journals as a valuable primary source to illuminate social, cultural, and gender change in China, there were few, if any, scholars working on early-twentieth-century Chinese women's magazines.

[36] Such a phenomenon anticipated that of 1990s China, a period of accelerating market reform when women's magazines increasingly advertised cosmetics and skin-whitening creams to entice the female consumer of "beauty" (Johansson, "White Skin, Large Breasts").

to the pervasive and reactionary influence of the country's gender ideology of *ryōsai kenbo* (i.e., *liangqi xianmu* good wife and virtuous mother).[37] In contrast, a contributor to *Women's World* in 1904 praised Japanese women's public-mindedness, claiming that Chinese women were not even the equal of lowly Japanese prostitutes, who at least demonstrated some inkling of patriotism by donating their valuables to help finance Japan's current war with Russia.[38] This unfavorable comparison with Chinese women was likewise emphasized by a contributor to a Chinese student journal published in Japan, *Zhejiang chao* (Tides of Zhejiang). The author expressed admiration for vigorous and outgoing Japanese female students in order to ridicule Chinese women of leisure "who were solely concerned with prettifying themselves and who spent the entire day mindlessly wriggling about like playthings or exhibits at a zoo."[39]

The early Republican women's press also presented complex and ambivalent images of Japanese women. Some May Fourth era journals such as *New Youth* highlighted the significance and influence of the Japanese feminist movement centered on *Seitō* (the Bluestocking Society). The group of writers who founded this society in 1911 identified themselves as "new women" (*atarashii onna*) and sought to promote free thinking in both their personal lives and literary works.[40] Zhou Zuoren (1885–1967), younger brother of Lu Xun, for example, published in *New Youth* in 1918 his translation of an essay ("On Chastity") written by one of *Seitō's* most celebrated members, Yosano Akiko (1878–1942), to buttress his condemnation of Chinese family and gender ideology. *Xin funü* (New woman), a journal published in Shanghai (1920–1921) and one of the first women's journals to include investigative reports on Chinese working women and publicize the case for birth control, presents a different view of Japanese women. One contributor, Fu Yanzhang, who had apparently lived in Yokohama for two years, emphasized what he saw as Japanese women's extreme subservience to men. In a 1920 article on Japanese women he observed that they were generally looked down upon in society. As a result of their lowly status, he maintained, Japanese women were obliged to walk behind male companions on the streets, give seating priority to men on public trams, and turn their faces away when addressing or talking to others. By way of contrast, he noticed in an aside, adolescent girls in Japan were more *ziran* (natural) than their Chinese counterparts. The latter were obsessed with superficial outward appearance, manifested in

---

[37] Chen Yiyi, "Nanzun nübei." See also Liu Jucai, *Zhongguo jindai funü*, 218. Chen Yiyi maintained that Japanese women's slavish deference to men was even more iniquitous than that of their Chinese counterparts subjected to the conventional Chinese notion of *nanzun nübei* (respect for the male, contempt for the female).

[38] Yate, "Lun zhuzao guomin mu."   [39] Tai Gong, "Dongjing zazhi shi."

[40] Bardsley, *The Bluestockings of Japan.*

their wearing of modish fashion items such as high-heeled shoes and fancy spectacles.[41]

In other instances, Japanese womanhood represented the Asian ideal in contradistinction to the Western Other.[42] Advertisements in the first issues of *The Ladies' Journal* describing the benefits of a brand of fortifying pills for women (*qingkuai wan*) are illustrated by the image of a *Japanese* woman in traditional dress (kimono) as the epitome of the *liangqi xianmu* (good wife and virtuous mother) who ensures her personal health in order to fulfill her duty as a diligent household manager (see Figure 13.1).

Did such complex and contradictory representations extend to other non-Western, and particularly Asian, women in the pages of the early Republican Chinese women's press? Very few articles were published, in fact, on the lives and experiences of non-Western women, and those that were consistently represented them as the "backward" and "primitive" Other. Thus, while earlier Chinese radicals and revolutionaries (however briefly) had sought common cause with Indian nationalists on the basis of their shared experience with imperialism, articles on India in the women's press attributed the "loss" of the country solely to weak, uneducated, and superstitious women. A long article on female customs in India in *The Women's Eastern Times* in 1916 warned that China would go the same way if women's education was not developed. Citing early Hindu religious texts such as *Manusmriti* (the laws of Manu), the author painted a dismal picture of Indian women. They were betrothed at the age of 6 and married before the age of 12, kept under close control and supervision at all times, regularly beaten, and expected to treat their husbands as gods. Since women were regarded as ornaments, the author continued, not only did they not possess any *ren'ge* (personhood), the only thing that occupied their minds was an obsessive hankering for material wealth. In more general terms, the article also referred to the custom of *sati* (widow suicide) to demonstrate "coldhearted cruelty" amongst the people, who shamefully had to wait for the "compassionate" intervention of the British before the custom was abolished.[43]

The author further declared that those sections in the laws of Manu dealing with a woman's duty to obey her father and husband had directly influenced the emergence of *sancong* (the three obediences) in China, according to which

---

[41] Fu Yanzhang, "Riben de funü." Copies of *Xin funü* (New woman) which was published in Shanghai are located in the Beijing University Library.

[42] In the "triangulation" of global forces (China, the West, Japan) referred to in Joan Judge's chapter in this volume, Japan may very well have served more as a "conduit" for the West than as a "bulwark" of the East, but perhaps a more detailed study of advertisements in the Chinese women's press might reveal more examples of the latter.

[43] Zhang Zhaosi, "Yindu nüzi fengsu tan." Curiously, having emphasized Indian women's subservience, the author also noted an alarming tendency amongst some of them (especially those from the lower classes) to fly into a rage and verbally abuse people in the street, a phenomenon, the author noted incredulously, that was not considered shameful at all.

Fig. 13.1 A notice by a Shanghai pharmacist advertising the benefits of *qingkuai wan*, a fortifying pill for women, *The Ladies' Journal* 1:5 (1915)
Note: Noting that all outstanding and heroic figures in the past and present in both China and the West were raised by "virtuous mothers," the advertisement insists that it is obligatory for "good wives and virtuous mothers" (*liangqi xianmu*) to ensure their own good health in order to perform their required tasks.

women obeyed their father when young, their husband when married, and their son when widowed. Several years later, another article in *The Ladies' Journal* on Indian women likewise observed that the low esteem in which women were held in China was directly linked to the influence of "Indian thought," with its valorization of female chastity, women's seclusion within the home, and absolute obedience to husbands.[44] While male intellectuals such as Liang Qichao in the 1890s or May Fourth radicals in the 1910s associated the "oppressed," "ignorant," and "pitiful" Chinese woman with Confucian patriarchy, these articles on India in the Chinese women's press located the source of Chinese women's plight in the thought and customs of a "backward" foreign (and Asian) Other. Moreover, while the likes of Tang Tiaonai earlier in

---

[44] Ke Shi, "Yindu de funü shenghuo." The early marriage of boys and girls in India was another aspect that Chinese commentators focused on. See "Kehai zhi zaohun."

the century had questioned the West's civilizational discourse as a cynical ploy to extend its control over "backward natives," as discussed above, a contributor to *The Ladies' Journal* in 1918 blamed those same "backward natives" as the key obstacle to social reform initiatives championed by Western missionaries and their followers to improve Indian women's lives.[45]

The particular discourse in the pages of the Chinese women's press on the "backwardness" of Indian women and the negative impact of Indian civilization on China anticipated the views of male intellectuals such as Hu Shi and Lin Yutang. These intellectuals would later argue that a major factor in the decline of women's status in China and the increasing restrictions imposed upon them during the Song period (tenth to thirteenth century) was the baneful influence of "Indian civilization" (in the guise of Buddhism). Such an assumption was shared in a 1931 essay by Zeng Baosun (1893–1978), great-granddaughter of the nineteenth-century statesman Zeng Guofan and the first Chinese woman to gain a university degree in England (in 1916). It was also echoed by Chen Hengzhe (1893–1976), China's first female university professor (at Peking University in 1920), in a 1943 essay, "The Influence of Foreign Cultures on Chinese Woman."[46] Their view was not, however, universal. Zhang Mojun (1884–1965), for example, daughter of a Qing dynasty official, recalled in her 1953 autobiography that at the age of nine she persuaded her mother not to bind her feet on the grounds that female Buddhist saints (bodhisattvas) worshipped by her mother all had "natural feet"[47] – the Indian "model" could work both ways, then.

Illustrations in *The Women's Eastern Times* suggest an evolutionary schema based on dress and marriage practices. In its second issue in 1911, a picture of a Chinese "traditional" wedding (with the bride veiled and hidden from view) is juxtaposed with a picture of a Western "free-style" wedding (in which the bride is noticeably taller than the groom) (see Figure 13.2). In the third issue of the magazine a picture of a large crowd at a Javanese royal wedding is juxtaposed with the image of a group of sophisticated European women in "new-style" dress. The following issue displays the photographs of two Javanese women in simple "native" dress (see Figures 13.3 and 13.4).[48] Such visual representations

---

[45] Jiang Xuehui, "Yindu nüjie jinwen."

[46] Tseng, "The Chinese Woman Past and Present"; Ch'en Heng-che, "The Influence of Foreign Cultures." Both Tseng and Ch'en, however, were very critical of those contemporary Chinese women, who, they believed, wilfully confused "liberty" with "license."

[47] Cited in Chang Mo-chün, "Opposition to Footbinding."

[48] Curiously, however, although several other images of Javanese women appear in later issues, there are no written articles on the women of the Dutch East Indies (Indonesia). One of the few illustrations of Asian women in *The Ladies' Journal* at this time (6:2, 1919, p. 12) depicts a Malay couple adorned in rich "native" dress. Photographs of topless Pacific islander women (one of which is juxtaposed with photographs of British and German royal princesses) are featured in *The Chung Hwa Women's Magazine* 1915:5 and 1915:7.

No.2

Fig. 13.2 Photographs of a "Chinese old-style wedding" (under the title "Preservation of the national essence"; right) and a "European new-style wedding" (under the title "The sweet taste of freedom"; left), *The Women's Eastern Times* 2 (July 26, 1911)

of the "Other" Asian woman in the Chinese women's press at this time thus foreshadow the orientalizing depiction of ethnic minority and rural women within China that became so ubiquitous by the end of the twentieth century.[49]

Just as articles on Indian women emphasized their seclusion, so the few references to Turkish women highlighted the isolated and restricted lives they led. In the view of one contributor to *The Women's Eastern Times*, oppressed Turkish women covered from head to foot in the *burqa* scarcely appeared as human. The article, in fact, conflated Turkish women with Muslim women in general, since it went on to describe the secluded lives of women in Morocco, where their lack of human contact had apparently given them the mentality of children.[50] *The Ladies' Journal*, which was able to draw on *direct* translations from Western sources within a few years of its first issue, translated an article in 1918 by an American teacher, Hester Jenkins, on the "pitiful" and bounded existence of Turkish women in the harem (*helun*).[51]

---

[49] Cf. Gladney, "Representing Nationality in China" and Mittler in this volume
[50] "Lun Tu'erqi nüzi."   [51] "Tu'erqi guisheng."

Fig. 13.3 A Javanese royal wedding (top) and fashionably dressed European women (bottom), *The Women's Eastern Times* 3 (September 22, 1911)

婦 貴 之 哇 爪   婦 富 之 哇 爪

Fig. 13.4 An aristocratic Javanese woman (left) and a wealthy Javanese woman (right), *The Women's Eastern Times* 4 (November 5, 1911)

A strangely contradictory image of women from the Philippines, whose anti-colonial struggle against the Spanish and then the Americans had been so much admired by early-twentieth-century Chinese revolutionaries, was presented in the pages of *The Ladies' Journal*. On the one hand, the Philippines was described as a place that had been *zhanran* (contaminated) by European mores; this had resulted in the practice of free-choice marriage and couples outrageously expressing their feelings openly and publicly.[52] On the other, the people were mired in native superstition (exacerbated by the influence of Catholicism). One such example of "superstitious" practice was the people's enthusiastic resort to the confessional in Catholic churches to absolve their guilt; even women, the article observed, come to church to openly admit their "crime" of adultery.[53]

Finally, looking further afield, the very few references to African women in *The Ladies' Journal* were similarly underpinned by the assumption of a "backward" Other. The only article specifically devoted to Africa in the magazine during the first decade of the Republic was a description (in 1921) of "strange marriage customs" amongst the Owambo people of southern

[52] Ya'e, "Feilübin xinnian zazhi."   [53] "Feilübin fengsu lüeshu."

Angola and northern South West Africa (present-day Namibia). Again, the emphasis was very much on the "primitive" nature of initiation rites among young women and the group celebrations and dancing that occurred before marriage.[54] One year earlier, in an article condemning the tendency of Chinese female students to flatten their breasts (with tight undergarments) and wear elaborate earrings in a "vain quest for beauty," the author noted that this was *especially* unacceptable because it made young Chinese women look like "backward" African women.[55] Yet a cartoon in a 1921 issue of *The Ladies' Journal* illustrating the difference between a "primitive" state and "civilization" by juxtaposing an image of a barely-clothed African woman and her child with that of a "modern" Western socialite couple might have contained a hidden message. It may have been created as a warning about the pitfalls of adopting Western gender norms, particularly among female students in China, who, in the view of many contributors to *The Ladies' Journal* in the 1910s, were guilty of superficial Westernization, championing absolute equality with men, and arrogantly refusing to assume their ordained roles as diligent, obedient, and capable household managers (see Figure 13.5).[56] The cartoon pictures the African woman and child deferentially and respectfully offering up food to a barely seen patriarch figure, while the man in the picture of the Western socialite couple wistfully (and hopelessly?) looks at a brash and confident woman who is casually walking away from him.

Conclusion

An exploration of how the foreign Other was discursively and visually represented in the early Republican Chinese women's press reveals two significant trends. First, the West generally served as the frame of reference for evaluating, critiquing, and even valorizing women's status and lives in China. Second, in contrast to a small group of early-twentieth-century Chinese revolutionaries and radicals who sought common ground with non-Western peoples, there was no attempt to imagine a particular *Asian* community of women based on shared experiences and notions of solidarity.[57] Thus Hu Binxia, who, as Siao-chen

---

[54] Feng Xiqing, "Feizhou jiehun qisu." The source of information for Feng's article is not given, although it is likely to have come from Western missionaries. Although some tribes of the Owambo (e.g., the Kwanyama) practised a matrilineal system in terms of inheritance and succession, this is not discussed in the article.

[55] Xu Shiheng, "Jinhou funü yingyou de jingshen."

[56] Bailey, *Gender and Education in China.*

[57] Early-twentieth-century Chinese revolutionaries had used the new term *Yazhou* for their "imagined" community; there is no reference to this term in the Chinese women's press. A few references are made to *Yadong* (another possible translation for "East Asia") in some women's journals such as *China Women's Journal* and the *China Women's News*, but invariably the author

FN22 7.7 (1921)

婦女雜誌　第七卷　第七號　世界改造與婦女

且女子既受高等教育則於子女的教育既能發揮多大的價值面
以之賞官吏就公職學識也可以不患不足了。

八　我國婦女的現狀

我國一般男子能發充分承認婦女的人格的很少而婦女能有
自覺心的也是鳳毛麟角不可多得男子多以玩物視婦人婦女也
居然以玩物自居而不以為羞婦女彷彿與煙酒等同到當作娛樂
品這種現狀實在是很可羞愁的推取我國婦女的地位所以不能
增進因為社交上沒有女性的要求故有人格的女子少出現於社
會這是斷來主張男治外女治內的結果與後受過教育的女子其
活動的範圍既不以家庭為限出面而與多數的男子交際則今後男
子的女性觀自可改變女子的地位也可因之而增進了。
總之婦女地位的增進須有女子自己努力而有向上探求的精神；
否則大學雖開女禁而來者寥寥或者程度太低不能與男子同班
有權利而無力享受實為可恥的事情所以為我國文化的將來計，
吾人當進而促婦女的自覺婦女的自己努力實為必要。

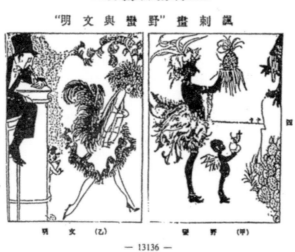

Fig. 13.5 Satirical cartoon illustrating "civilization" and "savagery," *The Ladies' Journal* 7:7 (1921)

Hu explains in her chapter, served as editor for *The Ladies' Journal* in 1916, blamed Chinese women for the country's lowly position in the international hierarchy of household hygiene and – even *worse* – for placing the country below *even* Iran, Turkey, and India.[58] Such an attitude persists to the present day. Thus, following the publication in 2002 of an international chart of "women in politics" by the Inter-Parliamentary Union that revealed that China had slumped from twelfth position (in 1994) to twenty-eighth, one official Chinese report noted gloomily that "we are not *even* as good as Vietnam or Cuba" (emphasis added).[59]

What most excited contributors and readers of the Chinese women's press in the early Republic were the deeds of derring-do performed by "active" Western women. These included the Frenchwoman Marie Marvingt (1875–1963), the world's first "great (female) athlete" (*da yundongjia*), who also flew air balloons, climbed mountains, and won awards in shooting and ski jumping. They also included the American Lillian Boyer (1901–1989), *shijie di-yi maoxian zhi nüzi* (the world's greatest female dare-devil), who performed aerial stunts and parachute jumps.[60] *The Ladies' Journal* also publicized the exploits of the American aviator Katherine Stinson (1891–1977), the first woman to carry the U.S. mail by air in 1913, who gave flying exhibitions in Beijing and Shanghai in 1917.[61]

Notwithstanding this fascination with Western women that characterized the Chinese women's press from its beginnings at the turn of the twentieth century, by the early years of the Chinese Republic in the 1910s it provided multiple and contradictory images of the West both as a model and as a source of "contagion."[62] This reflected how crucial, and controversial, the "woman

is referring to China only. See, for example, Ji Wei, "Puji jiaoyu yu nüzi jiaoyu." Likewise, the relatively new term *Dongfang* (the East) was invariably used to refer to China. See, for example, Wang Pingling, "Dongfang furen."

[58] Hu Binxia, "Hezhe wei wu funü." Having studied in Japan before 1911, it is more than likely that she would have at least been acquainted with the critique of Western civilization and the notion of a common Asian identity implied in the articles of Liu Shipei and He Zhen.

[59] Cited in Edwards, "Strategizing for Politics," 380. The Inter-Parliamentary Union was founded in 1889, and its headquarters are located in Geneva, Switzerland. By 2006 China had declined even further to forty-ninth position (Cuba and Vietnam were eighth and twenty-fifth, respectively).

[60] "Weixian zhi xinfu"; Liang Zijun, "Boye nüshi fangwenji." See also "Weixian zhi xinnü Mailimai," a collage of photographs in *Women's World* featuring Marie Marvingt in a plane, in a hot-air balloon, swimming, boxing, and rowing.

[61] See *Funü zazhi* 3:3 (1917) *yuxing*, 20. A Chinese newspaper report claimed that up to 40,000 people watched Stinson perform aerial stunts over Jiangwan, near Shanghai, in 1917. *Zhonghua xinbao* (China news), February 2, 1917. For more on Stinson in China, see Judge, *Republican Lens*, Chapter 7.

[62] It should be noted that some contributors to *Jiaoyu zazhi* (The educational review), an early specialized journal on education that began publication in 1909, like those in the women's press, also tended to draw lessons from Western practice that defy conventional notions of *the*

question" was at this time in grappling with issues of national and cultural identity and the making of Chinese modernity. In its "Othering" of the foreign Other, the early-twentieth-century Chinese women's press is, as Barbara Mittler demonstrates in the next chapter, a significant textual resource in delineating the trajectory of China's global modernity and the roots of contemporary Han Chinese representations of both Western women (as an ambiguous "fetish")[63] and ethnic minority women (as "exotic" figures situated on the lower rungs of a civilizational ladder). These representations have pervaded advertising, the media, and popular culture since the 1990s. Taking on certain historically contingent functions, they usually serve specific sociopolitical purposes that may lie far beyond the simple text of the media that carry them.

Western impact on Chinese intellectuals as the source of "democratic" or "progressive" thought. For example, in their advocacy of a more thoroughgoing official surveillance of a perceived "decadent" popular culture in China, contributors to *The Educational Review* hailed what they saw as efficient and rigorous state systems of censorship in Western countries.

[63] Johansson, "Consuming the Other." Johansson refers to a kind of "racial fetishism" in Chinese advertising during the 1990s that portrayed the "eroticized" Western woman as powerful, active, and self-confident (in contrast to the Chinese woman) while also lacking the inner beauty and modesty of the Chinese woman.

14   The New (Wo)man and Her/His Others: Foreigners on the Pages of China's Women's Magazines

Barbara Mittler

Periodicals are by nature ephemeral, each number marked clearly with its sell-by date. Yet to emphasize this momentary quality may obscure their impact both as a repository of cultural memory and as a catalyst of gendered action.[1] In China, women's magazines have already existed for more than a century. How important is their voice? Scrutinizing the presence of foreigners on the pages of Chinese women's journals throughout the long twentieth century, this chapter asks how their image and status changed and how this impacted (wo)manhood as an ideal and a lived reality. It will question the importance of these images to the making of the Chinese inflections to the grammar of global modernity-in-common. I will show that foreigners (particularly Westerners) were considered crucial as a frame of reference for evaluating the lives and works of China's *xin nü/nanxing* (New (Wo)men).[2] The chapter will read contemporary and historical women's magazines from different registers and addressed to different audiences – didactic *Nüzi shijie* (Women's world) (1904–1907), entertaining *Linglong – Linloon Magazine* (1931–1937), ideological *Zhongguo funü* (Woman of China) (1949–), and specialized *Nongjianü baishitong – Rural Women Knowing All* (1993–). Reading these journals, I discuss the changing functions of the foreign(er's) image. I will show that this image shifts between the poles of fascinating model of emulation and object of disgust, of fear and discrimination, and that it does so in accordance with particular and specific sociopolitical purposes that might lie far beyond the text of the journal itself, thus illustrating the important impact of these journals on the making of historical discourse and cultural memory. The foreign woman

---

Journal articles are cited by author (often anonymous) and title and are included in full in the works cited list at the end of this volume. In addition, this paper refers to more articles simply for additional reference, using the following shorthand: Journal volume year page (e.g., *Linglong* 244 (1936), 1000).

[1] Cf. the introduction to Beetham and Boardman, eds., *Victorian Women's Magazines*.

[2] In this paper, my use of "foreign" is primarily if not exclusively concerned with something these magazines would call *xifang* 西方 (the "West") and its import in women's journals throughout the long twentieth century. Differently, Paul Bailey's, Joan Judge's, and Xia Xiaohong's contributions in this volume point to the many important features of the "Eastern" and the "Southern" foreign in China's early women's magazines.

may at times appear both as an emblem of modernity and as a *femme fatale*, while the foreign man may be considered the highest authority as well as the meanest monster. While both extremes may at times appear asymmetrically prominently absent (or naturalized), their (non-)appearance always serves a purpose: not so much of describing the Other, but more of defining the Self.

China's print media, and women's journals among them, in spite of being cast in ephemeral form, thus have a primary significance in circulating meaning: they address their readers as consumers in search of entertainment but also as individuals in need of instruction in their various and ever-changing social roles. From the start, magazines that defined their readership as "women" took on, more or less overtly, the task of defining what it meant to be a "woman" (and, by comparison, a "man"). It is the purpose of this chapter to discuss how images of the foreign(er) contributed to the making of these identities and how they thus provide, in palatable form, a world of knowledge.

In a vertical reading, the chapter highlights some of the parallels and differences in depicting foreigners beginning with samples from China's earliest women's magazines, and considering magazines appearing through the years of the Republic, during the Maoist years, and in contemporary China. In analyzing the journals, the chapter takes a horizontal approach, juxtaposing visual matter such as photographs, advertising, and caricatures with different types of texts appearing between the same magazine covers. Throughout, I argue that the foreign(er) has a crucial role to play in the making of China's gendered (post)modernity, if only as a foil or mirror that transculturally reflects the self-assertion of China's new (wo)men. I emphasize two points: first, the foreign(er) is consciously used in Chinese women's magazines to teach a moral lesson, by prescribing what to do and what to avoid. Positive and negative foreign examples and an emphasis on the asymmetrical relations between China and these respective examples is crucial in the formation of a peculiarly Chinese (fe)male identity. Second, the foreign(er) is often naturalized in Chinese women's magazines. While foreign elements may well be apparent in a text or image at hand, they are not consciously acknowledged, nor is particular attention paid to them. Thus blurring the boundaries between Self and Other, this transcultural practice also serves to boost a particular Chinese sense of Self that is at once generalized ("we are just like everyone else") and valorized ("we are as good as everyone else").

Examining how the foreign appears on the pages of some of China's women's magazines in four snapshots of 1906, 1936, 1956/66, and 1996 (in thematic and not chronological order), we will find three modes of description: 1. the appeal to the venerated Other, 2. the warning against the abhorred Other, and 3. the acknowledgement of the Other in one's own midst and Self. The chapter describes these different modes of description as crucial parts of China's grammar of global modernity.

Fig. 14.1 As foreign as it gets, *Women's World* 10 (1904)–2 (1905)

Reading the Foreign

1.   Nüzi shijie – Women's World, 1906: Saturation

Women's World is full of the foreign(er). This is already visible in late 1904 when the journal stops carrying Qiu Jin's calligraphy on its cover, instead depicting a woman in foreign-style dress, who may or may not be Ilona Zrínyi (1643–1703), an important heroine in the struggle for national liberation of Hungary and Croatia (Figure 14.1).[3] We see her standing on a pillar in a huge garden in front of a house in classical European style, waving a Hungarian

---

[3] *Nüzi shijie* 1:10 (1904). After their defeat at the 1683 Battle of Vienna, both the Ottoman forces and Thököly's allied *kuruc* fighters had no choice but to retreat, and Thököly quickly lost one Rákóczi castle after another. At the end of 1685, the Imperial army surrounded the last remaining stronghold, Palanok Castle in Munkács. Ilona Zrínyi defended the castle for three years (1685–1688). Cf. Molnár, *A Concise History of Hungary*, 130, 134.

red-white-green flag. In addition, almost every article in a given volume of the journal deals with "the foreign" either explicitly, by quoting foreign sources or translating them,[4] or implicitly, by referring to Western science and technology.[5] In a horizontal reading of any volume of this journal, one finds that only very few articles make no mention of the foreign(er) at all.

Often, the gesture in which the foreign appears is one of veneration, where the asymmetrical relationship is between China as student and the foreigner as teacher. Looking through one edition of the journal horizontally, we find, in an essay entitled "On Female Danger" and written by Zhou Zuoren under the female penname Bingyun (Sick cloud),[6] that the author laments the dearth of Chinese biographies of good and wise women and the proliferation of stories elaborating "female danger." Zhou suggests going back to history and studying the lives of those maligned women,[7] recommending that their biographies should be compared with those of foreign women. Here as throughout the journal, the Other is used in a valorization of the Self. One editorial, entitled "Congratulations on the New Year,"[8] appeals repeatedly to the "women of China" (*Zhongguo funü* and *Zhongguo nüzi*) and calls upon them to stop footbinding, for example, in order to *ru wenming* (enter civilization), an idealized standard obviously set elsewhere, not in China.

Another article in the same volume explains how families should support children's engagement in sports and describes the reasons for China becoming the *yinruo de bingfu* (weak and sick man) of Asia,[9] an appellation first chosen by foreign observers, Hegel foremost among them. The article takes on this foreign moral judgement and constantly refers to *wu guo ertong* (my country's children), elaborating on their peculiar weaknesses, which can only be remedied if a rigorous practice of (foreign-style) sports and gymnastics is introduced. The foreign is held up, here, as a moral exemplar.

In another article from the same volume of the journal, "About Being Able to Speak but Not Act,"[10] this moral veneration mode continues, but ends in an intriguing twist. The author, using the pseudonym Baihua daoren Shoushi,[11]

---

[4] E.g., *Nüzi shijie* 2:4–5 (1906), 73–74, in an article about suffragettes in England; *Nüzi shijie* 2:4–5 (1906), 77–82, features a translated novel that is set in the United States; *Nüzi shijie* 2:4–5 (1906), 83–94, presents a translated novel set in Paris; *Nüzi shijie* 2:4–5 (1906), 95–106, is a report about a Chinese girls' school in Japan, including an exact curriculum (97) and an article on the Japanese schooling system for women.

[5] See, e.g., *Nüzi shijie* 2:4–5 (1906), 15–18, on the use of the five senses; on communication technologies and their use in warfare (pp. 19–22); and on how to use a camera.

[6] Bingyun, "Nühuozhuan."   [7] Ibid., 41.   [8] Zhi Qun, "Gonghe xinnian."

[9] Jing Hua, "Ertong jiaoyu hua," 27.   [10] Baihua daoren Shoushi, "Neng shuo bu neng xing."

[11] Baihua daoren is the pseudonym of Lin Baishui (1874–1926), who in 1901 became the main editor of the *Hangzhou baihuabao* (Hangzhou vernacular gazette). Shoushi, on the other hand, is probably Mrs Liang Aibao, who is also depicted in an image in *Linglong* 30 (1931), 1. The article is clearly written in a women's voice, but in the end, the identity of the author is not entirely clear.

sets out to explain "an expression frequently used by Westerners: words are the mother of deeds." The article complains that this is not so in China. Even though the Chinese have long since begun to talk about reform, education, or the constitution, everything "is the same as always, an old empire where autocracy reigns supreme." Why would the Chinese constantly say that they need to let their women's feet out, while nobody actually dared do so? The same was true with stopping the habit of smoking opium,[12] and with other ideas of freedom and emancipation of which "we speak all the time," but "never act" accordingly. Thus, diagnosing the "sickness of being able to say something but never to act upon it" (*neng shuo, bu neng xing de bibing*),[13] it concludes that this may also cause – and here, the focus suddenly changes direction completely – China's inability to act forcefully in the anti-American boycott. The article ends with an emotional appeal to join the boycott: "Finally we have our chance as women to do what we say."[14]

In this instance, the venerated, morally superior foreign West and its unquestionably accomplished "standards" are used to initiate an attack against China. Yet, in the end, this takes an unexpected turn: the foreign example is drawn upon to call on China's women to attack the foreigners. Here, then, the asymmetric relationship is reversed, as it is between China as the superior moral judge, the accuser, and the foreigner as the accused (and attacked through the boycott). While, as a whole, the article says very little about the West, the West appears whenever it is rhetorically convenient, both as a positive and as a negative foil, to discuss nothing but China and Chinese affairs. Here, the foreign(er) serves only as a commentary on questions of Chinese identity.

This mode of writing recurs in another article in the same volume, entitled "Admonition No. 3 to Debate the Treaty."[15] It proudly mentions the many different Japanese publications in praise of China's boycott against the Americans, thus using foreign standards to attack (other) foreigners – a typical example of the many triangulations taking place in the pages of these journals, as mentioned in Xia Xiaohong and Joan Judge's essays in this volume. Here, the Japanese are used as a yardstick against which to measure China's success. The article explains the need for the boycott, providing the background to the new immigration treaty to the United States. It stresses the importance of distinguishing American products from other *yanghuo* (foreign products) and

---

[12] Ibid., 13.   [13] Ibid., 14.

[14] There are some critical remarks in the article as well. It asks, for example, why the Chinese should begin to attack superstition and to destroy Buddha statues, while at the same time replacing them with Jesus?

[15] Zhi Qun, "Zhengyao zhi jinggao san." The Exclusion Act had first been drafted in 1882 and revised in 1884 to be in effect for ten years; it was extended for another ten years in 1894. The renewed revision of the treaty in 1904 sparked the discussions that led to the boycott in 1905 (cf. Remer and Palmer, *Chinese Boycotts*, 29). For a discussion of media responses to the boycott, see Mittler, *A Newspaper for China?* Chapter 6.

calls on women to check through their belongings and replace things that come from the United States with articles from China.[16]

The ubiquity of the foreign(er) (and most frequently the Westerner) on the pages of *Women's World* and its didactic effect is quite evident from this horizontal reading. But this foreign(er) as (moral) authority and (immoral) brute functions less to introduce the Other, but rather to instigate a redefinition of the Self, defining modern/new (wo)manhood in an emerging modern China.

2.   *Nongjianü baishitong – Rural Women Knowing All*, 1996: Denial

No contrast could be more pronounced than that between the earliest journal under scrutiny here, *Women's World*, and *Rural Women Knowing All*, first published in Beijing under the auspices of the Chinese Women's Federation in 1993. The editor, Xie Lihua (1951–), is fighting for the eradication of illiteracy, preventing suicides, and training women in rural self-government. She founded a vocational school for women in 1998 and her own NGO in 2001.

Her journal is specialized and targets rural women. Surveyed vertically, the covers throughout the year 1996 show country women at leisure – posing on the Great Wall[17] or playing on a boat in "traditional" dress (Figure 14.2), but also at work, their children always accompanying them (Figure 14.3).[18] While there is a clear emphasis on strong working women, the May cover also shows an attractive country woman with sexy flowery jacket and farmer's bamboo hat (Figure 14.4).

In spite of the fact that this journal targeted a very different readership from that of the urban-oriented *Women's World*,[19] the general (didactic) tone and the topics addressed are not all that dissimilar.[20] Going through one volume horizontally, one finds that this journal, too, gives voice to women's difficult plight. One article has a woman crying for help as her father drinks and gambles. Another is a personalized story of a peasant who refuses an arranged marriage because she is in love with a married man.[21]

---

[16] Ibid., 9.90   [17] *Nongjianü baishitong* 1 (1996).

[18] *Nongjianü baishitong* 4 (1996); 10 (1996).

[19] See remarks on readership in the contribution by Grace Fong to this volume.

[20] See, e.g., *Nüzi shijie* 2:4–5 (1905/6), 51–64 on women's education benefiting the country. It ends with a complaint echoed many times later on the pages of *Linloon Magazine* and other such journals that women are taken to be important as nothing but "playthings" *wei wannong zhi ju. Nüzi shijie* 2:4–5 (1906), 65–68 presents poetry about the hard fate of women, sent in by women.

[21] *Nongjianü baishitong* 2 (1996), 11; 17. Many other such stories are told: one deals with a woman who falls in love writing letters, but in the end never meets the man, not even sending him a picture of herself (p. 34); another is that of a woman from the countryside who becomes a worker in a factory, far away from home, describing the many difficulties her work entails (pp. 24–25). All of these share an extremely emotional tone, many mention women "sobbing and crying" (pp. 11, 48).

Fig. 14.2 Rural women at leisure, *Rural Women Knowing All* 2 (1996)

The editorial line is consistently didactic: women should stop complaining about the past and work on their inevitably brighter futures.[22] Many a success story is told, of peasant women from illiterate families aspiring and succeeding in entering university and becoming, for example, doctors.[23] It may appear paradoxical, but even though these stories all convey a great sense of longing not unlike the stories about women's education, health, sports, women's work, and women's suffrage in *Women's World*, in this 1990s journal, this longing does not include the world at large or thus the foreign(er) West.

We read about the necessity of improving working conditions for women with a brief side-cast to the International Women's League in an editorial on self-made eggs ("One Way to Wealth: Man-Made Eggs");[24] we see an article that argues that with the help of the Chinese Communist Party and its endorsement of the natural sciences, the lives of a mother and child have been saved ("Science Defeats the Midwife Devil").[25] But articles such as these

---

[22] *Nongjianü baishitong* 2 (1996), 51.   [23] Ibid., 17.   [24] "Zhifu zhi lu."
[25] Jiang Jinzhi, "Kexue dabaile chanfugui."

Fig. 14.3 Rural women at work, *Rural Women Knowing All* 4 (1996)

make only very implicit reference to foreign knowledge and technological achievements (which evidently have long since been naturalized, and have become part of the Chinese everyday, and thus stand out much less here than in *Women's World* some ninety years earlier).

A rare photograph of a foreign (Caucasian) woman, casually and provocatively dressed in shorts and heartily biting into an apple (Figure 14.5), stands out. The image appears embedded in the advice section of the journal, which makes no mention of foreign women, but instead has a Chinese country woman speak of her ideals and her dreams of owning her own bicycle.[26] The somewhat perplexing juxtaposition of this alluring, sexualized image and the practically oriented article juxtaposed with it may be deliberate and part of the didactic message of the journal, a cautionary tale about where falling for one's attractions or aspirations may lead to, but this is not entirely clear.

---

[26] "Ruguo wo shi ni."

Fig. 14.4 Rural women for (dis)play, *Rural Women Knowing All* 5 (1996)

For a foreign audience, the apple in the photograph (forbidden fruit since Eve) clearly points in a sexualized direction, and the photograph tallies with sexualized poses of foreign models in Chinese advertising of the time.[27] Yet read horizontally with all the other articles in the same issue, the function of the image remains ultimately ambiguous. Indeed, the foreign woman with the apple could even be seen as a moralistic, didactic warning. Then it could be read in conjunction with some of the other articles, where – not unlike in *Women's World* – the foreign appears to set standards, sometimes *ex negativo*, sometimes not. One article in the same issue actually suggests that one should offer certificates not just for intellectual or technical work but also for farm work, and to support this, cites examples of foreign university degrees in agriculture: here the foreign becomes a (rare) model to emulate ("If you want to do agriculture, please first get a 'green card'").[28]

---

[27] Cf. Johansson, "Consuming the Other," 379 for a description that fits almost exactly the illustration shown in the journal.

[28] Chen Benjian, "Yao zhong di qing."

Fig. 14.5 A rare foreign woman, *Rural Women Knowing All* 2 (1996), 52

Yet both in the negative and in the positive sense, the foreign is not the most important Other to be reckoned with in the pages of this journal. While *Rural Women Knowing All* is focused on female rural selves and their aspirations, these are contrasted less with foreigners and more with Chinese urban women, and it is this dichotomy that is most frequently illustrated[29] and discussed. It appears in a manner reminiscent of the arguments and illustrations used elsewhere in women's magazines to mark the indigenous from the foreign in the juxtaposition of *yangqi*, literally "foreign/Western-style," and *tuqi*, literally "rusticated" or "countrified," that is, "indigenous style" – or "trendy" and "outdated," respectively. Indeed, there is a certain interchangeability between these two asymmetrical binaries.

In the pages of the journal, urban women appear to have money, they can afford anything they want, and, even though they work, they have an easy life. Accordingly, they are always beautiful and well fed. Country women, on the other hand, are poor, and they have to work extremely hard.[30] Their aspirations

---

[29] *Nongjianü baishitong* 12 (1999), 24.   [30] Cf. illustration "Xiangxiaren chengliren."

for the city are what drives them.[31] The city, then, and not a foreign country, is described as the most adventurous place in the journal.[32]

In *Rural Women Knowing All*, then, the foreign(er) is but an extension of this urban Other, which becomes the more important exemplar and model). The journal is primarily concerned, however, with carrying information about improving work and life conditions for the rural female Self. The journal lives off rural women's very personal stories: of love and family care, of work and children, of how to find the best man and what is (not) a good match, and thus it fosters and prescribes gendered identities. The absence – denial – of the foreign(er) in the pages of the journal, evident from the horizontal and vertical readings engaged in here, serves an important function: in allowing a more intimate view of the rural self and her aspirations (and in juxtaposing these with the urban woman both as positive and as negative model), it helps to instigate a particular definition of rural (wo)manhood in a rapidly changing China, where to become urbanized is the ultimate aspiration.

3.   *Zhongguo Funü – Woman of China* 1956/1966: Confrontation

If *Women's World* and *Rural Women Knowing All* were at two extremes not only of the time spectrum we are considering here, but also in terms of their treatment of the foreign(er), *Woman of China*, the official publication of the All China Women's Federation in Beijing, can be said to stand somewhere in the middle, focusing less on the exemplary or the repelling Other, and more on the Other in one's midst, or one's Self "inmidst" the Other.

Women's primary function as mothers and caretakers is key in this journal: the last page usually contains a recipe, and the journal also teaches how best to educate children according to their age,[33] how to guide them to deal with money[34] and in language development,[35] and on how to keep good relations as a couple.[36] Didacticism is strong, and this trend continues into the 1960s. Next to practical information on what a woman needs to look after when she has her menstrual period,[37] and how to deal with children's scratches and fevers, one also learns why one gets pregnant, what a diaphragm does,[38] and what other means of contraception exist.[39] The journal advocates that children should be learning from model heroes such as altruistic Wang Jie (1942–1965), a famous platoon leader from the People's Liberation Army who had trained local militia in the use of landmines and, during an accidental explosion, had thrown himself into the blast and was killed – thus saving the lives of twelve people – and further instructs family heads on how best to

---

[31] Shi Jianling, "Mingyun kao ziji zhangwo."   [32] *Nongjianü baishitong* 1 (1996), 32.
[33] *Zhongguo funü* 1 (1956), 22–23.   [34] *Zhongguo funü* 1 (1956), 24, 25.
[35] *Zhongguo funü* 2 (1956), 24–25.   [36] *Zhongguo funü* 2 (1956), 16–18.
[37] *Zhongguo funü* 1 (1966), 23.   [38] *Zhongguo funü* 2 (1966), 30–32.
[39] *Zhongguo funü* 1 (1966), 24–25.

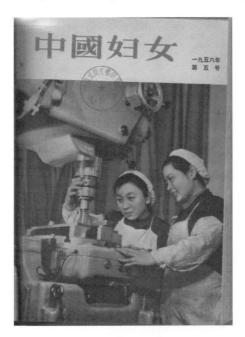

Fig. 14.6 Women at work, *Woman of China* 5 (1965)

teach children revolutionary ideas.[40] In all of this, however, the foreign(er) is conspicuously absent: role models are Chinese and not foreigners, and as for technologies and materialities, if they had originally been foreign, they are presented as naturalized and significantly transformed to serve the revolutionary goal.

The journal also focuses its attention on *laodong funü* (working women). It includes numerous images and texts to show the many different areas in which women set out to work in "New China": industry and agriculture among them. They are seen doing all kinds of jobs, but especially those where they could show their power and bodily strength, such as heavy industrial work:[41] They are seen working in the car industry, and as operators of large machines (Figure 14.6),[42] toiling away to change the course of a river[43] or "moving mountains" to build a new countryside together (Figure 14.7).[44]

The images and articles in this journal show, as one editorial puts it, that "women are changed as they are changing the world around them."[45] They have learned (and here we have an echo of earlier discussions in *Women's World*

[40] *Zhongguo funü* 1 (1966), 22, 26–27.   [41] *Zhongguo funü* 1 (1956), inside cover.
[42] *Zhongguo funü* 1 (1956), 10–13.   [43] *Zhongguo funü* 1 (1958), 12–13.
[44] *Zhongguo funü* 2 (1958), 10; 5 (1965), inside cover; 1 (1966), inside covers.
[45] *Zhongguo funü* 2 (1966), 2–5.

中 国 妇 女

1966

Fig. 14.7 Women moving mountains, *Woman of China* 1 (1966)

a good half century earlier) that "it is better to do things rather than to say things," as one representative of the women's league says.[46] While, in essence, the argument sounds very similar and calls for action, here no foreign model is invoked. Indeed, these women are inspired by none other than Mao himself, and many an article describes the wondrous effects of studying Mao even at home, as in the story of three sisters from Qingdao who have a weekly family session reading Mao together, thus learning that life is about more than being clothed well, eating well, and living well: *chuan de hao, chi de hao, zhu de hao*.[47]

On the rare occasions when foreigners appear, they are naturalized. One article that mentions the construction work Vietnamese women are involved in shows them carrying heavy bamboo poles.[48] Depicted as working extremely hard (with the support of some Chinese women), they are praised as an important backbone in the recovery of agriculture, handicraft work, and industry in Vietnam. Visually, though, they are not marked as Vietnamese.

[46] Zhou Jinsong, "Hua shuo qianbai bian."
[47] Tong Ziling, "Ting Mao Zhuxi de hua."   [48] Li Shichuan, "Yuenan funü."

An open "Othering" does not take place. If the foreign comes in at all, then (frequently as the Asian foreign) it often appears in the form of a Communist feminist *Internationale* or women's solidarity, women all working together and supporting each other as sisters – clearly, ideology comes first in this journal.[49]

An article on the first international Women's Conference, held in 1956, stresses the need to unite with women's movements all over the (Communist) world ("Women from all over the world actively prepare for the international women's conference").[50] Some of the countries singled out as partners for this unity are Japan, India, Argentina, and Australia. An additional article is specifically devoted to the USSR. Unification is necessary, it is argued, to address questions important to women all over the world: (1) raising salaries and wages and establishing equal rights for men and women in all of these fields, and (2) involving women in leadership positions.

This female sisterhood is the topic of many articles in *Woman of China*, as in a story about the reinstallation of railway tracks to Soviet Russia.[51] The idea finds its pictorial echo, too, as one inside cover assembles women's and children's movements worldwide.[52] Forming a feminist *Internationale* and emulating women, especially if not exclusively from the Communist world (e.g., learning about Soviet marriage and family life,[53] about women in Albania and Romania,[54] and about Algerian women's war efforts)[55] are the particular ways of negotiating between Self and Other that *Woman of China* introduces.

The journal contains the foreign in the form of translated texts, too, such as an essay on divorce by a Soviet lawyer.[56] The foreign Other is raised high to become a role model in the story, translated from a 1954 Soviet journal entitled *Working Women*, of a Russian female postal worker who had received the Lenin prize the day before the story begins. The reportage contains an extremely lyrical description of how the woman and her fellow postal workers are walking along the empty morning streets of Moscow and of how the emblem she has received is shining on her black uniform. While everybody wants to know what she received the prize for, she explains again and again – in a modest and thus politically correct manner – that she has not quite understood why she should have received it: "I am just a very ordinary citizen."[57]

The Other as model appears in the form of a few "inside Others" as differences between city and countryside or between Han and minorities are

---

[49] Cf. also *Zhongguo funü* 1 (1966), 18–20, about Vietnamese women's battalions and war victims. On Pan-Asian links see Bailey in this volume.
[50] Shi Meimei, "Geguo nügong jiji choubei."   [51] Fang Zong, "Heping youqi xinfu de lu."
[52] *Zhongguo funü* 3 (1956).   [53] *Zhongguo funü* 2 (1958), 18–19.
[54] *Zhongguo funü* 1 (1958), 20–21.   [55] *Zhongguo funü* 2 (1958), 19–20.
[56] *Zhongguo funü* 2 (1956), 14–15.   [57] Wa Ka'erlefusikaya, "Sanshiliu nian ru yi."

illuminated,[58] telling stories of how an illiterate woman learned how to read, or introducing books apt to be read by peasants.[59] But the negative Other is not absent either, for example, in an article that elaborates on the difficult situation of working women in the United States, entitled "The Tragic Life of American Working Women."[60] Even more pointedly, an article from 1966 states that since China is surrounded by enemies, the Chinese should retaliate by showing everyone their knife's tip in turn.[61] American imperialism is attacked harshly.[62] Americans in Taiwan are said to purposefully kill people in car accidents and to snatch children away from their parents.[63] The ideological function of introducing the Other is almost too obvious.

While in Maoist China, the foreign(er) appears most frequently as naturalized – particular knowledge or technological feats are introduced with no special reference to their foreign "origins" – in those rarer instances where the foreign (which is quite diverse, and can come in the form of a minority, as well as an Asian or Western "specimen") appears as a positive or negative role model, it serves a clearly demarcated and political function: it helps create an idealized image of the strong, independent woman who cares more about her work than about her looks and, in truly Maoist altruist fashion, more about everyone around her than about herself.

4.   *Linglong – Linloon Magazine*, 1936: Differentiation

Nothing could be more different, again, from *Woman of China* than *Linloon Magazine*.[64] Here, the foreign(er) and especially the Western foreign woman is a dominant presence. Going through *Linloon Magazine*'s tables of contents (which only highlight the most important articles), one finds that more often than not more than a third of the articles deal openly with foreign subjects (e.g., *Linloon Magazine* 225 [1936] with five out of twelve and *Linloon Magazine* 244 [1936] with five out of thirteen articles). As one reads the journal closely, one realizes that even articles that do not betray foreign substance in their titles deal with foreign themes. This is so, for example, in the section on general knowledge (*changshi*). Much of what is introduced here is in fact foreign knowledge. Foreign (in this case English) words are used nonchalantly throughout the text, for instance, in a discussion on hygiene in the children's section.[65] The same is true for the introduction of amenities for the "modern

---

[58] *Zhongguo funü* 2 (1956), 1–2.
[59] *Zhongguo funü* 2 (1956), 10–11, 27. On minorities (e.g., Mongolians) see *Zhongguo funü* 1 (1958), 18–19.
[60] Zhou Xiuqing, "Meiguo laodong funü."   [61] *Zhongguo funü* 2 (1966), 18.
[62] *Zhongguo funü* 2 (1966), 19.   [63] *Zhongguo funü* 2 (1966), 24–25.
[64] This discussion is based on a horizontal reading of *Linglong* 1936, issues 225, 244, and 262.
[65] *Linglong* 262 (1936), 2013. Also 244 (1936), 2012–13.

family home," which appear both in text and in images and obviously introduce furniture and settings that have, in some way or other, foreign "roots."[66] Yet, while it is obvious that "modern" is equal to "foreign," and "foreign" here is mostly "Western," this is nowhere highlighted in the journal's discourse. The furniture and the room sets described and depicted here, whatever their origins may be, appear as a naturalized presence; their foreignness is *not* their most important feature.[67] Only when an American camping trailer is described, combining all family life amenities in very little space, including running water, electric equipment, and nice furniture (even drapes on the windows), is the particular "foreign" quality of the "wondrous" object highlighted.[68]

A wide range of foreign countries appear in the pages of *Linloon Magazine*, then, but no immediately apparent distinction is made between them. We do not find an equivalent to the black and white depictions from the Maoist era. There are reports about Soviet women's exceptional beauty and how strong their bodies are, superior to those of China's women.[69] There are articles about New York women and their fashionable cars,[70] about strong women in Egypt quite able to *guanshu* (control) their men,[71] and about the Swedish anti-emancipist Ellen Key, who fights for the importance of motherhood, advocating that women should not go out into society, because this makes them become playthings of men.[72]

Then again, there are articles on "The Spirit of Gorky and the Women's Movement,"[73] arguing that women should learn from Gorky's fighting spirit and actively strive for freedom, equality, and emancipation. Against Ellen Key (and in a spirit that recalls changing attitudes toward *guo* and their ramifications for the makeup of gender roles in the earliest women's journals, as discussed by Qian Nanxiu), this article rejects the idea that women should stay home to serve as "good wives and virtuous mothers" and calls it *tuoxie zhuyi* (defeatism) to compromise oneself in such a way. It concludes, "The women's movement in China is flourishing (*fangxing wei'ai*). We have to take up the spirit of Gorky now and fight for freedom and equality. We must not be content to be mothers at home!"

There are empathetic reports about Hitler's cousin and her sad fate in Vienna – she did not find a job after it was found out who she was;[74] about Muslim women from Turkestan;[75] and about hat colors in Europe[76] and

---

[66] Cf. Maria af Sandeberg's chapter in this volume.

[67] E.g., *Linglong* 262 [1936], 3542; see also pp. 3543–44.   [68] *Linglong* 262 (1936), 3555–58.

[69] *Linglong* 225 (1936), 481–82. Another article explains that Russian women, leaving the factory, are putting on makeup: they used to be dressed in a very masculine way, but are now becoming more conscious that this need not be and argue how important it is that women stay feminine (*Linglong* 262 [1936], 3491–94).

[70] *Linglong* 225 (1936), 485–86.   [71] "Aiji de nüzi."

[72] You Ran, "Fan nüquan yundong."   [73] Wang Lanfang "Gao'erji jingshen."

[74] *Linglong* 225 (1936), 494.   [75] *Linglong* 225 (1936), 483–85.

[76] *Linglong* 225 (1936), 511.

women's self-sacrifice in India.[77] Most of these articles are somehow didactic: the foreign plays its role as model to emulate or beast to abhor. The article on India even does both: it teaches *ex negativo* and observes that women absolutely *mei you diwei* (have no status) in Indian society (echoing the negative press for Indian women already discussed by Paul Bailey). Deploringly, it describes practices such as *suttee* where women burn themselves on the deaths of their husbands. On the other hand, it mentions that English colonizers have tried to put to a stop this cruel practice – all to no avail.[78] The journal thus presents different views of different foreigners: they may be good or bad.

Often, the didactic message is quite clear: Russian women are described as feminine, but strong and sporty as well. They are held up as models to be matched or, even better, surpassed.[79] The many articles on German nudism, or *Freikörperkultur* (FKK), and on the importance of healthy bodies ultimately have the same function: they are calling upon China's women to look after their bodies and to become stronger in order to overcome foreign perceptions of China as sickly and weak.[80]

The foreign, or the *wai* (outside) example, both Asian and Western, thus provides the frames through which to view China, which, ultimately, wants to be seen as an equal on the international stage. This is why an article that reports the nomination of ten female "world orators," among them women from Russia, the United States, Britain, and France, but also Song Qingling from China, is quite buoyant.[81] If China is not perceived and viewed as an equal, eye to eye, on the other hand, *Linloon Magazine* is sure to complain: in one article, it blames Chinese men for what they have done to Chinese women by inventing footbinding, the memory of which continues to stick in the foreign mind. The article complains that although for twenty years women have been allowed to unbind their feet and to participate in sports, foreign countries still believe that footbinding continues to be practiced in China.[82] And indeed, in a collection of articles on Chinese women in American journals, which *Linloon Magazine* publishes, footbinding plays a prominent role.[83] The article notes that there is even an aestheticized discussion on the beauty of small shoes in some of these reports on China.[84] On the other hand, it is proud to say that China appears quite regularly on the pages of journals in the United States: according to their own statistics, at least one piece or so in an average U.S. journal deals with China.[85]

---

[77] *Linglong* 244 (1936), 1988–90.   [78] Luo Man, "Yindu de guafu."
[79] *Linglong* 225 (1936), 481–82.   [80] E.g., *Linglong* 262 (1936), 1975; 225 (1936), 463, 465.
[81] "Shijie shi da yanshuojia."   [82] *Linglong* 262 (1936), 3489–91.
[83] "Meiguo zazhi shang."   [84] Ibid., 3504.
[85] The article is gratified that American journals praise the New Life Movement. *Linloon Magazine* had been a fervent advocate of the movement. See Yen Hsiao-pei, "Body Politics."

Yet the constant and repeated emphasis, or should one say, foreign fascination with footbinding in many of these articles is considered humiliating.

The foreign appears to be, here as elsewhere, a standard to which one must somehow measure up. The foreign serves as the attractive and adored exemplar. But it also has a different function: in *Linloon Magazine* it often takes the form of the fascinating, alluring, but always slightly strange (and significantly sexualized) Other, one whose actions are marveled at and deliberated, if not condemned. Articles such as one dealing with a woman from Yugoslavia who had married eighteen times[86] or an American woman who had gotten divorced seven times[87] fit perfectly into the category of "strange stories from the West," which had been well established in China since the nineteenth century (while the "strange stories" genre as such dates back to the fourth century as a tradition).[88] This finds its reflection also in the column titles under which these entertaining stories appear, "Yiguo qingdiao" (Exotic sentiments) being one of them.[89]

The story of Mussolini's wife, a story of true love and devotion to the family by a former family maid who rises to become the wife of one of the most powerful politicians in Europe, must be read in this vein.[90] Mme Mussolini with her homely looks (a picture of her is included on the first page of the article; see Figure 14.8) may serve as a counter-model to the stereotyped "modern woman" who frequently appears, only to be criticized, in *Linloon Magazine* and who cares for herself and her looks but not for her family (and, by implication, her country). Yet, for the sake of appealing to the reader, this story of a homely woman is framed in sex scandal rumors about Mussolini and his (many) mistresses.

In an article about a former British sportswoman and feminist named Mary Edith Louise Weston (b. 1906) and her sex change, the same principle is at work.[91] The article plays on the extraordinary feat of this sex change. While calm and neutral in its language, the event is framed as scandalous, eye-catching, and titillating, to draw the reader's attention to the "strange customs" of the "foreign country" with an enigmatic title: "An English Sports Professional: Woman Turned into Man."

The same is true for the article explaining "American Women and Their Car Life," which sets out to explain why Americans love their cars and "never want to part with 'her,'" not least because cars are so convenient for making love in secret.[92] The (sexually) tantalizing, the alluring, and the strange and curious are stressed in these articles, often with at least an implicit slight sense

---

[86] *Linglong* 236 (1936), 3485–86.   [87] "Wei shenme yao."
[88] See Mittler, *A Newspaper for China?* Chapter 5.   [89] "Yiguo qingdiao."
[90] Jing Fang, "Mosuolini furen."   [91] "Shenglixue shang."
[92] "Meiguo nüzi yu qiche" 2033.

Fig. 14.8 Mussolini's wife, *Linloon Magazine* 225 (1936), 466

of condescension or criticism: the foreign appears as the fascinating, but also somewhat transgressive counterexample, a metaphoric *femme fatale*.[93]

In *Linloon Magazine*, not unlike *Rural Women Knowing All*, the Other also appears in contrasting city, countryside, and borderlands. When *Linloon Magazine* speaks of women from these regions, it describes them in terms of the well-established *jianmei* (healthy beauty) discourse of the time.[94] In a negatively reciprocal relation with *Rural Women Knowing All*, the exotic but strong beauties from the (Chinese) borderlands are described in the same vocabulary of strangeness as foreigners. They become a fascinating Other.

What is *Linloon Magazine*'s take on the foreigner, then? On the one hand, it is characterized by the proud acknowledgement that China is beginning to step out on the international stage, which goes along with the naturalization of much

---

[93] See Edwards, Louise. "The Shanghai Modern Women's American Dreams." See also an article in which a fifty-year-old American virgin is raped and murdered (*Linglong* 225 (1936), 531); and one on Japanese dress (*Linglong* 244 (1936), 2031).
[94] *Linglong* 262 (1936), 3505–7.

Fig. 14.9 Inviting positions, *Linloon Magazine* 222 (1936), 304

foreign knowledge. On the other hand, *Linloon Magazine* often betrays a sense of humiliation in view of what is so much better and more advanced elsewhere, while sometimes this is changed into a voluntarist spirit already observed by Paul Bailey. Then again, it includes ridiculing, critical attitudes toward the foreign Other, on the one hand, and an incredulous, overwhelmed fascination that borders on the naive, on the other. The visual images of foreigners included on the pages of *Linloon Magazine* augment this kind of polyphonic discourse. They contain the alluring foreign woman with gaze openly focused on the viewer[95] or titillatingly averted.[96] The foreign body appears clearly sexualized (held in inviting position, half-clad; see Figure 14.9),[97] but at the same time also as a model of health and agility, which is why she may, alternatively, be shown doing sports or standing (in extremely short shorts) with her bicycle (Figure 14.10) or doing exercises.[98] Foreign equipment and paraphernalia are emblematic of "the modern" as in an illustration of the "new family home's" living room,[99] although not always explicitly "rooted" as foreign.

---

[95] *Linglong* 262 (1936), 2559.   [96] *Linglong* 221 (1936), 221 and 215; 225 (1936), 417.
[97] *Linglong* 222 (1936), 304 and 303; see also 262 (1936), 2560.
[98] *Linglong* 244 (1936), 1977.   [99] *Linglong* 262 (1936), 3520.

Fig. 14.10 Healthy bodies, *Linloon Magazine* 221 (1936), 214

Rethinking the Foreign

"Othering" is a process often helpful or cataclysmic in identity construction. China in the long twentieth century is a world where through the unpredictable dynamic of asymmetrical cultural encounters, familiar difference and bizarre sameness are simultaneously articulated in multiple ways. Women's magazines constitute one site where this articulation takes place. This chapter set out to probe into the impact of women's magazines, to measure the importance of their voice in contributing to and serving as a repository for cultural memory and a catalyst for gendered action. It studied the presence of foreigners in the pages of Chinese women's magazines to see what – if their image and status changed – this could tell us about the making of modern (wo)manhood throughout this period of time. I have argued that by depicting the foreign(er) in particular ways, women's magazines engaged in a process of continuously (re-)making and (re-)defining China's New (Wo)men (*xin nü/nanxing*) and thus contributed to the grammar of gendered modernity in China

The chapter has shown that throughout the period studied here, foreigners (and Westerners in particular) held iconic status. Historical women's magazines such as *Women's World* and *Linloon Magazine* are plastered with textual and visual images of foreign (wo)men. Foreigners who are, in the pages of women's magazines today, clearly coveted as "standards of beauty"[100] as well as "of achievement" also served this function in late Qing and Republican times (and even much throughout the years of the People's Republic of China) as well.[101] We have seen that their depiction is not exclusively negative, as has sometimes been argued,[102] but also not as exclusively positive, as others have contended.[103] Indeed, since the nineteenth century, the foreign Other (and the Western Other in particular) has played a crucial, if ambiguous, but always didactic role in China's media. China was simultaneously attracted to and repulsed by the foreign as visible in its women's journals: this polar attraction becomes a trope reflecting a more or less torn collective psyche, constantly pondering the asymmetries and seemingly apparent superiorities involved in relations between "the West and the Rest."[104] The polarized and dichotomous interpretation of the foreign Other – hovering between admiration, on the one hand, and suspicion, on the other – which had already crystallized in the nineteenth century remains a valid and powerful tension to the present day.[105] Following the foreign was compared to following a dream, but doing so, and falling prey to foreign allure, was considered more or less dangerous. The potential conflation between Self and Other is deliberated and criticized repeatedly: it finds blatant expression in a series of vicious *Shenbao* caricatures from 1912, depicting how such "traitors" to Chinese purity come into being – and this is reflected in the negative depictions of Chinese following the wrong foreigners throughout the period under scrutiny here.[106] And yet this potential conflation is even more dangerous, as it is also almost inevitably complete, as shown by a caricature, from the satirical journal *Shidai manhua* (Modern sketch; see Figure 14.11), which portrays a man with deep-set eyes and a mustache, wearing stylish shoes in white and black, a newspaper around his waist, with a heavy, dark bowler hat, a nude statue under his arm. One might at first assume that this man must be the depiction of a foreigner. He bears some of the most important accoutrements that foreigners had brought to China: newspapers and nudes, airplanes and bombs. But from the caption, one finds that

---

[100] Johansson, "Consuming the Other," 381.

[101] On successful women entrepreneurs, see Evans, *The Subject of Gender*, 12–13.

[102] Johansson, "Consuming the Other."

[103] See Bailey in this volume, who argues that Western women, differently from Asian women, would generally be positively connoted.

[104] Mittler, *A Newspaper for China?* 358–59.

[105] Ibid., Chapter 5, especially 330–43. Even during the allegedly "xenophobic" Cultural Revolution (1966–1976), this somewhat schizophrenic attitude can be observed: the angel-like Canadian doctor Norman Bethune (1890–1939) stands in stark contrast to American (and Japanese!) traitors, who appear as devilish beings.

[106] For a selection of these images, see ibid., 348–50. Bailey, too, mentions a contributor to *The Women's Eastern Times* who warned that *Oufeng* (Europeanization) was gradually "infecting" or "contaminating" (*ran*) China's women.

Fig. 14.11 "The standard Chinese," *Shidai Manhua* 25 (20 January 1936), n.p.

he is not a foreigner, indeed, but nothing less than a *biaozhun Zhongguoren* (standard Chinese person). Discussions about the dangers of "wholesale Westernization" have punctuated China's long twentieth century, and even when it comes to rethinking gender relations in China, they are at the very forefront.

With all the arguments made about foreigners so far, this "standard Chinese person," who looks exactly like a foreigner, is not an exception but another rule and brings us to a third way of depicting foreigners in the print media: the blurring of boundaries between Self and Other. This is characteristic in the franchise world of body shapes exhibited in *Elle* and *Vogue China* today.[107] Yet the fluid, transcultural body shapes to be found there can in fact be seen throughout the twentieth century. The figure on the cover page of *Women's World*, depicting a woman in foreign-style dress, whom we had earlier conjectured to be Ilona Zrínyi (see Figure 14.1), with her black hair and small eyes, need not immediately and necessarily strike the Chinese reader as exotic and

---

[107] Laila Abu-Er-Rub and Annika Joest, in their dissertation work in Heidelberg (to be published in a volume on *Transcultural Sexualities in Transcultural Research – Heidelberg Studies on Asia and Europe in a Global Context*), presented several cases of comparison between the Chinese and the Indian *Elle* and *Vogue* under the auspices of the "Rethinking Trends" Project conducted at the Cluster "Asia and Europe in a Global Context," 2009–2012 (http://www.asia-europe.uni-heidelberg.de/en/research/b-public-spheres/b12.html).

Fig. 14.12 Transcultural types, *Linloon Magazine* 40 (1931), 1559

foreign, but could be native and Chinese as well. *The Ladies' Journal* regularly features the stylish woman in bobbed, sometimes curly hair and tight-fitting dress, typical of contemporary international, not just Chinese, fashions (see the illustrations in Julia F. Andrews' chapter). This same type appears, page after page, in *Linloon Magazine*,[108] most notably in the series "Ta yu ta" (She and he), which, as Liying Sun shows in her writings, probably originated in the United States but then traveled extensively throughout the world (see Figure 14.12).[109] Depending on their local situatedness, and their particular target audience, the images in this series take on different messages: in one, for example, the dialogue attached to the image of two stylish women and one man (he and one she, curiously, with blond hair, but otherwise a generic 1930s chic) consists of a (distinctly Chinese) debate about boycotting Japanese products (Figure 14.12). Only the text situates the image, which itself, in spite of the hair colors, is not strikingly "foreign." And indeed, contemporary Chinese audiences may or may not have been aware of the foreign origins of these images at all.

The use of such "naturalized" imagery continues in *Woman of China*. A mother depicted in one 1950s comic strip need not necessarily be from

---

[108] See also *Linglong* 225 (1936), 487; 145 (1934) 1253; and 145 (1934), 1256.

[109] See, e.g., *Linglong* 31 (1931), 1192; 29 (1931), 1064; 12 (1931), 416; 40 (1931), 1559; 29 (1931), 1064; 12 (1931), 416; 31 (1931), 1192. See also Liying Sun, "Body Un/Dis-Covered."

Fig. 14.13 The transcultural 1950s, *Woman of China* 9 (1956), 6

China (Figure 14.13): her dress, her shoes, and those of her little child are characteristic of a transcultural 1950s style that goes beyond specific localities. The same can be said for the mother who appears in *Rural Woman Knowing All* in 1996 (Figure 14.14), who simply looks like a generic "mother with child."

Presenting a distinct Chinese or a distinct foreigner, Self or Other, is by and large a matter of stereotyping and styling, yet popular Chinese print media often refrain from it. Reuses of the same visual material between media all over the world since at least the nineteenth century make this transcultural naturalization of the (fe)male phenotype possible. While Chinese history may be called a history of "Westernization,"[110] it may not always be adequate to

---

[110] See Chow, *Woman and Chinese Modernity*, 81–100, 84.

Fig. 14.14 Foreign or Chinese? Not always an easy distinction, *Rural Women Knowing All* 2 (1996), 54

insist on demarcations between "East" and "West": questions of "origins" are not necessarily the primary concerns of contemporary audiences.

Taking a transcultural perspective is fruitful here, as these images address not so much the dichotomies between Self and Other, but rather questions that are part of a feminine as well as a feminist *Internationale* and that have dominated discussions in China's women's magazines from their beginnings to the present day. More than anything else, these are questions about the female Self and about how to gender modernity. This gendered modernity is played out through discussions that range from the more serious to the seriously trivial – such as how to resolve the dilemma of women's economic independence and the working mother;[111] how best to arrange power relations within a marriage;[112] why women are always late (Figure 14.15) and men always interested in "only one thing" (i.e., sex; Figure 14.16);[113] why women are engrossed more in pretty clothes than in daily politics; and what one should do about female spendthrifts and male misers.[114]

To sum up: the foreign takes multiple forms in China's women's magazines. In journals such as *Women's World*, a greater part of the text either deals with the foreign or is translated from foreign texts; in *Rural Women Knowing All*, the foreign is conspicuously absent, or replaced by the city and urbanity;[115] in *Linloon Magazine* and *Woman of China* the foreigner can take on different roles, but throughout the foreigner also often appears as naturalized. The allure of the foreign (as well as the nude or the scientific) on the pages of China's women's magazines may have served as a titillating, attractive eye-catcher, perhaps even as an incentive to buy. Yet, even more importantly, the foreign(er) serves as a point of negotiating identity – China's national as well as her gender identity. Journals that defined their readership as "women" took on, more or less overtly, the task of defining what it meant to be a "woman" (and, by relation, a "man" as well) or what it meant to be a particular kind of woman: a mother, a lady with time and money (the Republican lady or *taitai* as discussed by Joan Judge), a working or, in China's case, a peasant woman (*nongjianü*), a *xin nüxing* ("New" Woman) or a *Zhongguo funü* or *Zhongguo nüzi* (Chinese woman),[116] and so on. In four snapshots from 1906, 1936, 1956/66, and 1996, we found how three different modes of representing the foreigner shaped ideals of (wo)manhood in memory and action: the venerated Other, the abhorred Other, as well as the transcultural Other in one's midst. All of these are found throughout the twentieth century in China, but are emphasized differently at different points in time, reflecting and at the same time shaping social realities to come by providing, in palatable form, a world of information (not just) about gender and gender relations. Evidence from this chapter, which engaged in horizontal, vertical, and integrated reading of women's journals, makes it possible to argue, in placing these journals within the sea of other popular print products throughout this period, that the strong and assertive woman figure emblematic of Cultural Revolution propaganda, one that is officially erased in propaganda posters by the end of

---

[111] Cf. *Zhongguo funü* 9 (1956), 6)   [112] Cf. *Zhongguo funü* 2 (1988); 1 (1998), 32.

[113] *Linglong* 29 (1931), 1064; 225 (1936), 487.

[114] Cf. *Linglong* 31 (1931), 1192. Mittler, *Portrait(s) of a Trope*, discusses many of these tropes and their visual and textual reflections.

[115] For an interesting study of cultural urbanity not related to women's magazines but to rural channels, see Ballew, "Xiaxiang for the '90s."

[116] Cf. in *Nüzi shijie* 2:4–5 (1905/6), 1–3: the editorial quite typically constantly refers to *Chinese nüzi* throughout the text. Journals from the Communist period, on the other hand, will use *funü*.

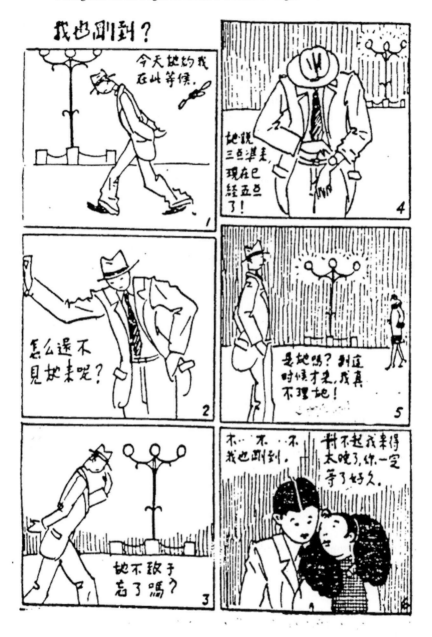

Fig. 14.15 Foreign or Chinese? Not always an easy distinction, *Linloon Magazine* 44 (1932), 1790

Fig. 14.16 Foreign or Chinese? Not always an easy distinction, *Linloon Magazine* 71 (1932), 970h

the 1970s, comes in "through the back door," can build on prior models, or in fact remains a presence throughout, by way of the assertive gestures of foreign (as well as Chinese) models to be seen all over the pages of China's women's magazines throughout this period.[117] Women's magazines also illustrate that although it is true that female images since the early 1980s have returned to a more "sweet and gentle femininity" that began to "eclipse the 'androgyny' of the Cultural Revolution years," as Harriet Evans puts it,[118] this move, which is evident in the changes of female shapes, forms, and colors on propaganda posters – a move from strong hands and bodies to small and lean feet and bodies, which echoes prominent imagery from the 1950s – curiously returns full circle to some of the ideals of "healthy beauty" from the 1930s advocated in journals like *Linloon Magazine*, through illustrations of foreign beauties but also through deliberations of strong and warrior-like women introduced in China's earliest women's magazines, such as Chen Xiefen's 1902–1903 *Journal of Women's Learning*. The predominance of this type of strong but beautiful foreign woman in advertising and illustrations in some of China's

[117] On foreign models, see Johansson, "Consuming the Other."
[118] Evans, *The Subject of Gender*, 12–13.

women's magazines in recent decades points to the role these images may have played in (re-)establishing this model.[119] Images of foreigners in China's women's magazines, then, are part of a mindmap of potentialities: by sedimenting themselves in cultural memory, they offer role models for later generations to draw on.

This answers the question with which this chapter began: the impact and importance of women's magazines within the circle of print media in China. The figure of the foreigner sets the borders, provides the frames, and offers transgressively abhorred counterexamples as well as attractive and adored exemplars to the Chinese reader. Although periodicals are by nature ephemeral, and women's journals are considered even less consequential, their impact both as a repository of cultural memory and as a catalyst of gendered action, as we have seen above, is significant. Reading images of (wo)manhood through the lens of depictions of the Other, we can see how important their voice is – inscribing itself in cultural memory and thus reforming the grammars of global modernity – in justifying and creating ever new directions for redefining and reenacting gender in China.

---

[119] For examples, see Mittler, "Von großen Händen. "

Conclusion: A Space of Their Own?
Concluding Reflections

Harriet Evans

Between the last years of the Qing dynasty and the early Republic, "woman" became a privileged site for debates about China's national independence and modernity. Alongside common assumptions about women's social and intellectual inferiority to men, "woman" was visualized and written about in the burgeoning print media as a metaphor for hopes and desires for social and political change, as well as for anxieties and fears about social instability and national weakness. She addressed interests across the political spectrum, from social reformers' concerns with women's education to revolutionary anarchists' critique of liberal perspectives on gender equality. Women's journals played a prominent role in promoting this public appearance of women. As noted in the introduction to this volume, between the first women's journal published in 1898 during the One Hundred Days Reform movement and 1911, some forty-four Chinese women's journals appeared in Shanghai and Japan, followed by thirty more between 1912 and 1915. Open the pages of a random selection of those published in the early Republican era and you will be confronted with a dizzying range of images and narratives: photographs of Western athletes, the latest designs for domestic interiors, instructions about how to be a good wife and mother, biographical sketches of poets, artists, educators, scientists, virtuous women, and national heroines, cautionary tales warning young women of the pitfalls of illicit love, guides to healthy childbirth, photographs of nude women, eugenicist arguments about the benefits of companionate marriages, heated debates about women's rights, marriage reform, female celibacy, and the "third sex," and much more.

That the figure of "woman" became inseparable from ideas about nationhood and modernity is, of course, a familiar theme in the historiography of modern China. Indeed, as Dorothy Hodgson argued, modernity is always gendered, though inflected differently across temporal and cultural boundaries.[1] Furthermore, the appearance of "woman" as a vector for the transmission of anxieties and fears at a moment of rapid social transformation is also by no means specific to China. It is equally important, however, to focus on the figure

[1] Hodgson, *Gendered Modernities.*

332

of "woman" as fertile ground for the generation and dissemination of ideas about gender difference and gender relations – how women should conduct themselves in public, for example, or the kinds of dress appropriate to women in different public contexts, or the kinds of employment considered appropriate for educated women. The collaborative research project out of which this collection of essays has emerged brings together print culture, modernity, and gender within a transcultural framework to shed new light both on the gendered inflexions of Chinese modernity as well as the gendered attributes of the modern Chinese woman.

Before reflecting further on these ideas, I want first to return to the vexed matter of definition that Margaret Beetham outlines in her Preface to this volume. What is meant by the term "women's journal" as applied to the publications explored in this volume? If understood to refer to publications that were edited and written by women, then the foregoing chapters make it clear that many, if not most, of those produced during the Republican era would not qualify. The gender of the writer was, moreover, often obscured by what Fong terms "literary cross-dressing," which drew both writer and reader into an imagined community of assumed but unverified identities. If understood to refer to the readership, the editorial intention was, so it seems, to target a predominantly female audience, although without more detailed evidence, this is difficult to ascertain. However, the research methodologies and analyses undertaken by the contributors to this volume afford a few glimpses of the kind of people who might have opened the pages of the journals in question. Julia F. Andrews describes the cover image of the first issue of *The Women's Eastern Times*, which depicted two girls, one holding a Western-style book under her arm, "looking happily at the cover of the inaugural issue of *The Women's Eastern Times*." Painted by a well-known artist of the time, this "striking conceit," as Andrews describes it, draws the reader into a world of enjoyment where there is little distinction between the magazine world and its contents, and "reality." Siao-chen Hu's chapter suggests that at least some of the readers were female educators and students who created friendships and social networks in the "textualized space" of *The Ladies' Journal* and *The Chung Hwa Woman's Magazine*. Novels of the period, as Ellen Widmer details, depicted excitable women reading women's journals as powerful sources of ideas about change, alongside male literati readers who worried about their incendiary impact. Grace Fong argues that *Women's World* enthusiastically solicited poetry written by women teachers and students who were in the vanguard of change, foregrounding women as the journal's intended readership. Thin though it is, such evidence is enough to allow us to imagine a new pleasure of social exchange, even intimacy, afforded by women's shared reading of the text and by their shared appreciation of the image.

Beetham suggests that in contrast to the gendered character of all periodical forms, the "women's magazine . . . makes the role of gender central and explicit." The journals explored in this book converge in an almost exclusive focus on the figure of the female, depicted in narratives, photographs, illustrations, and art. The male emerges by implication and omission, and sometimes in overt critique, but invariably as a standard against whom women's qualities and attributes are implicitly – and sometimes explicitly – measured. The character of the woman in question also shifts quite radically across the time frame of the journals. The early journals of the turn of the century were edited and written by politically motivated women and men committed to radical change, who called into being a new female readership, a universal category of "women" who were variously addressed as *jiemei* (sisters) or *nü tongbao* (female compatriots). The more commercially oriented magazines published after 1912 under the auspices of large publishing concerns, most notably the Shanghai Commercial Press, retreated from the radical stance of their predecessors to foreground a less threatening version of the "new style" woman who continued to exemplify the allegedly "traditional" qualities of the "virtuous wife and good mother."

The unstable, or unfixed, character of the "woman's journal" highlights the significance of the question mark in the subtitle of this book. If we cannot identify who the women were who read, who were imaged, or who even wrote in the pages of these journals – apart from in the most general social outline – how can we begin to suggest that they offered women a "space of their own"? In the remaining space available, to conclude this volume, I want to suggest some ways in which we might approach this question, on the one hand by trying to identify the range of female subjects variously constituted by the images and texts of these journals, and on the other by seeking to trace common elements or parameters to those images and texts across time. In what ways might the differences in the subjects interpellated by these journals be interpreted to suggest that the journals offered a separate space of reflection, critique and enjoyment? Or, on the contrary, might the differences be less important than certain shared characteristics suggestive of a hegemonic female subject across the twentieth century?

The French sinologist Jacqueline Nivard has noted that the publication of a women's journal at the turn of the century constituted a "revolutionary act" in itself.[2] According to Nanxiu Qian, the 1898 *Chinese Girl's Progress* version of *guo* (nation, country, state) and women's self-positioning made nationalistic men uneasy, for their "strong sense of subjectivity and sweeping demands to become the intelligent 'mother' of the world sounded shockingly unfamiliar to their patriarchal ears." However, by the second decade of the twentieth century, the main women's magazines were producing what, by today's standards, both Chinese and Western, would be conservative depictions of the bourgeois woman – as homemaker, responsible mother, decorative wife, or educator

---

[2] Nivard, "L'évolution de la presse feminine," 160.

specializing in home economics. Buttressed by a "scientific discourse" of modern domestic management, child development, and women's education, the ideal of what Maria af Sandeberg calls the "educational home" was an essential component in the "imagined community" of the new nation. So, while such images were far from transgressive – indeed, as af Sandeberg points out, the educational home represented an ideal life style, especially for husbands, fathers, and sons – nevertheless, only two short decades after the legitimate appearance of "woman" in public space, her public print presence alone constituted a challenge to conventional expectations of feminine behavior and its association with the domestic realm. In disturbing the boundaries between the domestic and the public, or the "inner" and the "outer," such a presence offered women the opportunity to reflect on their conventional roles from a position of relative detachment, just as much as it reasserted woman's association with the domestic realm.

The public gaze on "woman" in the women's journals of these decades facilitated other, more unconventional possibilities for the feminine subject. The appearance of hitherto taboo topics such as menstruation and childbirth, often in graphic and detailed form, as Joan Judge argues, foregrounded women's bodies in the constitution of a new femininity characterized by scientific knowledge about reproduction, health, and hygiene. The "women's art" that emerged in the pages of *The Women's Eastern Times* and *The Ladies' Journal* visualized a range of feminine bodies, from athletes, physicians, and musicians to "even hypnotists." Doris Sung argues that the photo portraits of women that appeared in every issue of these two journals opened up rich new worlds of imagination, aspiration, and desire to their audiences. On a very different note, *Eyebrow Talk* and *Linloon Magazine* offered their publics sudden and unprecedented access to the female nude, doubtless delighting many, women as well as men, as well as – in the case of *Eyebrow Talk*– provoking the moral outrage of others, the state censors included.

The radical character of the public presence of "woman," whatever her political or social views, in these early journals was also forcefully present in the dissenting voices of their contributors. Rachel Hsu looks at the women who took up the form of the argumentative essay, conventionally a male preserve, to challenge male editors' attempts to silence demands for gender rights by bracketing women's demand for emancipation as calls for love and sexual liberation. Some even took on the scientific establishment to critique the view that women were biologically structured to take on the responsibility for domestic duties. On a very different note, Chen Xuezhao, writing in *New Woman*, completely dismantled the idea that women's emancipation lay in romantic love by arguing that autonomy and economic independence were the foundation of women's equality with men. The anarchist-feminist He-Yin Zhen's *Journal of Natural Justice*, published in Japan between 1907 and 1908, was the platform for her elaboration of a complex and sophisticated theory of the political and economic conditions for gender equality, including sexual freedom, that not only contested the idea that monogamous marriage could bring about women's emancipation, but even questioned the legitimacy of nationalist revolution when the nation was founded on fundamentally unequal and unjust principles.[3]

Women's journals, therefore, afforded spaces where the female subject emerged in much more diverse, complex, and publicly engaged guises than the binaries of "tradition" and "modernity" often applied to the early women's movement in China would suggest. A cacophony of voices and a heteroglossia of textual tropes privileged women's journals as a new public space in which image and text, editor, writer, and reader talked with, back to, and against each other, both deferring precise identification of the female subject and constantly foregrounding her as a figure of innovation, challenge, and surprise.

From a different perspective, these journals actively participated in defining the parameters or limitations of womanhood, or the feminine subject. Follow up the early journals with a brief survey of some of their sister publications nearly a century later, including the Chinese editions of *Vogue* and *Elle*, and you will come across many similar themes, modified in language and form to correspond with the times. At first glance, the diversity of images and themes would seem to confound any attempt to discern common parameters. Yet across these differences emerges an exclusive notion of gender that, in my view, underwrites the epistemological boundaries of binary gender difference inscribed in a hegemonic transcultural modernity.

One of the visually most obvious lines marking differences of inclusion and exclusion emerges through depictions of the foreign Other. Mostly but by no means exclusively, the white, Western Other is a ubiquitous presence in these journals, either through explicit reference to the gendered attributes of woman considered appropriate to the scientific, educational, political, and physical features of modernity, by silent implication through reference to the weaknesses and failures of Chinese womanhood, or as a figure who transgressed acceptable standards of morality. As Joan Judge notes, the importation of figures from outside – notably the West and Japan – expanded the parameters of what could be seen and discussed in the pages of a respectable Chinese journal, as they both sanctioned the introduction of topics not normally broached in public, such as women's reproductive health, and deterred local critiques of such discussions. "Doubly mediated texts" meeting Chinese readers from the West via Japan made it possible for Chinese authors and translators to broach sensitive topics such as prostitution, female same-sex love, and gender discrimination. The "Western woman" acquired an "iconic stature" in the Chinese imaginary of the period, as Judge puts it, evidenced by the vast preponderance

[3] Liu, Karl, and Ko, *The Birth of Chinese Feminism.*

of photographs of Western women among the foreign portraits printed in *The Women's Eastern Times*. Her naked body in the pages of *Linloon Magazine* and *Eyebrow Talk* called up interests and longings that the absence of the Chinese nude left unarticulated. In contrast, the figure of the Japanese woman or the depiction of feminine characteristics of Indian and other Asian women (Bailey) offered an ambivalent and often negative counterpoint to the strong physique associated with the Western woman. Asian and other non-Western women were consistently represented as "backward," even "primitive," and Turkish and African women emerged in an even more adverse light. Reform-minded intellectuals such as Hu Shi and Lin Yutang referred to the dire influence of Buddhism, a foreign religion, in explaining the decline of women's status in China (Bailey). Such views were expounded at a time of political and intellectual ferment, and across different political fora, raising many questions about what happened to the solidarity shown to other Asian women by the radical women of the late Qing years. The focus on the Western woman as the standard by which to evaluate and critique women's status and lives in China cancelled out the possibility of imagining a particular *Asian* community of women based on shared experiences and notions of solidarity (Bailey, Mittler). Multiple and contradictory images upholding the West both as a model and as a source of "contagion" in the women's journals indicated how controversial the "woman question" was in grappling with issues of national and cultural identity. At the same time, however, it privileged the white, Western woman as the hegemonic standard of health, beauty, and consumerist attainment, which continues to crowd the pages of globally produced women's journals today.

Nevertheless, the boundaries between Western and Chinese women were not so clear. Liying Sun traces the spatial and temporal trajectories of the images of female nudes that appeared in the pages of *Linloon Magazine* and argues that there was a fluid appropriation of images that originated in tabloid gossip columns of the United States The potentially transgressive delights, as well as the regulatory zeal, that images of nude women in the pages of *Eyebrow Talk* evoked echoed broader debates at the time across China and the West about the moral dangers of obscene materials and "harmful fiction." The transcultural connections set up between China and the West in the women's press of this period therefore suggest a reimagining – a reconstitution – of Chinese woman not via simple contrast, affirmative or negative, with the foreign. Western woman emerges not as a category or standard in her own right, as it were, but as an inextricable part of Chinese womanhood, to the point that the Other (the Western) eventually becomes an unnoticed part of the self.

"Chinese woman" therefore emerges as a fluid though central subject of a colonial and postcolonial modernity in which "the West" necessarily has an inextricable part. At the same time, the journals discussed in this volume suggest a constitution of the Chinese feminine subject via a range of hierarchical inclusions and exclusions that signal limits to the multiplicity of possibilities discussed throughout this book. Across the decades spanning the late Qing and Republican eras, women's journals appealed to politically diverse constituencies, but were increasingly associated with a liberal and nationalist agenda. Disseminated by predominantly male editors and writers, and despite their differences of appeal and opinion, they converged in their focus on the urban, educated, youthful, and healthy female subject. The notion of Chinese women that emerged was an exclusive rather than a generic category.

A glimpse at the only publications that featured rural women – notably the communist *Woman of China* of the 1950s and early 1960s, and later, *Rural Women Knowing All* of the reform era – makes this clear (Mittler). Journals of the Republican period made little reference to either rural women or older women, both of whom featured in their absence as the silenced internal subalterns. In her changing fashions, aspirations, and cultural and consumerist desires, the modern Chinese woman constituted by these journals is premised on the silencing and absenting of the rural (and the old). If the women's press in the early Republican period saw the healthy bodies of Western women as the standard of national strength, then by the mid-1950s, communist publications looked instead to women of the nonaligned nations and the rural sector to support radically different gendered values appropriate to the new socialist woman (Mittler). Corresponding with the ideological leanings of the newly established government of the People's Republic, images of the female subject in *Woman of China*, the only women's journal of the Mao years, produced affirmative images of the rural female subject that did not, at first glance, imply a hierarchical relationship with her urban sister. Even so, while during the Mao era and subsequent decades, references to the rural woman are made, they appear within a teleological framework that privileges the urban standards and aims of socialist and postsocialist modernity.

Over the course of a century or so, the transcultural flows and passions inspiring the contents of these journals have therefore contributed to a construction of hierarchical notions of gender that mark key lines of advantage and disadvantage. They form part of a transcultural gendering of modernity, in which to be a modern woman is associated with clear, urban-centered features, produced across national and cultural boundaries, however differently they might be defined in a local context. The depictions of woman in these journals therefore also had their part to play in the genealogy of today's globalized, cosmopolitan femininity. How readers contributed to such a process in their reading practices, and how editors' publication decisions were influenced or determined by commercial interests, are themes to be followed up elsewhere. Engaging in deeper horizontal, vertical, situated, and integrated readings by looking at other journals published for a general readership and their interactions with different groups of readers identified by region, education, social status, and age, as well as gender, would enable us to probe further the notions of appropriate womanhood and gender that were informed by and contributed to the images of these journals. If, however, as the title of this volume suggests, we are to look at these journals as sites where women could exercise autonomous agency as well as the production of gender, then in what they omit and exclude as much as in what they address and include, they suggest significant markers of difference between various categories of woman, urging important questions about who the gendered subject of "Chinese women's" journals was and continues to be.

Appendix: Journal Data

This appendix provides a list, in alphabetical order, of the women's journals referred to in this volume, together with basic bibliographical information about each journal. Each entry refers back to the chapters in which the journal is discussed.

Funü gongming (The woman's resonance)
Founded in March 1929. Edited by women.
Mentioned in Chapter 7 by Hsu.

Funü ribao (Women's daily)
A supplement to *Diansheng* ("Movie and radio" or "Movie tone"), published around 1932 and edited by "Ms Chen Zhengling," most likely a pseudonym of Lin Zecang.
Mentioned in Chapter 2 by Sun.

Funü shibao – The Women's Eastern Times
Founded in 1911 as supplement to *Shibao – The Eastern Times*. Folded 1917. The first commercial women's journal in China and the only one to survive the transition from the Qing dynasty to the Republic. Published in Shanghai. Editors Bao Tianxiao and Chen Lengxue (ps. of Chen Jinghan). The contents of *The Women's Eastern Times* are fully searchable through the WOMAG database.
Mentioned in Chapter 1 by Andrews, in Chapter 5 by Sung, in Chapter 12 by Judge, and in Chapter 13 by Bailey.

Funü zazhi – The Ladies' Journal
Founded in 1915. Published by the Commercial Press in Shanghai. The last issue came out in December 1931, shortly before the Japanese bombing of Shanghai in January 1932, which caused heavy damage to the Commercial Press. The journal was not revived after that. Editors included Wang Yunzhang and Zhu Hu Binxia (1915–20), Zhang Xichen (1921–25), Du Jiutian (1926–30), Ye Shengtao and Yang Runyu (1930–31). Conventional periodization of the life span of the journal describes Zhang Xichen's editorship as the most progressive and feminist, and the earlier and later

periods as more conservative, yet a closer scrutiny of the variety of content of the journal does not bear this out. The most controversial issue of the journal was the January 1925 special issue on "new sexual morality," which led to Zhang Xichen losing his job. He then went on (together with Zhou Jianren) to edit *The New Woman* (see below). The contents of *The Ladies' Journal* are fully searchable through the WOMAG database.
Mentioned in Chapter 1 by Andrews, in Chapter 5 by Sung, in Chapter 7 by Hsu, and in Chapter 9 by af Sandeberg.

Funü zhoubao (Women weekly)
Published from 1923–1925 and edited by Xiang Jingyu (1895–1928). A supplement of the Shanghai daily *Minguo ribao* (Republican daily news). One of the rare women's journals that voiced views as radical as those of some Western female-edited journals.
Mentioned in Chapter 7 by Hsu.

Linglong – Linloon Magazine
Weekly illustrated magazine founded in Shanghai in March 1931. Ran for 298 issues until August 1937. A pocket-sized, lavishly illustrated magazine, uniquely printed so that half of each issue was readable from left to right and the other half from right to left. Very popular especially with a young female readership, as noted by Zhang Ailing, who famously wrote that in the 1930s "every female student had a copy of *Linloon Magazine* in her hand." The contents of *Linloon Magazine* are searchable through the WOMAG database.
Mentioned in Chapter 2 by Sun and in Chapter 14 by Mittler.

Meiyu (Eyebrow talk)
Founded in Shanghai in November 1914 with Gao Jianhua as editor-in-chief, supported by her husband Xu Xiaotian. Published by the New Learning Society (*Xinxue huishe*), which was mainly a publisher of school textbooks and had distributors throughout China. *Eyebrow Talk* was the first modern fiction journal edited by a woman, featuring relatively many female authors, and specifically targeted at a female readership. Its covers and illustrations included unprecedented amounts of nudity. A total of eighteen issues appeared, with the last issue appearing in April 1916, several months before the journal was officially banned by the Beijing government.
Mentioned in Chapter 3 by Hockx and in Chapter 6 by Huang.

Nongjianü baishitong – Rural Women Knowing All
The only Chinese women's magazine addressed specifically to women from the countryside, published in Beijing, under the auspices of the Chinese Women's Federation. The journal first appeared in 1993. Editor Xie Lihua (b. 1951), who had formerly (since 1985) edited *Zhongguo funü* (Chinese woman), initiated much activity in the countryside in fighting for the

eradication of illiteracy, preventing suicides, and training women in rural self-government. She founded a vocational school for women in 1998 and her own NGO in 2001. Since then, she has been engaged in creating some 100 book societies for rural women. Her journal estimates its readership as between sixteen and forty-five years old and with a primary school education or more.
Mentioned in Chapter 14 by Mittler.

Nübao (Women's journal)
Published in Shanghai and edited by Chen Xiefen. Four biweekly issues came out in late 1899. None are extant.
Mentioned in Chapter 11 by Xia. Qian mentions the continuation of this journal; see the entry *Xuchu nübao*; Qian also mentions another journal of the same name edited by Chen Yiyi slightly later.

Nü xuebao – Chinese Girl's Progress
Published in Shanghai and edited by Xue Shaohui. Twelve issues appeared between July and October 1898.
Mentioned in Chapter 10 by Qian and in Chapter 11 by Xia.

Nü xuebao (Journal of women's learning)
Published in Shanghai and edited by Chen Xiefen. Four issues appeared between February and November 1903 in continuation of the Chinese Girl's Progress and the Xuchu nübao.
Mentioned in Chapter 10 by Qian.

Nüzi shijie (Women's world)
Published in Shanghai between 1904 and 1907, under the editorship of Ding Chuwo. Starting out as a monthly, its publication frequency gradually decreased. The eighteenth and final issue came out in 1907 under the editorship of Chen Yiyi, a close associate of Qiu Jin. Although the editorial board was controlled by men and most contributors were male social and political reformers, the journal also attracted a good number of female contributors. The contents of *Women's World* are fully searchable through the WOMAG database.
Mentioned in Chapter 4 by Fong, in Chapter 11 by Xia, in Chapter 13 by Bailey, and in Chapter 14 by Mittler.

Shenzhou nübao (Women's journal of the divine continent, also China women's journal, different from 1912–1913 *Shenzhou nübao* below)
Published in Shanghai and edited by Chen Yiyi (see above). Three issues appeared between December 1907 and February 1908.
Mentioned in Chapter 10 by Qian.

Shenzhou nübao (China women's news, different from 1907–1908 *Shenzhou nübao* above)

Published in Shanghai from November 1912 to July 1913 and edited by Zhang
 Mojun.
Mentioned in Chapter 13 by Bailey.

Xin funü (New woman)
Published in Shanghai from 1920 to 1921. One of the first women's journals to
 include investigative reports on Chinese working women and publicize the
 case for birth control.
Mentioned in Chapter 13 by Bailey.

Xin nüxing (The new woman)
Founded in 1926 under the editorship of Zhang Xichen, after he was forced to
 leave his post as editor of *The Ladies' Journal* (see above). When Zhang set
 up the Kaiming Bookstore publishing house in 1927, *New Woman* became
 one of its journals. The journal focused mainly on issues related to love
 and sex and enjoyed a healthy circulation, possibly up to 10,000 copies
 per issue. The journal folded in December 1929 after a total of forty-eight
 issues.
Mentioned in Chapter 7 by Hsu.

Xuchu nübao (Continued publication of women's journal)
Published in Shanghai and edited by Chen Xiefen. Nine issues appeared
 between May and December 1902.
Mentioned in Chapter 10 by Qian and in Chapter 11 by Xia.

Zhongguo funü (Woman of China)
This journal, the voice and official organ of the Communist Chinese All China
 Women's Federation, was first published in Yan'an between 1939 and 1941,
 and revitalized in July 1949, then under the name *Xin Zhongguo funü* (New
 woman of China), which was changed back to *Zhongguo funü* (Woman of
 China) in 1956. Mao had always supported the journal and until today, his
 calligraphy graces its cover page. As with so many other publications, the
 journal did not appear between July 1968 and 1978.
Mentioned in Chapter 14 by Mittler.

Zhongguo nübao (Chinese women's journal)
Published in Shanghai and edited by Qiu Jin. Two issues appeared between
 January and March 1907.
Mentioned in Chapter 10 by Qian.

Zhongguo xin nüjie zazhi (Magazine of China's new world of women)
Launched in Tokyo in February 1907, this was the first overseas Chinese
 women's journal. The editor, Yan Bin, studied medicine at the Dōjin Hospital, connected to Waseda University. Six issues of the journal appeared, and
 it folded in November or December 1907.
Mentioned in Chapter 4 by Fong, Chapter 11 by Xia and Chapter 13 by Bailey.

Zhonghua funü jie – The Chung Hwa Women's Magazine
Founded in 1915, folded after eighteen issues in 1916. Published by the Chung
Hwa Bookstore (*Zhonghua shuju*), which published eight major journals,
devoted to topics such as Chinese education, industry, commerce, children,
and fiction. The editorship of all eight journals was nominally attributed to
Liang Qichao, but in practice each journal had its own editorial board.
Mentioned in Chapter 8 by Hu and in Chapter 13 by Bailey.

Glossary

Author names that appear in the bibliography in pinyin and characters are omitted here. Where an author has a pen name, both are given here.

Ainü zhong 哀女種
"Aiguo lun" 愛國論
Aiguo nüxiao 愛國女校
aiguo 愛國
An Lushan 安祿山
Ankaidi 安凱地
Anru 安如
Anzan tebiki: gokai kyōsei 安産手引: 誤解矯正
atarashii onna 新しい女
Baichuanwei 白川尾 (Qian Juntao 錢君匋)
baihua 白話
Baitou sao geng duan 白頭搔更短
Balishi 巴理士
Bankoku fujin kyōfukai 萬國婦人矯風會
bao jiangtu 保疆土
baofu xin 報復心
baogaoshu 報告書
baoguo, baozhong, baojiao 保國, 保種, 保教
bei shiguan 備史官
Beiyang 北洋
bianji shi 編輯室
"Bianji shi zhi tanhua" 編輯室之談話
bianji tiaoli 編輯條例
biao shifan 表師範
biaozhun Zhongguoren 標準中國人
Biluo *nüshi* 碧羅女士
Bingyun 病雲
Bisumaruku *fujin* ビスマルク夫人
Bozi 伯子 (Fan Dangshi 范當世)

buliang xiaoshuo 不良小說
cai 才
cai duo wei fu 才多為富
cai neng yinglai Zhongguo de xin shiji 才能迎來中國的新世紀
Cai Yuanpei 蔡元培
cainü 才女
caizi jiaren 才子佳人
Cang 藏
Cao Lengbing 曹冷冰
changshi 常識
channan 產難
chanpo xue 產婆學
chanpo xuexiao 產婆學校
chanyu 產育
Chao Yuen-ren 趙元任 (Zhao Yuanren)
Chen 陳
Chen Chao 陳超
Chen Fan 陳範
Chen Hengke 陳衡恪 (Shizeng 師曾)
Chen Jinghan 陳景韓
Chen Jitong 陳季同
Chen Lengxue 陳冷血
Chen Moruo 陳默若
Chen Qian 陳騫
Chen Shiwu 陳適吾
Chen Shoupeng 陳壽彭
Chen Zhenling 陳珍玲
cheng 成
Cheng Bojia 程伯葭
cheng yixia 稱義俠
chengji 成績
chengjian 成見
chengyi 誠意
Chongshi nüxiao 崇實女校
Choushu 仇書
chuan de hao, chi de hao, zhu de hao 穿得好,吃得好,住得好
chuangban zhe 創辦者
Chūjōtō (Zhongjiangtang) 中將湯
Chun wang 春望
Chunnong 蓴農
Chunqi 春綺
ci 慈

ci 詞

cibei 慈悲

cifu 慈父

cimu 慈母

da yundong jia 大運動家

Da Zhonghua zazhi 大中華雜誌

Dagongbao 大公報

Dahua zazhi gongsi 大華雜誌公司

Dalu bao 大陸報

danmei 耽美

Daodejing 道德經

Dasheng bian 達生編

daxue 大學

Deguo xiaoxuexiao jiashike zhong tiaoshi fa 德國小學校家事科中調食法

Denggao 登高

Di Baoxian 狄葆賢 (Chuqing 楚青, Pingzi 平子)

Diansheng ribao 電聲日報

Diansheng zhoukan 電聲週刊

Dianshizhai huabao 點石齋畫報

diaoke 雕刻

Ding Zuyin 丁祖蔭

dongfang 東方

Dongfang zazhi 東方雜誌

Dongya gongsi shuyaoju 東亞公司書葯局

Dongya/Yadong 東亞/亞東

Dongyuan 東原

Du Fu 杜甫

Du Jiutian 杜就田

Du Nüzi shijie yougan 讀女子世界有感

du qianhao 讀前號

Du Qingchi 杜清持 (also written 池)

duli fan 獨立旛

Dulü'en 杜律恩

Dushi xiangzhu 杜詩詳註

Dushu zazhi 讀書雜誌

duxi/moxi 毒習/魔習

duxing 毒性

duzhe julebu 讀者俱樂部

"Eguo nü waijiaojia (wuguan zhi quanquan dashi) Nabikefu furen" 俄 國 女 外交家(無官之全權大使)那俾可甫夫人

Eikoku bungaku shi 英國文學史

Erhe 爾和 (Tang Tiaonai 湯調鼐)

Ertong youxi yongshu 兒童游戲用書

"Faguo jiuwang nüjie Ruo'an zhuan" 法國救亡女傑若安傳

"Faguo xinwenjie zhi nüwang Yadan furen" 法國新聞界之女王亞丹夫人

Fan Dangshi 范當世 (Kentang 肯堂, Bozi 伯子)

Fan Xiaochang 范孝嫦

Fan Yunsu 范蘊素

fangwenji 訪問記

fangxing wei'ai 方興未艾

fanjia zhi ma 泛駕之馬

fei lian'ai yu fei fei lian'ai lunzhan 非戀愛與非非戀愛論戰

Feili 斐立

Feng Zikai 豐子愷

"Fenghuangtai shang yi chuixiao" 鳳凰臺上憶吹簫

fengsu 風俗

"Fude" 婦德

Fujin eisei 婦人衛生

Fujin risshi hen 婦人立志篇

Fujo shinbun 婦女 新聞

fuke 婦科

"Fukkoku kakumei no hana (Rōran fujin no den)" 佛國革命の花(ローラン
夫人の傳

"Fukkoku shinbunkai no joō (Adamu fujin)" 佛國新聞界の女王 (アダム夫
人)

Fumei'er nü jindan 福美爾女金丹

funü 婦女

Funü gongming 婦女共鳴

Funü jiating bao 婦女家庭報

Funü jiating zhi ban 婦女家庭之伴

Funü jiyi zaohua cailiao qiju yigai juquan 婦女技藝造花材料器具一概俱
全

Funü ribao 婦女日報

Funü shibao 婦女時報

funü wenti 婦女問題

Funü wenti yanjiuhui 婦女問題研究會

Funü zazhi 婦女雜誌

Funü zhoubao 婦女週報

Furen dushen shenghuo wenti 婦人獨身生活問題

Furen weisheng shu 婦人衛生書

fūren 夫人

fùren 婦人

"Furenjie zhi shuangbi" 婦人界之雙璧

fuyin 福音

gaizui suo 改罪所
Gao Buying 高步瀛
Gao Jianfu 高劍父
Gao Jianhua 高劍華 (Gao Qin 高琴)
Gao Mengdan 高夢旦
Gao Qifeng 高其峰
gaodeng nuli 高等奴隸
Ge Xianglan 戈湘嵐
geming 革命
geming sixiang jiaoyu haizi 革命思想教育孩子
geren renge 個人人格
Gongbei 鞏北/拱北
gonghe 共和
Gongsun Daniang 公孫大孃
gongyi 工藝
Gongyu ji 攻玉集
gou ri xin, riri xin, you ri xin 苟日新, 日日新, 又日新
Gu Erniang 顧二孃
Gu Mingdao 顧明道
Gu Renchai 顧紉茝
guafen 瓜分
Guangdong nüxuetang 廣東女學堂
Guangfu hui 光復會
Guanghua daxue 光華大學
Guangxue hui 廣學會
guanshu 管束
guixiu 閨秀
guiyuan 閨媛
Gulunna 古倫娜
guo 國
Guo Jianren 郭堅忍
guochi 國恥
guojia 國家
guojia zhuyi 國家主義
guomin zhi mu 國民之母
guomin/nüguomin 國民/女國民
guoshi ruo 國勢弱
guoti 國體
guowen fanzuo 國文範作
"Guying" 顧影
Haibo yao 海波藥
Haitian Duxiaozi 海天獨嘯子

Han Yuesu 韓約素
Hang Zhiying 杭穉英
Hangzhou 杭州
Hangzhou baihuabao 杭州白話報
Hanshou 漢壽
Hanzhang 含章
haokan de buliang xiaoshuo 好看的不良小說
Haoliang zhi leji 濠梁之樂記
He Chenghui 何承徽
He Yimei 何逸梅
Heiye zhi mingxing 黑夜之明星
helun 呵倫
Hongxue lun buyao 紅血輪補藥
Hongye ciren 紅葉詞人 (Lou Tong 婁桐)
Hou Hanshu 後漢書
Hu Dunfu 胡敦復
Hu Gangfu 胡剛復
Hu Mingfu 胡明復
Hu Xigui 胡錫圭
Huang Daopo 黃道婆
Huang Shiying 黃士英
huanqiu 環球
huaqian yuexia zhi liangban 花前月下之良伴
huatu 畫圖
huikeshi 會客室
huizhuo 穢濁
hundun 混沌
hunyin xun 婚姻訓
Jannu daruku 惹安達克
Ji Zonglan 計宗蘭
jia 家
Jiang Fengzi 蔣鳳子
Jiang Guancha Guanyun 蔣觀察觀雲
Jiang Weiqiao 蔣維喬 (Zhuzhuang 竹庄)
Jiang Yingqing 姜映清
Jiangnan shuishi xuetang 江南水師學堂
jianmei 健美
Jiaoyu gongbao 教育公報
Jiaoyu zazhi 教育雜志
Jiaoyubu quanguo meishu zhanlanhui 教育部全國美術展覽會
Jiaoyuguan 教育館
jiating jiaoyu 家庭教育

jiating xin zhishi 家庭新知識
Jiating xingqi 家庭星期
Jiating zazhi 家庭雜誌
jiaxue 家學
jiazheng 家政
jie 節
jiebai jiemei 結拜姐妹
"Jiehun wenti zhi yanjiu" 結婚問題之研究
jiemei 姐妹
jiepou xue 解剖學
Jigao jia fangming lu 寄稿家芳名錄
Jin Cheng 金城
Jin Meisheng 金梅生
Jin Ping Mei 金瓶梅
Jin Shaocheng 金紹城
Jin Taotao 金陶陶
Jin Xuechen 金雪塵
Jin Zhang 金章
jinbu 進步
Jing Yuanshan 經元善 (Shanxi Longsou 剡溪聾叟)
jingbi 經閉
Jinghua zhoukan 精華週刊
jingjiguan 京畿館
jingshui butiao 經水不調
Jingxiong 競雄
Jingzhi nüxuexiao 競志女學校
Jinjiang 晉江
Jinlü qu 金縷曲
jinshen 謹慎
jinshi 進士
"Jinshi di yi nüjie Luolan furen zhuan" (近世第一女傑) 羅蘭夫人傳
(*Jinshi Ou-Mei*) *haojie zhi xijun* (近世歐美) 豪傑之細君
jishi xingle 及時行樂
Jissen 實踐
jiufa 舊法
jiuguo jiuzhong 救國救種
jiupai 舊派
Jiyūron 自由論
jizai 記載
Jogaku sekai 女学世界
Jogaku zasshi 女学雑誌
Joshi bijutsu gakkō 女子美術学校

Joshi risshi hen 女子立志編
jujia 居家
"Jundui kanhufu Nandige'er zhuan" 軍隊看護婦南的辯爾傳
Junyue 君月
Junzi 君子
junzi zhi dao 君子之道
juzhi 沮止
Kaiming shudian 開明書店
kaishu 楷書
Kajita Hanko 梶田
Kang Tongbi 康同璧
Kang Youwei 康有為
Kangnashi 康納士
Kentang 肯堂 (Fan Dangshi 范當世)
kexue 科學
Kinbara Murako 金原村子
Kinbara Tomiko 金原富子
Kobayashi Haru 小林春
kouleqin 扣樂沁
kua jiyi 誇技藝
kuaile wubi 快樂無比
kundao 坤道
laodong funü 勞動婦女
laopo 老婆
Laozi 老子
Li Li 李麗
Li Licheng 酈荔丞
Li Yu 李煜
lian'ai 戀愛
lian'ai shensheng 戀愛神聖
"Lian'ai ziyou jieda kewen" 戀愛自由解答客問
"Lian'ai ziyou yu ziyou lian'ai de taolun" 戀愛自由與自由戀愛的討論
lian'ai ziyou 戀愛自由
Liang Aibao 梁愛保
Liang Guiqin 梁桂琴
Liang Guizhu 梁桂珠
Liang Xinxi 梁心璽
Liang Yongfu 梁永福
liangfu 良父
liangqi xianmu 良妻賢母
Liangyou 良友
Lianniang 蓮娘

Libailiu 禮拜六

Lidai funü zhuzuo kao 歷代婦女著作考

lie wenyuan 列文苑

Lienü zhuan 列女傳

Lie 烈

limao 禮貌

Lin Baishui 林白水

Lin Yuan Gaozi 林原高子

Lin Zeren 林澤人

Ling Shuren 凌樹人

Linglong congshu 玲瓏叢書

Linglong 玲瓏

Liu Fa qingong jianxue yundong 留法勤工儉學運動

Liu Peiyu 柳佩瑜

Liu Yazi 柳亞子 (Yalu 亞盧)

Liu Xihong 劉錫鴻

Liushi 劉氏

Lize 麗則

Longyang 龍陽

Lou Tong (Hongye ciren) 婁桐 (紅葉詞人)

Lu 陸

Lu Feikui 陸費逵

Lu Meiniang 盧眉孃

Lu Shouqian 盧壽錢

lu wugong 錄武功

Lu Xiaocang 陸曉滄

Lü Bicheng 呂碧城

Lü Huiru 呂惠如

Lü Yunqing 呂筠青

luan 亂

"Lun zhuzao guominmu" 論鑄造國民母

Lunshuo 論說

lunshuowen 論說文

Luo Lan 羅蘭

Luo Wei yaofang 羅威藥房

"Luolan furen zhuan" 羅蘭夫人傳

Ma Simei 馬嗣梅

Man 滿

Manjianghong 滿江紅

Mei Meng 梅夢

mei you diwei 没有地位

meili de zhuzhai 美麗的住宅

Meiqian nüshi 梅倩女史
"Meiren yima kanjiantu" 美人依馬看劍圖
"Meishi'er" 美世兒
meishu 美術
meishu lan 美術欄
meishu shenghuo 美術生活
meishuguan 美術館
Meiyu 眉語
mengnie chuxing 萌糵初興
minghua 名畫
mingmin tongda 明敏通達
Minguo ribao 民國日報
Mingzhu 名著
Minli bao 民立報
Minli nüzi zhongxuetang 民立女子中學堂
Mitsukoshi 三越
Mizuhara Zen 水原漸
Moli 茉莉
Mufan zazhi 母范雜志
"Mukan no Rokoku zenken taishi (Novikofu fujin)" 無官の露國全權大使
　　(ノヴイコフ夫人)
Nakesi 納克司
nan bu yan nei, nü bu yan wai 男不言内, 女不言外
Nantong 南通
Nanyang quanyehui 南洋勸業會
"Nanzimen shuo" 男子們說
neiwu bu 内務部
neiyan bu chu, waiyan buru 内言不出, 外言不入
"Neize" 内則
neng shuo, bu neng xing de bibing 能說不能行的弊病
Ni Wuzhai 倪無齋
ni'ai 溺愛
Nihon fujo kai 日本婦女会
Nihon shin fujin 日本新婦人
"Nonggongshangbu nüzi xiugongke zongjiaoxi" 農工商部女子繡工科總教
　　習
Nonggongshangbu 農工商部
Nongjianü baishitong 農家女百事通
nongjianü 農家女
"Nü cike Shalutu Ge'erdie zhuan" 女刺客沙魯土・格兒垤傳
nü junren 女軍人
"Nü qingnian yishujia" 女青年藝術家

nü tongbao 女同胞
Nü wenhao Haili'aide Feiqushi *zhuan* 女文豪海麗愛德・斐曲士傳
Nü xuebao 女學報
Nü xuehui 女學會
Nü xuetang 女學堂
Nü yu hua 女獄花
Nübao 女報
Nügong 女紅
nüjie 女傑
nüjie weiren 女界偉人
Nüjiebao 女界寶
Nülun 女論
"Nüquan shuo" 女權說
nüquan 女權
nüshi 女史
nüti 女體
Nüwa shi 女媧石
nuxing 奴性
Nüxue wencong 女學文叢
nüxuebu 女學部
Nüzi 女子
Nüzi canzheng xiejinhui 女子參政協進會
Nüzi chanke xuexiao 女子產科學校
"Nüzi dang you putong yixue zhishi" 女子當有普通醫學知識
Nüzi guomin bao 女子國民報
nüzi guomin yinhang 女子國民銀行
nüzi quan 女子權
Nüzi shijie 女子世界
nüzi wu cai bian shi de 女子無才便是德
Nüzi zazhi 女子雜志
Ō-Bei joshi risshin den 欧米女子立身伝
Ogata Masakiyo 緒方正清
Onna no sekai 女の世界
Ōsaka kōtō igakkō 高等医学校
Ōsaka mainichi shinbun 大坂每日新聞
"Ōshū seikai no san joketsu" 歐洲政界の三女傑
Ōshū sensō jikki 歐洲戰爭實記
Oufeng 歐風
Ouling 耦菱
Ou-Mei 歐美
Ou-Xi furen 歐西婦人
Ouyang pucun 歐陽浦存

Pan Jinlian 潘金蓮
Pan Yuliang 潘玉良
"Picha nüren zhuan" 批茶女士傳
pingdeng 平等
Pingquan 平權
Pudong 浦東
Pu-wei Yang Chao 楊步偉 [Yang Buwei]
Qian Jibo 錢基博
Qian Juntao 錢君匋 (Baichuanwei 白川尾, Bacceo)
Qian Weizhen 錢維貞
Qian Yifang 錢挹芳
Qian Zhongshu 錢鍾書
qiangzhong 強種
qiankun 乾坤
qin 琴
qingkuai wan 清快丸
Qingyibao 清議報
Qiu Canzhi 秋灿芝
Qiu Jin 秋瑾
Qiu Ping 秋蘋
Qiu Zhao'ao 仇兆鰲
Qiuxing bashou 秋興八首
qixue kuisun 氣血虧損
Qu shi fufu yiyuan 瞿氏夫婦醫院
ran 染
ren shicai 任使才
ren'ge 人格
renzhong lie 人種劣
Riben xinshiji 日本新式髻
ru wenming 入文明
"Ruguo wo shi ni" 如果我是你
"Rui Miseeru joshi" 路易美世兒女史
Ruiyun 瑞雲
ruo bu shengyi 弱不勝衣
ryōsai kenbo [*liangqi xianmu*] 良妻賢母
Saigoku risshi hen 西國立志編
Saishin kekkongaku 最新結婚学
sancong 三從
Sanhe gongsi 三和公司
"Seijika no tsuma" 政治家の妻
Seitō 青鞜
Sekai kokon meifu kagami 世界古今名婦鑑

Sha Xuemei 沙雪梅

shangdeng gei jiang 上等給獎

Shanghai manhua 上海漫畫

shangpin zhi nüzi 上品之女子

Shangwen yinshuasuo 尚文印書所

Shangyu 上虞

Shanxi Longsou 剡溪聾叟 (Jing Yuanshan 經元善)

shaonian 少年

Shaoying 少英

Shen Bochen 沈伯塵

Shen Shanbao 沈善寶

Shen Shou 沈壽 (Yu Shen Shou 余沈壽)

Shen Ying 沈瑛

Shenbao 申報

shengli xue 生理學

shengli 生理

Shengsheng gaoji zhuchan xuexiao 生生高級助產學校

Shengsi guantou juben 生死關頭劇本

shenjia zhuyi 身家主義

shenming zhi shanshu 神明之善書

Shenzhou nübao 神州女報

Shenzhou 神州

Sheying huabao 攝影畫報

"Sheying yanjiu lan" 攝影研究欄

shi 詩

Shi Shuyi 施淑儀

Shibao 時報

Shidai manhua 时代漫画

Shifu 實甫 (Yi Shunding 易順鼎)

shijie di-yi maoxian nüzi 世界第一冒險女子

shijie geming 詩界革命

"Shijie shi nüjie yanyi" 世界十女傑演義

Shijie shi nüjie 世界十女傑

shijie zhuyi 世界主義

shijie 世界

Shimen wenming nüshu 石門文明女塾

Shimoda Utako 下田歌子

Shin fujin 新婦人

Shin Nihon 新日本

shiyantan 實驗談

shiye zhi cixu 事業之次序

shiye 實業

shiyuan 施願
Shizeng 師曾 (Chen Hengke 陳衡恪)
shizhuan 史傳
Shouheizi 守黑子
Shoushi 壽氏
shuhao 書號
Shuo nümo 說女魔
Shuo qun 說羣
Shuoye 說腋
si zheng chang 思正長
sikepoluomeng 斯柯婆羅蒙
Siku Quanshu 四庫全書
Siqi Zhai 思綺齋
Sishu 四書
Song Shu 宋恕
Songling nüzi Pan Xiaohuang 松陵女子潘小璜
Su Bennan 蘇本楠
Su Benyan 蘇本㠛
Subao 蘇報
Sugiura Hisui 杉浦非水
Sun Qingwei 孫青未
Ta yu ta 她与他
Taisei fujo kikan 泰西婦女龜鑑
Taisei retsujoden 泰西列女傳
taitai 太太
Taixi lienü zhuan 泰西列女傳
Taizhou nüzi shixiao 台州女子師校
Takahashi Oden 高橋阿傳
Tang Jianwo 湯劍我
Tang Tiaonai 湯調鼐 (Erhe 爾和)
tang 堂
"Tangshi wo youle xiaohai" 倘使我有了小孩
tanhua hui 談話會
Tao Yuanqing 陶元慶
te mei xing 特美性
tebie jishi 特別記事
Teng Chao 滕超
Teng Zhuo 滕卓
Terada Shirō 寺田四郎
tianji suodan 天機所誕
Tianyi bao 天義報
Tianzu hui 天足會

Tiaonian mengying 髫年夢影

Tiyujia Tang Jianwo *nüshi xizhuang xiaoying* 體育家湯劍我女士西裝小影

Tokutomi Sohō 德富蘇峰

Tongcheng 桐城

Tongli 同里

Tongsu chanke sanbai yong 通俗產科三百咏

Tongsu jiaoyu yanjiuhui 通俗教育研究會

tongsu tushuguan 通俗圖書館

tongxun 通訊

tongzhong 同種

Tongzhou 通州

Tsumura Juntendō 津村順天堂

tu'an 圖案

tuhua 圖畫

tuhuabu 圖畫部

tuhuahua 圖畫化

tuoxie zhuyi 妥協主義

tuozhimian 脫脂棉

tuqi 土气

wai 外

waiguo 外國

waiyi 外夷

Wanfang 婉芳

Wang 王

Wang Changlu 汪長祿

Wang Jie 王杰

Wang Lingxi 王靈希

Wang Miaoru 王妙如

Wang Ruizhu 王瑞竹

Wang Yigang 王以剛

Wang Yunzhang 王蘊章

Wang Yuzhen 汪毓真

wangfei 王妃

wangguo 亡國

wangluo yinhui seqing xiaoshuo 網絡淫穢色情小說

Wanxian 婉仙

wei wannong zhi ju 為玩弄之具

weibi guaili you shang fengsu zhi xiaoshuo zazhi 猥鄙乖離有傷風俗之小說雜誌

Weilianshi dayisheng hongse buwan 韋廉士大醫生紅色補丸

weisheng 衛生

wenming 文明

wenpo 穩婆
wenrou 溫柔
Wenxue yanjiuhui 文學研究會
"Wenyi" 文藝
"Wenyuan" 文苑
"Wenyuan zhuan" 文苑傳
"Wenyuan: Yinhua ji" 文苑: 因花集
wenzhong 文中
Wu 武
Wu Baochu 吳保初
Wu Changshi 吳昌碩
Wu Dingchang 吳鼎昌
wu guo ertong 吾國兒童
Wu Jianlu 吳劍鹿
Wu Juenong 吳覺農
Wu Mengban 吳孟班
Wu Pingyun nüshi 吳萍雲女士
Wu Rulun 吳汝綸
Wu Ruonan 吳弱男
Wu Shujuan 吳淑娟
Wu Yanan 吳亞男
Wu Zhiying 吳芝瑛
Wu Zhuo 吳卓
Wu Zuxiang 吳祖襄
Wujiang 吳江
Wuxi 無錫
Wuzhou dayaofang 五洲大藥房
Xi'ou/Dong'ou 西歐/東歐
xiadeng jinzhi 下等禁止
"Xiandai nüzi de kumen wenti" 現代女子的苦悶問題
Xiang Jingyu 向警予
xiang nanzi jingong 向男子進攻
Xiangying lou shixuan 湘影樓詩選
xianqi liangmu 賢妻良母
xianshen 仙神
xianshu mingyuan 賢淑名媛
xianyan 鮮妍
xiao jiating 小家庭
xiao 孝
xiaobao 小報
xiaodumian 消毒棉
xiaoshuo gu 小說股

Xiaoshuo yuebao 小說月報

xiaoshuo 小說

xiaoxian 消閒

xiapin zhi nüzi 下品之女子

Xie Daoyun 謝道韞

Xie Jingqin 謝錦琴

Xie Lihua 謝麗華

Xie Youyun 謝幼韞

Xin funü 新婦女

xin guomin 新國民

xin nanxing 新男性

xin nüxing 新女性

Xin qingnian 新青年

xin qingshu 新情書

xin xingdaode 新性道德

Xin Zhongguo funü 新中國婦女

xinfa 新法

"Xingshi tu" 醒獅圖

Xingyi 星一

"Xinhai xia Minli Shanghai nüzhongxuetang benkesheng di-yi ci biye sheying"
辛亥夏民立上海女中學堂本科生第一次畢業攝影

xinju 新劇

Xinjun 欣君

Xinmin congbao 新民叢報

xinmin zhi zhi 新民之旨

xinxue 新學

Xinxue huishe 新學會社

Xixue 西學

Xiyangpai xin nüzi 西洋派新女子

Xu Baowen 許寶文

Xu Hemei 徐呵梅

Xu Jia'en 許家恩

Xu Jiaxing 許家惺

Xu Nianci 徐念慈

Xu Shangmu 徐尚木 (Xu Yitang 徐益棠)

Xu Xiaotian 許嘯天

Xu Yasheng 徐亞生

Xu Yishi 徐一士

Xu Yitang 徐益棠 (Xu Shangmu 徐尚木)

Xu Yongqing 徐詠青

Xu Yuhua 許毓華

Xu Zehua 許澤華

Xu Zhengshou 許正綬
Xu Zihua 徐自華
Xuchu nübao 續出女報
xue 學
Xue Jinqin 薛錦琴
Xue Shaohui 薛紹徽
Xuesheng zazhi 學生雜誌
xueyi 學藝
Xujiahui 徐家匯
Xu-Zhang Huiru 徐張蕙如
Yalu 亞盧 (Liu Yazi 柳亞子)
Yan Bin 燕斌
Yang Buwei (Pu-wei Yang Chao, Yang Pu-wei) 楊步偉
Yang Daquan 楊達權
Yang Pu-wei (Yang Buwei) 楊步偉
Yang Runyu 楊潤餘
yanghuo 洋貨
yangqi 洋气
yanyi 演義
Yao Shumeng 姚淑孟
Yao Ying 姚瑩
Yao Yingnai 姚英乃
Yao Yiyun 姚倚雲
Yao Yunsu 姚蘊素
yaofang 藥房
Yaoniang 窅娘
"Yashamen no jobosatsu (Rui Miseeru)" 夜叉面の女菩薩 (ルイ、ミセール)
Yazhou heqin hui 亞洲和親會
Ye Changchi 葉昌熾
Ye Feng 葉風
Ye Mengqing 葉孟青
Ye Qianyu 葉淺予
Ye Shengtao 葉聖陶
yeman 野蠻
Yi Mengwei 易孟微
Yi Shunding 易順鼎 (Shifu 實甫)
Yi Yu 易瑜 (Zhonghou 仲厚)
yi zhi jiajiang, yu ci shou zi 懿旨嘉獎, 御賜壽字
yi zu er dengfeng zaoquan 一足而登峰造全
yi 藝

Yichu 逸初

"Yiguo qingdiao" 异国情调異國情調

yihai 譯海

"Yinbingshi shihua" 飲冰室詩話

Yinbingzi 飲冰子

yinfu 淫婦

"Ying'er baoyu fa" 嬰兒保育法

"Yingguo da cishanjia Meili Jia'abinta zhuan" 英國大慈善家美利·加阿賓他傳

"Yingguo nüjie Niejike'er zhuan" 英國女傑涅几柯兒傳

"Yingguo xiaoshuojia Aili'atuo nüshi zhuan" 英國小說家愛里阿脱女士傳

yingxiong haojie zhi nüzi 英雄豪傑之女子

Yinhua ji 因花集

yinhui 淫穢

yinruo de bingfu 羸弱的病夫

yinshu 淫書

yinwei 淫猥

yishu 藝術

Yiwen 逸纹

yongjian 勇健

yongyi yufu 庸醫愚婦

Yosano Akiko 與野晶子

you suo si 有所思

youguo 憂國

youshi aiguo 憂時愛國

youxi 遊戲

Yu Mengban 于孟班

Yu Qing'en 俞慶恩

Yuan Shikai 袁世凱

Yuan Zhenniang 袁貞娘

yuefenpai 月分牌

Yuehen 越恨

yuejing dai 月經帶

yule 娛樂

Yunsu xuan shigao 蘊素軒詩稿

Yunxi nüshi 雲溪女士

Yuren 愚人

Zaisheng yuan 再生緣

zannan beinü 贊男卑女

zazu 雜俎

zhaimian 摘棉

zhaimian huahui 摘棉花卉

Zhan Kai 詹塏

zhandou 戰鬪

Zhang 張

Zhang Ailing 張愛玲

Zhang Binglin 章炳麟

Zhang Cixi 張次溪

Zhang Fangyun 張芳芸

Zhang Hongsheng 張宏生

Zhang Jianyao 張劍耀

Zhang Jian 張謇

Zhang Jiebin 張介賓

Zhang Lingtao 張令濤

Zhang Mojun 張默君 (Zhang Zhaohan)

Zhang Rentian 張任天

zhang wenheng 掌文衡

Zhang Xichen 章錫琛

Zhang Zhaohan 張昭漢 (Zhang Mojun)

Zhang Zhidong 張之洞

Zhanguo ce 戰國策

zhanran 沾染

Zhao Aihua 趙愛華

Zhao Yuanren 趙元任 (Chao Yuen-ren)

Zhejiang chao 浙江朝

Zhejiang Yude nüzhong 浙江育德女中

zhen ling 珍玲

zhen 貞

zhen, shan, mei 真善美

zhencao 貞操

Zheng Mantuo 鄭曼陀

Zheng Xuan 鄭玄

Zheng Zhenxuan 鄭振壎

Zhenling xinxiang 珍玲信箱

Zhenxiang huabao 真相畫報

Zhibai 知白

zhihua zhi gong 治化之功

Zhina 支那

Zhitang huixiang lu 知堂回想錄

Zhong-Fa lao yaofang 中法老藥房

Zhong-Xi dayaofang 中西大藥房

Zhongguo funü 中國婦女

Zhongguo furen hui 中國婦人會
Zhongguo nübao 中國女報
Zhongguo nüzi 中國女子
Zhongguo sheying xuehui 中國攝影學會
Zhongguo tongzijie 中國童子界
Zhongguo xin nühao 中國新女豪
Zhongguo xin nüjie zazhi 中國新女界雜誌
Zhonghou 仲厚 (Yi Yu 易瑜)
Zhonghua da zidian 中華大字典
Zhonghua ertong huabao 中華兒童畫報
Zhonghua funü jie 中華婦女界
Zhonghua jiaoyu jie 中華教育界
"Zhonghua Minguo funü yuejing diaocha biao" 中華民國婦女月經調查表
Zhonghua shuju 中華書局
Zhonghua yixue 中華醫學
Zhongjiangtang 中將湯
Zhongwai dashiji 中外大事記
Zhongwai yingxun 中外影訊
Zhongxue 中學
"Zhongyong" 中庸
Zhou Jianren 周建人
Zhou Jun 周峻
Zhou Shixun 周世勳
Zhou Shuren 周樹人
Zhou Zuoren 周作人
Zhu Deshang 朱德裳
Zhu Zongliang 祝宗梁
zhuangyuan 狀元
zhuanji 傳紀
Zhuo Hua 灼華
zhusu 鑄塑
Zhuzhuang 竹庄 (Jiang Weiqiao 蔣維喬)
zi lizhi 資吏治
zili 自立
ziran 自然
ziyou 自由
ziyou hua 自由花
ziyou lian'ai 自由戀愛
ziyou luntan 自由論壇
ziyou shen 自由身
zizhu 自主

Zong Weigeng 宗惟賡
Zou Shengwen 鄒盛文
zuidu furen xin 最毒婦人心
Zuixin jiehun xue 最新結婚學
"Zuojia jingyan tan" 作家經驗譚
zuoyeshi 作業室

Bibliography

ABBREVIATIONS

Funü zazhi FNZZ
Funü shibao FNSB
Zhonghua funüjie (The Chung Hwa Women's Magazine) *ZHFNJ*

NOTES ON STYLE IN ENTRIES

Page numbers in square brackets refer to page numbers in the reprint version of the
journal included in *Zhongguo jinxiandai nüxing huibian*.
Articles are listed under author names rather than pen names. Names that appear in
square brackets are the actual names; names not in brackets are the names under
which the articles were published.

DATABASES AND COLLECTIONS

"A New Approach to the Popular Press in China: Gender and Cultural Production,
1904–1937." www.womag.uni-hd.de/
"Chinese Women's Magazines in the Late Qing and Republican Periods" (Database).
http://womag.uni-hd.de/index.php
Diansheng 電聲 (*Diansheng ribao* 電聲日報, 1932–1933; *Diansheng zhoukan* 電聲
週刊, 1934–1941), Library of Institute of Chinese Studies, Heidelberg.
"Early Chinese Periodicals online" (Database). Ecpo.uni-hd.de
"Funü zazhi mulu ziliaoku" 《婦女雜誌》目錄資料庫 (Database of the tables of
contents of *Funü zazhi*). http://mhdb.mh.sinica.edu.tw/fnzz/
"Linglong Women's Magazine." Columbia University Library. www.columbia.edu/cu/
lweb/digital/collections/linglong/collection_index.html
Linglong 玲瓏 ("Lin Loon Magazine"). Shanghai, 1931–1937. Heidelberg; Columbia
University Library.
Shenbao Fulltext Database (via CrossAsia). http://crossasia.org/databases
Sheying huabao 攝影畫報 ("Pictorial Weekly"). Shanghai, 1925–1937. Heidelberg.

REFERENCES

Abe Isoo 安部磯雄. "Fujin yundô jyûgonen shi" 婦人運動十五年史 (Fifteen years of
the women's movement). *Shin Nihon* 5: 1 (1915), 41.
Acharya, Amitav. "Asia Is Not One." *Journal of Asian Studies* 69: 4 (2010), 1001–13.

Af Sandeberg, Maria. "Gender in Chinese Literary Thought of the Republican Period." Ph.D. dissertation, SOAS, University of London, 2005.

"Aiji de nüzi" 埃及的女子 (The women of Egypt). *Linglong* 262 (1936), 3504.

Al-Olayan, S. Fahad, and Kiran Karande. "A Content Analysis of Magazine Advertisements from the United States to the Arab World." *Journal of Advertising* 29: 3 (2000), 77–81.

Anderson, Benedict. *Imagined Communities: Reflections on the Origin and Spread of Nationalism*. London: Verso, 1983, 1991.

Anderson, Doris. *Rebel Daughter: An Autobiography*. Toronto: Key Porter, 1996.

Andrews, Julia F. "Commercial Art and China's Modernization." In *A Century in Crisis: Modernity and Tradition in the Art of Twentieth Century China*, edited by Julia F. Andrews and Kuiyi Shen, 181–97. New York: Guggenheim Museum, 1998.

Aoyagi Yūbi 青柳有美. *Jissen mutsū ansan pō, Fuku: Ijutsu no shinpo* 實驗無痛安産法 附・醫術の進步 (The practice of painless childbirth: Supplement on medical progress). Tokyo: Jitsugyô no sekaisha, 1915.

___ *Zui xin jiehunxue* 最新結婚學 (Latest studies in marriage). Translated by Chen Shiwu 陳適吾. Shanghai: Youzheng shuju, 1915.

Attwood, Lynne. *Creating the New Soviet Woman: Women's Magazines as Engineers of Female Identity, 1922–1953*. Basingstoke: Macmillan, 1999.

Atwood, Margaret. *Second Words: Selected Critical Prose*. Toronto: Anansi, 1982.

Aying 阿英. *Wanqing xiaoshuo shi* 晚清小說史 (History of the late Qing novel). Beijing: Dongfang chubanshe, 1996.

Bai Ben 白本. "He wei mofang? Yige ertong xinli de yanjiu" 何謂模仿? 一個兒童心理的研究 (What is imitation? A study in child psychology). *FNZZ* 12: 4 (1926), 33–40.

Baihua daoren Shoushi 白話道人壽氏. "Neng shuo bu neng xing" 能說不能行 (About being able to speak but not act). *Nüzi shijie* 2/4–5 (1905/6), 11.

Bailey, Paul. "Active Citizen or Efficient Housewife? The Debate over Women's Education in Early Twentieth Century China." In *Education, Culture and Identity in Twentieth Century China*, edited by Glen Peterson, Ruth Hayhoe and Yongling Lu, 318–47. Ann Arbor: University of Michigan Press, 2001.

___ *Gender and Education in China: Gender Discourses and Women's Schooling in the Early Twentieth Century*. London: Routledge, 2007.

___ *Reform the People: Changing Attitudes towards Popular Education in Early Twentieth-Century China*. Edinburgh: Edinburgh University Press, 1990.

___ "'Unharnessed Fillies': Discourse on the 'Modern' Female Student in Early Twentieth Century China." In *Wusheng zhi sheng: Jindai Zhongguo de funü yu wenhua* (Voices amid silence: Women and culture in modern China), edited by Lo Jiu-jiung and Lu Miaw-fen, 327–57. Taibei: Institute of Modern History, Academia Sinica, 2003.

Ballaster, Ros, Margaret Beetham, Elizabeth Frazer, and Sandra Hebron. *Women's Worlds: Ideology, Femininity and the Woman's Magazine*. London: Macmillan, 1991.

Ballew, Tad. "Xiaxiang for the '90s: The Shanghai TV Rural Channel and Post-Mao Urbanity amid Global Swirl." In *China Urban: Ethnographies of Contemporary Culture*, edited by Nancy Chen, Constance Clark, Suzanne Gottschang, and Lyn Jeffery, 242–73. Durham, NC: Duke University Press.

Bao Tianxiao 包天笑. "Bianji shi" 編輯室 (From the office of the editor). *FNSB* 2 (July 26, 1911), 56; *FNSB* 6 (May 1, 1912), 88; *FNSB* 9 (February 25, 1913), 92.

— "Bianji shi zhi tanhua" 編輯室之談話 (Conversation from the office of the editor). *FNSB* 19 (August 1916), 114.

Bao Yong'an 鮑永安 (ed.) and Su Keqin 苏克勤 (annot.). *Nanyang quanyehui wenhui* 南洋勸業會文匯 (Collected essays on the Nanyang Industrial Exposition). Shanghai: Shanghai jiaotong daxue chubanshe, 2010.

Bao Yong'an 鮑永安 (ed.) and Su Keqin 苏克勤 and Yu Jieyu 余洁宇 (compilers). *Nanyang quanyehui tushuo* 南洋勸業會圖說 (Illustrated archive of the Nanyang Industrial Exposition). Shanghai: Shanghai jiaotong daxue chubanshe, 2010.

Bao Zhen 寶貞 and Tai Guangdian 邰光典. "Xin jiating" 新家庭 (The new family). *FNZZ* 7: 1 (1921), 5–8 [19–22].

Baosun 豹孫. "Lixiang de zhuzhai: jia zai shanhuan shuirao zhong" 理想的住宅: 家在山環水繞中 (The ideal dwelling: Surrounded by mountains and streams). *FNZZ* 12: 11 (1926), 33–34.

Bardsley, Jan. *The Bluestockings of Japan: New Woman Essays and Fiction from Seitô 1911–1916*. Ann Arbor: Center for Japanese Studies, University of Michigan, 2007.

Baron, Beth. "Readers and the Women′s Press in Egypt." *Poetics Today* 15: 2 (1994), 217–40.

Beahan, Charlotte. "Feminism and Nationalism in the Chinese Women's Press 1902–1911." *Modern China* 1: 4 (1975), 379–416.

Beetham, Margaret. *A Magazine of Her Own? Domesticity and Desire in the Women's Magazine 1800–1914*. London: Routledge, 1996.

— "In Search of the Historical Reader: The Woman Reader, the Magazine and the Correspondence Column." *SPIEL* 1: 19 (2000), 89–104.

Beetham, Margaret and Boardman, Kay (eds.). *Victorian Women's Magazines: An Anthology*. Manchester: Manchester University Press, 2001.

"Benbao zhengwenli" 本報徵文例 (Submission guidelines for our magazine). *FNSB* 2 (1911).

"Benshe chuban shuji yugao" 本社出版書籍預告 (Advance notice from this society concerning books to be published), *Zhongguo xin nüjie zazhi* 5 (1907).

"Benshe tebie guanggao" 本社特別廣告 (Special notice of the [journal's] main office), *Zhongguo xin nüjie zazhi* 5 (1907).

"Bianji yulu" 編輯餘錄 (Editorial afterword). *FNZZ* 7:5 (1921), 108; *FNZZ* 7:7 (1921), 116; *FNZZ* 8:2 (1922), 120.

"Bianjishi de baogao" 編輯室的報告 (Reports from the editorial office). *FNZZ* 12:7 (1926), 259.

"Bianjishi zhuiyan" 編輯室贅言 (Additional comments from the editorial office). *FNZZ* 12:8 (1926), 134; *FNZZ* 15:7 (1929), 218.

Bianzhe 編者. "Feikan ci" 廢刊詞 (Announcement of termination [of *Xin nüxing*]). *Xin nüxing* 4:12 (1929), 1500.

— "Xiandai nüzi de kumen wenti" 現代女子的苦悶問題 (The dilemma of modern women). *Xin nüxing* 2:1 (1927), 21.

Bingyun 病雲 (Zhou Zuoren). "Nühuozhuan" 女禍傳 (On female danger). *Nüzi shijie* 2/4–5 (1905/6), 39–46.

"Bishimaike furen zhuan" 俾士麥克夫人傳 (Biography of Bismarck's wife). *Dalu bao* 3 (1903). Republished in *Nü xuebao* 3 (1903).

Bland, Lucy. *Banishing the Beast: English Feminism and Sexual Morality, 1885–1914.* London: Penguin, 1995.

"Bo'aizhuyi shixingjia Mode nüshi zhuan" 博愛主義實行家墨德女士傳 (Biography of Lucretia Mott). *Zhongguo xin nüjie zazhi* 5 (1907).

Boyd, Mary Sumner, and Marguerite Tracy. *Painless Childbirth: A General Survey of All Painless Methods, with Special Stress on "Twilight Sleep" and Its Extension to America.* New York: Frederick A. Stokes Company, 1915.

Braithwaite, Brian. *The Business of Women's Magazines: The Agonies and the Ecstasies.* London: Associated Business Press, 1979.

Brake, Laurel. *Subjugated Knowledges: Journalism, Gender and Literature in the Nineteenth Century.* London: Macmillan, 1994.

Brinckloe, William Draper. "The Home I'd Like to Have." *Ladies' Home Journal* 4 (1922), 27, 47.

Butler, Judith. *Gender Trouble: Feminism and the Subversion of Identity.* New York: Routledge, 1990.

Cai Yuanpei. "On Replacing Religion with Aesthetic Education." In *Modern Chinese Literary Thought, Writings on Literature, 1893–1945*, edited by Kirk A. Denton, 182–89. Stanford, CA: Stanford University Press, 1996.

Carr & Johnston Co. *Practical Homes.* St Paul, MN: Brown-Blodgett Company, 1926. [Online version: https://archive.org/details/PracticalHomes1926.]

Castro, Jan Garden. "An Interview with Margaret Atwood." In *Margaret Atwood: Visions and Forms*, edited by Kathryn VanSpanckenen and Jan Garden Castro, 215–32. Carbondale: Southern Illinois University Press, 1988.

Chang, Hao. *Liang Ch'i-ch'ao and Intellectual Transition in China, 1890–1907.* Cambridge, MA: Harvard University Press, 1971.

Chang, Mo-chün. *See* Zhang Mojun.

Changwen 長文. "Duan bi tou" 短筆頭 (Short pen). *Xin nüxing* 4: 2 (1929), 231–32.

Chaoran 超然. "Jiaoyu zinü de liyan" 教育子女的俚言 (Some simple remarks on the education of children). *FNZZ* 15: 9 (1929), 25–28 [47–50].

Chapman, Mary and Angela Mills, eds. *Treacherous Texts: U.S. Suffrage Literature, 1846–1946.* New Brunswick, NJ: Rutgers University Press, 2011.

Chen Benjian 陈本建. "Yao zhong di qing xian na 'lüka'" 要种地请先拿"绿卡" (If you want to do agriculture, please first get a greencard). *Nongjianü baishitong* 3 (1996), 6–9.

Chen Bochui 陳伯吹. "Ta de binggen zai niai" 她的病根在溺愛 (The root of her problem is over-indulgent love). *FNZZ* 13: 2 (1927), 30–32 [46–48].

Chen, Chaonan, and Yiyou Feng. *Old Advertisements and Popular Culture: Posters, Calendars and Cigarettes, 1900–1950.* San Francisco: Long River Press, in association with Shanghai People's Art Press, 2004.

Chen Duansheng 陳端生. *Zaisheng yuan* 再生缘 (Love reincarnate). 2 vols. Beijing: Huaxia chubanshe, 2000.

Ch'en, Heng-che [Chen Hengzhe]. "The Influence of Foreign Cultures on the Chinese Woman." In *Chinese Women through Chinese Eyes*, edited by Li Yu-ning, 73–86. New York: M. E. Sharpe, 1992.

Chen Sanli 陳三立. *Sanyuan jingshe shiwenji* 散原精舍詩文集 (Essays from the Sanyuan studio). Shanghai: Shanghai guji, 2003.

Chen Shuyu 陳漱渝. "Lu Xun yu tongsu jiaoyu yanjiuhui" 魯迅與通俗教育研究會 (Lu Xun and the Popular Literature Research Association). *Shandong shifan daxue xuebao* 5 (1977), 72–75.

Chen Xiaofeng 陳曉峰. "Yao Yiyun nüzi shifan jiaoyu sixiang yanjiu" 姚倚雲女子師範教育思想研究 (A study of Yao Yiyun's thoughts on women's teacher training). *Jiaoyu xueshu yuekan* 9 (2009), 77–81.

Chen Xiefen 陳擷芬. Aiguo nü'er chuanqi 愛國女兒傳奇 (Legend of patriotic girls). *Xuchu nübao* 6 (1902), "Nübao fujian" column, 1a–3b.

— "Jiang kai nüxuetang" 將開女學堂 (A new girls' school to be opened). *Xuchu nübao* 2 (1902), "Nübao xinwen" column, 5b–6a.

— "Nannü dou yao kan" 男女都要看 (Men and women all have to read!). *Xuchu nübao* 8 (1902), "Nübao yanshuo" column, 2a–3b.

— "Nüshu shenshao" 女塾甚少 (Girls' schools are too few). *Xuchu nübao* 1 (1902), "Nübao xinwen" column, 3b.

— "Nüxuehui timinglu" 女學會題名錄 (Members of the Women's Study Society). *Xuchu nübao* 2 (1902), "Nübao xinwen" column, 6a.

— "Nüxuetang di-yi kecheng yaojin" 女學堂第一課程要緊 (Curriculum is the most important for girls' schools). *Xuchu nübao* 6 (1902), "Baihua yanshuo" column, 1a–3a.

— "Sibada nüzi" 斯巴達女子 (Spartan women). *Xuchu nübao* 6 (1902), "Weiguo zhengwen lu" column, 1a–b.

— "Xuban *Nübao* shili" 續辦《女報》事例 (Models for the continuation of *Women's Journal*). Originally published in *Subao*. Reprinted in *Shishi caixin huixuan, juan* 3, April 21, 1902. N.p.

— "Yao you aiguo de xin" 要有愛國的心 (We must embrace patriotism). *Xuchu nübao* 3 (1902), "Nübao yanshuo" column, 1a–2b.

— "Zhongguo nüzi zhi qiantu" 中國女子之前途 (The future of Chinese women). *Nü xuebao* 4 (1903), 1–6.

Chen Xiefen [Chunan nüzi 楚南女子]. "Shijie shi nüjie yanyi" 世界十女傑演義 (Tales of ten world heroines). *Nü xuebao* 4 (1903).

Chen Xuezhao 陳學昭. "Gei nanxing" 給男性 (For men). *Xin nüxing* 1:12 (1926), 897–901.

Chen Xuezhao "Lü Fa tongxin" 旅法通信 (Correspondence during travel to France). *Xin nüxing* 2:11 (1927), 1263–67.

— "Xiandai nüzi de kumen wenti: Shi" 現代女子的苦悶問題: 十 (The dilemma of modern women: 10). *Xin nüxing* 2:1 (1927), 35–39.

— "'Xiandai nüzi kumen wenti' de weisheng: Yi" 「現代女子苦悶問題」的尾聲: 一 (Coda to "The dilemma of modern women": 1). *Xin nüxing* 2:3 (1927), 353–56.

Chen Yiyi 陳以益 "Nanzun nübei yu xianmu liangqi" 男尊女卑與賢母良妻 (Respect for men and contempt for women, and [the concept of] worthy mother and good wife). In *Xinhai geming qian shinian jian shilun xuanji*, edited by Zhang Nan and Wang Renzhi, vol. 3, 482–84. Beijing: Sanlian shudian, 1977.

— "Nübaojie zuixin diaochabiao" 女報界最新調查表 (Most updated investigation of periodicals for women). Published in *Shenzhou nübao* 3 (1908), reprinted in *Nülun*, 11–12.

Chen Yiyi [Chen Zhiqun 陳志群]. "*Shenzhou nübao* fakanci" 神州女報發刊詞 (Inaugural statement to the *Shenzhou nübao*). Originally published in *Shenzhou nübao* 1 (1907). Reprinted in *Nülun* 女論 (On women), a special issue of *Nübao* (1909), 9–10.

Chen Yiying 陳以英 of Jiyang 暨陽. "Shuhan wen" 書翰文 ([Open] letter). *FNSB* 6 (1912), 83.

Chen Zhiqun. *See* Chen Yiyi.

Cheng, Eileen. "'In Search of New Voices from Alien Lands': Lu Xun, Cultural Exchange and the Myth of Sino-Japanese Friendship." *Journal of Asian Studies* 73: 3 (2014), 589–618.

Chiang, Yung-chen. "Womanhood, Motherhood and Biology: The Early Phases of *The Ladies' Journal*, 1915–25." *Gender and History* 18: 3 (2006), 519–45.

Chin, Carol C. "Translating the New Woman: Chinese Feminists View the West, 1905–15." *Gender and History* 18: 3 (2006), 490–518.

Chinese National Association for the Advancement of Education. "Bulletins on Chinese Education" (Yingwen Zhongguo zuijin jiaoyu zhuangkuang 英文中國最近教育狀況), 1923. Shanghai: The Commercial Press, Rpt. 1925, 1–36.

Chow, Rey. *Woman and Chinese Modernity: The Politics of Reading between West and East*. Minneapolis: University of Minnesota Press, 1991.

Christmann, Barbara and Margarete Leppert. "Das Bild der Frau in den deutschen Frauenzeitschriften: Analyse und Bewertung bestehender Leitbilder anhand ausgewählter Zeitschriften." Thesis, Oldenburg Pädagogische Hochschule, 1973.

Chu Guoqing 初國卿. "Zhongguo jinxiandai nüxing qikan shulüe" 中國近現代女性期刊述略 (A brief introduction to modern Chinese women's journals). Preface to *Zhongguo jinxiandai nüxing qikan hubian*. Beijing: Xianzhuang shuju, 2006.

Chu Hui 儲禈. "Jiating tushushi wenti" 家庭圖書室問題 (The issue of the home library). *FNZZ* 13: 7 (1927), 57–64 [133–40].

Chu Qizhen 褚琦珍. "Jiating jiaoyu yu nüzi jiaoyuzhi guanxi" 家庭教育與女子教育之關系 (The relationship between home education and women's education). *FNSB* 3 (1911), 12–14 [40–42].

"Chuangban Zhongguo nübao zhi caozhang ji yizhi guanggao" 創辦中國女報之草章及意旨廣告 (Notice concerning the draft charter and intent of *Chinese Women's News*). In *Qiu Jin xianlie wenji*, edited by Zhongguo guomindang zhongyang weiyuanhui dangshi weiyuanhui 中國國民黨中央委員會黨史委員會, 147–48. Taibei: Zhongyang wenwu gongyingshe, 1982.

"Chuangshe wanguo hongshizi kanhufu duizhe Naitingge'er furen zhuan" 創設萬國紅十字看護婦隊者奈挺格爾夫人傳 (Biography of Florence Nightingale, founder of the Red Cross women nurses team). *Zhongguo xin nüjie zazhi* 1 (1907) and 2 (1907).

Chunan nüzi. *See* Chen Xiefen.

Chunnong. *See* Wang Yunzhang.

Cixous, Hélène. "The Laugh of the Medusa." *Signs* 1: 4 (1976), 875–93.

Clark, Caroline. "*Ms. Magazine*: An Ideological Vehicle in a Consumer Setting." Dissertation, McGill University, 1994.

Cooke, Nathalie, and Jennifer Garland. "Putting Questions to Images: The *Chatelaine* Project." *VRA Bulletin* 35: 2 (2008), 86–93.

Cross, Gary. *An All-Consuming Century: Why Commercialism Won in North America*. New York: Columbia University Press, 2000.

"Da shi ji" (Records of main events). *Jiaoyu zazhi* 7: 3 (1915), 19.

Dai Qiu 待秋. "Xinjiu de chongtu" 新舊的衝突 (The conflicts between the new and the old). *FNZZ* 9: 4 (1923), 24–30.

Dan Yuan 淡圜. "Mujiao de shili" 母教的勢力 (The power of maternal teaching). *FNZZ* 14: 10 (1928), 8–14 [26–32].

David, Elise J. "Making Visible Feminine Modernities: The Traditionalist Paintings and Modern Methods of Wu Shujuan." MA thesis, Ohio State University, 2012.

Daxia 大俠. "Nü cike Shalutu Ge'erdie zhuan" 女刺客沙魯土・格兒垤傳 (Biography of female assassin Charlotte Corday), *Nüzi shijie* 2 (1905).

Deng Tianyu 鄧天喬. "Wo xiang de hunzu" 我鄉的婚俗 (The marital custom of my hometown). *Xin nüxing* 1: 6 (1926), 445–50.

Dethier, Kathryn "The Spirit of Progressive Reform: The *Ladies' Home Journal* House Plans 1900–1902." *Journal of Design History* 6: 4 (1993), 229–45.

DiCenzo, Maria, Lucy Delap, and Leila Ryan. *Feminist Media History: Suffrage Periodicals and the Public Sphere*. New York: Palgrave Macmillan, 2011.

Dikötter, Frank. *Things Modern: Material Culture and Everyday Life in China*. London: Hurst, 2007.

(Ding) Chuwo [丁] 初我. "Ai nüzhong" 哀女種 (Lament for womankind). *Nüzi shijie* 6 (1906).

— "Furenjie zhi shuangbi: xingchang zhi baijin" 婦人界之双雙璧: 刑場之白菫 (Double jade piece in the world of women: The white flowers of the execution field). *Nüzi shijie* 12 (1904), 15–19.

— "Nü wenhao Haili'aide Feiqushi zhuan" 女文豪海麗愛德・斐曲士傳. (Biography of the great female writer Harriet Beecher). *Nüzi shijie* 1 (1905).

— "Nüquan shuo" 女權說 (On women's rights). *Nüzi shijie* 5 (1904).

— "Nüzi shijie songci" 女子世界頌詞 (Ode to women's world). *Nüzi shijie* 1 (1904).

— "Shuo nümo" 說女魔 (On the she-devil). *Nüzi shijie* 2 (1904).

Ding Shouhe 丁守和 (ed.). *Xinhai geming shiqi qikan jieshao* 辛亥革命時期期刊介紹 (Introduction to journals of the 1911 revolution period). 5 vols. Beijing: Renmin chubanshe, 1982.

Ding Xilun 丁錫綸. "Dui ertong wanju de yijian" 對兒童玩具的意見 (Suggestions concerning children's toys). *FNZZ* 6: 5 (1920), 14–18 [82–86].

Dongyuan 東原. "Du qianhao" 讀前號 (Reading the previous issue). *FNZZ* 9: 6 (1923), 123.

Dooling, Amy D. "Revolution in Reading and Writing: Women, Texts, and the Late Qing Feminist Imagination." Unpublished manuscript.

"Dou'an shi yangsheng lingyao/zhiyu jingbi xueku zhi zheng/qingxue buxue zhi-liangyao" 兜安氏養生靈藥/治癒經閉血枯之症/清血補血之良藥 (Doan's Elixir of Life/for curing blocked menses dried blood/a great medicine for anemia). *FNSB* 7 (1912).

Drège, Jean-Pierre. *La Commercial Press de Shanghai 1897–1949*. Paris: Institut des hautes etudes chinoises, 1978.

Du Jikun 杜繼琨. "Zai tan *Nü xuebao*" 再談女學報 (More about the *Chinese Girl's Progress*). *Tushuguan* 4 (1963), 55–56.

Du Qingchi 杜清池. "Guangdong Yifeng nü xuexiao xuyuan" 廣東移風女學校序言 (Preface to the Guangdong Transformation Girl's School). *Xuchu nübao* 6 (1902), "Nübao lunshuo" column, 1a–2b.

Duara, Prasenjit. "Asia Redux: Conceptualising a Region for Our Times." *Journal of Asian Studies* 69: 4 (2010), 963–83.

East Asian Publishing and Society. www.brill.com/publications/journals/east-asian-publishing-and-society.

Edwards, Louise. "Strategizing for Politics: Chinese Women's Participation in the One-Party State." *Women's Studies International Forum* 30: 5 (2007), 380–90.

— "The Shanghai Modern Woman's American Dreams: Imagining America's Depravity to Produce China's 'Moderate Modernity.'" *Pacific Historical Review* 81: 4 (2012), 567–601.

Elliot, Bridget, and Jo-Ann Wallace. *Women Artists and Writers: Modernist (Im) Positionings.* New York: Routledge, 1994.

Endres, Kathleen L. *Women's Periodicals in the United States: Consumer Magazines.* Westport, CT: Greenwood, 1995.

Enstad, Nan. *Ladies of Labor, Girls of Adventure: Working Women, Popular Culture, Everyday Lives and Labor Politics at the Turn of the Twentieth Century.* New York: Columbia University Press, 1999.

Eskridge, Melissa J. *How the Psychology of Women Is Presented in Women's Magazines: An Examination of Selected Articles from Ms., Cosmopolitan, Seventeen, Ladies' Home Journal, and Working Woman.* Thesis (M.S.), University of Tennessee, Knoxville, 1986.

Evans, Harriet. *The Subject of Gender: Daughters and Mothers in Urban China.* Lanham: Rowman and Littlefield, 2008.

"Fakanci" 發刊辭 (Inaugural essay). *FNSB* 1 (1911), 1.

Fan Beiqiang 范北強. "Nantong nüzi shifan gaishu" 南通女子師範概述 (An overview of Nantong women teachers' school). *Wenshi ziliao xuanji* 2 (1982), 93–100.

Fan Yao Yunsu 范姚蘊素. "Bu Chunqi he Shizeng daowang yuanyun" 步春綺和師曾悼亡原韻 (Following the original rhymes of the elegies by [Wang] Chunqi and [Chen] Shizeng). *ZHFNJ* 2: 5 (1916).

— "Chou Lü Huiru nü xiaozhang" 酬呂惠如女校長 (A return gift to the female principal Lü Huiru). *ZHFNJ* 1: 6 (1915), "Wenyi" column.

— "Die yun jihuai Zhonghou" 疊韻寄懷仲厚 (A vowel rhyme, in longing for Zhonghou). *ZHFNJ* 1: 12 (1915).

— "He Lü Huiru luohua shi yuanyun" 和呂惠如落花詩原韻 (Matching the original rhymes of Lü Huiru's poem about falling blossoms). *ZHFNJ* 1: 9 (1915), "Wenyi" column.

— "He Mengwei" 和孟微 (He Mengwei). *ZHFNJ* 2: 4 (1916).

— "He Yi Mengwei jihuai yuanyun" 和易孟微寄懷原韻 (Matching the rhymes of Yi Mengwei's [poems of] longing). *ZHFNJ* 1: 11 (1915).

— "Jihuai Yi Zhonghou Changsha" 寄懷易仲厚長沙 (Longing for Yi Zhonghou and Changsha). *ZHFNJ* 2: 5 (1916).

— "Lü Huiru xiaozhang jieyou qingliang shan deng saoye lou he qi tibi yuanyun yi zeng" 呂惠如校長偕遊清涼山登掃葉樓和其題壁原韻以贈 (Principal Lü Huiru accompanied me to Mount Qingliang to climb the Saoye Tower. I gifted her this poem which matches the rhymes of the wall inscription). *ZHFNJ* 2: 5 (1916).

__ "Taijiao" 胎教 (Prenatal education). *ZHFNJ* 1:6 (1915).

__ "Wen Zhonghou shu qi zhinü Mengwei zhi congying xi weide xiangjian jin yu qi antou deyue laishu yuan cong wu you du qi shi qingfen manzhi xi er ci qianyun jizeng" 聞仲厚述其姪女孟微之聰穎惜未得相見今於其案頭得閱來書願從吾遊讀其詩清芬滿紙喜而次前韻寄贈 (Upon hearing Zhonghou describe her niece's cleverness I regretted not having met her. Today on her table I saw a letter from her expressing her wish to associate with me. Her poems were full of purity and grace. Rejoicing, I followed her rhyme and gifted her this poem). *ZHFNJ* 1: 10 (1915).

__ "Yong bai hehua he Ye Mengqing hong hehua yuanyun" 詠白荷華和葉孟青紅荷華原韻 (Using a white lotus flower to match the original rhymes of Ye Mengqing's red lotus flower). *ZHFNJ* 1: 8 (1915).

__ "Yong Liangdang xuan zengyou yun ji Zhonghou" 用兩當軒贈友韻寄仲厚 (For Zhonghou, using the rhymes from the poems to friends in the Liangdang pavilion [collection]). *ZHFNJ* 1: 12 (1915).

__ "Zeng Wu Zhiying nushi" 贈吳芝瑛女士 (For Ms. Wu Zhiying). *ZHFNJ* 1: 6 (1915), "Wenyi" column.

__ "Zeng Yi Zhonghou gui Longyang xu" 贈易仲厚歸龍陽序 (Preface to "Seeing off Yi Zhonghou who is returning to Longyang"). *ZHFNJ* 1: 6 (1915).

__ "Zengbie Yi Mengwei" 贈別易孟微 (A parting gift to Yi Mengwei). *ZHFNJ* 2: 2 (1916).

__ "Zhiyan liubie zhusheng" 質言留別諸生 (Some truthful words as a departing gift to all the students). *ZHFNJ* 2: 6 (1916).

Fang Zong 方綜. "Heping youyi xinfu de lu" 和平友谊新福的路 (The road of peace, freedom and happiness). *Zhongguo funü* 2 (1956), 12–13.

Farquhar, Mary Ann. *Children's Literature in China: From Lu Xun to Mao Zedong.* Armonk, NY/London: M. E. Sharpe, 1999.

Fei Zhi 非指. "Mengtaisuoli jiaoyu fa shiyi" 蒙台梭利教育法釋義 (Explanation of the Montessori method of education). *FNZJ* 1: 4 (1915), 1–4 [113–16].

"Feilübin fengsu lüeshu" 菲律賓風俗略述 (Brief account of Philippine customs). *FNZZ* 7: 11 (1921), 91.

Feng, Jin. "'Addicted to Beauty': Consuming and Producing Web-based Chinese *Danmei* Fiction at Jinjiang." *Modern Chinese Literature and Culture* 21: 2 (2009), 1–41.

Feng Xiqing 封熙卿. "Feizhou jiehun qisu" 非洲結婚奇俗 (Strange marriage customs in Africa). *FNZZ* 7: 5 (1921), 65–67.

Feng Yuehua 馮月華. *Jiangsu funü yundong shi* 江蘇婦女運動史 (A history of the women's movement in Jiangsu). Beijing: Zhongguo funü chubanshe, 1995.

Fengzi 鳳子. "Lian'ai ziyou jie xupian: zai da YD xiansheng bing da Wang Pingling Zhang Xichen er wei xiangsheng guanyu lian'ai wenti de taolun" 戀愛自由解續篇——再答YD先生并答王平陵章錫琛二位先生關於戀愛問題的討論 (Sequel of discussion on freedom to love: Further response to Mr. YD and to Mr. Wang Pingling and Zhang Xichen's discussion on the issue of romantic love). *FNZZ* 9: 2 (1923), 43–45.

__ "Lian'ai ziyou jieda kewen di-yi" 戀愛自由解答客問第一 (Q & A on freedom to love: I). *FNZZ* 8: 8 (1922), 17–18.

__ "Lian'ai ziyou jieda kewen di-er" 戀愛自由解答客問第二 (Q & A on freedom to love: II). *FNZZ* 8: 8 (1922), 18–19.

— "Lian'ai ziyou jieda kewen di-san" 戀愛自由解答客問第三 (Q & A on freedom to love: III) *FNZZ* 8: 8 (1922), 19.

— "Lian'ai ziyou jieda kewen di-si" 戀愛自由解答客問第四 (Q & A on freedom to love: IV). *FNZZ* 9: 2 (1923), 40–41.

— "Nanyang tongxin: Nanyang huaqiao taolun lihun wenti de yimu" 南洋通信——南洋華僑討論離婚問題的一幕 (Correspondence from Southeast Asia: One facet of the discussions over divorce by Southeast Asian overseas Chinese). *Xin nüxing* 1: 1 (1926), 59–65.

— "Nüzi jiefang yu nüzi jiaoyu" 女子解放與女子教育 (Woman's liberation and women's education). *FNZZ* 10: 11 (1924), 1662–75.

— "Songxing" 送行 (Seeing someone off). *FNZZ* 11: 2 (1925).

— "Wo de lihun" 我的離婚 (My divorce). *FNZZ* 8: 4 (1922), 143–45.

— "Yige fengzi," 一個瘋子 (A lunatic). *FNZZ* 10: 12 (1924).

Fernsebner, Susan R. "A People's Playthings: Toys, Childhood, and Chinese Identity, 1909–1933." *Postcolonial Studies* 6: 3 (2003), 269–93.

— "Objects, Spectacle, and a Nation on Display at the Nanyang Exposition of 1910." *Late Imperial China* 27: 2 (2006), 99–124.

Fetterley, Judith. *The Resistant Reader: A Feminist Approach to American Fiction.* Bloomington: Indiana University Press, 1978.

Fong, Grace S. "Writing Self and and Writing Lives: Shen Shanbao's (1808–1862) Gendered Autobiographical Practices." *Nan Nü* 2: 2 (2000), 259–303.

Fraser, Hilary, Stephanie Green, and Judith Johnston. *Gender and the Victorian Periodical.* Cambridge: Cambridge University Press, 2003.

Frith, Katherine Toland. "Portrayals of Women in Global Women's Magazines in China." In *Mediasia: Global Media/tion in and out of Context*, edited by Todd Joseph Miles Holden, 149–69. London: Routledge, 2006.

Frodsham, J.D., trans. *The First Chinese Embassy to the West: The Journals of Kuo Sung-t'ao, Liu Hsi-hung and Chang Te-yi.* Oxford: Clarendon Press, 1978.

Fu Yanzhang 傅嚴長. "Riben de funü" 日本的婦女 (Japanese women). *Xin funü* 1: 5 (1920), 39–41.

Fujo shinbun o yomu kai '婦女新聞' お読む会 (ed.). *Fujo shinbun' to josei no kindai* 婦女新聞'と女性の近代 (Women's modernity and Fujo shinbun). Tokyo: Fuji Shuppan, 1997.

"Fumei'er nü jindan xinchu pin" 福美爾女金丹新出品 (New product: Fumeier pills for women). *FNSB* 18 (1916) and 19 (1916), front matter.

"Funü wenti yanjiuhui wei *Xin nüxing* feikan qishi" 婦女問題研究會為新女性廢刊啟事 (Announcement of the termination of *Xin nüxing* by the Association for Women's Issues). *Xin nüxing* 4:12 (1929).

"Funü yu zhiyan" 婦女與紙煙 (Women and cigarettes). *FNSB* 1 (1911), 81–82.

"Funü zazhi fakanci yi" 婦女雜誌發刊辭一 (Inaugural essay of *The Ladies' Journal* 1). *FNZZ* 1.1 (1915), 1–2.

Funü zazhi yanjiu zhuanhao 婦女雜誌研究轉好 (Special Issue on *Funü zazhi*). *Jindai Zhongguo funhuanhao enti* 近代中國婦女史研究 12 (2004).

Furth, Charlotte. *A Flourishing Yin: Gender in China's Medical History, 960–1665.* Berkeley: University of California Press, 1999.

Gao Jianhua 高劍華. "Luoti meiren yu" 裸體美人語 (The words of the nude beauty). *Meiyu* 1: 4 (1915), *Duanpian xiaoshuo* section, 1–6.

Gao Junyin 高竣尹. "Lun nüxuexiao dang zhuzhang jiashi ke" 論女學校當主張家事科 (Girls' schools should emphasize courses in domestic science). *Zhonghua jiaoyujie* 1: 3 (1913), 42–44.

Gao Shan 高山 [Zhou Jianren 周建人]. "Zhencao guannian de gaizao" 貞操觀念的改造 (Reforming views on chastity). *FNZZ* 8: 12 (1922), 2–5.

Gao Weixiang 高維祥. "*Sheying huabao* he sheying tongzhi" 攝影畫報和攝影同志 (*Pictorial Weekly* and photographic amateurs). *Sheying huabao* 6: 300 (1931), 400.

Gao, Yunxiang. "Nationalist and Feminist Discourses on *Jianmei* (Robust Beauty) during China's 'National Crisis' in the 1930s." *Gender and History* 18: 3 (2006), 546–73.

Gerth, Karl. *China Made: Consumer Culture and the Creation of the Nation.* Cambridge, MA: Harvard University Asia Center, 2004.

Gilmartin, Christina Kelley. *Engendering the Chinese Revolution: Radical Women, Communist Politics, and Mass Movements in the 1920s.* Berkeley: University of California Press, 1995.

Gimpel, Denise. *Lost Voices of Modernity: A Chinese Popular Fiction Magazine in Context.* Honolulu: University of Hawai'i Press, 2001.

Gladney, Dru. "Representing Nationality in China: Refiguring Majority/Minority Identities." *Journal of Asian Studies* 63: 1 (1994), 92–123.

Glosser, Susan L. *Chinese Visions of Family and the State.* Berkeley: University of California Press, 2003.

Gong Min 龔敏. "Fan Dangshi yu Chen Sanli de wenxue jiaowang" 范當世與陳三立的文學交往 (The literary contact between Fan Dangshi and Chen Sanli). *Gudian wenxue zhishi* 3 (2009), 75–80.

Gough-Yates, Anna. *Understanding Women's Magazines: Publishing, Markets and Readerships.* London: Routledge, 2003.

Graham, A. C. *Disputers of the Tao: Philosophical Argument in Ancient China.* La Salle, IL: Open Court, 1989.

Gu'an. *See* Xu Nianci.

Gu Yanling 顧燕翎 (ed.). *Nüxingzhuyi lilun yu liupai* 女性主義理論與流派 (Feminist theories and schools). Taibei: Nüshu wenhua gongsi, 2001.

"Guanggao: Shuaxin neirong jiandi jiage" 廣告: 刷新內容減低價格 (Advertisement: Content refreshed and price lowered). *FNZZ* 7:5 (1921).

Hagedorn, Nancy L. "'A Friend to Go between Them': The Interpreter as Cultural Broker during Anglo-Iroquois Councils, 1740–70." *Ethnohistory* 35: 1 (1988), 60–80.

Hansheng 漢聲 (Voice of the Han [Continuation of *Hubei xuesheng jie*]), Tokyo, June–July 1903. Rpt. Taibei: Zhongguo Guomindang, Zhongyang weiyuan hui, Dangshi shiliao bianzuan weiyuan hui 中國國民黨, 中央委員會, 黨史料編纂委員會, 1968.

Harada Minoru 原田實. "Chang muxing zunzhong lun de Ailunkai nüshi weisheme dushen" 唱母性尊重論的愛倫凱女士為什麼獨身 (Why Ellen Key, the promoter of protection of motherhood, remained single). Translated by You Tong 幼彤. *FNZZ* 8: 10 (1922), 12–15.

Harrell, Paula. *Sowing the Seeds of Change: Chinese Students, Japanese Teachers, 1895–1905.* Stanford, CA: Stanford University Press, 1992.

He Xiangning 何香凝. "Guomin geming shi funü weiyi de shenglu" 國民革命是婦女唯一的生路 (National revolution is the only life road for women). In *Shuangqing wenji 2*, edited by Shang Mingxuan and Yu Yanguang, 35–37. Beijing: Renmin chubanshe, 1985.

He Zhen 何震 and Liu Shipei 劉師培. "Lun zhongzu geming yu wuzhengfu geming zhi deshi" 論種族革命與無政府革命之得失 (On the pros and cons of racial revolution and anarchist revolution). In *Xinhai geming qian shinian jian shilun xuanji*, edited by Zhang Nan and Wang Renzhi, vol. 2.2, 947–59. Beijing: Sanlian shudian, 1963.

Helin 鶴林. "Lixiang de zhuzhai: yishuhua de leyuan" 理想的住宅: 藝術化的樂園 (The ideal dwelling: An artistic paradise). *FNZZ* 12: 11 (1926), 37–39.

Hermes, Joke. *Reading Women's Magazines: An Analysis of Everyday Media Use*. London: Polity Press, 1995.

Hill, Michael. "No True Men in the State: Pseudo/translation and 'Feminine' Voice in the Late Qing." *Journal of Modern Literature in Chinese* 10: 2 (2011), 125–48.

Ho, Clara Wing-chung [Liu Yongcong], ed. *Biographical Dictionary of Chinese Women: The Qing Period, 1644–1911*. Armonk, NY: M. E. Sharpe, 1998.

Hockx, Michel. *Questions of Style: Literary Societies and Literary Journals in Modern China, 1911–1937*. Leiden: Brill, 2003.

Hockx, Michel and Liying Sun. "Women and Scandal in Early Modern Chinese Literature: The Journal *Meiyu* (Eyebrow Talk, 1914–1916)." Public lecture. SOAS, University of London, March 9, 2010.

Hodgson, Dorothy (ed.). *Gendered Modernities: Ethnographic Perspectives*. New York: Palgrave, 2001.

Hong Jingfang 洪競芳. "Wo jiang zenmeyang zuo fumuqin: jiu jiating zhong de jingyan tan" 我將怎麼樣作父/母親: 舊家庭中的經驗談 (The kind of father/mother I want to be: About my experiences of the old style family). *FNZZ* 11:11 (1925), 1737–40 [63–66].

Hong Jun 洪鈞. "Duan bitou zhi xu" 短筆頭之續 (Sequel to short pen). *Xin nüxing* 4:2 (1929), 626–27.

Honma Hisao 本间久雄. "Xing de daode de xin qingxiang" 性的道德底新傾向 (The new tendency of sexual morality), translated by Selu 瑟廬. *FNZZ* 6: 11 (1920), 1–10.

hooks, bell. *Talking Back: Thinking Feminist, Thinking Black*. Boston: South End Press, 1989.

Howland, Douglas R. *Translating the West: Language and Political Reason in Nineteenth-Century Japan*. Honolulu: University of Hawaii Press, 2002.

Hu Binxia 彬夏. "Hezhe wei wu funü jinhou wushinian nei zhi zhiwu" 何者為吾婦女今後五十年內之職務 (What should be women's tasks in our country over the next fifty years?). *FNZZ* 2: 6 (1916), *sheshuo*: 1–5.

— "Meiguo jiating" 美國家庭 (American households). *FNZZ* 2: 2 (1916), *sheshuo*: 1–8.

Hu Shi 胡適. "Zhencao wenti" 貞操問題 (The issue of chastity). *Xin qingnian* 5: 1 (1918), 5–14.

Hu, Siao-chen. "The Construction of Gender and Genre in the 1910s New Media: Evidence from the Ladies' Journal." In *Different Worlds of Discourse: Transformations of Gender and Genre in Late Qing and Early Republican China*, edited by Nanxiu Qian and Richard Smith, 349–82. Leiden: Brill, 2008.

Hu, Siao-chen [Hu Xiaozhen 胡曉真]. *Xin lixiang, jiu tili, yu buke siyi zhi she-hui* 新理想、舊體例與不可思議之社會 (New ideas, old rules, and an unimaginable society). Taipei: Institute of Chinese Literature and Philosophy, Academica Sinica, 2011.

__ "Xingtan yu wentan: Qing-mo minchu nüxing zai chuantong yu xiandai jueze qingjing xia de jiaoyu yu wenxue zhiye" 杏壇與文壇——清末民初女性在傳統與現代抉擇情境下的教育與文學志業 (Lecterns and letters: Late Qing and early Republican women's educational and literary careers in the face of the choice between tradition and modernity). *Jindai Zhongguo funüshi yanjiu* 15 (2007), 35–75.

Hu Wanchuan 胡萬川. *Huaben yu caizi jiaren xiaoshuo zhi yanjiu* 話本與才子佳人小說之研究 (A study of *huaben* fiction and scholar–beauty romances). Taibei: Da'an chubanshe, 1994.

Hu Wenkai 胡文楷 and Zhang Hongsheng 張宏生 (eds.). *Lidai funü zhuzuokao (zengdingben)* 歷代婦女著作考 (增訂本) (Survey of women's works through the ages [revised edition]). Shanghai: Shanghai guji chubanshe, 2008.

Hu Xiaozhen. *See* Hu, Siao-chen.

Hu, Ying. *Burying Autumn: Death, Poetry and Friendship*. Cambridge, MA: Harvard University Asia Center, 2016.

__ "Naming the First 'New Woman.'" In *Rethinking the 1898 Reform Period: Political and Cultural Change in Late Qing China*, edited by Rebecca E. Karl and Peter Zarrow, 180–211. Cambridge, MA: Harvard University Asia Center, 2002.

__ "Reconfiguring *Nei/Wai*: Writing the Woman Traveller in the Late Qing." *Late Imperial China* 18: 1 (1997), 72–99.

__ *Tales of Translation: Composing the New Woman in China, 1899–1918*. Stanford, CA: Stanford University Press, 2000.

Hu Yingjian 胡迎建. *Minguo jiutishi shigao* 民国旧体诗史稿 (Draft history of classical-style poetry in the Republican period). Nanchang: Jiangxi renmin chubanshe, 2005.

Huang Fuqing [Huang Fu-ch'ing] 黃福慶. *Qingmo liu-Ri xuesheng* 清末留日學生 (translated by Katherine P.K. Whitaker as *Chinese Students in Japan in the Late Qing Period*). Taipei: Zhongyang yanjiu yuan, jindaishi yanjiu suo, 1975.

Huang Haitao 黃海濤 [Calvin H. T. Wong]. "Biefa yanghang kao: Jianlun jindai Zhongguo zhishifenzi yu Biefa yanghang" 別發洋行考: 兼論近代中國知識份子與別發洋行 (Kelly & Walsh and its relation with the Chinese intellectuals in modern China). In *Jiuxue xinzhi ji: Xianggang chengshi daxue Zhongguo wenhua zhongxin shizhounian lunwen ji*, edited by Zheng Peikai [Cheng Pei-kai] and Fan Jiawei [Fan Ka Wai], 213–55. Guilin: Guangxi Normal University Press, 2008.

Huang Jinzhu 黃錦珠 [Jin-Chu Huang]. *Nüxing shuxie de duoyuan chengxian: Qingmo Min-chu nü zuojia xiaoshuo yanjiu* 女性書寫的多元呈現: 清末民初女作家小說研究 (The multiple appearances of women's writing: Fiction by women writers of the late Qing and early Republic). Taibei: Liren shuju, 2014.

(Huang) Shouqu (黃) 守蕖, "Wuben nüxuetang keyi, du *Nübao* shuhou" 務本女學堂課藝.讀〈女報〉書後 (The curriculum at the Wuben Girls School, after reading the notice in *Nübao*). *Nübao* 7 (1902).

Huang Yi Yu 黃易瑜. "Ji Fan Yunsu Tongzhou shi fang de qi shoushu" 寄范蘊素通州時方得其手書 (Sent to Fan Yunsu, having received her letter only in Tongzhou). *FNZZ* 1: 9 (1915), "Wenyuan" column.

Hubei xuesheng jie 湖北學生界 (Students of Hubei), Tokyo, January 29, 1903–May 27, 1903. Rpt. Zhongguo guomindang, Zhongyang weiyuan hui, Dangshi shiliao bianzuan weiyuan hui 中國國民黨, 中央委員會, 黨史史料編纂委員會, 1968.

Hui 慧. "Nüzi canzheng yundong zhi zuijin shiwu nian shi" 女子參政運動之最近十五年史 (History of women's suffrage movements in the past fifteen years). *FNSB* 17 (1915), 5–14.

Hunt, Lynn. "Introduction: Obscenity and the Origins of Modernity, 1500–1800." In *The Invention of Pornography: Obscenity and the Origins of Modernity, 1500–1800*, edited by Lynn Hunt, 9–46. New York: Zone Books, 1996.

Hüntemann, Mechthild. "Der schöne Schein in der Massenkommunikation: Über Intention und Funktion von Frauenzeitschriften." Diploma thesis, Marburg University, 1976.

Idema, Wilt and Beata Grant. *The Red Brush: Writing Women of Imperial China*. Cambridge, MA: Harvard University Asia Center, 2004.

Ip, Manying. "A Hidden Chapter in Early Sino-Japanese Cooperation: The Commercial Press–Kinkôdô Partnership, 1903–1914." Sophia University Repository for Academic Resources (1986-01), 23–44. Available at http://jairo.nii.ac.jp/0165/00012673/en (accessed Jan. 26, 2013).

Iwasaki Sodō 岩崎徂堂 and Mikami Kifū 三上寄風 (eds.). *Sekai jūni joketsu* 世界十二女傑 (Twelve world heroines). Tokyo: Kōbundō shoten, 1902.

Iwasaki Sodō and Mikami Kifū. "Shaarotto Korudei jō" 沙鲁土·格尔垤嬢 (Ms. Charlotte Corday). In *Sekai jūni joketsu*, edited by Iwasaki Sodō and Mikami Kifū, 6. Tokyo: Kōbundō shoten, 1902.

Iwasaki Sodō and Mikami Kifū (eds.). *Shijie shi'er nüjie* 世界十二女傑 (Twelve world heroines). Translated by Zhao Bizhen 趙必振. Shanghai: Guangzhi shuju, 1903.

"Japanese Folk Medicines." *The British Medical Journal* 2: 2429 (1907), 165.

Jeffreys, Sheila. *The Spinster and Her Enemies: Feminism and Sexuality 1880–1930*. London: Pandora Press, 1985.

Ji Wei 季威. "Puji jiaoyu yu nüzi jiaoyu" 普及教育與女子教育 (Universal education and women's education). *Shenzhou nübao* 2: 5 (1913).

Jia Shumei 贾树枚 (ed.). *Shanghai xinwen zhi* 上海新闻志 (Record of the Shanghai press). Shanghai: Shanghai shehui kexue yuan chubanshe, 2000.

"Jia you juwan zhi fu/baoyang ziji jiankang/fuke liangyao Zhongjiangtang" 家有巨萬之富/保養自己健康/婦科靈藥中將湯 (Wealthy families, take care of (your) health/A magical elixir for gynecological problems, Chûjôtô Tsumura). *FNSB* 7 (1912).

Jiang Danshu 姜丹書. "Yishu niannian hualiangtou" 藝術廿年話兩頭 (A dialogue on art over a period of twenty years). *Yaboluo* [Apollo] 6 (1929), 94–96.

Jiang Guancha Guanyun. *See* Jiang Zhiyou.

Jiang Jinzhi 姜金枝. "Kexue dabaile chanfugui" 科学打败了产妇鬼 (Science defeats the midwife devil). *Nongjianü baishitong* 2 (1996), 56.

Jiang Renlan 江紉蘭. "Lun funü zuixin Xifa yi you jiezhi" 論婦女醉心西法宜有節制 (Women should curb their infatuation with Western ways of doing things). *FNSB* 3 (1911), 13–16.

— "Shuo nüzi canzheng zhi liyou" 說女子參政之理由 (On the reasons for women's suffrage). *FNSB* 8 (1912), 1–6.

Jiang Weiqiao 蔣維喬. "Lun nüxuexiao zhi jiashi shixi" 論女學校之家事實習 (On the concrete practice of domestic science in girls' schools). *Jiaoyu zazhi* 9:6 (1917), 105–11.

Jiang Xingde 蔣星德. "Wei xin zhufu suo dang wei" 為新主婦所當為 (What the new housewife should do). *FNZZ* 14: 12 (1928), 13–19 [31–37].

Jiang Xuehui 江學煇. "Yindu nüjie jinwen" 印度女界近聞 (Recent news on the world of Indian women). *FNZZ* 4: 5 (1918), *jishu*: 4–6.

Jiang Yan 蔣燊. "Ertong benwei yu minben zhuyi" 兒童本位與民本主義 (Child-centeredness and democracy). *FNZZ* 12: 8 (1926), 2–5.

Jiang Zhiyou 蔣智由. "Aiguo nüxuexiao yanshuo" 愛國女學校演説 (Speech at [the opening ceremony of] the Patriotic Girls' School). *Xuchu nübao* 9 (1902), 1a–4b.

Jiang Zhiyou 蔣智由 [Jiang Guancha Guanyun 蔣觀察觀雲 (Censor Jiang Guanyun)]. "Diyi ci Nüxuehui yanshuo" 第一次女學會演説 (Speech at the first meeting of the Women's Learned Society). *Xuchu nübao* 2 (1902). "Nüxuehui yanshuo" column, 2a–4a.

Jiangsu 江蘇 (Jiangsu journal). Tokyo, April 27, 1903–May 15, 1904. Rpt. Taibei: Zhongguo Guomindang, Zhongyang weiyuan hui, Dangshi shiliao bianzuan weiyuan hui 中國國民黨, 中央委員會, 黨史史料編纂委員會, 1968.

Jiaoxin 蕉心. "Nüzi dang you putong yixue zhishi" 女子當有普通醫學知識 (Women should have basic medical knowledge). *FNSB* 15 (1914), 3–5.

Jiezi 介子. "Nüzimen shuo" 女子們說 (Women said). *Xin nüxing* 4: 5 (1929), 623–25.

— "'Nanzimen shuo' yu 'Nüzimen shuo'" 「男子們說」與「女子們說」 ("Men said" and "women said"). *Xin nüxing* 4: 8 (1929), 1085–88.

Jin Jungwon 陳姃湲. "*Funü zazhi* (1915–1931) shiqi nian jianshi: *Funü zazhi* heyi mingwei funü 《婦女雜誌》 (1915–1931) 十七年簡史 – –《婦女雜誌》何以名為婦女 (Of the women, by the women, or for the women? – Rewriting a brief history of the seventeen-year run of the *Ladies' Journal*, 1915–1931). *Jindai Zhongguo funüshi yanjiu* 12 (2004), 1–36.

Jin Yi 金一. "*Nüzi shijie* fakanci 《女子世界》發刊詞 (*Women's world* inaugural statement). *Nüzi shijie* 1 (1904).

Jindai Zhongguo funü shi yanjiu 近代中國婦女史研究 12 (2004) (Special Issue on *Funü zazhi*).

Jing Fang nüshi 精芳女士. "*Mosuolini furen*" 莫索里尼夫人 (Mussolini's wife). *Linglong* 225 (1936), 466–72.

Jing Hua 競華. "Ertong jiaoyu hua" 兒童教育話 (Speaking about educating children). *Nüzi shijie* 2: 4–5 (1905/6), 27–30.

Jing Yuanshan 經元善 [Shan Xi longsou 剡溪聾叟 (The Deaf Old Man from the Shan Stream)]. "Diyi ci Nüxuehui yanshuo" 第一次女學會演說 (Speech at the first meeting of the Women's Learned Society). *Xuchu nübao* 2 (1902), "Nü xuehui yanshuo" column, 1a–2a.

"Jinyao xinwen yi: Jingshi jinshi" 緊要新聞一: 京師近事 (Important news 1: Recent events at the capital). *Shenbao*, July 15, 1911, 6.

Johansson, Perry. "Chinese Women and Consumer Culture: Discourses on Beauty and Identity in Advertising and Women's Magazines 1985–1995." Dissertation, Institute of Oriental Languages, University of Stockholm, 1998.

__ "Consuming the Other: The Fetish of the Western Woman in Chinese Advertising and Popular Culture." *Postcolonial Studies* 2: 3 (1999), 377–88.

__ "White Skin, Large Breasts: Chinese Beauty Product Advertising as Cultural Discourse." *China Information* 13: 2–3 (1998), 59–83.

Jones, Andrew F. *Developmental Fairy Tales: Evolutionary Thinking and Modern Chinese Culture*. Cambridge, MA: Harvard University Press, 2011.

__ "The Child as History in Republican China: A Discourse on Development." *positions: east asia cultures critique* 10: 3 (2002), 695–727.

Judge, Joan. "Between Nei and Wai: Chinese Female Students in Japan in the Early Twentieth Century." In *Gender in Motion: Divisions of Labor and Cultural Change in Late Imperial and Modern China*, edited by Bryna Goodman and Wendy Larson, 121–43. Lanham, MD: Rowman and Littlefield, 2005.

__ "Beyond Nationalism: Gender and the Chinese Student Experience in Japan in the Early 20th Century." In *Wusheng zhi sheng: Jindai Zhongguo de funü yu guojia*, ed. Lo Chui-jung, 359–93. Taipei: Institute for Modern History, Academia Sinica, 2003.

__ "Blended Wish Images: Chinese and Western Exemplars at the Turn of the Twentieth Century." *Nan Nü* 6: 1 (2004), 102–35.

__ "Mediated Imaginings: Biographies of Western Women and Their Japanese Sources in Late Qing China." In *Different Worlds of Discourse: Transformations of Gender and Genre in Late Qing and Early Republican China*, edited by Nanxiu Qian, Grace S. Fong, and Richard J. Smith, 147–66. Leiden: Brill, 2008.

__ "Portraits of Republican Ladies: Materiality and Representation in Early Twentieth Century Chinese Photographs." In *Visualizing China*, ed. Christian Henriot and Wen-hsin Yeh, 131–70. Leiden: Brill, 2013.

__ *Print and Politics: 'Shibao' and the Culture of Reform in Late Qing China*. Stanford, CA: Stanford University Press, 1996.

__ "Reforming the Feminine: Female Literacy and the Legacy of 1898." In *Rethinking the 1898 Reform Period: Political and Cultural Change in Late Qing China*, ed. Rebecca E. Karl and Peter Zarrow, 158–79. Cambridge, MA: Harvard University Asia Center, 2002.

__ *Republican Lens: Gender, Visuality, and Experience in the Early Chinese Periodical Press*. Berkeley: University of California Press, 2015.

__ "Talent, Virtue, and the Nation: Chinese Nationalisms and Female Subjectivities in the Early Twentieth Century." *American Historical Review* 106: 3 (2001), 765–803.

__ "The Fate of the Late Imperial 'Talented Woman': Gender and Historical Change in Early-Twentieth-Century China." In *Gender and Chinese History: Transformative Encounters*, edited by Beverly Bossler, 139–60. Seattle: University of Washington Press, 2015.

__ *The Precious Raft of History: The Past, the West, and the Woman Question in China*. Stanford, CA: Stanford University Press, 2008.

Juewo. *See* Xu Nianci.

Junyue 君月. "Lixiang de zhuzhai: kongzhong louge" 理想的住宅: 空中樓閣 (The ideal dwelling: Castles in the air). *FNZZ* 12: 11 (1926), 42–43.

Kang Tongwei 康同薇. "Nüxue libi shuo" 女學利弊說 (On the advantages and disadvantages of education for women). *Nü xuebao* 7 (September 1898), 2a–3b.

Karl, Rebecca. "Creating Asia: China in the World at the Beginning of the Twentieth Century." *American Historical Review* 103: 4 (1998), 1096–1118.

___ "On Women's Labor: He Zhen, Anarcho-feminism and Twentieth-Century China in the World." *Labrys/Etudes Féministes/Estudos Feministas* 15–16 (2009). www .labrys.net.br/labrys15/china/rebecca.htm.

___ *Staging the World: Chinese Nationalism at the Turn of the Twentieth Century.* Durham, NC: Duke University Press, 2002.

Katō Minryū 加藤眠柳. *Joshi risshi hen* 女子立志編 (On women's self-help). Tokyo: Naigai shuppan kyōkai, 1903.

Ke Huiling 柯惠鈴. "Xingbie yu zhengzhi: jindai Zhongguo geming yundong zhong de funü (1900s–1920s)" 性別與政治: 近代中國革命運動中的婦女 (1900s–1920s) (Gender and politics: Women in the modern Chinese revolutionary movement, 1900s–1920s). Ph.D. dissertation, National Chengchi University, 2004.

Ke San 克三. "Lixiang de zhuzhai: zhongdeng jieji de jihua" 理想的住宅: 中等階級的計劃 (The ideal dwelling: A middle class plan). *FNZZ* 12: 11 (1926), 36–37.

Ke Shi. *See* Zhou Jianren.

"Kehai zhi zaohun" 可駭之早婚 (The shocking custom of early marriage). *Shenzhou nübao* 2 (1913), *zazu*: 53.

Keller, Kathryn Urbanowitz. "Mothers and Work as Represented in Popular American Magazines, 1950–1989." Dissertation, New School for Social Research, 1991.

Key, Ellen. *Ertong de jiaoyu* 兒童的教育 (Children's education), translated by Shen Zemin 沈澤民. Shanghai: Shangwu yinshuguan, 1923.

___ *The Century of the Child.* New York: G. P. Putnam's sons, 1909.

Kindai Nihon shisō shi kenkyūkai 近代日本思想史研究会 (Research group on modern Japanese intellectual history). *Jindai Riben sixiang shi* 近代日本思想史 (Modern Japanese intellectual history), translated by Ma Cai 马采. Beijing: Commercial Press, 1983.

Kinkley, Jeffrey C. "Introduction." In *Surviving the Storm: A Memoir*, by Chen Xuezhao, translated by Ti Hua and Caroline Greene, vii–xxvi. Armonk, NY: East Gate, 1991.

Ko, Dorothy. *Cinderella's Sisters: A Revisionist History of Footbinding.* Berkeley: University of California Press, 2005.

___ *Teachers of the Inner Chambers: Women and Culture in Seventeenth-Century China.* Stanford, CA: Stanford University Press, 1994.

Kong Lingzhi [Kung Ling-Jr] 孔令芝. *Cong Linglong zazhi kan 1930 niandai Shanghai xiandai nüxing xingxiang de suzao* 從《玲瓏》雜誌看1930年代上海現代女性形象的塑造 (The construction of female images in 1930s Shanghai as seen in *Linloon Magazine*). Taibei: Daoxiang chubanshe, 2011.

Kong, Shuyu. *Consuming Literature: Best Sellers and the Commercialization of Literary Production in Contemporary China.* Stanford, CA: Stanford University Press, 2005.

Kong Xiangwo 孔襄我. "Dushen de wojian" 獨身的我見 (My opinion on celibacy). *FNZZ* 8:10 (1922), 9–11.

Korinek, Valerie J. "Roughing it in Suburbia: Reading *Chatelaine* Magazine, 1950–1969." Ph.D. dissertation, University of Toronto, 1996.

Kowallis, Jon E. von. *The Subtle Revolution: Poets of the "Old Schools" during Late Qing and Early Republican China*. Berkeley, CA: Institute of East Asian Studies, 2005.

Kuangfu. *See* Zheng Zhenun.

Kurtz, Joachim. "Messenger of the Sacred Heart: Li Wenyu (1840–1911) and the Jesuit Periodical Press in Late Qing Shanghai." In *From Woodblocks to the Internet: Chinese Publishing and Print Culture in Transition, Circa 1800–2008*, ed. Cynthia Brokaw and Christopher A. Reed, 81–110. Leiden/Boston: Brill, 2010.

Lackner, Michael, and Natascha Vittinghoff, eds. *Mapping Meanings: The Field of New Learning in Late Qing China*. Leiden/Boston: Brill, 2004.

Laing, Ellen Johnston. *Selling Happiness: Calendar Posters and Visual Culture in Early-Twentieth-Century Shanghai*. Honolulu: University of Hawai'i Press, 2004.

Latham, Sean, and Mark S. Morrison. "Introduction." *The Journal of Modern Periodical Studies* 1: 1 (2010), iii–v.

Leary, Patrick. *The Punch Brotherhood: Table Talk and Print Culture in Mid-Victorian Britain*. London: British Library, 2010.

Lee, Haiyan, *Revolution of the Heart: A Genealogy of Love in China, 1900–1950*. Stanford, CA: Stanford University Press, 2007.

Lee, Leo Ou-fan. *Shanghai Modern: The Flowering of a New Urban Culture in China, 1930–1945*. Cambridge, MA: Harvard University Press, 1999.

Lei Qin 泪沁. "Lixiang de zhuzhai: women de hezuo zhuyi de zhuzhaicun" 理想的住宅: 我們合作主義的住宅村 (The ideal dwelling: Our cooperative village). *FNZZ* 12: 11 (1926), 39–40.

Lei, Sean. "Moral Community of Weisheng: Contesting Hygiene in Republican China." *East Asian Science, Technology and Society: An International Journal* 3: 4 (2009), 475–504.

Levine, Alan J. *"Bad Old Days": The Myth of the 1950s*. New Brunswick, NJ: Transaction Publishers, 2008.

Li E 厲鶚. *Yutai shushi* 玉臺書史 (History of calligraphy from the Jade Terrace). Shanghai: Shanghai guji chubanshe, 2002.

Li Foru 李佛如. "Nüjie zhenyan" 女界箴言 (Exhortation to women's circles). *ZHFNJ* 10 (October 1915).

Li Guiyun 李癸雲. *Menglong, qingming yu liudong: lun Taiwan xiandai nüxing shizuo zhong de nüxing zhuti* 朦朧、清明與流動: 論台灣現代女性詩作中的女性主體 (Obscure, transparent, and fluid: On the female subject in poems by contemporary Taiwanese women). Taibei: Wanjuanlou tushu gongsi, 2002.

Li Huanqiu 李浣秋. "Jianming jiepouxue shuyao" 簡明解剖學述要 (A brief introduction to anatomy). *FNZZ* 2: 1–3 (1916).

Li Keqiang 李克強. "*Linglong* zazhi jiang'ou de modeng nüxing xingxiang" 《玲瓏》雜誌建構的摩登女性形象 (The image of modern women constructed in *Linloon Magazine*). *Ershiyi shiji shuangyuekan* 60 (2000), 92–98.

Li Rongzhang 李榮章. "Shujia nei de xiuye: ertong de leyuan" 暑假内的修業: 兒童的樂園 (Revision in the summer holidays: Children's paradise). *FNZZ* 13: 7 (1927), 41–43 [63–65].

Li Shichuan 黎氏釧. "Yuenan funü wei heping jianshe he tongyi zuguo er douzheng" 越南妇女为和平建设和统一祖国而斗争 (Vietnamese women struggling for peaceful reconstruction and unification of their motherland). *Zhongguo funü* 1 (1956), 18–19.

Li Songyao 李頌堯. "Jianei meizhuangfa de taolun" 家內美裝法的討論 (A discussion of interior decoration in the home). *FNZZ* 12: 1 (1926), 193–200.

Li, Xiaorong. "Engendering Heroism: Ming–Qing Women's Song Lyrics to the Tune *Man jiang hong*." *Nan Nü* 7: 1 (2005), 1–39.

Li Yuyi 李寓一. "Congsu yong meili de yanse zhuangshi ni de fangjian" 從速用美麗的顏色裝飾你的房間 (Decorate your home without delay using beautiful colours). *FNZZ* 14: 2 (1928), 17–27 [35–45].

— "Jiaoyubu quanguo meishu zhanlan canguan ji (san), (ba) Gongyi meishubu gaikuang" 教育部全國美術展覽參觀記 (三), (八)工藝美術部概況 (A visit to the Ministry of Education National Fine Arts Exhibition (3), (8) The section on arts and crafts). *FNZZ* 15: 7 (1929), 133.

— "Jiaoyubu quanguo meishu zhanlanhui canguan ji er: xihua bu zhi gaikuang" 教育部全國美術展覽會參觀記二: 西畫部之概況 (Report on the visit to the Ministry of Education National Art Exhibition 2: Overview of Western-style painting section). *FNZZ* 15: 7 (1929), 1–2.

Li Zhihong 李志宏. *Mingmo Qingchu caizi jiaren xiaoshuo xushi yanjiu* 明末清初才子佳人小說敘事研究 (A study of narration in scholar–beauty romances of the late Ming and early Qing). Taibei: Da'an chubanshe, 2008.

Lian Shi 蓮史. "Benshe wu da zhuyi yanshuo" 本社五大主義演說 (Speech on the five great principles of this society). *Zhongguo xin nüjie zazhi* 4 (1907).

— "Fakanci" 發刊詞 (Inaugural statement). *Zhongguo xin nüjie zazhi* 1 (1907).

— "Funü de feiren shidai: Cu putianxia nanxing fanxing," 婦女的非人時代 – 促普天下男性反省 (The age where women are not human: Urging men all over the world to reflect on themselves). *FNZZ* 9: 4 (1923), 44–46.

— "Ji Meiguo furen zhanshi zhi weiye" 記美國婦人戰時之偉業 (A record of the great deeds of American women in wartime). *Zhongguo xin nüjie zazhi* 4 (1907).

— "Liu-Ri nüxuejie jinshi ji" 留日女學界近事記 (Recent news from the Chinese women's student association in Japan). *Zhongguo xin nüjie zazhi* 1 (1907).

— "Luo Ying nüshi zhuan" 羅瑛女士傳 (Biography of Luo Ying). *Zhongguo xin nüjia zazhi* 5 (1907).

— "Mingyuxin yu zerenxin zhi guanxi" 名譽心與責任心之關係 (The relationship between fame and responsibility). *Zhongguo xin nüjie zazhi* 5 (1907).

Liang Hualan 梁華蘭. "Nüzi wenti" 女子問題 (The woman question). *Xin qingnian* 3: 1 (1917), 1–2.

Liang Lingxian 梁令嫻. "Suo wang yu wuguo nüzi zhe" 所望于吾國女子者 (What I expect from our country's women). *ZHFNJ* 1 (1915).

Liang Qichao 梁啟超. "Bianfa tongyi: Lun nüxue" 變法通議: 論女學 (Treatises on political reform: On women's education). In *Yinbing shi wenji*, 38–39. Taibei: Taiwan Zhonghua shuju, 1983.

— "Lun nüxue" 論女學 (On education for women). *Shiwu bao* 23 (1897), 1a–4a, and 25 (1897), 1a–2b.

— "Lun Zhongguo xueshu sixiang bianqian zhi dashi" 論中國學術思想變遷之大勢 (On the general trend in changes of Chinese academic thought). *Xinmin congbao* 3 (1902).

— "Luolan furen zhuan" 羅蘭夫人傳 (Biography of Madame Roland). Originally published in *Xinmin congbao* 17 & 18 (1902) under Liang's pseudonym, Zhongguo zhi xinmin 中國之新民 (A new Chinese citizen) and the title "Jinshi diyi nüjie Luolan furen zhuan" 近世第一女傑羅蘭夫人傳 (Biography of the most eminent modern heroine, Madame Roland). Reprinted in *Xuchu nübao* 8 (1902), 1a–2b and 9 (1902), 3a–4b, incomplete.

— *Yinbingshi heji* 飲冰室合集 (Collected essays from the ice drinker's studio). Beijing: Zhonghua shuju, 1989.

Liang Zijun 梁子駿. "Boye nüshi fangwenji" 波耶女士訪問記 (Record of an interview with Lillian Boyer). *FNZZ* 8: 12 (1922), 54–58.

Liao Chaoyang 廖朝陽. "Pipan yu fenli: dangdai zhuti wanquan cunhuo shouce" 批判與分離: 當代主體完全存活手冊 (Critique and separation: A survival guide for the contemporary subject). *Zhongwai wenxue* 25: 5 (1996), 119–53.

Liddle, Dallas. *The Dynamics of Genre: Journalism and the Practice of Literature in Mid-Victorian Britain*. Charlottesville: University of Virginia Press, 2009.

Light, Beth and Ruth Roach Pierson, eds. *No Easy Road: Women in Canada 1920s–1960s*. Toronto: New Hogtown Press, 1990.

Liji [zhengyi] 禮記[正義] ([Orthodox commentary on] *The Book of Rites*). *Zhu* 註commentary by Zheng Xuan 鄭玄 (127–200), and *shu* 疏 commentary by Kong Yingda 孔穎達 (574–648). In *Shisanjing zhushu*, edited by Ruan Yuan, 1: 1221–22: 1696. Reprint. Beijing: Zhonghua shuju, 1979 (original from 1826).

Lin Li 林立 [Lap Lam]. *Canghai yiyin: Minguo shiqi Qing yimin ci yanjiu* 滄海遺音: 民國時期清遺民詞研究 (Sounds left unrecognized: A study of song lyrics by Qing loyalists in the Republican period). Hong Kong: The Chinese University Press, 2012.

Lin Wenfang 林文方. "Wo jiang zenmeyang zuo fu/muqin: Yuan jiyi jiangqiu ziji de renge" 我將怎麼樣作父/母親: 願極意講求自己的人格 (The kind of father/mother I want to be: I want to strive to develop my character). *FNZZ* 11: 11 (1925), 1740–43 [66–67].

Lin Zecang 林澤蒼. "Sanhe gongsi shiwu zhounian jinian zhi huigu" 三和公司十五週年紀念之回顧 (Looking back on San Ho Company to commemorate the fifteenth anniversary). *Diansheng* 6: 1 (1937), 79–81.

Lin Zemin 林澤民. "Canguan Yingguo huangjia sheying xuehui ji" 參觀英國皇家攝影學會記 (A visit to the Royal Photographic Society of Great Britain). *Sheying huabao* 6: 271 (1931), 167.

Lin Zhongda 林仲达. "Dui Zhongguo qingnian funü tan ertong jiaoyu wenti" 對新中國青年婦女談兒童教育問題 (Talking to China's young women about children's education). *FNZZ* 16: 11 (1930), 2–14 [24–36]; 16: 12 (1930), 2–14 [22–34].

Linden, Roberta Barbara. "Media Images of Women and Social Change: A Feminist Perspective." Dissertation, University of Toronto, 1990.

Lingxi. *See* Wang Lingxi.

Link, E. Perry. *Mandarin Ducks and Butterflies: Popular Fiction in Early Twentieth-Century Chinese Cities*. Berkeley: University of California Press, 1981.

Liu Guiqiu 劉桂秋. "Bashi nian qian de jiaogai shiyan – Qian Jibo zai Lize nüxiao de zuowen jiaoxue" 八十年前的教改實驗——錢基博在麗則女校的作文教學 (An experiment in educational reform from eighty years ago: Qian Jibo's writing course at Lize Girls' School). *Xiezuo* 20 (2003), 12–14.

⎯ *Wuxi shiqi de Qian Jibo yu Qian Zhongshu* 無錫時期的錢基博與錢鍾書 (Qian Jibo and Qian Zhongsu during their time in Wuxi). Shanghai: Shanghai shehui kexue chubanshe, 2004.

Liu Heng 劉恒. "Yige shujiaqi zhong jiating jiaoxue sheshi de jingguo" 一個暑假期中家庭教學設施的經過 (My experience of arrangements for home teaching during the summer holidays). *FNZZ* 17. 6 (1931), 53–61 [81–89].

Liu Jianmei. *Revolution Plus Love: Literary History, Women's Bodies, and Thematic Repetition in Twentieth-Century Chinese Fiction*. Honolulu: University of Hawai'i Press, 2003.

Liu Jucai 劉巨才. *Zhongguo jindai funü yundong shi* 中國近代婦女運動史 (A history of the modern Chinese women's movement). Liaoning: Zhongguo funü chubanshe, 1989.

Liu, Lydia. *Translingual Practice: Literature, National Culture, and Translated Modernity – China, 1900–1937*. Stanford, CA: Stanford University Press, 1995.

Liu, Lydia, Rebecca E. Karl, and Dorothy Ko (eds. and trs.). *The Birth of Chinese Feminism: Essential Texts in Transnational Theory*. New York: Columbia University Press, 2013.

Liu Renpeng 劉人鵬. *Jindai Zhongguo nüquan lunshu – guozu, fanyi yu xingbie zhengzhi* 近代中國女權論述⸺國族、翻譯與性別政治 (The discourse of women's rights in modern China: Nationality, translation, and gender politics). Taipei: Taiwan xuesheng shuju, 2000.

Liu Sheng 劉王盛. "Zhongguo nüxue shifan lun" 中國女學師範論 (On women's normal schools in China). *ZHFNJ* 6 (1915).

Liu Shipei 劉師培. "Wuzhengfuzhuyi zhi pingdengguan" 無政府主義之平等觀 (The view of equality in anarchism). In *Xinhai geming qian shinian jian shilun xuanji*, edited by Zhang Nan and Wang Renzhi, vol. 2.2, 918–31. Beijing: Sanlian shudian, 1963.

Liu Xiang 劉向, ed. *Zhanguo ce* 戰國策 (Intrigues of the Warring States). 3 vols. Shanghai: Shanghai guji chubanshe, 1985.

Liu Xiaobo 劉孝伯. "Wojiang zenmeyang zuo fu/muqin: Menwaihan de yidian yijian" 我將怎麼樣作父/母親：門外漢的一點意見 (The kind of father/mother I want to be: Some suggestions from a non-expert). *FNZZ* 11: 11 (1925), 1712–16 [38–42].

Liu Yazi 柳亞子. "Zhongguo nü jianxia Hongxian Nie Yinniang zhuan" 中國女劍俠紅線聶隱娘傳 (Biographies of Hongxian and Nie Yinniang, Chinese female knights-errant). *Nüzi shijie* 4, 5, and 7 (1904).

Liu Yazi [Yalu 亞盧]. "Zhongguo di-yi nü haojie nü junrenjia Hua Mulan zhuan" 中國第一女豪傑女軍人家花木蘭傳 (Biography of Hua Mulan, China's first female hero and female soldier). *Nüzi shijie* 3 (1904).

Liu Yongcong 劉詠聰 [Clara Wing-chung Ho]. *De, cai, se, quan: Lun Zhongguo gudai nüxing* 德、才、色、權：論中國古代女性 (Virtue, talent, beauty, and power: Women in ancient China). Taipei: Maitian, 1998.

Liu Zengren 劉增人. *Zhongguo xiandai wenxue qikan shilun* 中國現代文學期刊試論 (Overview of modern Chinese literary journals). Beijing: Xinhua chubanshe, 2005.

Lu Cui 盧翠. "Nüzi aiguo shuo" 女子愛國說 (On women's patriotism). *Nü xuebao* 5 (1898), 2b–3a.

Lü Fangshang 呂芳上. "1920 niandai Zhongguo zhishifenzi youguan qing'ai wenti de jueze yu taolun" 1920 年代中國知識分子有關情愛問題的抉擇與討論

(The choices and discussions about the issue of love by Chinese intellectuals in the 1920s). In *Wu sheng zhi sheng (I): jindai Zhongguo de funü yu guojia*, ed. Lü Fangshang, 73–102. Nangang: Institute of Modern History, 2003.

Lu Jianbo 盧劍波 and Deng Tianyu 鄧天喬. "Xieci: Zhi Huang Zhong, Du Keming da yishi" 謝辭: 致黃鍾、杜克明大醫師 (Thank you note: To Drs. Huang Zhong and Du Keming). *Xin nüxing* 新女性 2: 9 (1927).

Lu Manyan 陸曼炎. *Zhongwai nüjie zhuan* 中外女傑傳 (Biographies of Chinese and foreign women). Chongqing: np, 1942.

Lü Peng 呂鵬. "Hushe yanjiu" 湖社研究 (A study of the Lake Society). Ph.D. dissertation, Central Academy of Fine Arts, 2007.

Lu Shouzhen 陸守真. "Lun Tu'erqi nüzi" 論土耳其女子 (On Turkish women). *FNSB* 4 (1911), 54–56.

Lu Xun 魯迅. "Shanghai wenyi zhi yipie: Bayue shier ri zai shehui kexue yanjiuhui jiang" 上海文藝之一瞥: 八月十二日在社會科學研究會講 (A glance at the literary arts in Shanghai: Lecture at the Social Sciences Research Association on August 12). In *Lu Xun quanji*, 4: 291–307. Beijing: Renmin wenxue chubanshe, 1981.

Lu Xun [Tang Si 唐俟]. "Wo zhi jielieguan" 我之節烈觀 (My view of chastity). *Xin qingnian* 5: 2 (1918), 92–101.

Lu Xun bowuguan 魯迅博物館 (ed.). *Zhou Zuoren riji* 周作人日记 (Diary of Zhou Zuoren). Zhengzhou: Daxiang chubanshe, 1996.

Luo Jialun 羅家倫. "Jinri Zhongguo zhi zazhi jie" 今日中國之雜誌界 (China's magazine world today). Reprinted in Zhang Jinglu, *Zhongguo xiandai chuban shiliao* 1, 79–89. Beijing: Zhonghua shuju, 1954.

Luo Man 羅曼. "Yindu de guafu xuexiao" 印度的寡婦學校 (The school for widows in India). *Linglong* 244 (1936), 1988–90.

Ma Yazhen [Ya-Chen Ma] 馬雅貞. "Cong 'Yutai shushi' dao 'Yutai huashi': nüxing yishujia chuanji de duli chengshu yu Zhexi de yiwen chuancheng 從《玉臺書史》到《玉臺畫史》: 女性藝術家傳記的獨立成書與浙西的藝文傳承 (From 'The Jade Terrace History of Calligraphy' to 'The Jade Terrace History of Painting': The separate compilation of women artists' biographies and the cultural tradition of western Zhejiang)." *Tsing Hua Journal of Chinese Studies*, 40: 3 (2010), 411–52.

Ma, Yuxin. *Women Journalists and Feminism in China, 1898–1937*. Amherst, MA: Cambria Press, 2010.

Maeyama Kanako 前山加奈子. "Chûgoku no josei muke teiki kankôbutsu ni tsuite–sono naiyô to tokuchô" 中国の女性向け定期刊行物について――その内容と特徴 (Chinese periodicals for women from 1898 to 1949: Their contents and characteristics). *Surugadai University Studies* 10 (1995), 115–45.

Mann, Susan. *Gender and Sexuality in Modern Chinese History*. New York: Cambridge University Press, 2011.

— *Precious Records: Women in China's Long Eighteenth Century*. Stanford, CA: Stanford University Press, 1997.

— "Review: *Mapping Meanings*, edited by Lackner and Vittinghoff." *China Review International* 12: 1 (2005), 147–51.

— *The Talented Women of the Zhang Family*. Berkeley: University of California Press, 2007.

Mao Xianglin 毛祥麟. *Duishan shuwu moyu lu* 對山書屋墨餘錄 (Notes taken in a mountain-facing studio). Vol. 5 in *Biji qibian* 筆記七編 (Seven collections of notes). Taipei: Guangwen chuju, 1991.

Matsuo Yōji 松尾洋二. "Ryō Keichō to shiden, Higashi Ajia ni okeru kindai seishin shi no honryū" 梁啓超と史伝: 東アジアにおける近代精神史の奔流 (Liang Qichao and historical biography, the rapid spread of the history of a modern spirit in East Asia). In *Ryō Keichō, Seiyō kindai shisō juyō to Meiji Nihon* 梁啓超: 西洋近代思想受容と明治日本 (Liang Qichao: Meiji Japan and the reception of modern Western thought), edited by Hazama Naoki 狭間直樹, 273–77. Tokyo: Misuzu shobō, 1999.

McCracken, Ellen. *Decoding Women's Magazines: From Mademoiselle to Ms.* NY: Palgrave Macmillan, 1992.

McMahon, Keith. *Polygamy and Sublime Passion: Sexuality in China on the Verge of Modernity*. Honolulu: University of Hawai'i Press, 2010.

Mei Zhu. 梅鑄. "Faguo jiuwang nüjie Ruo'an zhuan" 法國救亡女傑若安傳 (French heroine who saved the nation, Joan of Arc). *Zhongguo xin nüjie zazhi* 3 (April 1907).

"Meiguo nüzi yu qiche shenghuo" 美國女子與汽車生活 (American women and their car life). *Linglong* 244 (1936), 2032–34.

"Meiguo yibai xianqi zhi zishu" 美國一百賢妻之自述 (The personal stories of one hundred virtuous American wives). *ZHFNJ* 1: 8 (1915); 1: 9 (1915); 1: 12 (1915); 2: 1 (1916).

"Meiguo zazhi shang de Zhongguo nüzi" 美國雜誌上的中國女子 (Chinese women in American journals). *Linglong* 262 (1936), 3503–04.

Meiyu 眉語 (Eyebrow Talk). Reprint. Beijing: Quanguo tushuguan wenxian suowei fuzhi zhongxin, 2006.

"*Meiyu* xuanyan" 眉語宣言 (*Eyebrow Talk* manifesto). *Meiyu* 1 (1914), 2.

Meng Ping 夢萍. "Lixiang de zhuzhai: yu yuan yi zu" 理想的住宅: 於願已足 (The ideal dwelling: That is all I wish for). *FNZZ* 12: 11 (1926), 43–45.

Meng Yue 孟悅 and Dai Jinhua 戴錦華. *Fuchu lishi dibiao: Zhongguo xiandai nüxing wenxue yanjiu* 浮出歷史地表: 中國現代女性文學研究 (Rising above the horizon of history: A study of modern Chinese women's literature). Taipei: Shibao wenhua chuban gongshi, 1993.

Miaoyi 渺一. "Wo jiang zenmeyang zuo fu/muqin: lixiang shang yingyou de tiaojian" 我將怎麼樣作父/母親: 理想上應有的條件 (The kind of father/mother I want to be: The ideal conditions). *FNZZ* 11: 11 (1925), 1724–25 [50–51].

Millum, Trevor. *Images of Woman: Advertising in Women's Magazines*. London: Chatto and Windus, 1975.

Minick, Scott, and Jiao Ping. *Chinese Graphic Design in the Twentieth Century*. New York: Van Nostrand Reinhold, 1990.

Mishra, Pankaj. *From the Ruins of Empire: The Revolt against the West and the Remaking of Asia*. London: Allen Lane, 2012.

Mittler, Barbara. *A Newspaper for China? Power, Identity and Change in Shanghai's News Media (1872–1912)*. Cambridge, MA: Harvard University Press, 2004.

— "In Spite of Gentility: Women and Men in *Linglong* (Elegance), a 1930s Women's Magazine." In *The Quest for Gentility in China: Negotiations beyond Gender and Class*, edited by Daria Berg and Chloe Starr, 208–34. New York: Routledge, 2007.

—— *Portrait(s) of a Trope: New Women and New Men in Chinese Women's Magazines, 1898–2008*. Book manuscript in preparation.

—— "Von großen Händen und kleinen Füßen – Emanzipation auf Chinesisch." In *Frauenbilder/Frauenkörper – Inszenierungen des Weiblichen in den Gesellschaften Süd- und Ostasiens*, edited by Stephan Köhn and Heike Moser, 291–312. Wiesbaden: Harrassowitz, 2013.

Miyamoto Keisen 宮本桂仙. *Seiyō danjo kōsaihō* 西洋男女交際法 (Social interactions between men and women in the West). Tokyo: Hakubenkan, 1906.

—— "Xiyang nannü jiaoji fa" 西洋男女交際法 [Social interactions between men and women in the West], translated by Hui 慧. *FNSB* 17 (1915), 24–37; 18 (1916), 11–14; 19 (1916), 55–59; 20 (1916), 60–67; 21 (1917), 49–56.

Mo Xinghan 莫星漢. "'Gei nanxing' de fanying" 「給男性」的反應 (The response to "For men"). *Xin nüxing* 2: 1 (1927), 127–29.

Moeran, Brian. "On Entering the World of Women's Magazines: A Cross-Cultural Comparison of *Elle* and *Marie Claire*." In *Marketplace Anthropology*, edited by S. G. Taher, 187–209. Hyderabad: The ICFAI University Press, 2006.

Molnár, Miklós. *A Concise History of Hungary*, translated by Anna Magyar. Cambridge: Cambridge University Press, 2001.

Mudge, Bradford K. *The Whore's Story: Women, Pornography, and the British Novel, 1684–1830*. Oxford: Oxford University Press, 2000.

Muramatsu Rakusui 村松樂水. *(Jinshi Ou-Mei) haojie zhi xijun* (近世歐美) 豪傑之細君 (The wives of great heroes [in the modern West]). Translated by Ding Chuwo. Changshu: Haiyu tushuguan, 1903.

Murata Yûjirô 村田雄二郎 (ed.). *"Fujo zasshi" kara miru kindai Chûgoku josei* 「婦女雜誌」からみる近代中国女性 (Modern Chinese women from the perspective of *The Ladies' Journal*). Tokyo: Kanbun shuppan, 2005.

—— *"Fujo zasshi" sômokuroku, sakuin* 『婦女雜誌』総目録 – 索引 (*Funü zazhi*: General catalogue and index). Tokyo: Tōkyō daigaku "Fujo zasshi" kenkyûkai, 2006.

Nakamura Masanao 中村正直. *Saigoku risshi hen* 西國立志編. Translation of *Self-Help*, by Samuel Smiles. Tokyo: Kihira aiji, 1876.

—— "Saigoku risshi hen daijūichi hen jo" 〈西國立志編〉第十一編序 (Introduction to the eleventh essay in *Self-Help*). In *Saigoku risshi hen*, by Samuel Smiles, translated by Nakamura Masanao, 545. Tokyo: Kihira aiji, 1876.

Nakauchi Giichi 中内義一. *Jannu daruku* 惹安達克 (Jeanne d'Arc). No. 32 in series Sekai rekishi dan 世界歷史譚 (Discussions of world history). Tokyo: Hakubunkan, 1901.

Nemoto Tadashi 根本正. *Ō-Bei joshi risshin den* 欧米女子立身伝 (Biographies of successful European and American women). Tokyo: Yoshikawa kōbunkan, 1906.

Nivard, Jacqueline. "L'évolution de la presse féminine chinoise de 1898 à 1949." *Études chinoises* 5: 1–2 (1986), 157–84.

—— "Women and the Women's Press: The Case of *The Ladies' Journal* (*Funü zazhi*) 1915–1931." *Republican China* 10: 1b (1984), 37–56.

"Nongzhang xieji" 弄璋叶吉 (Birth of a son brings on luck). *FNSB* 3 (1911).

"Nüjie yaowen" 女界要聞 (News from the women's world). *FNZZ* 5: 7 (1919), *jishu*: 1–4.

Nülun 女論 (On women). Special issue of *Nübao*, edited and published by Chen Yiyi (Shanghai: Nübao she, 1909).

"Nüzi jianyi de tiyu" 女子簡易體育 (Women's basic physical education). *Nüzi shijie* 10 (1904), *jiaoyu*: 1–8.

Ogawa, Hiromitsu. "Regarding the Publication of the Meishu congshu (Fine Arts Series), the Introduction of the European Concept of 'Fine Arts' and the Japanese translated term Bijutsu." http://archiv.ub.uni-heidelberg.de/volltextserver/5810/1/Regarding_the_Publication_of_the_Meishu_Congsh_final.pdf.

Ou Peifen 歐培芬. "Jinggao zheng xuanjuquan zhi nütongbao" 敬告爭選舉權之女同胞 (Respectful words to our female compatriots fighting for the vote). *Minli bao*, June 7, 1912.

Ouling 耦菱. "Wo jiang zenmeyang zuo fu/muqin: suo fu de zeren bing bu qing" 我將怎麼樣作父/母親: 所負的責任卻不輕 (The kind of father/mother I want to be: A heavy responsibility). *FNZZ* 11: 11 (1925), 1736–37 [62–63].

"Paiwan Yihou" 排完以後 (After typesetting). *Xin nüxing* 1: 12 (1926).

Pan Tianzhen 潘天禎. "Tan Zhongguo jindai di-yi fen nübao – *Nü xuebao*" 談中國近代第一份女報 – – 《女學報》 (About the first women's journal in modern China – *Chinese Girl's Progress*). *Tushuguan* 3 (1963), 57–58.

Pan Yuliang 潘玉良. "Wo xi fenbi hua de jingguo tan" 我習粉筆畫的經過談 (My experience of learning how to paint with pastels). *FNZZ* 15: 7 (1929), 51.

Peng Shanzhang 彭善彰. "Jiejue funü zhiye de jige wenti" 解決婦女職業的幾個問題 (Solving some problems concerning women's occupations). *FNZZ* 13: 5 (1927), 7–10 [21–24].

Pflugfelder, Gregory M. "'S' is for Sister: Schoolgirl Intimacy and 'Same-Sex Love' in Early Twentieth Century Japan." In *Gendering Modern Japanese History*, edited by Barbara Molony and Kathleen Uno, 133–90. Cambridge, MA: Harvard University Asia Center, 2005.

Pickowicz, Paul, Kuiyi Shen, and Yingjin Zhang. *Liangyou, Kaleidoscopic Modernity and the Shanghai Global Metropolis, 1926–1945*. Leiden: Brill, 2014.

Probst, Ulrike. "Frauenzeitschriften: Mittel zur Emanzipation oder Fortschreibung traditionellen Rollenverhaltens – Exemplarische Untersuchung am Beispiel der *Cosmopolitan*." Ph.D. dissertation, Erlangen-Nürnberg University, 1994.

Qi Zhan 棨旃. "Yingguo xiaoshuojia Ailiatuo nüshi zhuan" 英國小說家愛里阿脫女士傳 (Biography of Ms. Eliot, British novelist). *Zhongguo xin nüjie zazhi* 4 (1907).

Qian Jianqiu 錢劍秋. "Falü shang nannü pingdeng zhi yuanze" 法律上男女平等之原則 (The principle of legal equality between the sexes). *FNZZ* 14: 4 (1928), 9–10 [29–30].

Qian Jibo 錢基博. "Lize nüxue guochi jinian beiyin" 麗則女學國恥紀念碑陰 (Inscription on the back of Lize Girls' School monument for national humiliation). *FNZZ* 1: 11 (1915).

— "Ni gai Tongcheng Wu Zhiying nüshi xie benxiao guochi jinian bei yin qi" 擬丐桐城吳芝瑛女士寫本校國恥紀念碑陰啟 (Drafting a letter to Madam Wu Zhiying of Tongcheng, asking for her calligraphy for the inscription on the back of our school's monument for national humiliation). *FNZZ* 1: 11 (1915).

— "Wujiang Lize nüzhongxue guowen jiaoshou xuanyanshu" 吳江麗則女中學國文教授宣言書 (Manifesto for teaching Chinese at the Lize Girls' School in Wujiang). *FNZZ* 1: 11 (1915), 1–5.

Qian Juntao 錢君匋. *Qian Juntao zhuangzhen yishu* 錢君匋裝幀藝術 (Qian Juntao's book cover design). Hong Kong: Shangwu yinshuguan, 1992.

Qian, Nanxiu 錢南秀. "'Borrowing Foreign Mirrors and Candles to Illuminate Chinese Civilization': Xue Shaohui's (1866–1911) Moral Vision in the *Biographies of Foreign Women*." *Nan Nü* 6: 1 (2004), 60–101.

— *Politics, Poetics, and Gender in Late Qing China: Xue Shaohui and the Era of Reform*. Stanford, CA: Stanford University Press, 2015.

— "Qingmo nüxing kongjian kaituo: Xue Shaohui bianyi *Waiguo lienü zhuan* de dongji yu mudi" 清末女性空間開拓: 薛紹徽編譯《外國列女傳》的動機與目的 (Expansion of women's space: Xue Shaohui's motivation and purpose of compiling the *Biographies of Foreign Women*). *Fanyi shi yanjiu* 翻譯史研究 1 (2011), 170–200.

— "Revitalizing the *Xianyuan* (Worthy Ladies) Tradition: Women in the 1898 Reforms." *Modern China* 29: 4 (2003), 399–454.

— "The Mother *Nü Xuebao* versus the Daughter *Nü Xuebao*: Generational Differences between 1898 and 1902 Women Reformers." In *Different Worlds of Discourse: Transformations of Gender and Genre in Late Qing and Early Republican China*, edited by Nanxiu Qian, Grace S. Fong, and Richard J. Smith, 257–92. Leiden: Brill, 2008.

Qian Yusun 錢鈺孫. "Guanyu ertong benneng de jiaoyu" 關於兒童本能的教育 (On education based on children's instincts). *FNZZ* 8: 1 (1922), 70–72.

Qianhui 乾慧 and Zhidu 智度 (trs.). "Yingguo nüjie Niejike'er zhuan" 英國女傑涅幾柯兒傳 (Biography of the British heroine Nightingale). *Nü xuebao* 4 (1903).

Qin Zong 琴宗 and Zhi Xin 知新 (trs.). "Wutong anchan fa" 無痛安產法 (Painless childbirth). *FNSB* 20 (1916), 46–54.

Qiu Ping 秋蘋. "Chanfu zhi xinde ji shiyan tan" 產婦之心得及實驗談 (Acquired knowledge and experience of women in childbirth). *FNSB* 1 (1911), 17–20.

Qiu Zhao'ao 仇兆鰲 (annot.). *Dushi xiangzhu* 杜詩詳註 (Du's poems with detailed commentary). 5 vols. Beijing: Zhonghua shuju, 1979.

Qu Jun 瞿鈞. "Diaocha funü yuejing qi" 調查婦女月經啟 (Investigation of the onset of menstruation). *FNSB* 16 (1915), 84–85.

— "Furen zhi weisheng zahua" 婦人之衛生雜話 (Miscellaneous comments on women's hygiene). *FNSB* 4 (1911), 17–28.

Qu Jun 瞿鈞 [Qu Shaoheng 瞿紹衡]. "Funü zhi weisheng yi ban: yuejing zhi zhuyi/renshen zhi baoyang" 婦人之衛生 一班- 月經之注意/妊娠之保養 (A lesson on women's hygiene: Attentiveness to menstruation/care during pregnancy). *FNSB* 3 (1911), 25–29.

Reed, Christopher A. *Gutenberg in Shanghai: Chinese Print Capitalism, 1876–1937*. Vancouver: University of British Columbia Press, 2004.

Remer, C.F. and William B. Palmer, *A Study of Chinese Boycotts with Special Reference to Their Economic Effectiveness*. Baltimore: Johns Hopkins Press, 1933.

Reynolds, Douglas R. *China, 1898–1912: The Xinzheng Revolution and Japan*. Cambridge, MA: Council on East Asian Studies, Harvard University, 1993.

(Riben) Xin nüzi zhi yi ren (日本) 新女子之一人 (A new [Japanese] woman). "Yu nanzi fa kangzhan" 與男子閥抗戰 (Wars of resistance against male domination). Translated by Jiang Su 江素. *FNSB* 16 (1915), 1–9.

Richter, Daniel K. "Cultural Brokers and Intercultural Politics: New York–Iroquois Relations, 1664–1701." *Journal of American History* 75: 1 (1988), 40–67.

Rogaski, Ruth. *Hygienic Modernity: Meanings of Health and Disease in Treaty-Port China*. Berkeley: University of California Press, 2004.

Röser, Jutta. *Frauenzeitschriften und weiblicher Lebenszusammenhang: Themen, Konzepte und Leitbilder im sozialen Wandel*. Opladen: Westdeutscher Verlag, 1992.

"Ruguo wo shi ni" 如果我是你 (If I were you). *Nongjianü baishitong* 2 (1996), 52.

Ruiyun 瑞雲. "Wo jiang zenmeyang zuo fu/muqin: wode tonghui yi chi" 我將怎麼樣作父/母親: 我的痛悔已遲了 (The kind of father/mother I want to be: It is too late for me to repent). *FNZZ* 11:11 (1925), 1719–21 [45–47].

Runge (ルンゲ氏), [Max], Mizuhara Zen 水原漸, and Chiba Toshijirô 千葉稔次郎. *Sankagaku* 産科学 (Obstetrics). Tokyo: Kanehara torasaku, 1899.

Sakamoto, Hiroko. "The Cult of 'Love and Eugenics' in May Fourth Movement Discourse." *positions: east asia cultures critique* 12 (2004), 329–76.

Sanetô Keishû 實藤專秀. *Chûgokujin Nihon ryûgaku shi zôho* 中国人日本留学史增補 (A history of Chinese students in Japan, enlarged edition). Tokyo: Kuroshio shuppan, 1970.

Sang, Tze-lan Deborah. *The Emerging Lesbian: Female Same-Sex Desire in Modern China*. Chicago: University of Chicago Press, 2003.

"Sanhe gongsi shiwu zhou jinian quanti zhiyuan sheying" 三和公司十五週紀念全體職員攝影 (A group photo of all staff of the San Ho Company on the occasion of its fifteenth anniversary). *Diansheng* 6: 1 (1937), 80.

Sanjiaojia 三腳架. "Li Li pai luoti zhao" 李麗拍裸體照 (Li Li took nude photographs). *Kaimaila* 110 (1932), 2.

Scanlon, Jennifer. *Bad Girls Go Everywhere: The Life of Helen Gurley Brown*. New York: Oxford University Press, 2009.

⸺ *Inarticulate Longings: The Ladies' Home Journal, Gender, and the Promises of Consumer Culture*. New York: Routledge, 1995

Schmidt, Jerry. *Within the Human Realm: The Poetry of Huang Zunxian, 1848–1905*. Cambridge: Cambridge University Press, 1994.

Schneider, Helen M. *Keeping the Nation's House: Domestic Management and the Making of Modern China*. Vancouver: University of British Columbia Press, 2011.

Selu. *See* Zhang Xichen.

Shan Xi longsou. *See* Jing Yuanshan.

Shanghai Funü zazhi she, ed. *Funü zazhi* 婦女雜誌 (The Ladies' Journal), 72 vols. Beijing: Xianzhuang shuju, 2006.

Shanghai jiefang qianhou wujia ziliao huibian 上海解放前後物價資料匯編 (Compilation of materials about commodity prices in Shanghai before and after liberation). Shanghai: Shanghai renmin chubanshe, 1959.

Shanghai meishu zhi 上海美術志 (A chronicle of art in Shanghai). Shanghai: Shanghai shuhua chubanshe, 2004.

Shanghai tushuguan 上海圖書館, ed. *Quanguo baokan suoyin* 全國報刊索引 (National periodicals index). Shanghai: Shanghai tushuguan, 1980.

Shanghai tushuguan 上海圖書館, ed. *Zhongguo jindai qikan bianmu huilu* 中國近代期刊編目彙錄 (Collected catalogues of modern Chinese periodicals). Shanghai: Shanghai renmin chubanshe, 1965, 1980.

Shanghai tushuguan 上海圖書館 and Zhu Junzhou 祝均宙, eds. *Shanghai tushuguan guancang jinxiandai Zhongwen qikan zongmu* 上海圖書館館藏近現代中文期刊總目 (Catalog of holdings of modern Chinese periodicals in the Shanghai Library). Shanghai: Shanghai kexue jishu wenxian chubanshe, 2004.

Shangmu. *See* Yu Xitang.

Shanzai 善哉. "Funü tongxing zhi aiqing" 婦女同性之愛情 (Same-sex love among women). *FNSB* 7 (1912), 36–38.

— "Xuanze wanju yu ertong jiaoyu" 選擇玩具與兒童教育 (On choosing toys and children's education). *FNSB* 7 (1912), 21–3.

— "Xuran yu furen" 鬚髯與婦人 (Facial hair and women). *FNSB* 7 (1912), 27–29.

Shao Yi 韶懿. "Lun changji zhi you baihai er wu yili" 論娼妓之有百害而無一利 (On the great harm and lack of benefits of prostitution). *FNSB* 5 (1912), 6–9.

Shaoying 少英. "Meishujia Wang Ruizhu nüshi de luezhuan" 美術家王瑞竹女士的略傳 (A short biography of artist Ms. Wang Ruizhu). *FNZZ* 12: 1 (1926), 19–20.

Shaoying 少英. "Zhu de wenti" 住的問題 (The housing problem). *FNZZ* 13: 2 (1927), 1–4 [53–56].

Shen Pengnian 沈鵬年. "Lu Xun zai 'wusi' yiqian dui wentan niliu de douzheng" 魯迅在'五四以前對文壇逆流的鬥爭 (Lu Xun's battle against the literary counter-current prior to 'May Fourth'). *Xueshu yuekan* 6 (1963), 24–40.

Shen Tongwu 沈同午 (Zhigong 職公). "Nü junren zhuan" 女軍人傳 (Biography of a female soldier). *Nüzi shijie* 1, 2, and 3 (1904).

Shen Yan 沈燕. "20 shiji chu Zhongguo nüxing xiaoshuo zuojia yanjiu" 20 世紀初中國女性小說作家研究 (A study of early twentieth-century Chinese female fiction writers). M.A. thesis, Shanghai shifan daxue, 2004.

Shen Yanbing 沈雁冰. *Wo zouguo de daolu* 我走過的道路 (The road I have taken). Hong Kong: Sanlian, 1981.

Shen Ying 沈瑛, Lai Mayi 賴媽懿, and the women trustees of the Shanghai Guishuli Nüxue Hui Shushu 上海桂墅里女學會書塾. "Zhongguo Nüxue ni zengshe baoguan gaobai" 中國女學擬增設報館告白 (Announcement of the establishment of a journal affiliated with the Chinese Girls' School). *Xinwen bao*, 17 May 1898; *Zhixin bao* 55 (9 June 1898), 26a; *Xiangbao* 87 (15 June 1898).

"*Shenglixue shang zhi qiji Yingguo nü yundongjia nü hua nan*" 生理學上之奇蹟 英國女運動家女化男 (The biological miracle: A female English sports professional turned into a man). *Linglong* 244 (1936), 2036–38.

Shevelow, Katherine. *Women and Print Culture: The Construction of Femininity in the Early Periodical*. London: Routledge. 1989.

Shi He 史和, Yao Fushen 姚福申, and Ye Cuidi 葉翠娣 (eds.). *Zhongguo jindai baokan minglu* 中國近代報刊名錄 (A list of modern Chinese periodicals). Fuzhou: Fujian renmin chubanshe, 1991.

Shi Jianling 史建玲. "Mingyun kao ziji zhangwo" 命运靠自己掌握 (Take your fate in your own hands). *Nongjianü baishitong* 1 (1996), 12.

Shi Meimei 史美枚. "Geguo nügong jiji choubei guojinügong huiyi" 各国女工积极筹备国际女工会议 (Women from all over the world actively prepare for the international women's conference). *Zhongguo funü* 1 (1956), 20.

Shiao, Ling A. "Printing, Reading, and Revolution: Kaiming Press and the Cultural Transformation of Republican China." Ph.D. dissertation, Brown University, 2009.

Shibusawa Tamotsu. *Taisei fujo kikan* 泰西婦女龜鑑 (Exemplary Western women). Tokyo: Hakubunkan, 1892.

"Shijie shi da yanshuojia" 世界十大演说者 (Ten greatest orators in the world). *Linglong* 1936 244: 1985–86.

Shijie shi nüjie 世界十女傑 (Ten world heroines). Changshu: Haiyu tushuguan, 1903.

Shimoda Utako 下田歌子. "Lun Zhongguo nüxue shi" 論中國女學事 (On education for Chinese women). Translated orally by Zhang Yingxu 張鍈緒 and transcribed by Yang Du 楊度. *Xuchu nübao* 9 (1902), "*Nübao* lunshuo" column, 1a–4a.

Shirose Waichirō 白勢和一郎. *Taisei retsujoden* 泰西列女傳 (Biographies of Western women). Shibata: Ryokujukan, 1876.

"Shishi wenda" 时事问答 (Questions and answers on current affairs). *Zhongguo funü* 2 (1966), 18.

Shu Xincheng 舒新城. *Zhongguo jindai jiaoyushi ziliao* 中國近代教育史資料 (Materials on the modern history of Chinese education), vol. 2. Beijing: Renmin jiaoyu chubanshe, 1961.

Skalli, Loubna H. *Through a Local Prism: Gender, Globalization, and Identity in Moroccan Women's Magazines*. Lanham: Lexington Books, 2006.

Sloan, Mark. *Birth Day: A Pediatrician Explores the Science, the History, and the Wonder of Childbirth*. New York: Ballantine Books, 2009.

Smith, Richard J. *The Qing Dynasty and Traditional Chinese Culture*. Lanham, MD: Rowman and Littlefield, 2015.

Sohō sei 蘇峰生 (Tokutomi Sohō 德富蘇峰). "Fujin risshi hen ni daisu" 婦人立志篇に題す (Dedication for *Fujin risshi hen*). In *Fujin risshi hen* by Takekoshi Takeyo, 2. Tokyo: Keiseisha, 1892.

Spiller, Gustav. *The Training of the Child: A Parent's Manual*. London and New York: T.C. and E.C. Jack Dodge Publishing, 1912.

Su Jianxin 蘇建新. *Zhongguo caizi jiaren xiaoshuo yanbian shi* 中國才子佳人小說演變史 (A history of the development of Chinese scholar–beauty romances). Beijing: Shehui kexue wenxian chubanshe, 2006.

Sudō Mizuyo 須藤瑞代. *Zhongguo "nüquan" gainian de bianqian – Qing-mo Min-chu de renquan yu shehui xingbie* 中國「女權」概念的變遷——清末民初的人權與社會性別 (The transformation of the concept of "women's rights" in China: Human rights and social gender in the late Qing and early Republic). Translated by Sudō Mizuyo and Yao Yi 姚毅. Beijing: Shehui kexue wenxian Chubanshe, 2010.

Suleiman, Michael W. "Changing Attitudes towards Women in Egypt: The Role of Fiction in Women's Magazines." *Middle Eastern Studies* 14: 3 (1978), 352–71.

Sun Liying. "An Exotic Self? Tracing Cultural Flows of Western Nudes in Pei-yang Pictorial News (1926–1933)." In *Transcultural Turbulences: Towards a MultiSited Reading of Image Flows*, edited by Christiane Brosius and Roland Wenzlhuemer, 271–300. Berlin and Heidelberg: Springer Verlag, 2011.

__ "Body Un/Dis-covered: *Luoti*, Editorial Agency and Transcultural Production in Chinese Pictorials (1925–1933)." Ph.D. dissertation, University of Heidelberg, 2015.

Sun Liying 孫麗瑩. "Cong *Sheying huabao* dao *Linglong*: qikan chuban yu Sanhe gongsi de jingying celüe (1920s–1930s)" 從《攝影畫報》到《玲瓏》: 期刊出版與三和公司的經營策略 (1920s–1930s) (From *Pictorial Weekly* to *Linloon Magazine*: Periodical publishing and the business strategies of the San Ho Company, 1920s–1930s). *Jindai Zhongguo funüshi yanjiu* 23 (2014), 127–81.

Sun, Liying and Matthias Arnold. "TS Tools." *Tijdschrift voor Tijdschriftstudies* 33 (2013), 73–78.

Sung, Doris, Liying Sun, and Matthias Arnold. "The birth of a database of historical periodicals: 'Chinese women's magazines in the late Qing and early Republican period.'" *Tulsa Studies in Women's Literature* 33: 2 (2014), 227–37.

Tai Gong 太公. "Dongjing zazhi shi" 東京雜事詩 (Poems on various topics relating to Tokyo). *Zhejiang chao* 2 (1903), 161–64.

"Taixi lienüzhuan" 泰西列女傳 (Biographies of Western women). *FNZZ* 3: 5 (1917), *jishumen*: 1–11; 3: 6 (1917), *jishumen*: 7–15; 3: 7 (1917), *jishumen*: 1–9; 3: 8 (1917), *jishumen*: 1–8; 3: 9 (1917), *jishumen*: 5–14; 3: 10 (1917), *jishumen*: 3–11; 3: 11 (1917), *jishumen*: 8–16; 3: 12 (1917), *jishumen*: 3–14.

Takekoshi Takeyo 竹越竹代 (compiler). *Fujin risshi hen* 婦人立志篇 (On women's self-help). Tokyo: Keiseisha, 1892.

Tang Jianwo 湯劍我. "Furen bing ji tazhong jibing zhi yundong liaofa" 婦人病及他種疾病之運動療法 (Exercises to cure gynecological problems and other illnesses). *FNSB* 4 (1911), 75–76.

__ "Shengticao" 繩體操 (Rope exercises [for the family]). *FNSB* 2 (1911), 71–76.

Tang Shuyu 湯漱玉 [Wang Tang Shuyu 汪湯漱玉]. *Yutai huashi* 玉臺畫史 (History of painting from the jade terrace). For the nineteenth century edition, see Qiantang 錢塘: Wangshi Zhenyitang 汪氏振綺堂, Daoguang 4 [1824]. Reprint: Shanghai: Shanghai guji chubanshe, 2002.

Tang Si. *See* Lu Xun.

Tang, Xiaobing. "'Poetic Revolution,' Colonization, and Form at the Beginning of Modern Chinese Literature." In *Rethinking the 1898 Reform Period: Political and Cultural Change in Late Qing China*, edited by Rebecca E. Karl and Peter Zarrow, 245–65. Cambridge, MA: Harvard University Asia Center, 2002.

Tang Yuan 唐沅, Han Zhiyou 韓之友, and Feng Shihui 封世辉 (compilers). *Zhongguo xiandai wenxue qikan mulu huibian* 中國現代文學期刊目錄彙編 (Collected Contents of Modern Chinese Literary Periodicals). 2 vols. Tianjin: Tianjin renmin chubanshe, 1988.

"Tianjin mingfu ceng huan weiji wei Weilianshi da yisheng hongse buwan suo zhiyu" 天津命婦曾患胃疾為韋廉士大醫生紅色補丸所治愈 (A woman from Tianjin had been suffering from stomach ache. She was cured by Dr. Williams' Pink Pills for Pale People). Weilianshi da yisheng hong se bu wan 韋廉士大醫生紅色補丸 [Dr. Williams' Pink Pills for Pale People]. *FNSB* 4 (1911).

Tianyu 天喬. *Funü jiaoyu yu funü jiefang* 婦女教育與婦女解放 (Women's education and women's liberation). Shanghai: Xinren shudian, 1939.

__ "Funü yu jiashi" 婦女與家事 (Women and housework). *Xin nüxing* 3: 2 (1928), 125–32.

___ "Funü yu wuyue" 婦女與五月 (Women and the month of May). *Xin nüxing* 3: 5 (1928), 485–500.

___ "Shidai xia xisheng de xin nüzi: bei mai yihou" 時代下犠牲的新女子: 被賣以後 (The current sacrifice of new woman: After being sold). *Xin nüxing* 3: 3 (1928), 271–77.

___ "Tangshi wo youle xiaohai: yi" 倘使我有了小孩: 一 (If I had children [1]). *Xin nüxing* 3: 1 (1928), 7–11.

___ "Women de jiehe" 我們的結合 (Our union). *Xin nüxing* 2: 1 (1927), 125–26.

Tianyu (ed.). "Nanchong jiage" 南充嫁歌 (Marriage songs of Nanchong). *Xin nüxing* 新女性 1: 9 (1926), 713–21.

Tokutomi Roka 德富芦花. *Sekai kokon meifu kagami* 世界古今名婦鑑 (Past and present world famous women exemplars). Tokyo: Min'yūsha, 1898.

Tong Ziling 童自玲. "Ting Mao Zhuxi de hua zuo geming de jiashu" 听毛主席的话做革命的家属 (Listening to Mao's words, becoming a member of the revolutionary family). *Zhongguo funü* 2 (1966), 8–10.

"Tongsu jiaoyu yanjiuhui zhi zhuzhong xiaoshuo" 通俗教育研究會之注重小說 (The Popular Education Research Association's focus on fiction). *Jiaoyu zazhi* 7: 12 (1915), 108–09.

Tseng, Pao-sun [Zeng Baosun]. "The Chinese Woman Past and Present." In *Chinese Women through Chinese Eyes*, edited by Li Yu-ning, 59–71. New York: M. E. Sharpe, 1992.

Tsugawa Iedachi 津川家立. "Cuimian shousheng fa" 催眠收生法 (Hypnosis for childbirth), translated by Wu Shu'an 吳淑安. *FNSB* 14 (1914), 17–20.

"Tu'erqi guicheng" 土耳其閨乘 (Turkey's control of the inner chambers). *FNZZ* 4: 1 (1918), *jishu*: 1–2; 4:2 (1918), *jishu*: 1–2.

Tuhua ribao 圖畫日報 (Daily pictorial). Shanghai, 1909. Reprint, 8 vols., Shanghai: Shanghai guji chubanshe, 1999.

Unschuld, Paul U. *Medicine in China: A History of Ideas*. Berkeley and Los Angeles: University of California Press, 1985.

Vitiello, Giovanni. "The Fantastic Journey of an Ugly Boy: Homosexuality and Salvation in Late Ming Pornography." *positions: east asia culture critique* 4: 2 (1996), 291–320.

Vurideeru Fujin ヴリデール婦人. "Kyô no haishô mondai" 今日の廢娼問題 (Today's problem of abolishing prostitution). *Jogaku sekai* 女学世界 (June 1, 1911), 158–64.

Wa Ka'erlefusikaya 瓦卡尔勒夫斯卡婭. "Sanshiliu nian ru yi" 三十六年如一 (Thirty-six years like one). *Zhongguo funü* 1 (1956), 21.

Waara, Carrie. "Invention, Industry, Art: The Commercialization of Culture in Republican Art Magazines." In *Inventing Nanjing Road: Commercial Culture in Shanghai, 1900–1945*, edited by Sherman Cochran, 61–90. Ithaca, NY: Cornell University East Asia Program, 1999.

Wagner, Rudolf G. "Joining the Global Imaginaire: The Shanghai Illustrated Newspaper *Dianshizhai huabao*." In *Joining the Global Public: Word, Image, and City in Early Chinese Newspapers, 1870–1910*, edited by Rudolf G. Wagner, 105–74. Albany: State University of New York Press, 2007.

___ "The Role of the Foreign Community in the Chinese Public Sphere." *China Quarterly* 142 (1995), 423–43.

Wagner, Rudolf G. (ed.). *Joining the Global Public: Word, Image, and City in Early Chinese Newspapers, 1870–1910*. Albany: State University of New York Press, 2007.

Wanfang 婉芳. "Lixiang de zhuzhai: Wo de jihua ruci" 理想的住宅: 我的計劃如此 (The ideal dwelling: Such is my plan). *FNZZ* 12: 11 (1926), 40–42.

Wang Changlu 汪長錄. "Fu de" 婦德 (On women's virtue). *ZHFNJ* 1 (1915).

Wang Chengbin 王成彬, Yang Shaohui 杨晓辉, and Sun Jing 孙静, "Fan Bozi yu Nantong Fan shi jiaoyu shijia" 范伯子與南通范氏教育世家 (Fan Bozi and the Fan family of educators from Nantong). *Nantong daxue xuebao* 21: 3 (2005), 62–69.

Wang, David Der-wei. *Fin-de-Siecle Splendor: Repressed Modernities of Late Qing Fiction, 1848–1911*. Stanford: Stanford University Press, 1997.

Wang, Gary. "Making 'Opposite-Sex Love' in Print: Discourse and Discord in *Linglong* Women's Pictorial Magazine, 1931–1937." *Nan Nü* 13: 2 (2011), 244–347.

Wang Jiting 汪集庭. "Funü yingyou zhi zhishi" 婦女應有之知識 (The knowledge women need to have). *FNZZ* 3: 1 (1917), *jiazhengmen*: 10–12.

Wang, Jun. *Merry Laughter and Angry Curses: The Shanghai Tabloid Press, 1897–1911*. Vancouver: University of British Columbia Press, 2012.

Wang Lanfang 王蘭芳. "Gao'erji jingshen yu fuyun" 高爾基精神與婦運 (The spirit of Gorky and the women's movement). *Linglong* 244 (1936), 1968–70.

[Wang] Lingxi (王)靈希. "Meiguo da jiaoyujia Lihen nüshi zhuan" 美國大教育家黎痕女士傳 (Biography of American educator Ms. Lyon). *Zhongguo xin nüjie zazhi* 2 (1907).

— "Meiguo da xinwenjia Asuoli nüshi zhuan" 美國大新聞家阿索里女士傳 (Biography of American reporter Ms. Ossoli). *Zhongguo xin nüjie zazhi* 1 (1907).

Wang Pingling 王平陵. "Dongfang furen zai falü shang de diwei" 東方婦人在法律上的地位 (East Asian women's standing under the law). *FNZZ* 8: 10 (1922), 23–30.

Wang Pingling 王平陵 and Zhang Xichen 章錫琛. "Tongxin: Lian'ai wenti de taolun" 通信: 戀愛問題的討論 (Correspondence: Discussion about the issue of romantic love). *FNZZ* 8: 9 (1922), 120–23.

Wang Qisheng 王奇生. "Minguo shiqi de Rishu Hanyi" 民国时期的日书汉译 (The translation of Japanese books into Chinese in the Republican period). *Jindaishi yanjiu* 6 (2008), 45–63.

Wang Yamin 王亞民 (compiler). *Nantong Fan shi shiwen shijia* 南通范氏詩文世家 (The literary Fan family from Nantong). Shijiazhuang: Hebei jiaoyu chubanshe, 2004.

Wang Yigang 王以剛. "Ertong e xiguan jiaozhengfa" 兒童惡習慣矯正法 (How to correct children's bad habits). *FNZZ* 8: 3 (1922), 84–86 [104–06].

Wang Yugang 汪于岡 and Qu Jun 瞿鈞 [Qu Shaoheng 瞿紹衡]. "Shengsi guantou juben" 生死關頭劇本 (Script for life-and-death crisis). In *Sili Shengsheng zhuchan xuexiao di-yijie biye jinian kan* 私立生生助產學校第一屆畢業紀念刊 (Commemorative publication in honor of the first graduating class of the private Shengsheng School of Obstetrics). N.p. 1935.

Wang Yunzhang 王蘊章. *Ranzhi yuyun* 然脂餘韻 (Ranzhi's leftover rhymes). Shanghai: Shangwu yinshuguan, 1918.

Wang Yunzhang [ps. Chunnong 蒪農]. "Yutai yicheng" 玉臺藝乘 (Arts of the jade terrace). *FNZZ* 1: 1 (1915), Meishu, 1–5, and 1: 2 (1915), Meishu, 1–6.

Wang Zheng. *Women in the Chinese Enlightenment: Oral and Textual Histories*. Berkeley, Los Angeles and London: University of California Press, 1999.

Weedon, Chris. *Nüxingzhuyi shijian yu houjiegouzhuyi lilun* 女性主義實踐與後結構主義理論 (Feminist practice and poststructuralist theory), translated by Bai Xiaohong 白曉虹. Taipei: Guiguan chubanshe, 1994.

"Wei shenme yao he qige zhangfu lihun?" 為甚麼要和七個丈夫離婚 (Why does one want to divorce seven husbands?). *Linglong* 262 (1936), 3552–54.

Weishisheng 衛士生. "Tai fuyu kexuejia secai de Zheng xiansheng" 太富於科學家色彩的鄭先生 (The overly scientific Mr. Zheng). *FNZZ* 9: 4 (1923), 50–53.

"Weixian zhi xinfu Mailimai" 危險之新婦麥麗麥 (The bride of danger, Marie Marvingt). *Nüzi shijie* 3 (1915), yizhu: 1–10.

White, Cynthia L. *Women's Magazines 1693–1968*. London: Michael Joseph Ltd., 1970.

Whitehorne, Oliver. *Cosmo Woman: The World of Women's Magazines*. Maidstone: Crescent Moon, 2007.

Widmer, Ellen. *The Beauty and the Book: Women and Fiction in Nineteenth-Century China*. Cambridge, MA: Harvard University Asia Center, 2006.

— *Fiction's Family: Zhan Xi, Zhan Kai, and the Business of Women in Late-Qing China*. Cambridge, MA: Harvard University Asia Center, 2015.

Williams, Henry Smith. *Twilight Sleep: A Simple Account of New Discoveries in Painless Childbirth*. New York: Harper, 1914.

Williams, Raymond. *The Long Revolution*. Harmondsworth: Penguin Books, 1961.

Winichakul, Thongchai. *Siam Mapped: A History of the Geo-body of a Nation*. Honolulu: University of Hawai'i Press, 1994.

Winship, Janice. *Woman Becomes an "Individual": Femininity and Consumption in Women's Magazines, 1954–69*. Birmingham: Centre for Contemporary Cultural Studies, University of Birmingham, 1981.

"Wo rufa fu le Luowei yaofang de guben zigong wan bing yong waizhi de shoushu wo zhongzhong shuo bu chu de bingzheng dou quanyu le zhenzhen shi fuke de lingdan miaofa ya" 我如法服了羅威藥房的固本子宮丸並用外治的手術我種種說不出的病症都痊癒了真真是婦科的靈丹妙法呀 (After I took the Luowei Pharmacy's Guben Medicine for the Uterus as directed and underwent [external treatment], all of my unmentionable diseases were cured. This is really a miraculous cure for women). *FNSB* 2 (1911).

Wu Bonian 吳伯年. "Yanjiu tuhua yijian" 研究圖畫意見 (Findings from research on painting). In *Nanyang quanyehui yanjiuhui baogaoshu* 南洋勸業會研究會報告書 (Reports by the research committee of the Nanyang Industrial Exposition), 1913. Reprinted in *Nanyang quanyehui baogaoshu*, edited by Bao Yong'an et al., 173–74. Shanghai: Shanghai jiaotong daxue chubanshe, 2010.

Wu Chongmin 伍崇敏. "Nannü ziyou pingdeng zhenjie" 男女自由平等真解 (A true explication of male–female equality). *ZHFNJ* 1 (1915).

Wu Juenong 吳覺農. "Jindai de zhencaoguan," 近代的貞操觀 (Modern views of chastity). *FNZZ* 8:12 (1922), 5–8.

Wu Juenong 吳覺農 [Y.D.]. "Wo de lihun qianhou" 我的離婚的前後 (Before and after my divorce). *FNZZ* 9: 4 (1923), 41–43.

___ "Ziyou lian'ai yu lian'ai ziyou: Dule Fengzi nüshi de 'dakewen' yihou" 自由戀愛與戀愛自由——讀了鳳子女士的『答客問』以後 (Free love and freedom to love: After reading Ms. Fengzi's 'Q and A'). *FNZZ* 9: 2 (1923), 41–43.

___ "Ziyou lian'ai yu lian'ai ziyou xupian: Zaida Fengzi nüshi" 自由戀愛與戀愛自由續篇——再答鳳子女士 (Sequel to free love and freedom to love: Further response to Ms. Fengzi). *FNZZ* 9: 2 (1923), 45–48.

Wu Jun 吳俊, Li Jin 李今, and Liu Xiaoli 劉曉麗 (eds.). *Zhongguo xiandai wenxue qikan mulu xinbian* 中國現代文學期刊目錄新編 (New edition of the catalog of modern Chinese literary periodicals). 3 vols. Shanghai: Shanghai renmin chubanshe, 2010.

Wu, Shengqing. *Modern Archaics: Continuity and Innovation in the Chinese Lyric Tradition, 1900–1937*. Cambridge, MA: Harvard University Asia Center, 2013.

Wu, Yi-li. *Reproducing Women: Medicine, Metaphor, and Childbirth in Late Imperial China*. Berkeley: University of California Press, 2010.

Wu Zuxiang 吳祖襄. "Wo jiang zenmeyang zuo fu/muqin: He dajia tantan keneng ba" 我將怎麼樣作父/母親: 和大家談談可能罷 (The kind of father/mother I want to be: Let's discuss the options). *FNZZ* 11: 11 (1925), 1722–24 [48–50].

"Wuben nüxuetang keyi" 務本女學堂課藝 (The curriculum at the Wuben Girls' School). *Nübao* 7–8 (1902).

Xia Xiaohong 夏曉虹 (ed.). *Nüzi shijie wenxuan* 女子世界文選 (Selected works from the *Women's world*). Guiyang: Guzhou jiaoyu chubanshe, 2003.

Xia Xiaohong. "*Shijie gujin mingfu jian* yu wan-Qing waiguo nüjie zhuan" 〈世界古今名妇鉴〉与晚清外国女杰传 (The *Sekai kokon meifu kagami* and biographies of foreign heroines in the late Qing). *Beijing daxue xuebao* 2, 2009.

___ "Tianyi bao and He Zhen's Views on 'Women's Revolution,'" translated by Hu Ying. In *Different Worlds of Discourse: Transformations of Gender and Genre in Late Qing and Early Republican China*, edited by Nanxiu Qian, Grace S. Fong, and Richard J. Smith, 293–314. Leiden: Brill, 2008.

___ "Wan-Qing liang fen *Nü xuebao* de qianshi jinsheng" 晚清兩份《女學報》的前世今生 (The previous and the present lives of the two late Qing *Nü xuebao*). *Xiandai zhongwen xuekan* 16 (2012), 25–33.

___ "Wan-Qing nüxing de xingbie guanzhao" 晚清女性的性別觀照 (A gender perspective on late Qing women). Introduction to *Nüzi shijie wenxuan*, ed. Xia Xiaohong, 45–52. Guiyang: Guzhou jiaoyu chubanshe, 2003.

___ *Wan-Qing nüxing yu jindai Zhongguo* 晚清女性与近代中国 (Late Qing women and modern China). Beijing: Beijing daxue chubanshe, 2004.

___ "Wu Mengban: Guozao xieshi de nüquan xianqu" 吳孟班: 過早謝世的女權先驅 (Wu Mengban: A feminist predecessor who died too young). *Wen shi zhe* 文史哲 299 (2007), 84–94.

___ "Xiandai nüzi de kumen wenti: Liu, shiqi" 現代女子的苦悶問題: 六、十七 (The dilemma of modern women: 6, 17). *Xin nüxing* 2: 1 (1927), 28–30, 53–55.

___ "Xiangxiaren chengliren" 鄉下人城裡人 (Country people, city people) (illustration). *Nongjianü baishitong* 7 (2001), n.p.

Xie Yinian 謝頤年. "Ertong shiqi de zhongyao yu jiating de gaizao" 兒童時期的重要與家庭的改造 (The importance of childhood, and family reform). *FNZZ* 17: 11 (1931), 29–34 [49–54].

"Xin lian'ai wenti" 新戀愛問題 (New issue of romantic love). *Xin nüxing* 3:12 (1928), 1347–1426.

Xingyi 星一. "Meiguo Bolingma'er Nüzi Daxue ji" 美國勃靈馬爾女子大學記 (Bryn Mawr Women's College in the United States). *FNSB* 1 (1911), 26–30.

— "Meiguo funü zatan" 美國婦女雜談 (Random reflections on American women). *FNSB* 2 (1911), 51–54.

— "Meiguo Huade furen yu qi nü Ana lun yinshi shu 美國華得夫人與其女阿娜論飲食書 (A letter on the topic of eating, from the American Mrs. Huade to her daughter Ana [Anna?]). *FNSB* 1 (1911), 30–31.

— "Meiguo hunjia zhi fengsu" 美國婚嫁之風俗 (Marriage customs in America). *FNSB* 2 (1911), 31–35.

Xinjun 欣君. "Nanzimen shuo" 男子們說 (Men said). *Funü gongming* 1 (1929), 35–36.

Xiong Yuezhi 熊月之 and Zhou Wu 周武 (eds.). *Sheng Yuehan daxue shi* 聖約翰大學史 (History of St John's University). Shanghai: Shanghai renmin chubanshe, 2007.

Xu Ang 徐昂. "Fan Yao Taifuren jiazhuan" 范姚太夫人家傳 (Family history of the dowager Fan Yao). In *Nantong Fan shi shiwen shijia*, compiled by Wang Yamin, *juan* 8–9. Shijiazhuang: Hebei jiaoyu chubanshe, 2004.

Xu Baowen 許寶文 homepage. www.xbaowen.cn/newpage5.htm.

— "Wo de jiating" 我的家庭 (My family). Accessed February 26, 2014. www.xbaowen .cn/newpage4.htm.

Xu Chan 許嬋. "Napolun zhi mu Liqixia zhuan" 拿破崙之母藜琪夏傳 (Biography of Letizia, mother of Napoleon). *FNSB* 12 (1914), 1–14.

— "Ou-mei geguo furen yuedan" 歐美各國婦人月旦 (An assessment of women in Europe and America). *FNSB* 7 (1912), 23–26.

Xu Dingyi 許定一. *Zuguo nüjie weiren zhuan* 祖國女界偉人傳 (Biographies of great women of our country). Yokohama: Xinminshe, 1906.

Xu Fu 許孚. "Chaozhou Yaoping xian Longdu Qianxi xiang nüxuetang ji" 潮州饒平縣隆都前溪女學堂記 (Record of the girls' school at Qianxi village, Longdu town, Yaoping county, Chaozhou prefecture). *Nü xuebao* 2 (1898), 3b–4a.

Xu Hemei 徐呵梅. "Pianjian de nanxing zhi pianjian: ze Kuangfu xiansheng" 偏見的男性之偏見 – 責曠夫先生 (The bias of biased men: Criticism of Mr. Kuangfu). *FNZZ* 9: 4 (1923), 46–50.

Xu Huiqi 許慧琦 [Rachel Hui-chi Hsu]. "*Funü zazhi* suo fanying de ziyou lihun sixiang jiqi shijian: cong xingbie chayi tanqi" 《婦女雜誌》所反映的自由離婚思想及其實踐——從性別差異談起 (Free divorce in thought and practice: Gender differences in the *Ladies' Journal*). *Jindai Zhongguo funüshi yanjiu* 12 (2004), 65–114.

Xu Huiqi. "1920 niandai de lian'ai yu xin xingdaode lunshu: cong Zhang Xichen canyu de sanci lunzhan tanqi" 1920 年代的戀愛與新性道德論述——從章錫琛參與的三次論戰談起 (Discourses on romantic love and new sexual morality of the 1920s: Exemplified by three debates in which Zhang Xichen took part). *Jindai Zhongguo funüshi yanjiu* 16 (2008), 29–92.

Xu Nianci (Gu'an 觚庵). "Jundui kanhufu Nandige'er zhuan" 軍隊看護婦南的辯爾傳 (Biography of the army nurse, Nightingale). *Nüzi shijie* 5 (1904), 6 (1904), 8 (1904).

— "Yingguo da cishanjia Meili Jia'abinta zhuan" 英國大慈善家美利‧加阿賓他傳 (Biography of Mary Carpenter, English humanitarian). *Nüzi shijie* 5 (1904), 6 (1904), 8 (1904).

Xu Shiheng 徐世衡. "Jinhou funü yingyou de jingshen" 今後婦女應有的精神 (The required outlook for women in the future). *FNZZ* 6: 8 (1920), *changshi*: 12–18.

Xu Xiaotian 許嘯天. "Xin qingshu shi shou" 新情書十首 (Ten new love-letters), *Meiyu* 1: 4 (1915), *suijin ji* section, 5–7.

Xu Xuewen 徐學文. "Wo jiang zenmeyang zuo fumuqin: ruhe cai suan bushi shize ne" 我將怎麼樣作父/母親: 如何才算不是失責呢 (The kind of father/mother I want to be: How to live up to the responsibility). *FNZZ* 11: 11 (1925), 1716–19 [42–45].

Xu Yasheng 徐亞生. "Ertong wanju de yanjiu" 兒童玩具的研究 (A study of children's toys). *FNZZ* 5 (1929), 13–16 [33–36].

Xu Yishi 徐一士. *Lingxiao Yishi suibi* 凌霄一士隨筆 (Notes by Lingxiao and Yishi). Taiyuan: Shanxi guji chubanshe, 1997.

Xu Yitang 徐益棠 [Shangmu 尚木]. "Ertong yu jiating tushushi" 兒童與家庭圖書室 (Children and the home library). *FNZZ* 13:7 (1927), 65–68 [141–144].

— "Gushi de jiangfa" 故事的講法 (The way to tell stories). *FNZZ* 13: 7 (1927), 69–71 [145–47].

Xu Yongqing 徐咏青. *Zhongxue yong qianbi huatie* 中學用鉛筆畫帖 (Pencil sketching for middle school students). Shanghai: Shangwu yinshuguan, 1902.

Xu Zhenya 徐枕亞. *Yuli hun* 玉梨魂 (The jade pear spirit). Vol. 70 in *Zhongguo jindai xiaoshuo daxi* 中國近代小說大系 (A compendium of modern Chinese fiction), Vol. 70. Nanchang: Baihuazhou wenyi chubanshe, 1993.

Xu Zhihao 許志浩. *Zhongguo meishu qikan guoyanlu* 中國美術期刊過眼路 (Brief list of art periodicals in China). Shanghai: Shanghai shuhua chubanshe, 1992.

Xue Haiyan 薛海燕. *Jindai nüxing wenxue yanjiu* 近代女性文學研究 (Research on modern women's literature). Beijing: Zhongguo shehui kexue chubanshe, 2004.

Xue Haiyan 薛海燕. "Minchu (1912–1919) xiaoshuo jie nüxing zuozhe qunti de shengcheng yanjiu" 民初 (1912–1919) 小說界女性作者群體的生成研究 (A study of the emergence of a community of female writers on the fiction scene of the early Republic [1912–1919]). *Henan jiaoyu xueyuan xuebao* 29: 6 (2010), 84–86.

Xue Shaohui 薛紹徽. "Chuangshe nüxuetang tiaoyi bing xu" 創設女學堂條議並敍 (Suggestions for establishing the Girls' School, with a preface). *Qiushi bao* 9 (1897), 6a–7b, and 10 (1897), 8a–b. Revised version, *Xinwen bao*, January 14–17, 1898. Abridged version, *Nüxue jiyi chubian*, 33a–35a.

— "Nü xuebao xu" 女學報序 (Preface to the *Chinese Girl's Progress*). *Nü xuebao* 1 (1898), 2b–3a.

— "Nüjiao yu zhidao xiangguan shuo" 女教與治道相關說 (On the connection between women's education and governance). *Nü xuebao* 3 (1898), 2a–b.

Xue Shaohui 薛紹徽 and Chen Shoupeng 陳壽彭 (trs. and eds.). *Waiguo lienü zhuan* 外國列女傳 (Biographies of foreign women). Nanjing: Jinling jiangchu bianyi zongju, 1906.

— "Xuebu zouding nüzi shifan xuetang zhangcheng" 學部奏定女子師範學堂章程 (Regulations for normal schools for women). In *Zhongguo jinxiandai yishu jiaoyu fagui huibian (1840–1929)*, edited by Zhang Xian and Zhang Yuan, 167–75. Beijing: Jiaoyu chubanshe, 1997.

— "Xuebu zouding nüzi xiaoxuetang zhangcheng" 學部奏定女子小學堂章程 (Regulations for elementary schools for women). In *Zhongguo jinxiandai yishu jiaoyu fagui huibian (1840–1929)*, edited by Zhang Xian and Zhang Yuan, 167–75. Beijing: Jiaoyu chubanshe, 1997.

Y.D. *See* Wu Juenong.

Ya'e 亞娥. "Feilübin xinnian zazhi" 菲律賓新年雜誌 (Random notes on the New Year in the Philippines). *FNZZ* 3: 1 (1917), *jishumen*: 9–10.

Yalu. *See* Liu Yazi.

Yamada, Nanako. *Woodblock Kuchi-e Prints: Reflections of Meiji Culture*. Honolulu: University of Hawai'i Press, 2000.

Yan Bin 燕斌. "Zhongguo liu-Ri nüxueshenghui chengli tonggaoshu" 中國留日女學生會成立通告書 (Announcing the founding of the Association of Chinese Women Students in Japan). *Zhongguo xin nüjie zazhi* 2 (1907).

Yan Juanying 顏娟英. "Buxi de biandong – yi Shanghai meishu xuexiao wei zhongxin de meishu jiaoyu yundong" 不息的變動—以上海美術學校為中心的美術教育運動 (Ceaseless changes – The art education movement centered on the art schools in Shanghai). In *Shanghai meishu fengyun – 1872–1948 Shenbao yishu ziliao tiaomu suoyin*, edited by Yan Juanying, 47–117. Taipei: Academia Sinica, 2006.

Yang Chao, Pu-wei. *Autobiography of a Chinese Woman*. New York: John Day Company, 1947.

Yao Yi 姚毅. *Kindai Chūgoku no shussan to kokka shakai: Yishi, josanshi, sesseiba* 近代中国の出産と国家社会: 医師, 助産士, 接生婆 (Nation, society, and childbirth in modern China: Doctors, midwives, and birth grannies). Tokyo: Kenbun shuppan, 2011.

"Yao Yiyun shiwen" 姚倚雲詩文 (Poetry and prose by Yao Yiyun). In *Nantong Fan shi shiwen shijia*, compiled by Wang Yamin, *juan* 16. Shijiazhuang: Hebei jiaoyu chubanshe, 2004.

Yate 亞特. "Lun zhuzao guomin mu" 論鑄造國民母 (On the forging of mothers of citizens). *Nüzi shijie* 7 (1904), *lunshuo*: 1–7.

Ye Changchi 葉昌熾. *Yuandu lu riji chao* 緣督廬日記抄 (Transcribed diaries from the hut overseeing the edge), vol. 14. http://ctext.org/library.pl?if=gb&res=2080.

Ye Shengtao 葉聖陶 [Ye Tao 葉陶]. "Ertong zhi guannian" 兒童之觀念 (Views on children). *FNSB* 3 (1911), 6–7 [36–37].

Ye Xiaoqing. *The Dianshizhai Pictorial: Shanghai Urban Life, 1884–1898*. Ann Arbor: University of Michigan Press, 2003.

Yen Hsiao-pei. "Body Politics, Modernity and National Salvation: The Modern Girl and the New Life Movement." *Asian Studies Review* 29 (2005), 165–86.

Yicheng 毅成. "Lixiang de zhuzhai: Yizhong de sheshi" 理想的住宅: 意中的設施 (The ideal dwelling: The desired arrangements). *FNZZ* 12: 11 (1926), 34–36.

"Yiguo qingdiao" 異國情調 (Exotic sentiments). *Linglong* 225 (1936), 481.

Yin, Tongyun. "From Painter to Artist: Representing Guohua Paintings, and Painters in Liangyou, 1926–1938." In *Liangyou: Kaleidoscopic Modernity and the*

Shanghai Global Metropolis, 1926–1945, edited by Paul G. Pickowicz, Kuiyi Shen, and Yingjin Zhang, 227–47. Leiden: Brill, 2013.

"Yingxiong taidu zhi Huashengdun mu" 英雄态度之华盛顿母 (The heroic mother of Washington). *FNSB* 5 (1911), 39–41.

Yiwen 逸纹. "Wo jiang zenmeyang zuo fu/muqin: chiluoluode chenshuo yixia" 我將 怎麼樣作父/母親: 赤裸裸的陳說一下 (The kind of father/mother I want to be: A sincere account). *FNZZ* 11: 11 (1925), 1730–32 [56–58].

Yosano Akiko 與謝野晶子. "Zhencao lun" 貞操論 (On chastity), translated by Zhou Zuoren. *Xin qingnian* 4: 5 (1918), 386–94.

You Jianming 游鑑明 [Yu Chien-ming]. "Qianshan wo duxing? Nian shiji qianbanqi Zhongguo youguan nüxing dushen de yanlun" 千山我獨行? 廿世紀前半期 中國有關女性獨身的言論 (All alone am I? Discussions of female single-hood in early twentieth century China). *Jindai Zhongguo funüshi yanjiu* 9 (2001), 121–87.

You Ran 悠然. "Fan nüquan yundong de Ailun Kai" 反女權運動的爱倫凱 (A woman against the women's movement: Ellen Key). *Linglong* 225 (1936), 490.

Young, William H., and Nancy K. Young. *The 1950s*. Westport, CT: Greenwood Press, 2004.

Yu Fuyuan 余福媛. "Guanyu *Nü xuebao* de kanqi he kanxingqi" 關於女學報的刊期 和刊行期 (About the journal *Chinese Girl's Progress* and its publication dates). *Tushuguan* 2 (1986), 52–53.

Yu Jing 余競. "Shujia nei de xiuye: lequ de canhen" 暑假内的修業: 樂趣的殘痕 (Revision in the summer holidays: Traces of happiness). *FNZZ* 13: 7 (1927), 44–45 [66–67].

Yu Tiansui 余天遂. "Yu zhi nüzi jiaoyu guan" 余之女子教育觀 (My views on Chinese women's education). *FNZZ* 1: 1 (1915), *lunshuo*: 1–3.

Yun Xuemei 云雪梅. *Jin Cheng* 金城 (Jin Cheng). Shijiazhuang: Hebei jiaoyu chuban-she, 2002.

Yuren 愚人. "Dule 'Nüzimen shuo' yihou" 讀了「女子們說」以後 (After reading "Women said"). *Funü gongming* 8 (1929), 35–36.

Zamperini, Paola. "Canonizing Pornography. A (Foolish?) Woman's Sexual Education in *Chipozi Zhuan*." Available at www.asia-europe.uni-heidelberg.de/ fileadmin/Documents/Research_Areas/Research_Project_B/B8_Rethinking_ Gender/Zamperini_Canonizing_Pornography.pdf.

Zhang Fengru 張鳳如. "Faqi nüzi guomin yinhang zhi shuoming" 發起女子國民銀行 之說明 (Explanation concerning the launch of a women citizens' bank). *Shenzhou nübao* 3 (1912), *zhuanjian*: 1–5.

Zhang Jinglu 張靜盧. "Shangwu yinshuguan dashi jiyao" 商務印書館大事紀要 (Summary of major events [in the history of] the Commercial Press). In Zhang Jinglu, *Zhongguo chuban shiliao, bubian*, 557–71. (Supplement to historical materials on Chinese publishing). Beijing: Zhonghua shuju, 1957.

Zhang Mojun 張默君. "Ziti meiren yima kanjian tu (shi tu wei youhua zuoyu sinian Jiuyue wuri)" 自題美人倚馬看劍圖 (是圖為油畫作於四年九月五日) (Colophon for my own painting "A beauty inspecting a sword while standing beside [her] horse" [The oil painting was done on September 5, 1915]). *FNSB* 21 (1917), 101–2.

Zhang Mojun [Chang, Mo-chün]. "Opposition to Footbinding." In *Chinese Women through Chinese Eyes*, edited by Li Yu-ning, 125–28. New York: M. E. Sharpe, 1992.

Zhang Shiyang 章士敭. "Zhang Xichen yu Kaiming shudian" 章錫琛與開明書店 (Zhang Xichen and Kaiming bookstore). *Chuban shiliao* 3 (2003), 76–85.

Zhang Xiantao. *The Origins of the Modern Chinese Press: The Influence of the Protestant Missionary Press in Late Qing China*. London: Routledge, 2007.

Zhang Xichen 章錫琛. "Cong shangren dao shangren" 從商人到商人 (From a merchant to a merchant). *Zhongxuesheng* 11 (1931), 99–112.

— "Du Fengzi nüshi he YD xiansheng de taolun" 讀鳳子女士和YD先生的討論 (Reading the discussions between Ms. Fengzi and Mr. YD). *FNZZ* 9: 2 (1923), 48–49.

— "Weiba yiwai zhi xu: fei fei lian'ai lun bing jiujiao yu zhuzhang zajiao zhujun" 尾巴以外之續－－非非戀愛論並就教於主張雜交諸君 (A sequel to the tail: Against anti-love theories, and seeking advice from those who advocate promiscuity). *Xin nüxing* 3:8 (1928), 886–92.

— "Wo de lian'ai zhencao guan: xiezai Qiandi Jianbo liang jun de wen hou" 我的戀愛貞操觀－－寫在謙弟劍波兩君的文後 (My view of chastity bound to love: After reading the texts by Qiandi and Jianbo). *Xin nüxing* 2:5 (1927), 533–36.

— "Xin xingdaode shi shime" 新性道德是什麼 (What is new sexual morality). *FNZZ* 11:1 (1925), 2–7.

Zhang Xichen [Selu 瑟廬]. "Ailun Kai ertong liangqin xuanze guan" 愛倫凱兒童兩親選擇觀 (Ellen Key's views on the choice of parents). *FNZZ* 9: 11 (1923), 31–35 [51–55].

— "Ailunkai nüshi yu qi sixiang" 愛倫凱女士與其思想 (Mrs. Ellen Key and her ideas). *FNZZ* 7: 2 (1921), 21–27.

— "Wenming yu dushen" 文明與獨身 (Civilization and singlehood). *FNZZ* 8: 10 (1922), 2–7.

Zhang Yanbing 張岩冰. *Nüquanzhuyi wenlun* 女性主義文論 (A feminist reader). Jinan: Shandong jiaoyu chubanshe, 1998.

Zhang Zhaosi 張昭泗. "Yindu nüzi fengsu tan" 印度女子風俗談 (A discussion of female customs in India). *FNSB* 20 (1916), 36–46.

Zhang Zhongmin 张仲民. *Chuban yu wenhua zhengzhi: Wan Qing de "weisheng" shuji yanjiu* 出版与文化政治: 晚清的卫生'书籍研究 (Publishing and cultural politics: Research on late Qing books on "hygiene"). Shanghai: Shanghai shudian chubanshe, 2009.

Zhao Yuan 趙媛. "Jiating jiaoyu lun" 家庭教育論 (On home education). *FNSB* 1 (1911), 6–12 [24–29].

Zheng Shiqu 鄭師渠. "Liang Qichao de aiguo lun" 梁啟超的愛國論 (Liang Qichao on patriotism). *Hebei xuekan* 25: 4 (July 2005), 174–83.

"Zheng tongling ruhe dechang xinyuan" 鄭統領如何得償心願 (How Commander Zheng got what he wanted). *FNSB* 11 (1913).

Zheng Yimei 鄭逸梅. *Yihai yishao xubian* 藝海一勺續編 (A dipper in the sea of art, continued). Tianjin: Guji chubanshe, 1996.

Zheng Zhenduo 鄭振鐸. "Ertong Shijie xuanyan" 兒童世界宣言 (Declaration of children's world) *FNZZ* 8: 1 (1922), 133–134.

Zheng Zhenxun 鄭振壎 [Kuangfu 曠夫]. "Wo ziji de hunyinshi" 我自己的婚姻史 (My own marriage history). *FNZZ* 9: 2 (1923), 7–24.

Zheng Zhenxun 鄭振壎 [Kuangfu 曠夫]. "Wo ziji de hunyinshi" 我自己的婚姻史 (My own marriage history). *FNZZ* 9: 2 (1923), 7–24.

Zhenguo 振幗. "Eguo nü waijiaojia (wuhuan zhi quanquan dashi) Nabikefu furen" 俄國女外交家(無官之全權大使)那俾可甫夫人 (Ms. Novikoff, Russian female diplomat and unofficial plenipotentiary). *Zhongguo xin nüjie zazhi* 6 (1904).

— "Faguo xinwenjie zhi nüwang Yadan furen" 法國新聞界之女王亞丹夫人 (Ms. Adam, queen of the world of French journalism). *Zhongguo xin nüjie zazhi* 6 (1904).

Zhi Qun 志羣. "Gonghe xinnian" 恭賀新年 (Congratulations on the New Year). *Nüzi shijie* 2: 4–5 (1905/6), 1–3.

— "Zhengyao zhi jinggao san" 爭約之警告三 (Admonition number three to debate the treaty) *Nüzi shijie* 2: 4 (1906), 7–11.

Zhi Xin 知新 and Qin Zong 琴宗 (trs.). "Wutong anchan fa xu" 無痛安產法 (續) (Painless childbirth [continued]). *FNSB* 21 (1917), 56–70.

"Zhifu zhi lu – Renzao biandan" 致富之路 – 人造变蛋 (One way to wealth: Man-made eggs). *Nongjianü baishitong* 2 (1996), inside cover.

Zhiyuan 致遠. "Deyizhi zhi nü" 德意志之女 (German women). *ZHFNJ* 7 (1915).

Zhong Tingxiu 鍾挺秀. "Shijie geguo funü canzheng yundong gaishu" 世界各國婦女參政運動概述 (A brief account of the women's suffrage movements in the countries of the world). *FNZZ* 15: 8 (1929), 13–19 [29–35].

Zhonggong zhongyang Ma-En-Lie-Si zhuzuo bianyiju yanjiushi 中共中央馬恩列斯著作編譯局研究室 (ed.). *Wu si shiqi qikan jieshao* 五四時期期刊介紹 (Introduction to journals of the May Fourth period). 3 vols. Beijing: Sanlian shudian, 1979.

Zhongguo jinxiandai nüxing qikan huibian 中国近现代女性期刊汇编 (Compilation of modern and contemporary Chinese women's journals). 85 vols. Beijing: Xianzhuang shuju, 2006.

Zhongguo xin nüjie zazhi 中國新女界雜誌 (Magazine of China's new world of women). Tokyo: Zhongguo xin nüjie zazhi she, 1907. Reprint, Taibei: Youshi wenhua shiye gongsi, 1977.

Zhou Chunyan 周春燕. *Nüti yu guozu: qiangguo qiangzhong yu jindai Zhongguo de funü weisheng (1895–1949)* 女體與國族: 強國強種與近代中國的婦女衛生 (1895–1949) (Female bodies and the nation: Strengthening the nation, strengthening the race and modern Chinese women's health [1895–1949]). Gaoxiong: Fuwen, 2010.

Zhou Jianren 周建人. "Xingdaode zhi kexue de biaozhun" 性道德之科學的標準 (The scientific standard for the new sexual morality). *FNZZ* 11: 1 (1925), 8–12.

— "Zhongguo nüzi de juexing yu dushen" 中國女子的覺醒與獨身 (Chinese women's awakening and singlehood). *FNZZ* 8: 10 (1922), 7–9.

Zhou Jianren [Ke Shi 克士]. "Aiqing de biaoxian yu jiehun shenghuo" 愛情的表現與結婚生活 (The expression of romantic love and marital life). *FNZZ* 9: 4 (1923), 22–24.

— "Yindu de funü shenghuo" 印度的婦女生活 (The lives of women in India). *FNZZ* 8: 10 (1922), 72–73.

Zhou Jinsong 周金宋. "Hua shuo qianbai bian buru daitou gan yibian" 话说千百遍不如带头干一遍 (To say something thousands of times is not as good as simply taking the lead and doing something once) *Zhongguo Funü* 2 (1966), 6–7.

(Zhou) Shoujuan (周) 瘦鵑 (tr.). "Funü zhi yuanzhi" 婦女之原質 (Women's nature). *FNSB* 8 (1912), 24.

Zhou Xiuqing 周修慶 "Meiguo laodong funü de beican shenghuo" 美國勞動婦女的悲慘生活 (The tragic life of American working women). *Zhongguo funü* 2 (1956), 19.

Zhou Zuoren 周作人. *Zhitang huixiang lu* 知堂回想錄 (Memoirs of the Hall of Knowledge). 2 vols. Hong Kong: Sanyu tushu wenju gongsi, 1971.

Zhu Baoliang 朱宝樑, comp. *Ershi shiji Zhongwen zhuzuo zhe biming lu* 20世纪中文著作作者笔名录 (Twentieth-century Chinese authors and their pen names). Guilin: Guangxi shifan daxue chubanshe, 2002.

Zhu Deshang 朱德裳. *Sanshi nian wenjian lu* 三十年聞見錄 (Record of things seen and heard in thirty years). Changsha: Yuelu shushe, 1985.

Zhu Yin 竹蔭. "Nüzi haomei shi buyong shuode" 女子好美是不用說的 (Needless to say, women are aesthetically inclined by nature). *FNZZ* 12: 1 (1926), 167–70.

Zhu Youhuan 朱有瓛 (ed.). *Zhongguo jindai xuezhi shiliao* 中國近代學制史料 (Historical materials on the modern Chinese education system). Shanghai: Huadong shifan daxue, 1983.

Zhu Zhidao 朱志道. "Wo jiang zenmeyang zuo fu/muqin: Shi'er tiao de yijian" 我將怎麼樣作父/母親: 十二條的意見 (The kind of father/mother I want to be: Twelve suggestions). *FNZZ* 11: 11 (1925), 1732–35 [58–61].

Zhuang Yu 莊俞 and Jiang Weigao 蔣維高. "Jiaoyuguan yanjiu yijianshu" 教育馆研究意见书 (Findings on the research of the education pavilion). In *Nanyang quanyehui baogaoshu*, edited by Bao Yong'an 鮑永安, Su Keqin 苏克勤, and Yu Jieyu 余洁宇, 49–51. Shanghai: Shanghai jiaotong daxue chubanshe, 2010.

Zhuo Hua 灼華. "Da yanshuojia Lifoma nüshi zhuan" 大演說家梨佛瑪女士傳 (Biography of the great speaker, Ms. Livermore). *Zhongguo xin nüjie zazhi* 4 (1907).

— "Houteng Qingzi xiaozhuan" 後藤清子小傳 (Short biography of Gotō Kiyoko). *Zhongguo xin nüjia zazhi* 6 (1907).

"Zi neiwu bu ju tongsu jiaoyu yanjiuhui chengqing zi jin Meiyu zazhi qing chazhao wen" 咨內務部據通俗教育研究會呈請咨禁眉語雜誌請查照文 (Request to the Ministry of the Interior to note the request from the Popular Education Research Association to ban the magazine *Eyebrow Talk*). *Jiaoyu gongbao* 3: 11 (1916), *gongdu* section, 12.

"Zigong bingxue zhi daoyao/Zhongjiangtang" 子宮病血之道藥/中將湯 (The Chūjōtō Tsumura, medicine for uterine blood disease). *FNSB* 6 (1912).

Zou Shengwen 鄒盛文. "Xiyang zaoyuan fa" 西洋造園法 (Western garden design). *FNZZ* 11: 5 (1925), 850–56 [169–75].

Zou Zhenhuan 鄒振環. "Tushanwan yinshuguan yu Shanghai yinshua chuban wenhua de fazhan" 土山灣印書館與上海印刷出版文化的發展 (Tushanwan Press and the development of the printing and publishing culture in Shanghai). In *Chongshi lishi suipian: Tushanwan yanjiu ziliao cuibian*, edited by Huang Shulin, 194–211. Beijing: Zhongguo xiju chubanshe, 2010.

Index

Note: Page numbers followed by *n* indicate a footnote with relevant number; illustrations are denoted by *fig*.